Integrated Approaches in Information Technology and Web Engineering:
Advancing Organizational Knowledge Sharing

Ghazi Alkhatib
Applied Science University, Jordan

David Rine
George Mason University, USA

INFORMATION SCIENCE REFERENCE

Hershey · New York

Director of Editorial Content:	Kristin Klinger
Director of Production:	Jennifer Neidig
Managing Editor:	Jamie Snavely
Assistant Managing Editor:	Carole Coulson
Typesetter:	Larissa Vinci
Cover Design:	Lisa Tosheff
Printed at:	Yurchak Printing Inc.

Published in the United States of America by
Information Science Reference (an imprint of IGI Global)
701 E. Chocolate Avenue, Suite 200
Hershey PA 17033
Tel: 717-533-8845
Fax: 717-533-8661
E-mail: cust@igi-global.com
Web site: http://www.igi-global.com

and in the United Kingdom by
Information Science Reference (an imprint of IGI Global)
3 Henrietta Street
Covent Garden
London WC2E 8LU
Tel: 44 20 7240 0856
Fax: 44 20 7379 0609
Web site: http://www.eurospanbookstore.com

Library of Congress Cataloging-in-Publication Data

Alkhatib, Ghazi, 1947-

 Integrated approaches in information technology and web engineering :

advancing organizational knowledge sharing / Ghazi Alkhatib and David Rine, editors.

    p. cm.

 Includes bibliographical references and index.

 Summary: "This book offers indepth research into Web Engineering (WE) systems and tools that support knowledge sharing among individuals within organizations as well as those belonging to virtual organizations"--Provided by publisher.

 ISBN 978-1-60566-418-7 (hardcover) -- ISBN 978-1-60566-419-4 (ebook) 1. Information technology--Handbooks, manuals, etc. 2. Computer software--Quality control--Handbooks, manuals, etc. 3. Application software--Development--Handbooks, manuals, etc. 4. Web services--Handbooks, manuals, etc. I. Rine, David C. II. Title.

 TK5105.888.A379 2008

 005.068'4--dc22

                        2008037395

British Cataloguing in Publication Data
A Cataloguing in Publication record for this book is available from the British Library.

All work contributed to this book is original material. The views expressed in this book are those of the authors, but not necessarily of the publisher.

Integrated Approaches in Information Technology and Web Engineering: Advancing Organizational Knowledge Sharing is part of the IGI Global series named *Advances in Information Technology and Web Engineering (AITWE)* Series, ISBN: pending

Advances in Information Technology and Web Engineering (AITWE) Series

ISBN: pending

Editor-in-Chief:
Ghazi I. Alkhatib, Applied Science University, Jordan
David C. Rine, George Mason University, USA

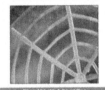

Integrated Approaches in Information Technology and Web Engineering: Advancing Organizational Knowledge Sharing

Ghazi I. Alkhatib, Applied Science University, Jordan & David C. Rine, George Mason University, USA
Information Science Reference * copyright 2009 * 361pp * H/C (ISBN: 978-1-60566-418-7) * US $195.00 (our price)

With the increasing proliferation of information technology and Web-based approaches to the implementation of systems and services, researchers, educators, and practitioners worldwide are experiencing a rising need for authoritative references to enhance their understanding of the most current and effective engineering practices leading to robust and successful solutions.

Integrated Approaches in Information Technology and Web Engineering: Advancing Organizational Knowledge Sharing presents comprehensive, research-driven insights into the field of Web engineering. This book collects over 30 authoritative articles from distinguished international researchers in information technology and Web engineering, creating an invaluable resource for library reference collections that will equip researchers and practitioners in academia and industry alike with the knowledge base to drive the next generation of innovations.

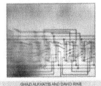

Agent Technologies and Web Engineering: Applications and Systems

Ghazi I. Alkhatib, Applied Science University, Jordan & David C. Rine, George Mason University, USA
Information Science Reference * copyright 2009 * 361pp * H/C (ISBN: 978-1-60566-618-1) * US $195.00 (our price)

In recent years, the emerging field of agent technologies has become mainstream in Web engineering. With constant field developments and updates, a reference source is needed that reflects the increased scope of agent technology application domains and development practices and tools.

Agent Technologies and Web Engineering: Applications and Systems presents the latest tools and applications addressing critical issues involved with information technology and Web engineering research. Covering topics such as next-generation networks, XML query processing, and Semantic Web services, this book provides cutting-edge research for practitioners and academicians involved in agent technology and Web engineering fields.

The Advances in Information Technology and Web Engineering (AITWE) Book Series aims to provide a platform for research in the area of Information Technology (IT) concepts, tools, methodologies, and ethnography, in the contexts of global communication systems and Web engineered applications. Organizations are continuously overwhelmed by a variety of new information technologies, many are Web based. These new technologies are capitalizing on the widespread use of network and communication technologies for seamless integration of various issues in information and knowledge sharing within and among organizations. This emphasis on integrated approaches is unique to this book series and dictates cross platform and multidisciplinary strategy to research and practice. The Advances in Information Technology and Web Engineering (AITWE) Book Series seeks to create a stage where comprehensive publications are distributed for the objective of bettering and expanding the field of web systems, knowledge capture, and communication technologies. The series will provide researchers and practitioners with solutions for improving how technology is utilized for the purpose of a growing awareness of the importance of web applications and engineering.

Hershey · New York

Order online at www.igi-global.com or call 717-533-8845 x 100 –
Mon-Fri 8:30 am - 5:00 pm (est) or fax 24 hours a day 717-533-8661

Table of Contents

Preface xviii

Section I
Platforms and Architectures

Chapter I

Integration of Libre Software Applications to Create a Collaborative Work Platform for
Researchers at GET.. 1

Olivier Berger, GET/INT, France

Christian Bac, GET/INT, France

Benoît Hamet, GET/INT, France

Chapter II

FLOSSmole: A Collaborative Repository for FLOSS Research Data and Analyses 18

James Howison, Syracuse University, USA

Megan Conklin, Elon University, USA

Kevin Crowston, Syracuse University, USA

Chapter III

Applying Social Network Analysis Techniques to Community-Driven Libre Software Projects 28

Luis López-Fernández, Universidad Rey Juan Carlos, Spain

Gregorio Robles, Universidad Rey Juan Carlos, Spain

Jesus M. Gonzalez-Barahona, Universidad Rey Juan Carlos, Spain

Israel Herraiz, Universidad Rey Juan Carlos, Spain

Chapter IV

Multi-Modal Modeling, Analysis, and Validation of Open Source Software Development Processes ... 51

Walt Scacchi, University of California, USA

Chris Jensen, University of California, USA

John Noll, University of California, and 2Santa Clara University, USA

Margaret Elliott, University of California, USA

Chapter V

An Empirical Study on the Migration to OpenOffice.org in a Public Administration 66
    B. Rossi, Free University of Bolzano-Bozen, Italy
    M. Scotto, Free University of Bolzano-Bozen, Italy
    A. Sillitti, Free University of Bolzano-Bozen, Italy
    G. Succi, Free University of Bolzano-Bozen, Italy

Chapter VI

Open Source in Web-Based Applications: A Case Study on Single Sign-On 83
    Claudio Agostino Ardagna, Università degli Studi di Milano, Italy
    Fulvio Frati, Università degli Studi di Milano, Italy
    Gabriele Gianini, Università degli Studi di Milano, Italy

Chapter VII

Engineering Wireless Mobile Applications 98
    Qusay H. Mahmoud, University of Guelph, Canada
    Zakaria Maamar, Zayed University, UAE

Chapter VIII

A Prediction Based Flexible Channel Assignment in Wireless Networks using Road Topology
Information 113
    G. Sivaradje, Pondicherry Engineering College, India
    R. Nakkeeran, Pondicherry Engineering College, India
    P. Dananjayan, Pondicherry Engineering College, India

Section II
Development

Chapter IX

High Performance Scheduling Mechanism for Mobile Computing Based on Self-Ranking
Algorithm (SRA) 127
    Hesham A. Ali, Mansoura University, Egypt
    Tamer Ahmed Farrag, Mansoura University, Egypt

Chapter X

Hierarchical Scheduling in Heterogeneous Grid Systems 143
    Khaldoon Al-Zoubi, Carleton University, Canada

Chapter XI

Object Grouping and Replication on a Distributed Web Server System 158
    Amjad Mahmood, University of Bahrain, Kingdom of Bahrain
    Taher S. K. Homeed, University of Bahrain, Kingdom of Bahrain

Chapter XII

On the Logarithmic Backoff Algorithm for MAC Protocol in MANETs 174

    Saher S. Manaseer, University of Glasgow, UK

    Mohamed Ould-Khaoua, University of Glasgow, UK

    Lewis M. Mackenzie, University of Glasgow, UK

Chapter XIII

Secure Online DNS Dynamic Updates: Architecture and Implementation 185

    Xunhua Wang, James Madison University, USA

    David Rine, George Mason University, USA

Chapter XIV

FSR Evaluation Using the Suboptimal Operational Values 203

    Osama H S Khader, The Islamic University of Gaza, Palestine

Chapter XV

Modeling Variant User Interfaces for Web-Based Software Product Lines 212

    Suet Chun Lee, BUSINEX, Inc., USA

Section III
Open Source

Chapter XVI

Experience Report: A Component-Based Data Management and Knowledge Discovery
Framework for Aviation Studies 244

    M. Brian Blake, Georgetown University and The MITRE Corporation, USA

    Lisa Singh, Georgetown University, USA

    Andrew B. Williams, Spelman University, USA

    Wendell Norman, The MITRE Corporation, USA

    Amy L. Sliva, Georgetown University, USA

Chapter XVII

Agile Development of Secure Web-Based Applications 257

    A. F. Tappenden, University of Alberta, Canada

    T. Huynh, University of Alberta, Canada

    J. Miller, University of Alberta, Canada

    A. Geras, University of Alberta, Canada

    M. Smith, University of Alberta, Canada

Chapter XVIII

Web Data Warehousing Convergence: From Schematic to Systematic 278

    D. Xuan Le, La Trobe Univerity, Australia

    J. Wenny Rahayu, La Trobe Univerity, Australia

    David Taniar, Monash University, Australia

Chapter XIX

Engineering Conceptual Data Models from Domain Ontologies: A Critical Evaluation 304

Haya El-Ghalayini, University of the West of England (UWE), UK
Mohammed Odeh, University of the West of England (UWE), UK
Richard McClatchey, University of the West of England (UWE), UK

Chapter XX

Modeling Defects in E-Projects 317

John D. Ferguson, University of Strathclyde, UK
James Miller, University of Alberta, Canada

Chapter XXI

Tool Support for Model-Driven Development of Web Applications 331

Jaime Gomez, University of Alicante, Spain
Alejandro Bia, University of Alicante, Spain
Antonio Parraga, University of Alicante, Spain

Compilation of References 345

Index 367

Detailed Table of Contents

Preface xviii

Section I
Platforms and Architectures

Chapter I

Integration of Libre Software Applications to Create a Collaborative Work Platform for
Researchers at GET.. 1

    Olivier Berger, GET/INT, France
    Christian Bac, GET/INT, France
    Benoît Hamet, GET/INT, France

Libre software provides powerful applications ready to be integrated for the build-up of platforms for internal use in organizations. The authors of this chapter describe the architecture of the collaborative work platform which they have integrated, designed for researchers at GET. They present the elements learned during this project in particular with respect to contribution to external libre projects, in order to better ensure the maintainability of the internal applications, and to phpGroupware as a framework for specific applications development.

Chapter II

FLOSSmole: A Collaborative Repository for FLOSS Research Data and Analyses 18

    James Howison, Syracuse University, USA
    Megan Conklin, Elon University, USA
    Kevin Crowston, Syracuse University, USA

This chapter introduces and expands on previous work on a collaborative project, called FLOSSmole (formerly OSSmole), designed to gather, share and store comparable data and analyses of free, libre, and open source software (FLOSS) development for academic research. The project draws on the ongoing collection and analysis efforts of many research groups, reducing duplication, and promoting compatibility both across sources of FLOSS data and across research groups and analyses. The chapter outlines current difficulties with the current typical quantitative FLOSS research process and uses these to develop requirements and presents the design of the system.

Chapter III

Applying Social Network Analysis Techniques to Community-Driven Libre Software Projects 28

Luis López-Fernández, Universidad Rey Juan Carlos, Spain

Gregorio Robles, Universidad Rey Juan Carlos, Spain

Jesus M. Gonzalez-Barahona, Universidad Rey Juan Carlos, Spain

Israel Herraiz, Universidad Rey Juan Carlos, Spain

Source code management repositories of large, long-lived libre (free, open source) software projects can be a source of valuable data about the organizational structure, evolution and knowledge exchange in the corresponding development communities. Unfortunately, the sheer volume of the available information renders it almost unusable without applying methodologies which highlight the relevant information for a given aspect of the project. Such methodology is proposed in this chapter, based on well known concepts from the social networks analysis field, which can be used to study the relationships among developers and how they collaborate in different parts of a project. It is also applied to data mined from some well known projects (Apache, GNOME, and KDE), focusing on the characterization of their collaboration network architecture. These cases help to understand the potentials of the methodology and how it is applied, but also show some relevant results which open new paths in the understanding of the informal organization of libre software development communities.

Chapter IV

Multi-Modal Modeling, Analysis, and Validation of Open Source Software Development Processes ... 51

Walt Scacchi, University of California, USA

Chris Jensen, University of California, USA

John Noll, University of California and 2Santa Clara University, USA

Margaret Elliott, University of California, USA

Understanding the context, structure, activities, and content of software development processes found in practice has been and remains a challenging problem. In the world of free/open source software development, discovering and understanding what processes are used in particular projects is important in determining how they are similar to or different from those advocated by the software engineering community. Prior studies have revealed that development processes in F/OSSD projects are different in a number of ways. In this chapter, the authors describe how a variety of modeling perspectives and techniques are used to elicit, analyze, and validate software development processes found in F/OSSD projects, with examples drawn from studies of the software requirements process found in the NetBeans. org project.

Chapter V

An Empirical Study on the Migration to OpenOffice.org in a Public Administration 66

    B. Rossi, Free University of Bolzano-Bozen, Italy

    M. Scotto, Free University of Bolzano-Bozen, Italy

    A. Sillitti, Free University of Bolzano-Bozen, Italy

    G. Succi, Free University of Bolzano-Bozen, Italy

The aim of this chapter is to report the results of a migration to Open Source Software (OSS) in one Public Administration. The migration focuses on the office automation field and, in particular, on the OpenOffice.org suite. The authors have analysed the transition to OSS considering qualitative and quantitative data collected with the aid of different tools. All the data have been always considered from the point of view of the different stakeholders involved, IT managers, IT technicians, and users.

The results of the project have been largely satisfactory. However the results cannot be generalised due to some constraints, like the environment considered and the parallel use of the old solution. Nevertheless, the authors think that the data collected can be of valuable aid to managers wishing to evaluate a possible transition to OSS.

Chapter VI

Open Source in Web-Based Applications: A Case Study on Single Sign-On 83

    Claudio Agostino Ardagna, Università degli Studi di Milano, Italy

    Fulvio Frati, Università degli Studi di Milano, Italy

    Gabriele Gianini, Università degli Studi di Milano, Italy

Business and recreational activities on the global communication infrastructure are increasingly based on the use of remote resources and services, and on the interaction between different, remotely located parties. In such a context, Single Sign-On technologies simplify the log-on process allowing automatic access to secondary domains through a unique log-on operation to the primary domain. This chapter evaluates different Single Sign-On implementations focusing on the central role of Open Source in the development of Web-based systems. This chapter outlines requirements for Single Sign-On systems and evaluate four existing Open Source implementations in terms of degree of fulfilment of those requirements. Finally, the authors compare those Open Source systems with respect to some specific Open Source community patterns.

Chapter VII

Engineering Wireless Mobile Applications 98

    Qusay H. Mahmoud, University of Guelph, Canada

    Zakaria Maamar, Zayed University, UAE

Conventional desktop software applications are usually designed, built, and tested on a platform similar to the one on which they will be deployed and run. Wireless mobile application development, on the other hand, is more challenging because applications are developed on one platform (like UNIX or Windows) and deployed on a totally different platform like a cellular phone. While wireless applications can be much smaller than conventional desktop applications, developers should think in the small in terms of the devices on which the applications will run and the environment in which they will operate instead of the amount of code to be written. This chapter presents a systematic approach to engineering wireless application and offers practical guidelines for testing them. What is unique about this approach is that it takes into account the special features of the new medium (mobile devices and wireless networks), the operational environment, and the multiplicity of user backgrounds; all of which pose new challenges to wireless application development.

Chapter VIII

A Prediction Based Flexible Channel Assignment in Wireless Networks using Road Topology Information 113

    G. Sivaradje, Pondicehrry Engineering College, India
    R. Nakkeeran, Pondicehrry Engineering College, India
    P. Dananjayan, Pondicehrry Engineering College, India

In this chapter, a novel prediction technique is proposed, which uses road topology information for prediction. The proposed scheme uses real time positioning information and road topology information, which matches with the real environment. The scheme uses flexible channel assignment to maintain a better tradeoff between forced termination and call blocking probabilities. For reservation of resources in advance, the information about future handoffs is obtained from the road topology prediction technique. To show the effectiveness of the prediction scheme and flexible channel assignment scheme, this work aims at simulation of other channel assignment strategies viz., fixed and dynamic channel assignment strategy with and without incorporating the prediction based on road topology information. It gives accurate prediction results which helps to maintain a better QoS and resource management.

Section II
Development

Chapter IX

High Performance Scheduling Mechanism for Mobile Computing Based on Self-Ranking Algorithm (SRA) 127

    Hesham A. Ali, Mansoura University, Egypt
    Tamer Ahmed Farrag, Mansoura University, Egypt

Due to the rapidly increasing of the mobile devices connected to the internet, a lot of research is being conducted to maximize the benefit of such integration. The main objective of this chapter is to enhance the performance of the scheduling mechanism of the mobile computing environment by distributing some of the responsibilities of the access point among the available attached mobile devices. To this aim, the authors investigate a scheduling mechanism framework that comprises an algorithm provides the mobile device with the authority to evaluate itself as a resource. The proposed mechanism is based on the proposing of "self ranking algorithm (SRA)" which provides a lifetime opportunity to reach a proper solution. This mechanism depends on event-based programming approach to start its execution in a pervasive computing environment. Using such mechanism will simplify the scheduling process by grouping the mobile devices according to their self -ranking value and assign tasks to these groups. Moreover, it will maximize the benefit of the mobile devices incorporated with the already existing grid systems by using their computational power as a subordinate value to the overall power of the system.

Chapter X
Hierarchical Scheduling in Heterogeneous Grid Systems 143
    Khaldoon Al-Zoubi, Carleton University, Canada

This chapter proposes hierarchal scheduling schemes for Grid systems: a self-discovery scheme for the resource discovery stage and an adaptive child scheduling method for the resource selection stage. In addition, the authors propose three rescheduling algorithms: (1) the Butterfly algorithm in order to re-schedule jobs when better resources become available, (2) the Fallback algorithm in order to reschedule jobs that had their resources taken away from the Grid before the actual resource allocation, and (3) the Load-Balance algorithm in order to balance load among resources. A hybrid system to combine the proposed hierarchal schemes with the well-known peer-to-peer (P2P) principle is also proposed. The authors compare the performance of the proposed schemes against the P2P-based Grid systems through simulation with respect to a set of predefined metrics.

Chapter XI
Object Grouping and Replication on a Distributed Web Server System 158
    Amjad Mahmood, University of Bahrain, Kingdom of Bahrain
    Taher S. K. Homeed, University of Bahrain, Kingdom of Bahrain

Object replication is a well-known technique to improve performance of a distributed Web server system. This chapter first presents an algorithm to group correlated Web objects that are most likely to be requested by a given client in a single session so that they can be replicated together, preferably, on the same server. A centralized object replication algorithm is then proposed to replicate the object groups to a cluster of Web-server system in order to minimize the user perceived latency subject to certain constraints. Due to dynamic nature of the Web contents and users' access patterns, a distributed object replication algorithm is also proposed where each site locally replicates the object groups based on the local access patterns. The performance of the proposed algorithms is compared with three well-known algorithms and the results are reported. The results demonstrate the superiority of the proposed algorithms.

Chapter XII
On the Logarithmic Backoff Algorithm for MAC Protocol in MANETs 174
    Saher S. Manaseer, University of Glasgow, UK
    Mohamed Ould-Khaoua, University of Glasgow, UK
    Lewis M. Mackenzie, University of Glasgow, UK

In wireless communication environments, backoff is traditionally based on the IEEE binary exponential backoff (BEB). Using BEB results in a high delay in message transmission, collisions and ultimately wasting the limited available bandwidth. As each node has to obtain medium access before transmitting a message, in dense networks, the collision probability in the MAC layer becomes very high when a poor backoff algorithm is used. The Logarithmic algorithm proposes some improvements to the backoff algorithms that aim to efficiently use the channel and to reduce collisions. The algorithm under study is based on changing the incremental behavior of the backoff value. The Binary Exponential Backoff (BEB) is used by the Local Area Networks standards, IEEE 802.11, Medium Access Control (MAC).

application and offers practical guidelines for testing them. What is unique about this approach is that it takes into account the special features of the new medium (mobile devices and wireless networks), the operational environment, and the multiplicity of user backgrounds; all of which pose new challenges to wireless application development.

Chapter VIII

A Prediction Based Flexible Channel Assignment in Wireless Networks using Road Topology Information 113
G. Sivaradje, Pondicherry Engineering College, India
R. Nakkeeran, Pondicherry Engineering College, India
P. Dananjayan, Pondicherry Engineering College, India

In this chapter, a novel prediction technique is proposed, which uses road topology information for prediction. The proposed scheme uses real time positioning information and road topology information, which matches with the real environment. The scheme uses flexible channel assignment to maintain a better tradeoff between forced termination and call blocking probabilities. For reservation of resources in advance, the information about future handoffs is obtained from the road topology prediction technique. To show the effectiveness of the prediction scheme and flexible channel assignment scheme, this work aims at simulation of other channel assignment strategies viz., fixed and dynamic channel assignment strategy with and without incorporating the prediction based on road topology information. It gives accurate prediction results which helps to maintain a better QoS and resource management.

Section II
Development

Chapter IX

High Performance Scheduling Mechanism for Mobile Computing Based on Self-Ranking Algorithm (SRA) 127
Hesham A. Ali, Mansoura University, Egypt
Tamer Ahmed Farrag, Mansoura University, Egypt

Due to the rapidly increasing of the mobile devices connected to the internet, a lot of research is being conducted to maximize the benefit of such integration. The main objective of this chapter is to enhance the performance of the scheduling mechanism of the mobile computing environment by distributing some of the responsibilities of the access point among the available attached mobile devices. To this aim, the authors investigate a scheduling mechanism framework that comprises an algorithm provides the mobile device with the authority to evaluate itself as a resource. The proposed mechanism is based on the proposing of "self ranking algorithm (SRA)" which provides a lifetime opportunity to reach a proper solution. This mechanism depends on event-based programming approach to start its execution in a pervasive computing environment. Using such mechanism will simplify the scheduling process by grouping the mobile devices according to their self -ranking value and assign tasks to these groups. Moreover, it will maximize the benefit of the mobile devices incorporated with the already existing grid systems by using their computational power as a subordinate value to the overall power of the system.

Chapter XV
Modeling Variant User Interfaces for Web-Based Software Product Lines 212
    Suet Chun Lee, BUSINEX, Inc., USA

Software product line (SPL) is a software engineering paradigm for software development. A software product within a product line often has specific functionalities that are not common to all other products within the product line. Those specific functionalities are termed "variant features" in a product line. SPL paradigm involves the modeling of variant features. However, little work in SPL investigates and addresses the modeling of variant features specific to user interface (UI). Unified Modeling Language (UML) is the de facto modeling language for object-oriented software systems. It is known that UML needs better support in modeling UIs. Thus, much research developed UML extensions to improve UML support in modeling UIs. Yet little of this work is related to developing such extensions for modeling UIs for SPLs in which variant features specific to UI modeling must be addressed. This research develops a UML extension -Web User Interface Modeling Language (WUIML) to address these problems. WUIML defines elements for modeling variant features specific to user interfaces for Web-based SPLs. The model elements in WUIML extend from the metaclass and BasicActivity of the UML2.0 metamodel. WUIML integrates the modeling of variant features specific to user interfaces to UML. WUIML defines a model element, XOR, to represent exclusive or conditions in a product line user interface model. WUIML would reduce SPL engineers' efforts needed in UI development. To validate the WUIML research, a case study was conducted. The results of indicate that modeling UIs for Web-based SPLs using WUIML is more effective and efficient than using standard UML.

Section III
Open Source

Chapter XVI
Experience Report: A Component-Based Data Management and Knowledge Discovery
Framework for Aviation Studies 244
    M. Brian Blake, Georgetown University and The MITRE Corporation, USA
    Lisa Singh, Georgetown University, USA
    Andrew B. Williams, Spelman University, USA
    Wendell Norman, The MITRE Corporation, USA
    Amy L. Sliva, Georgetown University, USA

Organizations are beginning to apply data mining and knowledge discovery techniques to their corporate data sets, thereby enabling the identification of trends and the discovery of inductive knowledge. Many times, traditional transactional databases are not optimized for analytical processing and must be transformed. This article proposes the use of modular components to decrease the overall amount of human processing and intervention necessary for the transformation process. The authors' approach configures components to extract data-sets using a set of "extraction hints". This framework incorporates decentralized, generic components that are reusable across domains and databases. Finally, the authors detail an implementation of their component-based framework for an aviation data set.

Chapter XVII

Agile Development of Secure Web-Based Applications 257

A. F. Tappenden, University of Alberta, Canada

T. Huynh, University of Alberta, Canada

J. Miller, University of Alberta, Canada

A. Geras, University of Alberta, Canada

M. Smith, University of Alberta, Canada

This article outlines a four-point strategy for the development of secure Web-based applications within an agile development framework and introduces strategies to mitigate security risks that are commonly present in Web-based applications. The proposed strategy includes the representation of security requirements as test cases supported by the open source tool FIT, the deployment of a highly testable architecture allowing for security testing of the application at all levels, the outlining of an extensive security testing strategy supported by the open source unit-testing framework HTTP Unit, and the introduction of the novel technique of security refactoring that transforms insecure working code into a functionally-equivalent secure code. Today, many Web-based applications are not secure, and limited literature exists concerning the use of agile methods within this domain. It is the intention of this article to further discussions and research regarding the use of an agile methodology for the development of secure Web-based applications.

Chapter XVIII

Web Data Warehousing Convergence: From Schematic to Systematic 278

D. Xuan Le, La Trobe University, Australia

J. Wenny Rahayu, La Trobe University, Australia

David Taniar, Monash University, Australia

This chapter proposes a data warehouse integration technique that combines data and documents from different underlying documents and database design approaches. The well-defined and structured data such as Relational, Object- oriented and Object Relational data, semi-structured data such as XML, and unstructured data such as HTML documents are integrated into a Web data warehouse system. The user specified requirement and data sources are combined to assist with the definitions of the hierarchical structures, which serve specific requirements and represent a certain type of data semantics using object-oriented features including inheritance, aggregation, association and collection. A conceptual integrated data warehouse model is then specified based on a combination of user requirements and data source structure, which creates the need for a logical integrated data warehouse model. To evaluate the conceptual integrated data warehouse model a case study is developed using prototype in a Web-base environment. The evaluation of the proposed integration Web data warehouse methodology includes the verification of correctness of the integrated data, and the overall benefits of utilizing this proposed integration technique.

Chapter XIX

Engineering Conceptual Data Models from Domain Ontologies: A Critical Evaluation 304

Haya El-Ghalayini, University of the West of England (UWE), UK

Mohammed Odeh, University of the West of England (UWE), UK

Richard McClatchey, University of the West of England (UWE), UK

This chapter studies the differences and similarities between domain ontologies and conceptual data models and the role that ontologies can play in establishing conceptual data models during the process of information systems development. A mapping algorithm has been proposed and embedded in a special purpose Transformation Engine to generate a conceptual data model from a given domain ontology. Both quantitative and qualitative methods have been adopted to critically evaluate this new approach. In addition, this chapter focuses on evaluating the quality of the generated conceptual data model elements using Bunge-Wand-Weber and OntoClean ontologies. The results of this evaluation indicate that the generated conceptual data model provides a high degree of accuracy in identifying the substantial domain entities along with their relationships being derived from the consensual semantics of domain knowledge. The results are encouraging and support the potential role that this approach can take part in the process of information system development.

Chapter XX
Modeling Defects in E-Projects 317
    John D. Ferguson, University of Strathclyde, UK
    James Miller, University of Alberta, Canada

It is now widely accepted that software projects utilizing the Web (e-projects) face many of the same problems and risks experienced with more traditional software projects, only to a greater degree. Further, their characteristics of rapid development cycles combined with high frequency of software releases and adaptations make many of the traditional tools and techniques for modeling defects unsuitable. This chapter proposes a model to explain and quantify the interaction between generic defect injection and removal processes in e-projects. The model is based upon published research and development from the field of quantitative ecological population modeling. This basic modeling approach is then subsequently tailored to fit the software production process within an e-project context.

Chapter XXI
Tool Support for Model-Driven Development of Web Applications 331
    Jaime Gomez, University of Alicante, Spain
    Alejandro Bia, University of Alicante, Spain
    Antonio Parraga, University of Alicante, Spain

This chapter describes the engineering foundations of VisualWADE, a CASE tool to automate the production of Web applications. VisualWADE follows a model-driven approach focusing on requirements analysis, high level design, and rapid prototyping. In this way, an application evolves smoothly from the first prototype to the final product, and its maintenance is a natural consequence of development. The chapter also discusses the lessons learned in the development of the tool and its application to several case studies in the industrial context.

Compilation of References 345

Index 367

Preface

The International Journal of Technology and Web Engineering (JITWE) outlines a critical dimension of Web Engineering (WE) systems and tools supporting knowledge sharing among individuals within organizations and members of virtual organizations. In an effort to facilitate and foster such dimensions and views about Web engineering concepts and practices, we selected related articles published in the first two volumes of JITWE and include them in this book: *Integrated Approaches in Information Technology and Web Engineering Advancing Organizational Knowledge Sharing.*

While we do not claim that these papers address all issues raised in WE research, these two volumes address several of these issues. We categorized all chapters in each of these two independent manuscripts into several sections, each of which outlines information technology and Web engineering research areas. The current volume includes foundational and timely articles addressing advancements in open source, platforms and architectures, and development. The following provides an overview of the contents of each section in this manuscript:

- **Section I—Open Source:** Research group support, open source development projects and environments.
- **Section II—Platforms and Architecture:** Wireless and mobile computing and networks, scheduling in mobile computing and grid systems, distributed Web servers and MANETs, secure DNS updates.
- **Section III—Development:** Software product lines, secure agile development, component based data management, data warehousing, WS discovery systems, defects in e-projects, web site performance, semantic service oriented manufacturing, web application tools.

Section I: Open Source

The July/August 2008 issue of Technology Review published by MIS (technology review, 2008) addressed an important area in open source and the Internet: the concept of social networks which brings people around the world to share and develop open source software and applications.

In another related strategic direction, both Microsoft and IBM are competing in the area of open source by making their corresponding products available for customers. (Microsoft, 2007)

Stimulated by this pervasive trend and other research in this area (Watson, et. al, 2008), this section includes all chapters based upon articles that appeared in a related special issue. Although, these articles could be reclassified, we decided to keep them in a separate section to reflect the research area's importance and its special characteristic to Web engineering. Early chapters expand on the concept of collaboration and social interaction using open source tools for research groups, while later chapters include an analysis of social networks as it applies to open source projects. Contributions in this section also present a method for the analysis and validation of software development process in an open source environment and explain the use of open source in the development and understanding of Web engineering systems and environments.

Section II: Platforms and Architectures

This section contains chapters based upon previous issue articles on platforms and architectures of Web engineering. These areas include wireless networks and mobile computing. Follow on chapters present scheduling algorithms in heterogeneous grid systems. An approach to object grouping and replication on a distributed Web server system is then presented. Chapters then present a Modified Backoff Algorithm for MAC Protocol in MANETs and an architecture and implementation on secure online DNS dynamic updates. Chapters then present FSR evaluation using the suboptimal operational values.

Section III: Development

This section contains chapters related to the development of Web engineering applications. The first chapters cover application development under varied environments and approaches, such as software product lines, component-based knowledge discovery, agile development for secure systems, Web data warehousing, ontology data modeling, Web Service Discovery Systems, and semantic service-oriented manufacturing. Later chapters present a new approach to using growth function for modeling defects in e-projects. This is followed by the presentation of research on Web site performance analysis and the explanation of a tool to support model-driven development of Web applications.

While these sections contain research related to knowledge sharing in organizations, future research should address issues related to integrating information technologies and Web engineering methods, such as agents, Virtual Private Network (VPN), peer-to-peer networks, ontology, semantic web, searching, and indexing, with the objective of building organization learning and memory through knowledge management systems. (Chan and Chao, 2008) (Yueh and Jsu, 2008) The Internet provides a seamless platform for the collection and dissemination of knowledge across organization boundaries linking enterprises, virtual teams, and members of virtual organizations.

REFERENCES

Chan, I., & Chao, C. (2008). Knowledge management in small and medium-sized enterprises. *Communications of the ACM, 51*(4), 83-88.

microsoft.com/presspass/press/ 2008/ feb08/ 02-21ExpandInteroperabilityPR.mspx, and http://www. nytimes.com/2007/ 09/18/technology/18blue.html)

technologyreview.com/magazine, accessed September, 2008.

Watson, R. T, et. al. (2008). The business of open source. *Communications of the ACM, 51*(4), 41-46.

Yueh, H., & Hsu, S. (2008). Designing a learning management system to support instruction. *Communications of the ACM, 51*(4), 59-63.

About the Editors

Ghazi Alkhatib is an assistant professor of software engineering in the College of Computer Science and Information Technology, Applied Science University (Amman, Jordan). In 1984, he obtained his Doctor of Business Administration from Mississippi State University in information systems with minors in computer science and accounting. Since then, he has been engaged in teaching, consulting, training, and research in the area of computer information systems in the U.S. and Gulf countries. In addition to his research interests in databases and systems analysis and design, he has published several articles and presented many papers in regional and international conferences on software processes, knowledge management, e-business, Web services and agent software, workflow, and portal / grid computing integration with Web services.

David Rine is Professor Emeritus, Volgenau School of Information Technology and Engineering, George Mason University Virginia, USA. He has been practicing, teaching and researching engineered software development for over 30 years. Prior to joining George Mason University he served in various leadership roles in the IEEE Computer Society and co-founded two of the technical committees. He joined George Mason University in 1985 and was the founding chair of the Department of Computer Science and one of the founders of the (Volgenau) School of Information Technology and Engineering. Rine has received numerous research, teaching and service awards from computer science and engineering societies and associations, including the IEEE Centennial Award, the IEEE Pioneer Award, the IEEE Computer Society Meritorious Service Awards, the IEEE Computer Society Special Awards, and the IEEE Computer Society 50th anniversary Golden Core Award, the historical IEEE Computer Society Honor Roll and Distinguished Technical Services Awards. He has been a pioneer in graduate, undergraduate and high school education, producing computer science texts and leading establishment of the international Advanced Placement Computer Science program for the nation's high school students, co-designer the first computer science and engineering curriculum (1976) and the first masters in software engineering curriculum (1978). He has been an editor of a number of prestigious software-oriented journals. During his tenure he has authored over 300 published works and has directed many PhD students. Complementing his work at GMU, he has worked on many international technology and relief projects in various countries and made many life-long international friendships. His past students are the most important record of his technical achievements.

Section I
Platforms and Architectures

Chapter I
Integration of Libre Software Applications to Create a Collaborative Work Platform for Researchers at GET

Olivier Berger
GET/INT, France

Christian Bac
GET/INT, France

Benoît Hamet
GET/INT, France

ABSTRACT

Libre software provides powerful applications ready to be integrated for the build-up of platforms for internal use in organizations. We describe the architecture of the collaborative work platform which we have integrated, designed for researchers at GET. We present the elements we have learned during this project in particular with respect to contribution to external libre projects, in order to better ensure the maintainability of the internal applications, and to phpGroupware as a framework for specific applications development.

INTRODUCTION

ProGET is a collaborative work platform, built out of a set of specialised libre software applications integrated together. ProGET is designed for the whole of teachers/researchers at GET. It provides every GET research project with the best features found in each application (wiki, mailing-lists management, shared WebDAV folders, Web portal, etc.).

We start with a description of the libre components that have been integrated and of the features that have been selected, as well as elements of architecture of the developed platform. We will then introduce the strategy for collaboration that we have devised for our contribution to phpGroupware. We finish with a first evaluation at the end of the initial development phase.

RESEARCH AT GET

The *Groupe des Écoles des Télécommunications*[1] (GET) is composed of several engineering and business schools together with research centers in Paris (ENST), Brest (ENST Bretagne), and Évry (INT), in France. The research teams are made up of more than 600 full-time research equivalents. The range of the researchers' expertise is from technologies to social sciences, and enables an integrated approach of characteristic of GET research and fosters its adaptability to new application sectors and new usages in response to current challenges in the fields of information and communication.

To give a clearer view of research at GET, the Research Office started to catalogue the activities from the different locations so that the research may be described in terms of research *projects* and *programmes*. A project is made-up of a group of people working together on closely related subjects. For example the authors belong to the "Collaborative Platforms for Research" (PFTCR) project. A programme associates different projects loosely related. For example our project is related to the "Web and Information Society" programme. Due to the fact that GET teams are located in different areas, the research office also decided to propose a Web platform to help researchers collaborate through groupware tools and animate their research work.

PROGET INTEGRATED PLATFORM FOR COLLABORATIVE WORK

ProGet has been launched in July 2003 with the following goals:

1. Provide all research teams in GET and their external partners (more than 1,250 users) with cutting-edge technologies in terms of Web based groupware tools
2. Allow the Research Office to manage the *administrative* records describing research projects
3. Generate a public *Web portal* based on information extracted from both previous components.[2] The home page of the Web portal is shown Figure 1.[3]

Groupware Tools for Researchers/ Teachers

The following features have been selected as corresponding to the basic needs for collaborative work in the context of research activities at GET:

Document sharing: People in the same project must have a way to share the documents they produce, whatever the type of document.

Asynchronous communication: Each project manages predefined *mailing lists* and may also create mailing lists as it needs.

Online editing: People in the same project group are allowed to write easily and collaborate on simple hypertext pages using their Web browsers, to create a collaborative Web, in a wiki-type tool.

Publishing short announcements: The project manager can write short news items about the project, and have the project news published online on the public Web portal very easily.

Figure 1. Homepage of the GET public research portal

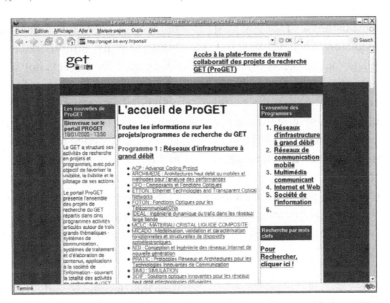

The platform must provide secure access, from any point on the Internet, to a set of tools. These tools will have to be accessible through a Web interface, to allow people to use them without the need to install any specific application on the computer from which they are connected.

Some features must also be accessible through non-Web client tools, in the Microsoft Windows™, or GNU/Linux environments. For instance, as explained in the section entitled, Project Documents Repository Accessible through WebDAV, access to the DAV repositories through DAV-compatible file managers. Information generated in this collaborative part of the platform may be made accessible to the public portal directly by the research teams, without further interaction with a Webmaster.

Tools for the Research Office

The Research Office is supervising the setup and evolution in time of the research projects and programs. In ProGET, it uses, for this purpose, a dedicated tool, which helps managing the life cycle of the *project description forms*.

This module does not provide a replacement for the research information system under development at the present time at GET. It only allows the management of information on the projects which are necessary for the other parts of the platform. It handles the initial list of persons participating in projects teams, people who are project managers, the projects' descriptions, and their yearly goals.

The project description forms are initially filled by the researchers who will be responsible for the projects. They are then validated by the research offices. This validation allows the creation of the collaboration projects in the platform. Those forms are also used to feed the contents of the research public Web portal.

Public Web Portal

The platform publishes a public Web portal which reflects the state of research activity at GET. This portal describes essential information relating to the research programmes and projects at GET. Figure 1 shows the home page of the portal.

This public Web site corresponds to a dynamic extraction of the contents of the project description forms stored in the database. That is why it will be updated immediately whenever the GET Research Office validates new projects creation, or updates the contents of existing forms.

Since the data extraction is dynamic, this portal Web site can be duplicated in several flavors according to the origin of the visit. So when the Web site is browsed from inside the GET intranet, it will provide more detailed information, including some facts about the research projects which are considered to be published to a restricted audience only (teams composition, detailed yearly goals of the projects, etc.).

PREVIOUS WORK WITH LIBRE SOFTWARE COLLABORATION TOOLS

As described by Cousin, Ouvradou, Pucci, and Tardieu (2001), we and other GET researchers and students contributed in the development of a collaborative platform called *PicoLibre*. This platform is targeted at collaborative software development, to help students in computer science curricula and researchers to develop and host their software projects. It provides the necessary collaboration tools (mailing lists, CVS repository, issue trackers, etc.) in a similar way to SourceForge. Another goal of the PicoLibre project was to foster the publication of projects as libre software, since it would be a way to introduce the users to the practice of the common tools used everyday by libre software developers.

This platform was created as a free software tool (published under the GNU GPL license[4]), using free software components and adapting them for PicoLibre. Several PicoLibre instances are in operation since Fall 2001 in GET sites and outside.

In some aspects, PicoLibre is a very successful project, since it allows GET to host a large number of software projects with a minimum burden for its administrators. It is also sometimes used for projects not specifically targeted at software development, for teams that need a collaboration space and associated *groupware* tools. The PicoLibre project has helped us attain a better knowledge of the specifics of the design and development, but also the administration, of a collaborative Web-based platform in the context of a higher education institution.

But PicoLibre also failed to certain extents, especially with respect to its maintainability, and in its capacity to be integrated into a libre software distribution. The project was done in such short time that developers only concentrated on the innovative parts and spent too few efforts in keeping the software they developed in the mainstream of the libre projects it was based on (in particular with respect to phpGroupware [phpgw]).

Although having been used intensively by teams of researchers or students investigating software development, PicoLibre was not well suited for generic needs of teams of nonsoftware developers. For example, the CVS[5] revision management repository is a central tool in PicoLibre. It is very useful for software development, but does not fit well for casual researchers' use. For example, although it is possible with CVS to manage the revisions of a document written with an office suite, it is not very convenient, since it requires installation of a specific CVS client program. Most nonsoftware developers (e.g., researchers in the field of finance or business administration) are thus not comfortable in using such a tool.

To build on top of our previous developments, and considering the aforementioned perspective, we proposed to start and build the ProGet platform using some of the free software modules that had been used to create PicoLibre, and to combine these modules with other existing libre software projects to fulfil new capabilities. We intended also to do our developments and the integration of the numerous applications necessary in a much more maintainable way.

STRUCTURE OF THE PLATFORM

The ProGET platform is composed of several specialised software applications, installed together on a dedicated machine running the GNU/Linux operating system (Debian). This article does not describe all of the components of the system, but only the modules which provide the highest level features, and the way they have been integrated into a single platform.

The development team has been participating for a long time in communities of research and practice in libre software: development of PicoLibre (see previous work with libre software collaboration tools), organisation of the *Autour du Libre* conference, participation in the *CALIBRE* FP6 European project,[6] and so forth. We have then naturally preferred to use exclusively libre software for the development of the platform, in order to ensure the complete control of all technical aspects, and the conformance to open standards.

Integration Principles

To deliver the required features, we have integrated different existing libre software applications that we will list in the section entitled, Integrated Libre Software High-level Applications. Most of these applications rely on the Apache Web server, in particular for the PHP execution engine.

Each one of the products, taken apart, was often not covering all required features. So instead of trying to add to one of these applications the missing features, we have preferred to integrate several rather specialised applications. We are therefore

able to take advantage of the best aspects of each, even if there is a risk of partial redundancy. For instance, phpGroupware provides a wiki module, but a rather limited one. We have preferred to plug phpGroupware and TWiki, an advanced wiki engine, instead of engaging in a tougher effort of enhancement of phpGroupware.

In each integrated libre software application, we have been careful to allow the possibility of a logical *partition* of the data stored in the application, to ensure that the research projects can be kept autonomous and enhance privacy (see data partition).

To make sure users will not have to deal with a set of authentication tokens (login + password), the authentication will be done in the same way in all the modules, although they may be operated by separate applications. This is done in a classical way, by relying on interaction with a dedicated directory implemented by OpenLDAP. Some components also share a database stored in a dedicated MySQL server.

Integration of the applications for the realisation of ProGET was done in a rather traditional way, by sharing the lowest layers (OpenLDAP, MySQL) and with adapters (code: *glue*), when the applications themselves were rather monolithic. It would have been preferable to take advantage of libre applications organised in a more modular way and supporting a Web service paradigm. But very few mature versions of libre software which may have been integrated offered such interoperability mechanisms at the start of our project. Even today, this kind of interface is not always entirely present, even if this approach seems to be preferred now for the future versions of projects like phpGroupware or Sympa, for instance.

Integrated Libre Software High-Level Applications

The main libre software applications that have been integrated in the ProGET platform are:

- **The Apache Web server.** The server provides the link between the client tools (browsers) and the Web applications.
- **A WebDAV repository.** The `mod_dav7`Apache module implements the shared Web folders which implement the documents repositories for the projects (see Project Documents Repository Accessible Through WebDAV).
- **The phpGroupware engine and applications.** PhpGroupware provides the Web interface of the "virtual desktop" of the collaborative workspace (see Researchers/teachers Virtual Desktop in phpGroupware), and brings in standard groupware components. It also serves as the basis for the software infrastructure of the public portal. In addition to standard phpGroupware modules, we have added two new modules developed for the needs of GET. One module which extracts information out of the collaborative work applications to deliver the public portal (see Public Web Portal) and a module which enables the administrative management for the Research Office (see Tools for the Research Office).
- **The Sympa mailing list manager (Sympa).** This powerful mailing-list manager provides some asynchronous communication means inside and outside of the projects.
- **The TWiki wiki server (Wiki).** This wiki system, among the most advanced, provides a whiteboard-like interface to implement the "knowledge base" of the projects.
- **The Agata Reports reporting tool.**[8] It helps the Research Office to issue queries on the projects description forms in order to answer internal or external requests about research activity at GET.

We hereafter describe some of the characteristics of the ProGET modules and the obtained features.

Researchers/Teachers Virtual Desktop in phpGroupware

Each researcher who connects to the platform gets access to the user's own "virtual desktop," provided through phpGroupware. Figure 2 shows this start page for a researcher who belongs to two research projects (here LICIP and PFTCR).

The user will then be provided directly, for each project the user belongs to, with a set of collaboration tools (with the corresponding links in the central column of Figure 2):

- Direct access to browsing of the contents of the documents repository of the project (see Project Documents Repository Accessible Through WebDAV);
- Web-based file manager (Web interface for the management of the contents of this repository);
- Mailing lists (access to the Web interface of Sympa for the lists of the project);
- News (management of the project's news displayed in the public portal);
- Project's wiki (see Project's Wiki);
- Project's specific Web pages (see Project Dedicated Web Sites);
- Access to the project's description page in the GET research portal (see Project Dedicated Web Sites;
- Shared address book and calendar (standard phpGroupware tool);
- Printable project form (including restricted access information).

Some of these tools are described in more detail hereafter.

Project Documents Repository Accessible Through WebDAV

As described in Dridi and Neuman (1999), WebDAV suits well to create a groupware portal that helps people share their documents. In ProGet each project is provided, for its internal use, with a unique secured documents repository, in the form of a specific Web folder. It is shared among members of the project team. It can be accessed via HTTPS for browsing or through

WebDAV (Goland, Whitehead, Faizi, & Jensen, 1999) (over HTTPS) for modification of contents of the repository. Figure 3 shows the contents of a repository through HTTPS in a Web browser (here, the `public _ html` subfolder in project PFTCR's folder).

Figure 2. ProGET Collaborative workspace start page

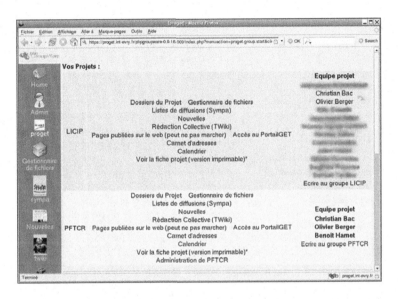

Figure 3. Contents of a project's DAV folder (Web folder)

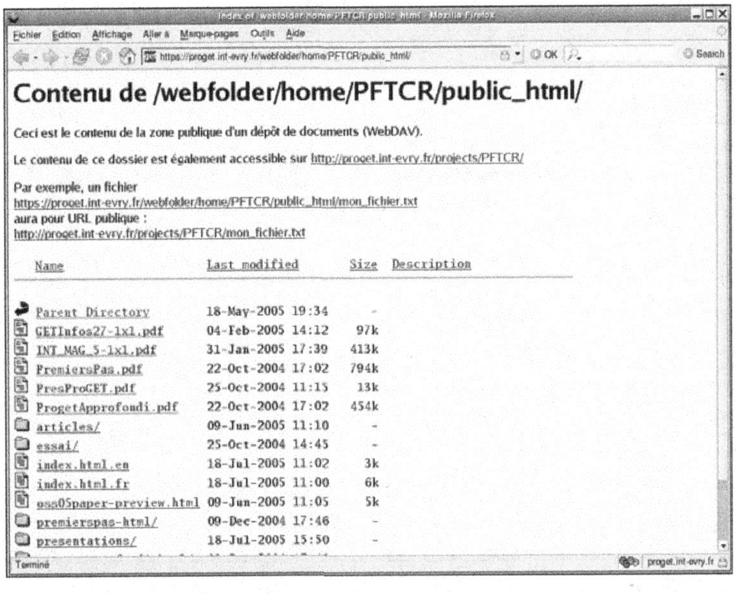

The use of the WebDAV protocol enables transparent access in browsing or modification in the office applications, allowing for instance drag-and-drop in file managers for uploading. The uploading is thus extremely simplified[9] compared to the use of protocols like FTP or CVS.

Figure 4. Contents of a project's DAV folder in KDE

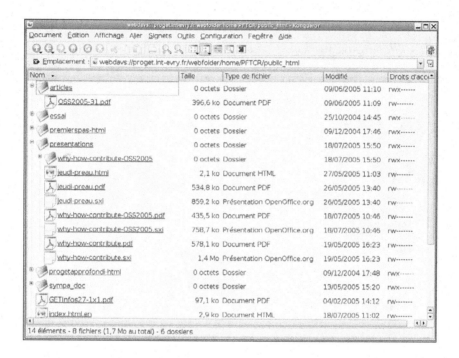

Figure 5. Most recent changes in a project's wiki

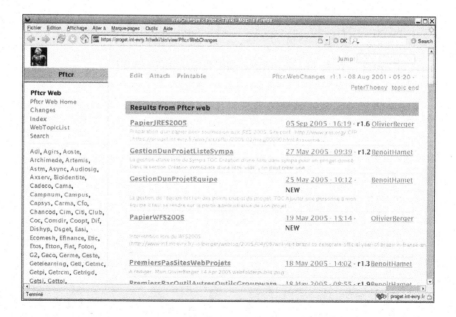

DAV compatible clients exist on all platforms, for instance, under KDE (see Figure 4) or on Windows XP.

A simple file manager is also available as a Web application in the phpGroupware collaborative work environment of the project, for cases where the nomad users will not have the possibility to access the repository with DAV clients.

A specific subsection of each project's documents repository, corresponding to the **public_html** subdirectory, may contain the public Web site specific to the project (see Project Dedicated Web Sites). This subtree can then host a set of public pages very easily maintained, in addition to the stereotyped information displayed in the project's form on the portal. Figure 3 shows the contents via DAV of this subdirectory, which is displayed, in this case, as the contents of a folder, a list of documents, instead of as a set of Web pages (pages would be displayed as in Figure 6).

Project's Wiki

Each project is provided, internally, with a *wiki*[10] which can be used to share, in an authenticated way, in the form of Web pages, a set of simple hypertext documents, not necessarily very structured up front.

This wiki can serve many uses. Each project may for example use it as a hypertext repository to set up a knowledge base, which will hold all elements of the project's life, its productions, and ongoing works. The wiki enables the progressive elaboration of information, in a way less structured and more open than by using the project's documents repository.

Of course, the TWiki wiki engine provides all classical features of these tools (most recent modifications list, notifications, search tool, backlinks, etc.) allowing users to better apprehend the mass of hypertextual information such a tool can host. Figure 5 shows an example of a list of most recent changes in a project's wiki.

A portion of the wiki can be used to put online hypertextual contents in the project's public Web site, in an automated way (see Project Dedicated Web Sites). To this end, the wiki pages must have been identified individually as *public*. This feature may be used for instance to prepublish on the Web some of the information being elaborated inside the project, which has not yet achieved a sufficiently finalised or structured form required for publication of the documents available on the project's Web site. This is a way to offer some means of transparency on the research works, by allowing the public to directly view the "lab notepads" of the projects.

Project Dedicated Web Sites

On the same platform, each research project benefits from several dedicated publication spaces, for its external communication on the Web.

Stereotyped Page in the Public Portal

This page describes briefly the research activity and the team. It represents a stereotyped description of a project which has been validated by the Research Office. In addition, the page contains a dedicated news zone for the project which is updated directly by each project manager. This zone helps spreading news about the life of the project. To this end, an RSS[11] feed comes alongside each project's news pages.

Project stereotyped pages are created in the research portal through a phpGroupware module named **sitemgr**. This module is configured specifically and relies on information extracted from the administrative database of project forms.

Specific Web Space

This Web site is made of static HTML pages. The content of this space is managed directly by each project, at will. It may be produced with the HTML editing software of its choice. The upload is made directly by members of the project via publications in the public_html12 subdirectory of the project's WebDAV folder (see Project Documents Repository Accessible Through WebDAV).

No specific competence is required in the teams to be able to contribute to the project's Web site. Figure 6 shows an example of such a Web page. The URL to access this Web space is stereotyped from the project's acronym: http://proget.int-evry.fr/projects/PROJECT_NAME/

Wiki Excerpts Publication Space

This space complements the previous spaces by allowing the direct publication of excerpts (pages declared *public*) of the resources elaborated by the project inside its internal wiki (see Project's Wiki). This may help with prepublishing, issuing short reference papers, providing a knowledge base, and so forth.

GET Research Projects Administrative Management Module

Whereas other modules of the platform existed previously as generic libre software tools fulfilling the classical needs of every organisation, this project administrative management module has been developed specifically for the needs of the GET Research Office. This module implements the workflow of the contents of research projects forms, during the life cycle of GET research projects (creation, approval, yearly updates, etc.). It was developed in PHP on top of the phpGroupware API, by using the **templates** component, which allows the creation of input masks and screens for the update of the data stored in the underlying MySQL database.

It also uses a set of query and report templates built with *Agata Reports*, a tool for creation of database queries without programming skills, in Web mode. An expert of the domain, who knows the database schema, can then improve the set

of queries initially integrated in ProGET, for instance, to produce complex reports in the form of spreadsheet files or even synthetic booklets in the form of word-processor or PDF files.

Data Partition

Inside the same collaborative work platform, each research project must be able to host its own information and documents, which may be confidential. Thus, a partition of the whole data handled by ProGET was set up, relative to the project groups. This applies in particular to the documents stored in the document repositories (including its dedicated Web site), the messages on the mailing lists in Sympa, the information from the projects description forms in restricted access, and some of the information in the php-Groupware tools.

In a classical way, the OpenLDAP directory is used to allow the authentication of the user's work sessions with a unique password for the different tools integrated in the same platform. The directory is also used as a reference for the description of project teams and their access authorisation for the data handled by the different applications. The system relies on persons and groups defined in a single place, in the LDAP directory. The information are managed through the users and groups management modules in phpGroupware.

A list of persons responsible for the project and a list of participants are associated to each research project. Members of the first group have the right to modify the list of members of the second group via the Web interface in phpGroupware, and to add new co-opted members in their group of responsible persons. The management of the teams for the collaborative work is then done directly in the projects, in an autonomous way, for a better reactivity.

In each of the applications integrated in the platform, access to the data relating to the research projects is controlled by checking if one belongs to

Figure 6. Dedicated project's Web site for project PFTCR

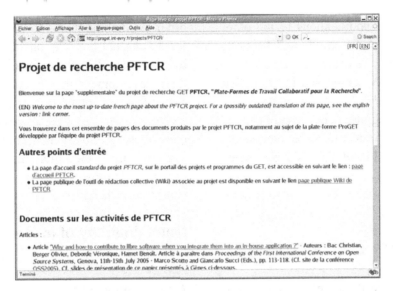

these groups. For instance, Sympa is configured to query OpenLDAP directly, which helps defining automatic subscription of members of a project group to a mailing list. That way, each research project receives automatically a discussion list whenever it is created. The record of discussions on this list is only accessible to its subscribers, the members of this research project.

For the phpGroupware tools (calendar, address book, news, etc.), the partition of the data is implemented on the basis of stereotyped php-Groupware *categories*. So each project group defined in the underlying OpenLDAP directory receives a corresponding phpGroupware category automatically, which is then used as an umbrella for classifying the information.

In TWiki, this principle is implemented through standard mechanisms which are devised to host several autonomous wikis on the same site (known as *Webs* in TWiki). All the pages of a project are contained in a TWiki Web, that is a dedicated autonomous wiki. The creation of this space is done at the time a group of users is created, and corresponding privileges are granted to this group (allowed to modify pages, to add new members to the group, etc.). Unlike the other

applications integrated in ProGET, it was not possible to let TWiki (at least the standard version we used) interface directly with the LDAP directory for the definition of groups of persons. An adapter module has been developed, to synchronise the groups defined in TWiki with the contents of the research project teams.

Modification and Customisation Efforts

Most of our software development effort has been targeted on:

- **phpGroupware custom components** for administrative management of research projects (see Tools for the Research Office) and Web portal (see Public Web Portal). These developments were very specific to the needs of GET, and should not be released.
- **phpGroupware low-level components.** We have in particular improved the interaction mechanisms between phpGroupware and OpenLDAP, and the code used to access WebDAV. These developments do not specifically fit only our own needs, and improve

in a sensible way the standard phpGroupware platform.

- **Bug fixes** and modifications to the other components. Many small modifications and bug fixes were necessary in particular on the WebDAV server, and in the LDAP server interface of Apache, or on the *TWiki* and *Sympa* programs. These modifications make it easier to integrate these components on top of OpenLDAP. These developments were contributed to the community in the form of patches when they were of general interest.

STRATEGY FOR CONTRIBUTION

This section deals with some methodological aspects of the development project of the ProGET platform. Our project is more an in-house project than an Open Source project and thus case studies like Mockus, Fielding, and Herbsleb (2002), do not always apply to it. Despite the fact that the project was not open to outsiders, it relies profoundly on libre software and we felt the need to set up a strategy for contributing to libre projects. The strategy was adopted in order to establish the conditions of a greater maintainability of the developed system and a clean integration of our patches and improvements to the original projects. These aspects have been described in more detail by the authors in a previous article; see Bac, Berger, Deborde, and Hamet (2005).

Benefits of Libre Software for Their Integration in In-House Applications

Libre software offer today an opportunity to lower the duration and cost of software projects. They also help to raise the quality of the applications (Bauer & Pizka, 2003). The software components are numerous and available for integration or adaptation in order to create applications that fit the needs of organisations (Wheeler, 2005). The development of the initial version of an in-house application can be done quickly, even in a "brutal" way, by modifying components in order to combine them. To be able to use them for its internal projects, one may not be forced to participate directly, or in an indirect way, to their development in the libre communities.[13] These tasks of integration can then be done in a classical way, as if the components had been completely developed internally, without trying to contribute to the initial "upstream" projects. But it is also possible, and even advisable, to contribute, whenever it is possible.

Maintainability of In-House Specific Developments

After the initial integration phase comes the issue of the midterm evolution of the obtained product. This issue becomes crucial when it becomes necessary to react to recurring external evolutions of the integrated components (for instance in case of a published fix for a security problem). We profess, out of the experience gained during this project, that it is necessary to define a policy for contributions on the most important integrated components.

This active contribution brings the possibility of transferring the evolutions that were required by the internal developments into the libre modules that were used. Once they have been adopted by the external projects, they will become part of all future releases of these components, which will remove the need to keep on applying internally some specific patches each time a new update is issued for the original module. In this respect, some amount of the maintenance effort for the internal solution is "outsourced" to the libre community, which helps lower the internal costs.

Strategy Adopted

To make some adaptation on phpGroupware components, we have not limited ourselves to only modifying internally this software (as it had been done before for PicoLibre), but on the contrary, we have decided to collaborate actively with the phpGroupware project. This led us to undertaking the process for the official application of a member of our team to the phpGroupware project, and the transfer of the copyright on our developments to the FSF which holds the rights for phpGroupware.

Again, our goal, by doing so, is to have our modifications integrated in the standard code base of phpGroupware, so that they will be part of future releases of the software, and we may not have to apply again and again the same changes whenever a new version of phpGroupware is released. This way, we intend to lower the cost for the future maintenance of ProGET.

FIRST OUTCOMES AND PROSPECTS

Even if integration of existing applications requires extensive adaptation (Adams, Boldtreff, Nutter, & Rank, 2005), the effort is far lower than what would have been necessary for a project entirely developed internally. The vast range of features that we thought necessary for our platform was only achievable at a reasonable cost by taking advantage of existing libre software. This platform brings generic tools for nonprogrammer researchers but also features appealing to the most demanding researchers, like DAV repositories or a wiki.

The ProGET platform is in production now and opened for its users since June 2005. The GET research portal and the projects administrative management application are already used on a day to day basis. It is however too early to proceed to an assessment of the use of collaborative work tools, which are still used regularly by only a few research projects.

The use of the collaborative work environment is at the present time proposed for volunteers. Its roll-out to the whole GET research teams is not yet envisioned, some uncertainties remaining on the general infrastructure to be set up, for instance, for the necessary training phase of the users, or the financial costs to ensure the maintenance of the production platform with maximum availability. Some findings can still be learned from the return on experience of the first users.

Conformance to Requirements

The tools which have been integrated offer a far range of features, which address most of the generic needs of the research teams at GET. The TWiki tool, quite versatile, provides in particular a great potential, although it requires some amount of training. Some shortcomings have however appeared during the first months of usage of the platform.

ProGET was devised by focusing on an organisation structured around the notion of research project with a clearly defined perimeter, validated by the GET Research Office. However, needs for collaborative work tools also come from contexts outside the precise boundaries of already validated research projects. Thus, during upstream exploratory phases leading to the creation of projects, for instance, some collaboration is often necessary between members of teams which have already been established independently, and who often work part-time on these exploratory activities. Several users have requested that the kind of tools available in ProGET be offered also for these upstream phases, where they could greatly facilitate participation, reactivity, and communication between various actors. It then seems necessary to be able to handle also collaborative work groups linked to exploratory phases, outside the rigid frame of validated research projects already approved for the GET research portal.

It was also identified, through the first steps of take-up of the tools by research teams, that the principle of partition of data that was implemented, based on a lowest granularity corresponding to the research projects, was not fitting that well.

Inside a GET research project, teams have to work for different research contracts, which all have their own list of partners, and their own privacy requirements. The granularity chosen for teams which have to access the same set of documents and information in the project is thus not well adapted in the current version of the platform. It seems necessary to be able to define, for collaborative work, some subprojects more or less autonomous in the realm of the same research project, which will each define a specific list of participants and associated access privileges.

Evolution Towards Other Collaborative Activities

The users of the platform are also participating, besides their research activities, in teaching activities, and numerous other work groups, for which Web-based collaborative work tools may not always be available, either at GET or at its partners.'

There is thus a need for the availability of one or more platforms supporting collaborative work, which would be as feature-full as the Pro-GET platform, but which may allow the easy and quick creation of projects and their work groups, progressively, in a loose environment, as was the case with the PicoLibre platforms.

Need for such a platform could lead to the creation of a "new generation" PicoLibre system, which could integrate the whole set of generic components that have been integrated in ProGET, together with a generic module for creation of collaborative work spaces, and which could be more maintainable than the previous generation.

The ProGET platform could then be split in two parts: on the one hand a module for the administrative management of GET research projects and a GET research Web portal, and on the other hand the use of a "PicoLibre V2" kind of platform, in which the groups corresponding to the GET research projects could be hosted, among others.

Constraints for Administration

The ProGET platform was devised in an effort for reuse and modularisation in integrating the existing libre components, in order to lower the maintenance efforts to be made internally (see Strategy for Contribution). However, the installation and maintenance tasks for such a platform are quite demanding and require specific competence (good knowledge of the internals of the various integrated software), which imply a necessary precise planning in the event of the outsourcing of its administration to the regular IT department which is in charge of the GET information systems.

In this respect, one first hypothesis for improvement would be the availability of the whole set of components in a standard packaging. It would be interesting to have all the components used, and their new adapters, available in the form of packages for the libre software distributions already known by the support teams. For instance, in the Debian distribution, the phpGroupware, Sympa, and TWiki tools are already packaged in the ordinary way. It would be interesting if all modules that have been developed for ProGET were packaged too. This could be achieved by taking advantage of the recent efforts made to package the modules of the PicoLibre application for Debian.

PhpGroupware for the Development of Custom Applications

Several findings can be stated, looking at the use of phpGroupware as the basis for the development of custom applications. PhpGroupware brings a large choice of components which have not all achieved a common level of quality. Some functions suffered from numerous bugs preventing them to be put into production as such, in particular regarding the conditions required for ProGET, for instance if using underlying OpenLDAP and WebDAV layers.

In addition, the structure of data in phpGroupware is in general organised from the perspective of one phpGroupware instance deployed in an organisation where, by default, the whole of the information handled by the system will be available to all the users. This may fit, for instance, to SMEs or very small virtual organisations where all actors have to be informed of everything happening in the organisation. This model happened however to be poorly convenient in our case which requires that projects hosted on the same phpGroupware platform be kept separate, and that a strong level of confidentiality be preserved on the information (see Data Partition).The use of phpGroupware categories partially helps to solve this kind of constraint, but by paying the price of some usage precautions which degrade the global usability of the application.

PhpGroupware provides an interesting API for the PHP developer, for Web based collaborative work applications that will be relatively simple. It happens to be somehow limited though, for advanced needs for the development of complex applications, in particular concerning the ACLs, the corresponding data model, and the independence of the lowest level modules. PhpGroupware lacks also of a module providing applicative workflow facilities.

The use of the *template* "RAD tool" integrated in phpGroupware turns out a poor choice in the case of a complex application, despite its ease of use for relatively simple needs. Indeed, its associate documentation and tutorial only scarcely refer to the *MVC* model which is however generalised in the more complex modules of phpGroupware. In the latest modules developed for ProGET, we thus have preferred to use these more classic MVC *patterns* and rely more on the HTML templating system, that happen to be more maintainable. This choice was made with a midterm vision, as the learning curve for developers is bigger in this case.

PhpGroupware is still an interesting project for a rather simple use of its existing modules. And although it provides rich and quite generic APIs, which allow the development of new applications, it cannot constitute a really generic application development *framework* like other libre environments (Zope, Apache Tomcat, etc.).

CONCLUSION

Although it may be enhanced on numerous aspects, the ProGET platform delivers a range of features without competition in existing libre software collaborative work platforms, for a modest development cost.

There are strong needs in higher-grade research and teaching institutions for tools supporting collaborative work. ProGET can then constitute a reference point for organisations wishing to integrate, for their custom needs, existing libre software applications for collaborative work.

Even if a policy is adopted for the contribution to the libre software projects used, in order to lower certain maintenance costs, the generalisation of the use of the present platform at GET and the future developments necessary to enhance it will only be possible through a substantial investment, which may be far more important than what was spent for the first initial developments.

One possibility for the reduction of these costs could be the mutualisation of the development between several organisations. It could be articulated around the industrialisation as well-packaged libre software programs of the most generic elements of ProGET, leading the way to a new generation PicoLibre platform.

REFERENCES

Adams, P., Boldyreff, C., Nutter, D., & Rank, S. (2005, May 17). *Adaptive reuse of libre software systems for supporting on-line collaboration*. In *Proceedings of the 5th Workshop on Open Source Software Engineering*, St. Louis, Missouri.

Bac, C., Berger, O., Deborde, V., & Hamet, B. (2005, July 11-15). *Why and how to contribute to libre software when you integrate them into an in-house application? In Proceedings of the First International Conference on Open Source Systems*, Genova.

Bauer, A., & Pizka, M. (2003). The contribution of free software to software evolution. In *Proceedings of the International Workshop on Principles of Software Evolution (IWPSE)*.

Cousin, E., Ouvradou, G., Pucci, P., & Tardieu, S. (2002). *PicoLibre: A free collaborative platform to improve students' skills in software engineering.* In *Proceedings of the IEEE International Conference on Systems, Man and Cybernetics.*

Dridi, F., & Neumann, G. (1999, June). How to implement Web-based groupware systems based on WebDAV. In *Proceedings of the IEEE 8th International Workshops on Enabling Technologies: Infrastructure for Collaborative Enterprises.*

Mockus, A., Fielding, R.T., & Herbsleb, J.D. (2002). Two case studies of open source software development: Apache and Mozilla. *ACM Transactions on Software Engineering Methodology, 11*(3), 309-346.

Goland, Y., Whitehead, E., Faizi, A., & Jensen, D. (1999). HTTP extensions for distributed authoring. In *Proceedings of WEBDAV*. Retrieved June 16, 2006, from http://Webdav.org/

Wheeler, D.A. (2005). Why open source software/free software (OSS/FS, FLOSS, or FOSS)? Look at the numbers! Retrieved June 16, 2006, from http://www.dwheeler.com/oss_fs_why.html

ADDITIONAL RESOURCES

Web site of the OpenLDAP project: http://www.openldap.org/

Web site for the phpGroupware project: http://www.phpgroupware.org/

Web site for project PicoLibre: http://www.pico-libre.org/

SourceForge project hosting platform: http://sourceforge.net/

Sympa project's Web site: http://www.sympa.org/

TWiki project's Web site: http://twiki.org/

"Wiki" article in the Wikipedia encyclopedia: http://fr.wikipedia.org/wiki/Wiki

ENDNOTES

[1] http://www.get-telecom.fr/
[2] The GET research portal can be accessed at http://proget.int-evry.fr/.
[3] The screenshots of the application provided in figures of this chapter display pages in French. Not all interface elements have been provided with a translation to English yet in the ProGET application.
[4] GNU General Public licence: http://www.gnu.org/copyleft/gpl.html
[5] Concurrent Versions System: http://www.nongnu.org/cvs/
[6] FP6 IST Project 00433 "Coordination Action for Libre Software": http://www.calibre.ie/
[7] DAV module for Apache: http://www.Web Webdav.org/mod_dav/
[8] http://agata.org.br/
[9] The counterpart of this simplification, compared to CVS in particular, is that the repository does not support documents versioning on its own. This could be enhanced in a future version of ProGET by using *Subversion* (http://subversion.tigris.org/) instead of the mod_dav module used today, which would bring the platform closer to what exists in the recent Trac software development platform (http://projects.edgewall.com/trac/), which combines a Wiki and Subversion.
[10] The authors assume that the reader is already familiar with this kind of tool which has

become very popular in the latest years
For more details, refer to (wiki) and to the
Wikipedia project which hosts it, for a good
example of application of wikis.

11 Really Simple Syndication: http://blogs.law.
harvard.edu/tech/rssVersionHistory

12 The name "public_html" is a convention
adopted after Web server Apache's naming
policy.

13 Note that contrary to some rumors, it is in
no way mandatory to publish the modifications that one has made on a libre software
program, as long as this software is not
distributed to third parties, even if it was
initially published under the GNU GPL.

Chapter II
FLOSSmole:
A Collaborative Repository for FLOSS Research Data and Analyses

James Howison
Syracuse University , USA

Megan Conklin
Elon University, USA

Kevin Crowston
Syracuse University , USA

ABSTRACT

This paper introduces and expands on previous work on a collaborative project, called FLOSSmole (formerly OSSmole), designed to gather, share and store comparable data and analyses of free, libre, and open source software (FLOSS) development for academic research. The project draws on the on-going collection and analysis efforts of many research groups, reducing duplication, and promoting compatibility both across sources of FLOSS data and across research groups and analyses. The paper outlines current difficulties with the current typical quantitative FLOSS research process and uses these to develop requirements and presents the design of the system.

INTRODUCTION

This article introduces a collaborative project called FLOSSmole,[1] designed to gather, share, and store comparable data and analyses of free and open source software development for academic research. The project draws on the ongoing collection and analysis efforts of many research groups. Our intent in developing FLOSSmole is to reduce duplication, and to promote compatibility both across sources of FLOSS data and across research groups and analyses.

Creating a collaborative data and analysis repository for research on FLOSS is important because research should be as reproducible, extendable, and comparable as possible. Research with these characteristics creates the opportunity to employ meta-analyses, exploiting the diversity of existing research by comparing and contrasting results to expand our knowledge. Unfortunately, the current typical FLOSS research project proceeds in a way that does not necessarily achieve these goals. These goals require detailed communal knowledge of the many choices made throughout a research project. Traditional publication prioritizes results, but masks or discards much of the information needed to understand and exploit the differences in our data collection and analysis methodologies. FLOSSmole was originally designed to provide resources and support to academics seeking to prepare the next generation of FLOSS research. Since its inception, FLOSSmole has also been a valuable resource for nonacademics who are also seeking good data about development practices in the open source software industry.

BACKGROUND OF PROBLEM

Obtaining data on FLOSS projects is both easy and difficult. It is easy because FLOSS development utilizes computer-mediated communications heavily for both development team interactions and for storing artifacts such as code and documentation. This way of developing software leaves a freely available and, in theory at least, highly accessible trail of data upon which many academics have built interesting analyses about optimal organization of development teams, economics of building software in the commons, and the like. Yet, despite this presumed plethora of data, researchers often face significant practical challenges in using this data to construct a col-

laborative and deliberative research discourse. In Figure 1, we outline the research process we believe is followed in much of the quantitative literature on FLOSS.

The first step in collecting online FLOSS data is selecting which projects and which attributes to study, two techniques often used in estimation and selection are census and sampling. (Case studies are also used but these will not be discussed in this article.)

Conducting a census means to examine all cases of a phenomena, taking the measures of interest to build up an entire accurate picture. Taking a census is difficult in FLOSS for a number of reasons. First, it is hard to know how many FLOSS projects there are "out there," and it is hard to know which projects should actually be included. For example, are corporate-sponsored projects part of the phenomenon or not? Do single-person projects count? What about school projects?

Second, the projects themselves, and the records they leave, are scattered across a surprisingly large number of locations. It is true that many are located in the major general repositories, such as Sourceforge[2] and GNU Savannah.[3] It is also true, however, that there are a number of other repositories of varying sizes and focuses (e.g., CodeHaus,[4] CPAN[5]), and that many projects, including the well-known and much-studied Apache and Linux projects, prefer to use their own repositories and their own tools. This diversity of location effectively hides significant portions of the FLOSS world from attempts at census. Even if a full listing of projects and their locations could be collated, there is also the practical difficulty of dealing with the huge amount of data — sometimes years and years of e-mails, CVS, and bug tracker conversations — required to conduct certain comprehensive analyses.

Do the difficulties with census-taking mean that sampling would be more effective? By saying sampling we mean taking a random selection of a small (and thus more manageable) subgroup of projects that can, through careful selection, represent the group as a whole. While this will go some way toward solving the manageability problem, sampling FLOSS projects is difficult for the same reason as census-taking: the total population from which to take the sample selection is not well-defined. Perhaps more importantly, sampling open source projects is methodologically difficult because everything FLOSS research has shown so far points to massively skewed distributions across almost all points of research interest (Conklin, 2004; Xu, Yongqin, Christley, & Madey, 2004). Selecting, even at random, from highly skewed distributions does not, in general, produce a representative sample. The difficulty of sampling is demonstrated in the tendency of FLOSS studies to first limit their enquiries to projects using one repository (usually Source-forge), and often to draw on samples created for entirely different purposes (such as top 100 lists as in Krishnamurthy, 2002), neither of which

is a satisfactory general technique. Selection of projects to study is further complicated by the fact that the public repositories contain a large number of projects that are dormant, relocated, or dead.

BACKGROUND: DATA COLLECTION DIFFICULTIES

Once the projects of interest have been identified and located, the actual project data must be collected. There are two techniques that prevail in the FLOSS literature for collecting data: Web spidering and obtaining database dumps.

Spidering data is fraught with practical complexities (Howison & Crowston, 2004). Because the FLOSS repositories are usually maintained using a database back-end and a Web front-end, the data model appears straightforward to repro-

Figure 1. The typical quantitative FLOSS research process (notice its noncyclical and noncollaborative nature)

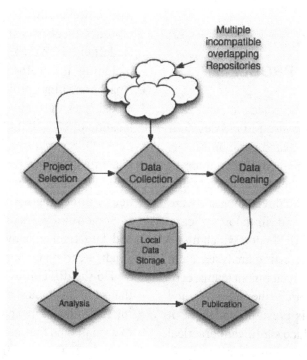

duce. The central limitation of spidering, however, is that the researcher is continually in a state of discovery. The data model is always open to being changed by whoever is controlling the repository, and there is usually no way that the researcher will know of changes in advance. Spidering is a time-intensive and resource-consuming process, and one that is being unnecessarily replicated throughout the world of FLOSS research.

Getting direct access to the database is clearly preferable, but not all repositories make their dumps available. (Some, such as Freshmeat, provide a nightly build containing several text files with the majority of their information included.) And understandably so because it is not a costless process to make data-dumps available. Dumps can contain personally identifiable and financial information (as with the Sourceforge linked donation system) and so the data must be anonymized or otherwise modified to protect this information. Repositories are facing an increasing number of requests for database snapshots from academics and are either seeking a scalable way to do releases or declining to release the data entirely. It is often unclear whether database dumps obtained by one research project can be shared with other academics, so rather than possibly breach confidentiality or annoy their subjects by asking for signed releases, it is understandable that academics who do get a database dump may not make those dumps easily available. Other projects, such as the Sourceforge dump available from Notre Dame[6], only provide the dumps to qualified academic researchers with editorial restrictions. It is unclear what effect this limitation will have on research efforts in the open source community, however, since research efforts are certainly not limited to academics.

Even when dumps are available it is necessary to interpret their database schema. This is not always as straightforward as one would expect. After all, the databases were designed to be used to build Web pages quickly, not to conduct academic analyses. Furthermore, they have been built over time and face the complexity that any schema faces when stretched and scaled beyond its original intended use: labels are obscured, extra tables are used, and there are inconsistencies between old and recently added data. The interpretation and transformation of this data into information semantically interesting to researchers is not a trivial process, and there is no reason to think that researchers will do this transformation in a consistent fashion.

Even pristine and labeled data from repositories is not sufficient because different repositories store different data. Different forges can have projects with the same names, different developers can have the same name across multiple forges, and the same developer can go by multiple names. Forges have different terminology for things like developer roles, project topics, and even programming languages. They often have fields which are named the same in multiple forges but which represent different data. Another problematic area is calculated fields, such as activity or downloads, for which there is incomplete publicly available information on their formula or correctness.

BACKGROUND: DATA CLEANING DIFFICULTIES

Once projects have been selected and the available data harvested, researchers must be confident that data adequately represent the activities of a project. For example, projects use repository tools to differing degrees. For example, many projects are listed on Sourceforge, and use the mailing lists and Web hosting provided there. But some of these same projects will shun the notoriously quirky "Tracker" bug-tracking system at Sourceforge, preferring to set up their own tracking systems using, perhaps, Bugzilla or RT software. Other projects host their activities outside Sourceforge but maintain a "placeholder" registration with little used mailing lists and out of date release information. It is very difficult, short of detailed examination of each project, to know whether a project is fully using a tool. Thus, it is difficult to state with confidence that the data collected about that tool is a reasonable depiction of the project's activities.

Complete accuracy is, of course, not required because in large-scale data analysis some "dirty data" is acceptably handled through statistical techniques. At a minimum, though, researchers contemplating the accuracy of their data must have some reason to believe that there are no systematic reasons that the data collected in the name of the group would be unrepresentative. Unfortunately, given the idiosyncrasies of FLOSS projects, confidence on this point appears to require project-by-project verification, a time-consuming process for individual researchers and projects, and one that is too frequently repeated by other researchers.

The conclusion we draw from this analysis is that each step of the typical FLOSS research process introduces variability into the data that underlies any quantitative analysis of FLOSS development. Decisions about project selection, collection, and cleaning are compounded throughout the cycle of research. FLOSS researchers have not, so far, investigated the extent to which this variability affects their findings and conclusions. In addition, the demands of traditional publication also mean that the decisions are not usually fully and reproducibly reported.

Our critique is not against the existence of differences in research methods or even difference in datasets. There is, rightly, more than one way to conduct research, and indeed this richness drives discovery. Rather, our critique is that the research community is currently unable to begin a meta-analysis phase or a reflective phase because the current process of FLOSS research introduces variability that is difficult to trace. The research process is also hampered by redundant, wasted effort in data collection and analysis. It is time to learn from the free and open source approaches we are studying and develop an open, collaborative solution to this problem.

PROPOSING A SOLUTION: FLOSSMOLE

The previous problem description motivates our attempt to build a system to support research into FLOSS projects. FLOSSmole (formerly OSSmole — the name was changed to reflect our inclusion of Free and Libre software in addition to open source software) is a central repository of data and analyses about FLOSS projects which have been collected and prepared in a decentralized manner. Data repositories have been useful in other fields; the presence of trusted datasets allows research communities to focus their efforts. For example, the TREC datasets have supported a community of information retrieval specialists facilitating performance and accuracy comparisons; the UMI machine learning repositories have been widely used in the development of new machine learning algorithms. There are numerous examples from biology and physics as well. The intention of FLOSSmole is to provide high-quality and widely used datasets, and to share standard analyses for validation, replication, and extension.

REQUIREMENTS OF THE FLOSSMOLE SYSTEM

Below we list some of our initial requirements for an optimal data and analysis clearinghouse for FLOSS data, and we note to what extent FLOSSmole has met each of these requirements. The next section expands on additional specific design attributes of the FLOSSmole system.

An optimal data and analysis repository for FLOSS data should be:

Collaborative. The system should leverage the collective effort of FLOSS researchers to reduce redundancies and to free researchers' time to pursue novel analyses. Thus, in a manner akin to the BSD rather than the GPL licensing model, FLOSSmole expects, but does not require, that those that use data contribute additional data and the analysis scripts that they obtain or use.

Available. The system should make the data and analysis scripts available without complicated usage agreements, where possible through direct unmonitored download or through interactive database queries. This should end the problem of data lockup, and will ease entry of new researchers with novel techniques. Freely available data also lowers the barriers to collegial replication and critique. FLOSSmole scripts and data are open-sourced and available to anyone via the FLOSSmole Sourceforge project page.[7]

Comprehensive and compatible. Given the fragmentation of FLOSS project storage identified previously, the system should cover more than just one repository. The system should be able to pull historical snapshots for purposes of replication or extension of earlier analyses. Compatibility requires that the system should translate across repositories allowing researchers to conduct both comprehensive and comparative analyses. (Currently FLOSSmole contains data from three repositories.) There exists the potential to develop an "interchange" format for FLOSSmole project collateral which projects themselves, which fear data and tool lock-in, might find convenient and useful as they experiment with new tools and repositories.

Of high quality. Researchers should be confident that the data in the system is of high quality. The origins and collection techniques for individual data-points must be traceable so that errors can be identified and not repeated. Data validation performed routinely by researchers can also be shared (for example, scripts that sanity-check fields or distributions) and analyses validated against earlier analyses. By implementing these requirements, FLOSSmole is potentially a large advantage over individual research projects working with nonvalidated single datasets because it implements the "many eyeballs" FLOSS methodology for quality assurance.

Able to support reproducible and comparable analyses. It is desirable that data extracted from the database for transformation be exported with verbose comments detailing its origins and how to repeat the extraction. The best way to ensure reproducible and comparable analyses is to have as much of the process as possible be script-driven, and in this goal, FLOSSmole excels. Optimally, the system should specify a standard application programming interface (API) for inserting and accessing data via programmed scripts. That would allow analyses to specify, using the API, exactly the data used.

A system that meets these requirements, we believe, will promote the discovery of knowledge about FLOSS development by facilitating the next phase of extension through replication, apposite critique, and well-grounded comparison.

ADDITIONAL DESIGN DETAILS

The FLOSSmole data model is designed to support data collection, storage, and analysis from multiple free and open source forges in a way that meets the previously stated requirements. This section lists some additional design details we have made in implementing our FLOSSmole system.

FLOSSmole is able to take both spidered data and data inserted from a direct database dump. The raw data is time stamped and stored in the database, without overwriting any data previously collected, including data from the same project and from the same forge. Finally, periodic raw and summary reports are generated and made publicly available on the project Web site.

The type of data that is currently collected from the various open source forges includes the full HTML source of the forge data page for the project, project name, database environments, programming languages, natural languages, platforms, open source license type, operating systems, intended audiences, and the main project topics. Developer-oriented information includes number of developers, developer information (name, username, e-mail), and the developer's role on the project. We have also collected issue-tracking data (mainly bugs), such as date opened, status, date closed, and priority. Data has been collected from Sourceforge, GNU Savannah, the Apache foundation's Bugzilla and Freshmeat. We are currently creating mappings between fields from each of these repositories and assessing how comparable the fields are. The forge-mapping task is extensive and time-consuming, but the goal is to build a dataset that is more complete and is not specific to only one particular forge.

FLOSSmole is constantly growing and changing as new forges are added. And because data from multiple collectors are both expected and encouraged, it is important that the database also store information about where each data record originally came from (i.e., script name, version, command-line options used, name and contact information of person donating the data, and date of collection and donation). This process ensures accountability for problematic data, yet encourages collaboration between data collectors. The information is stored inside the database to ensure that it does not get decoupled from the data.

Likewise, it is a general rule that data are not overwritten when project details change; rather, one of the goals of the FLOSSmole project is that a full historical record of the project be kept in the database. This will enable researchers to analyze project and developer changes over time and enable access to data that are difficult or impossible to access once they are no longer viewable from the repository's front-end interface.

Access to the FLOSSmole project is two-pronged: both data and scripts are continually made available to the public under an open source license. Anyone can download the FLOSSmole raw and summary data for use in their own research projects or just to get information about the state of the art in open source development. The raw data are provided as multiple text file "data dumps" from the FLOSSmole database. Summary files are compiled periodically, and show basic statistics. Examples of summary statistics that are commonly published would be the count of projects using a particular open source license type, or the count of new projects in a particular forge by month and year, or the number of projects that are written using each programming language. It is our hope that more sophisticated analyses will be continually be contributed by researchers, and that the system will provide dynamic and up-to-date results rather than the static pictures that traditional publication unfortunately leaves us.

The scripts that populate the FLOSSmole database are also available for download under an open source license. These scripts are given for two reasons: first, so that interested researchers can duplicate and validate our findings, and second, so that anyone can expand on our work, for example, by modifying a script to collect data from a new forge. Indeed this process has begun with the recent publication of a conference paper comparing and commenting on our spidering and summaries and beginning collaboration (Weiss, 2005). FLOSSmole expects and encourages contributions of additional forge data, and interested researchers should see the FLOSSmole project page and join the mailing list for information on how to contribute.

RESULTS

Because it is a regularly updated, publicly available data repository, FLOSSmole data have been used both for constructing basic summary reports about the state of open source, as well as for more complex social network analyses of open source development teams. For example, summary reports posted as part of the FLOSSmole project regularly report the number of open source projects, the number of projects per programming language, the number of developers per project, and so forth. These sort of descriptive data are useful for constructing "state of the industry" reports, or for compiling general statistical information about open source projects. The FLOSSmole collection methods are transparent and easily reproduced, so FLOSSmole can serve as a reliable resource for these metrics. Having a stable and consistently updated source of this information will also allow metrics to be compared over time. One of the problems with existing analyses of open source project data is that researchers will run a collection and analyze it once, publish the findings, and then never run the analysis again. The FLOSSmole data model and collection methodology was designed to support historical comparisons of this kind.

FLOSSmole data were used in a number of large-scale social network analyses of FLOSS project development. Crowston and Howison (2004) report the results of a SNA centralization analysis in which the data suggest that, contrary to the rhetoric of FLOSS practitioner-advocates, there is no reason to assume that FLOSS projects share social structures. Further FLOSSmole data were used in the preparation of Crowston, Howison, and Annabi (2006) which, in an effort to avoid the ambiguities of relying on ratings or downloads, develops a range of quantitative measures of FLOSS project success including the half-life of bugs. FLOSSmole makes available the full data and analysis scripts, which make these analyses fully reproducible, and, we hope, extendable.

FLOSSmole data were also used in a recent exploration of whether open source development teams have characteristics typical of a complex network (Conklin, Howison, & Crowston, 2004). This research investigated whether FLOSS development networks will evolve according to "rich get richer" or "winner take all" models, as other self-organized complex networks do. Are new links (developers) in this network attracted to the largest, oldest, or fittest existing nodes (project teams)? The FLOSSmole data were used to determine that there are indeed many characteristics of a complex network present in FLOSS software development, but that there may also be a mutual selection process between developers and teams that actually stops FLOSS projects from matching the "winner take all" model seen in many other complex networks.

Projects of a nonacademic nature are making use of FLOSSmole data as well. The Swik project from SourceLabs[8] is a wiki-driven system for managing facts about other open source software projects. Swik uses FLOSSmole data to populate its initial list of projects. Working independently, the Swik team was able to download FLOSSmole data and put them to use immediately to save time and effort during their development process. By using a dataset that was freely available and for which the provenance of all data was known and validated, Swik was able to accelerate their development cycle.

LIMITATIONS AND FUTURE WORK

There are, of course, limitations in the FLOSSmole project and in our approach. First, we are limited to collecting data available online, and we are limited to collecting data gathered as a direct result of documented project activities. Of course, electronically documented project activities are not the only interactions FLOSS team members have, and even these activities are not always available for perusal by outside parties. Thus while textual data like mailing lists, CVS comments, Forums, and IRC chat logs could be included[9], FLOSSmole does not aim to capture unlogged instant messaging, IRC, Voice-over-IP, or face-to-face interactions of FLOSS developers. Nor do we intend to store interviews or transcripts conducted by researchers that would be restricted by research ethics policies.

There are also dangers in this approach that should be acknowledged. The standardization implied in an academic repository, while valuable, runs the risk of reducing the valuable diversity that has characterized academic FLOSS research. We hope to provide a solid and traceable dataset and basic analyses that will support, not inhibit, interpretative and theoretical diversity. This diversity also means that research is not rendered directly comparable simply because analyses are based on FLOSSmole data or scripts; the hard intellectual work remains and hopefully FLOSSmole, by supporting baseline activities, leaves us more time for such work.

It is quite likely that a functional hierarchy could develop between cooperating projects, something akin to the relationship between FLOSS authors and distributions, such as Debian or Red Hat and their package management systems (i.e., apt and rpm). For example, such an arrangement would allow groups to specialize in collecting and cleaning particular sources of data and others to concentrate on their compatibility. Certainly, we expect that the existing communities of academics interested in FLOSS, such as opensource.mit.edu, will be a source of data and support.

Finally, we must also consider privacy issues. There is some discussion in the research community about breaching developer privacy in a large system of aggregated data like ours (Robles, 2005), specifically in terms of uniquely identifying developers and analyzing their work products. FLOSSmole should have the ability to hash the unique keys indicating a developer's identity. This effort will have to be researched, implemented, and documented for the benefit of our community.

CONCLUSION

Researchers study FLOSS projects in order to better understand collaborative human behavior during the process of building software. Yet it is not clear that current researchers have many common frames of reference when they write and speak about the open source phenomenon. As we study open software development, we learn the value of openness and accessibility of code and communications; FLOSSmole is a step towards applying that to academic research on FLOSS. It is our hope that by providing a repository of traceable and comparable data and analyses on FLOSS projects, FLOSSmole begins to address these difficulties and supports the development of a productive ecosystem of FLOSS research.

ACKNOWLEDGMENT

This research was partially supported by NSF Grants 03-41475, 04-14468, and 05-27457. Any opinions, findings, conclusions, or recommendations expressed in this material are those of the authors and do not necessarily reflect the views of the National Science Foundation. The authors thank the FLOSS developers who contributed to the research.

REFERENCES

Conklin, M. (2004, July 30). Do the rich get richer? The impact of power laws on open source development projects. In *Proceedings of the Open Source Conference (OSCON),* Portland, Oregon.

Conklin, M., Howison, J., & Crowston, K. (2005, May 17). Collaboration using OSSmole: A repository of FLOSS data and analyses. In *Proceedings of the Mining Software Repositories Workshop (MSR2005) of the 27th International Conference on Software Engineering (ICSE 2005),* St. Louis,

Missouri.

Crowston, K., Howison, J., & Annabi, H. (2006). Information systems success in free and open source software development: Theory and measures. *Software Process: Improvement and practice, 11*(2), 123148.

Crowston, K., & Howison, J. (2004). The social structure of open source software development teams. *First Monday, 10*(2). Retrieved from http://firstmonday.org/issues/issue10_2/crowston/.

Howison, J., & Crowston, K. (2004). The perils and pitfalls of mining sourceforge. In *Proceedings of the Mining Software Repositories Workshop at the International Conference on Software Engineering (ICSE 2004)*, Edinburgh, Scotland.

Krishnamurthy, S. (2002). Cave or community? An empirical examination of 100 mature open source projects. *First Monday, 7*(6). Retrieved from http://www.firstmonday.org/issues/issue7_6/krishnamurthy/

Robles, G. (2005, May 17). Developer identification methods for integrated data from various sources. In *Proceedings of the International Workshop on Mining Software Repositories (MSR2005) of the 27th International Conference on Software Engineering (ICSE2005)*, St. Louis, Missouri.

Weiss, D. (2005). Quantitative analysis of open source projects on SourceForge. In *Proceedings of the First International Conference on Open Source Systems (OSS 2005)*, Genova, Italy.

Xu, J., Gao, Y., Christley, S., & Madey, G. (2004). A topological analysis of the open source software development community. In *Proceedings of HICSS 2005*, Hawaii.

ENDNOTES

[1] FLOSSmole: http://ossmole.sf.net
[2] Sourceforge: http://www.sf.net
[3] Savannah: http://savannah.gnu.org
[4] CodeHaus: http://www.codehaus.org
[5] Comprehensive Perl Archive Network: http://www.cpan.org
[6] http://www.nd.edu/~oss/Data/data.html
[7] FLOSSmole: http://ossmole.sf.net
[8] Swik: http://swik.net/
[9] http://libresoft.urjc.es/Activities/WoP-DaSD2006

This work was previously published in Int. Journal of Information Technology and Web Engineering, Vol 1, Issue 3, edited by E. Damiani and G. Succi, pp. 17-26, copyright 2006 by IGI Publishing (an imprint of IGI Global).

Chapter III
Applying Social Network Analysis Techniques to Community-Driven Libre Software Projects

Luis López-Fernández
Universidad Rey Juan Carlos, Spain

Gregorio Robles
Universidad Rey Juan Carlos, Spain

Jesus M. Gonzalez-Barahona
Universidad Rey Juan Carlos, Spain

Israel Herraiz
Universidad Rey Juan Carlos, Spain

ABSTRACT

Source code management repositories of large, long-lived libre (free, open source) software projects can be a source of valuable data about the organizational structure, evolution and knowledge exchange in the corresponding development communities. Unfortunately, the sheer volume of the available information renders it almost unusable without applying methodologies which highlight the relevant information for a given aspect of the project. Such methodology is proposed in this paper, based on well known concepts from the social networks analysis field, which can be used to study the relationships among developers and how they collaborate in different parts of a project. It is also applied to data mined from some well known projects (Apache, GNOME, and KDE), focusing on the characterization of their collaboration network architecture. These cases help to understand the potentials of the methodology and how it is applied, but also show some relevant results which open new paths in the understanding of the informal organization of libre software development communities.

INTRODUCTION

Software projects are usually the collective work of many developers. In most cases, and especially in the case of large projects, those developers are formally organized in a well defined (usually hierarchical) structure, with clear guidelines about how to interact with each other, and the procedures and channels to use. Each team of developers is assigned certain modules of the project, and only in rare cases do they work outside that realm. However, this is usually not the case with libre software[1] projects, where only loose (if any) formal structures are acknowledged. On the contrary, libre software developers usually have access to any part of the software, and even in the case of large projects, they can move freely to a certain extent from one module to other, with only some restrictions imposed by common usage in the project and the rules on which developers themselves have agreed to.

In fact, during the late 1990s some voices started to claim that the success of some libre software projects was rooted in this different way of organization, which was referred to as the "bazaar development model," described by Eric Raymond (1997) and later complemented by some more formal models of nonhierarchical coordination (Elliott & Scacchi, 2004; Healy & Schussman, 2003). Some empirical studies have found that many libre software projects cannot follow this bazaar-style model, since they are composed of just one or two developers (Healy & Schussman, 2003; Krishnamurthy, 2002), but the idea remains valid for large projects, with tens or even hundreds of developers, where coordination is obviously achieved, but (usually) not by using formal procedures. These latter cases have gained much attention from the software engineering community during the last years, in part because despite apparently breaking some traditional premises (hard-to-find requirement studies, apparently no internal structure, global

software development, etc.) final products of reasonable quality are being delivered. Large libre software projects are also *suspicious* of breaking one of the traditional software evolution *laws*, showing linear or even superlinear growth even after reaching a size of several millions of lines of code (Godfrey & Tu, 2000; Robles, Amor, Gonzalez-Barahona, & Herraiz, 2005a). The *laws* of software evolution state that the evolution of a system is a self-regulating process that maintains its organizational stability. Thus, unless feedback mechanisms are appropriately introduced, the effective global activity tends to remain constant, and incremental growth declines. The fact that several studies on some large libre software projects show evidence that some of these *laws* are disobeyed may be indicative of an efficient organizational structure.

On the other hand, the study of several large libre software projects has shown evidence about the unequal distribution of the contributions of developers (Dinh-Trong & Bieman, 2005; Koch & Schneider, 2002; Mockus, Fielding, & Herbsleb, 2002). These studies have identified roles within the development community, and have discovered that a large fraction of the development work is done by a small group of about 15 persons, which has been called the "core" group. The number of developers is around one order of magnitude larger, and the number of occasional bug reporters is again about one order of magnitude larger than that of developers (Dinh-Trong & Bieman, 2005; Mockus et al., 2002). This is what has been called the *onion* structure of libre software projects (Crowston, Scozzi, & Buonocore, 2003). In this direction, it has also been suggested that large projects need to adopt policies to divide the work, giving rise to smaller, clearly defined projects (Mockus et al., 2002). This trend can be observed in the organization of the CVS[2] repository of really large libre software projects, where the code base is split into modules with their own maintainers, goals, and so forth. Modules are usually supposed to be built maintaining the interrelationships to a minimum, so that independent evolution is possible (Germán, 2004a).

In this article, a new approach is explored in order to study the informal structure and organization of the developers in large libre software projects. It is based on the application of well known social networks analysis (SNA) techniques to development data obtained from the versioning system (CVS). According to the classical Conway's *law*, organizations designing systems are constrained to produce designs which are copies of their communication structures (Conway, 1968). Following this line of reasoning, the relationships among modules will be studied, and the dual case of those among developers. Our target is the advancement of the knowledge about the informal coordination structures that are the key to understanding how these large libre software projects can work in the apparent absence of formalized structures, and where the limits are of those ways of coordinating and exchanging information. We have designed a methodology following this approach, and have also applied it to some well known projects. Although the aim of our approach is mainly descriptive, not proposing novel models for project evolution or agent behavior, just trying to describe in as much detail as possible the organizational structure of libre software projects, our work is illustrative of the power of the SNA techniques. To attain this goal, our approach is similar to that presented in Madey, Freeh, and Tynan (2002) and Xu, Gao, Christley, and Madey (2005): we consider libre software projects as complex systems and characterize them by using mathematical formalisms. As a result, some interesting facts related to the organizational structure of libre software projects have been uncovered.

The remainder of this article is organized as follows. The next section contains a basic introduction to SNA, and how we intend to apply its techniques to the study of libre software projects based on the data available in their CVS repositories. The third section specifies in detail the methodology for such a study, followed by the fourth section with a brief introduction to a set of classical social network analysis parameters. After that, the fifth section presents the main characteristics of the networks corresponding to the three projects used as case examples: Apache, GNOME, and KDE. This serves as an introduction to the more detailed comments on several aspects of those projects, presented in the sixth, seventh, eighth, ninth, and tenth sections. The final section offers some conclusions, comments on some related work, and discusses further lines of research.

APPLICATION OF SNA TO LIBRE SOFTWARE PROJECTS

The study and characterization of complex systems is a fruitful research area, with many interesting open problems. Special attention has been paid recently to complex networks, where graph and network analysis play an important role. This approach is gaining popularity due to its intrinsic power to reduce a system to its single components and relationships. Network characterization is widely used in many scientific and technological disciplines, such as neurobiology (Watts & Strogatz, 1998), computer networks (Albert, Barabási, Jeong, & Bianconi, 2000), or linguistics (Kumar, Raghavan, Rajagopalan, & Tomkins, 2002).

Although some voices argue that the software development process found in libre software projects is hardly to be considered as a new development paradigm (Fuggetta, 2003); without doubt, the way it handles its human resources differs completely from traditional organizations (Germán, 2004b). In both cases, traditional and libre software environments, the human factor is of key importance for the development process and how the software evolves (Gîrba, Kuhn, Seeberger, & Ducasse, 2005), but the volunteer nature of many contributors in the libre software case makes it a clearly differentiated situation (Robles, González-Barahona, & Michlmayr, 2005b).

Previous research on this topic has both attended to technical and organizational points of view. Germán used data from a versioning repository in time to determine feature-adding and bug-correcting phases. He also found evidence for developer territoriality (software artifacts that are mainly, if not uniquely, *touched* by a single developer) (Germán, 2004a).

The intention of other papers has been to uncover the social structure of the underlying community. The first efforts in the libre software world are due to Madey et al. (2002), who took data from the largest libre software projects repository, SourceForge.net, and inferred relationships among developers that contributed to projects in common. A statistical analysis of some basic social network parameters can also be found by López, Gonzalez-Barahona, and Robles (2004) for some large libre software projects. Xu et al. (2005) have presented a more profound topological analysis of the libre software community, joining in the same work characteristics from previous papers: data based on the SourceForge platform and a statistical analysis of some parameters with the goal of gaining knowledge on the topology of the libre software phenomenon. This has also been the intention of González-Barahona, López-Fernández, and Robles (2004), where a structure-finding algorithm was used to obtain the evolution in time of the organization of the Apache project. Wagstrom, Herbsleb, and Carley (2005) propose to use the knowledge acquired from analyzing libre software projects with SNA for the creation of models that help understand the underlying social and technical process.

METHODOLOGY

The first problem to solve when using SNA is getting the information to construct the network to analyze. One especially interesting kind of data sources is the records maintained by many computer based systems. For instance, Guimera, Danon, Diaz-Guilera, Giralt, and Arenas (2003) analyze informal networking on organizations using tracks of e-mail exchanges. Therefore, from the many kinds of records available about the activity of a libre software project, those provided by the CVS system where source code is stored have been the ones chosen. Those records offer information about who modified the code, and when and how, in many cases from the very beginning of the project, in some cases over a total period of time above 10 years.

The information in the CVS repository of a project includes an accurate and detailed picture of the organizational structure of the software, and of the developers working on it. When two developers work on the same project module, they have to exchange (directly or maybe indirectly) information and knowledge to coordinate their actions and produce a working result. It seems reasonable to assume that the higher their contributions to the module, the higher the strength of their informal connection.

Based on this assumption, a specific kind of social network has been considered, those called affiliation networks. They are characterized by showing two types of vertices: *actors* and *groups*. When the network is represented with actors as vertices, each one is usually associated with a particular person, and two of them are linked together when they belong to the same group. When the network is represented with groups as vertices, two groups are connected when there is, at least, one actor belonging, at the same time, to both groups. In our case, actors will be identified as developers, and groups as software modules. The "belong to" relationship will be in fact "has contributed to." This approach will result in a dual view of the same organization: as a network of modules linked by common developers, and as a network of developers linked by common modules. Similar approaches have been used for analyzing other complex organizations, like the network of scientific authors (Newman, 2001a, b) or the network of movie actors (Albert & Barabasi, 2002).

To finish the characterization of our networks, weighted edges are being considered. This means that it is not only taken into account whether a node has some relationship with any other, but also the strength of that relationship. In our case, the weight will be related to the size of contributions to common modules (in the case of developers) and to the size of contributions by common developers (in the case of modules). It should be noted that from the methodological point of view, the use of weights is a major contribution of this article in comparison with previous works describing SNA techniques applied to libre software (Madey et al., 2002; Wagstrom et al., 2005; Xu et al., 2005). As we will see in this article, the use of weights is indicated as the distribution of work follows a very unequal distribution, in the range of a Pareto distribution[3] (Ghosh & Prakash, 2000). Our assumption at this point is that considering a link between two major contributing developers that equals the one between two random chosen developers, introducing an important bias in the results regarding the distribution of work observed in libre software environments.

Once we have identified how we want to use SNA for libre software projects, a well defined methodology is proposed in order to apply those ideas to any libre software with a public CVS repository. The process begins by downloading the relevant information from the CVS repository.[4] This information includes, for each commit (modification in a file in the repository): the date, the identifier of the developer (commiter), and the number of lines involved. Using all those records, the following networks are defined for characterizing the organization of the project:

- **Modules network.** Each vertex represents a particular software module (usually a directory in the CVS repository) of the project. Two modules are linked together by an

edge when there is at least one commiter who has contributed to both. Those edges are weighted using a *degree of relationship* between the two modules, defined as the total number of commits performed by common commiters.

- **Commiters network.** In this case, each vertex represents a particular commiter (developer). Two commiters are linked by an edge when they have contributed to at least one common module. Again, edges are weighted by a *degree of relationship* defined as the total number of commits performed by both developers on modules to which both have contributed.

The definition being used for the *degree of relationship* is an attempt to measure the *closeness* of two vertices. The higher this parameter, the stronger the relationship between those vertices. In this sense, *cost of relationship* between any two vertices can also be defined as the inverse of their *degree of relationship*. In this sense, the *cost of relationship* defines a distance between vertices: the higher it is, the more difficult it is to reach one of them from the other. More formally, given a (connected) graph G and a pair of vertices i and j, we define the distance between them as $d_{ij} = \sum_{e \in P_s} c_r$, where e are all the edges in the shortest path P_s from i to j, and c_r is the *cost of relationship* of any of those edges.

Parameters

Once the networks are constructed based on the previous definitions, and the degrees and costs of relationship have been calculated for linked nodes, standard SNA concepts can be applied in order to define the following parameters of the network (the interpretation of the main implications of each parameter is also offered):

Degree. The degree, k, of a vertex is the number of edges connected to it. In SNA, this parameter reflects the popularity of a vertex, in the sense that most popular vertices are those maintaining the highest number of relationships. More revealing than the degree of single vertices is the distribution degree of the network (the probability of a vertex having a given degree). This is one of the most relevant characterizations because it provides essential information to understand the topology of a network (and if longitudinal data is available, the evolution of the topology). For example, it is well known that a random network follows a Poisson's distribution, while a network following a preferential attachment growth model presents a power law distribution (Albert & Barabasi, 2002). In our context, the degree of a commiter corresponds to the number of other commiters sharing modules with that committer, while the degree of a module is the total number of modules with which it shares developers.

- **Weighted degree.** When dealing with weighted networks, the degree of a vertex may be tricky. A vertex with a high degree is not necessarily well connected to the network because all its edges may be weak. On the other hand, a low degree vertex may be strongly attached to the network if its entire links are heavy. For this reason the weighted degree of a vertex, w, is defined as the sum of the weights of all the edges connected to it. The weighted degree of a vertex can be interpreted as the maximum capacity to receive information of that vertex. It is also related to the effort spent by the vertex in maintaining its relationships.

- **Clustering coefficient** (Watts & Strogatz, 1998). The clustering coefficient, c, of a vertex measures the transitivity of a network. Given a vertex v in a graph G, it can be defined as the probability that any two neighbors of v are connected (the neighbors of v are those vertices directly connected to v). Hence

$$c(v) = \frac{2E(v)}{k_v (k_v - 1)} \qquad (1)$$

where k_v is the number of neighbors of k_v and $E(v)$ is the number of edges between them. The intuitive interpretation of the clustering coefficient is somehow subtle. If the total number of neighbors of v is k_v, the maximum number of edges than can exist within that neighborhood is $k_v (k_v - 1)/2$. Hence, the clustering coefficient represents the fraction of the number of edges that really are in a neighborhood. Therefore it can be considered as a measurement of the tendency of a given vertex to promote relationships among its neighbors. In a completely random graph, the clustering coefficient is low, because the probability of any two vertices being connected is the same, independently on them sharing a common neighbor. On the other hand, it has been shown that most social networks present significantly high clustering coefficients (for instance, the probability of two persons being friends is not independent from the fact that they share a common friend) (Albert & Barabasi, 2002; Watts, 2003).

From an organizational point of view, the clustering coefficient helps to identify hot spots of knowledge exchange on dynamic networks. When this parameter is high for a vertex, that vertex is promoting its neighbors to interact with each other. Somehow it is fostering connections among its neighborhood. High clustering coefficients in networks are indicative for *cliques*. Besides, the clustering coefficient is also a measurement of the redundancy of the communication links around a vertex.

- **Weighted clustering coefficient** (Latora & Marchiori, 2003). The clustering coefficient does not consider the weight of edges. We may refine it by introducing the weighted clustering coefficient, c_w, of a vertex, which is an attempt to generalize the concept of clustering coefficient to weighted networks. Given a vertex v in a weighted graph G it can be defined as:

$$c_w(v) = \sum_{i \neq j \in N_G(v)} w_{ij} \frac{1}{k_v(k_v - 1)} \qquad (2)$$

where $N_G(v)$ is the neighborhood of v in G (the subgraph of all vertices connected to v), w_{ij} is the degree of relationship of the link between neighbor i and neighbor j ($w_{ij} = 0$ if there are no links), and k_v is the number of neighbors. The weighted clustering coefficient can be interpreted as a measurement of the local efficiency of the network around a particular vertex, because vertices promoting strong interactions among their neighbors will have high values for this parameter. It can also be seen as a measurement of the redundancy of interactions around a vertex.

- **Distance centrality** (Sabidussi, 1996). The distance centrality of a vertex, D_c, is a measurement of its proximity to the rest. It is sometimes called *closeness centrality* as the higher its value the closer that vertex is (on average) to the others. Given a vertex v and a graph G, it can be defined as:

$$D_c(v) = \frac{1}{\sum_{t \in G} d_G(v,t)} \qquad (3)$$

where $d_G(v,t)$ is the minimum distance from vertex v to vertex t (i.e., the sum of the costs of relationship of all edges in the shortest path from v to t). The distance centrality can be interpreted as a measurement of the influence of a vertex in a graph because the higher its value, the easier for that vertex to spread information through that network. Observe that when a given vertex is "far" from the others, it has a low degree of re-

lationship (i.e., a high cost of relationship) with the rest. So, the term $\sum_{t \in G} d_G(v.t)$ will increase, meaning that it does not occupy a central position in the network. In that case, the distance centrality will be low. Research has shown that employees who are central in networks learn faster, perform better, and are more committed to the organization. These employees are also less likely to turn over. Besides, from the point of view of information propagation, vertices with high centrality are like "hills" on the plain, in the sense that any knowledge is put on them is rapidly seen by the rest and spreads easily to the rest of the organization.

- **Betweenness centrality** (Anthonisse, 1971; Freeman, 1977). The betweenness centrality of a vertex, c, is a measurement of the number of shortest paths traversing that particular vertex. Given a vertex v and a graph G, it can be defined as:

$$B_c(v) = \sum_{s \neq v \neq t \in G} \frac{\sigma_{st}(v)}{\sigma_{st}} \qquad (4)$$

where $\sigma_{st}(v)$ is the number of shortest paths from s to t going through v, and σ_{st} is the total number of shortest paths between s and t. The betweenness centrality of a vertex can be interpreted as a measurement of the information control that it can perform on a graph, in the sense that vertices with a high value are intermediate nodes for the communication of the rest. In our context, given that we have weighted networks, multiple shortest paths between any pair of vertices are highly improbable. So, the term $\sigma_{st}(v)/\sigma_{st}$ takes usually only two values: 1, if the shortest path between s and t goes through v, or 0 otherwise. So, the betweenness centrality is just a measurement of the number of shortest paths traversing a given vertex. In the SNA literature vertices with high betweenness centrality are known to cover "structural holes." That is, those vertices glue together parts of the organization that would be otherwise far away from each other. They receive a diverse combination of information available to no one else in the network and have therefore a higher probability of being involved in the knowledge generation processes.

High values of the clustering coefficient are usually a symptom of *small world* behavior. The small world behavior of a network can be analyzed by comparing it with an equivalent (in number of vertices and edges) random network. When a network has a diameter (or average distance among vertices) similar to its random counterpart but, at the same time, has a higher average clustering coefficient, it is defined as a small world. It is well known (Watts, 2003) that small world networks are those optimizing the short and long term information flow efficiency. Those networks are also especially well adapted to solve the problem of searching knowledge through their vertices.

Table 1 summarizes the various SNA parameters that have been presented in this section, their meanings, and the information they provide. These parameters, and their distributions and correlations will characterize the corresponding networks. From their study, a lot can be learned about the underlying organization and structure that those networks capture. An attempt to illustrate this is found in the following sections by studying several cases on real libre software projects.

Table 1. Summary of the SNA parameters described in this article, their meaning and their interpretation

Parameter	Meaning	Interpretation
Degree of relationship	Common activity among two entities (measured in commits)	How strong the relationship is
Cost of relationship	Inverse of the degree of relationship	Gives the cost of reaching one vertex from the other
Degree	Number of vertices connected to a node	Popularity of a vertex
Distribution degree	Probability of a vertex having a given degree	Topology of the network (Poisson or power law distributions)
Weighted degree	Degree considering weights of the links among vertices	Maximum capacity to receive information for a vertex. Effort in maintaining the relationships
Clustering coefficient	Fraction of the total number of edges that could exist for a given vertex that really exist	Transitivity of a network: tendency of a vertex to promote relationships among its neighbors. Helps identifying hot spots of knowledge interchange in dynamic networks
Weighted clustering coefficient	Generalization of the clustering coefficient concept to weighted networks	Local efficiency of the network around a vertex. Redundancy of interactions around a vertex
Distance centrality	Measurement of the proximity of a vertex to the rest	Gives the influence of a vertex in a graph. The higher the value the easier it is for the vertex to spread information through the network
Betweenness centrality	Number of shortest paths traversing a vertex	Measurement of the information control. Higher values mean that the vertex is an intermediate node for the communication of the rest. Vertices with high values are known to cover "structural holes"
Small world	Diameter (or average distance among vertices) similar but higher average clustering coefficient than random network	Optimizes short and long term information flow efficiency. Especially well adapted to solve the problem of searching knowledge through their vertices

Table 2. Number of vertices and edges of the module networks in the Apache, GNOME, and KDE projects

Project name	Modules (Vertices)	Edges	Average	% of edges (avg)
Apache	175	2491	14.23	8.13
KDE	73	1560	21.37	29.27
GNOME	667	121,134	181.61	27.23

Table 3. Number of vertices and edges of the commiter networks in the Apache and KDE projects

Project name	Commiters (Vertices)	Edges	Commiters per module	Avg Number of edges
Apache	751	23,324	4.3	31.06
KDE	915	205,877	12.5	225.00
GNOME	869	N/A	1.3	N/A

CASE STUDIES: APACHE, KDE, AND GNOME

Apache,[5] KDE, and GNOME are all well known libre software projects, large in size (each one well above the million of lines of code), in which several subprojects (modules) can be identified. They have already been studied from several points of view (Germán, 2004a; Koch & Schneider, 2002; Mockus et al., 2002). Here, they will be used to show some of the features of our proposed methodology for applying SNA to software projects.

The use of versioning systems is fortunately the case for most large libre software projects. Some approaches on how to gather information from versioning repositories, in particular CVS (Germán, 2004a; Germán & Hindle, 2006; Zimmermann & Weißgerber, 2004; Zimmermann, Weißgerber, Diehl & Zeller, 2005), have been presented, and are used in this study. Therefore, focus is set on what to do once that information is available, and not on how to gather it.

Tables 2 and 3 summarize the main parameters of both. In the case of commiter networks the GNOME case has been omitted.

By comparing the data in both tables some interesting conclusions can already be drawn. It may be observed, for instance, that the average

number of commiters per module is greater in KDE (12.5) than in Apache (4.3), meaning more people being involved in the average KDE subproject. It can also be highlighted that the average degree on the commiters networks is in general larger than in the modules ones. This is especially true for KDE, which rises from a value of 21.4 in the latter case to 225 in the former. In the case of Apache it only raises from 14.2 to 31.1. Therefore, we can conclude that in those cases, commiters are much more linked than modules. The percentage of modules linked gives an idea of the synergy (in form of sharing information and experience) in a network as many modules have commiters in common. It can be assumed that this happens because of the technical proximity between modules. Regarding our case studies, KDE and GNOME show percentages near 30%, while the average Apache module is only linked to 8% of the other modules in the versioning system. So, Apache is specially fragmented in several module families that have no commiters in common. KDE and GNOME have a higher cohesion, while there is more dispersion in Apache.

In the following sections some specific aspects of all those networks will be studied, with the idea of illustrating both how the methodology is applied and which kind of results can be obtained from it.

Figure 1. Cumulative degree distribution for Apache (▽), KDE (+), and GNOME (·)

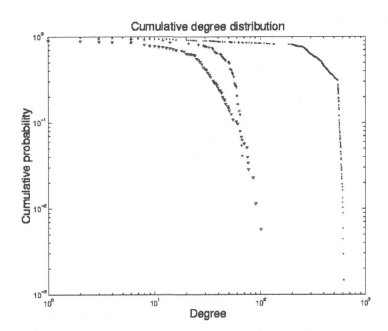

DEGREE IN THE MODULES NETWORK

Table 4 shows that the number of modules for Apache (175), KDE (73), and GNOME (667) differ significantly. These projects are similar in software size (at least in order of magnitude), so the number of modules depends mainly on the various strategies that the projects follow when creating a new module. KDE has a structured CVS; applications that belong together are usually grouped into one module (so, for instance, there exists the *kdenetwork* module for many network applications or the *koffice* module for the various office suite programs). Apache has modules at the application level. Finally, GNOME follows a more *chaotic* approach, resulting in many more modules. Almost every application, even components (there are almost a dozen different GIMP add-ons with their own module) can be found to be a module in themselves.

The most popular characterization of network degree is the distribution degree $P(k)$, which measures the probability of a given vertex having exactly k edges. However, the representation of $P(k)$ in networks of a small size like ours is usually messy.[6] In these cases, the specialized literature prefers to use an associated parameter called the *cumulative distribution degree*, $CP(k)$, which is defined as $CP(k) = \sum_{k}^{\infty} P(i)$ and is usually represented in a log-log scale.

Figure 1 shows the cumulative distribution degree for our three networks. As it can be observed, all of them present a sharp cut off, which is a symptom of an exponential fall of the distribution degree tail. From a practical point of view, this means that none of our networks follow a power law distribution. This is quite a remarkable finding, because the specialized literature has shown that most social networks present power laws for this parameter. This implies that the growth of the network does not follow the traditional random preferential attachment law. Thus, it is difficult to come to any conclusions at this point; maybe by using a weighted network approach, as shown later, we could infer more information about the network topology.

Figure 2. Assortativity (degree - degree distribution) for Apache (), KDE (+) and GNOME (·). Cumulative weighted degree distribution for Apache (▽), KDE (+) and GNOME (·)

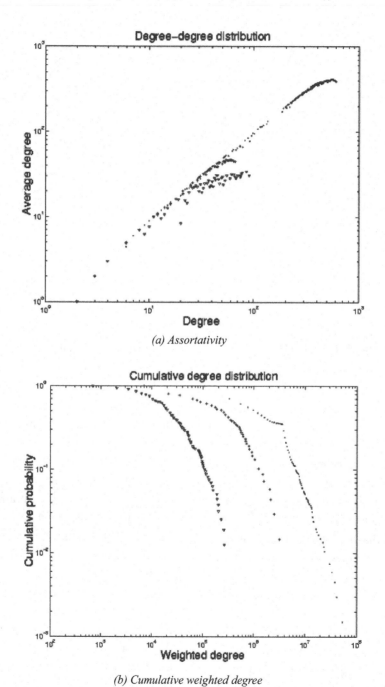

(a) Assortativity

(b) Cumulative weighted degree

Starting with the degree of the vertices, an analysis of assorts of the networks can also be carried out. The assorts measure the average degree of neighbors of vertices having a particular degree. For this reason it can also be called the *degree-degree distribution.*

Figure 2a represents this parameter for our networks. As can be observed, all three networks are elitist, in the sense that vertices tend to connect to other vertices having a similar degree ("rich" with "rich" and "poor" with "poor"). This is especially clear in the case of GNOME, where the curve approaches a linear equation with slope 1. Apache project deviates slightly from that behavior, showing some higher degree modules connected to other modules of a lower degree.

The previous analysis assumes unweighted networks. If weighted edges are considered now, similar conclusions are obtained. Figure 2b represents the cumulative weighted distribution degree of the networks. Comparing this picture with Figure 1, it may be remarked that the sharp exponential cut-offs have disappeared. This is especially clear in the case of GNOME, where the curve tail can be clearly approximated by a power law. The interpretation for this finding is that the growth of that network could be driven by a preferential attachment law based on weighted degrees. This means that the probability of a new module to establish a link with a given vertex is proportional to the weighted degree of that vertex. That is, the commiters of new modules are, with high probability, commiters of modules which are well connected (have high weighted degree) in the network. It should be noted that the use of weights has given a more realistic picture.

From Figure 1, it can be remarked that the sharp cut offs for Apache and KDE are close to each other. This means that the maximum numbers of relationships in both projects are similar. Nevertheless, observing Figure 2b, it can be seen that the KDE tail is clearly over the Apache tail. This fact implies that KDE weighted links are, on average, stronger than those of Apache. This can

be quantitatively verified: we have calculated the average edge weight for the three projects obtaining 1,409.27 for Apache, 11,136.82 for KDE, and 7,661.18 for GNOME.

If multiplied, the average edge weight and the number of modules, the figures obtained are the total amount of commits performed by developers that contribute to at least two modules: 105,695 for Apache, 812,988 for KDE, and 5,110,007 for GNOME. This gives an idea of the modularity of the modules as a lower number of commits is indicative for developer work being more focused on a low number of modules. While the figures for Apache are not surprising (we have already noticed with previous parameters that is a high level of structure in the Apache project), the difference between KDE and GNOME is astonishing. The organization of the KDE CVS repository yields in more independent modules than the ones found in the one for GNOME.

CLUSTERING COEFFICIENT IN THE MODULES NETWORK

For the analysis of the clustering coefficient, we have represented its distribution in Figure 3a.

In Table 4 the average distance $<d>$ among vertices are represented, together with the average clustering coefficients $<cc>$ for our three networks and their equivalent random counterparts ($<rd>$ is the random average distance and $<rcc>$ is the random average clustering coefficient). As can be observed, the three networks satisfy the small world condition, since their average distances are slightly above those of their random counterparts; but the clustering coefficients are clearly higher.

As can be observed, the average random clustering coefficients for KDE and GNOME are very close to the real ones, due to the high density of those networks. This could be an indication of over-redundancy in their links. That would mean that the same efficiency of information

Figure 3. Clustering coefficient distribution for Apache (∇), KDE (+) and GNOME (·). Average weighted clustering coefficient as a function of the degree of vertices for Apache (∇), KDE (+) and GNOME (.)

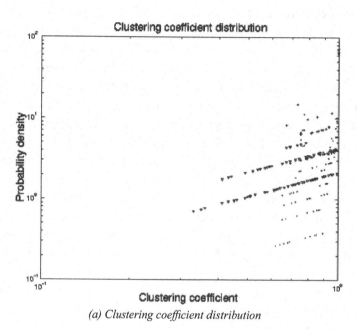

(a) Clustering coefficient distribution

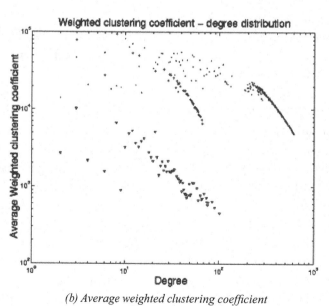

(b) Average weighted clustering coefficient

Table 4. Small world analysis for the module networks

Project name	$<d>$ / $<rd>$	$<cc>$ / $<rcc>$
Apache	2.06 / 1.47	0.73 / 0.19
KDE	1.31 / 1.11	0.88 / 0.65
GNOME	1.46 / 1.10	0.87 / 0.54

could be obtained with fewer relationships (i.e., eliminating many edges in the network without significantly increasing the diameter or reducing the clustering coefficient). In this sense, the Apache network seems to be more *optimized*. To interpret this fact, the reader may remember that links in this network are related to the existence of common developers for the linked modules. It should be noted that redundancy is probably a good characteristic of a libre software project as it may lose many developers without being affected heavily. It may be especially interesting to have over-redundancy in projects with many volunteers, as in those environments, turnover may be high. Future research should focus on investigating whether over-redundancy is a good or bad parameter in the case of libre software projects. On the other side, how much of this redundancy is due to the taking of a static picture of the project should be researched; it may well be that the redundancy we have observed is the result of different generations of developers working on the same file in different periods of time.

Some interesting conclusions can also be obtained by looking at the weighted clustering coefficient. In Figure 3b we can observe the average weighted clustering coefficient as a function of the degree of vertices (the weighted degree-degree distribution). As we have already noticed, the KDE and GNOME networks have a similar local redundancy, which is higher than the one of Apache. High redundancy implies more fluid information exchanges in the short distances for the first two projects. Besides, the weighted clustering coefficient lowers with the degree in all cases, according to a power law function. We can infer that highly connected vertices cannot maintain their neighbors as closely related as poorly connected ones. This happens typically in most social networks because the cost of maintaining close relationships in small groups is much lower than the equivalent cost for large neighborhoods.

DISTANCE CENTRALITY IN THE MODULES NETWORK

The analysis of the distance centrality of vertices is relevant because this parameter measures how close a vertex is to the rest of the network. In Figure 4a, the distance centrality distribution for our three networks can be observed. They follow multiple power laws, making higher values of the parameter most probable. This is an indication of well structured networks for the fast spread of knowledge and information.

We can also analyze the average distance centrality as a function of the degree (average distance centrality-degree distribution), which is shown if Figure 4b. It can be observed that in all three cases the average distance centrality grows with the degree following, approximately, a power law of low exponent. This means that, in terms of distance centrality, the networks are quite *democratic*, because there is not a clear advantage of well connected nodes compared to the rest. Curiously enough, the Apache and GNOME curves are quite similar, while the KDE one is clearly an order of magnitude over the rest. This could be an effect of the lower size of this network, but is also an indication of an especially well structured network in terms of information spread. So, even if KDE showed to be more modular as has been seen for a previous parameter, its structure seems to maximize information flow.

BETWEENNESS CENTRALITY IN THE MODULES NETWORK

The distance centrality of a vertex indicates how well new knowledge created in a vertex spreads to the rest of the network. On the other hand, betweenness centrality is a measurement of how easy it is for a vertex to generate this new information. Vertices with high betweenness centrality indexes are the crossroads of organizations,

Figure 4. Distance centrality distribution for Apache (∇), KDE (+), and GNOME (·); Average distance centrality as a function of the degree of vertices for Apache (∇), KDE (+), and GNOME (·)

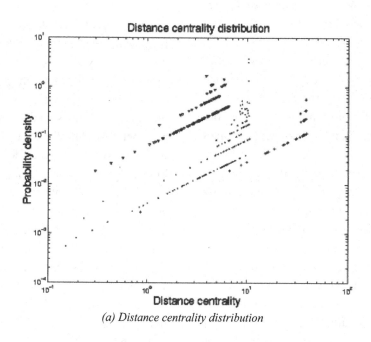

(a) Distance centrality distribution

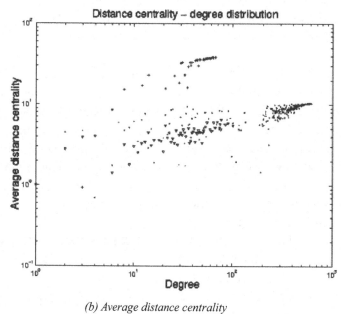

(b) Average distance centrality

Figure 5. Betweenness centrality distribution for Apache (∇), KDE (+) and GNOME (·). Average betweenness centrality distribution for Apache (∇), KDE (+) and GNOME (·)

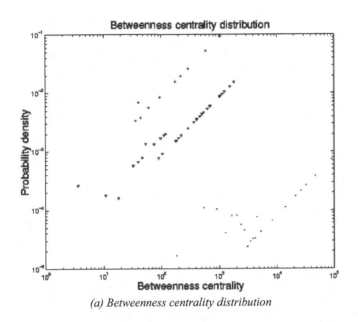

(a) Betweenness centrality distribution

(b) Average betweenness centrality distribution

Figure 6. Cumulative degree distribution for Apache (∇) and KDE (+); Cumulative weighted degree distribution for Apache (∇) and KDE (+)

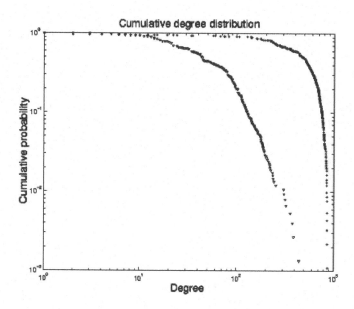

(a) Cumulative degree distribution

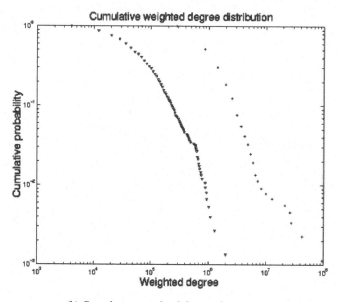

(b) Cumulative weighted degree distribution

Figure 7. Degree - degree distribution for Apache (▽) and KDE (+); Average weighted degree as a function of the degree for Apache (▽) and KDE (+)

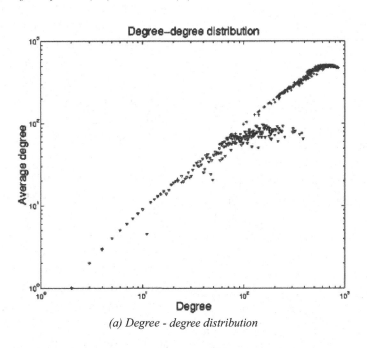

(a) Degree - degree distribution

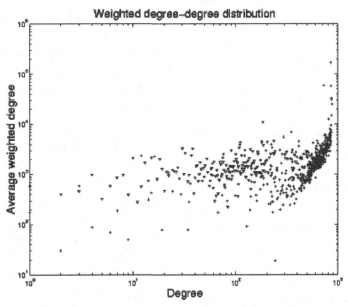

(b) Average weighted degree as a function of degree

Table 5. Small world analysis for commiter networks

Project name	$<d> / <rd>$	$<cc> / <rcc>$
Apache	2.18 / 1.60	0.84 / 0.08
KDE	1.47 / 1.10	0.86 / 0.52

where information from different origins can be intercepted, analyzed, or manipulated. In Figure 5a, the betweenness centrality distribution for our three networks can be observed. In the same way, this was the case for distance centrality, as it grows following a multiple power law. Nevertheless, there is a significant difference between the distributions of these two parameters. Although the log-log scale of the axis of Figure 5a does not allow visualizing it, the most probable value of the betweenness centrality in all three networks is zero. Just to show an example, only 102 out of 677 vertices of the GNOME network have a nonzero betweenness centrality. So, the distance centrality is a common good of all members of the network, while the betweenness centrality is owned by reduced elite. This should not be surprising at all, as projects usually have modules (i.e., applications) which have a more central position and attract more development attention. Surrounding these modules, other minor modules may appear.

This fact can also be visualized in Figure 5b, where we represent the average betweenness centrality as a function of the degree. It can be clearly seen that only vertices of high degree have nonzero betweenness centralities.

COMMITER NETWORKS

The analysis of commiter networks draw similar conclusions to those shown for module networks, and therefore they are not going to be commented on in detail. For instance, the cumulative degree distribution for the two commiter networks is shown in Figure 6a, which has clearly the same qualitative properties than for this parameter for the module networks shown in Figure 1. The same holds true for the commiter cumulative weighted degree distribution depicted in Figure 6b, or for the average degree as a function of degree, depicted in Figure 7a, where it can be noticed how both networks maintain the elitist characteristic also observed in the case of modules.

An interesting feature of commiter networks can be seen in Figure 7b. The average weighted degree of authors remains more or less constant for low values of the degree. Nevertheless, in the case of KDE, it increases meaningfully for the highest degrees. The implication is that commiters with higher degrees not only have more relationships than the rest, but also their relationships are much stronger than the average. This indicates that authors having higher degrees are more involved in the project development and establish stronger links than the rest. At the same time, as we observed in Figure 7a, they only relate to other commiters that are involved in the project to the same degree as they are. If this behavior is found in other large libre software projects, it could be a valid method to identify the leading "core" group of a libre software project. On the other hand, the Apache project seems to promote a single category of developers, given that the weighted degree does not depend so clearly on the degree of vertices. It may be also that because of the fragmentation of the Apache project in many *families* of modules, it is easy to developers to reach a point where they do not have the possibility to get to know more developers.

Table 5 digs into the small-world properties of commiter networks. As we can observe, both networks can still considered to be small world. The Apache case is especially interesting, because an increase in the average distance is observed. This characteristic plus the large value of the clustering coefficient may indicate that the network is forming cliques.

CONCLUSION, LESSONS LEARNED, AND FURTHER WORK

In this article an approach to the study of libre (free, open source) software projects has been presented, based on the quantitative and qualitative application of social networks analysis to the data retrieved from source code management repositories. Since most libre software projects maintain such repositories, and allow for public read-only access to them, this analysis can be repeated for many of them. However, given its characteristics, it will be most useful for large projects, well above the hundreds of thousands of lines of code and dozens of developers.

We have designed a detailed methodology which applies this SNA-based approach to the study of CVS data, and which can be automated. It starts by downloading the required information from CVS, and produces as an output several graphs and tables which can be interpreted to gain knowledge about the informal organization of the studied project. It is important to highlight a set of parameters in the output that are suitable for characterizing several aspects of the organization of the studied project, which makes it possible to gain a lot of insight on how a group of developers is managing coordination and information flow within the project. In addition, it has been shown that the introduction of weights in the relationships gives more realistic information about the projects under study.

It has also been shown how our methodology is applied to some important and well known projects: KDE, Apache, and GNOME. Although these studies are sketched just as case examples, some relevant results can also be extracted from them. For instance, it has been shown how all the networks that have been studied fulfill the requirements to be a small world. This has important consequences on their characterization, since small worlds have been comprehensively studied and are well understood in many respects. We have also not only found that the growth of the studied networks cannot be explained by random preference attachment (something that could be previously suspected). Moreover, it matches pretty well the pattern of preference attachment related to the weight (amount of shared effort) of links. Some other relevant results are the elitist behavior found in these projects with respect to the connectivity of modules and developers, which are indicators of an over-redundancy of links, and of a good structure for the flow of knowledge, and the absence of centers of power (in terms of information flux). All of these conclusions should be validated by studying more projects, and by analyzing with detail their microimplications before being raised to the category of characteristics of libre software projects, but that so far are good lines of further research.

There are some other studies applying similar techniques to libre software projects. For instance, Crowston and Howison (2003) suggests that large projects are more modular than small ones. However, to our knowledge the kind of comprehensive analysis shown in this article has never been proposed as a methodology for characterizing libre software projects and their coordination structure. In fact, after using it in the study of some projects, we believe that it has a great potential to explore informal organizational patterns, and uncovering nonobvious relationships and characteristics of their underlying structure of coordination.

REFERENCES

Albert, R., & Barabasi, A.-L. (2002). Statistical mechanics of complex networks. *Reviews of Modern Physics, 74*, 47–97.

Albert, R., Barabási, A.-L., Jeong, H., & Bianconi, G. (2000). Power-law distribution of the World Wide Web. *Science, 287.*

Anthonisse, J. (1971). The rush in a directed graph (Tech. Rep.). Amsterdam: Stichting Mathematisch Centrum.

Conway, M. (1968). How do committees invent? *Datamation, 14*(4), 28–31.

Crowston, K., & Howison, J. (2003). The social structure of open source software development teams. In *Proceedings of the ICIS.*

Crowston, K., Scozzi, B., & Buonocore, S. (2003). An explorative study of open source software development structure. In *Proceedings of the ECIS*, Naples, Italy.

Dinh-Trong, T.T., & Bieman, J.M. (2005). The FreeBSD project: A replication case study of open source development. *IEEE Transactions on Software Engineering, 31*(6), 481–494.

Elliott, M., & Scacchi, W. (2004). Mobilization of software developers: The free software movement (Tech. Rep.). Retrieved June 16, 2006, from http://opensource.mit.edu/papers/elliottscacchi2.pdf

Freeman, C. (1977). A set of measures of centrality based on betweenness. *Sociometry, 40*, 35-41.

Fuggetta, A. (2003). Open source software: An evaluation. *Journal of Systems and Software, 66*(1), 77–90.

Germán, D. (2004a). An empirical study of fine-grained software modifications. In *International Conference in Software Maintenance.*

Germán, D. (2004b). Decentralized open source global software development, the GNOME experience. *Journal of Software Process: Improvement and Practice, 8*(4), 201-215.

Germán, D.M., & Hindle, A. (2006). Visualizing the evolution of software using softChange. *Journal of Software Engineering and Knowledge Engineering, 16*(1), 5-21.

Ghosh, R.A., & Prakash, V.V. (2000). The Orbiten free software survey. *5*(7). Retrieved from http://www.orbiten.org/ofss/01.html

Gîrba, T., Kuhn, A., Seeberger, M., & Ducasse, S. (2005). How developers drive software evolution. In *Proceedings of the International Workshop on Principles in Software Evolution* (pp. 113–122), Lisbon, Portugal.

Godfrey, M.W., & Tu, Q. (2000). Evolution in open source software: A case study. In *Proceedings of the International Conference on Software Maintenance* (pp. 131–142), San Jose, California.

González-Barahona, J.M., López-Fernández, L., & Robles, G. (2004). Community structure of modules in the Apache project. In *Proceedings of the 4th Workshop on Open Source Software.*

Guimera, R., Danon, L., Diaz-Guilera, A., Giralt, F., & Arenas, A. (2003). Self-similar community structure in a network of human interactions. *Physical Review E 68, 065103(R).*

Healy, K., & Schussman, A. (2003). *The ecology of open-source software development.* (Tech. Rep.). University of Arizona.

Koch, S., & Schneider, G. (2002). Effort, cooperation and coordination in an open source software project: GNOME. *Information Systems Journal, 12*(1), 27–42.

Krishnamurthy, S. (2002). Cave or community? An empirical investigation of 100 mature open source projects. *First Monday, 7*(6).

Kumar, R., Raghavan, P., Rajagopalan, S., & Tomkins, A. (2002). The Web and social networks. *IEEE Computer, 35*(11), 32–36.

Latora, V., & Marchiori, M. (2003). Economic small-world behavior in weighted networks. *Euro Physics Journal, B32*, 249-263.

Lopez, L., Gonzalez-Barahona, J.M., & Robles, G. (2004). Applying social network analysis to the information in cvs repositories. In *Proceedings of the International Workshop on Mining Software Repositories, 26th International Conference on Software Engineering*, Edinburg, Scotland.

Madey, G., Freeh, V., & Tynan, R. (2002). The open source development phenomenon: An analysis based on social network theory. In *Proceedings of the Americas Conference on Information Systems (AMCIS2002)* (pp. 1806–1813), Dallas, Texas.

Mockus, A., Fielding, R.T., & Herbsleb, J.D. (2002). Two case studies of open source software development: Apache and Mozilla. *ACM Transactions on Software Engineering and Methodology, 11*(3), 309–346.

Newman, M.E.J. (2001a). Scientific collaboration networks: I. Network construction and fundamental results. *Physical Review, E64, 016131.*

Newman, M.E.J. (2001b). Scientific collaboration networks: Ii. Shortest paths, weighted networks, and centrality. *Physical Review, E64, 016132.*

Raymond, E.S. (1997). The cathedral and the bazar. *First Monday, 3*(3).

Robles, G., Amor, J.J., Gonzalez-Barahona, J.M., & Herraiz, I. (2005a). Evolution and growth in large libre software projects. In *Proceedings of the International Workshop on Principles in Software Evolution* (pp. 165–174), Lisbon, Portugal.

Robles, G., González-Barahona, J.M., & Michlmayr, M. (2005b). Evolution of volunteer participation in libre software projects: Evidence from Debian. In *Proceedings of the 1st International Conference on Open Source Systems* (pp. 100–107), Genoa, Italy.

Robles, G., Koch, S., & Gonzalez-Barahona, J.M. (2004). Remote analysis and measurement of libre software systems by means of the cvsanaly tool. In *Proceedings of the 2nd ICSE Workshop on Remote Analysis and Measurement of Software Systems (RAMSS), 26th International Conference on Software Engineering*, Edinburg, Scotland.

Sabidussi, G. (1996). The centrality index of a graph. *Psychometrika, 31*, 581-606.

Wagstrom, P.A., Herbsleb, J.D., & Carley, K. (2005). A social network approach to free/open source software simulation. In *Proceedings of the 1st International Conference on Open Source Systems* (pp. 100–107), Genoa, Italy.

Watts, D.J. (2003). *Six degrees.* New York: W.W. Norton & Company.

Watts, D.J., & Strogatz, S. (1998). Collective dynamics of small-world networks. *Nature, 393,* 440-442.

Xu, J., Gao, Y., Christley, S., & Madey, G. (2005). A topological analysis of the open source software development community. In *Proceedings of the 38th Hawaii International Conference on System Sciences*, Hawaii.

Zimmermann, T., & Weißgerber, P. (2004). Processing CVS data for fine-grained analysis. In *Proceedings of the International Workshop on Mining Software Repositories* (pp. 2–6), Edinburg, Scotland.

Zimmermann, T., Weißgerber, P., Diehl, S., & Zeller, A. (2005). Mining version histories to guide software changes. *IEEE Transactions on Software Engineering, 31*(6), 429–445.

ENDNOTES

* This work has been funded in part by the European Commission, under the CALIBRE CA, IST program, contract number 004337. Israel Herraiz has been funded in part by Consejeria de Educación of Comunidad de Madrid and European Social Fund under grant number 01/FPI/0582/2005.

[1] In this paper the term "libre software" will be used to refer to any software licensed under terms that are compliant with the definition of "free software" by the Free Software Foundation, and the definition of "open source software" by the Open Source Initiative, thus avoiding the controversy between those two terms.

[2] Concurrent Version System (CVS) is the source code management (also known as ver-

sioning) system used in most libre software projects, although lately a new generation of tools, including for instance Subversion, are gaining popularity. In those projects, the CVS repository is usually freely readable over the Internet.

[3] A Pareto distribution is known to be given when the 20% most active is responsible for 80% of the output.

[4] For downloading this information we have used the CVSAnalY tool described in Robles, Koch, and Gonzalez-Barahona (2004).

[5] Throughout this article, references to Apache cover all projects lead by the Apache Foundation and not just the HTTPd server, usually known as the Apache Web server.

[6] Social network analysis has been applied to networks with hundreds of thousands, sometimes millions of vertices. In this sense, our network is of a small size even if we are handling large libre software projects.

This work was previously published in Int. Journal of Information Technology and Web Engineering, Vol 1, Issue 3, edited by E. Damiani and G. Succi, pp. 27-48, copyright 2006 by IGI Publishing (an imprint of IGI Global).

Chapter IV
Multi–Modal Modeling, Analysis, and Validation of Open Source Software Development Processes

Walt Scacchi
University of California, USA

Chris Jensen
University of California, USA

John Noll
University of California, and 2Santa Clara University, USA

Margaret Elliott
University of California, USA

ABSTRACT

Understanding the context, structure, activities, and content of software development processes found in practice has been and remains a challenging problem. In the world of free/open source software development, discovering and understanding what processes are used in particular projects is important in determining how they are similar to or different from those advocated by the software engineering community. Prior studies have revealed that development processes in F/OSSD projects are different in a number of ways. In this paper, we describe how a variety of modeling perspectives and techniques are used to elicit, analyze, and validate software development processes found in F/OSSD projects, with examples drawn from studies of the software requirements process found in the NetBeans.org project.

INTRODUCTION

In the world of globally dispersed, free/open source software development (F/OSSD), discovering and understanding what processes are used in particular projects is important in determining how they are similar to or different from those advocated by the software engineering community. For example, in our studies of software requirements engineering processes in F/OSSD projects across domains like Internet infrastructure, astrophysics, networked computer games, and software design systems (Scacchi, 2002, 2004, 2005), we generally find there are no explicit software requirements specifications or documents. However, we readily find numerous examples of sustained, successful, and apparently high-quality F/OSS systems being deployed on a worldwide basis. Thus, the process of software requirements engineering in F/OSSD projects must be different than the standard model of requirements elicitation, specification, modeling, analysis, communication, and management (Nuseibeh & Easterbrook, 2000). But if the process is different, how is it different, or more directly, how can we best observe and discover the context, structure, activities, and content software requirements processes in F/OSSD projects? This is the question addressed here.

Our approach to answering this question uses multimodal modeling of the observed processes, artifacts, and other evidence composed as an ethnographic hypermedia that provides a set of informal and formal models of the software development processes we observe, codify, and document. Why? First, our research question spans two realms of activity in software engineering, namely, software development and software process modeling. So we will need to address multiple perspectives or viewpoints, yet provide a traceable basis of evidence and analysis that supports model validation. Second, given there are already thousands of self-declared F/OSSD projects affiliated with OSS portals like Source-Forge.net, Freshmeat.net, and Savannah.gnu.org,

then our answer will be constrained and limited in scope to the particular F/OSSD projects examined. Producing a more generalized model of the F/OSS development process studied requires multiple, comparative project case studies, so our approach should be compatible with such a goal (Scacchi, 2002). Last, we want an approach to process modeling that is open to independent analysis, validation, communication, and evolution, yet be traceable to the source data materials that serve as evidence of the discovered process in the F/OSSD projects examined (cf. Kitchenham, Dyba, & Jorgensen, 2004).

Accordingly, to reveal how we use our proposed multimodal approach to model requirements processes in F/OSSD projects, we first review related research to provide the foundational basis for our approach. Second, we describe and provide examples of the modeling modes we use to elicit and analyze the processes under study. Last, we examine what each modeling mode is good for, and what kind of analysis and reasoning it supports.

RELATED RESEARCH AND APPROACH

There is growing recognition that software requirements engineering can effectively incorporate multiple viewpoints (Finkelstein, Gabbay, Hunter, & Nuseibeh, 1994; Leite & Freeman, 1991; Nuseibeh & Easterbrook, 2000) and ethnographic techniques (Nuseibeh & Easterbrook, 2000; Viller & Sommerville, 2000) for eliciting, analyzing, and validating functional and nonfunctional software system *product* requirements. However, it appears that many in the software engineering community treat the *process* of requirements engineering as transparent and prescriptive, though perhaps difficult to practice successfully. However, we do not know how large distributed F/OSSD projects perform their development processes (cf. Curtis, Krasner, & Iscoe, 1998).

Initial studies of requirements development across multiple types of F/OSSD projects (Scacchi, 2002, 2004) find that OSS product requirements are continuously emerging (Gans, Jarke, Kethers, & Lakemeyer, 2003; Gasser, Scacchi, Penne, & Sandusky, 2003; Truex, Baskerville, & Klein, 1999) and asserted after they have been implemented, rather than relatively stable and elicited before being implemented. Similarly, these findings reveal requirements practice centers about reading and writing many types of communications and development artifacts as "informalisms" (Scacchi, 2002), as well as addressing new kinds of nonfunctional requirements like project community development, freedom of expression and choice, and ease of information space navigation. Elsewhere, there is widespread recognition that F/OSSD projects differ from their traditional software engineering counterparts in that F/OSSD projects do not in general operate under the constraints of budget, schedule, and project management constraints. In addition, OSS developers are also end users or administrators of the software products they develop, rather than conventionally separated as developers vs. users. Consequently, it appears that F/OSSD projects create different types of software requirements using a different kind of requirements engineering process, than compared to what the software engineering community has addressed. Thus, there is a fundamental need to discover and understand the process of requirements development in different types of F/OSSD projects.

We need an appropriate mix of concepts, techniques, and tools to discover and understand F/OSSD processes. We and others have found that process ethnographies must be empirically grounded, evidence-based, and subject to comparative, multiperspective analysis (Curtis et al., 1998; Finkelstein et al., 1994; Glaser & Strauss, 1967; Kitchenham et al., 2004; Nuseibeh & Easterbrook, 2000; Scacchi, 2002; Seaman, 1999). However, we also recognize that our effort to discover and

understand F/OSSD processes should reveal the experience of software development newcomers who want to join and figure out how things get done in the project (Scacchi, 2005).

As participant observers in such a project, we find that it is common practice for newcomers to navigate and browse the project's Web site, development artifacts, and computer-mediated communication systems (e.g., discussion forums, online chat, project Wikis), as well as to download and try out the current software product release. Such traversal and engagement with multiple types of hyperlinked information provide a basis for making modest contributions (e.g., bug reports) before more substantial contributions (code patches, new modules) are offered, with the eventual possibility of proposing, changing, or sustaining the OSS system's architecture. These interactive experiences reflect a progressive validation of a participant's understanding of current F/OSSD process and product requirements (Bolchini & Paolini, 2004; Narayanan & Hegarty, 2002). Thus, we seek a process discovery and modeling scheme that elicits, analyzes, and validates multimode, hypertext descriptions of a F/OSSD project's requirements process. Furthermore, the process descriptions we construct should span informal through formal process models, and accommodate graphic, textual, and computationally enactable process media. Finally, our results should be in a form open to independent analysis, validation, extension, and redistribution by the project's participants.

MULTIMODE PROCESS MODELING, ANALYSIS, AND VALIDATION USING ETHNOGRAPHIC HYPERMEDIA

An ethnographic hypermedia (Dicks & Mason, 1998) is a hypertext that supports comparative, cross-linked analysis of multiple types of qualitative ethnographic data (cf. Seaman, 1999). They are a kind of semantic hypertext used in coding, modeling, documenting, and explaining patterns of social interaction data and analysis arising in contemporary anthropological, sociological, and distributed cognition studies. The media can include discourse records, indigenous texts, interview transcripts, graphic or photographic images, audio/video recordings, and other related information artifacts. Ideally, they also preserve the form and some of the context in which the data appear, which is important for subsequent (re)analysis, documentation, explanation, presentation, and validation.

Ethnographic studies of software development processes within Web-based F/OSSD projects are the focus here. Ethnographic studies that observe and explain social action through online participant observation and data collection have come to be called "virtual ethnography" (Hine, 2000). Virtual ethnography techniques have been used to observe the work practices, compare the artifacts produced, and discover the processes of F/OSSD projects found on and across the Web (Elliott & Scacchi, 2003, 2005; Jensen & Scacchi, 2005a, b; Oza, Nistor, Hu, Jensen, & Scacchi, 2004; Scacchi, 2002, 2004, 2005). In particular, an important source of data that is examined in such studies of F/OSSD projects is the interrelated Web of online documents and artifacts that embody and characterize the medium and continuously emerging outcomes of F/OSSD work. These documents and artifacts constitute a particular narrative/textual genre ecology (Spinuzzi & Zachry, 2000) that situate the work practices and characterize the problem solving media found within F/OSSD projects.

We have employed ethnographic hypermedia in our virtual ethnographic studies of F/OSSD projects. What does this mean, and what challenges or opportunities for requirements elicitation, analysis, and validation have emerged along the way? These questions are addressed below

through examples drawn from a case study of the NetBeans.org OSSD project (Jensen & Scacchi, 2005a, b), which is one of the largest F/OSSD projects we have studied. The NetBeans.org project is a corporate sponsored OSSD project (Jensen & Scacchi, 2005a) focused on the development of an interactive development environment (IDE) for constructing application systems using Java enterprise beans technology. It is similar in size and scope to the Eclipse project founded by IBM, which is also developing a Java-based IDE.

As noted, the F/OSSD projects we study are found on the Web. Web sites for these projects consist of a network of hyperlinked documents or artifacts. Samples of sites we have studied include NetBeans.org, Mozilla.org, Apache.org, and GNUenterprise.org, among others (Elliott & Scacchi, 2003, 2004; Jensen & Scacchi, 2005a, b; Scacchi, 2002, 2004). A team of two to five researchers examines a project site (via browsing, searching, downloading, and cross-linking) over a period of 4-6 weeks initially, then periodically thereafter. The artifacts we examine include Web pages, e-mail discussion lists, bug reports, project to-do lists, source code files and directories, site maps, and more. These artifacts are an important part of the data we collect, examine, study, code, and analyze in order to identify F/OSSD work practices and development processes that arise in a given project.

We create a hypermedia of these artifacts in ways that allow us to locate the originating sources of data within the focal project's Web site. This allows us to maintain links to the source data materials that we observe as evidence of the process at hand, as well as to allow us to detect when these data sources have been updated or removed. (We also archive a local copy of all such data.) However, we create annotated and assembled artifacts that embed hyperlinks into these documents as part of our ethnographic hypermedia. As a result, multiple kinds of ethnographic records are created including annotated artifacts, rich hypermedia pictures, and ethnographic narratives. Juxtaposed about these records are other kinds of models including a process metamodel, attributed directed graph model, process domain ontology, and a formal, computationally enactable process model. Each is described next, and each is hyperlinked into an overall ethnographic hypermedia that provides cross-cutting evidence for the observed OSS requirements processes. This in turn provide us with an approach to mapping complex situations in various forms, which is consistent with recent advances in grounded theory approaches to ethnographic study (Clarke 2003).

Annotated Artifacts

Annotated artifacts represent original software development artifacts like (publicly available) online chat transcripts that record the dialogue, discussions, and debate that emerge between OSS developers. These artifacts record basic design rationale in an online conversation form. The textual content of these artifacts can be tagged, analyzed, hyperlinked, and categorized manually or automatically (Rao, 2003). However, these conversational contents also reveal much about how OSS developers interact at a distance to articulate, debate, and refine the continuously emerging requirements for the software system they are developing. For example, Elliott and Scacchi (2003, 2005) provide conversational transcripts among developers engaged in a debate over what the most important properties of software development tools and components to use when building free software. They provide annotations that identify and bracket how ideological beliefs, social values, and community building norms constrain and ultimately determine the technical choices for what tools to use and what components to reuse when developing OSS. The following is an example of an excerpt of an online chat transcript found in a F/OSSD project where the developer (here identified anonymously as "ByronC") who is an outsider to the project lurking on the chat

discussion and who advocates a strong belief for avoiding the use of nonfree software when developing F/OSS, as indicated by the (**boldface**) annotations we added.

```
<ByronC> Hello (Outsider Critique-1
<ByronC> Several images on the Web site
seem to be made with nonfree Adobe
software, I hope I'm wrong: it is quite
shocking. Does anybody know more on the
subject?
<ByronC> We should avoid using nonfree
software at all costs, am I wrong? (Ex-
treme belief in free software (BIFS)-1)
<ByronC> Anyone awake in here? Outsider
Critique-1)
```

Basic ethnographic data like this draws our attention to look for practices within F/OSSD efforts to see if such beliefs do in fact constrain the choice of software tools used within F/OSSD processes.

Navigational Rich Pictures

Rich pictures (Monk & Howard, 1998) provide an informal graphical scheme for identifying and modeling stakeholders, their concerns and beliefs, objects and patterns of interaction. We extend this scheme to form navigational rich pictures constructed as a Web-compatible hypertext image map that denotes the overall context as the composition and relationships observed among the stakeholder roles, activities, tools, and document types (resources) found in a F/OSSD project. In the example figures that follow, we display the stakeholders/roles using human-like icons, their concerns or beliefs as clouds associated to the icons, and the objects and patterns or interaction as hyperlinked entities. Figure 1 displays such a rich picture constructed for NetBeans.org. Furthermore, associated with each hyperlinked entity is a *use case* (Cockburn, 2001) that we have constructed to denote an observable activity per-

Figure 1. A rich picture image map of the requirements and release process in the NetBeans.org F/OSSD project

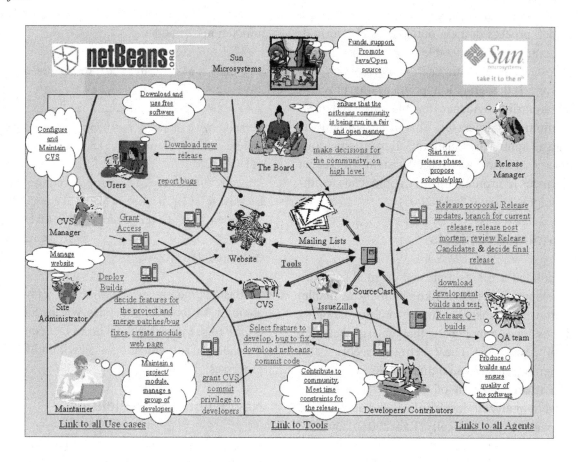

Figure 2. A hyperlink selection within a rich hypermedia presentation that reveals a corresponding use case

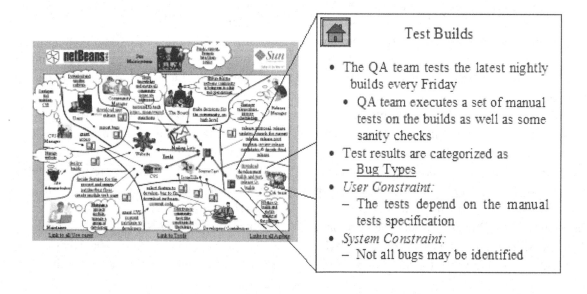

Figure 3. An attributed directed graph of the resource flow for the NetBeans.org requirement and release process. Boxes denote tasks/actions, ellipses denote resources/objects, dashed lines denote resource flows, and solid lines and labels denote agent/stakeholder roles performing tasks that transform input resources into output resources.

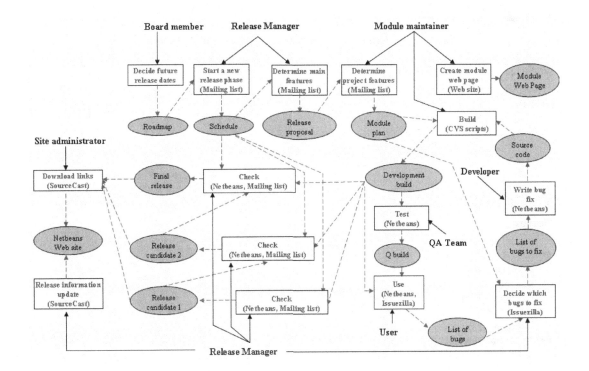

formed by an actor-role using a tool that consumes or produces a document/object type. An example use case is shown in Figure 2. Each other type of data also is hyperlinked to either a descriptive annotation or to a Web site/page where further information on the object type can be found.

Directed Resource Flow Graph

A directed resource flow graph denotes a recurring workflow pattern that has been discovered in an F/OSSD project. These workflows order the dependencies among the activities that actor-roles perform on a recurring basis to the objects/resources within their project work. These resources appear as or within Web pages on an F/OSSD project's Web site. For example, in the

NetBeans.org project, we found that software product requirements are intertwined with software build and release management. Thus, the "requirements and release process" entails identifying and programming new/updated system functions or features in the course of compiling, integrating, testing, and progressively releasing a stable composition of source code files as an executable software build version for evaluation or use by other NetBeans.org developers (Elliott & Scacchi, 2003, 2005; Oza et al., 2004). An example flow graph for this appears in Figure 3. The code files, executable software, updated directories, and associated e-mail postings announcing the completion and posting the results of the testing are among the types of resources that are involved. Last, the rendering of the flow

Figure 4. A view of the process domain ontology for the NetBeans.org software requirements and release process

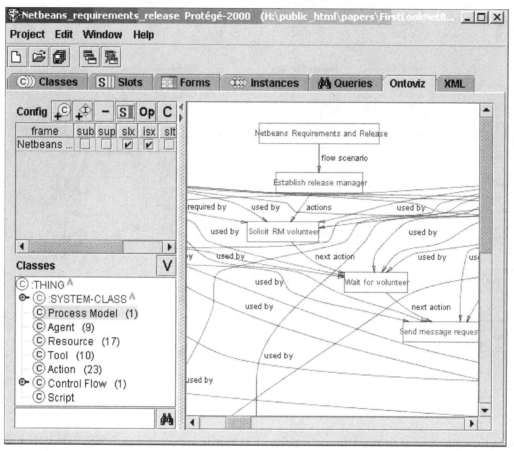

graph can serve as an *image map* to the online (i.e., on the NetBeans.org Web site) data sources from where they are observed.

Process Domain Ontology

A process ontology represents the underlying *process metamodel* (Mi & Scacchi, 1996; Noll & Scacchi, 2001) that defines the semantics and syntax of the process modeling constructs we use to model discovered processes. It provides the base object classes for constructing the requirements process (domain) taxonomies of the object classes for all of the resource and relation types found in the rich picture and directed resource flow graph. However, each discovered process is specific to

an F/OSSD project, and knowledge about this domain is also needed to help contextualize the possible meanings of the processes being modeled. This means that a process domain entails objects, resources or relations that may or may not be have been previously observed and modeled, so that it may be necessary to extend to process modeling constructs to accommodate new types of objects, resources, and relations, as well as the attributes and (instance) values that characterize them, and attached methods that operationalize them.

We use an ontology modeling and editing tool, Protégé-2000 (Noy, Sintek, Decker, Crubezy, Fergerson, & Musen, 2001), to maintain and update our domain ontology for OSS requirements processes. Using Protégé-2000, we can also visu-

Figure 5. An excerpt of the formal model of the Netbeans.org requirements and release process coded in PML

```
...
sequence Test {
 action Execute automatic test scripts {
 requires { Test scripts, release binaries }
 provides { Test results }
 tool { Automated test suite (xtest, others) }
 agent { Sun ONE Studio QA team }
 script { /* Executed off-site */ } }
action Execute manual test scripts {
 requires { Release binaries }
 provides { Test results }
 tool { NetBeans IDE }
 agent { users, developers, Sun ONE Studio QA team, Sun ONE Studio
developers }
 script { /* Executed off-site */ } }
iteration Update Issuezilla {
 action Report issues to Issuezilla {
   requires { Test results }
   provides { Issuezilla entry }
   tool { Web browser }
   agent { users, developers, Sun ONE Studio QA team, Sun ONE Studio
developers }
   script {
     <br><a href="http://www.netbeans.org/issues/">Navigate to Issuezilla </
a>
     <br><a href="http://www.netbeans.org/issues/query.cgi">Query Issuezilla
</a>
     <br><a href="http://www.netbeans.org/issues/enter _ bug.cgi">Enter issue
</a> } }
...
```

alize the structure of dependencies and relations (Grinter, 2003) among the objects or resources in a semantic Web manner. An example view can be seen in Figure 4. Furthermore, we can create translators that can transform syntactic form of the modeling representations into XML forms or SQL schema definitions, which enables further process modeling and tool integration options (cf. Jensen & Scacchi, 2005b).

Figure 6. A screenshot displaying the result of the PML-based reenactment of one step ("Action Report issues to Issuezilla") in the NetBeans.org requirements and release process

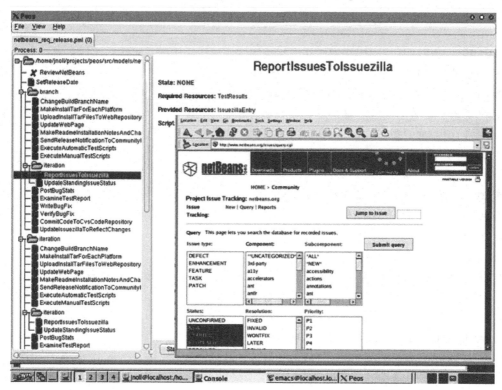

Formal Process Model and Its Enactment

A formal process model denotes a syntactically precise and semantically typed specification of the resource objects, flow dependencies, actor-roles, and associated tools that specifies an enactable (via interactive process-guided user navigation) hypertext representation we call an *organizational process hypertext* (Noll & Scacchi, 2001). This semantic hypertext, and its supporting run-time environment, enables the ability to walkthrough or simulate enactment of the modeled F/OSSD process as a process-guided, navigational traversal across a set of process linked Web pages. The semantic hypertext is automatically rendered through compilation of the process models that are output from the ontology editor in a process

modeling language called PML (Noll & Scacchi, 2001). A PML-based model specification can be automatically checked for inconsistencies can be detected at compile-time or run-time. An example of an excerpt from such a model is shown in Figure 5. The compiled version of the PML produced a nonlinear sequence of process-linked Web pages, each one of which corresponds to one step in the modeled process. An example showing the result of enacting a process (action) step specified at the bottom of Figure 5 appears in Figure 6.

Constructing an Ethnographic Hypermedia Narrative for Process Validation

An ethnographic narrative denotes a final ethnographic hypermedia view. This is an analytical

Figure 7. Getting captured and analyzed process models out for validation and possible evolution by NetBeans.org project participants

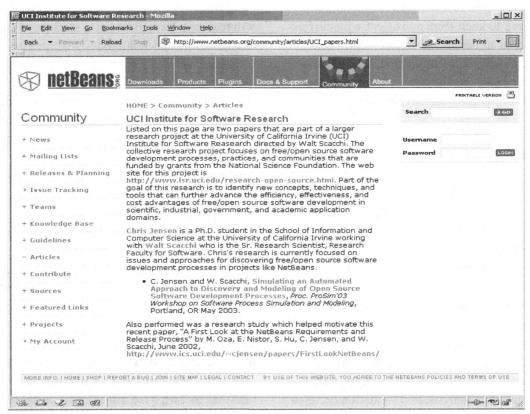

research narrative that is structured as a document that is (ideally) suitable for dissemination and publication in Web-based and printed forms. It is a composite model derived from selections of the preceding representations in the form of a narrative with embedded hyperlinked objects, and hyperlinks to related materials. It embodies and explains the work practices, development processes, resource types and relations, and overall project context as a narrative, hyperlinked ethnographic account that discovered at play within a given F/OSSD project, such as we documented for the NetBeans requirements and release process (Oza et al., 2004). In printed form, the narratives we have produced so far are somewhere between one-fourth to one-fifteenth the number of pages compared to the overall set of project-specific data

(documents) at the first two levels of hyperlink connectivity; said differently, if the ethnographic report is 30 or so printed pages (i.e., suitable for journal publication), the underlying ethnographic hypermedia will correspond to a hypermedia equivalent to 120-450 printed pages.

The narrative is in a form intended for external review and validation by those not involved in the collection, modeling, and analysis activities, such as members of the project under study (NetBeans. org; see Figure 7). These external reviewers can read through the narrative during validation to see if there are gaps or inconsistencies, or to pose questions to the narrative's authors. When such shortfalls are detected or reported, then the task is to determine if the problem arises from either a gap in the modeling effort, or in its narrative rendering. Finally, the narrative and its hypermedia components are envisioned as open and living documents, so that feedback from the community may serve to keep them consistent with current practice, or to detect and report inconsistencies that are in need of attention, update, or remediation, much like the software and artifacts found in the F/OSSD projects they describe.

DISCUSSION

We have learned a number of things based on applying and evaluating our approach to modeling development processes, such as those for software requirements, in different F/OSSD projects. First, no single mode of process description adequately subsumes the others, so there is no best process description scheme. Instead, different informal and formal descriptions respectively account for the shortcomings in the other, as do textual, graphic, and computationally enactable process representations. Second, incremental and progressive elicitation, analysis, and validation occur in the course of developing multimode requirements process models. Third, multimode process models are well-suited for discovery and understanding of complex software processes found in F/OSSD projects. However, it may not be a suitable approach for other software projects that do not organize, discuss, and perform software development activities in an online, persistent, open, free, and publicly accessible manner. Fourth, multimode process modeling has the potential to be applicable to the discovery and modeling of software product requirements, although the motivation for investing such effort may not be clear or easily justified. Process discovery is a different kind of problem than product development, so different kinds of approaches are likely to be most effective.

Next, we observed that the software product requirements in F/OSSD projects are continually emerging and evolving. Thus, it seems likely that the requirements process in such projects is also continuous. Thus, supporting the evolution of multimode models of OSS requirements processes will require either automated techniques for process discovery and multimode update propagation techniques, or else the participation of the project community to treat these models as *open source software process models*, that can be continuously elicited, analyzed, and validated along with other F/OSSD project assets, as suggested in Figure 7, which are concepts we are currently investigating. However, it seems fair to note that ethnographic accounts are situated in time, and are not intended for evolution.

Last, each of the methods we used for modeling processes found in F/OSSD projects has been previously applied and shown to be useful by other researchers. Our effort brings these diverse approaches together in order to demonstrate and compare their individual and collective value. Thus, we find the multimode approach to modeling, analyzing, and validating F/OSSD processes provides a new threshold for research and practice that in turn give rise to new insights and findings that none of the individual approaches can realize on their own. Finally, we believe the multimode approach can be readily adopted, taught, and put into practices to support not only F/OSSD projects, but any software development project that is distributed and supported across the Web/Internet.

CONCLUSION

Ethnographic hypermedia are an important type of semantic hypertext that are well-suited to support the navigation, elicitation, modeling, analysis, and report writing found in ethnographic studies of F/OSSD processes. We have described our approach to developing and using ethnographic hypermedia to support the modeling, analysis, and validation of software development processes in F/OSSD projects like NetBeans.org, where multiple modes of informal to formal representations are involved. We find that this hypermedia is well-suited for supporting qualitative research methods that associated different type of project data, together with comparative analysis of process descriptions rendered in graphic, textual, and computationally enactable descriptions. We provided examples of the various kinds of hypertext-based process descriptions and linkages that we constructed in moving from abstract, informal representations of the data through a series of ever more formalized process models resulting from our studies.

Based on our efforts and results reported here, it appears that free/open source software development projects can benefit from the discovery, modeling, and validation of the development processes they practice, and that ethnographic hypermedia based representations of these processes provides an innovative scheme for capturing, representing, and evolving these representations in a manner that can be maintained and evolved in an open source way.

ACKNOWLEDGMENT

The research described in this report is supported by grants #0083075, #0205679, #0205724, and #0350754 from the U.S. National Science Foundation. No endorsement implied. Mark Ackerman at University of Michigan, Ann Arbor; Les Gasser at University of Illinois, Urbana-Champaign; and others at ISR are collaborators on the research described in this article.

REFERENCES

Bolchini, D., & Paolini, P. (2004). Goal-driven requirements analysis for hypermedia-intensive Web applications. *Requirements Engineering, 9*, 85-103.

Clarke, A.E. (2003). Situational analysis: Grounded theory mapping after the postmodern turn. *Symbolic Interaction, 26*(4), 553-576.

Cockburn, A. (2001). *Writing effective use cases.* New York: Addison-Wesley.

Curtis, B., Krasner, H., & Iscoe, N. (1998). A field study of the software design process for large systems. *Communications of the ACM, 31*(11), 1268-1287.

Dicks, B., & Mason, B. (1998). Hypermedia and ethnography: Reflections on the construction of a research approach. *Sociological Research Online, 3*(3). Retrieved June 9, 2006, from http://www.socresonline.org.uk

Elliott, M., & Scacchi, W. (2003, November). Free software developers as an occupational community: Resolving conflicts and fostering collaboration. In *Proceedings of the ACM International Conference on Supporting Group Work* (pp. 21-30), Sanibel Island, Florida.

Elliott, M., & Scacchi, W. (2005). Free software development: Cooperation and conflict in a virtual organizational culture. In S. Koch (Ed.), *Free/open source software development* (pp. 152-172). Hershey, PA: Idea Group Publishing.

Finkelstein, A.C.W., Gabbay, D., Hunter, A., & Nuseibeh, B. (1994). Inconsistency handling in multi-perspective specifications. *IEEE Transactions on Software Engineering, 20*(8), 569-578.

Gans, G., Jarke, M., Kethers, S., & Lakemeyer, G. (2003). Continuous requirements management for organisation networks: A (dis)trust-based approach. *Requirements Engineering, 8*, 4-22.

Gasser, L., Scacchi, W., Penne, B., & Sandusky, R. (2003, December). Understanding continuous design in OSS projects. In *Proceedings of the 16th International Conference on Software & Systems Engineering and their Applications*, Paris, France.

Glaser, B., & Strauss, A. (1967). *The discovery of grounded theory: Strategies for qualitative research.* Chicago: Aldine Publishing Co.

Grinter, R.E. (2003). Recomposition: Coordinating a Web of software dependencies. *Computer Supported Cooperative Work, 12*(3), 297-327.

Hine, C. (2000). *Virtual ethnography.* Newbury Park, CA: Sage Publications.

Jensen, C., & Scacchi, W. (2005a, January). Collaboration, leadership, control, and conflict management in the NetBeans.org community. In *Proceedings of the 38th Hawaii International Conference on Systems Science,* Waikola Village, Hawaii.

Jensen, C., & Scacchi, W. (2005b, July-September). Process modeling across the Web information infrastructure. *Software Process--Improvement and Practice, 10*(3), 255-272.

Kitchenham, B.A., Dyba, T., & Jorgensen, M. (2004). Evidence-based software engineering. In *Proceedings of the 26th International Conference on Software Engineering* (pp. 273-281), Edinburgh, Scotland. IEEE Computer Society.

Leite, J.C.S.P., & Freeman, P.A. (1991). Requirements validation through viewpoint resolution. *IEEE Transactions on Software Engineering, 17*(12), 1253-1269.

Mi, P., & Scacchi, W. (1996). A meta-model for formulating knowledge-based models of software development. *Decision Support Systems, 17*(4), 313-330.

Monk, A., & Howard, S. (1998, March-April). The rich picture: A tool for reasoning about work context. *Interactions, 5*(2), 21-30.

Narayanan, N.H., & Hegarty, M. (2002). Multimedia design for communication of dynamic information. *International Journal on Human-Computer Studies, 57*, 279-315.

Noll, J., & Scacchi, W. (2001). Specifying process-oriented hypertext for organizational computing. *Journal of Network & Computer Applications, 24*(1), 39-61.

Noy, N.F., Sintek, M., Decker, S., Crubezy, M., Fergerson, R.W., & Musen, M.A. (2001, March-April). Creating semantic Web contents with Protégé-2000. *IEEE Intelligent Systems, 16*(2), 60-71.

Nuseibeh, B., & Easterbrook, S. (2000). Requirements engineering: A roadmap. In A. Finkelstein (Ed.), *The future of software engineering.* ACM and IEEE Computer Society Press.

Oza, M., Nistor, E., Hu, S. Jensen, C., & Scacchi, W. (2004, February). A first look at the Netbeans requirements and release process. Retrieved June 9, 2006, from *http://www.ics.uci.edu/cjensen/papers/FirstLookNetBeans/*

Rao, R. (2003, November). From unstructured data to actionable intelligence. *IT Pro*, pp. 29-35.

Scacchi, W. (2002, February). Understanding the requirements for developing open source software systems. *IEE Proceedings on Software, 149*(1), 24-39.

Scacchi, W. (2004, January). Free/open source software development practices in the computer game community. *IEEE Software, 21*(1), 59-67.

Scacchi, W. (2005). Socio-technical interaction networks in free/open source software development processes. In S.T. Acuña & N. Juristo (Eds.), *Peopleware and the software process (*pp. 1-27*).* World Scientific Press.

Seaman, C.B. (1999). Qualitative methods in empirical studies of software engineering. *IEEE Transactions on Software Engineering, 25*(4), 557-572.

Spinuzzi, C., & Zachry, M. (2000, August). Genre ecologies: An open system approach to understanding and constructing documentation. *ACM Journal of Computer Documentation, 24*(3), 169-181.

Truex, D., Baskerville, R., & Klein, H. (1999). Growing systems in an emergent organization. *Communications of the ACM, 42*(8), 117-123.

Viller, S., & Sommerville, I. (2000). Ethnographically informed analysis for software engineers. *International Journal Human-Computer Studies, 53*, 169-196.

ENDNOTE

*   Previous version appeared in *Proc. First Intern. Conf. Open Source Software*, Genova, Italy, 1-8, July 2005.

This work was previously published in Int. Journal of Information Technology and Web Engineering, Vol 1, Issue 3, edited by E. Damiani and G. Succi, pp. 49-63, copyright 2006 by IGI Publishing (an imprint of IGI Global).

Chapter V
An Empirical Study on the Migration to OpenOffice.org in a Public Administration

B. Rossi
Free University of Bolzano-Bozen, Italy

M. Scotto
Free University of Bolzano-Bozen, Italy

A. Sillitti
Free University of Bolzano-Bozen, Italy

G. Succi
Free University of Bolzano-Bozen, Italy

ABSTRACT

The aim of the paper is to report the results of a migration to Open Source Software (OSS) in one Public Administration. The migration focuses on the office automation field and, in particular, on the OpenOffice.org suite. We have analysed the transition to OSS considering qualitative and quantitative data collected with the aid of different tools. All the data have been always considered from the point of view of the different stakeholders involved, IT managers, IT technicians, and users. The results of the project have been largely satisfactory. However the results cannot be generalised due to some constraints, like the environment considered and the parallel use of the old solution. Nevertheless, we think that the data collected can be of valuable aid to managers wishing to evaluate a possible transition to OSS.

INTRODUCTION

Open Source Software (OSS) and Open Data Standards (ODS) emerged in recent years as a viable alternative to proprietary solutions. There are many cases in which the adoption of OSS has proven advantageous for companies deciding to adopt it in replacement or in conjunction with closed solutions. The limitation of these migrations for our point of view is that they were very often server-side oriented and not supported by empirical evidence of the benefits of the new solution. In this sense, there are very few case studies that report successful transitions on the desktop side (ZDNet, 2005) and some are still underway (Landeshauptstadt München, 2003; Stadt Wien, 2004). It is our opinion that the reason of the apparent different results in the two fields is due to the nature of OSS development (Feller & Fitzgerald, 2001) that leads to repercussions on the resulting usability (Nichols & Twidale, 2003).

When comparing OSS and proprietary software and when comparing software solutions in general, it is impossible to get a global index referring to quality in order to compare two solutions (Fenton & Pfleeger, 1997).

If we consider the most important aspects under which it is significant to analyse software, as:

- Reliability
- Performance
- Price
- Security
- Interoperability
- Usability
- Extendibility
- Functionalities
- Privacy protection

The categories have to be balanced with the requirements of the environment and users in which the solution is deployed. Where the aspects of security, reliability, and extendibility are of key importance, OSS has proven a valid solution, if not superior to proprietary solutions. Where functionalities, usability, and in general user interaction acquires importance as on the client side, OSS has yet to prove as a valid alternative. Price is a controversial issue as there is the need not only to evaluate the license price but also the software maintenance and other costs inherited from the migration. These considerations originated the study we propose.

The purpose of the study is to evaluate in a rigorous way the introduction of OSS in a working environment, following the criteria of a controlled experiment from the selection of the sample to the evaluation of the results. We selected a sample of 22 users from different offices in the public administration target of the experiment. We divided the sample in two groups, one to be migrated, the other to be used as a control group. The results obtained seem to report that the initial reduction of productivity is not as consistent as we thought, also taking into account that half of the users considered the introduced solution as offering less functionality than the proprietary one.

STATE OF THE ART

There are many studies available evaluating the Total Cost of Ownership (TCO) of OSS. The original model derived from the work of the Gartner Group in 1987 and has since then been inserted in different models. The TCO model helps managers by considering not only the cost of purchase but also further costs as maintenance or training.

All the studies are not unanimous as the savings that can be reached with the adoption of OSS (Robert Frances Group, 2002; The Yankee Group, 2005). One of the reasons is probably the different weight given to costs and benefits that are difficult to measure. Two of such measures are, for example, the risks of lock-ins and the development of local economies. The risks of entering a mechanism of lock-in, for example, by relying only on a single software supplier or storing massive amounts of data by means of closed data standards are real and must be considered in a TCO model evaluating a transition (Shapiro & Varian, 1999). On the other side, the adoption of OSS can be of benefit to local software companies that can exploit the possibility given by the available source code and open data standards. Also in this case, the amount of this kind of externality is difficult to quantify.

Considering OSS, there are many projects worth mentioning, we will name here two of the most famous and see how they perform on the market against proprietary solutions:

- the Apache Web server[1]
- the Mozilla Firefox Web browser[2]

Table 1 shows that the Apache Web server detains almost 70% of the whole market share (Netcraft Survey, 2005). As virus attacks of the last years have proven (CERT, 2001), one of the reason of such wide adoption is the security proposed by the Apache architecture.

Table 2 shows the market share of the Mozilla Firefox browser between January and April 2005. As it can be seen also in this case the software is gaining constant market shares in the last months. The software is still behind in market shares but it represents an important competitor for the market dominator, Microsoft Internet Explorer.

These are surely two of the most popular OSS that emerged during the last few years; there are many more that can compete with proprietary solutions. By looking at these and other examples, we can conclude that OSS already could represent an important alternative to proprietary software.

Another important consideration on OSS is represented by the cases in which a large migration has been performed or is in the process of being performed. Having a look at the different case studies available for the migration to OSS, we summarise the most famous during these years in Table 3; three are European, while one is U.S.-based.

One of the most remarkable deployments of OSS on the desktop side is surely the one of the Extremadura region in Spain, recently installing 80,000 Linux systems, 66,000 for the educational system and 14,000 for administrative workstations. The local administration created their Linux distribution called gnuLinex.[3] According to their IT department, the savings have been of the order of €18M (ZDNet, 2005). Another case of success is the one of the city of Largo, FL where the migration has involved 900 clients; the savings have been estimated at $300,000-$400,000 (Newsforge, 2002). The migration of the city of Munich and the one of the city of Vienna are currently underway (Landeshauptstadt München, 2003; Stadt Wien, 2004). As the delay of the Munich migration seems to demonstrate, a transition to OSS is not a process to underestimate. There are also cases where the proprietary solution has been considered as more convenient, like the city of Nürnberg, where according to their own migration study the transition from Windows 2000/Office 2000 to Windows XP/Office XP was considered €4.5M cheaper than the transition to Linux/OpenOffice. org (Stadt Nürnberg, 2004).

A final consideration on studies performed on OSS usability. Of certain interest for our study, albeit a little dated, is the experimentation conducted by the Berkeley University in November-December 2001 (Everitt & Lederer, 2001), comparing two different solutions in the office automation field, namely Sun StarOffice Writer 5.2 and Microsoft Word 2000. Authors report about an experiment on 12 users, regarding the user interface integration. As a result of the study, the two products were comparable, although the Microsoft solution proved to be more satisfactory and easier to use.

Table 1. Web servers in September and October 2005 (Netcraft Survey, 2005)

Developer	September 2005	Percent	October 2005	Percent	Change
Apache	49598424	69.15	52005811	69.89	0.74
Microsoft	14601553	20.36	15293030	20.55	0.19
Sun	1868891	2.61	1889989	2.54	-0.07
Zeus	584598	0.82	585972	0.79	-0.03

Table 2. Browsers market share ("Browser Market Share Study," itproductivity.org, 2005)

Browser	January 2005 (%)	April 2005 (%)
Internet Explorer	84.85	83.07
Firefox	4.23	10.28
Mozilla	4.48	3.81
Netscape	3.03	0.92
AOL	2.20	0.85
MSN	0.58	0.67
Opera	0.34	0.41
Total	99.71	100.01

Table 3. Large scale migrations to OSS of public administrations

Region	Clients to migrate	Side	Distribution
Extremadura	80,000	Desktop/Servers	gnuLinex
Munich	14,000	Desktop	Debian
Vienna	7,500	Desktop	Wienux (Debian/KDE)
Largo, FL	900	Desktop/Servers	Linux KDE 2.1.1

THE STUDY

Our study has been inserted into this framework; the intention is to contribute to the field with a solid and sound analysis of a real transition to OSS on the client side, specifically the analysis of a migration in the office automation field in one public administration.

In particular the study related the introduction of the OpenOffice.org[4] suite. The suite offers comparable functions as the one offered by Microsoft Office.[5] It is composed of several applications, a text-processor, a spreadsheet, software for presentations, for drawing operations and for the creation of formulae. The only functionality missing in the version installed was the possibility to create small local databases. In the organisation where we performed the study, this was a feature rarely employed by users and, in general, deprecated by

IT managers. We focused our analysis mainly on word-processors and spreadsheets.

The experiment was performed on 22 users of a public administration (PA) during the transition to OSS. In the following sections we expose the methodology adopted, the tools employed, and the main results obtained from the qualitative and quantitative data collected. The limitations and possible future additional work is listed at the end of the article. The overall sample of 22 users has been selected from three departments of the PA under exam. Some constraints had to be followed, for example, the fact that the head of the different offices posed a limitation on the number of the available workers per office. Table 4 represents the different groups, with two office directors per each group as part of the sample. The average age of participants to both groups was uniform between groups and has not influ-

Table 4. The selected sample and distribution among groups

Group	Women	Men	Total	Departments	Notes
Group 1	6	3	9	3	Only using MS Office
Group 2	9	4	13	3	Using MS Office and OpenOffice.org
Total	15	7	22	3	-

enced the results; users were selected from such departments in a random way with the limitations described previously. Regarding the protocol, the selection of the experimental groups has been done in a way to enable that the participants were, when possible, in some way in relation with each other, physically near and if possible coming from the same organisational units, to take advantage of possible network externalities that arise in terms of document exchange and reciprocal help (Shapiro & Varian, 1999).

One group experimented with the introduction of OpenOffice.org (our treatment X, in Figure 1), while the other group was used as a control group. The experimental design followed an experimental pretest-posttest control group design (Campbell & Stanley, 1990).

A questionnaire has been submitted to both groups before (O1) and after (O2) the introduction of OpenOffice.org to evaluate the effects of the experimentation on the attitude towards OSS. The activities of both groups have been constantly monitored by an automatic system for data collection (Sillitti, Janes, Succi, & Vernazza, 2003) that permitted the gathering of a series of objective process data (the series of observations O3,i).

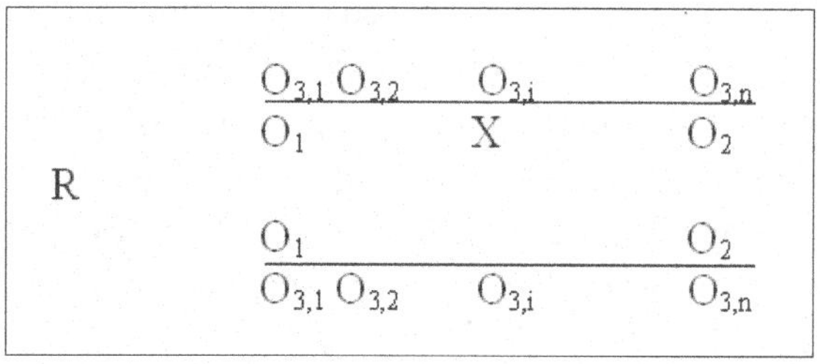

In some other cases where there has not been the possibility to have a control group and a proper randomisation of the sample, a "quasiexperimental" and a "one-shot" design have been employed (Campbell & Stanley, 1990). We are aware that in this way the results obtained are less extendible to the general case and more subject to exogenous effects.

TIME EVOLUTION OF THE EXPERIMENT

The experiment lasted for 32 weeks; during the first 10 only Microsoft Office was monitored and the different system dependencies were collected. OpenOffice.org was introduced in group 2 after week 10 and during the 23rd week of experimentation OpenOffice.org has been associated with Microsoft Office formats .doc and .xls. The results of the choice will be exposed in the subsequent sections. Figure 2 shows a graphical representation of the evolution of the experimentation.

In detail, the steps performed during the experimentation were the following:

1. Selection of the participants to the experiment;
2. Submission of the questionnaires on the attitude towards OSS;
3. Motivational seminar on the reasons of the experimentation;
4. Identification of the OpenOffice.org experimental group and control group;
5. Analysis of the most used documents and the possible software dependencies;

Figure 1. Experimental design adopted

Figure 2. Evolution of the experiment expressed in weeks

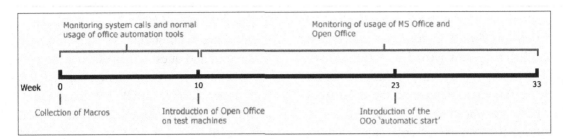

6. Installation of OpenOffice.org and translation in the OpenOffice.org format of the most used documents and on a per request basis;

7. Installation of the monitoring and data collection system to define the situation before the transition;

8. Training, performed on a single day, trying to focus on the different approach proposed by the new software; users were instructed on how to perform the usual office automation tasks;

9. Start of the OpenOffice.org data collection;

10. Support given to users through an online forum and a hotline;

11. Periodic verification meetings with users of OpenOffice.org to identify possible problems;

12. Automatic start of OpenOffice.org with files with Microsoft Office extension starting from week 23;

13. Submission of the final questionnaires.

Two types of questionnaires have been submitted to users. The first one identical before and after the experimentation, to understand the attitude towards OSS and the effects of the experimentation on such attitude; the second one has been submitted only at the end, where all the final results of the project have been collected and more information for the replication of the experiment have been determined. The Goal Question Metrics (GQM) paradigm (Basili, 1995) was employed in every phase of the project, from the overall design to the creation of the questionnaires. The GQM is a methodology that was developed at the University of Maryland in the mid-1980s that relates the goals of an organisation to a set of questions. Questions are further associated to a set of metrics. In this way it is always possible to evaluate whether a goal has been reached and what are the informational needs of a certain goal are.

SOFTWARE EMPLOYED

The tools used during the experimentation were useful to assess the evolution of the experiment and in particular to gather quantitative and objective data about the migration process. In particular, two applications were employed for the ex-ante analysis and one was continuously employed during the transition to monitor the usage of the proposed solutions.

*   PROM (PRO Metrics), a noninvasive monitoring tool was used to evaluate the usage of OpenOffice.org and Microsoft Office during all the transition process (Sillitti et al., 2003). Metrics of interest were the number of documents handled and time spent per single document. The software has been running during all weeks of the experimentation, permitting us to acquire objective data on the experimentation.

- DepA (Dependency Analyser) has been employed to evaluate at the beginning of the project the existing dependencies of Microsoft Office in terms of called and calling programs (Rossi & Succi, 2004). The program is a simple agent running on workstations to determine the calls from different applications, collecting in this way information on the different interrelations between applications. The program has been running on client desktops for the first 10 weeks.

- FLEA (FiLe Extension Analyser) has been used to perform a scan of the data standards available on the users' drives and analyse the eventual presence of macros. The software permits us to collect information on the type of extension, date of creation, date of last access, size of the file, and for particular extensions also information about the macros contained. The scan was performed at the beginning of the experimentation.

All tools deployed are not noninvasive in order not to bias the results. From the final questionnaires emerged that users did not notice the presence of any external software during the experimentation.

DATA ANALYSIS

In this section we report the results of the data collection activities. In particular we can distinguish the data collection across a temporal boundary (*ex-ante, during, and ex-post*) and between *qualitative* and *quantitative* data.

The biggest effort during the project has been to monitor constantly the users during the experimentation. To gather objective data on the migration, we used the PROM software. Data collected included the time spent on documents and the number of documents opened using the selected office automation suite. A more

fine-grained analysis on the function utilised has not been performed. During every phase of the project, the quantitative data collected has been backed with qualitative data coming from interviews and questionnaires. As a side effect, we noticed that the periodic meetings performed with users caused a small increase in the usage of the open source solution during the immediate subsequent days.

We will briefly review all the data collected, starting from the analysis of the existing situation, performed at the beginning of the experimentation.

EX-ANTE ANALYSIS

The aspects we analysed for an overview of the existing situation were concerned with the presence of interoperability issues in the users' environment and the presence of possible dependencies in the form of macros inside office automation documents. Macros are a series of commands inserted in the form of code inside documents, to perform a series of repetitive actions. They are generally very common in office automation documents, to permit the automation of repetitive tasks. As the usage in OpenOffice.org of macros written for Microsoft Office is not possible – at least at the time the experimentation was carried out – this is an interoperability issue. Macros need, in this way, to be completely rewritten.

The number of templates in the preexisting format represents another interoperability issue. Our software for data collection granted us the possibility to evaluate the number of this type of documents, but not the complexity, another factor to take into account when there is the need to migrate a document. The collection of such data has to be crossed with interviews with the IT personnel to evaluate the real relevance of the macros discovered and the real necessity of the conversion of templates.

Table 5. Type of data collected during the experimentation

	Ex ante	During	Ex-post
Qualitative	Interviews/questionnaires	Periodic meetings for feedback	Interviews/Questionnaires
Quantitative	Collection of data standards (FLEA), Collection of dependencies (DepA)	Monitoring of SW usage (PROM)	Number of OOo files created during the project.

The first step for performing the initial analysis of the experimentation environment was the one related to the presence of macros inside documents and the distribution of the documents. Another important issue was to find the number of templates available. This analysis has been performed statically at the beginning of the project. In the evaluation of macros impact, Microsoft Word and Microsoft Excel documents of the participants to the project were considered. Two different locations were considered:

- Users' drives
- Network drives

In the last location, both normal documents and templates were considered. Table 6 reports a summary of the results. We found 25.810 Word documents and 2.192 Excel documents. Among these, only 2 Word documents (0.01%) and 49 Excel documents (2.24%) contained macros. Moreover, our tool has identified a high number of Excel documents protected by password (near 16% of the total). In this case, it is not possible to determine whether they contain macros.

The second step has been the identification of the software dependencies that existed in the office automation environment. A dependency is either a call to an external application (outgoing call) or a call from an external application to the office automation suite (incoming call). As the dynamic evaluation of the calls, two different typologies have been considered:

- Applications that call Microsoft Word or Excel (Figure 3)

In this category we discovered that 80% of the times, Microsoft Word was called from explorer. exe which means a normal start from its icon or a file on the file manager. Furthermore, 12% of the times it was called from the e-mail client Outlook. Microsoft Excel was called 95% of the times by explorer.exe and 4% of the times from Outlook (for a total of 99% of the calls).

- Applications called from Microsoft Word or Excel (Figure 4)

74% of the global calls have been towards printer drivers. Almost 11% of the calls of Microsoft Word and Excel have been towards the program to report problems in Microsoft applications, and about 6% for the help guide.

Further interviews with IT managers confirmed the situation outlined by data collection tools. Globally, the system environment of the experimentation was less turbulent than we had thought initially. Templates, macros, and dependencies collected were not so critical to increase significantly the migration costs.

ONGOING EXPERIMENT ANALYSIS

The experimentation has been monitored constantly by PROM software. Figure 5 shows two different measures of productivity, the percentage of documents opened by using OpenOffice. org and the percentage of time spent within the OpenOffice.org suite. As an example, a percentage of 5% means that users spent in that week 95% of the time using Microsoft Office.

Table 6. Number of documents and macros during the pretransition phase; LOC = Lines of Code, CNO = Could Not Open

Location	Microsoft Word				Microsoft Excel			
	Files	Macros	LOC	CNO	Files	Macros	LOC	CNO
Users' driver	19144	2	12	-	1367	8	1070	14
Network driver	4484	-	-	-	816	43	21482	331
Network drives (templates)	2182	-	-	-	9	3	10197	-

From the data collected, we can notice, in particular, two effects:

- As expected, the level of adoption of the new software has been increased by the decision to associate the Microsoft Office file formats with OpenOffice.org. We expected to have complaints and reports of incompatibilities deriving from this decision. What happened was instead that users learned when it was convenient for compatibility reasons to adopt one solution or the other.
- Even after 32 weeks of experimentation, the time spent with OpenOffice.org was below 25% of the total time dedicated to the two suites for office automation. Also to note is the fact that the time and documents of Figure 5 are inclusive of the Microsoft Office documents opened with OpenOffice.org.

It is noteworthy that, during the experimentation, we did not benefit fully from the network effect that can be raised by the growing number of documents in one format and the subsequent exchange between users (Shapiro & Varian, 1999). In a broader migration such effects can also have an impact increasing the usage of the new platform proposed. In our experimentation users were in some way constrained in the adoption of the new format, as they could not exchange the documents with the users not participating in the experimentation.

We also posed two questions to evaluate the impact on productivity, according to the GQM methodology.

a) Did the usage of OpenOffice.org caused a reduction in the number of documents used per day? We studied the correlation between the number of documents used each day and

Figure 3. Number of incoming dependencies of Microsoft Word (left) and Microsoft Excel (right)

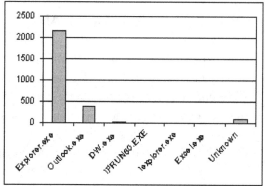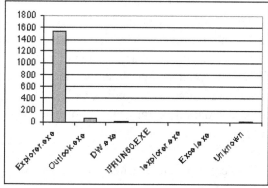

Figure 4. Number of outgoing dependencies for Microsoft Word/Excel

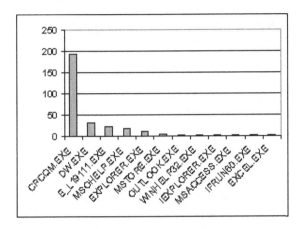

number of documents opened with OpenOffice.org. A negative effect on the usage of OpenOffice.org had to produce a negative impact on the usage of the office automation documents and a significant negative correlation between these two variables; that is, the more documents are handled with OpenOffice.org, the less they are globally handled. The correlation in question has been of -0.08, therefore we exclude that the usage of OpenOffice.org has reduced the number of documents handled daily.

b) Did the usage of OpenOffice.org caused an increase in the time devoted to each document? We studied the correlation between the time spent managing all the documents and the OpenOffice.org ones. A negative effect on the usage of OpenOffice.org has to create a significant positive correlation; that is, it should be evident that the more time spent with OpenOffice.org, the more time is spent globally managing documents, as OpenOffice.org required more time to accomplish the same tasks. This correlation has been determined in -0.04, therefore it has to be excluded that the usage of OpenOffice.org has increased the global effort to handle documents. The comparison with the control group confirmed furthermore that the evolution of the usage of documents among the test group and the control group has been consistent, excluding the presence of exogenous factors.

EX-POST ANALYSIS

At the end of the experimentation, the evaluation of the attitude towards OSS and in general the evaluation of the project has been performed. We submitted one questionnaire to users in order to evaluate their attitudes towards OSS and the knowledge that was acquired after the transition. We submitted also the same questionnaire to the control group to ensure that no exogenous effects biased the results. The questionnaire was designated to answer to the following two questions:

- What is the user perception of OSS at the end of the experiment?
- Has the user modified his/her perception of OSS at the end of the experiment?

All figures of this section represent the ex-ante situation on the left and the ex-post situation on the right. In this way it should be easier to evaluate the change of users' attitudes.

The *first question* that has been submitted was whether the Open Source concept has become more familiar after the experimentation. The result in this case is quite obvious; at the end the users had a clearer idea of the concept of OSS. It may be surprising the initial number of users claiming to know OSS, but this is due to the preproject meetings with IT managers explaining the reasons of the experimentation.

The *second question* enters the heart of the matter, questioning about the perception of OSS. In this case an interesting phenomenon has been discovered. At the beginning one group had no opinion on OSS (almost half of the interviewed). At the end of the experiment, almost all users have an opinion: those that were positive maintained the same opinion and the uncertain were divided

Figure 5. Increase in OpenOffice.org usage. On the X-axis there is the week of the project; OpenOffice.org has been inserted during week 10; and the automatic association has been activated during week 23. In blue the percentage of opened files using OpenOffice.org is represented and in orange the percentage of average time devoted to OpenOffice.org among users that effectively used OpenOffice.org.

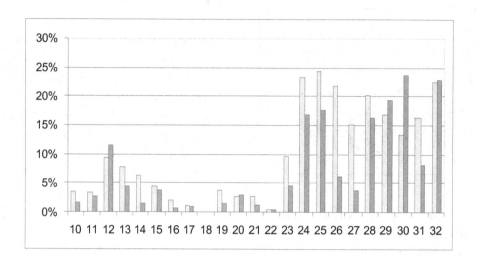

into three groups almost of the same size, those with a positive opinion, those with a negative one, and those that had no opinion. Nevertheless, at the end of the experiment only a small part of the participants had a negative opinion on OSS.

The *third question* focuses on the importance of the diffusion of the software in use. In this answer we have a strong movement towards a bigger knowledge; for example, the category "very important" has gone from 0 to almost 40%. The experimentation in the usage of OpenOffice.org has strongly increased the consciousness of the participants on the importance of the usage of well established software.

The *fourth question* poses the problem of the direct substitution and asks the user how much the user is reluctant to abandon the application in use in favour of an OS solution. In this case the user in favour maintained the same opinion, while reluctant people became more reluctant; also in this case users had a clearer idea of OSS after the experimentation. More than half of the interviewed users were still positive towards a possible transition.

The *fifth* and *sixth questions* present a slightly different nature. The aim is to find whether the experimentation changed the perception on the requirements of the software to be adopted and used. Question 5 focuses on the factors to consider when a new product is adopted and question 6 discusses the more important aspects of an efficient usage. In both cases the role of the training and support is evidenced as important, while other aspects as security, privacy, and availability of source code are considered less important. We can conclude that the effect of the OpenOffice.org introduction has increased the perception of the importance of the training. From one side, this can be obvious: the introduction of a new instrument requires always a training period, especially if it partially substitutes an old one. We must also point out that all the interviewed people had already performed their training with the office automation tools some time before, therefore such perception should already be present. It can be concluded that OSS has additionally stimulated the curiosity of participants, to the point to ask more questions about the tools used; such ap-

Figure 6. Question 1 – How familiar are you with the expression Open Source Software?

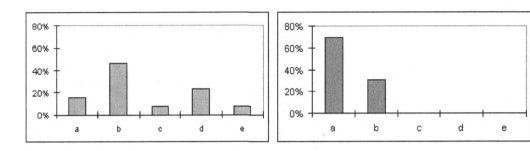

Figure 7. Question 2 – How do you perceive the expression Open Source Software?
Possible answers: (a) as something negative, (b) as something positive, (c) neither positive nor negative.

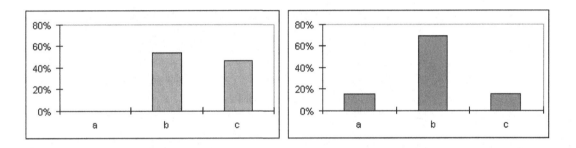

Figure 8. Question 3 - How important is it that the application you use is established and widely used?
Possible answers: (a) very important, (b) important, (c) of moderate importance, (d) of little importance, (e) not important.

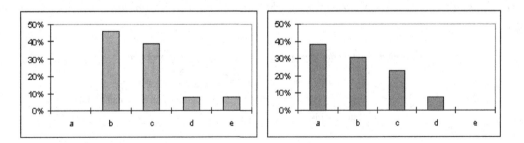

proach, if confirmed, can go in favour of people who claim that the adoption of OSS brings more "shared" knowledge.

The *last question* proposed before and after the experimentation is a sort of summary and deals with the motivations that the user would have to use OSS. It is interesting to note that near OSS supporters a new group emerged also absorbing neutral users towards a more negative opinion.

Some questions about the overall evolution of the migration have been submitted to users at the end of the project. Two questions are interesting

Figure 9. Question 4 – You are reluctant to give up the use of application software that you are using to in favour of an OSS alternative! Possible answers: (a) totally agree, (b) agree, (c) neither, (d) disagree, (e) totally disagree.

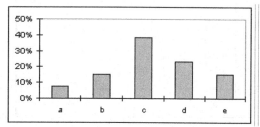 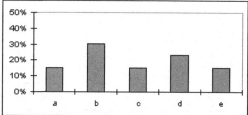

Figure 10. Question 5 – How important do you find the following factors when you use a new IT-platform? Factors considered are: (a) support and training, (b) easiness of use, (c) interoperability, (d) source code available, (e) functionalities, (f) security, (g) privacy.

Position	Before the experiment	After the experiment
1	Easiness of use	Easiness of use
2	Functionalities	Support and training
3		Functionalities
4	Support and training, interoperability, security	Interoperability
5		Security
6	Privacy	Privacy
7	Source code available	Source code available

Figure 11. Question 6 – The biggest advantages you perceive with OSS are:
Factors considered: (a) better support and training, (b) it is easier to use, (c) stability, (d) better functionalities, (e) better security.

Position	Before the experiment	After the experiment
1	Easiness of use	Easiness of use
2	Better functionalities, more stable	Better support and training
3		Better functionalities, more stable
4	Better support and training	
5	Better security	Better security

for our evaluation of the migration, both related to the functionalities of OpenOffice.org and the possible full migration to the new solution proposed. We must point out that the experimentation has been performed with version 1.1.3 of OpenOffice. org; the latest release would, probably, obtain better results.

Question 8 faces the problem of the choice between the two proposed solutions in a general way. It asks whether the functionalities offered by the two suites are equivalent. Some users answered that Microsoft Office offers more functionalities than OpenOffice.org 1.1.3. In some way, the surprise may be that half of the users considered the set of functionalities offered equivalent.

Figure 12. Question 7 – Which motivations do you have to use Open Source Software? Possible answers:
(a) You believe it is right to support OSS initiatives, (b) You find that today's market dominance of a single
software vendor is wrong, (c) other: specify, (d) I have no motivation to use Open Source Software.

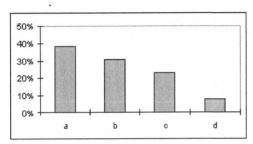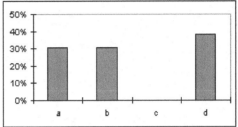

Figure 13. Question 8 – How do you evaluate the functionalities of OpenOffice.org with respect to the
Microsoft Office ones? Possible answers: (a) widely superior, (b) superior, (c) equal, (d) inferior, (e)

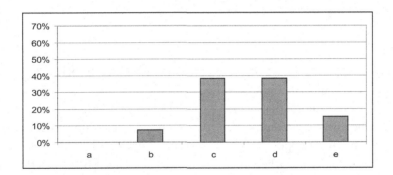

Question 9 contextualises the problem. It tries to evaluate the impact of a possible substitution of Microsoft Office with OpenOffice.org. In this case almost all the participants in the test considered the migration as possible, even though the majority sustained later that this operation requires some effort and is not only a simple substitution.

A final evaluation of the experimentation has been performed on the number of files generated by the users adopting the new data standard supplied by OpenOffice.org. Table 7 contains a summary of all the different files created during the experimentation in the two different formats proposed by the OpenOffice.org suite for text

processors and spreadsheets. Obviously this kind of static analysis represents only a small subset of the usage of the open solution, as users had also the freedom to open Microsoft Office proprietary formats using OpenOffice.org. For technical reasons FLEA could not be employed in this type of scan to give us more fine-grained data.

LIMITATIONS

This study represents the results of a single experience and such results cannot be systematically generalised, as the essential comparative aspect

Figure 14. Question 9 – In this moment, if Microsoft Office is removed, are you still able to perform the same tasks? Possible answers: (a) yes, (b) yes but with some problems, (c) no.

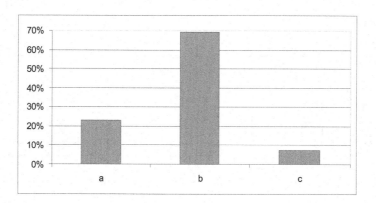

Table 7. Number of documents created during the experimentation

	Writer documents	Calc documents
Department 1	27	2
Department 2	223	34
Department 3	164	12
Total	414	48

is missing. As already mentioned, the PA under exam has imposed some constraints on the selection of the sample. The office automation field, in particular, may not be fully comparable to other desktop environments where open source solutions are not as strong as OpenOffice.org. Furthermore, this study does not focus on a complete substitution of the old solution, rather on the evaluation of the coexistence of both solutions. A further step might be the evaluation of the effects deriving from a complete migration.

CONCLUSION

The migration to OSS described in this article has to be taken with care before generalising the results to other similar cases. In particular the migration has been restricted to the OpenOffice.org platform and to the PA field. The migration approach has been the more gradual as possible,

maintaining the proprietary solution in parallel with the new one.

The results obtained from the experimentation have been encouraging for the introduction of OSS on the desktop-side. Data collected during the experimentation shows that the usage of the new platform increased during the whole period, reaching at the end 25% of the total office automation tasks. Proprietary software remained the preferred solution for users. The impact on productivity has been minimal also due to the similarities of the software considered. Users acquired a better understanding of OSS after the experimentation and tended to have, in general, a positive vision of the whole movement. Software used has been considered adequate for the transition, although a sort of lack of functionalities emerged from the opinions of the users. More recent releases of OpenOffice.org should solve these problems.

ACKNOWLEDGMENT

We acknowledge Dr. Hellmuth Ladurner for his precious help and support. Acknowledgments also go to all the users involved, participants in the experiment, technical personnel, and supervisors; without their constant effort and their availability, this study would not have been possible.

REFERENCES

Basili, V. (1995). Applying the goal/question/metric paradigm. Experience factory. In *Software quality assurance and measurement: A worldwide perspective* (pp. 21-44). International Thomson Publishing Company.

Campbell, D.T., & Stanley, T.D. (1990). *Experimental and quasi-experimental design*. Houghton Mifflin Company.

CERT. (2001). Advisory CA-2001-19: Code Red Worm. Retrieved June 15, 2006, from http://www.cert.org/advisories/CA-2001-19.html

Everitt, K., & Lederer, S. (2001). *A usability comparison of Sun StarOffice Writer 5.2 vs. Microsoft Word 2000*. Retrieved June 15, 2006, from http://www.sims.berkeley.edu/courses/is271/f01/projects/WordStar/

Feller, J., & Fitzgerald, B. (2001). *Understanding Open Source Software development*. Addison-Wesley.

Fenton, N.E., & Pfleeger, S.L. (1997). *Software metrics: A rigorous and practical approach* (2nd ed.). PWS Publishing Company.

Gartner Inc. (2003). *Distributed computing chart of accounts*. Retrieved June 15, 2006, from http://www.gartner.com/4_decision_tools/modeling_tools/costcat.pdf

Landeshauptstadt München. (2003). *Clientstudie der Landeshauptstadt München*. Retrieved June 15, 2006, from http://www.muenchen.de/aktuell/clientstudie_kurz.pdf

Netcraft Survey. (2005). Retrieved June 15, 2006, from http://news.netcraft.com/archives/Web_server_survey.html

Newsforge. (2002). *Largo loves Linux more than ever*. Retrieved June 15, 2006, from http://www.newsforge.com/print.pl?sid=02/12/04/2346215

Nichols, D.M., & Twidale, M.B. (2003, January). The usability of Open Source software. *First Monday, 8*(1). Retrieved June 15, 2006 from http://www.firstmonday.org/issues/issue8_1/nichols/

Robert Frances Group. (2002). *Total cost of ownership for Linux Web servers in the enterprise*. Retrieved June 15, 2006, from http://www.rfgonline.com/subsforum/LinuxTCO.pdf

Rossi, B., & Succi, G. (2004). *Analysis of dependencies among personal productivity tools: A case study*. Undergraduate Thesis, Free University of Bolzano-Bozen.

Shapiro, C., & Varian, H.R. (1999). *Information rules: A strategic guide to the network economy*. Harvard Business School Press.

Sillitti, A., Janes, A., Succi, G., & Vernazza, T. (2003, September 1-6). Collecting, integrating and analyzing software metrics and personal software process data. In *Proceedings of EUROMICRO 2003*, Belek-Antalya.

Stadt Nürnberg. (2004). *Strategische Ausrichtung im Hinblick auf Systemunabhängigkeit und Open Source software*. Retrieved June 15, 2006, from http://online-service.nuernberg.de/eris/agendaItem.do?id=49681

Stadt Wien. (2004). *Open Source software am Arbeitsplatz im Magistrat Wien*. Retrieved June 15, 2006, from http://www.wien.gv.at/ma14/pdf/oss-studie-deutsch-langfassung.pdf

The Yankee Group. (2005). 2005 *North American Linux TCO survey.* Retrieved June 15, 2006, from http://www.yankeegroup.com

ZDNet. (2005). *Extremadura Linux Migration case study.* Retrieved June 15, 2006, from http://insight.zdnet.co.uk/software/linuxunix/0,39020472,39197928,00.htm

ENDNOTES

[1] Apache Software Foundation, http://www.apache.org

[2] The Mozilla Firefox project, http://www.mozilla.com/

[3] gnuLinex, http://www.linex.org/

[4] OpenOffice.org, http://www.openoffice.org

[5] Microsoft Office, http://www.microsoft.com/office/editions/prodinfo/default.mspx

This work was previously published in Int. Journal of Information Technology and Web Engineering, Vol 1, Issue 3, edited by E. Damiani and G. Succi, pp. 64-80, copyright 2006 by IGI Publishing (an imprint of IGI Global).

Chapter VI
Open Source in Web–Based Applications:
A Case Study on Single Sign–On

Claudio Agostino Ardagna
Università degli Studi di Milano, Italy

Fulvio Frati
Università degli Studi di Milano, Italy

Gabriele Gianini
Università degli Studi di Milano, Italy

ABSTRACT

Business and recreational activities on the global communication infrastructure are increasingly based on the use of remote resources and services, and on the interaction between different, remotely located parties. In such a context, Single Sign-On technologies simplify the log-on process allowing automatic access to secondary domains through a unique log-on operation to the primary domain. In this paper, we evaluate different Single Sign-On implementations focusing on the central role of Open Source in the development of Web-based systems. We outline requirements for Single Sign-On systems and evaluate four existing Open Source implementations in terms of degree of fulfilment of those requirements. Finally we compare those Open Source systems with respect to some specific Open Source community patterns.

INTRODUCTION

The global information infrastructure connects remote parties, such as users and resources, through the use of large scale networks. Many companies focus on developing e-services, business, and recreational activities, such as e-government services, remote banking, and airline reservation systems (Feldman, 2000; Damiani, Grosky, & Khosla, 2003). In such a context, where the huge number of resources and services accessible on the Web leads to multiple log-on processes and identity profiles, a solution is needed to give to the users at least the illusion of having a single identity and a single set of credentials.

Furthermore, several regulations affecting e-services, such as the Sarbanes Oxley (SOX) directive and the Health Insurance Portability and Accountability Act (HIPAA), mandate provisions for maintaining the integrity of user profile data as an essential component of an effective security policy. HIPAA, for example, explicitly states that the companies are required to assign a unique pro-

file for tracking user identities to each user. Also, it mandates procedures for creating, changing, and safeguarding profiles. Traditional authentication policies do not even come close to fulfilling these requirements. Single Sign-On (SSO) (De Clercq, 2002) systems are aimed at simplifying log-on process, managing the multiple identities of each user, and presenting their credentials to network applications for authentication.

In the following, we put forward the idea of enriching existing e-services with a fully functional Open Source Single Sign-On (Buell & Sandhu, 2003) solution, allowing users to manage a single identity to access systems and resources. The motivation for focusing on Open Source software is that it is increasingly adopted as an alternative to proprietary solutions.

Many Web-based projects, in fact, are affected by budget, transparency, vendor lock-in, integration, and interoperability limitations that represent major crucial problems. The adoption of an Open Source approach can overcome these limitations. First, Open Source Software, although

Figure 1. User log-on to multiservice domain

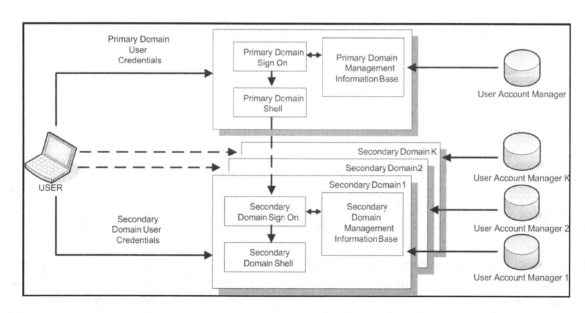

not necessarily free, is in most cases cheaper than proprietary software. Second, Open Source Software often adheres to open standards and it is conducted in public forums. Then, Open Source paradigm also guarantees supplier independence and avoids the lock-in problem: a lock-in situation, in fact, arises when software is proprietary; with Open Source Software data are not stored in a proprietary format, and it is possible for users to change between several different systems and suppliers. Finally, customization and re-use are simply addressable because source code is freely available and modifiable. Based on the above proprietary solution limitations, we can suggest that an important nonfunctional requirement for Web-based system could be implementing the entire application following the Open Source approach.

However, experience has shown that in some deployed systems based on Open Source operating system platforms a substantial amount of the application code, mostly used for access control and authentication related features, may belong to a proprietary application server (Ardagna, Damiani, Frati, & Montel, 2005). SSO systems need to be carefully operated to avoid becoming a single failure point for the whole infrastructure.

In this article, we describe a general model for Single Sign-On architectures focusing on the central role of Open Source implementations. We delineate a set of requirements that Single Sign-On solutions should satisfy and then evaluate four different fully functional Open Source Single Sign-On implementations: our system, called CAS++, developed as an extension to Yale University's CAS (Aubry, Mathieu, & Marchal, 2004; Central Authentication Service, 2003), the Liberty Alliance implementation named SourceID (Liberty Alliance Project, 2004; SourceID, 2005), Shibboleth (Shibboleth Project, 2004), and finally Java Open Single Sign-On (JOSSO) (Java Open Single Sign-On Project, 2005). The analysis is finally summarized in a comparison table.

Figure 2. User single sign-on to multiservice domain

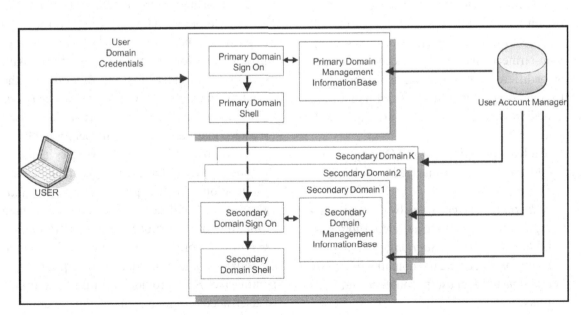

SINGLE SIGN-ON TECHNOLOGIES

The great amount of services available on the Net causes the proliferation of user accounts. Users typically have to log-on to multiple systems that require an equivalent number of log-on operations, each of which involves different usernames and authentication information. Each system has to manage its own user accounts and system administrators have to grant the integrity of security policies enforcement (Single Sign-On, 2003).

Within a scenario of multiservice domain, users have to manage different account profiles and perform a log-on action for each requested service. This approach is illustrated in Figure 1. These components act as independent domains and the user interacts with a primary domain to establish a session with it, providing a set of credentials applicable to that domain. When the user tries to interact with services of other logical domains, the user has to provide another set of applicable credentials to gain access to them.

Hence, the user has to manage separate log-on processes, which may be cumbersome and error-prone. Also, from a management point of view, we will need independent identities and accounts management for each domain and different authentication mechanisms. In this scenario, usability and security concerns arise and the need is felt for coordinating and, where possible, integrating user log-on mechanisms and user account management for different domains. A service/architecture that provides such coordination and integration is named *Single Sign-On* (Galbraith et al., 2002) (see Figure 2).

The advantages given by a SSO adoption are manifold and can be summarized as follows:

- *reduction* of (1) *time spent* by the users during log-on operations to individual domains, (2) *failed log-on transactions*, (3) *time used to log-on* to secondary domains, (4) *costs and time* used for users profiles administrations;

- *improvement of users security,* since the number of username/password each user has to manage is reduced;[1]
- *secure and simplified administration* because with a centralized administration point, system administrators reduce the time spent to add and remove users or modify their rights;
- *improved system security* through the enhanced ability of system administrators to maintain the integrity of user account configuration including the ability to change an individual user's access to all system resources in a coordinated and consistent manner;
- *improvement to services usability* because the user has to interact with the same login interface.

The advantages list clearly highlights that both users and management aspects of the services take great improvements by the adoption of SSO mechanism. In the SSO approach, the primary domain is responsible for collecting and managing all user credentials used during the authentication process, to gain access to each domain that the user may potentially require interaction with.

The information provided by the user to the Primary Domain can be used in several ways to log-on to a secondary domain: (1) *directly*, the user information is forwarded to a secondary domain as part of a secondary log-on; (2) *indirectly*, the user information is used to retrieve other user identification, in turn this information is used for a secondary domain log-on operation; (3) *immediately*, to establish a session with a secondary domain as part of the primary domain session initialization. Client applications are automatically invoked and communications performed at the time of the primary log-on operation; (4) *temporarily* stored or cached and used when the secondary domain services are requested. To summarize, SSO provides a uniform interface to user accounts management thus enabling a coordinated and synchronized management of the component domains.

REQUIREMENTS OF A SINGLE SIGN-ON SYSTEM

The requirements that a Single Sign-On system should satisfy are more or less well known within the security community, and several SSO projects published partial lists of them (De Clercq, 2002; Pashalidis & Mitchell, 2003).[2] A first step before implementing an innovative SSO system is spelling out these requirements, taking into account the lessons learned from previous projects. Our analysis brought us to formulate the following requirements (Ardagna, Damiani, De Capitani di Vimercati, Frati, & Samarati, 2006).

Authentication. The main feature of a SSO system is to provide an authentication mechanism. Usually the authentication is performed through the classic username/password log-in, whereby a user can be unambiguously identified. Authentication mechanisms should usually be coupled with a logging and auditing process to prevent or identify malicious attacks and unexpected behaviours. From a software engineering point of view, authentication is the only "necessary and sufficient" functional requisite for a SSO architecture.

Strong Authentication. For high security environments, the traditional username/password authentication mechanism is not enough. Malicious users can steal a password and act in place of the user. New approaches are therefore required to better protect services against unauthorized accesses. A good solution to this problem could integrate username/password with strong authentication mechanisms based on biometric properties of the user (fingerprints, retina scan, and so on).

Authorization. After the authentication process, the system can determine the level of information/services the requestor can see/use. While application based on domain specific authorizations can be defined and managed locally at each system, the SSO system can provide support for managing authorizations (e.g., role or profile acquisitions) that apply to multiple domains.

Provisioning. Provisions are those conditions that need to be satisfied or actions that must be performed before a decision is taken (Bettini, Jajodia, Sean Wang, & Wijesekera, 2002). A provision is as a precondition; it is the responsibility of the user to ensure that a request is sent in an environment satisfying all the preconditions. The nonsatisfaction of a provision implies a request to the user to perform some actions.

Federation. The concept of *federation* is strictly related to the concept of *trust*. A user should be able to select the services that the user wants to federate and defederate to protect the user's privacy and to select the services to which the user will disclose the user's own authorization assertions.

C.I.M. (Centralized Identity Management). The centralization of authentication and authorization mechanisms and, more in general, the centralization of identity management implies a simplification of the user profile management task. Users profiles should be maintained within the SSO server thus lowering the burden for local administrators. This allows a reduction of user profiles administration costs and time and improves administrators control on user profiles and authorization policies.

Client Status Info. The SSO system architecture implies the exchange of user information between SSO server and services to fulfil authentication and authorization processes. In particular, when the two entities communicate, they have to be synchronized on what concerns the user identity; privacy and security issues need to be addressed. Different solutions (Samar, 1999) of this problem could be adopted involving either the transport (e.g., communication can be encrypted) or the application layer.

Single Point of Control. The main objectives of a SSO implementation are that of providing a unique access control point for users who want to request a service, and that of delegating some features to an authentication server. This point of control should be unique to clearly separate the authentication point from business implementations, avoiding the replication, and the ad-hoc implementation of authentication mechanisms for each domain. Note that every service provider will eventually develop its own authentication mechanism.

Standard Compliance. It is important for wide range applications to support well-known and reliable protocols to make possible communications and integrations between different environments. In a SSO scenario, there are protocols for exchanging messages between authentication servers and service providers, and between technologies, within the same system, that can be different. Hence, every entity can use standard technologies (e.g., X.509 (Public-Key Infrastructure, 2002), SAML (Security Assertion Markup Language, 2003) for expressing and exchanging authentication information and SOAP (Simple Object Access Protocol, 2003) for data transmission) to interoperate with different environments.

Cross-Language Availability. The widespread diffusion of the global Internet as an infrastructure for accessing services has spawned the definition of different languages/technologies used to develop these applications. In this scenario, a requisite of paramount importance is the development of SSO solutions that allow the integration of

services implementation based on different languages, without substantial changes on services code. The first step in this direction is the adoption of standard communication protocols based on XML.

Password Proliferation Prevention. A well-known motivation for the adoption of SSO systems is the prevention of password proliferation so as to improve security and simplify user log-on actions and system profiles management.

OPEN SOURCE IMPLEMENTATIONS

After the definition of the requirements that a SSO framework has to fulfil, we evaluate four major Open Source SSO implementations with respect to these requirements.

Our Solution: CAS++

Our SSO implementation CAS++, that is an extension of Yale University's Central Authentication Service (CAS) (Aubry et al., 2004; Central Authentication Service, 2003), integrates the user authentication framework with PKI (Public Key Infrastructure) and strong authentication mechanisms, through the use of X.509 (Public-Key Infrastructure, 2002) identity certificates, smart cards, and fingerprint readers. Below, after a brief introduction about Yale's solution, we explain our improvement to CAS implementation fully integrated with JBoss security layer (Ardagna et al., 2005; JBoss, 2003; Scott, 2003).

Central Authentication Service (CAS)

Central Authentication Service (CAS) (Aubry et al., 2004; Central Authentication Service, 2003) is an Open Source framework developed by Yale University; it implements a SSO mechanism to provide a *Centralized Authentication* to a single server and *HTTP redirections*. CAS authentication model is loosely based on classic Kerberos-style authentication. When an unauthenticated user sends a service request, this request is redirected from the application to the CAS authentication server, and then back to the application after the user has been authenticated. The CAS Server is therefore the only entity that manages passwords to authenticate users and transmits and certifies their identities. The information is forwarded by the authentication server to the application, during redirections, by mean of session cookies (see CAS++ data flow in Figure 4).

CAS is composed of pure-Java servlets and can run over any servlet engine, and it provides a very basic Web-based authentication service. Its major security features are:

1. passwords travel from browsers to the authentication server via an encrypted channel;
2. reauthentications are transparent to users if they accept a single cookie, called *Ticket Granting Cookie* (TGC). This cookie is opaque (i.e., TGC contains no personal information), protected (it uses SSL), and private (it is only presented to the CAS server);
3. applications know user's identity through an opaque one-time Service Ticket (ST) created and authenticated by CAS Server.

Furthermore, CAS credentials are proxiable. At start-up, distributed applications get a *Proxy-Granting Ticket* (PGT) from CAS. When the application needs access to a resource, it uses the PGT to get a proxy ticket (PT). Then, the application sends the PT to a back-end application. The back-end application confirms the PT with CAS Server, and also gains information about who proxied the authentication. This mechanism allows "proxy" authentication for Web portals, letting users authenticate securely to untrusted sites (e.g., student-run sites and third-party vendors) without supplying a password. CAS works seamlessly with existing Kerberos authentication infrastructures and can be used by nearly any Web-application development environment (JSP, Servlets, ASP, Perl, mod-perl, PHP, Python, PL/SQL, and so forth) or as a serverwide Apache module. Also, it is freely available from Yale University (with source code).

CAS++ Implementation

We developed an Open Source SSO system, called CAS++, based on the use of identity certificates and fully integrated with the JBoss security layer (JBoss, 2003). Our solution integrates the CAS system with the authentication mechanism implemented by a Public Key Infrastructure (PKI). CAS++ implements a fully multidomain single point of control that provides a simple, efficient, and reliable SSO mechanism through HTTP redirections, focused on user privacy (opaque cookies) and security protection. CAS++ permits a centralized management of user profiles granting access to all services in the system with a unique log-on process. The profiles repository is stored inside the SSO server that is the only point where users credentials/profiles are accessed, thus reducing information scattering. In our implementation, services do not need an authentication layer because this feature is managed by CAS++ itself.

CAS++ is a fully J2EE compliant application that can be integrated with services coded in any Web-based implementation language. CAS++ relies on standard protocols such as SSL, for secure communications between the parties, and X.509 digital certificates for credentials exchange.

To strictly adhere to emergent standard protocols is highly recommended integration with SAML protocol that is the base language for security tokens communication and exchange. This improvement is planned for the next version of CAS++. Federation is not yet included in CAS++ features, because its first objective is the development of good and stable SSO framework.

Besides being a "pure-Java" module like its predecessor, CAS++ is a fully J2EE compliant application and can be integrated with services coded in any Web-based implementation language. It enriches the traditional CAS authentication process through the integration of biometric identification (by fingerprints readers), identity certificates, and smart-card technologies in addition to traditional username/password mechanism, enabling two authentication levels. Our strong authentication process flow is composed of the following steps (see Figure 3):[3]

1. the user requests an identity certificate to the CA (Certification Authority);
2. the user receives from the CA a smart card that contains a X.509 identity certificate, signed with the private key of the CA, that certifies the user identity. The corresponding user private key is encrypted with a symmetric algorithm (e.g., DES) and the key contained inside the smart card can be decrypted only with a key represented by user fingerprint (KFingerprintUser);
3. to access a service the public key certificate, along with the username/password pair, is encrypted with the CAS++ public key (KPuCAS++) and sent to CAS++;
4. CAS++ decrypts the certificate with its private key, verifies the signature on the certificate with the CA public key, and verifies the validity of this certificate by interacting with the CA;
5. CAS++ retrieves from the CA information about the validity of the user certificate;
6. if the certificate is valid, CAS++ extracts the information related to the user, creates the ticket (TGC, Ticket Granting Cookie), and returns it to the user encrypted with the public key of the user (KPuUser). At this point, to decrypt the TGC, the user must retrieve the private key stored inside the smart card by mean of the user's fingerprint. As soon

as the card is unlocked, the private key is extracted and the TGC decrypted. This ticket will be used for every further access, in the same session, to any application managed by the CAS++ Single Sign-On server.

At this point, for every further access in the session, the user can be authenticated by the service providing only the received TGC without any additional authentication action. In particular, the service access flow, that takes place over secure channels and is similar to the one in CAS implementation, is composed of the following steps (see Figure 4):

1. the user, via a Web browser, requests access to the service provider;
2. the service provider requests authentication information through a HTTP redirection to the CAS++ Server;
3. the CAS++ Server retrieves the user TGC and the service requested URL. If the user has been previously authenticated by CAS++ and has the privilege to access the service, a Service Ticket is created;
4. the CAS++ Server redirects the user browser to the requested service along with the ST;
5. service receives the ST and check its validity sending it to the CAS++ Server;
6. if ST is valid the CAS++ Server sends to the Service an XML file with user's credentials;
7. the user gains the access to the system.

To summarize, this mechanism provides a secure multilevel authentication and a centralized and application independent account management. The advantages of this approach are that the account management is centralized and separated by the real application, the traditional authentication process is improved through the integration of biometric identification (by fingerprints readers),

Figure 3. CAS++ certificate-based authentication flow

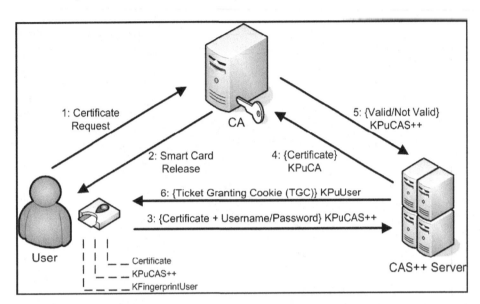

identity certificates, and smart card technologies in addition to traditional username/password mechanism. The introduction of smart cards and fingerprints readers does not affect the system performance and does not require huge additional costs. Finally, CAS++ tries to develop a first solution to address the authorization feature, managing the association of users identity with roles and relying on the specific service for task to define and manage the authorization policies.

SourceID

The second solution analyzed is SourceID, a SSO implementation of Liberty Alliance project specifications. The Liberty Alliance project (Liberty Alliance Project, 2004) is a business and technology consortium of more than 130 global organizations that was established in 2001 (Galbraith et al., 2002). Its mission is to provide a framework to protect business transaction granting privacy and security of the involved parties. Liberty Alliance is focused on (1) enabling consumers to protect privacy and security of their identity information; (2) enabling businesses to maintain and manage their customer relationships without third-party participation; (3) providing an open Single Sign-On standard that includes the centralized authentication from multiple providers; (4) creating an identity infrastructure supporting network access devices.

This infrastructure then is based on the following concepts:

- **Circle of Trust.** It is a set of Service Providers (SP) and Identity Providers (IdP) that have trusted business relationships, based on Liberty architecture, and operational agreements and can transact business in a secure and, apparently, seamless environment.
- **Identity Federation.** When an user authenticates him/herself to a particular service, the provider supplies the user with an assertion of the authentication event. An identity federation is said to exist between the provider and other service providers, when they are in the same Circle of Trust. The authentication assertion is used to link user identity across business boundaries.

Figure 4. CAS++ information flow for service request evaluation

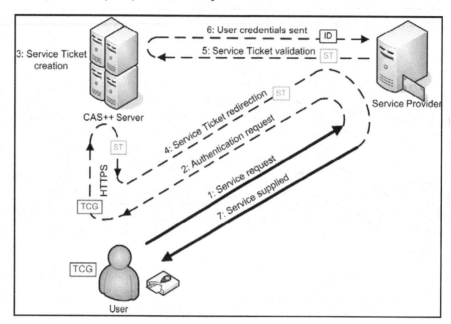

SourceID Implementation

SourceID, originated in 2001 by the Ping Identity Corporation, is an Open Source multiprotocol project for enabling identity federation and cross-boundary security. SourceID focuses on simple integration and deployment within existing Web applications and provides high-level developer functionalities and customization. SourceID-SSO is the subsystem implementing Liberty Single Sign-On specification and it is a framework that integrates Internet SSO services into new and existing Web portals. The lower level implementation of Liberty specifications, as for instance SOAP, SAML, Liberty features, protocols, and metadata schemas, are transparent for Web developers. SourceID-SSO provides, in fact, high-level servlets/JSP APIs for developers that are responsible for Web applications core business logic only.

From the architectural point of view, SourceID-SSO system is composed by three modules plugged into Web applications to provide SSO

facilities: *Profile* implements the Liberty Single Sign-On features, as for instance Federation, Single Sign-On and Log-Out; *Message* provides features to create specific XML messages (for instance Liberty protocol and authentication); and, finally, *Utility* provides functionality as Exception Handling, Data Format encoding, and decoding.

With respect to the listed requirements, SourceID is not a single point of control, because services maintain their own authentication layer to permit log-on actions before federation time. Hence, there is a lack of centralization in identity management: this will increase the time and the costs used to administrate user profiles and accounts. However, major advantages of SourceID implementation are the support of federation and the adherence to Liberty Alliance protocol and specification. SourceID is fully integrated with standard communication protocols used for messages exchange like SAML and SOAP. Finally, SourceID uses encrypted nonopaque cookies containing SP username, security assertion validity, and current domain.

Shibboleth

The third implementation evaluated is Shibboleth (Shibboleth Project, 2004), an Open Source implementation, of Internet2/MACE, aimed at developing architectures, policy structures, practical technologies, to support sharing of Web resources, subject to access control. Shibboleth is not only a SSO implementation, but it is a more general architecture that tries to protect privacy and in general to manage user credentials. However, in this article we only focus on Shibboleth's SSO implementation.

Within Shibboleth, SSO implementation is very closed to Liberty Single Sign-on specification. We can, in fact, highlight three main actors: Identity Provider (IdP), Service Provider (SP), and Requestor. The lower level implementation relies on different standards as HTTP, XML, XML Schema, XML Signature, SOAP, and SAML. As in Liberty Alliance approach, Shibboleth uses the federation concept, named Shibboleth club, between Identity and Service Providers.

Below, we briefly present the flow of Shibboleth authentication process (see Figure 5):

1. the User requests an access to a Shibboleth-protected resource on SP;
2. the SP requests user authentication;
3. the SP's authentication request is transparently redirected to user's IdP;
4. the IdP's requests user's local credentials to fulfil log-on process; these credentials could be simply username/password;
5. the User sends his/her local credentials to IdP;
6. the IdP verifies the credentials and generates the handle that identifies the user;
7. the IdP sends the generated handle to the SP;
8. the SP uses the received handle to ask for needed user attributes;
9. the IdP verifies the handle and sends the attributes to SP.

Note that, after the first user authentication, SP generates a security context to authenticate the user during further request without any authentication process. In the case in which a user already authenticated to IdP requests for another service, the process is the same as depicted above, except for point 4 and 5 that are not performed.

With reference to the requirements stated in the third section, Shibboleth has no single point of control. However a great advantage of Shibboleth, as for the SourceID implementation, is that of providing support of federation and also the full integration with standard communication protocols used for messages exchange like SAML and SOAP.

Shibboleth provides only traditional authentication mechanism with no strong authentication functionalities. On the other side, it supports authorization and provisioning features through an ad-hoc implementation inside SPs.

Java Open Single Sign-On

Java Open Single Sign-On (JOSSO) is an Open Source J2EE-based SSO infrastructure aimed at providing a solution for centralized platform-neutral user authentication (Java Open Single Sign-On Project, 2005). In the JOSSO architecture we can identify three main actors:

*   the **Partner application**, that is a Web application that uses SSO Gateway services to authenticate users;
*   the **SSO Gateway**, that represents the SSO server and provides authentication services to users who need authentication with partner applications;
*   the **SSO Agent**, that is a SSO Gateway client installed on managed services. It intercepts every access requests and administrates communication between partner applications and SSO Gateway.

Figure 5. Shibboleth process flow

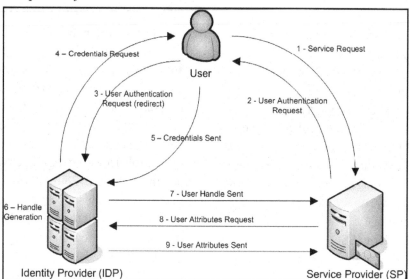

More in detail, JOSSO is (1) *a components-based framework*, since it provides a component oriented infrastructure to support multiple authentication schemes, credential, and session stores; (2) *providing support for integration* with Tomcat Web container, without requiring code customization, (3) *it is cross-platform*, allowing integration with Java and non-Java applications, using standard solutions such as JAAS, SOAP, EJB, servlet/JSP, and Struts; and (4) *provides support for strong authentication*, through the use of X.509 certificates.

The JOSSO authentication process flow is quite similar to the Shibboleth one (see Figure 5); the difference is that all the communications involving Partner Applications are intercepted and managed by a SSO Agent, that acts on behalf of the services. The main steps of the flow can be summarized as:

- the User requests an access to a protected resource within a partner application;
- the SSO Agent intercepts the request and redirects the user to the SSO Gateway authentication form;

- the user enters his/her credentials (for instance a pair username/password or a certificate);
- the SSO Gateway checks user credentials. If credentials are valid, it generates a SSO session token and redirects the user to the requested resource;
- the SSO Agent intercepts the session token and asks for its validation, via SOAP Web services, to the SSO Gateway;
- if validation succeeds, the SSO Gateway sends to the SSO Agent the user credentials;
- the user accesses the requested service.

JOSSO fulfils most of the requirements stated in the third section. It has a single point of control, provides a centralized identity management, and supports standard communication protocols used for messages exchange like SAML and SOAP and standard technologies, such as Web services. However, currently, JOSSO does not support federation. Finally, JOSSO can be completely integrated with different environments.

COMPARISON SUMMARY

In this section we provide a comparison of the Open Source communities behind the four presented implementations taking in account the metrics defined in Ardagna, Damiani, Frati, and Reale (2006). Note that a full comparison between the analyzed systems, with reference to the identified requirements, is not possible because all the requirements listed in the third section depend on the business/trust model adopted by each system, that are outside of the scope of this article (Ardagna et al., 2006).

First of all, we remark that while CAS, SourceID, and JOSSO are fully dedicated SSO systems, Shibboleth is a more comprehensive framework which contains, among other things, a SSO implementation. Focusing on the comparison, all the analyzed systems are quite stable due to the fact that their startups happened more than a year ago. However, CAS implementation stands out because it started about five years ago.

A common characteristic of the projects is that they are managed by a consolidated core group that gives stability to the project and coordination to Open Source community. Also the level of documentation is quite similar and it is included between 6.80 MB of JOSSO and 10.05 MB of CAS. Although CAS seems the more lively project due to the great number of releases, we argue that the more active and viable implementation is JOSSO, because it provides a new release every 21 days, while CAS implementation only provided a release every 79 days. This gap could give to adopters of the JOSSO framework a higher assurance of the project's reliability, because continuous releases keep the implementation up to date and resistant to new technologies and vulnerabilities. However, JOSSO's short update time is also influenced by the fact that the project is the youngest; in the next year, the average update time is likely to rise. Shibboleth and JOSSO are both supported by SourceForge (The Sourceforge Project, 2002).

CONCLUSION

In this article we illustrated the central role of Open Source in Web-based applications. In particular, first, we put forward the idea of developing fully Open Source applications, then we explained Single Sign-On technologies, and finally we discussed functional requirements for Single Sign-On architectures. We described CAS++, developed by our group at University of Milan, SourceID, distributed by Ping Identity Corporation, Shibboleth, a project of Internet2/MACE and JOSSO, developed by Novascope S.A. and JOSSO team, evaluating them against the listed requirements. Finally, we provide a comparison of the analyzed frameworks with respect to Open Source community aspects.

ACKNOWLEDGMENT

This work was supported in part by the European Union within the PRIME Project in the FP6/IST Programme under contract IST-2002-507591 and by the Italian MIUR within the KIWI and MAPS projects.

REFERENCES

Ardagna, C.A., Damiani, E., De Capitani di Vimercati, S., Frati, F., & Samarati, P. (2006). CAS++: An open source single sign-on solution for secure e-services. In *Proceedings of 21st IFIP International Information Security Conference "Security and Privacy in Dynamic Environments"*, Karlstad, Sweden.

Ardagna, C.A., Damiani, E., Frati, F., & Montel, M. (2005). Using open source middleware for securing e-gov applications. In *Proceedings of the First International Conference on Open Source Systems (OSS 2005)*, Genova, Italy.

Ardagna, C.A., Damiani, E., Frati, F., & Reale, S. (2006). Adopting open source for mission-critical applications: A case study on single sign-on. In *Proceedings of the Second International Conference on Open Source Systems (OSS 2006)*, Como, Italy.

Aubry, P., Mathieu, V., & Marchal, J. (2004). ESUP-Portal: Open source single sign-on with CAS (Central Authentication Service). In *Proceedings of EUNIS04 - IT Innovation in a Changing World*, Bled, Slovenia.

Bettini, C., Jajodia, S., Sean Wang, X., & Wijesekera, D. (2002). Provisions and obligations in policy management and security applications. In *Proceedings of the 28th VLDB Conference*, Honk Kong, China.

Buell, D.A., & Sandhu, R. (2003, November-December). Identity management. *IEEE Internet Computing, 7*(6), 26-28.

Central Authentication Service. (2003). Retrieved June 16, 2006, from http://tp.its.yale.edu/tiki/tiki-index.php?page= CentralAuthenticationService

Damiani, E., Grosky, W., & Khosla, R. (2003). Human-centered e-business. MA: *Kluwer Academic Publishers*.

De Clercq, J. (2002, October 1-3). Single sign-on architectures. In G.I. Davida, Y. Frankel, & O. Rees (Eds.), *Proceedings of the International Infrastructure Security Conference* (p. 4058), Bristol, United Kingdom. Lecture Notes in Computer Science 2437. Springer-Verlag.

Feldman, S. (2000). The changing face of e-commerce. *IEEE Internet Computing, 4*(3), 82–84.

Galbraith, B., et al. (2002). *Professional Web services security*. Wrox Press.

Java Open Single Sign-On Project. (2005). Retrieved June 16, 2006, from http://www.josso.org

JBoss, Open Source Application Server. (2003). Retrieved June 16, 2006, from http://www.jboss.org

Liberty Alliance Project. (2004). Retrieved June 16, 2006, from http://www.projectliberty.org/

Pashalidis, A., & Mitchell, C.J. (2003). A taxonomy of single sign-on systems. In *Proceedings of ACISP 2003* (pp. 249-264). LNCS 2727.

Public-Key Infrastructure (X.509), The Internet Engineering Task Force. (2003). Retrieved June 16, 2006, from http://www.ietf.org/ html.charters/pkix-charter.html

Samar, V. (1999). Single sign-on using cookies for Web applications. In *Proceedings of the 8th IEEE Workshop on Enabling Technologies: Infrastructure for Collaborative Enterprises* (pp. 158–163), Palo Alto, California.

Scott, S. (2003). *The JBoss Group: JBoss administration and development* (3rd ed., 3.2.x Series). JBoss Group, LLC.

Security Assertion Markup Language, OASIS Security Services (SAML) TC. (2003). Retrieved June 16, 2006, from http://www.oasis-open.org/committees/tc_home.php?wg_abbrev=security

Shibboleth Project. (2004). Retrieved June 16, 2006, from http://shibboleth.internet2.edu/

Simple Object Access Protocol (SOAP), The World Wide Web Consortium (W3C). (2003). Retrieved June 16, 2006, from http://www.w3.org/TR/soap/

Single Sign-On, The Open Group. (2003). Retrieved June 16, 2006, from http://www.opengroup.org/security/sso/

The Sourceforge Project. (2002). Retrieved June 16, 2006, from http://sourceforge.net/

SourceID, Open Source Federated Identity Management. (2005). Retrieved June 16, 2006, from http://www.sourceid.org/index.html

ENDNOTES

[1]   It is worth noticing that, while improving security since the user has less accounts to manage, SSO solutions may also result in greater exposure from attacks: if an attacker getting hold of a single credential can in principle compromise the whole system.

[2]   For an early attempt to collect SSO requirements see http://middleware.internet2. edu/Webiso/docs/draft-internet2-Webiso-requirements-07.html

[3]   Note that the first two actions are performed only once when the user requests the smart card along with an identity certificate.

This work was previously published in Int. Journal of Information Technology and Web Engineering, Vol 1, Issue 3, edited by E. Damiani and G. Succi, pp. 81-94, copyright 2006 by IGI Publishing (an imprint of IGI Global).

Chapter VII
Engineering Wireless Mobile Applications

Qusay H. Mahmoud
University of Guelph, Canada

Zakaria Maamar
Zayed University, UAE

ABSTRACT

Conventional desktop software applications are usually designed, built, and tested on a platform similar to the one on which they will be deployed and run. Wireless mobile application development, on the other hand, is more challenging because applications are developed on one platform (like UNIX or Windows) and deployed on a totally different platform like a cellular phone. While wireless applications can be much smaller than conventional desktop applications, developers should think in the small in terms of the devices on which the applications will run and the environment in which they will operate instead of the amount of code to be written. This paper presents a systematic approach to engineering wireless application and offers practical guidelines for testing them. What is unique about this approach is that it takes into account the special features of the new medium (mobile devices and wireless networks), the operational environment, and the multiplicity of user backgrounds; all of which pose new challenges to wireless application development.

INTRODUCTION

The general mobile computing model in a wireless environment consists of two distinct sets of entities (Figure 1): Mobile Clients (MCs) and fixed hosts. Some of the fixed hosts, called Mobile Support Stations (MSSs), are enhanced with wireless interfaces. A MSS can communicate with the MCs

Figure 1. Mobile Computing Model

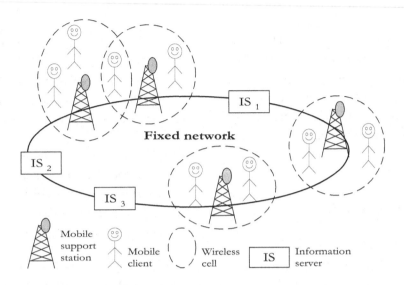

within its radio coverage area called wireless cell. A MC can communicate with a fixed host/server via a MSS over a wireless channel. The wireless channel is logically separated into two sub-channels: an uplink channel and a downlink channel. The uplink channel is used by MCs to submit queries to the server via an MSS, whereas the downlink channel is used by MSSs to disseminate information or to forward the responses from the server to a target client. Each cell has an identifier (CID) for identification purposes. A CID is periodically broadcasted to all the MCs residing in a corresponding cell.

A wireless mobile application is defined as a software application, a wireless service or a mobile service that can be either pushed to users' handheld wireless devices or downloaded and installed, over the air, on these devices. Such applications must work within the daunting constraints of the devices themselves:

• *Memory*: Wireless devices such as cellular phones and two-way pagers have limited amounts of memory, obliging developers to consider memory management most carefully when designing application objects.

• *Processing power*: Wireless devices also have limited processing power (16-bit processors are typical).

• *Input*: Input capabilities are limited. Most cell phones provide only a one-hand keypad with twelve buttons: the ten numerals, an asterisk (*), and a pound sign (#).

• *Screen*: The display might be as small as 96 pixels wide by 54 pixels high and 1 bit deep (black and white). The amount of information that can be squeezed into such a tight screen is severely limited.

In addition, the wireless environment imposes further constraints: (i) wireless networks are unreliable and expensive, and bandwidth is low; (ii) they tend to experience more network errors than wired networks; and (iii) the very mobility of wireless devices increases the risk that a connection will be lost or degraded. In order to design and build reliable wireless applications, designers need to keep these constraints in mind and ask themselves what impact do wireless devices with limited resources have on application design?

The motivation for this paper is provided in part by the above characteristics that form some of the foundations for pervasive computing environments. Such characteristics pose several challenges in designing wireless mobile applications for mobile computing. This paper provides a detailed treatment of the impact of these characteristics on engineering wireless mobile applications and presents a systematic approach for designing them. In addition, it offers practical design techniques for wireless application design and development.

WIRELESS APPLICATIONS

Wireless applications can be classified into two streams (Beaulieu, 2002; Burkhardt et al., 2002):

1. *Browser-based:* Applications developed using a markup language: This is similar to the current desktop browser model where the device is equipped with a browser. The Wireless Application Protocol or WAP (http://www.wapforum.org) follows this approach (Open Mobile Alliance, 2005).
2. *Native applications*: Compiled applications where the device has a runtime environment to execute applications. Highly interactive wireless applications are only possible with the latter model. Interactive applications, such as mobile computer games, are a good example. Such applications can be developed using the fast growing Java 2 Micro Edition (J2ME) platform (http://java.sun.com), and they are known as MIDlets.

Another stream is the hybrid application model that aims at incorporating the best aspects of both streams above. The browser is used to allow the user to enter URLs to download native applications from remote servers, and the runtime environment is used to let these applications run on the device.

WAP Might be Dead, But What Did We Learn?

WAP and J2ME MIDP solve similar problems but each can learn a couple of things from the other. There are special features that are available in WAP but not in MIDP and *vice versa*. These features are summarized as follows:

*   MIDP provides a low-level graphics APIs that enable the programmer to have control over every pixel of the device's display. This is important for entertainment applications (such as games) in a wireless environment.
*   MIDP is the way to go for games. The nature of MIDlets (they exist on the device until they are explicitly removed) allows users to run them even when the server becomes unavailable (support for disconnected operations).
*   WML provides tags and possible presentation attributes, but it doesn't define an interaction model. For example, WML defines a SELECT tag for providing a list. Some WAP-enabled devices interpret the SELECT tag as a popup menu list while others interpret it as a menu that can be used for navigation. Therefore, there is no standard interaction model defined for this element. If a developer uses it, the application may run well on some devices and poorly on others. MIDlets, on the other hand, provide a clearly defined standard for interaction using commands.

A Micro Browser is Needed

MIDlets combine excellent online and offline capabilities that are useful for the wireless environment, which suffers from low bandwidth and network disconnection. Integrating WAP and MIDP opens up possibilities for new wireless

Figure 2. Combining WAP and J2ME

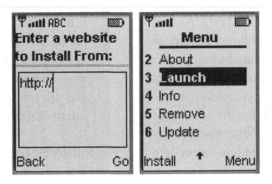

applications and over the air distribution models. Therefore, WAP and MIDP shouldn't be viewed as competing but rather as complementing technologies. In order to facilitate downloading wireless applications over the air, there is a need for some kind of an environment on the handset that allows the user to enter a URL for a MIDlet Suite, for example. This environment could very well be a WAP browser as shown in Figure 2.

Similar to Java Applets that are integrated into HTML, MIDlets can be integrated into a WML or an XHTML page. Such a page can then be called from a WAP browser and the embedded MIDlet gets downloaded and installed on the device. In order to enable this, a WAP browser is needed on the device. Another alternative approach for over the air provisioning is the use of Short Message Service (SMS) as have been done by Siemens where the installation of MIDlets is accomplished by sending a corresponding SMS. If the SMS contains a URL to a Java Descriptor (JAD) file specifying a MIDlet Suite, then the recipient can install the application simply by confirming the SMS.

DESIGN CHALLENGES AND POSSIBLE SOLUTIONS

In this paper we are more concerned with native interactive applications that can be developed using the J2ME platform or a similar technology. J2M2-based wireless applications can be classified into local (stand-alone) and network applications. Local applications (or stand-alone) perform all their operations on a handheld wireless device and need no access to external data sources through a wireless network. Examples include calculators and single-player games. Network applications, on the other hand, consist of some components running on a wireless device and others running on a network, and thus depend on access to external resources. An example would be an email application, with a client residing on a wireless phone interacting with a Simple Mail Transfer Protocol (SMTP) server to send/receive e-mail messages. A major difference between local and networked applications is in the way they are tested. Local applications are easier to test than network applications. For example, a calculator application can run on a wireless device even when it is not connected to any network, but an email client will not work without a connection to mail servers.

Challenges

The constraints discussed earlier pose several crucial challenges, which must be faced in order for wireless applications to function correctly in the target environment.

- **Transmission Errors:** Messages sent over wireless links are exposed to interference (and varying delays) that can alter the content received by the user, the target device, or the server. Applications must be prepared to handle these problems. Transmission errors may occur at any point in a wireless transaction and at any point during the sending or receiving of a message. They can occur after a request has been initiated, in the middle of the transaction, or after a reply has been sent. While wireless network protocols may be able to detect and correct some errors, error-handling strategies that address all kinds of transmission errors that are likely to occur are still needed.

- **Message Latency:** Message latency, or the time it takes to deliver a message, is primarily affected by the nature of each system that handles the message, and by the processing time needed and delays that may occur at each node from origin to destination. Message latency should be taken into account and users of wireless applications should be kept informed of processing delays. It is especially important to remember that a message may be delivered to a user long after the time it is sent. A long delay might be due to coverage problems or transmission errors, or the user's device might be switched off or have a dead battery. Some systems keep trying, at different times, to transmit the message until it is delivered. Other systems store the message, then deliver it when the device is reconnected to the network. Therefore, it is important to design applications that avoid sending stale information, or at least to make sure that users are aware it is not up to date. Imagine the possible consequences of sending a stock quote that is three days old, without warning the user!

- **Security:** Any information transmitted over wireless links is subject to interception.

Some of that information could be sensitive, like credit card numbers and other personal information. The solution needed really depends on the level of sensitivity. To provide a complete end-to-end security solution, you must implement it on both ends, the client and the server, and assure yourself that intermediary systems are secure as well.

Possible Solutions

Here are some practical hints useful to consider when developing mobile applications.

- *Understand the environment.* Do some research up front. As with developing any other software application, we must understand the needs of the potential users and the requirements imposed by all networks and systems the service will rely on.

- *Choose an appropriate architecture.* The architecture of the mobile application is very important. No optimization techniques will make up for an ill-considered architecture. The two most important design goals should be to minimize the amount of data transmitted over the wireless link, and to anticipate errors and handle them intelligently.

- *Partition the application.* Think carefully when deciding which operations should be performed on the server and which on the handheld device. Downloadable wireless applications allow locating much of an application's functionality of the device; it can retrieve data from the server efficiently, then perform calculations and display information locally. This approach can dramatically reduce costly interaction over the wireless link, but it is feasible only if the device can handle the processing the application needs to perform.

- *Use compact data representation.* Data can be represented in many forms, some more compact than others. Consider the available representations and select the one that requires fewer bits to be transmitted. For example, numbers will usually be much more compact if transmitted in binary rather than string forms.

- *Manage message latency.* In some applications, it may be possible to do other work while a message is being processed. If the delay in appreciable – and especially if the information is likely to go stale – it is important to keep the user informed of progress. Design the user interface of your applications to handle message latency appropriately.

- *Simplify the interface.* Keep the application's interface simple enough that the user seldom needs to refer to a user manual to perform a task. To do so: reduce the amount of information displayed on the device; make input sequences concise so the user can accomplish tasks with the minimum number of button clicks; and offer the user selection lists.

AD-HOC DEVELOPMENT PROCESS

An ad-hoc development process for wireless applications comprises three steps:

1. Write the application: Several Integrated Development Environments (IDEs) are available for developing Java-based wireless applications, e.g. Sun's J2ME Wireless Toolkit, and Metrowerks CodeWarrior.

2. Test the application in an emulation environment: Once the application compiles nicely, it can be tested in an emulator.

3. Download the application to a physical device and test it. Once application's performance is satisfactory on one or more emulators, it can be downloaded to a real device and tested it there. If it is a network application, it is tested on a live wireless

network to ensure that its performance is acceptable.

It is clear that many important software engineering activities are missing from this ad-hoc development process. For example, there is no formal requirements analysis phase, and so following an ad-hoc development process may lead to building a product different from the one the customers want, and also testing an application without knowing its requirements is not an easy task. In addition, issues related to the operating environment such as network bandwidth should be considered during the design so that the performance of the application will be satisfactory.

WIRELESS SOFTWARE ENGINEERING

While wireless application development might appear to have less need for the coordination that a process provides, aspects of development, testing, evaluation, deployment, and maintenance of a wireless application have to be integrated in the design process throughout the full development lifecycle. We have put forward a systematic approach to developing wireless applications, which is compatible with the Rational Unified Process or RUP (Jacobsen et al., 2000) in the sense that it is iterative and responsibility-driven. We have developed this systematic approach based on our experience designing and building wireless applications. We recognized that the development of a wireless application is not a one-shot task, and testing wireless applications is more challenging than testing conventional desktop software applications, and therefore an ad hoc development process cannot be used.

Development Activities

Our software engineering approach to wireless application development consists of a set of

Figure 3. Wireless application development activities

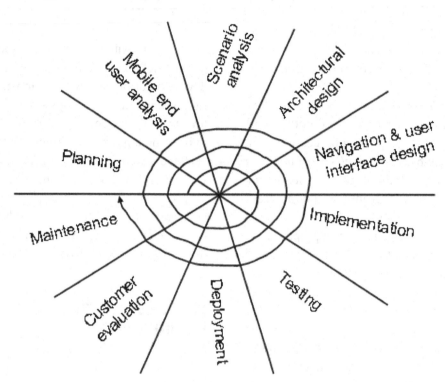

manageable activities that if followed properly leads to reliable and maintainable wireless applications. The activities of our approach are shown in Figure 3.

- **Planning**. This iterative process begins with a planning phase, which is an activity that identifies the objectives of the wireless application and specifies the scope of the first increment. In addition, the costs of the overall project are estimated, the risks are evaluated, and a tentative schedule is set.
- **Mobile User Analysis**. First, we must understand the audience of the application and the environment in which it will operate. As an example, if the application is a wireless network-aware application such as a multiplayer game, the study will include the users of the application and how they plan to use it.

The output at the end of this phase is a wireless application plan document that serves as the mobile end user requirement.

- **Scenario Analysis**. This phase is similar to conventional software requirements analysis, and therefore concepts and principles of requirements analysis can be applied here (Pressman, 2005). In this phase, the mobile end user, an interaction designer, and a developer sit together to come up with a complete scenario analysis model that takes into account the following types of scenario analysis:

  ○ **Screen and Interaction Analysis**: The basic unit of interaction between the user and the mobile device is the screen, which is an object that encapsulates device-specific graphic user input. Therefore, the content to be displayed on the screen is identified. Content may include text fields, menus, lists, and graphics. Interaction analysis specifies how the user interacts with the application. In order to find out how the user will interact with the application, UML (Booch et al., 2000) use cases are developed.

° **Usage Analysis**: The use case model developed during screen and interaction analysis is mainly related to how users interact with the application through the screen. The whole functionality of the application should be described with use cases.

° **Environment Analysis**: The environment in which the application will operate should be described in details. This includes the different wireless networks and backend systems used. In addition, target mobile devices such as cellular phones and PDAs on which the application will run should be described in details.

The output of this phase is an information analysis model document produced by the interaction designer and developer that outlines the functional requirements of the application and the constraints of the environment. This document is reviewed by developers and other stakeholders and modified as required.

• **Architectural Design**. This phase is concerned with the overall architecture (or structure) of the wireless application. Architecture is very important for any application, and no optimization techniques will make up for an ill-considered architecture. Design patterns can be used in this phase to reuse experience in order to come up with an extensible, high-performance architecture.

Some of the most important design goals should be to minimize the amount of data transmitted over the wireless link, and to anticipate errors and handle them intelligently. Other design and architecture issues include:

° *Application partitioning*. Designers need to think carefully when deciding which operations should be performed on the server and which on the wireless device. J2ME allows designers to locate much of an application's functionality on the device; it can retrieve data from the server efficiently, then perform calculations and display information locally. This approach can dramatically reduce costly interaction over the wireless link, but it is feasible only if the device can handle the processing your application needs to perform.

° *Message latency*. In some applications, it may be possible to do other work while a message is being processed. If the delay is appreciable – and especially if the information is likely to go stale – it is important to keep the user informed of progress.

The outcome of the architectural design phase is a design document that details the system architecture.

Navigation and User Interface Design. Once the application architecture has been established and its components identified, the interaction designer prepares screen mockups and navigation paths that show how the user moves from one screen to another to access services. Figure 4 shows a simple example where the user will have to login before she is able to check her messages.

The user interface is the face of the application to users. A poorly designed user-interface will

Figure 4. Screen Mockups

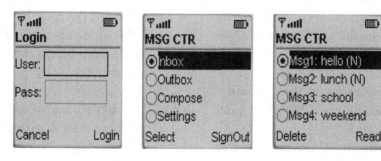

scare the user away, and a well-designed user interface will give a good first impression and improves the user's perception of the services offered by the application. The user interface must be well-structured and easy to use. Here are some guidelines that can help in designing simple, but yet effective user interfaces for mobile devices with tiny screens.

- Keep the application's interface simple enough that the user seldom needs to refer to a user manual to perform a task.
- Reduce the amount of information displayed on the device.
- Make input sequences concise so the user can accomplish tasks with the minimum number of button clicks.
- Offer the user selection lists.
- Do not depend on any specific screen size.

The output of this phase is a user manual that describes the screen mockups and the navigational paths.

Implementation. In this phase development tools are used to implement the wireless application. There are several tools available for building wireless applications such as Sun's J2ME Wireless Toolkit. We would recommend using a tool that allows installing the application in various emulation environments. Conventional implementation strategies and techniques such as coding standards and code reviews can be used in this phase.

Testing. Software testing is a systemic process to find differences between the expected behavior of the system specified in the software requirements document and its observed behavior. In other words, it is an activity for finding errors in the software system and fixing them so users can be confident that they can depend on the software. Errors in software are generally introduced by people involved in software development (including analysts, architects, designers, programmers, and the testers themselves). Examples of errors include mismatch between requirements and implementation.

Many developers view the subject of software testing as "not fashionable," and as a result too few of them really understand the job software testers do. Testing is an iterative process and should start from the beginning of the project. Software developers need to get used to the idea of designing software with testing in mind. Some of the new software development methodologies such as eXtreme Programming (XP) (Beck, 1999) stress incremental development and testing. XP is ideally suited for some types of applications, depending on their size, scope, and nature. User interface design, for example, benefits highly from rapid prototyping and testing usability with actual users.

Wireless applications, like all other types of software, must be tested to ensure functionality and usability under all working conditions. Testing is even more important in the wireless world because working conditions vary a lot more than they do for most software. For example, wireless applications are developed on high-end desktop machines but deployed on handheld wireless devices with very different characteristics.

One way to make testing simple is to design applications with testing in mind. Organizing the system in a certain way can make it much easier to test. Another implication is that the system must have enough functionality and enough output information to distinguish among the system's different functional features. In our approach, and similar to many others, the system's functional requirements (features that the system must provide) are described using the Unified Modeling Language (Booch et al., 2000) to create a use case model, then detailing the use cases in a consistent written form. Documenting the various uses of the system in this way simplifies the task of testing the system by allowing the tester to generate test scenarios from the use cases. The scenarios represent all expected paths users will traverse when they use the features that the system must provide.

Deployment. Deploying and running applications in an emulation environment is a very good way to test the logic and flow of your application generally, but you won't be certain it will satisfy users until you test it on a real physical device connected to a wireless network. Your application's performance may be stunning in the emulator, which has all the processing power and memory of your desktop machine at its command, but will it perform well on the handheld device, with its limited memory and processing power, low bandwidth, and other constraints? In this phase, the application is deployed on a live network and evaluated.

Customer Evaluation. Once the application has been deployed, it is ready to be downloaded by users for evaluation and usage. In this phase, users start using the deployed application and report any problems they may experience to the service provider.

Maintenance. Software maintenance encompasses four activities: error correction, adaptation, enhancement, and reengineering (Pressman, 2005). The application will evolve over time as errors are fixed and customers request new features. In this phase, users report errors to and request new features from the service provider, and developers fix errors and enhance the application.

TESTING ISSUES AND TESTING ACTIVITIES

The wide variety of mobile devices such as wireless phones and PDAs results in each device running a different implementation of the J2ME environment. Varying display sizes add to the complexity of the testing process. In addition, some vendors provide proprietary API extensions. As an example, some J2ME vendors may support only the HTTP protocol, which the MIDP 1.0 specification requires, while others support TCP sockets and UDP datagrams, which are optional. Here are some guidelines for testing wireless applications.

Validating the Implementation. Ensuring that the application does what it is supposed to be is an iterative process that you must go through during the implementation phase of the project. Part of the validation process can be done in an emulation environment such as the J2ME Wireless Toolkit (Sun Microsystems, 2005), which provides several phone skins and standard input mechanisms. The toolkit's emulation environment does not support all devices and platform extensions, but it allows making sure that the application looks appealing and offers a user-friendly interface on a wide range of devices. Once the application has been tested on an emulator, you can move on to the next step and test it on a real device, and in a live network.

Usability Testing. In usability testing, the focus is on the external interface and the relationships among the screens of the application. As an example, consider an email application that supports entry and validation of a user name and password, enables the user to read, compose, and send messages, and allows maintenance of related settings, using the screens shown in Figure 3, among others.

In this example, start the test at the Login window. Enter a user name and a password and press the soft button labeled Login. Enter a valid user name and password. The application should display the main menu. Does it? The main menu should display a SignOut button. Does it? Press the SignOut button. Does the application return to the Login screen? Write yourself a note to raise the question, "Why does the user 'log' in but 'sign' out?" Now enter an invalid user name or password. The program should display a meaningful message box with an OK button. Does it? Press the OK button. Does the application return to the Login screen?

You need to test the GUI navigation of the entire system, making notes about usability along the way. If, for example, the user must traverse several screens to perform a function that's likely to be very popular, you may wish to consider moving that particular function up the screen layers. Some of the questions you should ask during usability testing include: is the navigation depth (the number of screens the user must go through) appropriate for each particular function, does the application minimize text entry (painful on a wireless phone) or should it provide more selection menus, can screens of all supported devices display the content without truncating it, and if you expect to deploy the application on foreign devices, does it support international character sets?

Network Performance Testing. The goal of this type of testing is to verify that the application performs well in the hardest of conditions (for example, when the battery is low or the phone is passing through a tunnel). Testing performance in an emulated wireless network is very important. The drawback with testing in a live wireless network is that so many factors affect the performance of the network itself that you can't repeat the exact test scenarios. In an emulated network environment, it is easy to record the result of a test and repeat it later, after you have modified the application, to verify that the performance of the application has improved.

Server-Side Testing. It is very likely that wireless applications communicate with server-side applications. If your application communicates with servers you control, you have a free hand to test both ends of the application. If it communicates with servers beyond your control (such as *quotes. yahoo.com*), you just need to find the prerequisites of use and make the best of them. You can test server-side applications that communicate over HTTP connections using testing frameworks such as HttpUnit (http://httpunit.sourceforge.net)), and measure a Web site's performance using httperf (http://citeseer.nj.nec.com/mosberger98httperf. html), a tool designed for measuring the performance of Web servers.

Testing Checklists

Here we provide checklists that are useful when testing your application, in both emulation and live environments. These checklists include tests that are usually performed by certification programs offered by Nokia and Motorola (Motorola Application Certification Program).

Navigation Checklist. Here are some items to check for when testing the navigational paths of wireless applications:

- *Successful startup and exit*: Verify that your application starts up properly and its entry point is consistent. Also make sure that the application exits properly.
- *Application name*: Make sure your application displays a name in the title bar.
- *Keep the user informed*: If your application does not start up within a few seconds, it should alert the user.

- For large applications, it is a good idea to have a progress bar.
- *Readable text*: Ensure that all kinds of content are readable on both grayscale and color devices. Also make sure the text does not contain any misspelled words.
- *Repainting screens*: Verify that screens are properly painted and that the application does not cause unnecessary screen repaints.
- *Soft buttons*: Verify that the functionality of soft buttons is consistent throughout the application. Verify that the whole layout of screens and buttons is consistent.
- *Screen Navigation*: Verify that the most commonly used screens are easily accessible.
- *Portability*: Verify that the application will have the same friendly user interface on all devices it is likely to be deployed on.

Network Checklist. Some of the items that should be inspected when testing wireless applications are:

- *Sending/Receiving data*: For network-aware applications, verify that the application sends and receives data properly.
- *Name resolution*: Ensure that the application resolves IP addresses correctly, and sends and receives data properly.
- *Sensitive data*: When transmitting sensitive data over the network, verify that the data is being masked or encrypted.
- *Error handling*: Make sure that error messages concerning network error conditions (such as no network coverage) are displayed properly, and that when an error message box is dismissed the application regains control.
- *Interruptions*: Verify that, when the device receives system alerts, Short Message Service (SMS) messages, and so on while the application is running, messages are properly displayed. Also make sure that when the message box is dismissed the application continues to function properly.

PROVISIONING WIRELESS APPLICATIONS

Developers usually build, test, and evaluate an application on a platform similar to the one on which it will be deployed and run. Development of wireless applications is more challenging because they typically are developed on one platform (such as Solaris or MS Windows) but deployed on a totally different one (such as a cell phone or PDA). One consequence is that, while emulators enable developers to do some of their testing on the development platform, ultimately they must test and evaluate the application in the very different environment of a live wireless network.

Wireless applications fall into two broad categories:

Local applications (also called *stand-alone applications*) perform all their operations on a handheld wireless device and need no access to external data sources through a wireless network. Examples include calculators and single-player games.

Network applications consist of some components running on a wireless device and others running on a network, and thus depend on access to external resources. An example would be an email application, with a client residing on a wireless phone that interacts with a Simple Mail Transfer Protocol (SMTP) server to send messages.

Although these two types of applications are different, they are deployed in the same way. The big difference shows up later: Local applications are easier to test than network applications. For example, a calculator application can run on a wireless phone even when it is not connected to any network, but an email client won't work without a connection to the SMTP server that actually transmits the messages.

Figure 5. Over the air provisioning

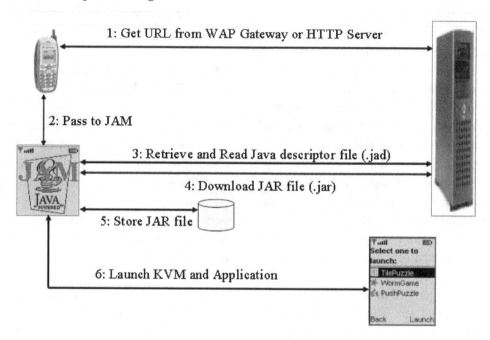

Over the Air Provisioning

For some time, wireless portals in Europe such as Midletcentral have allowed customers to download applications directly to their phones, over the air. Over-the-air provisioning of wireless applications (OTA) is finally available in North America. Nextel customers, for example, can download network-aware wireless applications without an update data cable. OTA is the deployment of wireless Java applications (*MIDlet suites*) from the Internet to wireless devices over a wireless network. Users need not connect their devices to the desktop with a data cable or visit a service center to install or upgrade software. To take advantage of OTA, you must equip your handheld device with a mechanism to discover MIDlet suites available for download, using the device's browser (such as a WAP browser) or a resident application written specifically to identify downloadable MIDlet suites. The process of

downloading MIDlets over the air is illustrated in Figure 5.

RELATED WORK

The explosive growth of the wireless mobile application market raises new engineering challenges (Morisio & Oivo, 2003); what is the impact of the wireless Internet on engineering wireless mobile applications for the new wireless infrastructure and wireless handheld devices? Due to the limited experience with wireless technologies and developing wireless applications, little work has been in the area of wireless software engineering. We found a special issue in the IEEE Transactions on Software Engineering on 'Software Engineering for the Wireless Internet' (Morisio & Oivo, 2003). However, out of the six papers accepted in the special issue only two papers deal with the development process. Ocampo et al., (2003) provided an initial reference process for developing wireless Internet applications, which does not differ significantly from traditional iterative process models but includes domain-specific guidance on the level of engineering processes. Satoh (2003) developed a framework for building and testing networked applications for mobile computing. The framework is aimed to emulate the physical mobility of portable computing devices through the logical mobility of applications designed to run on them; an agent-based emulator is used to perform application-level emulation of its target device.

More recently, Chen (2004) proposed a methodology to help enterprises develop business strategies and architectures for mobile applications. It is an attempt to formulate a life-cycle approach to assisting enterprises in planning and developing enterprise-wide mobile strategies and applications. This methodology is more concerned with business strategies rather than technical details and thus it is targeted at managers rather than developers. And finally, Nikkanen (2004) presented the development work of a browser-agnostic mobile e-mail application. It reports on experiences porting a legacy WAP product to a new XHTML-based browser application, and offers guidelines for developing mobile applications.

Our work is different in the sense that we provide a detailed treatment of the impact of the characteristics of mobile devices and the wireless environment on engineering wireless mobile applications; we discuss the challenges and offer practical solutions for developing mobile applications. We present a systematic approach for designing wireless mobile application. Our approach is iterative just like in (Ocampo et al., 2003), but differs in the sense that our process has more focus on requirements elicitation and more importantly scenario analysis. We do not provide a testing framework, but our testing strategy and checklist is more practical than using just an emulated environment. Finally, unlike the work reported

in (Chen, 2004) our methodology is targeted at developers and researchers rather than managers. And, unlike the work in (Nikkanen, 2004), our guidelines and systematic approach is not limited to WAP-based applications, but can be applied to engineering any wireless application.

CONCLUSION AND FUTURE WORK

As the wireless Internet becomes a reality and software developers become comfortable with the methods and processes required to build software, we recognize that the methods developed for conventional systems are not optimal for wireless applications. In particular, wireless application development doesn't always fit into the development model originated to cope with conventional large software systems. Most wireless application systems will be smaller than any medium size project; however, a software development method can be just as critical to a small software project success as it is to that of a large one. In this paper we have presented and discussed a systematic approach to wireless application development, and presented practical guidelines for testing wireless applications. The proposed approach takes into account the special features of the wireless environment. We have successfully used the approach presented to develop various wireless applications ranging from a stock portfolio management application to a mobile agent platform for mobile devices (Mahmoud, 2002). Our future work includes evaluating the effectiveness of the proposed methodology, documenting wireless software design patterns, and building tools to automate the task of testing wireless applications.

There are several interesting research problems in the emerging area of wireless mobile applications and services. Some of these research issues include: Novel mobile services in the area of m-commerce and health care; Security and privacy issues; Mobile agents for mobile services; Discovery and interaction of mobile services;

Enabling roaming of applications and profiles between different wireless standards; Location-aware and context-aware mobile services. We are currently addressing some of these research problems and research results will be presented in future articles.

ACKNOWLEDGMENT

The authors would like to thank the anonymous reviewers for the many helpful suggestions for improving this paper. This work was supported in part by the Natural Sciences and Engineering Research Council of Canada (NSERC) Discovery Grant No. 045635.

REFERENCES

Beaulieu, M. (2002). Wireless Internet Applications and Architecture, Addison-Wesley.

Beck, K. (1999). Extreme Programming Explained: Embrace Change. Addison-Wesley.

Booch, G., Rumbaugh, J., & Jacobsen, I. (2000). The Unified Modeling Language User Guide, Addison-Wesley.

Burkhardt, J, Henn, H., Hepper, S., Rintdorff, K., & Schack, T. (2002). Pervasive Computing Technology and Architecture of Mobile Internet Applications, Addison-Wesley.

Chen, M. (2004). A methodology for building mobile computing applications. International Journal of Electronic Business, Vol. 2, No. 3, pp. 229-243.

Jacobsen, I., Booch, G., & Rumbaugh, J. (2000). The Unified Software Development Process. Addison-Wesley.

Httperf. citeseer.nj.nec.com/mosberger98httperf. html.

HttpUnit. http://httpunit.sourceforge.net.

Mahmoud, Q. (2002). MobiAgent: An Agent-based Approach to the Wireless Internet. Journal of Internet Computing, special issue on Wireless Internet, pp. 156.162.

Morisio, M., & Oivo, M. (2003). Guest Editors Introduction: Software Engineering for the Wireless Internet. IEEE

Transactions on Software Engineering, Vol. 29, No. 12, pp. 1057-1058.

Motorola Application Certification Program. http://qpqa.com/motorola/iden.

Nikkanen, M. (2004). User-centered development of a browser-agnostic mobile e-mail application. Proceedings of the third Nordic conference on Human-computer interaction, Tampere, Finland, pp. 53-56.

Ocampo, A., Boggio, D., Munch, J., & Palladino, G. (2003): Towards a Reference Process for Developing Wireless Internet Services. IEEE Transactions on Software Engineering, Vol. 29, No. 12, pp. 1122 – 1134.

Open Mobile Alliance. http://www.wapforum. org.

Pressman, R.S. (2005). Software Engineering: A Practitioner's Approach. Sixth Edition, McGraw Hill.

Satoh, I. (2003). A Testing Framework for Mobile Computing Software. IEEE Transactions on Software Engineering, Vol. 29, No. 12, pp. 1112-1121.

Sun Microsystems J2ME: http://java.sun.com/ j2me.

Sun Microsystems J2ME Wireless Toolkit: http:// java.sun.com/products/j2mewtoolkit.

This work was previously published in Int. Journal of Information Technology and Web Engineering, Vol 1, Issue 1, edited by G. Alkhatib and D. Rine, pp. 59-75, copyright 2006 by IGI Publishing (an imprint of IGI Global).

Chapter VIII

A Prediction Based Flexible Channel Assignment in Wireless Networks using Road Topology Information

G. Sivaradje
Pondicherry Engineering College, India

R. Nakkeeran
Pondicherry Engineering College, India

P. Dananjayan
Pondicherry Engineering College, India

ABSTRACT

In this paper, a novel prediction technique is proposed, which uses road topology information for prediction. The proposed scheme uses real time positioning information and road topology information, which matches with the real environment. The scheme uses flexible channel assignment to maintain a better tradeoff between forced termination and call blocking probabilities. For reservation of resources in advance, the information about future handoffs is obtained from the road topology prediction technique. To show the effectiveness of the prediction scheme and flexible channel assignment scheme, this work aims at simulation of other channel assignment strategies viz., fixed and dynamic channel assignment strategy with and without incorporating the prediction based on road topology information. It gives accurate prediction results which helps to maintain a better QoS and resource management.

INTRODUCTION

Today's navigation systems are mostly based on a quite complex positioning system involving multi-sensor systems (differential odometers, gyros, and magnetic field sensors) in the mobile vehicle coupled with a global positioning system (GPS). Mobility prediction for mobile terminal (MT) traveling in a road is possible through GPS but that is not accurate and indeed not available in all areas. However, research shows that 85% of mobility activities in road traffic occur in urban areas where the availability of GPS signals is around 15 to 40%. Rare availability of satellite means due to masking and multi-path effects in urban areas, magnetic disturbances, wheel slips, and unfavorable error propagation lead to loss of position and in principle to total system failures. To make positioning systems available for every mobile vehicle (cars, motorbike, bicycle, pedestrian), development of navigation systems based on a personal digital assistant (PDA), digital maps, mobile phones, and GPS module are initiated (Zhao, 1997; Kyamakya, et al., 2002; Syrjärinne, 2001; Kaplan, 1996; Schwarz, & El-Sheimy, 1999).

Mobility prediction is an exciting research area in which mobile positioning is extremely valuable. The use of real-time positioning information for mobility prediction could potentially give rise to better accuracy and greater adaptability to time-varying conditions than previous methods (Adusei, et. al., 2002; Hellebrandt, Mathar, & Scheibenbogen, 1997; Hellebrandt & Mathar, 1999). The availability for a practical and accurate mobility prediction technique could open the door to many applications such as resource reservation, location tracking and management, location-based services, and others that have yet to be identified. If the system has prior knowledge of the exact trajectory of every MT, it could take appropriate steps to reserve resources so that quality of service (QoS) may be guaranteed during the MT's connection lifetime (Pathirana, Svkin,

& Jha, 2004). However, such an ideal scenario is very unlikely to occur in real life. Instead, much of the work on resource reservation has adopted a predictive approach (Aljadhai & Znati, 2001; Soh & Kim, 2001; Choi & Shin, 1998). A generalized framework for both describing the mobility and updating location information is considered based on a state-based mobility model (Song, Kang, & Park, 2005), and by caching and batch processing (Lee, Zhu, & Hu, 2005). Semantics prefetching strategy is developed, which, utilizes users' information to manage location dependent data's (Sang, Song., Park, & Hwang, 2005). Indexing schemes for location dependent queries (Waluyo, Srinivasan, & Taniar, 2005a) and data broadcasting are introduced in (Waluyo, Srinivasan, & Taniar, 2005b; Waluyo, Srinivasan, Taniar, & Rahayu, 2005). Management of data items in mobile databases and broadcasting system is proposed (Waluyo, Srinivasan, & Taniar, 2004). A mobile query processing approach is proposed when the user's location moves from one base station to another (Jayaputera & Taniar, 2005).

The use of GPS has been advocated as a promising choice for avoiding the poor network utilization due to unnecessary reservations (Erbas, Kyamakya, Steuer, & Jobmann, 2002). According to Zhao (2002), it is very reasonable to expect assisted GPS positioning methods to yield an accuracy of less than 20 m over 67% of the time period. Predicting the trajectory of mobile terminals (Chiu & Bassiouni, 2000) and call-level QoS (Soh & Kim, 2003) to perform resource reservations based on geographic information system (GIS) information is suitable for uniform traffic pattern only. Unfortunately, however, there exist some situations in which part of the GPS signal may be obstructed to the extent that the GPS receiver may not "see" enough satellites for positioning. This signal-obstruction problem was successfully overcome by integrating GPS with other positioning systems (Wang, et al., 2000). Augmenting GPS is not limited to sensor integration but it is possible with computer-based tools, such as GIS, for efficient data collection and analysis.

GPS/GIS Integration

The GIS is a computer-based tool capable of acquiring, storing, manipulating, analyzing, and displaying spatially referenced data (Drane, Macnaughtan, & Scott, 1998; Hofmann-Wallenhnohof, Lichtenegger, & Collins, 1997). Spatially referenced data is identified according to its geographic location (e.g., features such as streets, light poles, and fire hydrants). Spatial or geographic data can be obtained from a variety of sources such as existing maps, satellite imagery, and GPS. Once the information is collected, GIS stores it as a collection of layers in the GIS database. The GIS can then be used to analyze the information and decisions can be made efficiently. If this GPS/GIS is incorporated in the MT, it will be possible to accurately predict the user movements and resource reservations made based on this prediction would be quite appropriate.

GPS/Cellular Integration

Wireless network operators can either use the network-based location or the handset-based location. Most network-based caller location systems employ either the time difference of arrival (TDOA) approach or the angle of arrival (AOA) approach to determine the caller's location. Handset-based location technology integrates GPS with cellular communication through the installation of a GPS chipset in the handset of the wireless phone. Unlike network-based technology, handset-based location technology is very simple to implement and does not require the installation of additional equipment at the base stations (e.g., GPS timing receivers etc.). This method is simple, cost-effective, and flexible and hence, it will be the probable choice in future.

In cellular networks, MT that is carried in vehicles would encounter more frequent handoffs;

they are the ones that would benefit most from mobility predictions. In reality, mobile terminals move according to the presence of highways, streets, and roads. The mobile terminals do not move randomly, rather they follow some patterns that are somewhat predictable. Therefore, incorporation of road topology information into the prediction algorithm could potentially yield better accuracy (Östergren & Juhlin, 2005). Safar (2005) proposed an approach to efficiently and accurately evaluate nearest neighbor queries in mobile information systems that use GPS- and GIS-based spatial network databases, which is computationally expensive to compute the distances between objects. Most of the works in the literature have considered cell boundary to regular hexagon, which doesn't match with reality due to terrain characteristics and the existence of obstacles that interfere with radio wave propagation (Aljadhai, et al.; Choi et al.; Liu, Bahl, & Chlmtac, 1998).

Proposed algorithm utilizes the real-time positioning information obtained from augmented GPS for mobility prediction and the associated bandwidth reservation considering a fuzzy type of cell with irregular boundaries. This integrated framework assumes base stations (BS) are equipped with road-map information and that the mobile terminals are equipped with GPS devices. Prediction accuracy, blocking probability, handoff probability, and forced termination are obtained for the proposed algorithm and are compared with the existing algorithms.

SYSTEM DESCRIPTION

A cellular network with two-dimensional cell layout is considered in which each cell is adjacent to several other cells. The minimum granularity of bandwidth resources that could be allocated to any call is assumed to be one bandwidth unit (BU). Each BS has a capacity $C(j)$, which is assumed to be constant for flexible channel assignment (FCA). In DCA, the total capacity of the system C_T is shared by all the base stations; in FCA scheme, there are both fixed number of channels $C(j)$ for BS in reserve to the dynamic channels, which is common for all the cells. Given the bandwidth demand of individual connections, the BS performs admission control to ensure that the total demand of all active connections are below or equal to $C(j)$. Although it is suggested that some adaptive applications might be able to accept a lower bandwidth at the expense of lower call quality during congestion, that is considered here. Such an assumption is likely to reduce probability of forced termination (P_{FT}), but it may make harder to visualize the advantages of using mobility predictions, which is the main aim of this work.

In order to prioritize handoffs over new calls, each cell must reserve some bandwidth that can only be utilized by incoming handoffs. Specifically, each BS shall have a "reservation target" R_{target} that is being updated regularly based on mobility predictions. A new call request is accepted if the remaining bandwidth after its acceptance is at least R_{target}, for example,

$$C(j) - \left(\sum b_{x,j} + b_{new} \right) \geq R_{target}(j) \qquad (1)$$

where,

b_{new} is the bandwidth required by the new call request.

$b_{x,j}$ is the bandwidth currently being used by an existing connection x in cell j.

The BS can only attempt to meet this target by rejecting new call requests while waiting for some existing calls within the cell to release bandwidth when they are terminated or handed off to other cells. For a handoff request, the admission control rule is more lenient--it is admitted so long as there is sufficient remaining capacity for the handoff, regardless of the value of $R_{target}(j)$

$$C(j) - \sum b_{x,j} \geq b_{handoff} \qquad (2)$$

where,

$b_{handoff}$ is the bandwidth needed by the handoff.

When a new call request is rejected, it is assumed that it is cleared. Subsequent new call requests are assumed to be independent of previous requests. When the BS has insufficient bandwidth to accommodate an incoming handoff-request, it is assumed that it is forced to terminate. Handoff queuing is not assumed, although it would likely improve the performance of proposed scheme, such extensions may make it difficult to visualize the advantages of using mobility predictions.

ROAD TOPOLOGY-BASED PREDICTION SCHEME

In this technique, the serving BS receives regular updates about each active MT's position for every ΔT (say 1 sec). The output of each prediction has the form of a 3-tuple: target cell, prediction weight, and prediction limit. The target cell is the MT's predicted handoff cell. The prediction weight is a real number between 0 and 1 that indicates how likely the prediction is correct. The lower prediction limit (LPL) gives a statistical bound for the actual remaining time from handoff. Each MT may have more than a single 3-tuple to represent different paths from its current position that may lead to a handoff within the threshold time, T_{th}.

The prediction tasks are assigned to individual BSs, which are expected to have sufficient computational and storage resources. In order to incorporate the road information into mobility predictions, each BS needs to keep a database of the roads within its coverage area. The road between two neighbouring junctions is treated as a road segment, and each segment is identified using a junction pair (J_1, J_2), where a junction can be interpreted as an intersection of roads (e.g., T-junction). The approximate coordinates of each junction are to be stored in the database. Since the road segment may contain bends, it can be broken down further into piecewise-linear line segments. The coordinates defining these line segments within each road segment are also recorded. All the previous coordinates could be easily extracted from existing digital maps previously designed for GPS-based navigational devices. Infrequent updates to these maps are foreseen because new roads are not constructed very often, while existing road layouts are seldom modified. The database also stores some important information about each road segment. Since two-way roads would probably have different characteristics for each direction, the database shall store information corresponding to opposite directions separately. To summarize, the base station has the following information that is stored in the database.

1. Identifying of neighbouring segments at each junction.
2. Probability that a MT traveling along a segment would select each neighbouring segment. Note that this transition probability could be easily computed from the previously observed paths of other MTs.
3. Statistical data of time taken to transit each segment.
4. Statistical data about possible handoffs along each segment, such as probability of handoff, time in segment before handoff and handoff positions.

With the exception of the first item listed above, the other database entries will be updated periodically since they are dependent on current traffic conditions. In reality, the transition probabilities among road segments would probably vary with time and traffic conditions. For stochastic processes whose statistics vary slowly with time, it is often appropriate to treat the problem as a succession of stationary problems. The transition between road segments is modeled as a first-order Markov process, and it is assumed stationary between database update instances so as to simplify the computations.

Based on this model, the conditional distribution of a MT chooses, a neighboring segment,

Figure 1. Utilization of road topology information for mobility prediction

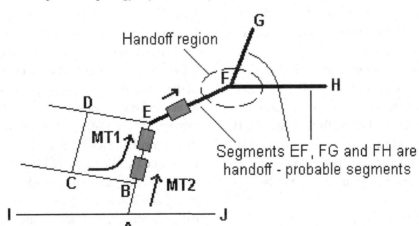

Figure 2. Road topology-based prediction algorithm flowchart

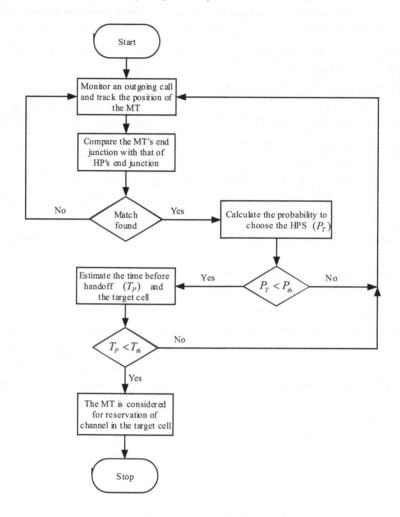

given all its past segments that are assumed to be dependent only on the current segment and the immediate prior segment.

Using the road topology shown in Figure 1 as an illustration, consider two MTs (MT1 and MT2) that are currently traveling from junction B towards junction E. MT1 came from segment CB previously, while MT2 came from segment AB. Based on the assumed model, the conditional probability of MT1 going to segment EF will be

$$P[s_{k+1} = EF \mid s_k = BE] \qquad (3)$$

where, s_k is the current segment that the MT transits.

The stationary assumption implies that the previous conditional probabilities are independent of the value of "k." A road segment is described as a "handoff-probable segment" (HPS) if MTs have previously requested handoffs while traveling through it. For each HPS, the handoff probability is obtained as the ratio of MTs that made handoff requests and the segment. Also, for those MTs that made handoff-requests, their target handoff cell is recorded, and information about the time

Figure 3. Procedure performed for every $T_{predict}$ to reserve bandwidth

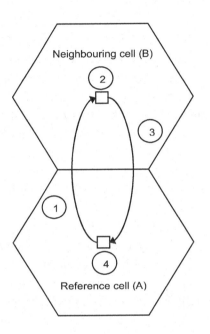

Table 1. Sequence of actions performed to reserve bandwidth

Step Number	Actions
1	Reference cell A sends $T_{th}(A)$ to neighbouring cell B
2	Neighbouring cell B performs predictions
3	Neighbouring cell B returns MT_ID, bandwidth requirement, prediction limit for MTs likely to handoff to reference cell A within $T_{th}(A)$
4	Reference cell A computes $R_{target}(A)$

Figure 4. Block diagram of the proposed integrated framework

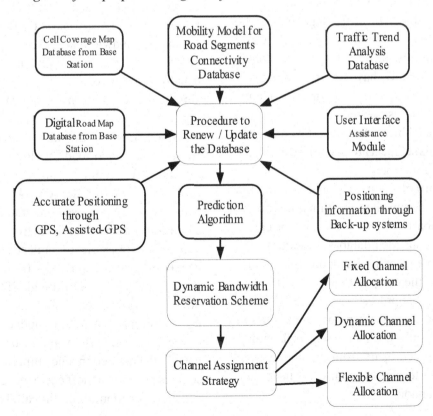

spent by them in the HPS before handoffs is collected, as well as their handoff positions. Using the model previously described, the conditional probabilities of handing off at each of the HPSs from segments that are several hops away is determined via the chain rule. It is also possible to predict the remaining time before handoff for each of these possible paths, using previously collected statistical information from each segment along the path.

In between database updates, the BS collects all the relevant data required for the subsequent update. The procedure begins by emptying both set of handoff-probable segments (S_{HPS}) and set of segments in which MTs may be considered for reservations (S_{RSV}) so that they can be regenerated based on the newly collected data. Each and every road segment within the BS's coverage area is sequentially examined one at a time. Then the first order transition probabilities are evaluated from the segment examined to its neighboring segments. After that, it evaluates the average speed of the MT in the particular segment so the time spent by MTs in the segment can be obtained. Then the probability that a MT would request a handoff while transiting the segment is computed. If handoffs have occurred along this segment previously, then the segment is identified as a HPS, and is entered into both S_{HPS} and S_{RSV}. Its membership in S_{RSV} signifies that MTs traveling in this segment are potential candidates for resource reservation.

One important point to emphasize for the previous database update algorithm is that all the previous database entries only need to be calculated once during each database update, which occurs very infrequently. Therefore, they should be well within the computational capability of a dedicated, average processor at the BS. Figure 2 shows the flowchart of the road topology-based prediction algorithm, which is self-explanatory. It should be noted apart from predicting MTs probable route to handoff it also estimates the time before handoff.

ROAD TOPOLOGY INFORMATION-BASED CHANNEL RESERVATION

In the proposed scheme, it is assumed that the system is having a perfect knowledge about future handoffs up to time T_{th} and an incoming handoff into the current cell will lead to a positive change in the bandwidth used, while an outgoing handoff will lead to a negative change. By summing up all the bandwidth changes over the time interval $(0, T_{th})$, it is realized that the maximum peak bandwidth to be reserved ($R_{target}(j)$) is fixed as one BU.

The predictions used to compute $R_{target}(j)$ are made periodically every $T_{predict}$. If the predictions are performed very frequently, they are more accurate but a more powerful processor will be required at each BS. On the other hand, their accuracy may deteriorate if they are far apart, causing the tradeoff between P_{FT} and P_{CB} to become less efficient. A two-cell structure is considered for bandwidth reservations as shown in Figure 3 and the sequences of actions performed to reserve bandwidth are listed in Table 1. In an actual cellular network, several neighboring cells usually surround each cell; Steps 1, 2, and 3 are simultaneously performed for every neighbouring cell.

Based on the bandwidth reservation obtained from the proposed road topology-based prediction algorithm, channels can be assigned through FCA, DCA, and FLCA. Figure 4 gives a detailed overview of the proposed integrated framework. The information is received from the mobility model for road segments connectivity, cell coverage, digital road map details from base station, positioning information through GPS systems and other backup systems, traffic trend analysis, and user information is used to update the database of the proposed system. Based on the database details, the prediction algorithm reserves the resources prior to handoff occurrence then flexible channel allocation admits the call. This combined

Figure 5. Simulated road map of Pondicherry Boulevard (India)

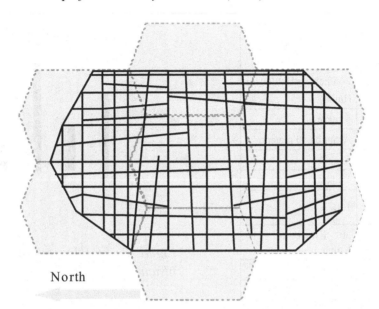

North

frame of real time data is from various sources, prediction analysis, and flexible channel allocation will provide a better trade-off between call dropping and call blocking probability, thereby improving the resource utilization and system performance.

SIMULATION RESULTS AND DISCUSSION

To facilitate the evaluation of the proposed scheme, a novel simulation model is designed and generated whenever an MT reaches the end of a road segment; it randomly selects the next junction from the array and moves along the selected segment until it reaches the selected junction. In the simulation, MTs new position is updated every second when it moves from one position to other, which is determined by computing the distance moved using the speed of the MT and slope of the road segment in which the MT is traveling. This step is repeated until the simulation is ended for each user.

Figure 5 shows a simulated road map model of Pondicherry Boulevard (India). Although the cell layout shown in the background adapts hexagonal cell model for determining BS locations, the simulation model does not assume handoffs occur at the hexagonal boundary. Instead, it identifies N points around each BS, which influences handoff and is viewed as handoff influence points (HIP). When the MT comes to one or more of these HIPs, handoff will occur during its transit through this region. Parameters used for simulations are listed in Table 2.

Figure 6 shows the predicted and actual handoffs at each time instant for a cell. Figure 7 shows the consolidated prediction result. It is inferred that predicted handoff is higher than the actual handoff in most of the cases. This clearly indicates the handoff-dropping probability will be the minimum possible if this prediction algorithm is incorporated.

Figure 8 depicts the blocking probability at each time instant and Figure 9 shows the average blocking probability for the proposed flexible channel assignment scheme with prediction. It is

Table 2. Parameters used for simulation

PARAMETER	DETAILS
Area simulated	PondicherryBoulevard (India)
Total area	5 sqkm
Radius of cell	Around 600 meters
Number of cells	5
Area of each cell	1 sqkm
Number of channels	100
Velocity	30 Kmph to 110 Kmph
Call holding time	25 s to 125
Call arrival	Poisson Distribution
Selection of Road segment at junction	Random
Position update	Every 1 s

Figure 7. Consolidated prediction result

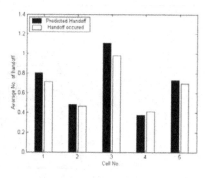

Figure 8. Blocking probability at each time instant

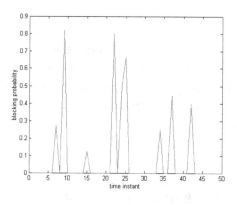

Figure 6. Prediction result at each time instant

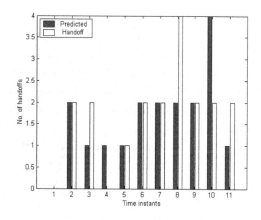

Figure 9. Average blocking probability

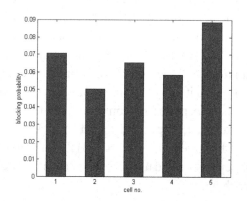

inferred that the blocking probability is always less than 0.1 and hence the proposed scheme is more efficient.

Figure 10 shows forced termination probability of the reference cell at each time instant and Figure 11 shows average forced termination probability for different cells. Here also it is in-

Figure 10. Forced termination probability at each time instant

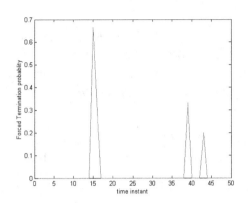

Figure 11. Average forced termination probability

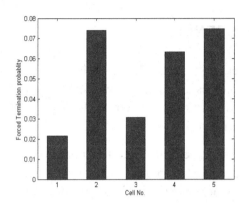

Figure 12. Probability of forced termination Vs call blocking

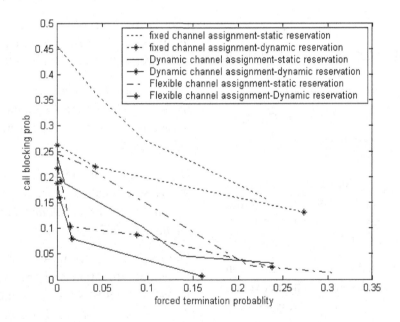

ferred that proposed scheme is better and offers optimum QoS.

CONCLUSION

In this article, a novel prediction technique is introduced, which uses GIS,GPS, and cellular integration based on road topology information prediction, which matches with the real environment. Flexible channel assignment implemented using the information obtained from this integrated prediction framework offers better tradeoff between forced terminations and call blocking probabilities. It gives accurate prediction results which helps to maintain a better QoS and resource management.

REFERENCES

Adusei, I. K., et. al. (2002). Mobile positioning technologies in cellular networks: An evaluation of their performance metrics. *MILCOM 2002,* California, USA.

Aljadhai, A., & Znati, T. (2001). Predictive mobility support for QoS provisioning in mobile wireless environments. *IEEE JSAC, 19*(10), 1915-30.

Chiu, M. H., & Bassiouni, M. A. (2000). Predictive schemes for handoff prioritization in cellular networks based on mobile positioning. *IEEE JSAC, 18*(3), 510-522.

Choi, S., & Shin, K. G. (1998). Predictive and adaptive bandwidth reservation for handoffs in QoS-sensitive cellular networks. In *Proceedings of ACM SIGCOMM '98* (pp. 155-166),

Drane, C. R., Macnaughtan, M., & Scott, C. (1998). Positioning GSM telephones. *IEEE Commun. Mag., 36*(4), 46-59.

Erbas, F., Kyamakya, K., Steuer, J., & Jobmann, K. (2002). On the user profiles and the prediction of user movements in wireless networks. In *Proceedings of PIMRC 2002.*

Hellebrandt, M., & Mathar, R. (1999). Location tracking of mobiles in cellular radio networks. *IEEE Trans. On Vehicular Technology, 48*(5).

Hellebrandt, M., Mathar, R., & Scheibenbogen, M. (1997). Estimating position and velocity of mobiles in a cellular radio network. *IEEE Trans. On Vehicular Technology, 46*(1).

Hofmann-Wallehnhof, B., Lichtenegger, H., & Collins, J. (1997). *Global positioning system: Theory and practice.* New York: Springer-Verlag.

Jayaputera, J., & Taniar, D. (2005). Data retrieval for location-dependent queries in a multi-cell wireless environment. *Mobile Information Systems, 1*(2), 91-108.

Kang, S., Song, M., Park, K., & Hwang, C. (2005). Semantic prefetching strategy to manage location dependent data in mobile information systems. *Mobile Information Systems, 1*(3), 149-166.

Kaplan, E. D. (1996). *Understanding GPS: Principles and applications.* Artech House Inc.

Kyamakya, K. et al. (2002). A navigation system using Cell-ID-based positioning and signal strength-based movement detection in cellular systems. *International Conference on Wireless Networks (ICWN 2002),* Las Vegas.

Lee, D. L., Zhu, M., & Hu, H. (2005). When location-based services meet databases. *Mobile Information Systems, 1*(2), 81-90.

Liu, T., Bahl, P., & Chlmtac, I. (1998). Mobility modeling, location tracking, and trajectory prediction in wireless ATM networks. *IEEE JSAC, 16*(6), 922-36.

Östergren, M., & Juhlin, O. (2005). Road talk: A roadside location-dependent audio message system for car drivers. *Journal of Mobile Multimedia, 1*(1), 047-061.

Pathirana, P. N., Svkin, A. V., & Jha, S. (2004). Location estimation and trajectory prediction for cellular networks with mobile base stations. *IEEE Transactions of Vehicular Technology, 53*(6), 1903-1913.

Safar, M. (2005). K nearest neighbor search in navigation systems. *Mobile Information Systems, 1*(3), 207-224.

Schwarz, K. P., & El-Sheimy, N. (1999). Future positioning and navigation (POS/NAV) technologies technical study. Study performed under Scientific Services Agreement with U.S. Topographic Engineering Center, Fort Belvoir, VA.

Soh, W. S., & Kim, H. S. (2003). QoS provisioning in cellular networks based on mobility prediction techniques. *IEEE Communication Magazine, 41*(1), 86-92.

Soh, W. S., & Kim, H. S. (2001). Dynamic guard bandwidth scheme for wireless broadband networks. In *Proceedings of the IEEE INFOCOM '01* (pp. 572-581), Anchorage, AK.

Song, M., Kang, S., & Park, K. (2005). On the design of energy-efficient location tracking mechanism in location-aware computing. *Mobile Information Systems, 1*(2), 109-127.

Syrjärinne, J. (2001). *Studies of modern techniques for personal positioning.* Doctor of Technology thesis work, Tampere University of Technology.

Waluyo, A. B., Srinivasan, B., & Taniar, D. (2005a). Efficient broadcast indexing scheme for location-dependent queries in multi channels wireless environment. *Journal of Interconnection Networks (JOIN), Special Issue on Advanced Information Networking: P2P Systems and Distributed Applications, 6*(3), 303-321.

Waluyo, A. B., Srinivasan, B., & Taniar, D. (2005b). Indexing schemes for multi channel data broadcasting in mobile databases. *International Journal of Wireless and Mobile Computing, 1*(6).

Waluyo, A. B., Srinivasan, B., & Taniar, D. (2004). Allocation of data items for multi channel data broadcast in mobile databases. *Embedded and Ubiquitous Computing, Lecture Notes in Computer Science* (Vol. 3207, pp. 409-418), Springer-Verlag.

Waluyo, A. B., Srinivasan, B., Taniar, D., & Rahayu, J. W. (2005). Incorporating global index with data placement scheme for multi channels mobile broadcast environment. *Embedded and Ubiquitous Computing, Lecture Notes in Computer Science* (Vol. 3824, pp. 755-764), Springer-Verlag.

Wang. J., et al. (2000). Integrating GPS and Pseudolite signals for position and attitude determination: Theoretical analysis and experiment results. *Proceedings of ION GPS 2000, 13th International Technical meeting, Satellite Division* (pp. 19-22), Institute of Navigation, Salt Lake City, UT.

Zhao, Y. (2002). Standardization of mobile phone positioning for 3G systems. *IEEE Commun. Mag.*, 108-16.

Zhao, Y. (1997). *Vehicle, location, and navigation systems: Intelligent transportation systems.* Boston; London: Artech House Publishers.

This work was previously published in Int. Journal of Information Technology and Web Engineering, Vol 1, Issue 4, edited by G. Alkhatib and D. Rine, pp. 37-48, copyright 2006 by IGI Publishing (an imprint of IGI Global).

Section II
Development

Chapter IX
High Performance Scheduling Mechanism for Mobile Computing Based on Self-Ranking Algorithm (SRA)

Hesham A. Ali
Mansoura University, Egypt

Tamer Ahmed Farrag
Mansoura University, Egypt

ABSTRACT

Due to the rapidly increasing of the mobile devices connected to the internet, a lot of researches are being conducted to maximize the benefit of such integration. The main objective of this paper is to enhance the performance of the scheduling mechanism of the mobile computing environment by distributing some of the responsibilities of the access point among the available attached mobile devices. To this aim we investigate a scheduling mechanism framework that comprises an algorithm provides the mobile device with the authority to evaluate itself as a resource. The proposed mechanism is based on the proposing of "self ranking algorithm (SRA)" which provides a lifetime opportunity to reach a proper solution. This mechanism depends on event-based programming approach to start its execution in a pervasive computing environment. Using such mechanism will simplify the scheduling process by grouping the mobile devices according to their self-ranking value and assign tasks to these groups. Moreover, it will maximize the benefit of the mobile devices incorporated with the already existing grid systems by using their computational power as a subordinate value to the overall power of the system. Furthermore, we evaluate the performance of the investigated algorithm extensively, to show how it overcomes the connection stability problem of the mobile devices. Experimental results emphasized that, the proposed SRA has a great impact in reducing the total error and link utilization compared with the traditional mechanism.

INTRODUCTION

Mobile computing and commerce are spreading rapidly, replacing or supplementing wired computing. Moreover, the wireless infrastructure upon which mobile computing is built may reshape the entire IT field. Therefore, it is fair to say that the mobile devices have a remarkable high profile in the most common communication devices nowadays. Individuals and organizations around the world are deeply interested in using wireless communication, because of its flexibility and its unexpected and fast development. The first solution to the need for mobile computing was to make computers small enough so that they could be easily carried. First, the laptop computer was invented; later, smaller and smaller computers, such as 3G, PDAs (personal digital assistants) and other handhelds, appeared. Portable computers, from laptops to PDAs and others are called mobile devices. In recent years a great development took place on the Internet and mobile technologies. Consequently, the next step will be merging these two technologies leading to the Wireless Internet.

The Wireless Internet will be much more than just internet access from mobile devices; the Wireless Internet will be almost invisible, as people will use mobile services and applications directly. On the other hand these services and applications will be acting as our agents, conducting searches and communicating with other services and applications to satisfy our needs. Not only will the integration of mobile technology and the Internet paradigm reinforce the development of the new context-aware applications, but also it will sustain traditional features such as user preferences, device characteristics, properties of connectivity and the state of service and usage history. Furthermore, the context includes features strictly related to user mobility such as user's current geospatial location (time and/or space). As direct use of existing Internet applications in a mobile environment is usually unsatisfactory; services and applications need to take into account the specific characteristics of mobile environments. The next section will introduce an overview of mobile devices as well as the present relation model between mobile devices and the grid.

Table 1. Worldwide wireless LAN equipment shipments (1000s of units) (Navrati Saxena 2005)

Product Segment	2001	2002	2003	2004	2005	2006
Adapters	6890	12599	21333	30764	41417	50415
Access Points	1437	1965	3157	3919	4851	5837
Broadband Gateways	552	850	1906	3365	5550	7941
Other WLAN Equipment	47	59	82	105	132	158
Total	8926	15473	26478	38153	51950	64351

Mobile Devices Development

The number of individuals and organizations relying on wireless devices is continually increasing. Table 1 represents a statistical study of the current and the future increase in the sales of wireless equipments and the considerable growth in the sales of mobile phones.

The mentioned table shows the rapid growth in the sales rates of wireless equipment, and they serve the purpose of being as a good metric of the flourishing future of the mobile computing. From 2001 to 2005, investments on mobile devices are expected to increase by 41% and reach $31 billion. In 2004, the laptops on the market reached 39.7 millions. On the other hand, not only did the number of mobile devices and wireless equipment increase, but also the computational power and the memory storage. As a result of such situation mobile computing and wireless Internet became a very important research area. This paper will approach it from the computational grid viewpoint.

Mobile Devices and the Computational Grid

The interaction between the mobile devices and the computational grid such as depicted in figure 1 can be classified into two models:

(I)   Mobile as a user of grid resources: The development in the computational power of the mobile devices such as (smart phones, PDAs...) will be limited due to its size, battery life, bandwidth and storage of data. However, when this integration occurs all of the huge computational power and stored data of the grid will be available to the mobile client. The mobile clients send their requests to the access point (AP) which can be considered as the grid gateway; the scheduler is responsible for finding a suitable resource

to perform the incoming request (Mustafa Sanver , 2004)

(II)   Mobile as a grid Resource: When one mobile device is considered a resource, it will be a very inferior and low ranking resource when compared with a PC. Meanwhile, because of the large number of the mobile devices that can be used, it can be a worth computational power. Also because of its large geographical distribution it can be considered as a very excellent data collector which can be used in many applications such as (geographical information systems, weather news...). Relatively, there are two approaches to integrate the mobile device into the existed grid; the first is that all the information of every mobile device is recorded in the scheduler, so every device is considered to be one grid resource. The second approach is the one in which the information of the mobile devices is hidden from the scheduler, it considers all the devices connected to an access point as one grid resource and the access point responsible for scheduling tasks on the mobile devices is also connected to it.

This paper introduces "self ranking algorithm" (SRA) that will be used to build a mobile comput-

Figure 1. an overview of integration of mobile devices with computational grid

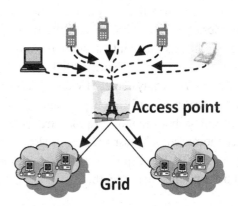

ing scheduling mechanism. Before introducing the proposed algorithm, an overview about the related work in the scheduling mechanism in the grid is given in section 2, detailed description of the targeted problem will be presented at hand in section 3, and a proposed framework is explained in section 4. Moreover, the proposed SRA will be introduced in section 5, the simulation used to state the proposed algorithm is available in section 6, finally, the results of that simulation will be analyzed in section 7.

RELATED WORK

Before starting to elaborate on the problem, five of the most recent systems especially on the scheduling algorisms are studied (Xiaoshan He 2003; Rajkumar Buyya 2003; Arun A. Somasundara 2004; F. Berman; H. Casanova 2005). Although they have very different parameters and concepts, all of them have two main objectives. The first objective is to increase the utilization of the system, while the second one is to find a suitable resource (as the economic cost, QoS, deadline…).

Table 2 shows a comparison between the most recent systems. Undoubtedly, one of the common problems that face any system when dealing with a large number of resources is "Load Balancing". Due to the fact that the ranking value of the resources is different, each of these systems endeavors to solve the problem which is illustrated in table 2. Another problem is how the system will deal with the mobility of clients and resources. The noticed remark is the limitation of researches that take into account the mobility of the resources (Daniel Nurmi 2004 ; Sang-Min Park 2003) .The study of these five systems shows that they are based on different parameters to rank the resource, but the most popular are QoS and the economic cost (Xiaoshan He 2003 ; Rajkumar Buyya 2003). The expressions used in Table 2 will be explained underneath:

Backfilling: it is a technique that tries to fill the gaps in the scheduling operation by executing the low priority functions in the low ranking resources that have not been used for a long time. This increases the system overall utilization and makes a kind of load balancing between the resources (Arun A. Somasundara , 2004).

Resource usage Accounts (Quotas): each resource must be assigned to certain functions according to its usage account. So, that preventing the resource from not being used can be caused by of the presence of high QoS resources. This approach gives the scheduler force more functions to be assigned to a certain resource by maximizing its Quota (Jang-uk In , 2004) .

Job Proxy: is created when the mobile user submits a job, it is responsible for the interaction between the mobile device and the system. It can also simulate the mobile action in case of mobile disconnecting. It does this until the mobile is connected again. If the mission is accomplished and the mobile is still disconnected, it stores the result for certain time-out duration (Sang-Min Park, 2003).

QoS Guided: the QoS Guided scheduler is the kind of scheduler that has a kind of intelligence as not to consume the high QoS resource in performing the jobs that need low QoS. It does this to save its power to the other tasks that need this high QoS (Xiaoshan He ,2003) .

SCHEDULING AND CONNECTION STABILITY PROBLEM

The new approach in the computing area is the Internet computing. It uses the already existing infrastructure of the Internet, and builds its own grid using devices interconnected to the Internet (Frontier, 2004). This is a very economical approach, because of the needless of building a special infrastructure. On the other hand, a lot of questions and issues raise, such as: "Do we

Table 2. Comparison between Referenced Systems

Project Features	Condor (Arun A. Somasundara, 2004)	Sphinx (Jang-uk In , 2004)	DDC (Rajkumar Buyya, 2003)	Disconnected operation service (Sang-Min Park, 2003)	QoS Guided Scheduling (Xiaoshan He 2003)
Mobility	---	---	---	Job Proxy	---
Load Balancing	Backfilling	Resource usage Accounts and Users Quotas	Improved by considering Time deadline addition to Cost	---	QoS Guided improve but not direct solution
Long Beginning Time	Backfilling	Resource usage Accounts (Quotas)	Improved by considering Time deadline and Cost	---	---
Resource Ranking Parameters	By The User	Percent of resource usage account used	Cost	disconnection rate and the reconnection rate	Availability of required QoS
Multi Scheduler	supported	---	---	supported	---
Resource Reservation	Future work	supported	Future work	---	---
QoS support	---	supported	Future work	---	supported
Scheduling Constrains	FIFO, user priorities	user priorities	Budget, deadline	---	QoS (one dimensional)

need to build a new infrastructure of a grid to integrate the mobile devices as a grid user or as a grid resource?" and also "What about the already existing grid projects?" (Peter Gradwell, 2003; Holly Dail, 2002; James Frey, 2001; F. Berman, 2005). Figure 2 shows how the already existing infrastructure can be ordered and organized to create an infrastructure that helps to integrate the mobile devices with the existing grid systems like (Condor, GriPhyN, Grid2003). This infrastructure aims at using the huge computational power due to the large number of internet users. It also aims at using the different services and resources available in the already existing grid projects. Above all, the main objective is to use the internet network to connect the mobile devices to the other parts of this infrastructure and to put all these services and computational power available to the mobile device. Finally, it aims at increasing the computational power and number of services of the system by integrating all that large number of mobile devices distributed around the world (Navrati Saxena , 2005).

The most important problem that can face any grid system is to develop a scheduling mechanism to manage such integration. The previous scheduling mechanisms depended on QoS (Xiaoshan He, 2003), cost (Rajkumar Buyya, 2002; Alexander Barmouta, 2003) or hybrid between some of other parameters (Jang-uk In, 2004; Atsuko Takefusa, 2001) to select the best scheduling decision. Due to this integration and the mobility of the device, a new parameter appeared. This parameter represents the stability of the connection established between the devices and the access point, in other words the rate of disconnecting and the rate of reconnecting. All the already existing systems make the scheduler monitor and evaluate the performance and the availability of its attached resources. This was acceptable with the PCs, but because of the huge number of mobile devices expected to attach to the scheduler, a very high overload on the scheduler can happen. So, the scheduler slows down more and more as the number of the attached resources increases.

Figure 2. the System Infrastructure organization

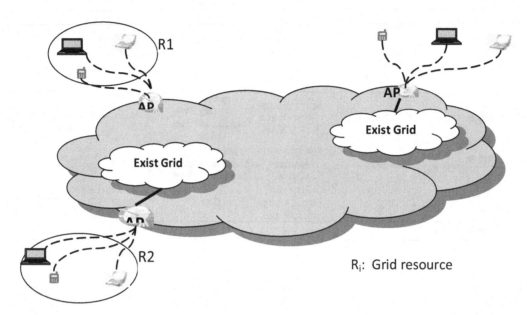

Plan of Solution

To overcome the overhead resulted from collecting the data at the access point scheduler and storing the historical ones of the mobile device performance, a SRA will be investigated. This algorithm has two key points, the first is to provide the mobile device with authority to evaluate and rank itself and remove this task from the central point (scheduler). The second one is considering the mobility of the resource as important metrics in such environment. Therefore, the main aim of this algorithm is to calculate a ranking value for each attached mobile device, which may be considered as a metric of the mobile performance. Moreover, it will be used to classify the mobile devices into groups to make the process of scheduling simpler and faster.

PROPOSED FRAMEWORK

Figure 3 depicts the framework and system components relationship for the given organization in figure 2. The following design guidelines are required to be adhered: (I) Use opportunistic schedulers which introduced in the Condor (Arun A. Somasundara , 2004), because it is a very excellent idea to make a good load balancing between high ranking resources and low ranking ones (e.g. Mobile devices). (II) Use the mobile proxy which is introduced in (Sang-Min Park, 2003) but we changed its name from job proxy to our proposed name "mobile proxy" which will be the interface between the mobile client and the other components of the system. (III) Use multi Schedulers because of the distribution of the considered infrastructure.

Proposed Framework Entities

In the following, the entities participating in the given framework are defined, their functions, and how they interact with each other as well.

The Task Farming Engine (TFE): it is responsible for partitioning the requested job into small tasks which will be assigned to resources to perform them using the scheduler and the dispatcher.

Figure 3. Mobile Dev. Scheduling Framework and components relationship

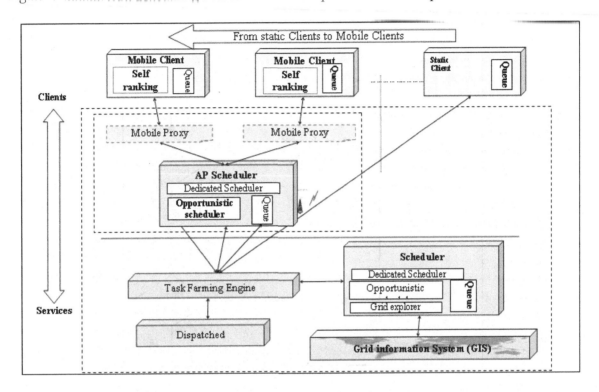

The Scheduler: it is responsible for resource discovery, resource trading, resource selection, and tasks assignment. The Dispatcher: it is responsible for the actual assigning of tasks to the resources decided by the scheduler, monitoring the execution of the tasks and controlling the process of collecting the different partitions of the job. Finally, it sends the overall result to the job requester. Grid information System (GIS): it can be considered as the resources characteristics database used by scheduler to find a suitable resource to perform the requested tasks using the resource QoS, Cost, rank. Dedicated Scheduler: each resource is assigned to one dedicated scheduler who has all the rights to use the resource at any time except if the resource owner needs his resource. This monopoly may leads to dis-functioning of some resources because they are in the resources list of certain Dedicated Scheduler beside other high ranked resources. So, these high ranked resources will be preferred to the scheduler. This problem may be resolved by the temporary claiming of the resource to other type of scheduler named "opportunistic scheduler". This problem causes holes in the scheduling operation. Opportunistic scheduler: when the dedicated scheduler claims some of its resources because they were idle for a long time or they had a low ranking value which made them useless for a long time. The Opportunistic scheduler tries to use this resource to execute some small tasks that may end before the dedicated scheduler needs the resource again. This operation is named "Backfilling", it is noted that this method will maximize the utilization of overall system.

Now, if a mobile client is connected to an access point, the first step is to create a mobile proxy object, which will be considered as a simulation of the mobile device. So, it may store the hardware specification of the mobile and its current loca-

Figure 4. Request processing flow

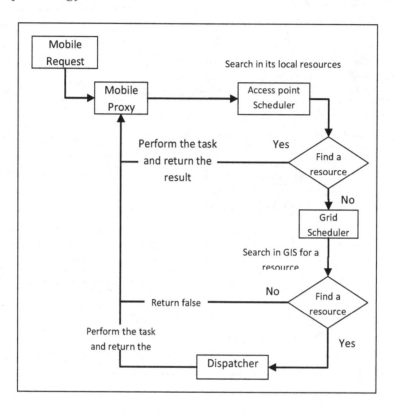

tion and it may also monitor the movement of the mobile from access point to another. This mobile proxy information will be the base knowledge on which the scheduler builds its work

Figure 4 depicts a request processing scenario. If the mobile client makes a request, this request will be stored in the mobile proxy. Then, it goes to a scheduler using the scheduling mechanism trying to find a suitable resource to perform this request from its local connected resources. But if the access point scheduler does not find a suitable resource it forwards this request to a higher level scheduler which usually has static PCs which have more computational power. This scheduler uses the GIS to find a suitable resource, when the resource is located the dispatched assigns the requested task to this resource. When the task is performed the outcome returns to the mobile proxy which is responsible for sending this result to the mobile clients in their current location.

PROPOSED "SELF RANKING ALGORITHM" SRA

The idea of the "Self ranking Algorithm" is to reduce the dependability on the access point scheduler and to distribute this overhead among the attached mobile devices. This can be done by making every mobile able to evaluate itself. Then, the access point can use this ranking value in the process of the scheduling.

The triggering to start this algorithm execution depended on the event based programming approach. The events that were taken into account are, (I) the event of disconnecting the mobile device and its scheduler because this event means the end of the last connected period, (II) the event of reconnecting the mobile device to its scheduler because this event means the end of the last disconnected period, (III) the event of finishing a task because this event changes the value of

Figure 5. Rank metric map

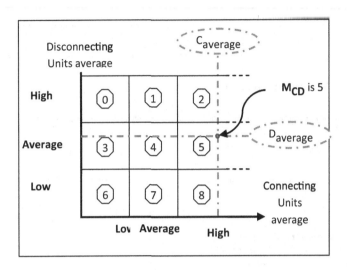

the mobile utilization. The self ranking value (R) has two parts: the first is the Connectivity metric (MCD) which can be considered as a metric of performance and connectivity of the mobile device as well. While, the second part which is the utilization metric (U) can be considered as a metric of the success of the mobile device in performing the assigned task. When the mobile client has a new ranking value, this value must be sent to the mobile proxy to be entered as a parameter in the scheduling process.

The considered parameters which are be used in the SRA are: The average number of time units being connected continually (Caverage), the average number of time units being disconnected continually (Daverage), and the previous utilization history metric (U). The calculated values of Caverage and Daverage will be used as a key to the proposed ranking map which is used to calculate the first part of the rank value that measures the mobile performance and connectivity. The overall ranking value is assumed to be between 1 and 10. This part represents 80% of this value; this percentage can be changed according to the schedulers' administrators. Figure 5 shows the rank metric map which is based on two roles, first as the Caverage value increases,

the rank must increase also. Second Daverage value increases the rank must decrease. The Caverage and Daverage is used to calculate values. It works as a coordinator of the Connectivity metric (MCD) on the rank metric map. The second part of the ranking value is the metric of the utilization of the mobile devices. So, it is calculated by the ratio between the number of the successful tasks and the number of all tasks. Summation of the two parts will generate the overall ranking value of the mobile device. Figure 6 shows the proposed algorithm.

SIMULATION MODEL

Validation of the proposed algorithm is done via simulation. The investigated simulation program is composed of three modules. The first one is responsible for generating a random movement path for the mobile devices, while the second is responsible for tracking the generated path, and this will be done through the access point. Finally, the third is responsible for tuning of critical parameters values and collecting outputs parameters, which are required to calculate Caverage and Daverage.

Figure 6. Self Ranking Algorithm for determine the mobile device ranking value

> **0**   Imports the prestored values :
>
> t_s : the start of the last reconnection event. t_e: the end of the connection period .
>
> T_u :Time unit defined by the scheduler N_c : number of reconnecting event occurring.
>
> N_D: number of disconnecting event occurring.
>
> $C_{average}$: The average number of time units to being connecting continually
>
> $D_{average}$: the average number of time units being disconnecting continually
>
> N_s : the number of successfully performed tasks   N : total number of tasks assigned to the device.
>
> **1**   Wait for incoming event and check it.
> **2**   *if the event is Disconnecting Event at time (t) then :*
>   2.1 Replace the prestored value t_e with the new value t : $t_e = t$
>   2.2 Calculate the Connection Period P_c by using the stored value of t_s and t_e: $P_c = t_e - t_s$
>   2.3 Calculate number of time units X_c of the connection period P_c by using T_u provided by the Scheduler :
>   2.4 Calculate the new value of $C_{average}$ by using the prestored value of $C_{average}$ and the prestored N_c:
>
> $$C_{average(new)} = C_{average\ (old)} * N_c + X_c/N_c + 1$$
>
>   2.5 $N_c = N_c + 1$.
>   2.6 Calculate the connectivity metric M_{CD} by using the new calculated $C_{average}$ and the prestored $D_{average}$ as coordinates of a point in the "rank metric map".
> **3**   *if the event is reconnecting Event at time (t) then :*
>
>   3.1 Replace the prestored value t_s with the new value t :$t_s = t$
>   3.2 Calculate the disconnection Period P_D by using the stored value of t_s and t_e: $P_D = t_s - t_e$
>   3.3 Calculate number of time units X_D of the disconnection period P_D by using T_u provided by the Scheduler :
>
> $$X_D = P_D / T_u$$
>
>   3.4 Calculate the new value of $D_{average}$ by using the prestored value of $D_{average}$ and the prestored N_D:
>
> $$D_{average(new)} = D_{average\ (old)} * N_D + X_D/N_D + 1$$
>
>   3.5 $N_D = N_D + 1$.
>   3.6 Calculate the connectivity metric M_{CD} by using the new calculated $D_{\ldots\ldots}$ and the prestored

Mobile Device Movement Mechanism

The mobile device movement path that will be generated is based on a mechanism that guarantees a random path as follows:

1. Generate random black and white areas as shown in Figure 7-a, white areas imply that there is an available connection between the mobile device and the scheduler access point, on the other hand black areas depict

Figure 7. steps of Random movement path generation

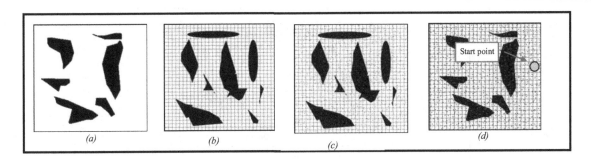

Figure 8. choose a random direction from eight

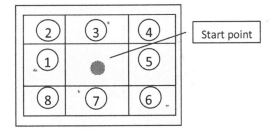

disconnection.

2. Divide the whole area into small rectangular areas as shown in Figure 7-b.
3. Generate a point within each rectangle at random position as shown in Figure 7-c.
4. Save the position of the generated points in an array.
5. Select one point from the previous array in random fashion to be the starting point

of the movement path as shown in Figure 7-d.

6. Select one of the possible eight directions shown in Figure 8 for the next hop.
7. Continue the movement towards the previous selected direction for a random number of hops.
8. Repeat step 6 and 7 until having the required length of the movement path.
9. Store all the selected points in step 6, 7 and 8 to represent a path for a mobile device movement.
10. Repeat steps from 2-9 to generate another mobile movement path.

Figure 9 illustrates some examples of the generated random mobile movement paths based on the previous mechanism.

Figure 9. Examples of the random mobile movement paths

Figure 10. AP monitoring of the mobile device movement process

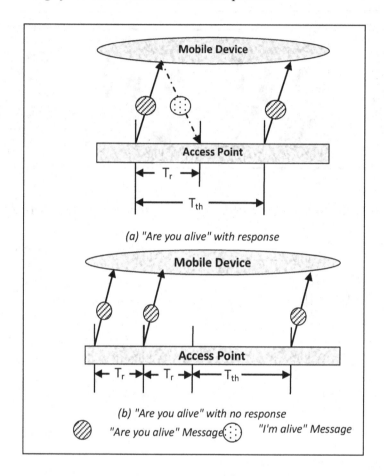

AP and Monitoring the Mobile Device

This module, as stated before, simulates the AP monitoring of the mobile device movement process. In such process AP sends "Are you alive?" message. If there is an available connection, the mobile device responses by an "I'm alive" message. The time between sending and receiving is called the response time Tr, this time can be determined experimentally, the AP waits for another threshold time Tth before sending the next monitoring message . On the other hand, if there is no response for Tr, the access point will send a message again. According to the response of the previous simulation the AP reports the mobile device status. Figure 10 shows this process.

At this point we have to notice that reducing Tth will lead to more accurate results, but on the other hand, the number of messages will increase which means high link usage which is considered from the application point of view to be a bad usage.

Parameters Setting, Collecting and Calculating

The different parameters, which are required for comparing the self ranking against the traditional AP ranking from network utilization and accuracy point of view, are calculated in this module.

Firstly, the speed of the mobile device movement and Tth and Tr is tuned. Some parameters

Figure 11 Total error and link utilization at no of mobiles = 50

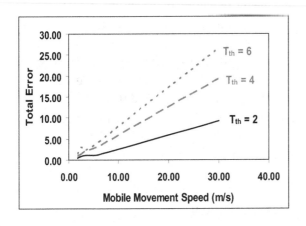
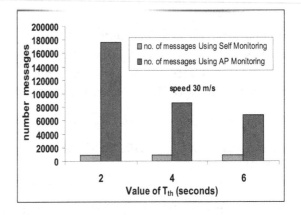

Figure 12. Total error and link utilization at no of mobiles = 75

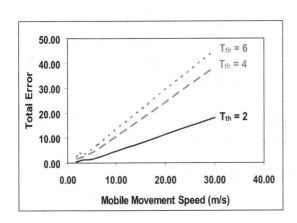
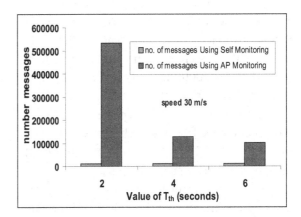

Figure 13. Total error and link utilization at no of mobiles = 100

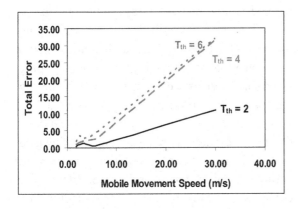
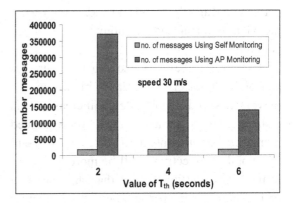

from the first and second modules are collected and stored including: the length of the generated path, the number of connection and the disconnection during the movement on the path, the total number of "Are you alive?" messages, and the number of messages with and without response. So, Caverage and Daverage can be calculated.

PERFORMANCE ANALYSIS AND DISCUSSION

Based on the previous discussion, on the change of the number of mobile devices used during the experiment (50, 75 and 100 mobiles) or on the change of the value of Tth (2, 4 and 6 seconds) various experiments are performed. There are another two factors were constant; the first is the length of the movement path witch selected to be long relatively (10000 hop). The second is Tr which is selected to be small relatively (0.5 second). Each of these experiments will be repeated for different movement speed from low mobility (with average movement speed 2 m/s) to high mobility (with average movement speed 30 m/s).

The average error in calculating the Caverage and Daverage has been calculated for each experiment at each used speed and their summation represents the total error in the experiment. Also, the number of network messages exchanged between AP and the mobile device, in both cases the AP monitoring and self monitoring, has been counted.

Figures 11, 12 and 13, show that the percentage of the total error increases rapidly as the movement speed of mobile device increases. This result is expected because as the movement speed increases the ability of AP to sense the change in the mobile connectivity will be more and more limited. Also, the figures show that when the value of Tth increases the percentage of the total error increases also while the number of the exchanged network messages decreases. This result is expected because Tth represents the time between two monitoring messages, as this time increases that means reduction in the ability of AP to sense the change in the mobile connectivity. The figures show the comparison between the number of exchanged messages between AP and mobile devices in the case of self monitoring and case of AP monitoring. It is noted that, in case of AP monitoring the number approximately doubled more than 70 times compared to the case of self monitoring.

CONCLUSION

This paper points out an overview of the issues of mobile devices integration with the existing grid. It shows that when some of authorization is impeded within the mobile client, every mobile can evaluate its performance by itself. The traditional method makes an overhead on the scheduler to perform a historical evaluation to the mobile performance which makes it busy in a secondary task and leaves its main task of scheduling. So, the "self ranking algorithm" will be the base of a scheduling mechanism which will schedule the tasks on the mobile devices. The originality of the proposed mechanism concentrates on mobile cooperating with services at the access point (AP). Using such mechanism will lead to minimizing the calculation time consumed in mobile ranking and evaluating before starting the scheduling process. Moreover, it will lead also to minimizing the amount of the stored data at the scheduler and to simplifying the scheduling process by grouping the mobile devices according to their self ranking value and assign tasks to these groups. Finally, it will result in maximizing the profit of the mobile devices integrated with the already existing grid systems by using their computational power as an addition to the system overall power. In brief the outcome will be maximizing the system utilization and making the system more flexible to integrate any new devices without any affright to increase the system complexity.

In this paper we present the newly emerging technical issues for realizing this mobile grid system, and particularly focus on the job scheduling algorithm to achieve more reliable performance. However, there are still challenging problems such as limited energy, device heterogeneity, security, and so on. We will tackle on these issues in future works and develop a prototype of mobile grid system.

REFERENCES

Alexander Barmouta & Rajkumar Buyya (2003), "GridBank: A Grid Accounting Services Architecture (GASA) for Distributed Systems Sharing and Integration ", Parallel and Distributed Processing Symposium, Nice, France, IEEE Computer Society.

Anthony Sulistio & Chee Shin Yeo & and Rajkumar Buyya (2003), Visual Modeler for Grid Modeling and Simulation (GridSim) Toolkit, International Conference on Computational Science (ICCS) 2003: Saint Petersburg, Russia / Melbourne, Australi .

Arun A. Somasundara & Aditya Ramamoorthy & Mani B. Srivastava (2004), Mobile Element Scheduling for Efficient Data Collection in Wireless Sensor Networks with Dynamic Deadlines , 25th IEEE International Real-Time Systems Symposium (RTSS'04) .

Atsuko Takefusa (2001) , A Study of Deadline Scheduling for Client-Server Systems on the Computational Grid, 10th IEEE Symposium on High Performance and Distributed Computing (HPDC'01), San Francisco, California.

Daniel Nurmi & Rich Wolski & John Brevik (2004), ModelBased Checkpoint Scheduling for Volatile Resource Environments, University of California Santa Barbara, Department of Computer Science, Technical Report, Santa Barbara.

Dantong Yu (2003), Divisible Load Scheduling for Grid Computing, Conference on Parallel and Distributed Computing and Systems (PDCS 2003).

F. Berman & H. Casanova (2005), "New Grid Scheduling and Rescheduling Methods in the GrADS Project", International Journal of Parallel Programming.

Frontier (2004), The Premier Internet Computing Platform, Whitepaper, http://www.parabon.com/clients/clientWhitePapers.jsp.

Holly Dail & Henri Casanova & Fran Berman (2002), A Decoupled Scheduling Approach for the GrADS Program Development Environment, IEEE/ACM SC2002 Conference.

James Frey (2001), Condor-G: A Computation Management Agent for Multi-Institutional Grids, IEEE.

Jang-uk In & Paul Avery (2004), "Policy Based Scheduling for Simple Quality of Service in Grid Computing", 18th International Parallel and Distributed Processing Symposium (IPDPS 2004),Santa Fe, New Mexico, USA. IEEE Computer Society.

Mustafa Sanver & Sathya Priya Durairaju & Ajay Gupta (2004), "Should one incorporate Mobileware in Parallel and Distributed Computation?", 10th International Conference on High Performance Computing (HiPC 2003) , Hyderabad, India.

Navrati Saxena & Kalyan Basu & Sajal K. Das & Christina M. Pinotti (2005), "A Dynamic Hybrid Scheduling Algorithm with Clients' Departure for Impatient Clients in Heterogeneous Environments" , 19th IEEE International Parallel and Distributed Processing Symposium (IPDPS'05), April - Rhodes Island, Greece.

Navrati Saxena (2005) , New Hybrid Scheduling Framework for Asymmetric Wireless Environments with Request Repetition , Third International Symposium on Modeling and Optimization in Mobile, Ad Hoc, and Wireless Networks.

Peter Gradwell (2003), Overview of Grid Scheduling Systems, Located at http://www.peter.me.uk/phd/writings/computing-economy-review.pdf

Rajkumar Buyya & Manzur Murshed (2002), GridSim: a toolkit for the modeling and simulation of distributed resource management and scheduling for Grid computing, The Computing Research Repository (CoRR).

Rajkumar Buyya & David Abramson & Jonathan Giddy (2002), Economic Models for Resource Management and Scheduling in Grid Computing, The Journal of Concurrency and Computation: Practice and Experience (CCPE).

Rajkumar Buyya & Manzur Murshed & and David Abramson (2003), A Deadline and Budget Constrained Cost-Time Optimization Algorithm for Scheduling Task Farming Applications on Global Grids, The Computing Research Repository (CoRR).

Sang-Min Park & Young-Bae Ko & Jai-Hoon Kim (2003) , Disconnected Operation Service in Mobile Grid Computing, International Conference on Service Oriented Computing ICSOC 2003: Trento, Italy.

Xiaoshan He (2003), A QoS Guided Scheduling Algorithm for Grid Computing, Journal of Computer Science and Technology, Special Issue on Grid Computing, 18(4).

This work was previously published in Int. Journal of Information Technology and Web Engineering, Vol 1, Issue 2, edited by G. Alkhatib and D. Rine, pp. 43-59, copyright 2006 by IGI Publishing (an imprint of IGI Global).

Chapter X
Hierarchical Scheduling in Heterogeneous Grid Systems

Khaldoon Al-Zoubi
Carleton University, Canada

ABSTRACT

This paper proposes hierarchal scheduling schemes for Grid systems: a self-discovery scheme for the resource discovery stage and an adaptive child scheduling method for the resource selection stage. In addition, we propose three rescheduling algorithms: (1) the Butterfly algorithm in order to reschedule jobs when better resources become available, (2) the Fallback algorithm in order to reschedule jobs that had their resources taken away from the Grid before the actual resource allocation, and (3) the Load-Balance algorithm in order to balance load among resources. We also propose a hybrid system to combine the proposed hierarchal schemes with the well-known peer-to-peer (P2P) principle. We compare the performance of the proposed schemes against the P2P-based Grid systems through simulation with respect to a set of predefined metrics.

INTRODUCTION

The current status of computation is equivalent in some respects to the status of electricity circa 1910s (Foster & Kesselman, 2004). At that time, electrical power was generated by generators for specific individuals or organizational needs.

Truly, the real influence of electricity in our lives was born with the creation of the electric power grid, which was provided via sharing generators. The "grid computing" term was adopted from the electricity grid to *amplify computational power* via *sharing* computational resources, since both grids are similar with respect to their infrastructure and purpose. The term "the grid" started in the mid-1990s (Foster, 2001; Foster & Kesselman, 2004) to portray the infrastructure of both scientific and commercial computing communities and has been gaining popularity ever since. The "grid" can be defined as a parallel and distributed system that enables a large collection of geographically distributed heterogeneous systems that usually span several organizations to share a variety of resources dynamically, depending on their availability, capability, user's requirements, and any other predefined rules set by local systems and resources owners. The type of sharing in the grid gives the impression of a powerful self-managing virtual computer. The Internet is an ideal choice to link thousands or millions of computers, since it already connects the whole world—if a node's IP address is known, it can then receive data from another node. Benefits of grids can be extensive. They include: (1) expanding computing power, since grids unleash the hidden computing power that is not being used most of the time (e.g., most machines in a typical organization are busy less than 5% of the time (Berstis, 2002)), (2) improving productivity and collaboration among organizations (i.e., wider audience) in a dynamic and geographically distributed manner to form one powerful computing system, and (3) solving complex problems that were previously unsolvable.

The rest of the article is organized as follows. In the next section, grid scheduling stages and some of the grid challenges are described. Then, the self-discovery method is presented. It is used in the resource discovery stage and the adaptive hierarchical scheduling (AHS) method, which is used in scheduling jobs on selected resources. Note that the AHS method is based on the AHS method for parallel and cluster systems presented in Dandamudi (2003). In addition, we present three rescheduling dynamic algorithms: the butterfly, the fallback, and the load-balance. Next the simulation model and samples of the results are given. Refer to Al-Zoubi (2006) for more a more

in-depth discussion of the presented schemes and the complete set of results. The results are followed by conclusions.

GRID SCHEDULING STAGES

Grid characteristics must be taken into account in order to perform efficient scheduling. Grid schedulers must make scheduling decisions in a very challenging environment that includes: (1) no control over the resources, since they don't own them; (2) distributed resources; (3) a dynamic existence of resources (i.e., resources may be added or removed from the grid at any time); (4) a dynamic information collection; (5) heterogeneous resources (jobs must match appropriate resources in order to be executed as requested by the users); and (6) tentative scheduling until the allocation of actual resources (i.e., resources may be taken from the grid before a job actually uses them).

In general, grid scheduling is performed in three stages (Nabrzyski, Schopf, & Weglarz, 2004). First is the resource discovery stage, which produces a set of matched resources. Schedulers are expected to collect static information (e.g., operating systems) from local schedulers or general information systems (GIS), in order to perform job matching. In the next stage, resources are selected (i.e., resource selection stage) from the list obtained during the first stage and are expected to meet user's imposed constraints (e.g., deadlines). Then schedulers are expected to collect dynamic information (e.g., system load) for the third stage and transfer jobs to selected resources (i.e., job execution stage).

HIERARCHAL SCHEDULING IN GRID SYSTEMS

Grid schedulers, in our proposed schemes, are structured in a tree form that we call a grid tree, as shown in Figure 1, where grid schedulers (GS) are placed into the tree according to their geographical locations. Users submit their jobs, in the form of requests to the grid via the grid system scheduler (GSS), which is the root node of the grid tree. A user's request describes the job in terms of the job minimum requirements (JMR) (e.g., operating system) in order to be matched to resources and includes any other constraints imposed by the user (e.g., completion deadline). A leaf grid scheduler (LGS), which is a node on top of local scheduler(s), connects directly with the user's workstation, brings the physical job to the grid (once a job is about to be mapped to the selected resources), and serves as middleware between the user's workstation and the allocated resources. Note that LGSs may be combined with local schedulers in one unit.

Theoretically, a scheduler, in our proposed systems, can break grid jobs into several subjobs to be executed in parallel and on different children's partitions. However, the art of automatic transformation into parallelism of an arbitrary job is in its infancy stage (Berstis, 2002). In our case, we assume whole jobs are submitted to resources.

Resource Discovery Stage

In this stage, we propose the *self-discovery* method. The purpose of this method is to produce a set of logical channels to be used as paths by jobs (in the next scheduling stage) to get to their physical resources. Logical channels serve as a map for jobs so that they know how to reach resources that can meet their computational requirements. The self-discovery method omits irrelevant dissimilarities between resources of different sites. The principle behind this method is that resources are equivalent to each other, if they match the same set of jobs. For example, one site advertises INTEL architectures and another site advertises AMD architectures. Now, suppose the grid has a set of jobs that can be executed on either INTEL or AMD platform. In this case, the grid system

considers architecture INTEL as equivalent to architecture AMD for those jobs in the set, since they can be executed on either platform. However, suppose now another set of jobs only requires architecture AMD in order to execute. In this case, the grid system considers architecture INTEL as nonequivalent to architecture AMD for the later set of jobs, since those jobs can only be executed on the AMD platform.

LGSs collect and store all static information about resources, either directly from local schedulers or from a GIS. Thus, information about local resources is distributed across the grid, which leads to (1) increasing system scalability and (2) maintenance of up-to-date databases. LGSs also initiate the resource discovery stage at system start up or when no jobs in the grid tree match their advertised resources, by issuing the request for job matching (RFJM) message to their parents, which in turn forwards the RFJM messages to the grandparents, and so on, until the RFJM message is received by the GSS, enabling it to initiate resource discovery to all of its raw jobs (i.e., new jobs that have not previously been through resource discovery stage). However, if the GSS has no raw jobs, it will then backlog the RFJM message until receiving new jobs.

The GSS starts the resource discovery stage by: (1) broadcasting a special message to all of its children to destroy all channels in the system and (2) passing all raw jobs to all of its children as one block. The children, in turn, pass the raw jobs as one block to the grandchildren, and so on, until they reach the LGSs at the bottom of the grid tree. LGSs match raw job requirements to their local resources and insert all raw jobs that match resources in their bags. They will then pass a copy of their bags (along with any previous matched jobs) to their parents. Note that (1) LGSs save all requests that they receive from their parents, whether they have matched or not, enabling LGSs to perform rematching, if needed, due to resources change (i.e., the GSS removes all stored requests from all bags once they are executed);

Figure 1. A grid tree with two channels

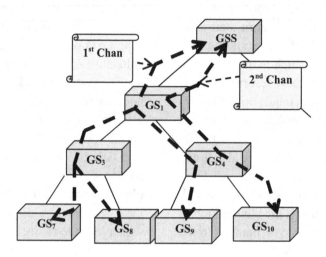

(2) intermediate schedulers (GS) always pass one RFJM message to their parents on behalf of their children and suppress other RFJMs, preventing the GSS from initiating any unnecessary resource discovery; and (3) a logical channel is created for every unique job bag.

Once a scheduler receives a bag (from one of its children) that is similar to another bag of an existing channel, it will then: (1) create a new branch from its existing channel and bind it with the child's channel; (2) recalculate its channel's processing power based on the new created branch; (3) inform the child of its channel's port number; and (4) update the parent, if needed, with the new processing power of its channel. However, if the received bag is distinctive, the scheduler will then: (1) create a new channel with a new port number; (2) create a new branch from its new channel and bind it with the child's channel; (3) initialize the channel processing power, based on the newly created branch; (3) inform the child with the channel's port number; and (4) update the parent, if needed, with the new bag and the channel's port number.

Now consider, as an example, the grid tree shown in Figure 1. Suppose the GSS pass six raw jobs, J_1 through J_6, as one block to all of its children. Suppose further that J_4, J_5, and J_6 do

not match resources at GS_{10}. In this case, the GSS ends up with two channels (via GS_1), where all jobs may use the first channel. On the other hand, J_1, J_2, and J_3 are the jobs that can only use the second channel.

Resource Selection Stage

The grid AHS scheduling method, in this stage, uses *self-scheduling* by exploring the parent-child relationship. When a nonroot GS wants some work to do, it initiates self-scheduling by sending a request for computation (RFC) message to its parent (via a channel), requesting computation from it. If the parent GS does not have computations that can be pushed to that child's channel at the time of receiving the RFC, it, in turn, generates its own RFC and sends it to its parent on the next level of the grid tree. This process is recursively followed until either the RFC reaches the GSS or a GS with computations is encountered along the path. Note that intermediate schedulers send one RFC message per channel to their parents but still mark all branches from which they have received RFCs. Upon receiving an RFC message from a channel's branch of a child, a scheduler uses a space-sharing policy to distribute computations among channels as follows:

$$B_{share} = \lceil B_{rate} \times N \rceil, \qquad (1)$$

where B_{share} is the branch's share of all jobs within the scheduler's subtree; B_{rate} is the branch's transfer rate; and N is the number of jobs within a scheduler's subtree. B_{rate} is calculated as follows:

$$B_{rate} = \frac{B_{pwr}}{\sum_{i=1}^{M} (C_{pwr})_i}, \qquad (2)$$

where B_{pwr} is the branch's processing power; C_{pwr} is the channel's processing power (i.e., total processing power for all of its branches); and M is the number of channels in a scheduler. Note that, in our case, the channel's processing power is the number of central processing units (CPUs) that reside under that channel; since we assume that our computational resources are parallel computers (see the Simulation Model and Results section). However, in reality, we expect processing power to consider more factors, such as RAMs, bandwidth, and so forth.

Now, once a scheduler determines the number of jobs that will be pushed onto a channel's branch, it builds a list of those jobs as one block and pushes them onto that branch. Suppose, as an example, that GS_1, in Figure 1, has nine jobs, upon receiving an RFC message from the first branch of the first channel (i.e., via GS_3). Suppose further that the three branches that connect GS_1 with its two children have equivalent processing power. In this case, GS_1 may then push up to three jobs onto that branch.

Schedulers perform the following steps to collect the jobs (in order to be pushed onto a channel's branch): (1) they invoke the butterfly algorithm; (2) they collect jobs from the unassigned (i.e., unpushed) jobs; and (3) they invoke the load-balance algorithm. Note that we expect schedulers, in practice, to collect more dynamic information related to performance (e.g., load) or economics (e.g., prices).

Butterfly Algorithm

The principle behind this scheme is to reschedule jobs to better resources (with respect to predefined metrics), when they become available. Note that this algorithm can be extended to any soft conditions imposed by a user, where soft conditions are the ones that the user is willing to live without until they become available (or if they ever become available). In our case, we consider the geographic closeness of resources with respect to work stations as our metric (we use IP addresses to determine location nearness). Interestingly, a job may keep jumping (like a butterfly) among children's partitions, until it settles on the closest resources. In this algorithm, after a scheduler receives an RFC message from a child, the scheduler will then (1) cancel any assigned jobs from other children (if the new child is closer to those jobs' work stations) and (2) push them into the new available child's partition.

Fallback Algorithm

The fallback algorithm is intended to reschedule jobs that become incomputable because of the grid losing its required resources on its scheduled partitions. When an LGS detects resource change, it performs rematching for all saved requests. Now, if an LGS ends up with the same job bag, this resource change is then irrelevant. However, if it produces a different bag, it will then pass it on to its parent.

Schedulers handle received bags in this stage as previously described in the resource discovery stage. Additionally, schedulers mainly have to carry out the following (of course, parents will also be updated): (1) remove any jobs that become incomputable; (2) recalculate modified channels processing power; and (3) delete any broken channels. For example in Figure 1, assume GS_{10} changes resources and produces a bag similar to GS_9's bag. In this case, GS_4 will then connect GS_{10} to the first channel and inform its parent (GS_1) of two things: (1) the first channel with new updated processing power and (2) the broken second channel. Now if GS_4 has jobs that become incomputable, it will then remove them and update GS_1. Note that GS_1 reschedules those returned jobs (if they still computable on its partition) with a priority (in our case, the lesser the sequence number, the higher the priority). For instance, GS_1 may swap some of those returned jobs with assigned jobs in GS_3's partition, in order to execute jobs in the same order of their arrival to the grid.

Load-Balance Algorithm

As stated earlier, schedulers determine the number of jobs (that will be pushed into a channel's branch) by considering all jobs within their subtrees. They will then collect those jobs by invoking the butterfly algorithm and from queued unassigned jobs. Schedulers will then balance the load among the channels by canceling already assigned jobs and then reschedule them on the channel's branch that just requested more work. Schedulers are always responsible for balancing all assigned jobs among their children's channels within their subtrees, since a parent may cause a child's subtree to get imbalanced (i.e., of course, parents do not know how assigned jobs are distributed within their children's subtrees). For example, assume that each of GS_7 and GS_8 in Figure 1 has four queued jobs (of course, GS_1 assumes that all eight jobs are still queued at GS_3). Suppose now that GS_1 decides to cancel four jobs to reschedule them on a GS_4's channel, in order to balance its subtree. Now, if GS_1 cancels the four jobs queued at GS_8, it imbalances the GS_3's subtree. In this case, GS_3 will balance its subtree upon receiving an RFC message from GS_8 (or will forward the RFC message to GS_1, if the RFC message is received from GS_7).

Hybrid System

The hierarchal system (one grid tree) has major drawbacks: (1) All requests are submitted to the GSS, which may become overwhelmed with too many requests; (2) it is difficult to bring in many organizations and have them agree on things, such as constructing the grid tree, controlling GSS policies (e.g., security) and dealing with new joined organizations; and (3) it is difficult to convince companies to replace their peer-to-peer (P2P) based grid systems.

The hybrid system, which is several grid trees that act also as peers to each other, as shown in Figure 2, does not only overcome the above drawbacks but does provide organizations with more efficient ways to manage their own resources, such as stamping foreign requests with low priority, isolating their resources swiftly from the entire grid without pumping out their pending requests of using their resources, and so forth.

In the hybrid system, a GSS in a grid tree also acts as a peer GSS (PGSS) that forwards requests (after decrementing hop count) to its neighbors. Of course neighbors can be part of any other system types (e.g., P2P system). The P2P system can be viewed as a hybrid system, where each grid tree has only one scheduler; and the hierarchal system can be viewed as a hybrid system with one peer. In our case, we assume that (1) requests are always forwarded to neighbors (i.e., a request dies when

Figure 2. Hybrid system example

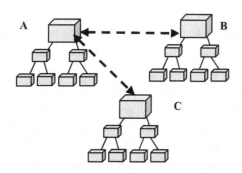

hop count reaches 0), hence, grid trees also serve as backups to each other; and (2) foreign and home requests are queued in the same fashion.

SIMULATION MODEL AND RESULTS

This section presents the simulation model and samples of the preliminary results. Readers are encouraged to refer to Al-Zoubi (2006) for the complete set of results and a more in-depth discussion.

The grid simulation model is broken into three submodels—communication, node, and system models—each of which is described below.

Communication Model

The communication model, which is used by nodes (i.e., node model) to communicate with each other, consists of 2,400 nodes that span across four backbones. Each backbone (600 nodes) consists of four nets, where each net consists of 10 networks and each network consists of 15 nodes. Therefore, there are four backbones, four nets, 10 networks, and 15 nodes, which add up to 2,400 nodes in total in the model. The communication model uses the discrete event simulation (DEVS) CD++ simulator (Al-Zoubi, 2006; Wainer, 2002) to simulate all of the communication aspects among all nodes.

The model presented numerous of challenges that we had to address to bring it closer as much as possible to the actual communication over the Internet, which is almost an impossible job to do, since the Internet is a very large unpredictable public network. We've assumed that 10% of the model's capacity accounts for the external Internet load and the routers processing time based on the studies in (Al-Zoubi, 2006; Odlyzko, 2003), which were based on actual statistics by the Internet Service Providers (ISP). We've also assumed 64 kilobytes TCP window size to control data flow

(Al-Zoubi, 2006). Backbones in the model are connected with 1000 km, 9.0 Gb/s (e.g. OC-192 link) cables, Nets/sites are connected with 50 km, 155 Mb/s (e.g. OC3 link) cables (Al-Zoubi, 2006; Odlyzko, 2003), and nodes within a site are connected with 100 MBytes/s (Al-Zoubi, 2006) cables.

Node Model

A node, in the communication model, is simply a computer with an IP address. On the other hand, the node component contains the implementation of the proposed schemes for the grid systems in this article. A node can be configured to operate as a peer, local scheduler, intermediate GS, LGS, GSS, PGSS, or a work station. Note that the node's configuration determines the system model type.

System Model

The grid model can be configured to a (P2P, a hierarchal (one grid tree), or a hybrid (several grid trees) system model, as discussed below. The P2P systems are distributed systems and the only ones, to our knowledge, that are currently well thought-out by researchers (Al-Zoubi, 2006; Nabrzyski et al., 2004; Shan, Smith, Oliker, & Biswas, 2004) to replace the centralized systems. As a result, it is a reasonable choice to be compared against the proposed hierarchal systems in this article.

P2P System

Once a job request is received at a peer that meets its requirement, it contacts the work station to offer its service and amount of time for the work station response (100 ms, in our case). Work stations may accept peer service by responding to it or may refuse peer service by simply not responding to it. If a peer cannot accept a work station request, it decreases the hop count (1,000

Table 1. Computational resources

Server number	Number of Nndes	CPUs per node
1	184	16
2	305	4
3	144	8
4	1,024	4
5	64	2
6	512	4
7	128	2

in our case) in the message and forwards it to its neighbors. In our model, peers accept requests if they meet their deadline, which is three times the estimated execution time for that job. To improve P2P performance, we would suggest that: (1) if a workstation doesn't get a service offer within two minutes, it resubmits the job request to the grid; and (2) neighbors are manually configured to be geographically close. However, this may not be the case in reality.

Hierarchal System

The heirarchal system has one grid tree. The tree is constructed by connecting the GSS to four children, where each child holds one backbone. Each backbone's root has four children, where each child holds one net. Each net's root has two children, where each child holds five sites.

Hybrid System

The hybrid system has several grid trees acting as peers to each other. We use two hybrid systems in our simulation: four grid trees system (Hybrid-4T) and 16 grid trees system (Hybrid-16T). In the Hybrid-4T system, the grid tree of the hierarchal system is broken into four grid trees, where each backbone has one grid tree. In the Hybrid-16T (16 grid trees), each net has one grid tree.

Grid Jobs

A work station submits a job to the grid via its grid entry (e.g., GSS) as a request that defines the JMR for that job. Jobs are assumed to be executed until completion of their predefined requirements (operating systems, in our case). Gaussian distribution is usually used to simulate the required time to run a job on a server (Al-Zoubi, 2006; Hotovy, 1996; Shan et al., 2004; Takefusa, 2001) with respect to the input job size and the server's processing power. Therefore, we assume job sizes are correlated to the amount of work performed by each job, where the input data size is expressed by Gaussian distribution with the mean $\mu = b * cpus * wall$ time in seconds, and where $b = 100$ (Shan, 2004). We also assume a job produces output data five times the original input job size.

Computational Resources

We assume all resources (i.e., servers) are parallel machines that consist of a number of interconnected nodes with a number of CPUs within a node as in Al-Zoubi (2006) and Shan et al. (2004). Table 1 shows the servers used in the simulation experiments, which are originally based on real machines (Al-Zoubi, 2006; Hotovy, 1996; Shan et al., 2004).

Those servers are duplicated in all the 160 sites in a range of two to six servers per site. The

Figure 3. A sample of AWT in experiment 1

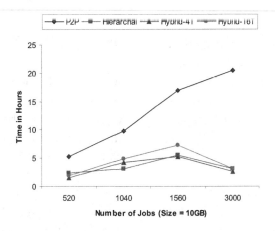

Figure 4. A sample of TRTime in experiment 1

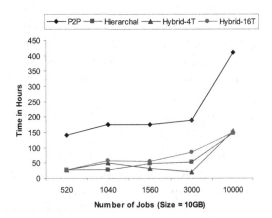

Figure 5. A sample of AET for large-sized jobs in experiment 1

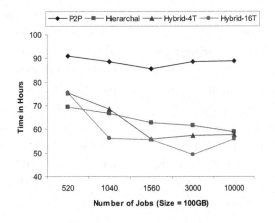

type of server and the operating system (Windows, UNIX, or LINUX) arc picked at random. We assume 0.1 local loads (i.e., not related to the grid) on all computational resources at all times, as the typical case in most studies like Hotovy (1996). Note that the simulation model consists of 520 servers versus about 1,880 work stations throughout all experiments for a ratio of 1:3.6.

Workloads

Unfortunately it was difficult to find real traces for grid computing. However we were able to base our workloads on real traces for parallel machines and scientific applications (Al-Zoubi, 2006; Feitelson, 2005; Hotovy, 1996; LTTR, 2000; Shan et al., 2004). Jobs in the workloads, that are relevant to this article, use input average sizes of 1GB, 10GB, and 100GB over the following number of jobs: 520, 1,040, 1,560, 3,000, and 10,000 jobs. Refer to Al-Zoubi) (2006) for the complete set of workloads. We use Poisson distribution to generate input data sizes for submitted jobs to the grid, where the Poisson mean is set to the desired average input size. In this way, jobs are generated with different sizes but with the desired average input size, which is close to the typical case in reality.

Performance Metrics

We use three performance metrics to compare systems: total response time, average waiting time, and average response time.

The total response time (TRT) is the time from submitting first job request until the completion of all jobs in a workload. For example, suppose that the first request was submitted to the grid at 5 p.m. and the last job of a workload was completed at 10 p.m, the total response time will then be five hours. The purpose of this metric is to show the degree of parallelism in the grid, since we view the grid as a huge virtual parallel machine. The total response time (TRT) is calculated as follows:

$$TRT = (LJC - FRS), \qquad (3)$$

where LJC (last job completion time) is the time that of the output (i.e., at workstation) of the last completed job in the workload is received FRS (first request submission) is the time of transmission of the first request by a work station.

The waiting time (WT) for a job is the time from submitting the job's request to the grid until the start of the actual job transfer to the selected resources. For example, if a work station submits a request to the grid at 5 p.m. and gets a service offer from a resource at 6 p.m., the waiting time for that job is one hour. The purpose of this metric is to measure the scheduling time (i.e., the time it takes until a resource is allocated to that job). The average waiting time (AWT) is calculated as follows:

$$AWT = \frac{1}{N}\sum_{j=1}^{N}(SJTT - RT)_j \qquad (4)$$

where N (job count) is the number of jobs in a workload. SJTT (start job transferring time) is the time when a workstation receives a service offer from a resource and starts transferring the physical job. RT (request time) is the time when a workstation submits that job request to the grid.

The execution time (ET) is the time from submitting the actual job to the grid until the job's output is received at the submitter's work station. For example, a work station receives a service offer from a resource at 5 p.m. Suppose now that the work station receives the output of the job at 6 p.m., then the execution time is one hour. Although all systems, in our model, function the same way when a request is mapped to a resource, we still need this metric to measure the location of where a job was executed. The average execution time (AET) is calculated as follows:

$$AET = \frac{1}{N} \sum_{j-1}^{N} (JCT - SJTT)_j \,,\qquad (5)$$

where JCT (job completion time) is the time when the job's output is received at the work station.

Simulation Experiments

We present, in this section, a sample of the experimental results to compare the performance over different scenarios. Refer to Al-Zoubi) (2006) for the complete set of results. Note that regardless of the configured system or experiment, the following assumptions still apply:

1. The computational power in the grid is maintained (i.e., 520 servers all the times);
2. a job is submitted by one work station and executed by one server. Note that a work-station is called active if it has a pending request in the grid. Otherwise, it is called inactive;
3. a work station that submits jobs according to a stochastic rate, only operates at that rate while it is inactive. For example, a work station submits jobs to the grid with the rate of 12 hours. Now, when that work station becomes inactive, it waits, according to that Poisson distribution, with a mean of 12 hours before it submits another job;
4. All results are obtained by averaging 20 different runs. Note that the difference between the worse and the best case runs is in the range of 5-15%. Perhaps, this is because of having too many nodes in the model.

First Experiment

In this experiment work stations submit jobs one after another until the entire workload is completed. This scenario is possible when an organization, for instance, executes a number of jobs one after another automatically as a set. The workload in this experiment is already distributed among sites by the submission approach. For example, it site A has three work stations and site B has six work stations. Most likely, site B will submit twice as many requests as site A.

The AWT and the TRT showed a substantial improvement against the P2P system, regardless of the number of used grid trees, workload, or scenario, as shown in Figures 3, 4, 6, and 9. Interestingly, the AWT starts declining when the hybrid system contains too many grid trees. Perhaps, this is because it gets closer and closer to the P2P system as a result of the increased number of trees in the system. The AET is almost the same for small jobs (1GB) but starts to differ when job size increases (100GB), as shown in Figures 5 and 7, which makes sense, since the model is built with high-performance links.

Second Experiment

In this experiment, work stations operate at different stochastic submission rates, where each work station selects, at random, one of the following rates: 10 minutes, 30 minutes, one hour, five hours, one day, or one week. Furthermore, a workload in this experiment is not already distributed among sites, as in the case of the first experiment. Furthermore, in this scenario, sites also have different probabilities when generating a job. For example, if site A has three workstations and site B has six, it is not necessarily true that site B is going to submit twice the number of requests that will be submitted from site A. On the other hand, it is quite possible that all requests will be submitted from site A.

Observations of the first experiment also are supported by this experiment. Furthermore, both the butterfly and the load-balance algorithms showed a significant influence on the performance of the hierarchal system, as shown in Figure 8. In fact, the more jobs in a workload the worse it gets. If the subject algorithms are disabled, hence, the more jobs, and the more performed rescheduling.

Figure 6. A sample of AWT in experiment 2

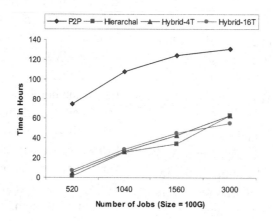

Figure 7. A sample of AET for small-sized jobs in experiment 2

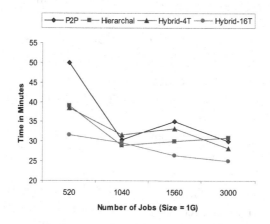

Figure 8. A sample of algorithms influence on the AWT in experiment 2

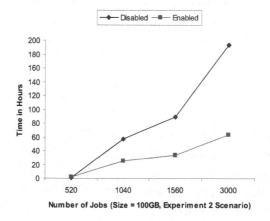

Figure 9. A sample of AWTime in experiment 3

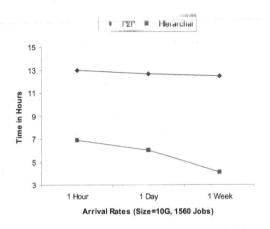

Figure 10. A sample of AWT in experiment 4

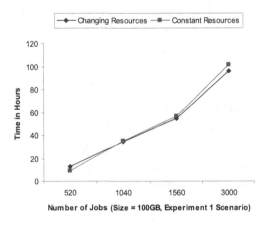

Third Experiment

In this experiment work stations submit jobs with the same stochastic rate (e.g., a one hour rate for all work stations in the grid). A workload in this experiment is already distributed among the sites, as in the case of the first experiment. We studied the systems with three different rates: one hour, one day, and one week.

Observations of the previous experiments also are supported by this experiment. In addition, the AWT tends to decline with a big slope in the hierarchal systems, when jobs arrive into the grid with

a larger mean rate. However, it decreases slightly in the P2P system, as shown in Figure 9.

Fourth Experiment

In this experiment, resources change according to one of the following stochastic changing-rates: one day, three days, one week, one month, three months, or six months. Note that the changing rate also is reselected at random, along with the advertised resources. For example, a server selects a six-month changing rate and reselects a three-month changing rate when it changes its advertised resources.

Now, when resource change is a possibility during job scheduling, the AWT turns out the same as when when resources are constant, as shown in Figure 10. This makes sense, since the fallback algorithm reschedules jobs, while resources are busy executing other jobs.

CONCLUSION

Many studies jump over the resource discovery stage into the second scheduling stage by assuming that all jobs can be executed anywhere in the grid or by simply assuming that resources will be discovered using the P2P approach. However, as we have shown, those stages have to be dealt with in a sequence because of their dependence on each other. The hierarchal approach has not only shown substantial improvement over the P2P system but also the ability to be combined with it in one hybrid system. Both the AWT and the TRT metrics showed a large improvement with the hierarchal approach in contrast to the P2P system, regardless of the number of grid trees, workload, or scenarios used. The AET metric also showed a significant improvement when not using the P2P system for large-sized jobs, but the numbers were almost the same for small-sized jobs. This makes sense, since the model is built with high-performance links. The three rescheduling algorithms showed a big contribution in the overall performance of the system. The fallback algorithm allowed some jobs to be executed despite resource change and maintained the same system performance when resources were constant. Both the butterfly and load-balance algorithms prevented the system from performing poorly when the number of jobs in workloads was increased.

Observably, the P2P approach puts the burden of discovering resources on the jobs. Peers "blindly" forward requests to their neighbors with the hope that those jobs will find appropriate resources. However, as was shown in this article, the hierarchal approach gives schedulers more "say" in discovering resources for jobs and in distributing the jobs among resources. This is not a trivial issue if we want to gain the full benefits of the grid systems. Therefore, grid schedulers, in the future, need to break grid jobs into subjobs and execute them in parallel on multiple resources. Currently, we do not see how peers in the P2P-based grid system can carry out this task. However, in theory, any grid scheduler in a grid tree may break a job into subjobs and execute that job in parallel among its children's partitions. For a more in-depth discussion, see Al-Zoubi (2006).

REFERENCES

Al-Zoubi, K. (2006). *Hierarchical scheduling in grid systems*. Unpublished master's thesis, Carleton University, Ottawa, Canada.

Berstis, V. (2002). *Fundamentals of grid computing*. Retrieved from http://www.redbooks.ibm.com/redpapers/pdfs/redp3613.pdf

Dandamudi, S. (2003). *Hierarchical scheduling in parallel and cluster systems*. Kluwer Academic Publishers.

Feitelson, D. (2005). *Parallel workloads archive*. Available from http://www.cs.huji.ac.il/labs/parallel/workload/

Foster, I. (2001). The anatomy of the grid: Enabling scalable virtual organizations. In *Proceedings of the 1st International Symposium on Cluster Computing and the Grid*. Retrieved from http://csdl2.computer.org/comp/proceedings/ccgrid/2001/1010/00/10100006.pdfFoster, I., & Kesselman, C. (2004). *The grid: Blueprint for a new computing infrastructure*. Morgan Kaufmann.

Hotovy, S. (1996). Analysis of the early workload on the Cornell theory. *ACM SIGMETRICS*, 272-273.

LTTR. (2000). *Long term technology review of the science & engineering base.* Available from http://www.rcuk.ac.uk/lttr/

Nabrzyski, J., Schopf, J., & Weglarz, J. (2004). *Grid resource management: State of the art and future trends.* Kluwer Academic Publishers.

Odlyzko, A. (2003). Internet traffic growth: Sources and implications. *Proceedings of the SPIE, 5247,* 1-15. Retrieved from http://www.dtc.umn.edu/~odlyzko/doc/itcom.internet.growth.pdf

Shan, H., Smith, W., Oliker, L., & Biswas, R. (2004). *Job scheduling in a heterogeneous grid environment.* Retrieved from http://www-library.lbl.gov/docs/LBNL/549/06/PDF/LBNL-54906.pdf

Takefusa, A. (2001). Bricks: A performance evaluation system for scheduling algorithms on the grids. *JWAITS, .*

Wainer, G. (2002). CD++: A toolkit to develop DEVS models. *Software: Practice and Experience, 32*(13), 1261-1306.

This work was previously published in Int. Journal of Information Technology and Web Engineering, Vol 2, Issue 1, edited by G. Alkhatib and D. Rine, pp. 1-16, copyright 2007 by IGI Publishing (an imprint of IGI Global).

Chapter XI
Object Grouping and Replication on a Distributed Web Server System

Amjad Mahmood
University of Bahrain, Kingdom of Bahrain

Taher S. K. Homeed
University of Bahrain, Kingdom of Bahrain

ABSTRACT

Object replication is a well-known technique to improve performance of a distributed Web server system. This paper first presents an algorithm to group correlated Web objects that are most likely to be requested by a given client in a single session so that they can be replicated together, preferably, on the same server. A centralized object replication algorithm is then proposed to replicate the object groups to a cluster of Web-server system in order to minimize the user perceived latency subject to certain constraints. Due to dynamic nature of the Web contents and users' access patterns, a distributed object replication algorithm is also proposed where each site locally replicates the object groups based on the local access patterns. The performance of the proposed algorithms is compared with three well-known algorithms and the results are reported. The results demonstrate the superiority of the proposed algorithms.

INTRODUCTION

The phenomenal growth in the World Wide Web (Web) has brought about a huge increase in the traffic to poplar Web sites. This traffic occasionally reaches the limits of the sites' capacity, causing servers to be overloaded (Chen, Mohapatra, & Chen, 2001). As a result, end users either experience a poor response time or denial of a service (time-out error) while accessing these sites.

Since these sites have a competitive motivation to offer better service to their clients, the system administrators are constantly faced with the need to scale up the site capacity. There are generally two different approaches to achieving this (Zhuo, Wang, & Lau, 2003). The first approach, generally referred to as *hardware scale-up*, is the use of powerful servers with advanced hardware support and optimized server software. While hardware scale-up relieves short-term pressure, it is neither a cost effective nor a long-term solution, considering the steep growth in clients' demand curve. Therefore, the issue of scalability and performance may persist with ever increasing user demand.

The second approach, which is more flexible and sustainable, is to use a distributed Web-server system (DWS). A DWS is not only cost effective and more robust against hardware failure, but it is also easily scalable to meet increased traffic by adding additional servers when required. In such systems, an object (a Web page, a file, etc.) is requested from various geographically distributed clients. As the DWS spreads over a metropolitan area network (MAN) or wide area network (WAN), movement of documents between server nodes is an expensive operation (Zhuo, Wang, & Lau, 2003). Maintaining multiple copies of objects at various locations in a DWS is an approach for improving system performance, such as latency, throughput, availability, hop counts, link cost, and delay (Kalpakis, Dasgupta, & Wolfson, 2001; Zhuo, Wang, & Lau, 2003).

There are two techniques used in maintaining multiple copies of an object: caching and replication. In Web caching, a copy of an object is temporarily stored at a site that accesses the object. The intermediate sites and proxies also may cache an object when it passes through them en route to its destination site. The objective of Web caching is to reduce network latency and traffic by storing commonly requested documents as close to the clients as possible. Since Web caching is not based on users' access patterns, the maximum

cache hit ratio achievable by any caching algorithm is bounded under 40-50% (Abrams, Standridge, Abdulla, Williams, & Fox, 1995). In addition, cached data have a time to live (TTL), after which the requests are brought back to the original site. Object replication, on the other hand, stores copies of an object at predetermined locations to achieve a defined performance level. The number of replica to be created and their locations are determined by users' access patterns. Therefore, the number of replicas and their locations may change in a well-controlled fashion in response to changes in the access patterns.

In most existing DWS, each server keeps the entire set of Web documents/objects managed by the system. Incoming requests are distributed to the Web server nodes via domain name system (DNS) servers or request dispatchers (Cardellini, Colajanni, & Yu, 1999; Colajanni & Yu, 1988; Kwan, Mcgrath, & Reed, 1995; Baker & Moon, 1999). Although such systems are simple to implement, they could easily result in uneven load among the server nodes, due to caching of IP addresses on the client side. To achieve better load balancing as well as to avoid disk wastage, one can replicate part of the documents on multiple server nodes, and requests can be distributed to achieve better performance (Li & Moon, 2001; Karlsson & Karamanolis, 2004; Riska, Sun, Smimi, & Ciardo, 2002). Choosing the right number of replicas and their locations is a nontrivial and nonintuitive exercise. It has been shown that deciding how many replicas to create and where to place them to meet a performance goal is an NP-hard problem (Karlsson & Karamanolis, 2004; Tenzakhti, Day, & Olud-Khaoua, 2004). Therefore, all the replica placement approaches proposed in the literature are heuristics that are designed for certain systems and work loads.

This article proposes two algorithms for replicating objects in a DWS environment. The first algorithm is centralized in the sense that a central site/server determines the allocation of objects. The distributed algorithm (DA), however, does not require a central server, except for determining the object groups. A detailed formulation of cost model and constraints is presented. Since most of the requests in a Web environment are read requests, our formulation is in the context of read-only requests. We also propose an object grouping algorithm to group objects, which are likely to be accessed in a single session by a client, to improve the efficiency and performance of the proposed replication algorithm. It should be noted that other issues, such as consistency and fault tolerance, that generally arise in distributed systems have not been addressed in this article and have been dealt with elsewhere (Agrawal & Bernstein, 1991; Anderson, Breitbart, Korth, & Wool, 1998; Wolfson, Jajodia, & Huang, 1997). Wolfson et al. (1997) also proposes how one copy serializability can be ensured by combining the data replication algorithms with two-phase-locking protocol in the presence of read-write requests.

The article proceeds in the following section with a discussion of the related work. It then describes our system model, followed by the proposed algorithms for grouping of highly correlated objects and object replication in a DWS environment. Subsequent sections present the results of our simulation study and conclusions.

SOME RELATED WORK

The object replication problem presented in this article is an extension of the classical data allocation problem (DAP) and file allocation problem (FAP) (Apers, 1998; Dowdy & Foster 1982). Both FAP and DAP are modeled as a 0-1 optimization problems and solved using various heuristics, such as the knapsack solution (Ceri, Martella, & Pelagatti, 1982) branch-and-bound (Fisher & Hochbaum, 1980), and network-flow algorithms (Chang & Liu, 1982). Most of the previous work on FAP and DAP is based on the assumption that access patterns are known a priori and remain unchanged. However, some solutions for dynamic

environments also were proposed (Gavish & Sheng, 1990; Loikopoulos & Ahmed 2000). The work presented in this article differs from both FAP and DAP in a number of ways. First, FAP and a large number of DAP consider that each object (a file, a relation, a fragment of a relation) is read and updated independently, and, hence, each object can be replicated independently. Whereas, we consider the objects that are most likely to be accessed (read) together in a single session as a unit of replication. Apers (1998) addresses the replication of object in the presence of join queries. His algorithm not only finds the sites where the relations should be allocated but also decides where the join operations should be performed. However, in the context of a Web, there is no join operation as such. Rather a user navigates a set of pages following the hyperlinks and, hence, does not require a join operation. In addition, both FAP and DAP deal with the replication and deletion of files in response to a sequence of read and write requests to optimize communication costs. Since most Web requests are read requests, we provide a detailed formulation in the context of read queries only. In addition, our second algorithm dynamically reallocates objects when users' access patterns change.

The problem of replica placement in communication networks has been extensively studied in the literature. Wolfson et al. (1997) proposed an adaptive data replication algorithm, which can dynamically replicate objects to minimize the network traffic due to "read" and "write" operations. They showed that the dynamic replication leads to convergence of the set of nodes that replicate the object. It, however, does not consider the issue of multiple object replications. Further, given that most objects in the Internet do not require "write" operations, the cost function based on "read" and "write" operations might not be ideal for such an environment.

Bestavros (1995) considered the problem of replicating contents of multiple Web sites at a given location. The problem was formulated as a constraint maximization problem, and the solution was obtained using the Lagrange multiplier theorem. However, the solution does not address the issue of selecting multiple locations through the network to do replication. Tensakhti et al. (2004) present two greedy algorithms, static and dynamic, for replicating objects in a network of Web servers arranged in a tree-like structure. The static algorithm assumes that there is a central server that has a copy of each object, and then a central node determines the number and location of replication to minimize a cost function. The dynamic version of the algorithm relies on the usage statistics collected at each server node. A test is performed periodically at each site holding replicas to decide whether there should be any deletion of existing replicas, creation of new replicas, or migration of existing replicas. Optimal placement of replicas in trees also has been studied by Kalpakis at el. (2001). They considered the problem of placing copies of objects in a tree network in order to minimize the cost of serving read and write requests to objects, when the tree nodes have limited storage and the number of copies permitted is limited. They proposed a dynamic programming algorithm for finding optimal placement of replicas.

The problem of document replication in extendable geographically DWSs is addressed by Zhuo et al. (2003). They proposed four heuristics to determine the placement of a replica in a network. In addition, they presented an algorithm that determined the number of copies of each documents to be replicated, depending on its usage and size. In Zhuo, Wang, & Lau (2002), the authors also proposed to replicate a group of related documents as a unit instead of treating each document as a replication unit. They also presented an algorithm to determine the group of documents that have high cohesion, that is, they are generally accessed together by a client in a single session.

Xu, Li, and Lee (2002) discussed the problems of replication proxy placement in a tree and data

replication placement on the installed proxies given that maximum M proxies are allowed. The authors proposed algorithms to find the number of proxies needed, where to install them, and the placement of replicas on the installed proxies to minimize the total data transfer cost in the network. Heddaya and Mirdad (1997) have presented a dynamic replication protocol for the Web, referred to as the Web wave. It is a distributed protocol that places cache copies of immutable documents on the routing tree that connects the cached documents home site to its clients, thus enabling requests to stumble on cache copies *en route* to the home site. This algorithm, however, burdens the routers with the task of maintaining replica locations and interpreting requests for Web objects. Sayal, Breitbart, Scheurermann, and Vingralek (1998) proposed selection algorithms for replicated Web sites, which allow clients to select one of the replicated sites that is close to them. However, they do not address the replica placement problem itself. Mahmood (2005a, b) proposed a series of algorithms to place objects in a DWS in a tree-like topology.

THE SYSTEM MODEL

A replicated Web consists of many sites/servers interconnected by a communication network. A unit of data to be replicated is referred as an *object*. An object can be an XML/HMTL page, an image file, a relation, and so forth. Each object is identified by a unique identifier and may be replicated on a number of sites/server. The objects are managed by a group of processes called replicas, executing at replica sites. We assume that the network topology can be represented by a graph $G(V, E)$, in which $N=|V|$ is the number of nodes or vertices, and $|E|$ denotes the number of edges (links). Each node in the graph corresponds to a router, a switch, or a Web site. We assume that out of those N nodes, there are n Web servers as the information provider. Associated with every node $v \in V$ is a set of nonnegative weights, and each of the weights is associated with one particular Web server. This weight can represent the traffic traversing this node v and going to Web server i ($i = 1,2,...,n$). This traffic includes the Web access traffic generated at the local site that node v is responsible for and, also, the traffic that passes through it on its way to a target Web server. Associated with every edge is a nonnegative distance, which can be hop count, data transmission rate, or the economic cost of the path between two nodes.

A client initiates a read operation for an object k, by sending a read request for k. The request goes through a sequence of hosts via their attached routers to the server that can serve the request. The sequence of nodes that a read request goes through is called a routing path, denoted by π. The requests are routed up the tree to the home site (i.e., root of the tree). Focusing on a particular sever i, the access traffic from all nodes leading to a server can be represented best by a tree structure, if the transient routing loop is ignored (Li, 1999; Tenzakhti et al., 2004). Therefore, for each Web server i, a spanning tree T_i, rooted at i, can be constructed. Hence, m spanning trees rooted at m Web servers represent the entire network.

Object Replication Model

In this article, we consider two object replication models: centralized and distributed. In a centralized model, a central arbitrator determines the number and placement of replicas. Upon determining the placement of replicas for each object, the central arbitrator reconfigures the system by adding and/or removing replicas, according to the new placement determined by the arbitrator. The location of each replica is broadcast to all the sites. In a distributed model, the central arbitrator only performs the global grouping of objects that is broadcast to all the sites. Each site itself periodically determines which object groups should be replicated locally to minimize the lo-

cally perceived latency. In both models, each site i keeps the following information:

$C_k^{i,j}$: The cost of accessing object k at site i from site j.

$f_k^{i,j}$: The access frequency of object k at site i from site j.

N_k : The set of sites that have a replica of object k.

The traffic frequency, $f_k^{i,j}$, is the number of read requests for a certain period of time t issued at site i for object k to site j. This frequency includes the number of requests issues from site i and the request for object k passing through in its way to j. This traffic can easily be monitored and recorded by using the existing technologies.

There are a number of methods that have been proposed to calculate cost (latency) (Tenzakhti et al. 2004). To determine the cost (latency), our preferred algorithm proceeds as follows. Each replica site j maintains a count c of the total number of requests it receives in a period of time t. The arrival rate, λ, at the replica is given by $\lambda = c/t$. Assuming that each replica site has an exponential service time with an average service rate of μ, then the time T that a request will spend at the replica site (waiting + processing time) is the well-known $M/M/1$ queuing result $T = 1/(\mu - \lambda)$. Periodically, each replica site computes its T and broadcasts it to all the sites in its tree. Upon receiving this value from site j, site i would add to it the average latency involved in receiving data from j and broadcast this new value to its neighbors other than j. The latency will reach at all the sites in a recursive way. The added communication cost (latency) can be obtained by having each site periodically query its neighbors and determining this cost.

The Cost Model

Suppose that vertices of $G(V,E)$ issue read requests for an object and copies of that object can be stored al multiple vertices of G. Suppose that there are total n sites (Web servers) and m objects. Let X be an $n \times m$ matrix, whose entry $x_{ik}=1$, if object k is stored at site i and $x_{ik}=0$, otherwise then the cost of serving object k at site i from site j, denoted by TC_k^i is given by:

$$TC_k^i = \sum_{j=1}^{n} x_{jk} f_k^{i,j} C_k^{i,j} \tag{1}$$

The cost of serving requests for all the m objects at site i, denoted by TC^i, is given by:

$$TC^i = \sum_{k=1}^{k=m} TC_k^i = \sum_{k=1}^{k=m} \left[\sum_{j=1}^{n} x_{jk} f_k^{i,j} C_k^{i,j} \right] \tag{2}$$

The cumulative cost, TC, of serving all the objects over the whole network can be written as:

$$TC(X) = \sum_{i=1}^{n} \sum_{k=1}^{m} \sum_{j=1}^{n} x_{jk} f_k^{i,j} C_k^{i,j} \tag{3}$$

If b_k, s_k, TS_i, L_{ik}, and P_i denote the minimum number of safety copies of object k, size of object k, total storage capacity at site i, processing load of object k, and total processing capacity of site i, respectively, then the replica placement problem can be defined as a 0-1 decision problem to find X that minimizes Equation 3, subject to storage capacity, processing capacity, and minimum copy constraints. That is, we want to:

$$\min TC(X) = \min \sum_{i=1}^{n} \sum_{k=1}^{m} \sum_{j=1}^{n} x_{jk} f_k^{i,j} C_k^{i,j} \tag{4}$$

Subject to

$$\sum_{i=1}^{i=n} x_{ik} \geq b_k \text{ for all } 1 \leq k \leq m; \tag{5}$$

$$\sum_{k=1}^{m} x_{ik} s_k \leq TS_i \text{ for all } 1 \leq i \leq n; \tag{6}$$

$$\sum_{k=1}^{m} x_{ik}.L_{ik} < P_i \text{ for all } 1 \leq i \leq n; \tag{7}$$

$$x_{ik} \in \{0,1\}, \text{ for all } i, j \tag{8}$$

In Equation 5, the minimum number of safety copies for object k should be equal or greater than 1 (i.e., $b_k \geq 1$). This is necessary in case some failure of the servers occurs, and/or we want a different minimum number of copies for each object. Note that each object should have at least one copy in the network. The second constraint specifies that the total size of all the objects replicated at node i should not exceed its storage capacity. The third constraint specifies that the processing load brought by all the objects assigned at node i should not exceed the total processing capacity of a node.

OBJECT GROUPING

Almost all the proposed object/document placement and replication algorithms for Web servers decide the placement/replication of a complete Web site or individual objects comprising a Web site. Both of these methods are not realistic. It has been shown in various studies that each group of users generally accesses a subsets of related pages during a single session. Therefore, it is logical to group documents that have high correlation—that is, the documents that are very likely to be requested by a client in a single session. This would reduce the HTTP redirection throughout an HTTP session and, hence, improve the response time. Each group then can be replicated on Web servers as a unit, hence reducing the search space.

In this section, we propose an algorithm to group objects that are highly correlated in the sense that they have high probability of being

Figure 1. Object grouping algorithm

```
Step 1. Process the log file (as explained below)
Step2. Create a correlation matrix (as explained below)
Step 3. Create a clique using:

R = {vertices connected to at least one edge}
while (R ≠ φ) {
  Find the longest edge in R with vertices O₁ and O₂
  V = { O₁ , O₂}
  G = R \ V, C = φ
  l=maximum size of V
  while ( |V| ≤ l ) {
        for (each vertex O in G) {
            if (O is connected to all vertices in V){
                Record shortest edge between O and vertices in V
                Add O to V
            } // if
        } // for
        if (C ≠ φ ) {
            Choose the vertex O whose shortest edge to V is longest
            Add O to V
            Delete O from G and R
            C = φ
            l=l+1
        }
        else {
                delete O₁ and O₂ O₁ and O₂ from G and R
                break
        }
  } // while
Construct a group for each remaining vertex
```

accessed by a client in a single session. The proposed algorithm is an adaptation of the algorithm proposed in Perkowitz and Etzioni (1998). The major difference is that the algorithm in Perkowitz and Etzioni produces nonoverlapping groups, that is, each document is placed in a single group, but the proposed algorithm may include an object in more than one group. This is particularly important, since different users may request different correlated objects during each session. Also, we use multiple sessions, instead of a single session, originating from a client to obtain object groups for the reasons explained.

The proposed algorithm (Mahmood, 2005a) groups the objects into correlated object clusters based on the user's access patterns, which are stored in the system access log files. An access log file typically includes the time of request, the URL requested, and the machine from which the request originated (i.e., IP address of the machine). The complete algorithm is given in Figure 1.

Below, we explain the major steps in the algorithm.

1. First the log file is processed and divided into sessions, where a session is a chronological sequence of document requests from a particular machine in a single session. We assume that each session spans over a finite amount of time. It is important to note that the log file may have multiple sessions for the same user. This gives a better picture of the usage pattern of a user. Also, note that we have to make sure that each request from a machine is recorded in the log file to obtain an accurate access pattern of users. This can be accomplished by disabling caching, that is, every page sent to a machine contains a

header saying that it expires immediately and, hence, browsers should load a new copy every time a user views that page.

2. At Step 2, we create a correlation matrix. The correlation between two objects O_1 and O_2 is the probability that they are accessed in the same user session. To calculate the correlation between O_1 and O_2, we scan the log file and count the number of distinct sessions in which O_1 was accessed after O_2 ($count(O_1,O_2)$) and calculate $p(O_1|O_2)= count(O_1,O_2)/ s(O_1)$, where $p(O_1|O_2)$ is the probability of a client visiting O_1, if it has already visited O_2 and $s(O_1)$ is the number of sessions in which O_1 was accessed by a client. Similarly, we compute $p(O_2|O_1)= count(O_2, O_1)/s(O_2)$, where $p(O_2|O_1)$ is the probability of O_2 being accessed after O_1 in a session; $count(O_2, O_1)$ is the number of sessions in which O_2 is accessed after O_1, and $s(O_2)$ is the total number of sessions in which O_2 is accessed. The correlation between O_1 and O_2 is the $min(p(O_1|O_2), p(O_2|O_1))$ to avoid mistaking a asymmetric relationship for a true case of high correlation.

3. At Step 3, we first create a graph corresponding to correlation matrix in which each object is a vertex and each nonzero cell of the correlation matrix is mapped to an edge. The length of an edge is equal to the correlation probability between two vertices. The edges with a small value are removed from the graph. We then group documents by identifying cliques in the graph. A clique is a subgraph in which each pair of vertices has an edge between them. The algorithm to identify cliques is given in Figure 1. The algorithm always starts with a pair of vertices that have the longest edge between them. Both of these vertices are included in the group and edge is removed. Then we examine the rest of the vertices that have not been included in the group and select the next best vertex (a vertex with the highest edge value) that is connected to the

vertices already included in the group and include it in the group. In this way, we choose the objects that are highly correlated. The size of the clique is bounded by the longest session of its members since there is no need for including an object in a group if it is not accessed in the longest session. Each vertex that is not included in any of groups is included in a separate group having that vertex as its only member.

OBJECT REPLICATION ALGORITHMS

The replica placement problem described in the previous section reduces to finding 0-1 assignment of the matrix X that minimizes the cost function subject to a set of constraints. The time complexity of this type of problems is exponential. In the next section, we present our proposed centralized as well as distributed object replication algorithms.

The proposed centralized algorithm is a polynomial time greedy algorithm that is executed at a central server/arbitrator and decides the placement of replicas for each object. The algorithm proceeds as follows. First, all of the object groups are organized in descending order of their density values to make sure that the objects that are heavily accessed are assigned to the best server. For each object, we determine the number of replicas that should be assigned to various servers, using the algorithm proposed in Zhuo et al. (2002) where R_k denotes the number of replica each object k should have. The first object in a group is assigned to most suitable server, and then all the other objects in the same group are allocated to the same server, if it has enough capacity. The idea is that the documents in the same group have high probability of being accessed in the same session by a client; therefore, keeping them together will improve the response time. If an object cannot be assigned to the same server then we find a server with minimum access

Figure 2. Proposed centralized replication algorithm

```
Group objects using object group algorithm
Arrange object groups in descending order of their density
Arrange objects in each group in descending order of their density
Determine the number of replicas for each object
for (k=1; k<= no_of_objects; k++) replica_assigned_k=0
for g = 1 to no_of_groups {
        while (G_i ≠ φ ) {
                k = first_object_in _G_i
                A = k // set of objects allocated to j
                if (k has not been allocated) {
                        j = site with minimum value of (2) such that no constraint is violated if a replica of k is allocated to j
                        Allocate k at j
                        replica_assigned_k = replica_assigned_k + 1
                }
                G_i = G_i - k
                while (j has capacity and G_i ≠ φ and ) {
                        k = first_object_in _G_i
                        Allocate k at j
                        replica_assigned_k = replica_assigned_k + 1
                        G_i = G_i - k
                        A= A ∪ k
                } // while
                for ( each k in A )
                for (r= replica_assigned_k;  r ≤ R_k ; r++) {
                        Find a site i not having a replica of k and has minimum value of        and if a replica of k is assigned at j
                        and no constraint is violated
                        Assigned k at j
                        replica_assigned_k = replica_assigned_k + 1
                } // for
        } // while
} // while
```

cost and assign the object to that server. After a copy of an object is assigned, then we assign the remaining replica of each object to best servers not having a copy of that object and having the capacity for that object. The complete algorithm is given in Figure 2.

In the second proposed algorithm, a central arbitrator is used to group the objects using the object grouping algorithm. These groups are sent to each site using any of the available techniques, such as push technology (Franklin & Zdonik, 1998). Each site then determines which groups should be locally replicated ,based on the object usage statistics collected locally. The DA first removes all the objects previously replicated at a site, except those objects that do not have a replica at any other site. It then sorts the object groups in descending order of their local density

values, where the local density value for a group G_i is calculated as:

Density(G_j)=(Total size of objects in G_j)/(Total local read requests for objects in G_j)

(9)

The object groups are allocated one at a time (in the sorted order), provided enough space is available on the server, and no other constraint is violated. In case there is not enough space available to accommodate the whole group, some of the objects with high local access frequency are replicated. The complete algorithm is given in Figure 3.

In the proposed DA, the central arbitrator performs object regrouping either after a predefined time interval or on specific events (such a predefined time period elapses after addition

Figure 3. Proposed distributed replication algorithm

```
//At each server
Remove all the locally replicated objects having at least one more replica
Calculate local density of each object group
Sort object groups in descending local density values
t=total_no_of_groups
i=1
while (Size(G_i) <= Avaiable_space && i <= t) {
    Replicate G_i provided no other constraint is violated
    i++
}
if (i <= t && Available_space >= size_of_smallest_object in G_i) {
    Sort objects in G_i in descending value of their local density
    Replicate objects one by one in the determined order subject to storage and other constraints
}
```

or removal of new objects), making the object groups more adaptive to the changing access patterns and objects. Each site also periodically determines the new replication schemes when it observes changes in the local access patterns. Each site also can perform object grouping based on the local logs, hence eliminating the need of a central arbitrator altogether.

EXPERIMENTAL RESULTS

Comparing the performance of the proposed algorithm to the optimal solution obtained by an exhaustive search would have been the best way to illustrate the merits of our algorithms. An exhaustive search, though, is able to provide the optimum solutions, within a reasonable running time, only for small-sized problems. Since small problem sizes have little practical meaning, we followed the approach used by other researchers and compared our results with those obtained by other well-known algorithms. These algorithms are the random allocation algorithm (Kangasharju, Roberts, & Ross, 2002), the greedy algorithm (Tenzakhti et al. 2004), and a DA also proposed in Tenzakhti et al. (2004). In the random placement, replicas are placed at random with uniform probability among all the sites in the network. It can be considered as an "upper bound" placement method in a sense that an efficient replica

placement method should always be better than the random placement (Radoslavov, Govindan, & Estrin, 2001).

In our simulation, we used trees having 100-600 nodes with a maximum degree of 15 (a tree with a higher number of nodes has a higher degree). Objects to be replicated were created so as to resemble a generic Web work load (Braford, Bestarov, Bradley, & Crovella, 1999), that is, object sizes followed a pareto distribution and their popularity followed the Zipf law (Zipf, 1949). The minimum object size was 4K. The total number of objects to be replicated varied from 500-2,500, depending on the number of sites in the network. The total number of requests considered for large network instances were 1 million, while for medium sized networks, it was 100,000. Two distinct cases were considered for request generation. In the first case, each site had the same probability of requesting an object, while in the second case requests were normally distributed in order to measure the performance of the algorithms at the presence of hot spots. We created log files by generating requests for objects for multiple sessions. These log files were used to group objects. The same log files were used by the proposed algorithms to collect various statistics. Total site capacity was taken proportional to the total size of all the objects, which was a random value between $(T/4)\%$ and $(3T/2)\%$, where T is total size of all the objects.

Figure 4. Mean latency for different tree sizes

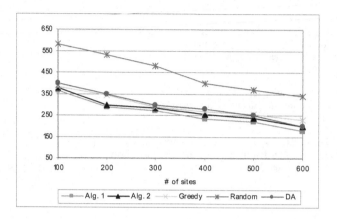

Figure 5. Average latency for all simulation runs

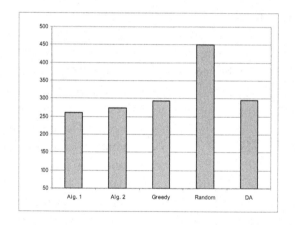

Figure 6. Effect of site capacity on mean latency for the proposed algorithms

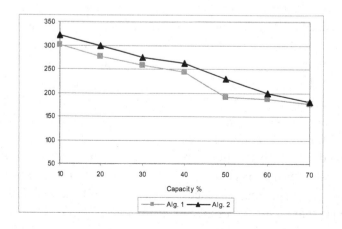

Figure 7. Effect of number of objects on mean latency for the proposed algorithms

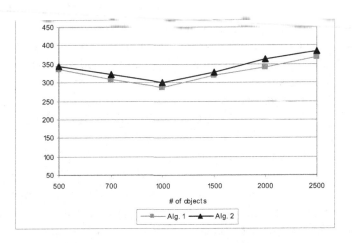

Figure 8. Average % improvement achieved by the proposed algorithms

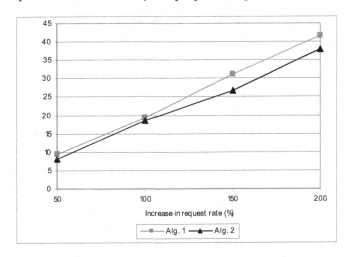

Figure 9. Performance of the proposed grouping algorithm

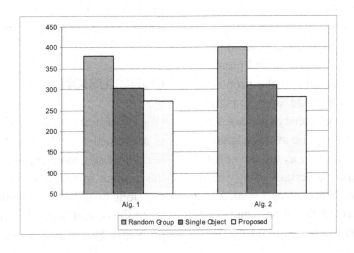

We used the average latency (i.e., average time required to serve a read request) as a measure of performance. The latency for accessing an object k from node i to node j is calculated as follows. During a simulation run, each site keeps a count c of the total number of requests it receives for an object. The latencies are updated periodically for each replica using the formula $T=1/(\mu-\lambda)$, where λ is the average arrival rate and μ is the average service time. Exponential service time is assumed with an average service rate of 100 to 150 transactions/second for different servers. The cost (latency) is computed at the end of each simulation run as discussed in the object replication model.

In the first set of experiments, we assessed the performance of the proposed algorithms as compared to other algorithms mentioned before. We fixed the site capacity to $T=30\%$. Figure 4 shows the average latencies for all the simulation runs for different tree sizes. The figure shows that the average latency decreases for all the algorithms as the number of sites increases in the system. This is because of the fact that as the number of sites increases, more replicas of an object can be placed. Also, note that the performance of proposed algorithms is better than all other algorithms. Also, note that the performance of the proposed DA is comparable to the centralized algorithm. Figure 5 shows the average performance of the algorithms for all the system configurations. It is evident that the proposed algorithms perform, on average, better than the other algorithms.

In the second set of experiments, we investigated the impact of site capacity and number of objects on solution quality of the proposed algorithms in terms of average latency. Figure 6 shows that the average latency decreases as the site capacity increases. The average latency tends to decrease significantly as the site capacity increases, while after a certain point where most read intensive objects are replicated, adding more storage space results in only marginal performance improvements. A similar trend was

seen when the number of objects were increased, while keeping other parameters constant. Figure 7 shows the effect of increasing the number of objects for a network of 100 sites (similar results were obtained for other configurations).

In the third set of experiments, we investigated the impact of the increase in the request frequencies. We periodically increased the access frequencies of each site-object pair randomly by 40-200%. The proposed algorithm is then run to determine the new replication schemes. We observed the improvement in latency, first by calculating the latency if no reallocation of objects is done and then by allowing the algorithm to adjust the replication using the statistics. The average percentage improvement in the latency is shown in Figure 8. It can be observed that the algorithms improve the replication schemes every time access frequencies are changed by adding, removing, or migrating objects to more appropriate sites.

We also investigated the effectiveness of the grouping algorithm. The objects were grouped randomly, using the proposed algorithm and putting a single object in each group. The proposed algorithms were run for each type of grouping. The results are shown in Figure 9. It can be seen in the figure that we obtained better replications when objects were grouped using the proposed algorithm. Random grouping of objects performed the worst while the performance of allocating a single object (i.e., groups with one object only) was better than the randomly grouping of objects.

CONCLUSION

Object replication on a cluster of Web servers is a promising technique for achieving better performance. However, one needs to determine the number of replicas of each object and their locations in a DWS. Choosing the right number of replicas and their locations are nontrivial problems. In this article, we presented an object grouping algorithm and two object replication algorithms. The object grouping algorithm groups Web objects based on the users' access patterns stored in Web log file. The documents that are highly correlated and have high probability of being accessed by a client in a single session are put into the same group so that they can be allocated, preferably, on the same server. The first proposed object replication algorithm is a centralized one, in the sense that a central site determines the replica placement to minimize a cost function subject to the capacity and other constraints. The second proposed algorithm is a distributed one, allowing each site to determine its locally optimal replication schemes, based on locally collected statistics. Taking each algorithm individually, simulation results show that each algorithm improves the latency of the transactions performed at different sites as the number of sites is increased. A comparison of the proposed algorithms with greedy, random, and DA demonstrates the superiority of the proposed algorithms.

REFERENCES

Abrams, M., Standridge, C. R., Abdulla, G., Williams, S., & Fox, E. A. (1995). Caching proxies: Limitations and potentials. In *Proceedings of the 4th International World Wide Web Conference,* Boston, (pp. 119-133).

Agrawal, D., & Bernstein, A. J. (1991). A nonblocking quorum consensus protocol for replicated data. *IEEE Transactions on Parallel and Distributed Systems, 2*(2), 171-179.

Anderson, T., Breitbart, Y., Korth, H. F., & Wool, A. (1998). Replication, consistency and practicality: Are these mutually exclusive? *ACM SIGMOD'98,* Seattle.

Apers, P. G. M. (1998). Data allocation in distributed database systems. *ACM Transactions on Database Systems, 13*(3), 263-304.

Baker, S. M., & Moon, B. (1999). Scalable Web server design for distributed data management. In *Proceedings of the 15th International Conference on Data Engineering,* Sydney, (pp. 96-110).

Bestavros, A. (1995). Demand-based document dissemination to reduce traffic and balance load in distributed information systems. In *Proceedings of the IEEE Symposium on Parallel and Distributed Processing,* pp. 338-345.

Braford, P., Bestarov, A., Bradley, A., & Crovella, M. (1999). Changes in Web client access patterns: Characteristics and caching implications. *WWW Journal, 2*(1), 15-28.

Cardellini, V., Colajanni, M., & Yu, P. S. (1999). Dynamic load balancing on Web-server systems. *IEEE Internet Computing, 3*(3), 28-39.

Ceri, S., Martella, G., & Pelagatti, G. (1982). Optimal file allocation in a computer network: A solution method based on knapsack problem. *Computer Networks, 6*(11), 345-357.

Chang, S. K., & Liu, A. C. (1982). File allocation in distributed database. *International Journal of Computer Information Science, 11*(2), 325-340.

Chen, X., Mohapatra, P., & Chen, H. (2001). An admission control scheme for predictable server response time for Web accesses. In *Proceedings of the 10th WWW Conference,* Hong Kong, (pp. 45-54).

Colajanni, M., & Yu, P. S. (1988). Analysis of task assignment policies in scalable distributed Web server systems. *IEEE Trans. on Parallel and Distributed Systems, 9*(6), 585-600.

Dowdy, L., & Foster, D. (1982). Comparative models of the file assignment problem. *Computer Surveys, 14*(2), 287-313.

Fisher, M. K., & Hochbaum, D. S. (1980). Database location in computer networks. *Journal ACM, 27*(10), 718-735.

Franklin, M. J., & Zdonik, S. B. (1998). Data in your face: push technology in perspective, *ACM SIGMOD Conference on Management of Data,* Seattle, (pp. 29-34).

Gavish, B., & Sheng, O. R. L. (1990). Dynamic file migration in distributed computer systems. *Comm. of ACM, 33*(1), 177-189.

Heddaya, A., & Mirdad, S. (1997). Web wave: Globally load balanced fully distributed caching of hot published documents. In *Proceedings of the 17th IEEE International Conference on Distributed Computing Systems,* (pp. 160-168).

Kalpakis, K, Dasgupta, K., & Wolfson, O. (2001). Optimal placement of replicas in trees with read write and storage costs. *IEEE Trans. on Parallel and Distributed Systems, 12*(6), 628-637.

Kangasharju, J., Roberts, J., & Ross, K. W. (2002). Object replication strategies in content distribution networks. *Computer Communications, 25*(4), 367-383.

Karlsson, M., & Karamanolis, C. (2004). Choosing replica placement heuristics for wide-area systems. *International Conference on Distributed Computing Systems (ICDCS) 2004.* Retrieved from http://www.hpl.hp.com/personal/Magnus_Karlsson

Kwan, T. T., Mcgrath, R. E., & Reed, D. E. (1995). NCSA's World Wide Web server: Design and performance. *IEEE Computer, 28*(11), 68-74.

Li, B. (1999). Content replication in a distributed and controlled environment. *Journal of Parallel and Distributed Computing, 59*(2), 229-251.

Li, Q. Z., & Moon, B. (2001). Distributed cooperative Apache Web server. In *Proceedings of the 10th International World Wide Web Conference, Hong Kong* (pp. 555-564).

Loikopoulos, T., & Ahmed, I. (2000). Static and dynamic data replication algorithms for fast information access in large distributed systems.

In *Proceedings of the 20th IEEE Conference on Distributed Computing Systems, Taipei,* (pp. 385-392).

Mahmood, A. (2005a). Object grouping and replication algorithms for World Wide Web. *Informatica, 28*(3), 347-356.

Mahmood, A. (2005b). Object replication algorithms for World Wide Web. *Computing and Informatics, 24,* 371-390.

Perkowitz, M., & Etzioni, O. (1998). Adaptive Web sites: Automatically synthesizing Web pages. In *Proceedings of the AAAI'98,* 722-732.

Radoslavov, P., Govindan, R., & Estrin, D. (2001). Topology informed internet replica placement. *Proceedings of the 6th International Workshop on Web Caching and Content Distribution, Boston,* Retrieved from http://www.cs.bu.edu/techreports/2001-017-wcw01-proceedings

Riska, A., Sun, W., Smimi, E., & Ciardo, G. (2002). ADATPTLOAD: Effective load balancing in clustered Web servers under transient load conditions. *Proceedings of the 22nd International Conference on Distributed Systems, Austria,* (pp. 89-97).

Sayal, M., Breitbart, Y., Scheurermann, P., & Vingralek, R. (1998). Selection of algorithms for replicated Web sites. *Performance Evaluation Review, 26*(1), 44-50.

Tenzakhti, F., Day, K., & Olud-Khaoua, M. (2004). Replication algorithms for the word-wide Web. *Journal of System Architecture, 50,* 591-605.

Wolfson, O, Jajodia, S., & Huang, Y. (1997). An adaptive data replication algorithm. *ACM Trans. Database Systems, 22*(2), 255-314.

Xu, J., Li, B., & Lee, D. L. (2002). Placement problems for transparent data replication proxy services. *IEEE Journal on Selected Areas in Communications, 20*(7), 1383-1398.

Zhuo, L., Wang, C L., & Lau, F. C. M. (2002). *Document replication and distribution in extensible geographically distributed Web servers.* Retrieved from http://www.cs.hku.hk/ ~clwang/ papers/ JPDC-EGDWS-11-2002.pdf

Zhuo, L., Wang, C-L., & Lau, F. C. M. (2003). Document replication and distribution in exten-

sible geographically distributed Web servers. *Journal of Parallel and Distributed Computing,* *63*(10), 927 944.

Zipf, G. K. (1949). *Human behavior and the principle of least-effort.* Cambridge: Addison-Wesley.

This work was previously published in Int. Journal of Information Technology and Web Engineering, Vol 2, Issue 1, edited by G. Alkhatib and D. Rine, pp. 17-33, copyright 2007 by IGI Publishing (an imprint of IGI Global).

Chapter XII
On the Logarithmic Backoff Algorithm for MAC Protocol in MANETs

Saher S. Manaseer
University of Glasgow, UK

Mohamed Ould-Khaoua
University of Glasgow, UK

Lewis M. Mackenzie
University of Glasgow, UK

ABSTRACT

In wireless communication environments, backoff is traditionally based on the IEEE binary exponential backoff (BEB). Using BEB results in a high delay in message transmission, collisions and ultimately wasting the limited available bandwidth. As each node has to obtain medium access before transmitting a message, in dense networks, the collision probability in the MAC layer becomes very high when a poor backoff algorithm is used. The Logarithmic algorithm proposes some improvements to the backoff algorithms that aim to efficiently use the channel and to reduce collisions. The algorithm under study is based on changing the incremental behavior of the backoff value. The Binary Exponential Backoff (BEB) is used by the Local Area Networks standards, IEEE 802.11, Medium Access Control (MAC). BEB uses a uniform random distribution to choose the backoff value; this often leads to reducing the effect of window size increment. This paper carries out a deeper study and analysis of the logarithmic backoff algorithm that uses logarithmic increment instead of exponential extension of window size to eliminate the degrading effect of random number distribution. Results from simulation experiments reveal that the algorithm subject to study achieves higher throughput and less packet loss when in a mobile ad hoc environment.

INTRODUCTION

Since their emergence, wireless networks have become increasingly popular in the computing industry. This is particularly true within the past decade, which has seen wireless networks being adapted to enable mobility. There are currently two variations of mobile wireless networks (IEEE, ANSI/IEEE Standard 802.11, 1999), infrastructure, and ad hoc wireless networks.

Infrastructured networks, that is, those networks with fixed and wired gateways, have bridges known as base stations. A mobile unit within these networks connects to, and communicates with, the nearest base station within its communication radius. Typical applications of this type of network include wireless local area networks (WLAN) (IEEE, ANSI/IEEE Standard 802.11, 1999).

Mobile ad hoc networks (MANETs) are getting more and more attention. Unlike wired networks, MANETs are easily deployed, and need no infrastructure (Fang, Bensaou, & Wang, 2002). Such networks can be useful in disaster recovery, where there is not enough time or resources to configure a wired network. Ad hoc networks also are used in military operations, where the units are moving around the battlefield in a random way, and a central unit cannot be used for synchronization (Fang et al., 2002).

In MANETs, a central station is not needed to control the different types of operations taking place allover the network (Sundaresan & Sivakumar, 2004). A node participating in an ad hoc network must have the ability to act as a client, a server, and a router (Fang et al., 2002). Nodes also should have the ability to connect to the network and to automatically configure to start transmitting data over the network. This is the reason why ad hoc protocols, in general, function in a distributed manner (Manaseer & Ould-Khaoua, 2005). The distributed coordination function (DCF) is used for synchronous, contention-based, distributed access to the channel (Bononi et al., 2004). MANETs use a shared medium to transfer data between its nodes.

It is unrealistic to expect a MANET to be fully connected, where a node can communicate directly with every other node in the network. Typically nodes must use a multihop path for transmission, and a packet may traverse multiple nodes before being delivered to its destination.

The wireless medium used by MANETs has a number of problems, including bandwidth sharing, signal fading, noise, interference, and so forth. With such a shared medium, an efficient and effective MAC is essential for sharing the scarce bandwidth resource (Cali, Conti, & Gregori, 1998; Fang et al., 2002). Based on the features mentioned, the design of the MAC protocol is a significantly affects a MANET.

As a part of an efficient MAC protocol, a backoff algorithm is used to avoid collisions, when more than one node tries to access the channel (Manaseer & Ould-Khaoua, 2005). Only one of the nodes is granted access to the channel, while other contending nodes are suspended into a backoff state for some period (Goodman, Albert, Madras, & March, 1985). Many backoff algorithms have been developed in the literature (Sundaresan & Sivakumar 2004; Xu, Gerla, & Bae, 2002). One example is the multiplicative increase linear decrease (MILD) algorithm (Sakakibara, Sasaki, & Yamakita, 2005). This algorithm improves the total throughput of the network, but the cost of this improvement is the need of a perfect knowledge about collisions happening over the network, which is high cost, hard-to-acquire knowledge.

In a normal LAN, the total number of nodes of the network is easily obtained. However, as nodes in MANETs are mobile, knowing the number of nodes may incur a high cost, since this knowledge needs to be updated. One approach to update and keep the knowledge coherent is by exchanging "hello" packets between neighboring nodes (Manaseer & Ould-Khaoua, 2005). Broadcasting "hello" packets over the network generates extra traffic load over the network, consumes a part of the network resources, causes a longer delay, requires more control processing, and even gives more work to the backoff algorithm itself. Other backoff algorithms have tried to find a fixed optimum backoff value to use. But, even though, the distributed functioning was not complete (Bao & Garcia-Luna-Aceces, 2001).

Many researchers have proposed the mechanism of channel sensing, or packet sensing, to avoid collision. The sensing mechanisms typically rely on the transmitter and receiver performing a handshake prior to the transmission of the data packet (Bharghavan, Demers, Shenker, & Zhang, 1994). More specifically, the medium access collision avoidance (MACA) method, proposed by Karn (1990), implements the handshake via a pair of request-to-send (RTS) and clear-to-send (CTS) messages. When a node has to send data to another, it first sends a short RTS packet to the destination. The receiver responds with a CTS packet (Bharghavan et al., 1994). On receipt of the CTS, the sender sends its queued data packet(s). All other nodes overhearing the CTS message will not send out any packet, until the predicted transmission period indicated in the CTS packet is passed. Any node that overhears the RTS signal but not CTS is allowed to send out packets in a certain time period, as either the RTS/CTS handshake is not completed or it is out of range of the receiver.

In the IEEE 802.11 standard MAC protocol, the BEB is used. This algorithm functions in the following way (Xu et al., 2002).

When a node over the network has a packet to send, it first senses the channel, using a carrier sensing technique. If the channel is found to be idle and not being used by any other node, the node is granted access to start transmitting. Otherwise, the node waits for an interframe space, and the backoff mechanism is invoked. A random backoff time will be chosen in the range [0, CW-1]. A uniform random distribution is used here, where CW is the current contention window size.

The following equation is used to calculate the backoff time (BO):

$$BO = (Rand\ ()\ MOD\ CW)* aSlotTime.$$

$$(1)$$

The backoff procedure is preformed then, by putting the node on a waiting period of length BO. Using carrier sense mechanism, the activity of the medium is sensed at every time slot. If the medium is found to be idle, then the backoff period is decremented by one time slot.

$$(BO)\ new = (BO)\ old - aSlotTime$$

$$(2)$$

If the medium is determined to be busy during backoff, then the backoff timer is suspended, meaning that the backoff period is counted in terms of idle time slots. Whenever the medium is determined to be idle for longer than an interframe space, backoff is resumed. When backoff is finished with a BO value of zero, a transfer should take place. If the node succeeded in sending a packet and receiving an acknowledgment for that packet, then the CW for this node is reset to the minimum, which is equal to 31 in the case of BEB. If the transfer fails, the node goes into another backoff period. When going for another backoff period again, the CW size is exponentially increased with a maximum of 1,023 (Zhai & Fang, 2003).

BEB has a number of disadvantages. One major disadvantage is the problem of fairness. BEB tends to prefer last contention winner and new contending nodes over other nodes when allocating channel access. This is done by choosing a random backoff value from a CW, which has a smaller size for new contending nodes and contention winners. This behavior causes what is known as the "channel capture effect" in the network. Another problem with BEB is stability. BEB has been designed to be stable for large numbers of nodes. Studies have shown that it is not.

Figure 1, CW increase in logarithmic algorithm

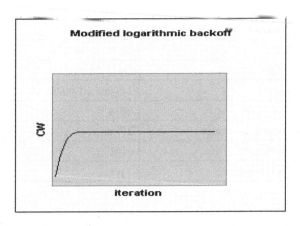

Figure 2. The logarithmic backoff algorithm.

> *Step 0:*   *set BO to initial value*
> *Step 1:*   *while BO ≠ 0 do*
>   *For each time slot*
>   *If channel is idle then BO = BO-1*
>   *If channel idle for more than IDFS then*
>   *Send*
>   *Else*
>   *BO = log(BO) * BO*
>   *Go to step 1*
> *Step 2:* *S top*

In this paper, we perform a deeper study and analysis of the logarithmic backoff algorithm proposed in a previous published work (Manaseer & Ould-Khaoua, 2005). Some additional factors, such as mobility speed of nodes, are taken into consideration. Moreover, more topologies are studied to investigate the performance of the subject algorithm.

The rest of this paper is organized as follows. The next section describes the modified logarithmic backoff algorithm. Then simulation environment and the results compared to IEEE 802.11 BEB algorithm and discussed. The paper ends with a conclusion and discussion of future work.

THE MODIFIED BACKOFF ALGORITHM

In IEEE 802.11 MAC protocol, the BEB algorithm exponentially increases the size of CW. BEB uses the following equation to increase the CW size

$$BO = (Rand () \ MOD \ CW) * aSlotTime.$$

$$(3)$$

The logarithmic backoff algorithm has used the logarithm of the current BO as the incremental factor to calculate the next backoff. The following formula is used to give this result (Manaseer & Ould-Khaoua, 2005):

Table 1. Simulation parameters

Parameter	Value
Nodes	20,40,...,100
Speeds (ms^{-1})	2,4,...,20
Area	1,000m X 1,000m
Simulation time	900 s
Transmission range	250 m
Traffic type	CBR
Packet send rate	1 p/s

$$(BO)_{new} = (\log (BO)_{old}) * (BO)_{old} * aSlotTime. \quad (4)$$

The used formula provides different outcome for backoff times, the behavior of the new formula can be seen in Figure 1. The further we go with backoff; the closer are the new values to the old values generated by the modified algorithm (Manaseer & Ould-Khaoua, 2005).

The main idea behind choosing such an equation for calculating BO is that instead of going on a backoff period for X time slots , the node goes into two consecutive backoff periods, say i_1 and i_2, where $i_1 + i_2 \approx X$, when the node is on a backoff period for a consecutive number of times. This allows the node a chance to access the channel and transmit in a way, for example, if backoff is stopped in the middle of the backoff period X (Manaseer & Ould-Khaoua, 2005).

Reducing the channel capture effect (Bensaou, Wang, & Ko, 2000) is another perspective of the new algorithm. In BEB, when a node loses in contention for channel access, there is a relatively high possibility that the next backoff timer will be double the current value; this assigns the node a higher probability of losing in the next contention against new arrivals and contention winners (Hastad, Leighton, & Rogoff, 1987). When using the logarithmic algorithm, the difference between the two backoff periods is smaller, so the chance

of losing the contention is not dramatically increased by the logarithmic algorithm. The modified algorithm also has stopped using the uniform random distribution. This, as we show in the next section, hides the effect of the incremental behavior of the CW.

SIMULATION RESULTS AND ANALYSIS

The logarithmic algorithm has been evaluated and compared against the standard BEB using the network simulator NS 2.29 (Fall & Varadhaa, 2002). The original standard MAC protocol has been modified to implement the logarithmic algorithm. Modifications have mainly targeted the mac802_11.h and mac802_11.cc files. Several topologies and mobility scenarios have been created to test the algorithm as intensively as possible.

Firstly, we have varied the total number of nodes in the network. Changing the number of nodes is used to predict the performance of our algorithm for all size networks. Simulations have been carried out for networks having a total number of nodes varying between 20 and 100 mobile nodes. Secondly, in order to address the main drawback of MANETs, we have used different values for mobility speed. Testing for speed values, ranging from 2 ms^{-1} to 20 ms^{-1},

Figure 3. Throughput of BEB versus modified algorithm

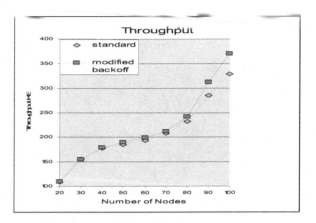

Figure 4. Throughput of two versions of the modified algorithm

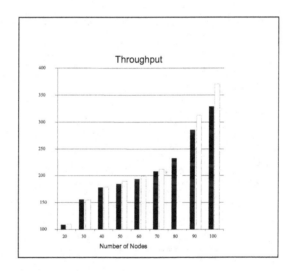

Figure 5. Throughput of the standard algorithms against the modified algorithm for different speeds

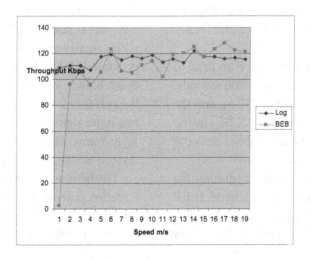

Figure 6. Dropped packets of the standard algorithms against the modified algorithm for different speeds

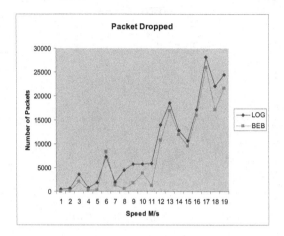

Figure 7. Throughput of the standard algorithms against the modified algorithm for different speeds

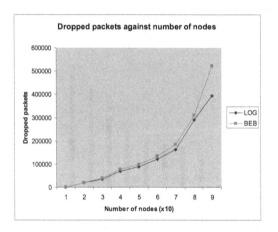

has given us useful information concerning the efficiency of our algorithm for static and highly mobile MANETs, as well.

Other simulation parameters are an area of 1,000m×1,000m, simulation time of 900 seconds, and nodes transmission range of 250 m, and the traffic generated is constant bit rate (CBR) traffic at a rate of 1 packet per second. Table 1 summarizes simulation parameters.

Figure 3 displays the results of running the modified algorithm against the standard IEEE 802.11 binary exponential backoff algorithm. The figure shows that the throughput is higher for the modified algorithm. A network with a larger number of nodes has a better throughput, than one with a small number of nodes. The reason for this is that for a larger number of nodes, contention is much higher, so it is more probable for a node to backoff for more consecutive periods. This leads to a more significant effect of the behavior of the logarithmic algorithm, and the backoff values start to be closer.

The BEB uses a uniform random number distribution generator. The random distribution used covers the effect of CW incremental behavior. The reason for excluding the random number distribu-

Figure 8. Forwarded data packets for LOG against BEB

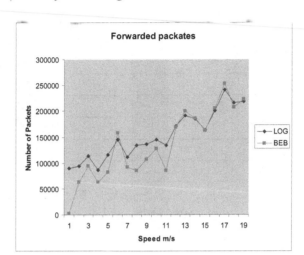

Figure 9. Average network delay for network size of 70 nodes

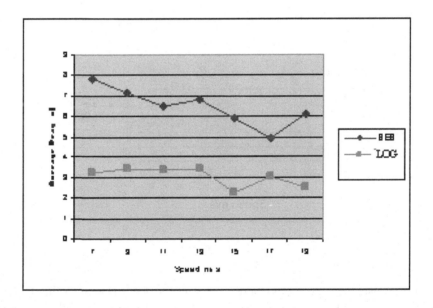

tion in our algorithm is that a formal distribution only benefits from the window size increment by 50% of the generated random values, which is useless in the case of the modified algorithm. The graph in Figure 4 shows a comparison of the same modified algorithm with another version of itself, where a random number distribution is used in the same way it is used by the standard binary exponential backoff algorithm. While

many researches try to analyze and understand the incremental behavior of a backoff algorithm, the effects of all the changes made are reduced by the random number distribution used.

Figure 5 shows that over different speeds, the exponential algorithm gives higher throughput at some speeds. But the value of the overall throughput in the network is unstable, that is, changing the speed from 4 m/s to 6 m/s, for example, increases

Figure 10. Average network delay for network size of 80 nodes

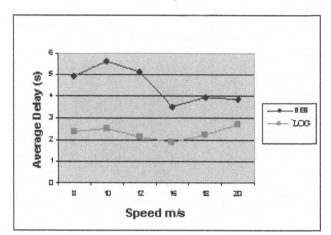

Figure 11. Average network delay for network size of 90 nodes

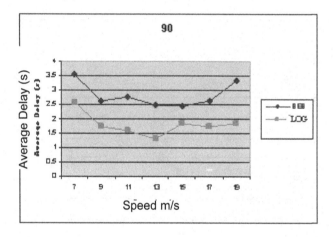

the throughput by 30%. Moreover, at speeds where BEB is accomplishing higher throughput, the difference in throughput is not of a significant value. By using the logarithmic algorithm, the maximum throughput change is 15% compared to a 45 % increment for networks using BEB.

Figure 6 is used to demonstrate that, for speeds from 7 m/s to 12 m/s, using BEB leads to less packet drops over the network. Although again the gap between the results of the two algorithms is not wide, the backoff algorithm used is not the only factor that affects the number of dropped packets; queue size is another factor, for example. Generally, the two algorithms drop approximately the same amount of data for this network topology with only 50 nodes.

Figure 7 presents evidence on the improvement the logarithmic algorithm is achieving. The results plotted in Figure 6 were obtained using only 50 nodes. As mentioned before, the logarithmic algorithm tends to achieve better results with larger networks. As shown in Figure 7, increasing the number of nodes over the network leads to less packet loss for the logarithmic algorithm.

Figure 8 shows the packet forwarding count as an indicator of node activity and channel usage. Once again, the logarithmic algorithm achieves a higher number of forwarded packets almost over all values of speed used for this experiment.

In the final part of the simulation, we studied the effect of mobility speed on average node-to-node delay. As expected, the BEB exponential increment causes longer idle time, increasing the average delay over the network. As seen in Figure 9, LOG has reduced average delays by 75%. Increasing network size leads to a larger number of CW size increments, since there are more colliding nodes. The same results are demonstrated in Figure 10.

Analyzing simulation results has shown an unpredictable behavior for BEB, when it comes to average delay. Examining the figures, results in a relatively stable performance for logarithmic algorithm. This can be seen in Figures 10 and 11. A deeper study of this observation is left for the future work of our research.

CONCLUSION AND FUTURE WORK

The BEB is used by the IEEE 802.11 MAC protocol. BEB uses uniform random distribution to choose the backoff value. In this paper, we have studied a modified logarithmic backoff algorithm, which uses logarithmic increments, instead of the exponential extension of window size to eliminate the effect of random number distribution. Results from simulations have demonstrated that the modified algorithm increased the total throughput of the MANETs, especially when the system size is large. Moreover, the tested algorithm also has shown stable network throughput over different speeds of nodes and increased packet forwarding over the network. Added to that, the logarithmic algorithm also has decreased the average node-to-node delay, especially when the system size is

large. Moreover, the same effect was observed for highly mobile networks.

One drawback of the studied algorithm is a slight increment in the number of dropped packets during simulation time. But this drawback is caused by other factors as well. Studying these factors is left for future work.

REFERENCES

Bao, L., & Garcia-Luna-Aceces, J. J. (2001). A new approach to channel access scheduling for ad hoc networks. *ACM MOBICOM*, 210-221.

Bensaou, B., Wang, Y., & Ko, C. C. (2000). Fair medium access in 802.11 based wireless ad-hoc networks. *IEEE/ACM MobiHOC, Boston, MA*.

Bharghavan, V., Demers, A., Shenker, S., & Zhang, L. (1994). MACAW: A media access protocol for wireless LAN's. In *Proceedings of the Conference on Communications Architectures, Protocols and Applications* (pp. 210-225).

Bononi, L., Budriesi, L., Blasi, D., Cacace, V., Casone, L., & Rotolo, S. (2004). A differentiated distributed coordination function MAC protocol for cluster-based wireless ad hoc networks. In *Proceedings of the 1st ACM International Workshop on Performance Evaluation of Wireless Ad Hoc, Sensor, And Ubiquitous Networks* (pp. 77-86).

Cali, F., Conti, M., & Gregori, E. (1998). IEEE 802.11 wireless LAN: Capacity analysis and protocol enhancement. In *Proceedings of INFOCOM'98, San Francisco,* (pp. 142-149).

Fall, K., & Varadhaa, K. (2002). NS notes and documentation. *The V l N l Project.* University of California-Berkeley.

Fang, Z., Bensaou, B., & Wang, Y. (2002). Performance evaluation of a fair backoff algorithm for IEEE 802.11 DFWMAC. *International Symposium on Mobile Ad Hoc Networking & Computing,* (pp. 48–57).

Goodman, J., Albert G. Madras, N., & March, P. (1985). Stability of binary exponential backoff. *Journal of the ACM, 35*(3), 579–602.

Hastad, J., Leighton, T., & Rogoff, B. (1987). Analysis of backoff protocols for multiple access channels. In *Proceedings of the Nineteenth Annual ACM Conference on Theory of Computing* (pp. 241-253).

IEEE, ANSI/IEEE Standard 802.11. (1999). *Edition (R2003), Part 11: Wireless LAN medium access control (MAC) and physical layer (PHY) specifications* (pp. 138-153)

Karn, P. (1990). MACA—A new channel access method for packet radio. *ARRL/CRRL Amateur Radio 9th Computer Networking Conference,*(pp. 134–140).

Manaseer, S., & Ould-Khaoua, M. (2005). A new backoff algorithm for MAC protocol in MANETs. *21ˢᵗ Annual UK Performance Engineering Workshop,* (pp. 159-164).

Sakakibara, K., Sasaki, M., & Yamakita, J. (2005). Backoff algorithm with release stages for slotted ALOHA systems. *ECTI Transactions on Electrical Engineering, Electronics, and Communications, 3*(1), 59-70.

Sauer, C., & Mac Nair, E. (1983). *Simulation of computer communication systems.* Prentice-Hall, Inc.

Sundaresan, K., & Sivakumar, R. (2004). A unified MAC layer framework for ad-hoc networks with smart antennas. In *Proceedings of the 5th ACM international symposium on mobile ad hoc networking and computing* (pp. 244–255).

Tobagi, F., & Kleinrock, L. (1975a). Packet switching in radio channels: Part I—Carrier sense multiple-access modes and their throughput-delay characteristics. *IEEE Transactions on Communications, 23*(12), 1400-1416.

Tobagi, F., & Kleinrock, L. (1975b). Packet switching in radio channels: Part II—The hidden terminal problem in carrier sense multiple-access and the busy-tone solution. *IEEE Transactions on Communications, 23*(12), 1417-1433.

Wu, C., & Li, V. O. (1987). Receiver-initiated busy-tone multiple access in packet radio networks. In *Proceedings of the ACM workshop on frontiers in computer communications technology* (pp. 336–342).

Xu, K., Gerla, M., & Bae, S. (2002). How effective is the IEEE 802.11 RTS/CTS handshake in ad hoc networks. *IEEE Global Telecommunications Conference, 1,* 72-76.

You, T., & Hassanein, H. (2002). Infrastructure-based MAC in wireless mobile ad-hoc networks. *27th Annual IEEE Conference on Local Computer Networks,* 821-830.

Zhai, H., & Fang, Y. (2003). Performance of wireless LANs based on IEEE 802.11 protocols. In *Proceedings of the 14ᵗʰ IEEE International Symposium on Personal, Indoor and Mobile Radio Communication,* 2586-2590.

This work was previously published in Int. Journal of Information Technology and Web Engineering, Vol 2, Issue 1, edited by G. Alkhatib and D. Rine, pp. 34-46, copyright 2007 by IGI Publishing (an imprint of IGI Global).

Chapter XIII
Secure Online DNS Dynamic Updates:
Architecture and Implementation

Xunhua Wang
James Madison University, USA

David Rine
George Mason University, USA

ABSTRACT

Domain Name System (DNS) is the system for the mapping between easily memorizable host names and their IP addresses. Due to its criticality, the Internet Engineering Task Force (IETF) has defined a DNS Security Extension (DNSSEC) to provide data-origin authentication. In this paper, we point out two drawbacks of the DNSSEC standard in its handling of DNS dynamic updates: 1) the on-line storage of a zone security key, creating a single point of attack for both inside and outside attackers, and 2) the violation of the role separation principle, which in the context of DNSSEC requires the separation of the roles of zone security managers from DNS name server administrators. To address these issues, we propose an alternative secure DNS architecture based on threshold cryptography. Unlike DNSSEC, this architecture adheres to the role separation principle without presenting any single point of attack. To show the feasibility of the proposed architecture, we developed a threshold cryptography toolkit based on the Java Cryptography Architecture (JCA) and built a proof-of-concept prototype with the toolkit. Our running results of the prototype on a representative platform show that the performance of our proposed architecture ranges from one to four times of DNSSEC's performance. Thus, through small performance overhead, our proposed architecture could achieve very high level of security.

INTRODUCTION

The Domain Name System (DNS) is a distributed database used in the Internet to map easily memorizable host names to their respective IP addresses (Mockapetris, 1987a, 1987b; Mockapetris & Dunlap, 1986, 1988, 1995).The DNS name space is organized into a hierarchy. Top-level domains include .com, .edu, .org, .biz, .info, .mil, .gov, .net, two-letter country codes like .ae and .jo (Postel, 1994). Second-level domain names typically designate individual institutions. For instance, Google Inc. is assigned a second-level domain name "google" under the top-level domain .com. In the domain name hierarchy, the subspace that is under a single administrative control is called a *zone*. In each zone, several predefined resources can be associated with a given domain name. Two example domain name resources are IP address and mail exchange server. The association of a domain name with a resource is called a *resource record* (RR). The most important RR of a domain name is the "type A" RR, which contains the host IP address of the domain name. All the RRs within a zone are stored in a *master file* to be published by the *primary name server* of that zone. Each zone also supports zero or more *secondary* name servers, which obtain RRs from the primary server. Secondary servers act as backup of the primary name server and can also reduce the workload of the primary server; they send appropriate RRs to clients in response to queries but are not involved in the maintenance of the master file.

Unfortunately, the DNS, a critical infrastructure component of the Internet, was designed without security considerations. In particular, the original DNS architecture provides no way for a client to authenticate a received RR. This loophole enables many security attacks (Bellovin, 1995; Schuba, 1993; Vixie, 1995). For example, an attacker in the middle can modify a DNS response to include a fake RR. By providing an incorrect IP address for the requested domain name (for instance, www.ebay.com), a malicious third party could cause the loss of business to the domain name owner (eBay Inc. in the example).

In response to the above concerns, the *DNS Security Extension (DNSSEC)* was developed by the Internet Engineering Task Force (IETF) (Arends, Austein, Larson, Massey, & Rose, 2005a, 2005b, 2005c). Throughout this article we use the terms IETF DNSSEC and DNSSEC interchangeably. The DNSSEC provides RR authentication by the use of digital signatures (Diffie & Hellman, 1976; Rivest, Shamir, & Adleman, 1978). With DNSSEC, each zone is equipped with a public/private key pair. Resource records of a zone with the same name are organized into RR sets (*RRset*) and the zone private key is used to digitally sign all the RRsets in that zone. For each RRset, its digital signature is stored in a newly defined resource record called *RRSIG RR*. The response to a DNS query comprises the requested RRsets and the corresponding RRSIG RR. The zone public key is disseminated through *DNSKEY RR*, a new RR defined by DNSSEC, and DNS clients use this key to verify RRSIG RRs. (Obviously, a zone's DNSKEY RR should be also authenticated and this is accomplished by a corresponding RRSIG RR by its parent zone.)

A major security goal of the DNSSEC is the *role separation* (Sandhu, Bhamidipati, & Munawer, 1999; Sandhu, Coyne, Feinstein, & Youman, 1996): It differentiates the roles of the DNS zone manager from the DNS name server administrator. In DNSSEC, it is the DNS zone manager, not the DNS name server administrator, who is responsible for the security of a zone. A DNS server is just a place to publish the digitally signed DNS zone data. With this separation, the compromise of secondary servers in a zone or even that of the primary server itself (assuming the zone private key is kept off line) will not necessarily affect the degree of assurance that a DNS client receives (Arends et al., 2005a). Role separation is consistent with the restriction idea in the design of secure systems (Saltzer & Schroeder, 1975) and meets the principle of least privilege and the principle of separation of privilege (Saltzer & Schroeder, 1975). (The principle of least privilege states that a subject should be given only those privileges that it needs to complete its task (Bishop, 2002, p. 343). The principle of separation of privilege states that a system should not grant permission based on a single condition (Bishop, 2002, p. 347).) This role separation design in DNSSEC also introduces management flexibility: it enables multiple zones to share a single DNS server to publish their zone data while each individual zone manager enforces the security of its respective zone independently. When zone data needs updating, the zone manager will digitally sign the new zone data off-line.

Motivation

The idea of keeping a zone's private key off-line and computing the signatures of RRsets off-line (Arends et al., 2005a; Eastlake, 1999a) is based on the assumption that RRs in a DNS zone are relatively static. Indeed, in some situations we can expect that the bindings between domain names and IP addresses do not change frequently. However, it has been pointed out that DNS dynamic updates, which enable real-time changes (i.e., add, delete, or update) in name/address bindings, are useful under many circumstances (Liu, 1999;Vixie, Thomson, Rekhter, & Vound, 1997). (DNS dynamic update is supported in the Berkeley Internet Name Domain [BIND] 8 and BIND 9 [Albitz & Liu, 2001].) For example, Dynamic Host Configuration Protocol (Albitz & Liu, 2001; Droms, 1997) allows one to assign IP addresses dynamically and simplifies network management. When a DHCP server authorizes a DHCP request (from a DHCP client), it changes some (name, IP address) pairs in that zone. To keep up, DNS needs to support the dynamic addition and deletion of records. For a dynamic RR update to take effect immediately and securely, the signature of the updated RRset has to be computed online. (BIND 9 name server is

capable of signing dynamically updated records on the fly.) It is worthwhile to note that although a DNS dynamic update requestor is communicating with a name server, the name server itself has no rights to update the zone data. Following the role separation principle, it is the zone private key, instead of the name server's private key, that is needed in a dynamic update.

In the earlier version of IETF's DNS dynamic update scheme (Eastlake, 1997), two modes were defined to achieve the above goal. In mode A, the zone private key is kept off-line and any dynamic requests will be authorized by a dynamic update key that is kept online. However, in this mode, since the zone private key is not kept online, "zone transfer security is not automatically provided for dynamically added RRs, where they could be omitted, and authorization is not provided for the server denial of the existence of a dynamically added type" (Eastlake, 1997). In this sense, this mode does not support genuine dynamic updates. In mode B, on the other hand, the zone private key is kept online at the zone primary name server and, thus, any legitimate DNS dynamic updates can be in effect immediately.

Both of the above modes require that a zone security related private key be kept on line at the primary name server. This practice raises security concerns (Eastlake, 1997). First, it makes the primary name server a single point of attack to both outside and inside attackers. Should the primary server be compromised, the online private key will be exposed, rendering dynamic RRs insecure in mode A or, even worse, all RRs in the entire zone insecure in mode B. Second, as an insider, the name server administrator has access to this private key, compromising the role separation principle and making it possible for the name server administrator to abuse his/her power. The latest version of IETF's dynamic update solution is defined in (Wellington, 2000), which specifies that all zone dynamic update policies are "configured by the zone administrator and enforced by the zone's primary name server." We observe that the new specification still retains the two aforementioned problems.

Our Contribution

The contribution of this article is an alternative architecture to the secure online DNS dynamic update problem. Through the introduction of zone-security servers and the application of threshold cryptography, our proposed architecture enforces the role separation principle and supports genuine, secure dynamic updates. The proposed architecture is also highly configurable, which allows it to achieve different levels of security. By giving concrete examples we show how our architecture can achieve intrusion tolerance against both outsider and insider attacks. A prototype implementation based on an Java Cryptography Architecture (JCA) extension is given to validate the proposed architecture.

The remainder of this article is organized as follows: we first give the related work and review an important building block of our solution, namely, threshold cryptography. We then present our proposed architecture and discuss the security levels that can be achieved through configurations. Next, we describe the design of a toolkit to implement our proposed architecture. A prototype is built and run to compare the performances of IETF's DNSSEC and our proposed architecture. Conclusions of this study are given in the end.

RELATED WORK

The design of the DNS system can be found in (Mockapetris, 1987a, 1987b; Mockapetris & Dunlap, 1986, 1988, 1995). Bellovin (1995) pointed out the authentication problem in DNS lookup response and explored how this flaw might be used to break into DNS-based systems

and applications. Schuba (1993) gave a detailed security analysis of the DNS system. Using the popular DNS software, Berkeley Internet Name Domain (BIND), as an example, Vixie (1995) discussed how to improve the security of various implementation aspects of DNS, such as caching. DNS dynamic updates were described in (Albitz & Liu, 2001; Vixie et al., 1997).

Arends et al. (2005a, 2005b, 2005c) described the IETF DNS security extension (DNSSEC) and defined the RRSIG RR (the resource record to store digital signature) and DNSKEY RR (the resource record to store public key). Eastlake (1999c, 2001) defined the RSA/SHA-1 RRSIGs—the RRSIG RRs implemented with SHA-1 hash algorithm (NIST, 2002) and RSA digital signature algorithm (Rivest et al., 1978)—and RSA DNSKEYs, the DNSKEY RRs to store RSA public keys. Eastlake (1999b) defined DSA DNSKEYs, the DNSKEY RRs to store DSA public keys, and DSA RRSIGs, the RRSIG RRs generated with the NIST DSA algorithm (NIST, 2000).

Secure dynamic update schemes were first proposed in (Eastlake, 1997) and then updated in (Wellington, 2000), which did not explore the details of zone private key management for DNS dynamic update. DNS dynamic updates are supported by BIND starting from version 9 (Wellington et al., 2002).

IETF also defined SIG(0) (Eastlake, 2000), a public key-based transaction level authentication mechanism, and TSIG (Vixie, Gudmundsson, Eastlake, & Wellington, 2000) a symmetric key-based transaction level authentication mechanism. Both of them can be used to authenticate the originators of DNS dynamic update requests.

Ateniese and Mangard (2001) proposed a symmetric key-based DNS security extension. In contrast, the secure dynamic update architecture of this article is proposed within the context of the public key-based DNSSEC (Arends et al., 2005a), which is more scalable.

BACKGROUND: THRESHOLD CRYPTOGRAPHY

Threshold cryptography is a branch of cryptography that enables a group of n members, 1, 2, ..., n, to act as a single communication party, using one pair of public and private keys (Desmedt, 1988, 1994, 1997). Similar to the traditional public key cryptography, the public key is known to the public. Unlike the traditional public key cryptography, the private key of the group, $K_{private}$, does not exist as a whole. Rather, each member i, $1 \le i \le n$, will be assigned ω_i key shares of the private key. Thus the total number of key shares in a threshold cryptosystem is $\sum_{i=1}^{n} \omega_i$. To perform a cryptographic computation f (such as decryption, signing, identification, etc.) on message m without reconstructing $K_{private}$, b, $(b \le n)$, or more group members will be required. Let $B = \{\pi_1, \pi_2, \dots, \pi_a\}$, $a \ge b$, $1 \le \pi_i \le n$, $1 \le i \le a$, be such a group. Each member π_i will compute a partial result $g_{\pi_i}(m, k_{\pi_i})$ where k_{π_i} is one key share owned by π_i. Subsequently, the partial results are combined to produce the final result, i.e., $f(m, K_{private}) = C_B (g_{\pi_i}(m, k_{\pi_i}), g_{\pi_2}(m, k_{\pi_2}), \dots, g_{\pi_a}(m, k_{\pi_a}))$, where C_B is the combination function. (For digital signature, this phase does not need to be performed by trusted entities.) Note that during this whole process the shared private key, $K_{private}$, is never reconstructed. Further, threshold cryptography requires that the shared private key cannot be reconstructed from any $t < b$ or less group members and any t or less group members cannot construct a valid signature by $K_{private}$ either. Thus, a threshold cryptography scheme is characterized by its underlying public-key cryptography technology, a key sharing mechanism, the number of participants, n, and t. It is worth mentioning that, given a threshold cryptography scheme, b, the number of participants in a threshold cryptographic computation, is determined by n and t. The exact relationship among b, n, and t varies from scheme to scheme. However, $b \ge t + 1$ must hold.

Research on threshold cryptography mainly concentrates on the design of threshold RSA (Desmedt, Di Crescenzo, & Burmester, 1994; Desmedt & Frankel, 1994; Frankel & Desmedt, 1992; Rabin, 1998; Shoup, 2000) and threshold DSA (Gennaro, Jarecki, Krawczyk, & Rabin, 1996b; Gennaro, Rabin, & Rabin, 1998; Langford, 1995). Threshold RSA can be used for both decryption and digital signing while threshold DSA is only used for digital signing.

For our purpose, we will use the threshold RSA primitive given in Desmedt et al. (1994), called the DDB94 primitive, for its simplicity and the threshold DSA primitive given in (Gennaro et al., 1996b; Gennaro, Jarecki, Krawczyk, & Rabin, 2001), called the GJKR96DSA primitive. (It should be noted that the original threshold DSA primitive published in Gennaro et al., 1996b, was further revised in Gennaro et al., 2001.)

- Threshold RSA. Throughout this article, N is used to denote the RSA modulus, which is the product of two primes, p and q. (N, e) and d are a pair of RSA public and private keys, respectively, such that, e and d are relatively prime to $\varphi(N) = (p-1) \times (q-1)$ and $e \times d \equiv 1 \mod \varphi(N)$. In RSA, for both decrypting and signing, $f(m, d) = m^d \mod N$.

Desmedt, Di Crescenzo, and Burmester described an elegant threshold RSA scheme in (Desmedt et al., 1994), where $b = t + 1$. A simple example of this threshold RSA scheme is the case of $n = 3$ and $t = 1$ (thus $b = 2$). Let A, B and C be the 3 members. A will be assigned a random number, d_1, B will be given 2 values, d_2 and d_3, and C will be given 2 values, d_2 and d_4, where $1 < d_i < \varphi(N)$ for $1 \le i \le 4$, $d = d_1 + d_2 \mod \varphi(N)$ and $d = d_3 + d_4 \mod \varphi(N)$. Thus, A has one key share and B and C have two key shares. Any two of them will be able to perform the cryptographic computation $f(m, d)$. For example, $f(m, d)$ can be computed by members A and B in two steps. First, A computes

$\tau_A = g_A (m, d_1) = m^{d_1} \bmod N$, and B computes $\tau_B = g_B (m, d_2) = m^{d_2} \bmod N$. Second, the partial results produced in the first step are combined to produce $\tau_A \times \tau_B \bmod N = (m^{d_1} \bmod N) \times (m^{d_2} \bmod N) = m^d \bmod N = f(m,d)$. Since C also possesses d_2, the above computation can also be performed collectively by A and C. Moreover, the above result can also be produced as $(m^{d_3} \bmod N) \times (m^{d_4} \bmod N)$, which can be performed by B and C.

- Threshold DSA. Threshold DSA is more complex than threshold RSA due to the structure of the DSA algorithm (NIST, 2000). Assume p, q and g are the DSA system parameters ($2^{159} < q < 2^{160}$, q divides $(p-1)$, $2^{511+64i} < p < 2^{512+64i}$ for some i, $0 \leq i \leq 8$, p and q are primes; g is a generator of the unique cyclic group of order q in $\mathbb{Z}_p^*$). x is the private key ($0 < x < q$) and $y = g^x \bmod p$ is the corresponding public key.

To our knowledge, the best result of threshold DSA is to have $t < n/2$ and $b = 2t + 1$ (Gennaro et al., 1996b, 2001). In the GJKR96DSA primitive, each participant is assigned a key share, x_i, $1 \leq i \leq n$, which is derived from x using the (t, n)-Shamir secret sharing scheme (Shamir, 1979). (Throughout this article, in a (t, n)-Shamir secret sharing scheme, any $(t+1)$ or more secret shares can be used to recover the shared secret while any t or less cannot. That is, $(t+1)$ is the threshold. This notation is slightly different from (Shamir, 1979) and (Stinson, 1995) where t is the threshold.) (Note that in this case, $\omega_i = 1$, $1 \leq i \leq n$). Compared to DDB94 RSA primitive, GJKR96DSA primitive is highly interactive: first, the a, $a \geq b$, participants collectively compute the (t, n)-secret shares of two random numbers u and δ, whose values are unknown to any one of them, and two $(2t, n)$-secret shares of 0 mod q. Let $(u_1, u_2, ..., u_a)$, $(\delta_1, \delta_2, ..., \delta_a)$, $(\lambda_1, \lambda_2, ..., \lambda_a)$, $(\zeta_1, \zeta_2, ..., \zeta_a)$ be the respective secret shares. Then, each participant π_i, $1 \leq i \leq a$, will compute $v_i = u_i \times \delta_i + \lambda_i \bmod q$ and $w_i = g^{\delta_i} \bmod p$. Then, μ is collectively computed from $(v_1, v_2, ..., v_a)$ using the Lagrange interpolation formula and

β is collectively computed from $(w_1, w_2, ..., w_a)$ using the Lagrange interpolation in the exponent (Gennaro et al., 2001). Let $\gamma = \beta^\mu \bmod p \bmod q$. Each participant will compute $s_i = u_i \times (m + x_i\gamma) + \zeta_i \bmod q$. In the end s is collectively computed from $(s_1, s_2, ..., s_a)$ using the Lagrange interpolation formula and s is exactly the DSA signature of m by x.

Other research on threshold cryptography can be found in (Boneh & Franklin, 1997; Catalano, Gennaro, & Halevi, 2000; Frankel, Gemmell, MacKenzie, & Yung, 1997; Frankel, MacKenzie, & Yung, 1998; Gennaro, Jarecki, Krawczyk, & Rabin, 1996a; Gilboa, 1999; MacKenzie & Reiter, 2001; Miyazaki, Sakurai, & Yung, 1999).

THE PROPOSED ARCHITECTURE

In this section, we present an architecture that supports genuine and secure DNS dynamic updates and, at the same time, separates the zone manager role and the name server administrator role. Moreover, the architecture is highly configurable to achieve intrusion tolerance against both outsider attacks and insider attacks.

The Architecture

Depicted in Figure 1 is the proposed secure DNS architecture. In our architecture, we assume that there exist n, $n \geq 2$, machines in a given DNS zone that are under the control of the zone manager, but not under the control of the name server administrators. We call these machines the *zone-security servers*. Using a threshold cryptography scheme with $n > t \geq 1$, the zone private key is shared among the n zone-security servers. Let $b > t$ be the number of zone private key shares needed in the computation of the signature of an RR. Since $b \geq 2$, any change to the zone data will need the cooperation of more than one zone-security server; the name server administrator will have no way to modify the digitally signed zone data. Thus, the role separation principle holds. Moreover, the

Figure 1. The proposed secure DNS architecture

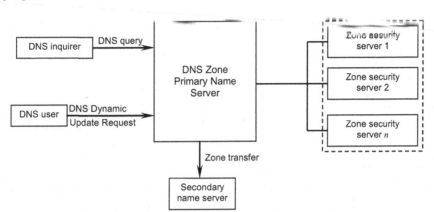

above architecture enhances intrusion tolerance of DNS (Wu, Malkin, & Boneh, 1999).

A DNS system is said to be *l-intrusion-tolerant* against an entity, E, with respect to confidentiality if breaking into *l* zone-security servers that are outside E's control will not help E gain any knowledge of the zone private key. Similarly, a DNS system is said to be *l-intrusion-tolerant* against E with respect to availability if breaking into *l* zone-security servers that are outside E's control will not help E deny the dynamic update service. Intrusion tolerance with respect to availability improves the survivability of DNS dynamic update service against both accidental failures and malicious attacks (Gennaro et al., 1996b). A DNS system is said to be *intrusion tolerant* against an outside (inside) attacker if it is at least 1-intrusion-tolerant against the outside (inside) attacker with respect to both confidentiality and availability. In our architecture, the zone private key cannot be recovered from any single location, thus, making the system intrusion tolerant against outside and inside attackers with respect to confidentiality. That is, even when an attacker manages to corrupt *l*, $l \leq t$, of relevant servers, secrecy of the zone private key is still maintained. Intrusion tolerance with respect to availability can be achieved through the selection of *n*.

Arends et al. (2005a); Eastlake (1999b, 2001) define two types of RRSIG records, the DSA RRSIG and the RSA/SHA-1 RRSIG. (RSA/MD5 RRSIG defined in (Eastlake, 1999c) was retired due to the weaknesses of the MD5 algorithm.) The DSA RRSIG uses the NIST DSA signature algorithm and the RSA/SHA-1 RRSIG uses the SHA-1 hash algorithm and the RSA digital signature algorithm. The important configuration and implementation details of our proposed architecture with respect to these two types of RRSIGs are given next.

Configurations

We now discuss the configuration of the proposed architecture, that is, the selection of *t* and *n* values:

- The value of *t*: $t > 1$ will make the DNS system intrusion tolerant against both inside and outside attackers with respect to confidentiality.
- The value of *n* (the number of group members): This value is determined by the underlying threshold cryptography algorithm. For threshold RSA, $n \geq t + 1$; to have intrusion tolerance with respect to availability,

Table 1. Example configurations in terms of t-n

Security Level	RSA/SHA-1 RRSIG		DSA RRSIG	
	1-2	1-3	1-3	1-4
Intrusion tolerant with respect to confidentiality (Y/N)	Y	Y	Y	Y
Intrusion tolerant (Y/N)	N	Y	N	Y

n should be larger than $t + 1$. For threshold DSA, however, the best known result is $n \geq 2t + 1$; to have intrusion tolerance with respect to availability, n should be larger than $2t + 1$.

In Table 1, we give the representative configurations to achieve the above security levels in different application cases. Additional details regarding these configurations are provided below. In the discussion, the n zone-security servers will be referred to as servers 1, 2, ..., n.

More Details

The DSA RRSIG

In this case, for a t-n configuration (such as the 1-3 and 1-4 configurations), the zone manager will generate n key shares of the zone private key and distribute them to the n servers using a (t, n)-Shamir secret sharing scheme (Shamir, 1979). When the zone data needs updating, $(2t + 1)$ or more servers are required to jointly compute the DSA RRSIG RR, using the GJKR96 DSA primitive described earlier in the Background section.

The RSA/SHA-1 RRSIG

Using the DDB94RSA primitive, we now discuss how the zone private key, d, is shared and how to generate a RSA/SHA-1 RRSIG RR.

- The ($t = 1, n = 2$) case. In this case, the zone manager generates a random, d_1, $1 < d_1 < \varphi(N)$, and computes d_2, $d_2 = d - d_1 \mod \varphi(N)$. Values d_1 and d_2 are sent securely to the zone-security server 1 and 2 respectively. To generate a RSA/SHA-1 RRSIG of m, where m is the SHA-1 digest of an RR (To be more precisely, m is the EMSA-PSS encoding of m. See (RSA Laboratories, 1999) for more details), these two servers will compute $m^{d_1} \mod N$ and $m^{d_2} \mod N$ respectively. Then, any one of them can combine the partial results as $m^{d_1} \times m^{d_2} \mod N = m^{d} \mod N$, the digital signature of m by the zone private key.

- The ($t = 1, n = 3$) case. This is exactly the case that we have describe in the background section where A, B, and C are the three zero security servers. One can revisit the background section for the details of key share distribution and signature generation.

IMPLEMENTATION TOOLKIT

In this section, we will describe the design of a toolkit to implement the proposed architecture. The toolkit design (Huang, Rine, & Wang, 2001) is based on the Java Cryptography Architecture.

In the literature, it has been reported that (Wu et al., 1999) implemented the DDB94 threshold RSA, in C language, and (Barak, Herzberg, Naor, & Shai, 1999) implemented the GJKR96 threshold

DSA in Java language. In DNSSEC, both RSA/SHA-1 RRSIG and DSA RRSIG are mandatory (Eastlake, 1999b, 2001) and it would be more appropriate to have a unified implementation framework for threshold RSA and threshold DSA. Such a framework should be extensible in that other threshold primitives, such as (Shoup, 2000), can be easily integrated. For this purpose, we extended the Java Cryptography Architecture (JCA) (Sun Microsystems, 2004b) to integrate threshold cryptography and, under such a framework extension, implemented two example providers, one for the DDB94 RSA primitive and the other for the GJKR96 DSA primitive.

Java Cryptography Architecture

The goal of JCA is not to provide concrete cryptography services. Instead, it aims at a framework that would allow various implementations (providers [Sun Microsystems, 2004a]) from different vendors to be plugged seamlessly into the framework and allow a JCA-based application to switch its cryptographic providers at run-time without changing its source codes. JCA achieves algorithm independence and implementation independence by adopting a 3-layer architecture: applications, the JCA framework and cryptographic providers. On the top of this 3-layer architecture are the JCA-based applications; the JCA framework sits below these applications but above a security provider. The JCA framework provides upward to applications with a uniform security interface consisting of a set of abstract classes, called engine classes, which are the abstraction of many cryptography concepts. The JCA framework also defines a downward interface, called Service Provider Interface (SPI) to which all security providers would supply the actual cryptographic service.

The JCA engine classes are included in the java.security and javax.crypto packages. We would like to explain briefly those relevant classes here. The Signature is the interface for digital signature signing and verification; Cipher represents the interface for encryption/decryption; KeyPairGenerator defines the interface to generate a public/private key pair. JCA defines two types of keys, opaque and *transparent* keys. An opaque key representation is a key in which an application has no direct access to the key material that constitutes the key; a transparent representation of keys allows an application to access each key material value individually. Key, PrivateKey and PublicKey are defined for opaque keys while KeySpec for transparent keys. The KeyFactory engine class provides the conversions between them.

The JCA Extension for Threshold Cryptography

The JCA framework extension for threshold cryptography comprises the TC primitive extension, the key share extension and other extensions.

Threshold Cryptography Primitive Extension

A cryptographic *primitive* is a basic mathematical operation on which cryptographic schemes can be built (Kaliski, 1998; RSA Laboratories, 1999). Conventional public key cryptography defines four types of primitives: encryption, decryption, signature and verification (RSA Laboratories, 1999). For example, conventional RSA has the following four primitives: RSAEP, RSADP, RSASP1 and RSAVP1 (Kaliski, 1998; RSA Laboratories, 1999). A *scheme*, on the other hand, combines cryptographic primitives and other techniques (such as the PSS-encoding; RSA Laboratories, 1999) to achieve a particular security goal.

In threshold cryptography, for an outsider, the group of users act as a single entity. Thus, the encryption and signature verification are the same as those defined in conventional public key cryptography. Decryption and signature, however, are different. Threshold cryptography introduces two new types of primitives for threshold RSA algorithm, TCRSADP and TCRSASP1, and one new type of signature primitive, TCDSASP, for threshold DSA algorithm.

Two new engine classes, TCCipher and TCSignature, are defined to introduce these services into the JCA framework. It should be noted that these definitions are abstract to all threshold cryptographic primitives rather than based on any concrete threshold primitives. TCCipher defines the generic threshold decryption operation and TCSignature defines the generic threshold signature. Unlike the JCA Cipher and Signature engine class, the TCCipher and TCSignature require more information for a threshold decryption/signature, mainly the information about the subset of the group of the entities who will participate in the threshold decryption/signature.

In correspondence with the two new engine classes, two new SPI classes, TCCipherSpi and TCSignatureSpi, are defined and they should be implemented by threshold cryptography service providers.

The Key Share Extension

In the conventional public key cryptography, there are two types of key, public key and private key. Public key remains the same in threshold cryptography. However, the (group) private key does not exist as a whole and is shared among a group of users. The sub-keys owned by the users are called *key shares*. A *key group* is defined as a collection of all key shares of a shared (group) private key. The number of key shares by a user and the form of key shares vary from primitives to primitives.

In the extension for threshold cryptography, some new interfaces and classes are introduced for key shares and key group. TCPrivateKeyShare is an interface to represent a generic key share and TCPrivateKeyGroup is an interface to a key group. TCKeyGroup is defined as the container of a public key and the corresponding TCPrivateKeyGroup.

Other Extensions

Since the key share generation process of threshold cryptography is different from the conventional public/private key pair generation process, a TCKeyGroupGenerator engine class is defined and its corresponding SPI class, TCKeyGroupGeneratorSpi, is introduced.

Two Example Providers

We now give the details of two example providers, the DDB94threshold RSA (Desmedt et al., 1994) and GJKR96threshold DSA (Gennaro et al., 1996b, 2001), which are developed under the above framework and will be used to implement the RSA/SHA-1 RRSIG and DSA RRSIG.

The DDB94 Provider

We first give the details of the DDB94 threshold RSA example provider.

The DDB94 Threshold RSA Key Share We use the Abstract Syntax Notation One (ASN.1), a standard for describing data objects (ITU, 1994), as the expression language. Formal names in ASN.1 are written without spaces, and separate words in a name are indicated by capitalizing the first letter of each word except the first word. Furthermore, we use the Distinguished Encoding Rules (DER), a widely used encoding rule in cryptographic community, to store the key shares persistently.

The DDB94 threshold RSA private key share contains the following information $\{N, e, n, t,$ key share values$\}$, which can be expressed as follows:

```
TCRSADDB94PrivateKeyShare ::=
SEQUENCE {
    version         INTEGER,
    modulus         INTEGER,      -- N
    publicExponent  INTEGER,      -- e
    groupSize       INTEGER,
    trustLimit      INTEGER       -- t
```

```
      keyId        INTEGER,
      subKeys      TCRSADDB94SubKeys
}

TCRSAD4SubKeys ::=
    SET OF TCRSADDB94SubKey

TCRSADDB94SubKey ::= SEQUENCE {
    subKeyValue INTEGER,
    keyshareList TCRSADDB94List
}

TCRSADDB94DDB94List ::=
    SEQUENCE OF DDB94BasicList

DDB94BasicList ::= SEQUENCE {
    start INTEGER,
    end INTEGER
}
```

The framework SPI implementation The example DDB94 provider has the following SPI concrete classes:

- TCRSADDB94Cipher extends TCCipherSpi and implements the DDB94 threshold RSA algorithm. It is used in the DDB94 threshold decryption and in the DDB94 threshold co-signing as well.
- TCRSADDB94Signature extends TCSignatureSpi and provides the DDB94 threshold signature service.
- TCRSADDB94KeyGroupGenerator is defined to extend TCKeyGroupGeneratorSpi and used to generate key shares using the DDB94 algorithm.
- TCRSADDB94PrivateKeyGroup extends TCPrivateKeyGroup and houses a collection of TCRSADDB94PrivateKeyShares defined earlier in this section.
- TCRSADDB94KeyFactory extends the KeyFactorySpi class.

The GJKR96 Threshold DSA Provider

The GJKR96DSA provider implements the GJKR96 threshold DSA algorithm and can only be used for threshold signature.

The GJKR96 Threshold DSA KeyShare The GJKR96 threshold DSA key share contains the following information $\{p, q, g, y, n, t, x_i\}$ whose ASN.1 format is as follows:

```
GJKR96DSAPrivateKeyShare := SEQUENCE {
    version     INTEGER,
    p           INTEGER,
    q           INTEGER,
    g           INTEGER,
    groupSize   INTEGER,
    trustLimit  INTEGER,
    keyId       INTEGER,    -- the ID of this key
share
    subKey   INTEGER        -- x_i,the key share
}
```

The GJKR96 Framework SPI Implementation The GJKR96 provider has the following concrete classes to implement the SPI interface:

- GJKR96DSA extends TCSignatureSpi and provides the GJKR96 threshold DSA signature service.
- GJKR96DSAKeyGroupGenerator is defined to extend TCKeyGroupGeneratorSpi and used to generate key shares using the GJKR96 DSA algorithm.
- GJKR96DSAPrivateKeyGroup extends TCPrivateKeyGroup and houses a collection of GJKR96DSAPrivateKeyShares defined in earlier in this section.
- GJKR96DSAKeyFactory extends the KeyFactorySpi class.

EXPERIMENTAL RESULTS

Using the toolkit described in the last section, we implemented the proposed architecture on a platform that comprised several Sun Sparc workstations (with dual CPUs of 360 MHz or 450MHz) running SunOS 5.9. A 10Mbps local area network link with less than 1 ms round-trip time connected the machines.

There are several goals for our experimentation. First, we would like to compare the performance of our proposed architecture with the IETF DNSSEC. Second, we want to investigate the performance impact of the distributed computing introduced in our proposed architecture. Third, for our proposed architecture we would like to get some indicative data on the performance impact of t and key size.

In our experimentation, for both RSA/SHA-1 RRSIG and DSA RRSIG, we tested the (t, n) combinations given in Table 1, that is, (t, n) as (1, 3) and (2, 4) for RSA/SHA-1 RRSIG and (t, n) as (1, 4) and (2, 6) for DSA RRSIG. For each (t, n) combination of the RSA/SHA-1 RRSIG, we tested two cases, one for 1024-bit (the size of N) RSA key and the other for 2048-bit RSA key. For each (t, n) combination of the DSA RRSIG, we also tested two cases, one with 512-bit (the size of p) DSA key and the other for 1024-bit DSA key. To make the results more comparable, for the cases of same key size, the same public/private keys are used for various (t, n) combinations.

Some Implementation Details

We note that the timing data depend on both the threshold cryptography primitives and our computing platform. In this regard some implementation details are given before we present the performance data.

The DDB94 Provider

- Compared to conventional RSA digital signature, Chinese Remainder Theorem (CRT), which makes conventional RSA digital signature four time faster (Koc, 1994; Quisquater & Couvreur, 1982), is not applicable in the DDB94 threshold RSA anymore. This is due to the fact that p and q do not exist as a whole any longer. This alone will make our RSA/SHA-1 RRSIG computation four times slower.
- The parallel computation. In our DDB94 example provider implementation, after send-

ing out the message to be digitally signed, the combiner performs its local computation, then waits for responses (partial results) from other participating servers and, in the end, combines all received partial results into the final result. This sequence will maximize the parallel computation between the combiner and other servers.

- Message size. For the case of 1024-bit RSA key, the size of a message (either a request or a response) sent between the combiner and a DDB94 distributed server is about 192 bytes. It is about 322 bytes for 2048-bit RSA keys.

The GJKR96 Provider

- The parallel computation. To maximize the parallel computation of the distributed servers, the GJKR96 DSA distributed servers start the local computation of the two Joint-Shamir-RSSs and two Joint-Shamir-ZSSs (Gennaro et al., 2001) once they receive the initial message from the combiner. This strategy significantly improves the computational parallelism. Indeed, most of the steps in GJKR96 DSA can be precomputed, which is not implemented in our experimentation (see the Performance Discussion section for more details).
- The number of messages. To reduce the number of messages exchanged between the distributed servers, the two Joint-Shamir-RSSs and two Joint-Zero-ZSSs are executed in batch. The values of v_i and w_i are also exchanged in a single message.

Performance Comparison over LAN

Table 2 gives the performance data of our proposed architecture in a local area network (LAN), where the round trip time for an IP packet between the zone-security servers is less than 1 millisecond.

Table 2. Experimental results (time in milliseconds)

Key Size (bits)	RSA/SHA1 RRSIG				DSA RRSIG			
	1024		2048		512		1024	
(t, n)	(1, 3)	(2, 4)	(1, 3)	(2, 4)	(1, 4)	(2, 6)	(1, 4)	(2, 6)
Our architecture over LAN	565.0	610.2	4265.5	4280.2	100.4	162.4	315.3	447.0
DNSSEC [Non CRT] (CRT)	[559.4] (160.5)		[4220.9] (1126.9)		31.1		101.7	

For comparison, it also gives the time to compute a RSA/SHA-1 RRSIG and DSA RRSIG on one machine under the same condition, using or not using Chinese Remainder Theorem (CRT).

From Table 2 one can observe that, compared to the IETF DNSSEC without CRT, our proposed architecture almost has the same performance. This can be explained in that the only additional overhead of our proposed architecture in terms of time is the communications among the servers, which is largely negligible in DDB94 RSA since the zone-security servers compute in parallel. However, since CRT is not applicable in our proposed architecture, its performance is about four times slower than the IETF DNSSEC with CRT.

For DSA RRSIG, our approach without precomputation is considerably costlier than the IETF DNSSEC DSA. (See the Performance Discussion section on how to use precomputation to speed up the DSA RRSIG computation in our proposed architecture.) When (t, n) = (1, 4), it is about three times slower than the IETF DNSSEC and, for the case of (t, n) = (2, 6) it is four times slower.

However, it is our belief that the high security level of our approach outweighs its performance penalty, especially in critical DNS zones, such as the .com zone.

Performance Comparison over the Internet

In some cases where high-level security is required, the zone-security servers may be geo-graphically distributed (for example, to survive military strikes). Therefore, it is meaningful to investigate the impact of the communication latency on the performance of our proposed architecture. For this purpose, artificial delays—deliberate delays introduced at each zone-security server at the places where messages are sent out—are introduced to simulate the network communication latency. In our experimentation, the following artificial delays, {0, 50, 100, 200, 300, 400, 500} milliseconds, are used.

Shown in Figure 2 is the performance of the RSA/SHA-1 RRSIG, implemented with the DDB94 algorithm, under various communication delays. In this figure four horizontal lines are drawn to represent the IETF DNSSEC RSA/SHA-1 performances which do not depend on communication delays. From it we can see that, in our proposed architecture, key size dominates t and the communication latency. When *t* increases, the performance does degrade but not at a significant level.

Shown in Figure 3 is the performance of the DSA RRSIG implemented with the GJKR96 algorithm. In this figure two horizontal lines are drawn to represent the IETF DNSSEC DSA performances which do not depend on communication delays. In our proposed architecture, the DSA RRSIG is highly sensitive to the communication latency and the performance degrades significantly when the communication latency increases.

Figure 2. Performance of RSA/SHA-1 RRSIG Using DDB94 (experiments denoted by (t, n)-key size)

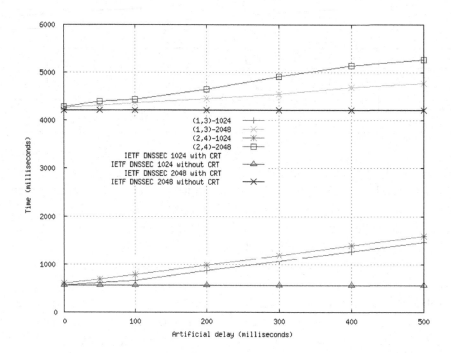

Figure 3. Performance of DSA RRSIG Using GJKR96 Without Precomputation (experiments denoted by (t, n)-key size)

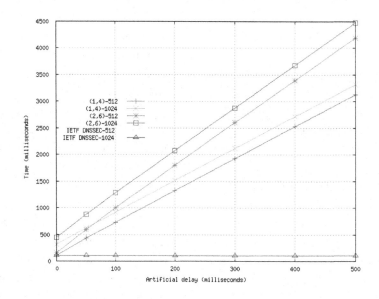

Performance Discussion

The above experimentation results have shown that the RSA/SHA-1 RRSIG performance of our proposed architecture is almost the same as that of the DNSSEC RSA/SHA-1 RRSIG without CRT and about four times of the DNSSEC RSA/SHA-1 RRSIG performance with CRT.

For DSA RRSIG, our proposed architecture's performance can be significantly improved through precomputation. Note that, in GJKR96DSA, the first steps through the generation of γ, which are the most time-consuming steps, are message independent and can be precomputed. This precomputation will make the performance of our proposed architecture in LAN almost the same as DNSSEC DSA RRSIG. It will also reduce the impact of the communication latency on our proposed architecture in the case of wide area network.

We also notice that, for small t, through some storages (to store values $w_i w_j$, $w_i w_j w_k$, ..., $\prod_{j \in \Gamma} w_j$ where Γ is the participant set and $i, j, k \in \Gamma$), the computation of Exp-Interpolate (the Lagrange interpolation in the exponent) of the GJKR96 algorithm can be performed in a single modulo exponentiation, as opposed to the $(t + 1)$ modulo exponentiations noted in (Gennaro et al., 2001).

CONCLUSION AND FUTURE RESEARCH

We have proposed an architecture in which genuine, secure DNS dynamic update is supported and the role separation of the zone manager and the name server administrator holds. The proposed architecture can be configured to achieve intrusion tolerance. Implementation details and experimental results about the DSA RRSIG and RSA/SHA-1 RRSIG are given. A JCA-based toolkit has been developed for validating the proposed architecture. Our running results of this toolkit on a representative platform show that the performance of our proposed architecture ranges from one to four times of the DNSSEC performance. Hence, through small performance overhead, our proposed architecture could achieve very high level of security.

In our performance comparison study, we measured the running time of our toolkit on a representative platform. It constitutes one of our future research topics to develop more rigorous standard-oriented benchmark test suites for DNS dynamic updates and use them to assess the performance of our proposed architecture.

ACKNOWLEDGMENT

Part of this work was done while the first author was taking Yvo Desmedt's Network security course at University of Wisconsin–Milwaukee. We would like to thank Yih Huang for the discussions and for reviewing the early draft of this article.

REFERENCES

Albitz, P., & Liu, C. (2001). *DNS and BIND* (4th ed.). O'Reilly & Associates.

Arends, R., Austein, R., Larson, M., Massey, D., & Rose, S. (2005a). *DNS security introduction and requirements*. Internet RFC 4033.

Arends, R., Austein, R., Larson, M., Massey, D., & Rose, S. (2005b). *Protocol modifications for the DNS security extensions*. Internet Request for Comments (RFC) 4035.

Arends, R., Austein, R., Larson, M., Massey, D., & Rose, S. (2005c). *Resource records for the DNS security extensions*. Internet RFC 4034.

Ateniese, G., & Mangard, S. (2001). A new approach to DNS security (DNSSEC). In *Proceedings of the Eighth ACM Conference on Computer and Communications Security* (pp. 86-95). New York: ACM Press.

Barak, B., Herzberg, A., Naor, D., & Shai, E. (1999). The proactive security toolkit and applications. In *Proceedings of the Sixth ACM Conference on Computer and Communications Security* (pp. 18-27).

Bellovin, S. M. (1995). Using domain name system for system break-ins. In *Proceedings of theFifth Usenix UNIX Security Symposium*. Salt Lake City, UT.

Bishop, M. (2002). *Computer security: Art and science*. Addison-Wesley.

Boneh, D., & Franklin, M. (1997). Efficient generation of shared RSA keys. In *Proceedings of the Advances in Cryptology (Crypto '97)* (pp. 425-439).

Catalano, D., Gennaro, R., & Halevi, S. (2000). Computing inverses over a shared secret modulus. In Proceedings of *Advance in Cryptology (Eurocrypt 2000)* (pp. 190-206).

Desmedt, Y. (1988). Society and group oriented cryptography: A new concept. In *Proceedings of Advances in Cryptology (Crypto '87)* (pp. 120-127).

Desmedt, Y. (1994). Threshold cryptography. *European Trans. on Telecommunications, 5*(4), 449-457.

Desmedt, Y. (1997). Some recent research aspects of threshold cryptography. In *Information security* (pp. 158-173).

Desmedt, Y., Di Crescenzo, G., & Burmester, M. (1994). Multiplicative nonabelian sharing schemes and their application to threshold cryptography. In *Proceedings of Advances in Cryptology (Asiacrypt '94)* (pp. 21-32).

Desmedt, Y. G., & Frankel, Y. (1994). Homomorphic zero-knowledge threshold schemes over any finite abelian group. *SIAM Journal on Discrete Mathematics, 7*(4), 667-679.

Diffie, W., & Hellman, M. E. (1976). New directions in cryptography. *IEEE Transactions on Information Theory, 22*(6), 644-654.

Droms, R. (1997). *Dynamic host configuration protocol*. Internet RFC 2131.

Eastlake, D. (1997). *Secure domain name system dynamic update*. Internet RFC 2137.

Eastlake, D. (1999a). *DNS security operational considerations*. Internet RFC 2541.

Eastlake, D. (1999b). *DSA KEYs and SIGs in the domain name system (DNS)*. RFC 2536.

Eastlake, D. (1999c). *RSA/MD5 KEYs and SIGs in the domain name system (DNS)*. Internet RFC 2537.

Eastlake D. (2000). *DNS request and transaction signatures (SIG(0)s)*. Internet RFC 2931

Eastlake, D. (2001). *RSA/SHA-1 SIGs and RSA KEYs in the domain name system (DNS)*. IETF Internet RFC 3110.

Frankel, Y., & Desmedt, Y. (1992). *Parallel reliable threshold multisignature* (Tech. Rep. Nos. TR–92–04–02). Milwaukee: University of Wisconsin–Milwaukee, Deptartment of EE & CS.

Frankel, Y., Gemmell, P., MacKenzie, P. D., & Yung, M. (1997). Proactive RSA. In *Advances in Cryptology (Crypto '97)* (pp. 440-454).

Frankel, Y., MacKenzie, P. D., & Yung, M. (1998). Robust efficient distributed RSA-key generation. In *Proceedings of the 30th Annual ACM Symposium on Theory of Computing* (pp. 663-672). Dallas, TX.

Gennaro, R., Jarecki, S., Krawczyk, H., & Rabin, T. (1996a). Robust and efficient sharing of RSA functions. In *Advances in Cryptology (Crypto '96)* (pp. 157-172).

Gennaro, R., Jarecki, S., Krawczyk, H., & Rabin, T. (1996b). Robust threshold DSS signatures. In *Advances in Cryptology (Eurocrypt '96)* (pp. 354-371).

Gennaro, R., Jarecki, S., Krawczyk, H., & Rabin, T. (2001). Robust threshold DSS signatures. *Information and Computation, 164*(1), 54-84.

Gennaro, R., Rabin, M. O., & Rabin, T. (1998). Simplified VSS and fast-track multiparty computations with applications to threshold cryptography. In *Proceedings of the 17th annual ACM symposium on Principles of Distributed Computing* (pp. 101-111).

Gilboa, N. (1999). Two party RSA key generation. In *Advances in Cryptology (Crypto'99)* (pp. 116-129). Santa Barbara, CA:

Huang, Y., Rine, D., & Wang, X. (2001). A JCA-based implementation framework for threshold cryptography. In *Proceedings of the 17th Annual Computer Security Applications Conference* (pp. 85-91). New Orleans, LA: IEEE Computer Society Press.

ITU. (1994). *Information technology – abstract syntax notation one (ASN.1) – specification of basic notation* (ITU–Telecommunication Standardization Sector, Recommendation X.680).

Kaliski, B. S., Jr. (1998). Emerging standards for public-key cryptography. In *Lectures on Data Security* (pp. 87-104). Springer.

Koc, C. K. (1994). *High-speed RSA implementation* (Tech. Rep.). RSA Laboratories.

Langford, S. K. (1995). Threshold DSS signatures without a trusted party. In *Proceedings of Advances in Cryptology (Crypto '95)* (pp. 397-409).

Laurie, B., Sisson, G., Arends, R., & Blacka, D. (2006). *DNSSEC hashed authenticated denial of existence*. Retrieved from IETF Internet-Draft draft-ietf-dnsext-nsec3-08

Liu, C. (1999). *Securing an Internet name server*. Retrieved from http://www.acmebw.com/papers/securing.pdf

MacKenzie, P., & Reiter, M. (2001). Two-party generation of DSA signatures (Extended abstract). In *Proceedings of Advance in Cryptology (Eurocrypt 2001)* (pp. 137-154).

Miyazaki, S., Sakurai, K., & Yung, M. (1999). On threshold RSA-signing with no dealer. In *Proceedings of the Second International Conference on Information Security and Cryptology (ICISC'99)* (pp. 197-207). Seoul, Korea: Springer.

Mockapetris, P. (1987a). *Domain names—Concepts and facilities*. Internet RFC 1034.

Mockapetris, P. (1987b). *Domain names—Implementation and specification*. Internet RFC 1035.

Mockapetris, P., & Dunlap, K. (1986). Implementation of the domain name system. In *Proceedings of the ACM SIGOPS European Workshop on Making Distributed Systems Work* (pp. 1-2). Amsterdam, The Netherlands:

Mockapetris, P., & Dunlap, K. J. (1988). Development of the domain name system. *ACM SIGCOMM Computer Communication Review, 18*(4), 123-133.

Mockapetris, P. V., & Dunlap, K. J. (1995). Development of the domain name system. *ACM SIGCOMM Computer Communication Review, 25*(1), 112-122.

NIST. (2000). *Digital signature standard (DSS)*. FIPS 186–2.

NIST. (2002). *Secure hash standard (SHS)*. FIPS 180–2.

Postel, J. (1994). *Domain name system structure and delegation*. Internet RFC 1591.

Quisquater, J.-J., & Couvreur, C. (1982). Fast decipherment algorithm for RSA public-key cryptosystem. *Electronic Letters, 18*(21), 905-907.

Rabin, T. (1998). A simplified approach to threshold and proactive RSA. In *Proceedings of Advances in Cryptology (Crypto'98)* (pp. 89-104).

Rivest, R., Shamir, A., & Adleman, L. (1978). A method for obtaining digital signature and public key cryptosystems. *Communications of the ACM, 21*(2), 120-126.

RSA Laboratories. (1999). *PKCS #1 v2.1: RSA cryptography standard.*

Saltzer, J., & Schroeder, M. (1975). The protection of information in computer systems. *Proceedings of the IEEE, 23*(9), 1278-1308.

Sandhu, R., Bellare, M., & Ganesan, R. (2002). Password enabled PKI: Virtual smartcards vs. virtual soft tokens. In *Proceedings of the First Annual PKI Research Workshop* (pp. 89-96).

Sandhu, R., Bhamidipati, V., & Munawer, Q. (1999). The ARBAC97model for role-based administration of roles. *ACM Transactions on Information and Systems Security, 2*(1), 105-135.

Sandhu, R., Coyne, E., Feinstein, H., & Youman, C. (1996). Role-based access control models. *IEEE Computer, 29*(2), 38-47.

Schuba, C. (1993). *Addressing weaknesses in the domain name system protocol.* Unpublished master's thesis, Purdue University, West Lafayette, IN.

Shamir, A. (1979). How to share a secret. *Communications of the ACM, 22*(11), 612-613.

Shoup, V. (2000). Practical threshold signatures. In *Proceedings of Advance in Cryptology (Eurocrypt 2000)* (pp. 207-220).

Stinson, D. R. (1995). *Cryptography: Theory and practice.* Boca Raton, FL: CRC.

Sun Microsystems. (2004a). *How to implement a provider for the Java cryptography architecture.*

Retrieved from http://java.sun.com/j2se/1.5.0/docs/guide/security/HowToImplAProvider.html

Sun Microsystems. (2004b). *Java cryptography architecture API specification & reference.* Retrieved from http://java.sun.com/j2se/1.5.0/docs/guide/security/CryptoSpec.html

Vixie, P. (1995). DNS and BIND security issues. In *Proceedings of the Fifth Usenix Security Symposium.* Salt Lake City, UT.

Vixie, P., Gudmundsson, O., Eastlake, D., III, & Wellington, B. (2000). *Secret key transaction authentication for DNS (TSIG).* Internet RFC 2845.

Vixie, P., Thomson, S., Rekhter, Y., & Vound, J. (1997). *Dynamic update in the domain name systems (DNS update).* Internet RFC 2136.

Wang, X., Huang, Y., Desmedt, Y., & Rine, D. (2000). Enabling secure online DNS dynamic update. In *Proceedings of the 16th Annual Computer Security Applications Conference* (pp. 52-58). New Orleans, LA: IEEE Computer Society Press.

Wellington, B. (2000). *Secure domain name system (DNS) dynamic update.* Internet RFC 3007.

Wellington, B., Massey, D., Blacka, D., Lewis, E., Akkerhuis, J., Schlyter, J., et al. (2002). *Secure dynamic DNS howto.* Retrieved from http://ops.ietf.org/dns/dynupd/secure-ddns-howto.html

Wu, T., Malkin, M., & Boneh, D. (1999). Building intrusion tolerant applications. In *Proceedings of the Eighth Usenix Security Symposium* (pp. 79-91).

This work was previously published in Int. Journal of Information Technology and Web Engineering, Vol 2, Issue 3, edited by L. Zhang, pp. 17-36, copyright 2007 by IGI Publishing (an imprint of IGI Global).

Chapter XIV
FSR Evaluation Using the Suboptimal Operational Values

Osama H S Khader
The Islamic University of Gaza, Palestine

ABSTRACT

In mobile ad hoc networks, routing protocols are becoming more complicated and problematic. Routing in mobile ad hoc networks is multi-hop because of the limited communication range of wireless radios. Since nodes in the network can move freely and randomly, an efficient routing protocol is needed in order for such networks to be able to perform well in such an environment. In this environment the routing strategy is applied such that it is flexible enough to handle large populations and mobility and be able to minimize the use of the battery. Also it should be designed to achieve maximum packet delivery ratio. Further more, the routing protocol must perform well in terms of fast convergence, low routing delay, and low control overhead traffic. In this paper an improved implementation of the Fisheye State Routing (FSR) protocols is presented, where a new selection routing criteria that utilizes a minimum number of hops is a selection metric. The results obtained from simulation indicate that the fewer number of hops used the better and more efficient the output for packet delivery ratio was generated

INTRODUCTION

A mobile ad-hoc network is a collection of mobile nodes with no pre-established infrastructure. Each of the nodes has a wireless interface and communicates with others over radio frequency (RF). Laptop computers and personal digital assistants that communicate directly with each other are some examples of nodes in an ad-hoc network. Nodes in the ad-hoc network are often mobile but also can consist of stationary nodes. An ad-hoc network uses no centralized administration. This ensures that the network will not cease functioning just because one of the mobile nodes moves out of the range of the others. Nodes should be able to enter and leave the network as they wish. Ad hoc networks are often characterized by a dynamic topology, due to the fact that nodes change their physical location by moving around. Another characteristic is that a node has limited central processing unit (CPU) capacity, storage capacity, battery power, and bandwidth. This means that power usage must be limited, leading to a limited transmitter range. Every node in an ad hoc network must be willing to forward packets for other nodes. Thus every node acts both as a host and as a router. The topology of ad-hoc networks varies with time as nodes move, join, or leave the network. This topological instability requires a routing protocol to run on each node to create and maintain routes among the nodes.

The rest of the article is organized as follows. A survey of most existing wireless routing protocols is given in the MANET Routing Protocols section The next section describes the FSR protocol. This followed by the performance results section. The last two sections are the conclusion and future work.

MANET ROUTING PROTOCOLS

Existing wireless routing schemes can be classified into four categories: (a) distance vector based, (b) link state (LS) based, (c) on-demand based, and (d) location based. Historically, the first type of routing scheme used in early packet networks, such as the ARPANET, was the distance vector type. The main advantages of the distance vector approach are simplicity and computation efficiency. However, this approach suffers from slow convergence and a tendency to create routing loops. While several approaches were proposed that solve the looping problem (Murthy & Garcia-Luna Aceves, 1996; Bhagwat, 1994). None of them overcome the problem of slow convergence. The solutions to both convergence and looping come in the form of the LS approach. LS is the

preferred scheme for wired nets. In LS, global network topology information is maintained in all routers by the periodic flooding of LS updates by each node. Any link change triggers an immediate update. As a result, the time required for a router to converge to the new topology is much less than in the distance vector approach. Due to global topology knowledge, preventing a routing loop is also easier.

Unfortunately, as LS relies on flooding to disseminate the update information, excessive control overhead may be generated, especially when mobility is high and frequent updates are triggered. In addition, the small update packets make for inefficient use of the wireless medium access control (MAC) layer. When mobile ad hoc network (MANET) size and mobility increase (beyond certain thresholds), current proactive routing schemes (i.e., the distance vector and LS) become infeasible, since they will consume a large part of network capacity and node processing power to transmit update control messages just to keep up with the topology changes. The most recent addition to the family are the on-demand routing schemes. These have been specifically introduced in order to overcome some limitations of the proactive protocols in mobile environments. Examples include ad hoc on-demand deistance vector by Perkins and Royer (1999), temporally ordered routing algorithm by Park and Corson (1997), and dynamic source routing by Zhong and Yuan (2003). The basic idea behind these reactive protocols is that a node discovers a route in an "on demand." It computes a route only when needed. In on-demand schemes, query/response packets are used to discover (possibly more than) one route to a given destination. These control packets are usually smaller than the control packets used for routing table updates in proactive schemes, causing less overhead. However, since a route has to be entirely discovered prior to the actual data packet transmission, the initial search latency may degrade the performance of interactive applications (e.g., distributed database queries).

Moreover, it is impossible to know in advance the quality of the path (e g , bandwidth, delay, etc.) prior to call setup. Such a priori knowledge is very desirable in multimedia applications, since it enables more effective call acceptance control. If the route breaks down because of mobility, a packet may need multiple route discoveries on the way to destination. Since flooding is used for query dissemination and route maintenance, on-demand routing tends to become inefficient when traffic load and mobility are high and network size grows large. A recent proposal that combines on-demand routing and conventional routing is zone routing protocol (ZRP) (Haas, 1997; Pearlman, 2000). For routing operations inside a local zone, an arbitrary proactive routing scheme (e.g., distance vector) can be applied. For interzone routing, on-demand routing is used. The advantage of zone routing is its scalability, as "global" routing table overhead is limited by zone size. Yet, the benefits of global routing are preserved within each zone. The performance of ZRP is dependent on a key parameter: the zone radius. The choice of radius is determined by network characteristics (e.g., node density, relative node velocity, etc.), which dynamically change in MANET.

Moreover the inter-one route discovery packets may loop back into zones already queried. This must be avoided to prevent overhead, which can be potentially worse than for flooding based queries. The advent of (GPS) global positioning system has made it possible to provided reliable and accurate information for the nodes mobility. For example (Kaplan,1996) has proposed a routing protocol based in this technology (GPS). With the knowledge of node position, routing can be more effective at the cost of overhead that is required to exchange location information. They broadcast to the nodes in the direction of the destination using only location information stored at the sender.

FSR

Topology Representation in FSR

The MANET is modeled as an undirected graph $G = (V, E)$, where V is a set of $|V|$ nodes and E is a set of $|E|$ undirected links connecting nodes in V. Each node has a unique identifier and represents a mobile host with a wireless communication device with transmission range R and large storage space. Nodes may move around and change their speed and direction independently. An undirected link (i, j) connecting two nodes i and j is formed, when the distance between i and j becomes less than or equal to R. Link (i, j) is removed from E, when node i and j move apart and out of their transmission ranges.

In the FSR routing implementation, for each node i, one list and three tables are maintained. They are: a neighbor list A_i, a topology table TT_i, a next hop table $NEXT_i$, and a distance table D_i. A_i is defined as a set of nodes that are adjacent to node i. Each destination j has an entry in table TT_i that contains two parts: $TT_i.LS(j)$ and $TT_i.SEQ(j)$. $TT_i.LS(j)$ denotes the LS information reported by node j. $TT_i.SEQ(j)$ denotes the time stamp indicating the time node j has generated this LS information . Similar, for every destination j, $NEXT_i(j)$ denotes the next hop to forward packets destined to j on the shortest path, while $D_i(j)$ denotes the distance of the shortest path from i to j.

Description of FSR Protocol

FSR is an implicit hierarchical routing protocol. It uses the "fisheye" technique proposed by Kleinrock and Stevens (1971), where the technique was used to reduce the eye of a fish captures with high detail the pixels near the focal point. The detail decreases as the distance from the focal point increases. In routing, the fisheye approach translates to maintaining accurate distance and path quality

Figure 1. Scope of fisheye

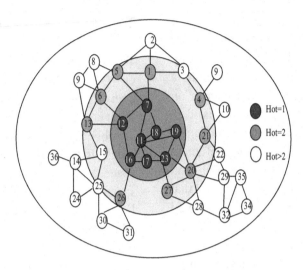

Figure 2. Message reduction using fisheye

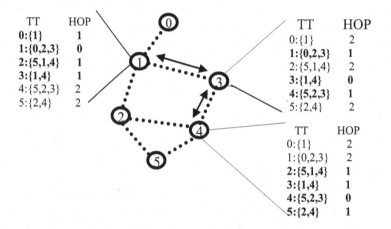

information about the immediate neighborhood of a node, with progressively less detail as the distance increases. FSR is functionally similar to LS routing in that it maintains a topology map at each node. The key difference is the way in which routing information is disseminated. In LS, LS packets are generated and flooded into the network whenever a node detects a topology change. In FSR, LS packets are not flooded. Instead, nodes maintain a LS table based on the up-to-date information received from neighboring nodes, and periodically exchange it with their local neighbors only (no flooding). Through this exchange process, the table entries with larger sequence numbers replace the ones with smaller sequence numbers. The FSR periodic table exchange resembles the vector exchange in a distributed Bellman-Ford (DBF) (or, more precisely, destinaion-sequenced distance vector[DSDV]), where the distances are updated according to the time stamp or sequence number assigned by the node originating the update. However, in FSR , LSs rather than distance vectors are propagated. Moreover, like in LS, a full topology map is kept at each node and shortest paths are computed using this map.

In a wireless environment, a radio link between mobile nodes may experience frequent disconnects and reconnects. The LS protocol releases a LS update for each such change, which floods the network and causes excessive overhead. FSR avoids this problem by using periodic, instead of event driven, exchange of the topology map, greatly reducing the control message overhead. When network size grows large, the update message could consume a considerable amount of bandwidth, which depends on the update period. In order to reduce the size of update messages without seriously affecting routing accuracy, FSR uses the fisheye technique. Figure 1 illustrates the application of fisheye in MANET. The circles with different shades of grey define the fisheye scopes with respect to the center node (node 11). The scope is defined as the set of nodes that can be reached within a given number of hops. In our case, three scopes are shown for 1, 2, and > 2 hops, respectively. Nodes are color coded as black, gray, and white, accordingly. The number of levels and the radius of each scope will depend on the size of the network.

The reduction of routing update overhead is obtained by using different exchange periods for different entries in the routing table. More precisely, entries corresponding to nodes within the smaller scope are propagated to the neighbors with the highest frequency.

In Figure 2, entries in bold are exchanged most frequently. The rest of the entries are sent out at a lower frequency. As a result, a considerable fraction of LS entries are suppressed in a typical update, thus reducing the message size.

This strategy produces timely updates from near stations, but creates large latencies from stations afar. However the imprecise knowledge of the best path to a distant destination is compensated by the fact that the route becomes progressively more accurate as the packet gets closer to destination. As the network size grows large, a "graded" frequency update plan must be used across multiple scopes to keep the overhead low.

The FSR concept originates from global state routing (GSR) (Iwata, Chiang, Pei, Gerla, & Chen, 2000). GSR can be viewed as a special case of FSR, in which there is only one fisheye scope level, and the radius is ∞. As a result, the entire topology table is exchanged among neighbors. Clearly, this consumes a considerable amount of bandwidth when network size becomes large. Through updating LS information with different frequencies, depending on the scope distance, FSR scales well to large-sized networks and keeps overhead low, without compromising route computation accuracy when the destination is near.

By retaining a routing entry for each destination, FSR avoids the extra work of "finding" the destination (as in on-demand routing) and, thus, maintains low single packet transmission latency. As mobility increases, routes to remote destinations become less accurate. However, when a packet approaches its destination, it finds increasingly accurate routing instructions as it enters sectors with a higher refresh rate.

PERFORMANCE EVALUATION OF ROUTING SELECTION CRITERIA

This section is devoted to studying packet delivery ratio versus mobility speed. Recent simulation studies show that the FSR protocol, which uses the shortest path, suffers from performance degradation as the network mobility increases. After extensive simulation studies and performance comparisons with other routing selection methods, it was found that the reason behind this degradation is that FSR uses the shortest path as a routing selection method, so when the mobility increases the number of hops increases. Therefore, it has a better chance of having route breaks.

A New Route Selection Criteria

In this section, a new scheme for route selection is introduced. In this scheme, the node selects the route with a minimum number of hops, instead of the shortest path. When there are multiple routes that have the same number of hops, the destination selects the route with the shortest path. Figure 3 describes each scheme. The shortest path scheme simply adds the routing distance of each intermediate node and selects the route with the least sum. For example, Figure 3 has three routes from the source S to the destination D; route X has the sum of 17 (i.e., $6 + 4 + 3 + 4 = 17$); route Y has the sum of 14 (i.e., $2 + 2 + 3 + 2 + 2 + 3 = 14$); and route Z has the sum of 16 (i.e., $5 + 3 + 3 + 2 + 3 = 16$). Therefore, route Y is selected and used as the route between source S and destination S.

The minimum number of hops scheme is similar to the shortest path scheme, however, instead of using the least sum as a routing method, it selects the route with the minimum number of hops.

Considering Figure 3 again, route X has 3 intermediate nodes (B, F, I) from the source S to the destination D; route Y has five intermediate nodes (A, E, H, J, L) from the source S to the destination D; and route Z has four intermediate nodes (C, G, K, M) from the source S to the destination D.

Therefore, route X is selected and used as the route between source S and destination S.

SIMULATION MODEL

The following configuration was used in a GloMoSim simulator (UCLA, 2001). IEEE 802.11 MAC protocol with distributed coordination function (DCF) (Nadeem & Agrawala, 2004; Buttyan & Hubaux 2003) is assumed as the MAC media access control layer. The simulation study is conducted for networks of 100, 200, and 300 mobile hosts; each of them is migrating within a range of 300x300 and 500x500 meters. The radio transmission range is assumed to be 120 meters; and the channel capacity is 2 Mbps. The random waypoint model is used in the simulation runs.

In this model, a node selects a destination randomly within the roaming area and moves towards that destination at a predefined speed. Once the node arrives at the destination, it pauses at the current position for five seconds. The node then selects another destination randomly and moves towards it, pausing there for five seconds, and so on. Note that the pause time is not considered in

Figure 3. Example network

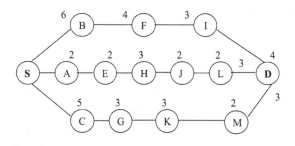

Route *X* : (S, B, F, I, D)

Route *Y* : (S, A, E, H, J, L, D)

Route *Z* : (S, C, G, K, M, D)

Figure 4. Packet delivery ratio of shortest path versus minimum number of hops in case of old parameters

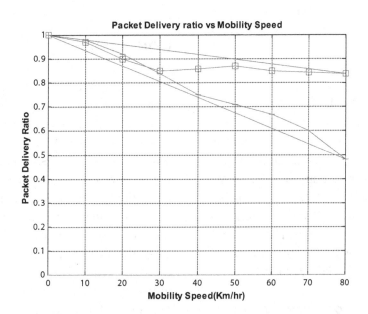

Figure 5. Packet delivery ratio of shortest path versus minimum number of hops in case of new parameters

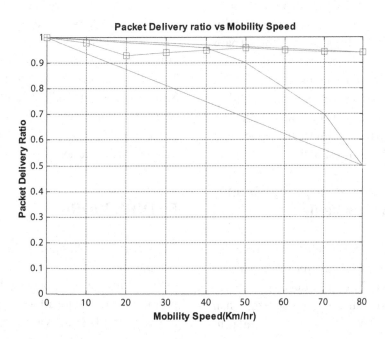

computation of node speed. The size of data payload is 512 bytes. Each simulation was executed for 600 seconds of simulation time. Multiple runs with different seed numbers were conducted for each scenario; and measurements were averaged over those runs

SIMULATION RESULTS

The two schemes were evaluated by comparing the performance with the new scheme that uses the minimum number of hops and the second scheme, which uses the shortest path, taking into account the old operational parameter values and the new values. The new values for FSR protocols where explored and proposed in previous work by El-Gamal, El-Adb and, Khader (2003).

Minimum Number of Hops by Means of Old Parameters Values

Figure 4 shows the packet delivery ratio versus the mobility speed of each scheme using the old parameter values of FSR.

As it is clear from the figure that the shortest path scheme does not perform when the mobility speed increases. This is because the shortest path method is not appropriate when the mobility speed increases. In the second scheme, the minimum number of hops performs well when the mobility increases, however in the very low mobility the new scheme performs at almost the same level of the one using the shortest path.

Minimum Number of Hops by Means of New Parameters Values

Figure 5 reports the packet delivery ratio versus the mobility speed of each scheme using our new parameters values of FSR, introduced previously Khader (2003). We can easily recognize, when viewing Figure 5, that the results are similar to

the previous experiment, however, the new used parameters values have a much better performance than the old parameter values.

CONCLUSION

Wireless ad-hoc networks can be deployed in areas where a wired network infrastructure may be undesirable or unavailable. What makes FSR perform well under large network sizes and high mobility rates is that FSR generates accurate routing decisions by taking advantage of the global network information. However, this information is disseminated in a method to reduce overhead control traffic caused by traditional flooding. Instead, it exchanges information about closer nodes more frequently than it does about nodes farther away. So, each node gets accurate information about neighbors, and the detail and accuracy of information decreases as the distance from the node increases. A performed evaluation of different styles of FSR protocols was conducted in this article. FSR was analyzed in diverse network scenarios to assess its relative strength and weakness. The results gave meaningful indications to protocol designers in this area. A novel routing selection criteria that considers the minimum number of hops was introduced in this article. This scheme was applied to the FSR protocol. Simulation results indicate that the new scheme performs much better than the shortest path, especially when the mobility rate is high and the network size is large.

FUTURE WORK

Researches are designing MANET protocols, comparing and improving existing MANET protocols. However, it is not clear that any particular protocol is the best for all scenarios; each protocol has definite advantages and disadvantages and is well suited for certain situations.

Future work can test performance of other routing protocols, such as DSDV, DSR, and hybrid ad-hoc routing approaches against the FSR protocol. In order to optimize the use of constrained resources in an ad-hoc network, mobility prediction and battery power conservation techniques can be developed and experimented to test the effect of these ad-hoc routing protocols in a real application.

REFERENCES

Buttyan L., & Hubaux, J. (2003). Simulating cooperation in self-organizing mobile ad hoc networks. *ACM/Kluwer Mobile Networks and Applications, 8*(5)

El-Gamal, Y., El-Abd, A. E., & Khader, O. H. S. (2003). Improving FSR protocol using the optimal performance operational parameters. In *ICCTA' International Conference on Computer Theory and Application,* (pp. 38-45).

Haas, Z. J. (1997). A new routing protocol for the reconfigurable wireless networks. In *Proceedings of IEEE ICUPC'97* (pp. 562-566). San Diego

Haas, Z. J., & Pearlman, M. R. (2000). Determining the optimal configuration for the zone routing protocol. *IEEE Journal on Selected Areas in Communications,*1395-1414.

Kaplan, E. D. (1996). *Understanding the GPS: Principles and applications.* Boston: Artech House.

Kleinrock, L., & Stevens, K. (1971). *Fisheye: A lenslike computer display Transformation* (Tech. Rep.) UCLA, Computer Science Department.

Murthy, S., & Garcia-Luna Aceves, J. J. (1996). An efficient routing protocol for wireless networks. *ACM/Baltzor Mobile Networks and Applications, 1*(2), 183-197.

Nadeem, T., & Agrawala, A. (2004). IEEE 802.11 DCF enhancements for noisy environments. *The 15th IEEE international Symposium on Personal, Indoor, and Mobile Radio Communications (PIMRC'04), Barcelona.*

Park, V. D., & Corson, M. S. (1997). A highly adaptive distributed routing algorithm for mobile wireless net works. In *Proceedings of IEEE IN-FOCOM'97* (pp. 1405-1413). Japan: Kobe.

Perkins, C. E., & Bhagwat, P. (1994). Highly dynamic destination sequenced distance vector routing (DSDV) for mobile computers. *Proceedings of ACM SIGCOMM'94, London, UK,* (pp. 234-244).

Perkins, C. E., & Royer, E. M. (1999). Ad hoc on-demand distance vector routing. In *Proceedings of IEEE WMCSA'99* New Orleans, LA (pp. 90-100).

UCLA Parallel Computing Laboratory, University of California. *About GloMoSim.* Retrieved from http://pcl.cs.ucla.edu/projects/glomosim/

Xu, K., Hong, X., & Gerla, M. (2002). An ad hoc network with mobile backbones. In *Proceedings of IEEE ICC,* New York.

Zhong, Y., & Yuan, D. (2003). Dynamic source routing protocol for wireless ad hoc networks in special scenario using location information. In *Communication Technology Proceedings, ICCT, International Conference, 2,* (pp. 1287-1290).

This work was previously published in Int. Journal of Information Technology and Web Engineering, Vol 2, Issue 1, edited by G. Alkhatib and D. Rine, pp. 47-56, copyright 2007 by IGI Publishing (an imprint of IGI Global).

Chapter XV
Modeling Variant User Interfaces for Web–Based Software Product Lines

Suet Chun Lee
BUSINEX, Inc., USA

ABSTRACT

Software product line (SPL) is a software engineering paradigm for software development. A software product within a product line often has specific functionalities that are not common to all other products within the product line. Those specific functionalities are termed "variant features" in a product line. SPL paradigm involves the modeling of variant features. However, little work in SPL investigates and addresses the modeling of variant features specific to user interface (UI). Unified Modeling Language (UML) is the de facto modeling language for object-oriented software systems. It is known that UML needs better support in modeling UIs. Thus, much research developed UML extensions to improve UML support in modeling UIs. Yet little of this work is related to developing such extensions for modeling UIs for SPLs in which variant features specific to UI modeling must be addressed. This research develops a UML extension -Web User Interface Modeling Language (WUIML) to address these problems. WUIML defines elements for modeling variant features specific to user interfaces for Web-based SPLs. The model elements in WUIML extend from the metaclass and BasicActivity of the UML2.0 metamodel. WUIML integrates the modeling of variant features specific to user interfaces to UML. For example, in a Web-based patient registration software product line, member products targeting British users may use British date format in the user interface, while member products targeting United States users may use United States date format in the user interface. Thus, this is a variant feature for this product line. WUIML defines a model element, XOR, to represent such exclusive or conditions in a product line user interface model. WUIML would reduce SPL engineers' efforts needed in UI development. To validate the WUIML research outcome, a case study was conducted. The results of this empirical study indicate that modeling UIs for Web-based SPLs using WUIML is more effective and efficient than using standard UML.

INTRODUCTION

Software product line (SPL) (Chastek, Donohoe, Kang, & Thiel, 2001; Clements & Northrop, 2002; SEI, 2005a) is a software engineering paradigm to develop software products. One important step in the SPL paradigm is the modeling of the functional features of software products across the product line. The features are called common core. An even more important step in the SPL paradigm is the modeling of the specific functional features within a particular member product in a product line. These specific functional features are called variant features because they are the features that differentiate member products in the product line. Then based on the model, a product is 'assembled' by reusing the common core and selected variant features.

Unified Modeling Language (UML) (OMG, 2003b, 2004) (Rumbaugh, Jacobson, & Booch, 2005) is a standard object-oriented modeling language. UML includes multiple views and diagram types to capture software functionalities from user perspective. However, UML seems to have not been developed for modeling user interface specific issues (Kovacevic, June 1998; Silva & Paton, 2003). One of the usages of user interface models is that in model-based user interface management systems (MB-UIMSs) (Pedro A. Szekely, Piyawadee Noi Sukaviriya, Pablo Castells, Jeyakumar Muthukumarasamy, & Salcher, 1996; Tony Griffiths et al., September 1999), user interface models can be used to generate user interface codes. There are extensions of UML (Blankenhorn & Jeckle, 2004) (Nunes, 2003) (Silva, 2002) to make UML better support user interface modeling. Yet these extensions often assume the modeling of a single system instead of a SPL. On the other hand, although standard UML (OMG, 2003b, 2004) seems to have not been developed to support the modeling of SPLs, there are works (Gomaa, 2004; Gomaa & Gianturco, 2002; Tewfik Ziadi, Loïc Hélouët, & Jézéquel, May 2004) on extending UML to improve UML

supports in modeling SPLs. Yet these works do not focus on user interface modeling. Currently, many software products are Web based. However, some (Silva, 2002) observe that there are specific modeling challenges for modeling user interfaces of Web-based software systems.

Thus, it is not clear how to model variant features for user interface specific issues in Web-based software product lines. This is an important barrier to overcome if software product line development of Web-based products is to take greater advantage of software reuse objectives: increased quality, decreased effort, or decreased time to market. Therefore, this paper is concerned with reporting research about developing a UML extension, Web User Interface Modeling Language (WUIML) that decreases effort by increasing effectiveness and efficiency needed in using UML to model user interfaces for Web-based software product lines. User interface development has been found (Myers, 1989) to account for a significant amount of overall software development work. WUIML would improve SPL software engineering paradigm in the user interface development perspective by reducing engineers' efforts needed in user interface modeling.

BACKGROUND AND RELATED WORK

Unified Modeling Language

Unified Modeling Language (UML) (Booch, Rumbaugh, & Jacobson, 1999; OMG, 2003b, 2004; Scott, 2004) is a graphical language for specifying software systems. UML is a standard of Object Management Group (OMG) (see http://www.omg. org). The most current version for UML is UML 2.0 (OMG, 2003b, 2004). This research considers UML in UML 2.0 context.

UML is a standardized notation for object-oriented development. UML consists of views, diagrams, model elements, and general mechanisms. Views are used to present different aspects of complex systems from both the 'system' in the problem and the 'system' in the solution. Tacitly, UML defaults to 'system' as meaning the system in the solution. This is consistent with the classical use cases modeling and design process model. Therefore, whenever the term 'system' is used in this paper, this usual UML use cases default as 'system in the solution' is implied. Moreover, each view requires a number of diagrams, such as use case diagram, class diagram, and interaction diagrams. Each diagram captures a particular aspect of a system. Views that are often used with UML include: use case view, logical view, implementation view, process view, and deployment view. Use case views describe the functionality a system should deliver from external actors' point of view. An actor is a human user or another system external to the system. A use case is often used to describe functions requested for a system. Logical views are used to describe a system's functionality. Use cases often are the first set of models being created for a system. However, some found common pitfalls in use cases for one who is new to use case modeling (Lilly, 2000; Rosenberg & Scott, 2001).

Modeling concepts are captured in model elements. Example model elements are class, object, state, node, package, and component (Eriksson, Penker, Lyons, & Fado, 2004). Model elements are used in diagrams. A model element can have a visual representation. There are rules that limit types of model elements for different diagrams. Relationships between model elements are specified by relationships, such as association, generalization, dependency, and aggregation.

Additional information that cannot be represented using model elements is represented using UML general mechanisms, such as adornments, comments, tagged values, and properties (Eriksson et al., 2004). Adornments are used to add visual impact to the element. For example, "underline" an instance of a type is an adornment. Comments can be placed anywhere in a diagram. Comments often contain explanations or questions to resolve issues at a later time. Model elements have properties to store data values about an element. A property is defined with a name and a value called a tagged value. Properties are used to add additional specifications about element instances that are not normally shown in the diagram.

UML can be extended or adapted by its extension mechanisms: stereotype, tagged values, and constraints. A stereotype defines a new kind of model element based on existing model elements. A stereotype is described by placing its name as a string and within a pair of guillemots. For example, a class with the stereotype <<Radio>> is read as "a class of the Radio stereotype," meaning that it is a radio type of class. The particular characteristics of a Radio class must have been defined when the stereotype is defined. A constraint is a restriction on an element that limits the usage of the elements. A constraint is enclosed in a curly bracket. For example, {student = "Dorothy"}. Alternatively, constraints can be written in Object Constraint Language (OCL) (OMG, 2003a). A UML profile (OMG, 2003b) is a stereotyped package that contains model elements that have been customized for a specific purpose using extension mechanisms, such as stereotypes, tagged values, and constraints. A profile can only extend an existing UML model element using stereotypes, tagged values, or constraints. A profile cannot create new model elements that were not previously defined in the UML 2.0 infrastructure specification (OMG, 2003b).

UML 2.0 is defined in Meta-Object-Facility (MOF) (OMG, 2002). MOF is an abstract language for defining modeling languages. Therefore, another way to extend UML is using MOF. MOF extends UML by defining new metamodel elements. This approach is often called metamodel approach. In metamodel approach, new model elements can be created. With metamodel approach, one can also create model elements that change UML symbols and semantics.

Software Product Line

Software product line (SPL) (SEI, 2005a) is a software engineering paradigm (SEI, 2005b). The paradigm mainly includes two software engineering processes: product line engineering and member product engineering. The product line engineering process involves a number of techniques in software engineering, such as domain analysis, requirements engineering, product architecture, and component development (Clements & Northrop, 2002). The product engineering process involves the configuration ('assemble') of member products from the product line assets. The SPL paradigm depends on the notion of variability and variability mechanisms. In SPL, the term variability is used to indicate the extent of differences in user visible software properties among member products. A user visible software property is a feature. A feature of a member product that is different from other member products is a variant feature. Therefore, a variant feature is a feature only to one or more (but not all) products in a SPL. Variability mechanisms are a set of methods and steps that can be applied to develop variant features for SPLs.

The user interface of member products of a SPL may vary in one or more user interface specific features. Example user interface specific features are the layout of the user interface, the functionality of the user interface, the interaction of the user interface to and from the user, etc. The user interface specific variant features, like other non-user interface specific features, also need to be captured in a SPL model.

It seems that issues in user interface developments have been largely ignored by the SPL researches. It is not clear how to go about applying the software product line paradigm in user interface modeling. WUIML developed in this research is differentiated from other related works (Gomaa, 2004; Gomaa & Gianturco, 2002; Shin, 2002; Webber, 2001), (Tewfik Ziadi et al., May 2004) in SPL researches in that WUIML is addressing

the modeling of user interfaces in a SPL using UML. It is known (Silva & Paton, 2003) that UML needs better support in modeling user interfaces. The related works extend UML to improve support on modeling SPL, yet those works have not addressed the modeling issues in user interfaces for SPL. User interface development has been found to (Myers, 1989) account for a significant amount of overall software development work. WUIML would improve SPL software engineering paradigm in the user interface development perspective by reducing engineers' efforts needed in user interface modeling.

Web User Interface Modeling

User interface is a computer-based media to facilitate communication between users and a software system (Marcus, 2002). Early user interfaces in software systems are text or form-based. Modern software systems however use graphical user interfaces (GUI) implemented according to programming packages, such as Java Swings classes (Eckstein, Loy, & Wood, 1998). More recently, HTML is used to create Web-based user interfaces that can be rendered by Internet browsers (Sommerville, 2001).

The user interfaces of a Web-based software product are called Web user interface (WUI) in this research. The modeling of a WUI is the development of an abstract understanding of the requirements of the WUI and represents it in an abstract notation. The modeling of WUI using WUIML does not provide a visual look of a WUI, thus, WUI modeling is not the design of a WUI. Currently, a major use of WUI modeling is to provide inputs for WUI code generation. In particular, WUI models resulting from WUI modeling are fed into a model-based tool. The tool either auto-generates (or semi-auto-generates) WUI implementations for the WUI models (Behrens, Ritter, & Six, 2003) (Gómez & Cachero, 2003).

UML-Based User Interface Modeling

One approach to user interface modeling and specification methods is to extend UML notations (Jacobson, Christerson, Jonsson, & Overgaard, 1992) (Phillips, Kemp, & Kek, 2001) (Scogings & Phillips, 2001) (Silva & Paton, 2003) (Nunes, 2003) (Blankenhorn & Jeckle, 2004) (Hennicker & Koch, 2001), (Behrens et al., 2003).

A Web UI development method is proposed in (Behrens et al., 2003). The method consists of two tasks: UI requirements modeling and mapping UI requirements model to UI architecture. The modeling of UI requirements includes the specification of use cases (called 'work units' in the paper) and then the work units are modeled using user-defined UML stereotypes representing user interface elements. A UI element is modeled as a <<scene>>. A <<scene>> may consist of zero or more <<class view>>. A user interface is then the composition of different <<scene>> elements. The navigations between user interfaces are based on the parent-child relationship between the user interfaces, domain requirements, and usability aspects. In (Hennicker & Koch, 2001), a UML profile for modeling user interfaces for Web applications is proposed. The UML profile includes UML stereotypes to model the presentation ('look and feel') and navigation aspects of Web UIs. The Object-Oriented Hypermedia (OO-H) Method (Gómez & Cachero, 2003) extends UML with a set of new views for modeling Web interface model. In (Silva & Paton, 2003), a UML extension, UMLi, was developed to support user interface modeling for interactive systems. However, UMLi has yet to address Web UI as indicated in (Silva, 2002) that there are additional user interface modeling properties for Web applications.

The major difference between this work and the related works (Gómez & Cachero, 2003) (Hennicker & Koch, 2001) (Behrens et al., 2003) (Silva, 2002) (Silva & Paton, 2003) (Jacobson et al., 1992) in user interface modeling is that WUIML addresses the modeling of user interfaces for SPLs and the related works focus on the modeling of user interfaces for a single system. In addition, the modeling elements in WUIML capture the Web user interface properties specific to Web software products according to important Web standards (Bos, Celik, Hickson, & Lie, 2004; Dubinko, Leigh, Klotz, Merrick, & Raman, 2002; Jonny Axelsson et al., 2003; Lie & Bos, 1999; Meyer, 2000, May 2000; W3C). WUIML improves SPL software engineering paradigm by reducing efforts needed by SPL engineers in user interface modeling for SPLs.

WEB USER INTERFACE MODELING LANGUAGE (WUIML)

WUIML improves UML support on user interface modeling for Web-based software product lines. User interface modeling falls into the scope of user interface development. The user interface models specified in WUIML form one generic user interface software product line asset for the entire main software product line. The idea is to have user interface models as core assets. Then to develop user interfaces for member products one would reuse all common user interface components and reuse selectively the variant user interface components.

In this research, the requirements analysis process for user interfaces is as follows. Given software requirements for a software product line, user interface related use cases from product line requirements are derived. A use case that is user interface related can be developed into many user interface scenarios. Each scenario is due to one or more variant user interface aspects. A user interface scenario involves one or more user interfaces. Any interaction between a human user and a user interface or between a user interface and a back-end application is also captured in the use case scenario. Once the user interfaces are identified, one can decide on the user interface components. After eliciting and describing the scenarios, the next step is to identify the relationships between user interfaces. The interacting relationships between user interfaces are captured in extended activity diagrams where nodes in the activity diagrams can represent variant user interfaces. The extended activity diagram shows the variant interactions between user interfaces.

In order to specify common and variant features for user interfaces, WUIML defines stereotyped relationships between modeling elements. These new relationships are selected syntheses and extensions from Jacobson, Griss, and Jonsson (Jacobson, Griss, & Jonsson, 1997) and Anastasopoulos' (Anastasopoulos & Gacek, 2001) variability mechanisms. In addition, the variant notations and rules of the FODA (Cohen, Stanley, Peterson, & Krut Jr., 1992) technique have been adopted and incorporated into WUI-ML. In addition, this research developed a new variability mechanism called WUIAggregation. WUIAggregation models a WUI that is an aggregation of different parts of other WUIs. For example, a portal WUI is a WUIAggregation of a number of other WUIs. The difference between WUIAggregation and the UML aggregation is that WUIAggregation limits its aggregated components to be instances of WUIComposite or specific WUIElements while the standard UML aggregation does not have this restriction. This restriction helps modelers on deciding what components are appropriate for the aggregation. The variability mechanisms are used to generate variants on user interface aspects. User interface aspects include (but not limited to) user functional requirements, style, presentation, layout, events, data model, and constraints.

The structural contents of WUIML are built from various World Wide Web Consortium (W3C) (see http://www.w3c.org) specifications: XHTML (Altheim, Boumphrey, McCarron, Schnitzenbaumer, & Wugofski, 2001; Altheim & Shane McCarron, 2001; Jonny Axelsson et al., 2003; Powell, 2003; Raggett, Hors, & Jacobs, 1999; Sauers & Wyke, 2001; W3C, 2002), XForms (Dubinko, 2003; Dubinko et al., 2002; Khare, 2000), and Cascading Style Sheets (CSS) (Bos et al., 2004, Lie & Bos, 1999; Meyer, 2000, 2003, Schengili-Roberts, 2004; Schmitt, 2003).

WUIML is also built on the UML 2.0 specifications (OMG, 2003b, 2004) and is an extension to the metamodeling approach of the UML 2.0. In particular, WUIML extends metaclass and BasicActivity of the UML 2.0 metamodel. The metaclass extension is achieved via stereotype extension mechanism. The extension to the BasicActivity is achieved via MOF.

A WUI structurally consists of multiple user interface elements, such as user interface visual elements (such as a button, a checkbox, etc.), hypertext links, images, text, etc. These elements are 'mapped' to stereotyped UML classes that extend the UML2.0 metaclass.

Events (sometimes termed 'triggers') occur when user interface elements interact with user actions. Actions are mapped to UML interfaces. An interface defines a set of operations triggered by events. Events and actions characterize a user interface interaction. Events and actions are modeled as operations of metamodel elements. Interactions between user interfaces are modeled using UML activity diagrams. In addition, UML activity diagram is extended to model variant interactions in WUIML.

Basic WUIML Elements

Figure 1 defines the Basic WUIML Elements in UML 2.0 notations. These model elements extend from the metaclass of the UML2.0 metamodel. These model elements have attributes and operations. The attributes are used to model the static features of user interfaces; for example, an attribute can be used to describe the background color of a user interface element. The operations are used to model the dynamic aspects of user interfaces, for example, events (e.g., a user clicks a button can be tracked by an event listener) and actions (e.g., an error message box popup can

Figure 1. Basic WUIML elements

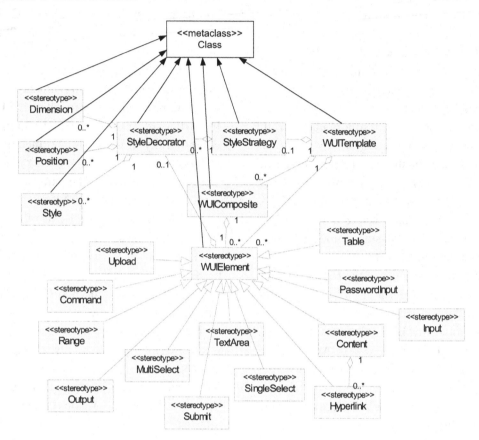

be implemented by a method) can be modeled as operations. Figure 2 shows the class diagram of the WUIElement and the Command model elements.

A WUI is modeled as a WUITemplate. A WUITemplate may be composed of one or more of WUIComposite. A WUITemplate may also be composed of one or more WUIElement and one or more WUIComposite. A WUIComposite has one or more specific WUI modeling elements (such as Submit, Input, etc.) that extend from the WUIElement. The style, layout, and position within a WUI of a WUIElement can be described using the StyleDecorator model element. A StyleDecorator composes of a number of Dimension element, Position element, and the Style element. The Dimension (how large or small the WUI element is), Position (where the WUI

element is positioned within a WUI), and Style (such as what is the foreground color of the WUI element) elements together model abstractly the style of a WUI element. A set of StyleDecorator elements forms a StyleStrategy. A StyleStrategy element describes the style of a WUIComposite element. A set of StyleStrategy elements models the style of a WUITemplate.

These WUIML elements integrate Web properties according to important Web standards (Bos et al., 2004; Dubinko et al., 2002; Jonny Axelsson et al., 2003; Lie & Bos, 1999; Meyer, 2000, May 2000; W3C) to the modeling of Web-based user interfaces for SPLs. With regard to the modeling of the static aspects of user interfaces, what WUIML adds to the standard UML is like what application programming interfaces (APIs) add to a programming language. For example, the Swing

Figure 2. The WUIElement and the Command element

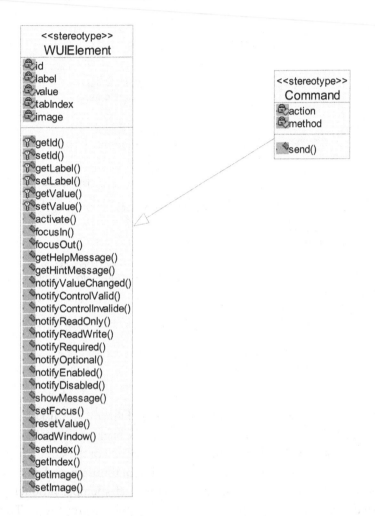

API (Eckstein et al., 1998) provides the building blocks for programmers to code user interfaces. Similarly, WUIML provides the building blocks for modelers to model user interfaces. When using Swing, a programming does not have to construct fundamental user interface elements, such as textboxes, radio buttons, etc. The programmer would just use them. Similarly, when using WUIML, a modeler does not have to model the fundamental user interface elements, such as textboxes, radio buttons, etc. When using standard UML, those fundamental user interface elements must be modeled first. In addition, WUIML provides a way to conveniently model the layout, size, and position (where it is within a user interface) for a particular user interface element. Currently, there are no standard way in using UML to model the layout and style of a Web-based user interface. WUIML defines a way for modeling the layout and style of a Web-based user interface.

Example I: Web User Interface Modeling Using Basic WUIML Elements

In a SPL, a user interface feature may vary among the member products. For example, consider a SPL of online patient registration systems. A member product to be deployed for US customers would have a user interface customized for US address

Figure 3. An example WUI model using WUIML basic elements

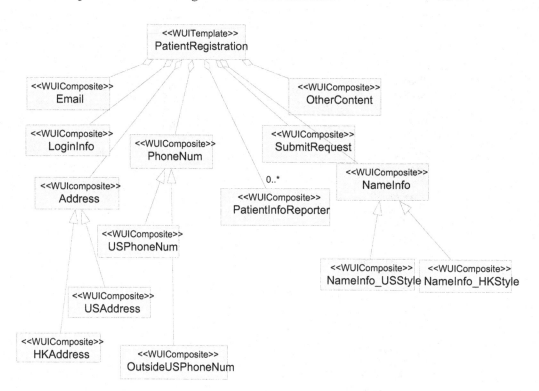

format. On the other hand, member products to be deployed for Hong Kong customers would have a user interface customized for Hong Kong address format.

Figure 3 shows a product line Web user interface model that consists of instances of <<WUIComposite>> elements. An instance of <<WUIComposite>> may compose of a number of fundamental user interface elements (such as a textbox, an input box, a listbox, etc.) but they are not shown in Figure 3. A <<WUIComposite>> can be considered as a portion of a user interface called user interface fragment in this research. A user interface is composed of a number of user interface fragments.

Modeling Variant Interactions

WUIML defines elements to model the different interactions between a user interface and its backend process. If a MVC architecture (Gamma, Helm, Johnson, & Vlissides, 1995) is the example, then the back-end application is the controller and the model. For the same functional task, such as a WUI for remittance of an online banking service SPL, each member product may implement it in a slightly different way. The difference would lead to differences in the WUI related to the task among member products. The differences in WUI would in turn lead to different patterns of user interactions to the WUI as well as different implementation of backend processes. For example, to send money to a foreign country, the WUI must collect the destination country (as country code) and currency (currency code) information from the user. On the other hand, to send money domestically within United States, the WUI does not need to collect country code or currency information. The different user interactions to a user interface in a SPL are called variant interactions. User actions, such as clicking a submit button in a WUI may trigger transitions between WUIs. In this research, UML activity diagram is used to model the interactions between WUIs.

WUIML defines two new metamodel elements using MOF to model variant interactions. The two new elements are VariantAction and SPLAction. In UML, a node in an activity diagram is represented by the ActivityNode element. The ActivityNode element has three children: ExecutableNode, ObjectNode, and ControlNode. Object Nodes represent the objects involved in the activity diagram. The ControlNode signifies the control flow on the activity diagram; for example, a fork bar is a ControlNode. The ExecutableNode has a child, the Action element. The Action element in UML is the representation of a node that characterized by one or more actions. Since interactions are characterized by actions, WUIML extends the UML Action element to model variant interactions.

Figure 4 shows the new metamodel elements: VariantAction and SPLAction and how they relate to other elements in the activity class diagram. The VariantAction element is a specialization of the UML Action element. The SPLAction is a specialization of the Element metamodel element from the UML2.0 kernel package. A SPLAction element contains one or many Variant Action elements. An UML Activity is now also consisting of one or more of the SPLAction and VariantAction elements.

Suppose we have an activity called 'submit order'. The 'submit order' activity is very common in Web-based shopping applications because a user must submit an order so that the order can be processed. But there are variants in 'submit order' activity. For example, most online shopping sites accept only credit card payments, thus, those applications may want 'submit credit card order'.

Figure 4. Extension to UML 2.0 Activity

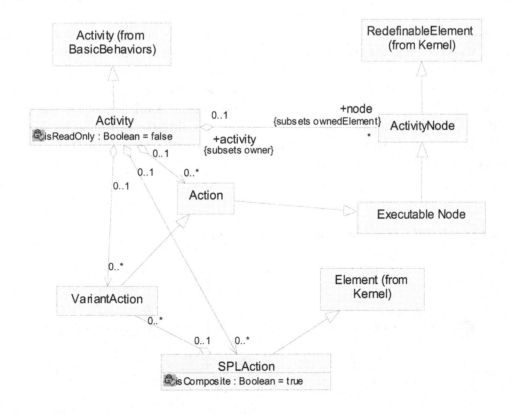

Figure 5. SPLAction symbol

In other case, corporate purchasing often submits purchase orders, and then pays the bill after receiving the invoice. In this case, 'submit purchase order' may be desired. Yet another variant is in the case where customer wants to receive the purchase and check it first before make any payment, these customers may want 'submit Cash-On-Delivery (COD) order'. Yet some merchants may offer a combination of these payment methods. There are a number of variants in the 'submit order' activity and we need to be able to model the variants. This paper extends UML activity diagram to model the requirements as follows.

Figure 5 shows a graphical symbol for the SPLAction. The symbol exposes the base action and its four variants actions. The shape of the base 'submit order' action is filled, while the variants are not. The base Submit Order action defines the common logics that are applicable across all the variants. Each variant differs from

other variants by some features. Our concern is on user interface modeling, it is clear that the user interface to collect information on a credit card order is different from the user interface to collect a COD order in some way.

Sometimes there are variant logics and behaviors within a variant member product that capture different execution scenarios. Those logics and behaviors can be modeled using standard UML activity diagrams. For example, suppose there is a WUI that provides user interface elements to accept either credit card based order option or purchase order option. If a customer chooses credit card order, the next WUI displayed is to collect the customer's credit card information. If a customer chooses purchase order based order option, then the next WUI displayed is to collect the customers purchase order related information. Thus, the software's behavior varies due to different execution scenarios. This variant is within a product.

These variant logics and behaviors due to different execution scenarios often easy for one to confuse with the product line variant logics and behaviors. To identify the product line variants, one must consider the same particular variant logics and behaviors across multiple member products at the same time. If the variant logics and behaviors work the same across the member products, then the variant logics and behaviors are not a product line variant.

Figure 6a. Exemple SPL variant interactions

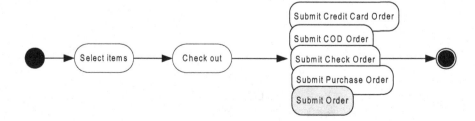

Figure 6b. Example member product variant interaction

Example II: Modeling Variant Interactions

Figure 6a shows an activity diagram for a SPLAction for an online e-retailer SPL. The SPLAction is about 'Submit Order'. The SPLAction consists of four variant actions: 'Submit Credit Card Order', 'Submit COD Order', 'Submit Check Order', and 'Submit Purchase Order'. A member product of this product line would have the same activity but with only one variant of the submit order action. Figure 6b shows the activity diagram for a member product that allows users to submit Credit Card Orders.

WUIML Elements for Variability Mechanisms

Figure 7 shows the WUIML elements for variability mechanisms that are based on Jacobson, Griss, and Jonsson (Jacobson et al., 1997) and Anastasopoulos' (Anastasopoulos & Gacek, 2001) variability mechanisms and the variant notations and rules of the FODA (Cohen et al., 1992) technique. Delegation, WUIDerive, WUIExtend, Use, TemplateInstantiation, and RequirePresenceOf are stereotypes extended from Dependency metaclass. WUIAggregation, Configuration, and Parameterization are defined as stereotypes of Class stereotype. WUIGeneralization is a stereotype of the Generalization metaclass. OptionalElement is a constraint to express that an element is optional in the model. XOR and OR are Constraints. A Parameterization element is composed of one or more Property. A Configuration element is composed of one or more Property and zero or more Constraint.

The Use model element is used to specify that the source user interface element (e.g. a user interface fragment to capture the travel date) depends on the target user interface element (e.g., a user interface of a calendar for setting a travel date). The Configuration model element models a set of parameters and rules. These parameters and rules manipulate the composition of the software component of a software system or the setting of software components or software systems, so that variants can be created. The Parameterization model element models a set of parameters that vary the features of a software product. The TemplateInstantiation model element is a special case of the Parameterization model element. In TemplateInstantiation, the parameters are templates. WUIExtend allows small extensions in functionality or 'look' to a user interface due to new requirements. WUIDerive extends UML derive stereotype to apply on all basic WUIML elements. Delegation is used to model the situation in which a Web user interface is acting as a representative of another Web user interface in performing certain operations. WUIAggregation allows one to model the situation in which various user interface fragments from various Web user interfaces are used to compose another Web user interface based on a business goal. WUIAggregation differs from UML aggregation in that the aggregated components in WUIAggregation must be instance of WUIComposte or specific WUI elements. WUIGeneralization models the 'is-a-kind-of' relationship between two user interfaces. WUIGeneralization differs from UML generalization in that the generalization in WUIGeneralization applies to specific WUI elements only. OptionalElement is used to specify that a

Figure 7. Model elements for variability mechanisms

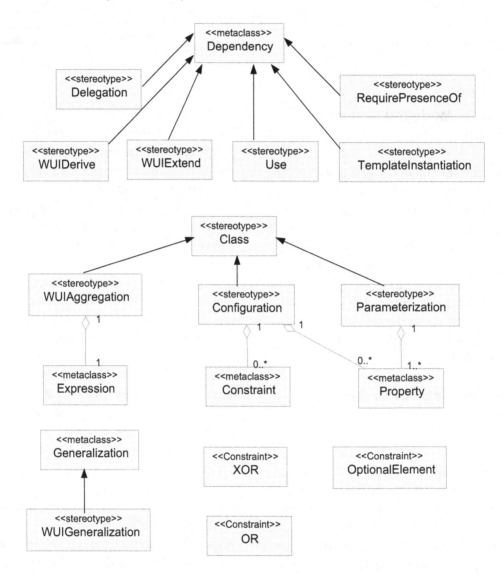

user interface element is optional in the model. OR models the inclusive or constraint. XOR models the exclusive or constraint. RequirePresenceOf models the situation in which a user interface feature depends on the presence of another user interface feature. For example, to model the style of a column within a table, it requires the presence of a table element.

Example III: Modeling Variant Web User Interface Features

To illustrate WUIML for modeling variant WUI features, let us continue the example shown in Figure 3. But this time, we apply the variability mechanisms and using the corresponding variability mechanism model elements defined in WUIML. Figure 8 shows a more detail WUIML model for the online patient registration systems

SPL. Figure 3 shows the common user interface features across the product line. Figure 8 shows the variant user interface features among member products within the product line in addition to the common features across the product line.

Applying variability mechanisms and the corresponding WUIML notations, variant WUI features are specified in Figure 8. The variant notations in WUIML are only used in product line WUIML models to show the variant features among member products. Thus, the variant notations in WUIML are not to appear in the WUIML model of a member product. For example, notice that the USAddress and HKAddress WUIComposite elements appear in Figure 3 are now specified with exclusive or constraint. This indicates that if a member product's WUI uses USAddress format, then it will not use the HKAddress format. TemplateInstantiation vari-

ability mechanism is used to create two variant WUIComposites of PatientInfoReporter. The patient information report can be in graphic format or summary format.

Modeling Dynamic Aspects of Web User Interfaces

In addition to interactions as described in the section above named 'Modeling Variant Interactions', the dynamic aspects of WUIs also include events and actions. In this paper, event literally means "something that takes place; an occurrence." (See American Heritage® Dictionary of the English Language, Fourth Edition, Houghton Mifflin Company.). In this paper, an event means an occurrence that takes place in the user interface. Example occurrence may be a mouse click on a button, a selection on a selection box, etc. The

Figure 8. WUIML model of the online patient registration systems SPL

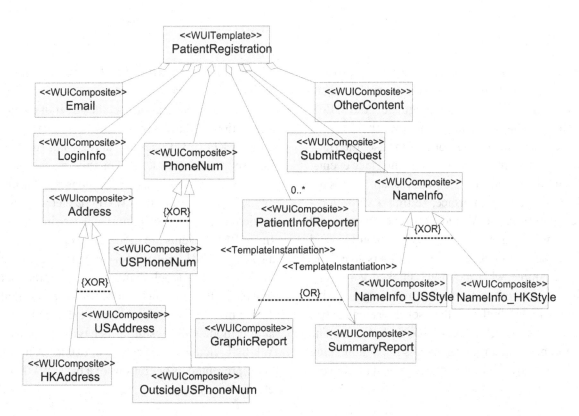

Figure 9. Patient Registration WUIML Model

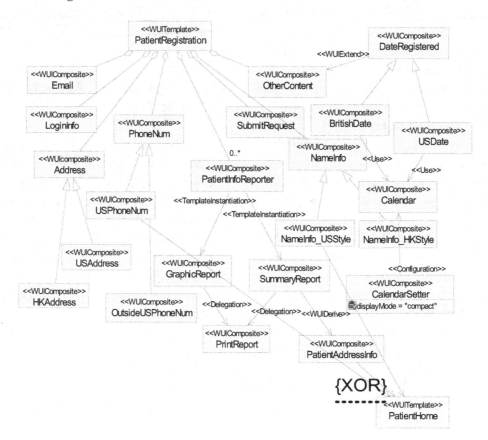

term action literally means "the state or process of acting or doing" (See American Heritage® Dictionary of the English Language, Fourth Edition. Houghton Mifflin Company, 2000.) In this paper, an action means doing some user interface related tasks in response to user interface events. Example action may be popping up a message box on the user interface, setting a value for a text input box, etc. Moreover, an event is observed by a user interface control, such as a button, and then the user interface control triggers an action. For example, when a button is clicked, a message box is popped up to display a message. In this scenario, the button is the user interface control that is observing the event: clicking the button. The popping up of a message box is the action being triggered by the button click event. The concept of events and actions described in this section are built on the XForms specification.

XForms specification includes a set of events and actions. Many events and actions have to do with XForms processing and are not suitable for use at modeling level. For this reason, only a selected set of events and actions are taking as the bases for building WUIML elements for modeling the dynamic nature of a user interface. In WUIML, events are modeled as operations of a basic WUIML metamodel element. Each basic WUIML metamodel element has a distinct set of events. Extra events can be added as needed by the modeler at design time as extensions. An action models the resulting behavior of a basic WUIML element in response to events. Actions are represented as operations of a basic WUIML element.

Example IV: Modeling Product Web User Interface Using WUIML

Figure 9 shows an even more detail WUIML model for the online patient registration systems SPL than Figure 8. In Figure 9, more variability mechanisms are applied to create variants. In addition to the variability mechanisms shown in Figure 8, the variability mechanisms applied in Figure 9 include WUIExtend, Use, Configuration, WUIAggregation, Delegation, and WUIDerive. Once we have a SPL WUIML model, we can derive product WUIML model from the SPL WUIML model. A product WUIML model is a WUIML model that reuses all the common features of a SPL WUIML model but reuses only selected variant features from a SPL WUIML model. Figure 10 and Figure 11 show two product WUIML models derived from Figure 9.

The variant patient registration WUIML model shown in Figure 10 is created by taking all the common model elements (i.e., Email, LoginInfo, Address, PhoneNum, NameInfo, OtherContent, PatientInfoReporter, and SubmitRequest) and selected variant user interface features (i.e., USAddress, USPhoneNum, and NameInfo_US-Style) from Figure 9.

Figure 11 shows another variant product WUIML model derived from Figure 9. Compare Figure 11 with Figure 10, Figure 11 shows more variant user interface features. Figure 11 includes the BritishDate WUIComposite that is extended from DateRegistered WUIComposite.

VALIDATION

The goal of this research is to improve UML support in modeling user interfaces for Web-based SPLs. The improvement goal is to have the new WUIML method exhibit decreased effort needed by increasing effectiveness and efficiency. The

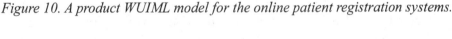

Figure 10. A product WUIML model for the online patient registration systems.

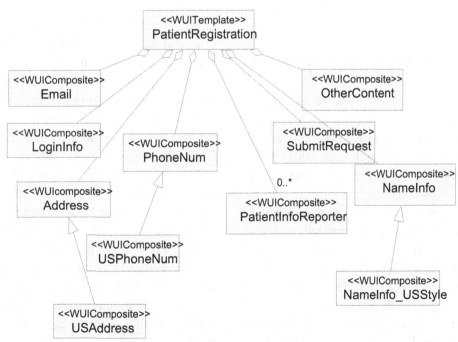

Figure 11. Variant Patient Registration Web User Interface

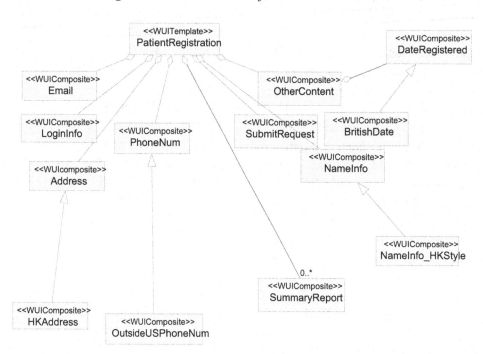

improvement will reduce the SPL engineers' efforts needed for developing user interfaces. To exhibit that this improvement goal is met a case study research validation method is applied to supply supporting evidence for the thesis (research hypothesis).

Case Study Research Method

Using case study (Lynch, 1999; Tellis, 1997a, 1997b; Yin, 2003) as an empirical research validation method has increasingly been adopted in software engineering research (Lee, 2004). This research uses a case study research method to validate the research hypothesis.

The rationale of a case study research method is the notion of 'analytical generalization'. Analytical generalization depends on whether the findings of a case study can be replicated. If the findings of a case can be replicated, an analytical generalization may be drawn.

In analytical generalization, the results of a case study should be compared with a proposi-

tion. For example, in this case study, the results of a multiple-case study are to compare with proposition 1 and proposition 2 (proposition 1 and proposition 2 will be discussed later.) Multiple cases are needed to test a proposition through replications of findings in order to lead to an analytical generalization (Yin, 2003). Many research methods, such as a survey, depend on statistical generalization (Yin, 2003). In statistical generalization, an inference is made about a population (or universe) base on the empirical data collected about a sample (i.e., surveys) (Yin, 2003). Since a case study is not based on statistical generalization, a sampling logic should not be used in a case study research method. As a result, the number of cases in a multiple-case design and the typical criteria regarding sample size are irrelevant (Yin, 2003).

The evidence from multiple-case studies makes the overall study more robust (Yin, 2003). In this empirical study, multiple case studies were conducted. In a multiple-case study, each case must be selected to predict similar results (a literal replication) or to produce contrasting results but for predictable reasons (a theoretical replication) (Yin, 2003). A literal replication explains the conditions under which a particular phenomenon is likely to be found. A theoretical replication explains the conditions when it is not likely to be found. This empirical study relies on literal replications. The two case studies conducted are expected to predict similar results. The study is trying to show that under the condition (i.e. using WUIML in modeling WUIs for a SPL), a particular phenomenon (i.e. increased modelers' effectiveness and efficiency in modeling) is likely to be found. For each case in the multiple-case study, the study indicates the way a particular proposition was demonstrated (or not demonstrated). Across cases in the multiple-case study, the study indicates the extent of the replication logic and the reasons on the prediction of supporting or contrasting results (Yin, 2003).

Case Study Design

The goal of this empirical study is to investigate the effectiveness and efficiency of WUIML. This empirical study uses a case study research method (Lee, 2004; Tellis, 1997a, 1997b; Yin, 2003) as the validation method. The design of a case study is characterized by five important case study components (Yin, 2003): a study's research questions, study propositions, units of analysis, the logic linking data (results) to the propositions, and the criteria for interpreting the findings.

Study's Research Questions

The study's research questions define the validation goal of a case study. The study's research questions should be clarified precisely (Yin, 2003). For example, in this empirical study, the study's research question is "Does Web user interface modeling for a Web-based medical SPL using WUIML increase SMEs' modeling efficiency

and effectiveness (thus decreases work)?" This study's research question needs to be clarified further because the notion of efficiency and effectiveness need further clarification. This study's' research question can be decomposed into a set of propositions.

Study Propositions

Study propositions are derived from the study's research questions (Yin, 2003) but are more specific than the study's research questions. Study propositions quantify the quality variables (indirect metrics) in a study's research question into directly measurable quantitative metrics (direct metrics or indicators). For example, in this multiple-case study, the study's research question is decomposed into two propositions:

1. SMEs are able to correctly model a larger number of required modeling items using WUIML than standard UML in modeling WUIs for a Web-based medical SPL in approximately the same amount of person-hours.
2. SMEs are able to correctly model larger numbers of required modeling items via reuse using WUIML than standard UML in modeling WUIs for a Web-based medical SPL in approximately the same amount of person-hours.

In this multiple-case study, for each WUI, the investigator has identified from the requirements a set of modeling items, called required modeling items that must be modeled by the SMEs. The resulted models produce by SMEs are inspected by the investigator. The investigator first checks the models for required modeling items. Then, base on his modeling experience, the investigator decides the correctness of the required modeling items found in the resulted models.

Units of Analysis

Units of analysis are materials such as documents or other resources that the subject matter experts (SMEs) use as inputs or materials to apply the method or tools being validated. In this study, the method under investigation is WUIML. The units of analysis are the Web user interface requirements for a medical SPL.

In the first case study, the requirements for the Pediatric Medical Profile Login WUI, the Adolescent Medical Profile Login WUI, and the Adult Medical Profile Login WUI are provided. These WUIs are each from a different member product (Pediatric Medical Management System, Adolescent Medical Management System, and Adult Medical Management System) of a medical product line (Medical Management Systems). The WUIs to model are extracted from three Web-based medical products under development in BUSINEX Inc.

The WUIs for the medical Web software products are based on actual medical forms from health-care providers in the United States. For the first case study, three member products of the product line are considered for WUI modeling. In particular, this case study requires the SMEs to model the Medical Profile Login WUI and a related activity across three member products of the product line. This WUI is chosen because it allows one to exercise the modeling of commonality and variability found in product lines.

In the second case study, the requirements for the Pediatric Exercise Record WUI, the Adolescent Exercise Record WUI, and the Adult Exercise Record WUI are provided. These WUIs are each from the same member products in the same product line as in the first case study. These requirements are the units of analysis for the second case study.

Note that within each case study, there are two SMEs. One SME applies WUIML to the requirements to generate results while the other SME applies standard UML to the requirements to generate results. The results generated by applying standard UML are used as the baseline for analyzing the results generated by applying WUIML.

In this research, the SMEs are well trained in software engineering; they are professional software engineers with experience ranging from seven to fifteen years. Their specialties are focused on user interface development. They are representative users for the new WUIML. The investigator provides training on WUIML to the SMEs before they begin conducting the case studies. In each case, all SMEs participate in the case study only once. Not having the same SME to participate in more than one case is to prevent the introduction of bias due to the familiarity of WUIML by SMEs participating in multiple case studies. The SMEs are to carry out the case study without help from the investigator. The SMEs are also not given information on the expected results of the case study. This is to prevent bias by the SMEs in performing the case studies.

Table 1 shows the required modeling items for the Pediatric Medical Profile Login WUIs. The result of whether these items are correctly modeled by SMEs, the number of correctly modeled items over total number of required modeling items by SMEs with or without product line reuse, and the approximate person-hours spent will be used to support/reject the study propositions 1 and 2. There are specific required modeling items for Adult Medical Profile Login WUI, Pediatric Medical Profile Login WUI, Adult Exercise Record WUI, Adolescent Exercise Record WUI, and Pediatric Exercise Record WUI, for brevity they are not shown here.

Linking Data to Propositions

Data analysis is done in the step of linking data (results) to propositions. In a case study, data are collected using formal case study worksheets. A case study worksheet consists of specific concrete questions associate with each one of the study

Table 1. Required modeling items for Pediatric Medical Profile Login WUI

Required modeling items for Pediatric Medical Profile Login WUI
Page title: "Pediatric Medical Profile Login"
Label 1: "Profile ID:"
A textbox for label 1.
Label 2: "Password:"
A textbox for label 2.
Label 3: "Role:"
A radio button.
The radio button must default to be checked.
A label for the radio button: "Parent/Guardian". (Only parent or legal guardian who are previously registered with the health provider can login for the child.).
A submit button with name "Login".
The Page title must placed on the top of the page.
The Profile ID and its related textbox must be immediately next to each other.
The Password and its related textbox must be immediately next to each other.
The Role and its related radioButton must not be immediately next to each other.
Profile ID must be placed on top of the Password and its related textbox.
The Role and the radio button must be on a line that is on top of the Login button.
The Login button must be placed at the lower left hand side of the page.
The activity diagram should include an action node: Pediatric Medical Profile Login.
The activity diagram should include an action node: Login Error.
The activity diagram should include an action node: Parent Welcome.
The activity diagram should include an action node: Customer Service.
The activity diagram should include a start node.
The activity diagram should include an end node.
The activity diagram should include a decision node: whether validation is successful.
The activity diagram should indicate the condition that "Profile ID, Password, and Role" values are available.

propositions. The answers to those questions are measures to concrete criteria metrics that can be analyzed to support (or reject) the propositions. Thus, the most concrete criteria metrics are measure terms found within the questions on the case study worksheets. Figure 12 shows a case study worksheet used in the first case study for modeling the Pediatric Medical Profile Login WUI. In Figure 12, each concrete criteria metrics in questions that link to propositions is identified by a name formed by three sections. For example, "Pediatric_WUIML_personHours"

is the metric about person-hours spent in using WUIML to model the Pediatric Medical Profile Login WUI. The same format is used in naming other metrics found in the questions in other case study worksheets in the case studies.

Table 2 summarizes the evidence collected through the case study worksheets in the case study about Medical Profile Login WUIs.

In each case study, WUIML and standard UML are applied to the units of analysis (that is the Web user interface requirements of a Web-based medical SPL) respectively. The results, that

Figure 12. Case study worksheet for modeling Pediatric Medical Profile Login WUI using WUIML

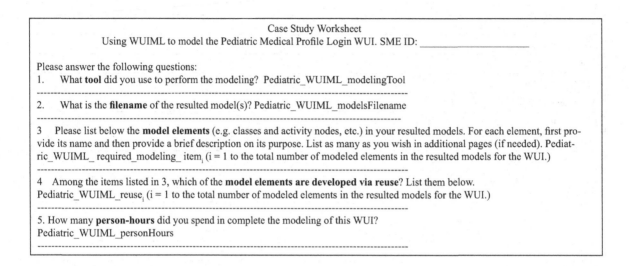

Case Study Worksheet
Using WUIML to model the Pediatric Medical Profile Login WUI. SME ID: _____

Please answer the following questions:
1. What **tool** did you use to perform the modeling? Pediatric_WUIML_modelingTool

----

2. What is the **filename** of the resulted model(s)? Pediatric_WUIML_modelsFilename

----

3   Please list below the **model elements** (e.g. classes and activity nodes, etc.) in your resulted models. For each element, first provide its name and then provide a brief description on its purpose. List as many as you wish in additional pages (if needed). Pediatric_WUIML_ required_modeling_ item$_i$ (i = 1 to the total number of modeled elements in the resulted models for the WUI.)

----

4   Among the items listed in 3, which of the **model elements are developed via reuse**? List them below. Pediatric_WUIML_reuse$_i$ (i = 1 to the total number of modeled elements in the resulted models for the WUI.)

----

5. How many **person-hours** did you spend in complete the modeling of this WUI? Pediatric_WUIML_personHours

----

is the resulting models and the completed use case worksheets, are analyzed to find out the following: D1) How many of the required modeling items are correctly modeled when the modeling was done in WUIML? D2) how many of the required modeling items are correctly modeled when the modeling was done in standard UML? D3) how many of the required modeling items are correctly modeled via reuse when the modeling was done in WUIML? To model via reuse is to create new models by re-using previously created models or model elements. For example, suppose one previously created a model that includes a class representing fruit. Now one can reuse the fruit class to create a class that represents a specific fruit, such as an apple, by extending the fruit class. Both standard UML and WUIML allow SMEs to model via reuse. D4) how many of the required modeling items are correctly modeled via reuse when the modeling was done in standard UML? D5) how many person-hours spent to generate the WUIML models? D6) how many person-hours spent to generate the standard UML models? D7) the total number of required modeling items. D1, D2, D5, D6, and D7 link to proposition 1. D3, D4, D5, D6, and D7 link to proposition 2.

Criteria for Interpreting a Case Study's Findings

In this empirical study, the criteria for interpreting a case study's findings correspond to the metric and measures used in evaluating the results of applying WUIML and standard UML respectively to the units of analysis. "A measure provides a quantitative indication of the extent, amount, dimension, capacity, or size of some attribute of a product or process(Pressman, 2004)." A metric is an important directly measurable attribute of a software product, a software service, a software process or a software resource. Direct metrics may be either used as indicators (predictors), or of other more valuable outcomes that are indirect metrics. For example, the indirect metrics in this case study are efficiency and effectiveness. The direct metrics are: m1) number of the required modeling items that are correctly modeled when the modeling was done in WUIML; m2) number of the required modeling items that are correctly modeled when the modeling was done in standard UML; m3) number of the required modeling items that are correctly modeled via reuse when the modeling was done in WUIML; m4) number

Table 2. Evidence collection through the case study worksheets

Questions (Units)	Evidence captured	Propositions to support/reject
Pediatric_WUIML_modelingTool	The modeling tool used to perform the modeling in WUIML for the Pediatric Medical Profile Login WUI.	Proposition 1 and Proposition 2
Pediatric_WUIML_modelsFilename	The name of the software copy of the resulted models in WUIML for the Pediatric Medical Profile Login WUI.	Proposition 1 and Proposition 2
Pediatric_WUIML_required_modeling_item$_i$	The correctly modeled required modeling items in WUIML for the Pediatric Medical Profile Login WUI.	Proposition 1
Pediatric_WUIML_reuse$_i$	The correctly modeled required modeling items via reuse in WUIML for the Pediatric Medical Profile Login WUI.	Proposition 2
Pediatric_WUIML_personHours	The person-hours spent to model the Pediatric Metrical Profile Login WUI using WUIML.	Proposition 1 and Proposition 2
Pediatric_UML_modelingTool	The modeling tool used to perform the modeling in UML for the Pediatric Medical Profile Login WUI.	Proposition 1 and Proposition 2
Pediatric_UML_modelsFilename	The name of the software copy of the resulted models in UML for the Pediatric Medical Profile Login WUI.	Proposition 1 and Proposition 2
Pediatric_UML_required_modeling_item$_i$	The correctly modeled required modeling items in UML for the Pediatric Medical Profile Login WUI.	Proposition 1
Pediatric_UML_reuse$_i$	The correctly modeled required modeling items via reuse in UML for the Pediatric Medical Profile Login WUI.	Proposition 2
Pediatric_UML_personHours	The person-hours spent to model the Pediatric Metrical Profile Login WUI using UML.	Proposition 1 and Proposition 2
Adolescent_WUIML_modelingTool	The modeling tool used to perform the modeling in WUIML for the Adolescent Medical Profile Login WUI.	Proposition 1 and Proposition 2
Adolescent_WUIML_modelsFilename	The name of the software copy of the resulted models in WUIML for the Adolescent Medical Profile Login WUI.	Proposition 1 and Proposition 2
Adolescent_WUIML_required_modeling_item$_i$	The correctly modeled required modeling items in WUIML for the Adolescent Medical Profile Login WUI.	Proposition 1
Adolescent_WUIML_reuse$_i$	The correctly modeled required modeling items via reuse in WUIML for the Adolescent Medical Profile Login WUI.	Proposition 2
Adolescent_WUIML_personHours	The person-hours spent to model the Adolescent Metrical Profile Login WUI using WUIML.	Proposition 1 and Proposition 2
Adolescent_UML_modelingTool	The modeling tool used to perform the modeling in UML for the Adolescent Medical Profile Login WUI.	Proposition 1 and Proposition 2
Adolescent_UML_modelsFilename	The name of the software copy of the resulted models in UML for the Adolescent Medical Profile Login WUI.	Proposition 1 and Proposition 2
Adolescent_WUIML_required_modeling_itemi	The correctly modeled required modeling items in UML for the Adolescent Medical Profile Login WUI.	Proposition 1
Adolescent_UML_reuse$_i$	The correctly modeled required modeling items via reuse in UML for the Adolescent Medical Profile Login WUI.	Proposition 2
Adolescent_UML_personHours	The person-hours spent to model the Adolescent Metrical Profile Login WUI using UML.	Proposition 1 and Proposition 2

continued on following page

Table 2. continued

Adult_WUIML_modelingTool	The modeling tool used to perform the modeling in WUIML for the Adult Medical Profile Login WUI.	Proposition 1 and Proposition 2
Adult_WUIML_modelsFilename	The name of the software copy of the resulted models in WUIML for the Adult Medical Profile Login WUI.	Proposition 1 and Proposition 2
Adult_WUIML_required_modeling_item$_i$	The correctly modeled required modeling items in WUIML for the Adult Medical Profile Login WUI.	Proposition 1
Adult_WUIML_reuse$_i$	The correctly modeled required modeling items via reuse in WUIML for the Adult Medical Profile Login WUI.	Proposition 2
Adult_WUIML_personHours	The person-hours spent to model the Adult Metrical Profile Login WUI using WUIML.	Proposition 1 and Proposition 2
Adult_UML_modelingTool	The modeling tool used to perform the modeling in UML for the Adult Medical Profile Login WUI.	Proposition 1 and Proposition 2
Adult_UML_modelsFilename	The name of the software copy of the resulted models in UML for the Adult Medical Profile Login WUI.	Proposition 1 and Proposition 2
Adult_UML_required_modeling_item$_i$	The correctly modeled required modeling items in UML for the Adult Medical Profile Login WUI.	Proposition 1
Adult_UML_reuse$_i$	The correctly modeled required modeling items via reuse in UML for the Adolescent Medical Profile Login WUI.	Proposition 2
Adult_UML_personHours	The person-hours spent to model the Adult Metrical Profile Login WUI using UML.	Proposition 1 and Proposition 2

of the required modeling items that are correctly modeled via reuse when the modeling was done in standard UML; m5) person-hours spent to generate the WUIML models; m6) person-hours spent to generate the standard UML models; m7) the total number of required modeling items.

The Case Study Procedure for both Case Studies

0. For those SMEs that need to perform the modeling in WUIML, teach them WUIML.
1. Identify the required modeling items from the software requirements.
2. Provide SMEs who are to conduct the modeling using WUIML with the software requirements.
3. Provide SMEs who are to conduct the modeling using standard UML with the software requirements.

4. Collect the results (WUIML models and the data from the completed case study worksheets) generated from step 2.
5. Collect the results (standard UML models and the data from the completed case study worksheets) generated from step 3.
6. Perform data analysis on the results and data collected from step 4 to find out the following: a) number of the correctly modeled required modeling items when the modeling was done in WUIML (the measure of m1); b) number of the correctly modeled required modeling items via reuse when the modeling was done in WUIML (the measure of m3); c) person-hours spent to generate the WUIML models (the measure of m5).
7. Perform data analysis on results and data collected from step 5 to find out the following: a) number of the correctly modeled required modeling items when the modeling was done in standard UML (the measure

of m2); b) number of the correctly modeled required modeling items via reuse when the modeling was done in standard UML (the measure of m4); c) person-hours spent to generate the standard UML models (the measure of m6).

8. Evaluate the outcome from step 6 to determine whether or not the proposition 1 is supported or rejected.

9. Evaluate the outcome from step 7 to determine whether or not the proposition 2 is supported or rejected.

RESULTS AND ANALYSIS

WUIML is developed to improve SPL software engineering paradigm in modeling user interfaces for Web-based SPLs. The improvement provided by WUIML should decrease the work needed by the SPL engineers in the WUI modeling perspective.

In the first case study, each SME has to model the WUIs for three product lines: Pediatric Medical Profile Login, Adolescent Medical Profile Login, and Adult Medical Profile Login. One SME is asked to model each WUI using WUIML while the other SME is asked to model the WUIs using standard UML. Each WUI is from a different member product (Pediatric Medical Management System, Adolescent Medical Management System, and Adult Medical Management System) of a medical product line (Medical Management Systems).

Table 3 shows the results for modeling Pediatric Medical Profile Login WUI using standard UML and WUIML respectively. The last row in Table 3 shows the ratio of the number of correctly modeled required modeling items to the total number of required modeling items in standard UML and WUIML respectively.

Note that in each case study, there are two SMEs. One SME is asked to model using standard UML while the other SME is asked to model using WUIML. In the following tables (Table 4, 5, 6, and 7), the numbers shown in the second column from the left were derived from the models created by the SME who was asked to model using standard UML. The numbers shown in the third column from the left were derived from the models created by the SME who was asked to model using WUIML. The sample size is irrelevant in case study research method because case study research method is based on analytical generalization instead of statistical generalization (Yin, 2003). However, the results shown in these tables must replicate (or be replicated by) the results from the second case study in order to lead to an analytical generalization.

Table 4 shows the ratio of the number of correctly modeled required modeling items to the total number of required modeling items in modeling the three WUIs and the person-hours spent on each approach. Notice that the person-hours spent for modeling the Pediatric Medical Profile Login WUI was more than the person-hours spent for Adolescent Medical Profile Login WUI and Adult Medical Profile Login WUI respectively in WUIML approach. This is because to model the WUIs for a member product (such as the Pediatric Medical Profile Login WUI), one must first develop the WUI models for the SPL.

Table 5 shows the number of correctly modeled required modeling items per person-hours for the models in UML and WUIML for the three member products' WUIs respectively.

Table 6 shows the ratio of the number of correctly modeled required modeling items via reuse (or product line reuse when WUIML is used) to the total number of reusable required modeling items in modeling the three WUIs and the person-hours spent on each approach.

Table 7 shows the number of correctly modeled required modeling items per person-hours via reuse for the models in UML and WUIML respectively.

The data in Table 3 show that 18 out of 25 required modeling items were correctly modeled

Table 3. Results for modeling the Pediatric Medical Profile Login WUI

Required modeling items for Pediatric Medical Profile Login WUI	Modeled correctly in Standard UML	Modeled correctly in WUIML
Page title: "Pediatric Medical Profile Login"	Yes	Yes
Label 1: "Profile ID:"	Yes	Yes
A textbox for label 1.	Yes	Yes
Label 2: "Password:"	Yes	Yes
A textbox for label 2.	Yes	Yes
Label 3: "Role:"	Yes	Yes
A radio button.	Yes	Yes
The radio button must default to be checked.	Yes	
A label for the radio button: "Parent/Guardian". (Only parent or legal guardian who are previously registered with the health provider can login for the child.).	Yes	Yes
A submit button with name "Login".	Yes	Yes
The Page title must placed on the top of the page.		Yes
The Profile ID and its related textbox must be immediately next to each other.		Yes
The Password and its related textbox must be immediately next to each other.		Yes
The Role and its related radioButton must not be immediately next to each other.		Yes
Profile ID must be placed on top of the Password and its related textbox.		Yes
The Role and the radio button must be on a line that is on top of the Login button.		Yes
The Login button must be placed at the lower left hand side of the page.		Yes
The activity diagram should include an action node: Pediatric Medical Profile Login.	Yes	Yes
The activity diagram should include an action node: Login Error.	Yes	Yes
The activity diagram should include an action node: Parent Welcome.	Yes	Yes
The activity diagram should include an action node: Customer Service.	Yes	Yes
The activity diagram should include a start node.	Yes	Yes
The activity diagram should include an end node.	Yes	Yes
The activity diagram should include a decision node: whether validation is successful.	Yes	Yes
The activity diagram should indicate the condition that "Profile ID, Password, and Role" values are available.	Yes	Yes
	18/25	24/25

for the Pediatric Medical Profile Login WUI using standard UML. On the other hand, the data in Table 3 show that 24 out of 25 required modeling items were modeled for the same Pediatric Medical Profile Login WUI using WUIML. This result in Table 3 indicates that a SME was able to correctly model more required modeling items using WUIML than using standard UML. Table 4 shows

Table 4. Ratio of correctly modeled required modeling items to the total number of required modeling items

WUI	Standard UML (Person-hours)	WUIML (Person-hours)
Pediatric	18/25 (8)	24/25 (7)
Adolescent	23/30 (10)	29/30 (4)
Adult	18/25 (7)	24/25 (2)

Table 5. Number of correctly modeled required modeling items

	Standard UML model	WUIML model
Pediatric	2.25	3.4
Adolescent	2.3	7.25
Adult	2.57	12
Average	2.37	9.08

Table 6. Number of correctly modeled required modeling items via reuse

WUI	Standard UML (Person-hours)	WUIML (Person-hours)
Pediatric	0/10 (8)	10/11 (3+4)
Adolescent	8/10 (10)	10/11 (4)
Adult	8/10 (7)	10/11 (2)

Table 7. Number of correctly modeled required modeling items via reuse (or product line reuse) per person-hours

	Standard UML model	WUIML model
Pediatric	0	1.43
Adolescent	0.8	2.5
Adult	1.14	5
Average	0.65	2.98

the correctly modeled required modeling items and the approximate person-hours for modeling the Pediatric, Adolescent, and Adult Medical Profile Login WUI respectively in standard UML and WUIML. Table 5 shows the calculated value of modeled items per person-hour based on the data from Table 4. The data in Table 5 shows that when using WUIML, a SME was able to correctly model about four times more required modeling items per person-hour (i.e. 9.08) than that in standard UML (i.e. 2.37). Thus, this result indicates WUIML is more efficient than standard UML in modeling user interfaces for Web-based SPL, therefore, this result supports proposition 1.

Table 6 shows the number of correctly modeled required modeling items via reuse (or product line reuse) and its corresponding person-hours used. For example, using standard UML to model the

Pediatric Medical Profile Login WUI, a SME was not able to reuse any model items out of the ten reusable items in the WUI model. For approximate eight person-hours, the SME has to model without reuse. This is because the Pediatric Medical Profile Login WUI was the first WUI for a SME to model. There is nothing to reuse yet. Notice that the number of reusable required modeling items is only a sub-set of the total number of required modeling items in a WUI model because some items are unique to a particular WUI and cannot be reused.

On the other hand, using WUIML, across all three WUIs (Pediatric Medical Profile Login, Adolescent Medical Profile Login, and Adult Medical Profile Login.), as shown in Table 6, number of correctly modeled required modeling items via reuse are consistent. This is because in WUIML, a SME is to first develop the product line WUI model. The WUI model for the SPL encapsulated all model items for its member product WUI models. Therefore, reusing the items in the product line WUI model creates the WUI model for a member product. As shown in Figure 7, the average number of correctly modeled required modeling items via reuse per person-hours using WUIML (i.e. 2.98) is about four times to that when using standard UML (i.e. 0.65). This result indicates that WUIML enables higher level of reuse than standard UML, thus it indicates increased effectiveness when using WUIML than using standard UML. Therefore, this result supports proposition 2.

The results of the second case study are not shown due to the limitation of the space in the paper. The second case study was conducted by another two SMEs. The units of analysis for the second case study were the software requirements for the Pediatric Exercise Record WUI, the Adolescent Exercise Record WUI, and the Adult Exercise Record WUI. The results from the second case study show that using WUIML to model the Exercise Record WUIs for the three member products of the SPL increases the modeler's efficiency and effectiveness in modeling. This result is similar to the result from the first case study. The results of the two case studies literally replicate. Based on the results, the analytical generalization that WUIML increases modelers' efficiency and effectiveness in model WUIs for SPL is drawn in this study.

The generalization thus provides a positive answer to the study's research question that Web user interface modeling for a Web-based medical SPL using WUIML increases SMEs' modeling efficiency and effectiveness (thus decreases work).

CONCLUSION AND FUTURE WORK

In standard UML, there is no standard way to model user interface and no standard way to model variant features of user interfaces for a SPL. WUIML defines elements to propose a standard way to model user interfaces as well as variant user interface features of Web-based SPLs. WUIML improves UML in terms of modeling of user interfaces and use interfaces for SPL.

Case study research method has been applied to investigate whether WUIML method increases modelers' efficiency and effectiveness on modeling a Web-based medical SPL when compared to standard UML method. The results indicate that modeling WUIs for SPL using WUIML is more effective and efficient than using standard UML.

There are many ways to model software using UML. Because UML is not formally defined, a human is needed to make the "best" judgment on the correctness of a UML model. In this empirical study, the way to determine whether a required modeling item is modeled correctly or not relies on a human's modeling experience. Since the same human is using his same modeling experience to make the judgment on all models, the bias due to human judgment should be insignificant.

Since the SMEs are of similar backgrounds and technical experience, the impact on modeling efficiency and effectiveness due to individual SME's capability should be insignificant. Since the same requirements are given for both approaches (WUIML and standard UML), the reuse opportunity base on application logics (according to the requirements) should be the same for all SMEs.

Future work is to develop a tool to support using WUIML to model WUIs for SPLs and to extend WUIML beyond the Web platform.

REFERENCES

Altheim, M., Boumphrey, F., McCarron, S., Schnitzenbaumer, S., & Wugofski, T. (Eds.). (2001). *Modularization of XHTML*.

Altheim, M., & Shane McCarron, S. (Eds.). (2001). *XHTML 1.1 - Module-based XHTML*.

Anastasopoulos, M., & Gacek, C. (2001). Implementing Product Line Variabilities. *ACM SSR '01*, 109-117.

Behrens, H., Ritter, T., & Six, H.-W. (2003). Systematic Development of Complex Web-Based User Interfaces. *Computer Science in Perspective, 2598*, 22-38.

Blankenhorn, K., & Jeckle, M. (2004). A UML Profile for GUI Layout. *Net.ObjectDays*, 110-121.

Booch, G., Rumbaugh, J., & Jacobson, I. (1999). *The Unified Modeling Language User Guide*: Addison Wesley Longman, Inc.

Bos, B., Celik, T., Hickson, I., & Lie, H. W. (Eds.). (2004). *Cascading Style Sheets, level 2 revision 1 CSS 2.1 Specification. W3C Candidate Recommendation. Available online: http://www.w3.org/TR/2004/CR-CSS21-20040225*.

Chastek, G., Donohoe, P., Kang, K. C., & Thiel, S. H., A. (2001). *Product Line Analysis: A Practical Description (CMU/SEI-2001-TR-001)*. Pittsburgh, PA. Software Engineering Institute, Carnegie Mellon University.

Clements, P., & Northrop, L. (2002). *Software Product Lines: Practices and Patterns*. (2nd ed.): Addition-Wesley.

Cohen, S. G., Stanley, J. J. L., Peterson, A. S., & Krut Jr., R. W. (1992). *Application of Feature-Oriented Domain Analysis to the Army Movement Control Domain* (CMU/SEI-91-TR-28). Pittsburgh, PA: Software Engineering Institute, Carnegie Mellon University.

Dubinko, M. (2003). *XForms Essentials*: O'Reilly & Associates, Inc.

Dubinko, M., Leigh, L., Klotz, J., Merrick, R., & Raman, T. V. (2002). *XForms 1.0*. Available: http://www.w3.org/TR/xforms/.

Eckstein, R., Loy, M., & Wood, D. (1998). *Java Swing*. (1st. ed.). Sebastopol, CA: O'Reilly and Associates, Inc.

Eriksson, H.-E., Penker, M., Lyons, B., & Fado, D. (2004). *UML 2 Toolkit*: Wiley Publishing, Inc.

Gamma, E., Helm, R., Johnson, R., & Vlissides, J. (1995). *Design Patterns* (1st ed.): Addison-Wesley Professional.

Gomaa, H. (2004). *Designing Software Product Lines with UML : From Use Cases to Pattern-Based Software Architectures*: Addison-Wesley Professional.

Gomaa, H., & Gianturco, M. (2002). Domain Modeling for World Wide Web Based Software Product lines with UML. *IEEE ICSR-7, LNCS, 2319*, 78-92.

Gómez, J., & Cachero, C. (2003). OO-H Method: Extending UML to Model Web Interfaces, *Information Modeling for Internet Applications* (pp. 144-173). Hershey, PA, USA: Idea Group Publishing.

Hennicker, R., & Koch, N. (2001). *Modeling the User Interface of Web Applications with UML.* Paper presented at the In Practical UML-Based Rigorous Development Methods - Countering or Integrating the eXtremists, Workshop of the pUML-Group at the UML 2001, Gesellschaft für Informatik, Köllen Druck+Verlag.

Jacobson, I., Christerson, M., Jonsson, P., & Overgaard, G. (1992). *Object-Oriented Software Engineering: a Use Case Driven Approach.* Reading, MA: Addison-Wesley.

Jacobson, I., Griss, M., & Jonsson, P. (1997). *Software Reuse: Architecture, Process, and Organization for Business Success.* Reading, MA: Addison-Wesley Longman.

Jonny Axelsson, Beth Epperson, Masayasu Ishikawa, Shane McCarron, Ann Navarro, & Steven Pemberton (Eds.). (2003). *XHTML™ 2.0. W3C Working Draft 6 May 2003.*

Khare, R. (2000). Can XForm Transform the Web? Transcending the Web as GUI, Part II. *IEEE Internet Computing*(March-April), 103-106.

Kovacevic, S. (June 1998). *UML and User Interface Modeling.* Paper presented at the UML'98, Mulhouse, France.

Lee, S.-W. (2004). *Proxy viewpoints model-based requirements discovery.* Unpublished doctoral, George Mason University, Fairfax, VA. U.S.A.

Lie, H. W., & Bos, B. (1999). *Cascading Style Sheets, level 1* (11 Jan 1999). Available: http://www.w3.org/TR/REC-CSS1 [2003, June 28, 2003].

Lilly, S. (2000). *How to Avoid Use-Case Pitfalls.* Available: http://www.sdmagazine.com/print/ [2005, April 9, 2005].

Lynch, C. L. (1999). *A Methodological Framework For Interface Requirements Identification and Specification.* Unpublished Doctoral, George Mason University, Fairfax, VA, U.S.A.

Marcus, A. (2002). Dare We Define User-Interface Design? *Interactions, 9*(5), 19-24.

Meyer, E. A. (2000). *Cascading Style Sheets: The Definitive Guide.* USA: O'Reilly & Associates, Inc.

Meyer, E. A. (2003). *Eric Meyer on CSS: Mastering the Language of Web Design* (2nd ed.): New Riders Publishing.

Meyer, E. A. (May 2000). *Cascading Style Sheets: The Definitive Guide.*: O'Reilly.

Myers, B. A. (1989). User-Interface Tools: Introduction and Survey. *IEEE Interface Systems*(January 1989), 15-23.

Nunes, N. J. (2003). Representing User-Interface Patterns in UML. *Lecture Notes in Computer Science,, 2817*, 142 - 151.

OMG. (2002). *Meta Object Facility (MOF) Version 1.4.* Available: http://www.omg.org/technology/documents/formal/mof.htm.

OMG. (2003a). *UML 2.0 OCL Specification, ptc/03-10-14*: Object Management Group.

OMG. (2003b). *Unified Modeling Language: Infrastructure, version 2.0 (3rd revised submission to OMG RFP ad/00-09-01)*: Object Management Group.

OMG. (2004). *Unified Modeling Language: Superstructure, version 2.0. ptc/04-10-02.*

Pedro A. Szekely, Piyawadee Noi Sukaviriya, Pablo Castells, Jeyakumar Muthukumarasamy, & Salcher, E. (1996). *Declarative Interface Models for User Interface Construction Tools: the MASTERMIND Approach.* Paper presented at the In Engineering for Human-Computer Interaction, Chapman & Hall, London, UK.

Phillips, C., Kemp, E., & Kek, S. M. (2001). Extending UML Use Case Modelling to Support

Graphical User Interface Design. *Proceedings of Software Engineering Conference, 48 - 57.*

Powell, T. (2003). *HTML & XHTML: The Complete Reference* (4th ed.): McGraw-Hill/Osborne.

Pressman, R. S. (2004). 15 Product Metrics for Software, *Software Engineering: A Practitioner's Approach* (6th ed.): McGraw-Hill.

Raggett, D., Hors, L. E., & Jacobs, I. (1999). *HTML 4.01 Specification.* Available: http://www.w3.org/TR/REC-html40/.

Rosenberg, D., & Scott, K. (2001). *Top Ten Use Case Mistakes.* Available: http://www.sdmagazine.com/print/ [2005, April 1, 2005].

Rumbaugh, J., Jacobson, I., & Booch, G. (2005). *The Unified Modeling Language Reference Manual* (2nd ed.): Addison Wesley.

Sauers, M., & Wyke, R. A. (2001). *XHTML essentials.* New York: Wiley Computer Publishing.

Schengili-Roberts, K. (2004). *Core CSS: Cascading Style Sheets* (2nd ed.): Prentice Hall PTR, NJ.

Schmitt, C. (2003). *Designing CSS Web Pages* (2nd ed.): New Riders Publishing.

Scogings, C., & Phillips, C. (2001). A method for the early stages of interactive system design using UML and Lean Cuisine+. *Proceedings. Second Australasian User Interface Conference, 2001. AUIC 2001, 69 -76.*

Scott, K. (2004). *Fast Track UML 2.0: UML 2.0 Reference Guide*: Springer Verlag.

SEI. (2005a). *A Framework for Software Product Line Practice, Version 4.2.* Software Engineering Institute. Available: http://www.sei.cmu.edu/productlines/framework.html [2005, March 23].

SEI. (2005b). *Software Product Lines.* Available: http://www.sei.cmu.edu/productlines/ [2005, March 23, 2005].

Shin, E. M. (2002). *Evolution in Multiple-View Models of Software Product Families.* George Mason University, Fairfax, VA.

Silva, P. P. d. (2002). *Object Modelling of Interactive Systems: The UMLi Approach.* Unpublished Doctoral, University of Manchester, United Kingdom.

Silva, P. P. d., & Paton, N. W. (2003). User Interface Modeling in UMLi. *IEEE Software* (July/August 2003), 62-69.

Sommerville, I. (2001). Chapter 15 User Interface Design, *Software Engineering*: Addison-Wesley.

Tellis, W. (1997a). Application of a Case Study Methodology. *The Qualitative Report, 3*(3).

Tellis, W. (1997b). Introduction to Case Study. *The Qualitative Report, 3*(2).

Tewfik Ziadi, Loïc Hélouët, & Jézéquel, J.-M. (May 2004). Towards a UML Profile for Software Product Lines. *Lecture Notes in Computer Science, 3014*, 129 - 139.

Tony Griffiths, Peter J. Barclay, Jo McKirdy, Norman W. Paton, Philip D. Gray, Jessie B. Kennedy, Richard Cooper, Carole A. Goble, Adrian West, & Smyth, M. (September 1999). *Teallach: A Model-Based User Interface Development Environment for Object Databases.* Paper presented at the UIDIS'99, Edinburgh, UK.

W3C. *The Extensible Stylesheet Language (XSL).* Available: http://www.w3.org/Style/XSL/ [2003, May 3].

W3C. (2002). XHTML 1.0: The Extensible Hypertext Markup Language (second edition).

Webber, D. L. (2001). *The Variation Point Model For Software product Lines.* George Mason University, Fairfax, VA, U.S.A.

Yin, R. K. (2003). *Case Study Research: Design and Methods* (3rd ed. Vol. 5). Thousand Oaks: Sage Publications, Inc.

This work was previously published in Int. Journal of Information Technology and Web Engineering, Vol 1, Issue 1, edited by G. Alkhatib and D. Rine, pp. 1-34, copyright 2006 by IGI Publishing (an imprint of IGI Global).

Section III
Open Source

Chapter XVI
Experience Report:
A Component–Based Data Management and Knowledge Discovery Framework for Aviation Studies

M. Brian Blake
Georgetown University and The MITRE Corporation, USA

Lisa Singh
Georgetown University, USA

Andrew B. Williams
Spelman University, USA

Wendell Norman
The MITRE Corporation, USA

Amy L. Sliva
Georgetown University, USA

ABSTRACT

Organizations are beginning to apply data mining and knowledge discovery techniques to their corporate data sets, thereby enabling the identification of trends and the discovery of inductive knowledge. Many times, traditional transactional databases are not optimized for analytical processing and must be transformed. This article proposes the use of modular components to decrease the overall amount of human processing and intervention necessary for the transformation process. Our approach configures components to extract data-sets using a set of "extraction hints". Our framework incorporates decentralized, generic components that are reusable across domains and databases. Finally, we detail an implementation of our component-based framework for an aviation data set.

INTRODUCTION

Over the past decade, government and industry organizations have enhanced their operations by utilizing emerging technologies in data management. Advances in database methodology and software (i.e. warehousing of transactional data) has increased the ability of organizations to extract useful knowledge from operational data and has helped build the foundation for the field of knowledge discovery in databases (KDD) (Fayyad, 1996; Sarawagi, 2000; Software Suites supporting Knowledge Discovery, 2005). KDD consists of such phases as *selection*, *pre-processing*, *transformation*, *data mining*, and *interpretation/evaluation*. Selection involves identifying the data that should be used for the data mining process. Typically, the data is obtained from multiple heterogeneous data sources. The pre-processing phase includes steps for data cleansing and the development of strategies for handling missing data and various data anomalies. Data transformation involves converting data from the different sources into a single common format. This step also includes using data reduction techniques to reduce the complexity of the selected data, thereby simplifying future steps in the KDD process. Data mining tasks apply various algorithms to the transformed data to generate and identify "hidden knowledge". Finally, the area of interpretation/evaluation focuses on creating an accurate and clear presentation of the data mining results to the user.

Excluding the data mining phase, where there are a plethora of automated algorithms and applications, the other phases are mostly human-driven. Data experts are required to complete the tasks related to the majority of steps in the KDD process as explained below.

- **Data Formatting, Loading, Cleaning and Anomaly Detection**. In the pre-processing phase, data experts must correct and update incorrect data values, populate missing data values, and fix data anomalies.

- **Adding Important Meta-Data to the Database**. In the data transformation phase, data must be integrated into a single model that supports analytical processing. This typically involves adding meta-data and converting data sets from text files and traditional relational schemas to star or multidimensional schemas.

- **User and Tool-Generated Hints**. In the final phases (i.e. data mining and evaluation), general approaches are needed to assist users in preparing knowledge discovery routines and analyzing results. These general approaches must allow the user to manually specify potential correlation areas or "hints". In the future, the suggestion of new hints may be automated by intelligent software mechanisms.

These human-driven tasks pose problems since the initial data set, which we will refer to as the *raw data,* is large, complex and heterogeneous. Our work attempts to reduce the amount of time required for human-driven tasks in the KDD setting. General reusable components may represent a feasible solution to assist in the execution of the time-consuming processing tasks underlying KDD. In this paper, specific tasks suitable for such components are identified and characterized. In addition, a component-based framework and corresponding process are described to address these tasks.

The paper proceeds in the following section with a discussion of related work with respect to component-based KDD. The paper then introduces the Component-Based Knowledge Discovery in Databases (C-KDD) framework. Subsequent sections provide specific low-level technical details of the C-KDD framework and, in the final sections, the C-KDD is used in an aviation-based study.

RELATED WORK

In practice, the application of KDD to the aviation domain has been done in a limited number of studies. In fact, there are few approaches known by the authors that use data mining techniques in the aviation domain. Earlier aviation studies (Nazeri, 2002; Callahan, 2001) use static, specialized techniques for aviation security and studies in weather. These earlier approaches do not leverage current data modeling approaches or follow a general purpose design. With respect to KDD-related research, there are many approaches that investigate the data mining phase (Aggrawal, 1996; Netz, 2001), but few approaches that address the human efforts particularly using component-based development. Bueno (1998) discusses the benefit of using components to assist with the KDD process. However, similar to

other KDD-related research, Bueno focuses on the components for the data mining stage of the process. Bueno does not significantly detail the connection of their components to the underlying database. C-KDD focuses on all KDD stages with an emphasis on the tedious human-driven data collection phase.

Chattratichat (1999) and Engels (1999) describe component architectures to assist human users in KDD. Chattratichat (1999) addresses data mining across different organizational regions and Engels (1999) focuses on assisting in the selection of data mining algorithms. Neither project considers support for the human-driven steps required to initially capture the data.

Kim (2002) describes Chamois, a component-based framework implemented by composing a number of third-party software packages. The goal of Chamois is similar to C-KDD; however,

Figure 1. The C-KDD framework for KDD

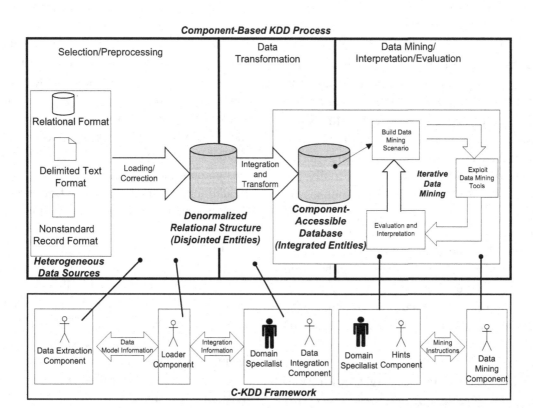

the focus is not on the integration of component capabilities at the specification level from the top-down, instead it focuses on building up a framework based on existing applications. The C-KDD approach focuses on the communication channels, particularly from human-to-component. The innovation of C-KDD is the formal data transfer specifications which have not been found in related frameworks supporting the full KDD process.

C-KDD FRAMEWORK

C-KDD is a component-based framework designed to support KDD phases. Five distinct KDD components were chosen to realize the various phases of the KDD process. These KDD components are the *Data Extraction Component, Loader Component, Data Integration Component, Data Mining Component,* and *Hints Component.* The Data Extraction Component and Loader Component combine to extract data from several heterogeneous data sources and populate a central relational data repository. A human, domain specialist identifies common fields between relational entities, and the Data Integration Component transforms these entities into the new component-accessible model. Finally, in the Data Mining, Interpretation, and Evaluation Phases, a human, domain specialist initiates a data mining scenario with the help of the Hints and Data Mining Components. The Hints Component presents the available data model to the domain specialists and accepts the human instructions to submit specialized studies to be executed by the Data Mining Component. The C-KDD framework is illustrated in Figure 1.

In the scope of this paper, we highlight the C-KDD specification techniques that allow human, domain experts to program components and automate portions of the KDD process. The following three sub-sections discuss how domain experts can specify data extraction/loading directives, data transformation instructions, and knowledge discovery instructions.

Component Specification for Data Extraction and Loading

In the Selection and Pre-processing phases of KDD, various data sources must be identified and the underlying data must be captured in machine-readable format. The approach taken in this work is to perform a component-mediated step that collects heterogeneous data and populates that data in several relational database tables using traditional approaches (i.e. existing data transformation techniques are embedded in component (Chawathe, 1998; Nodine 1998)).

The C-KDD framework considers several types of data formats. It was not possible in the initial investigations to consider every possible format, but samples of data were taken from the initial deployment domain (i.e. aviation studies). There were several types of structured and semi-structured data considered as listed below:

- Delimited Data in Row Format
- Delimited Data in Non-Fixed Row Format
- Relational Database Information
- Name/Value Format
- Mark-Up Format (i.e. XML and HTML)

Delimited Data in Row Format, Relational Database Format, Name/Value Format, and Mark-Up Language Format are standard structured formats for capturing data. Using general functions and minimal human intervention, the aforementioned formats are extracted with ease by the Data Extraction Component. Human intervention can be defined in two tasks. The first column in most input files contains the column headings. With respect to human intervention in this case, the human is required to confirm these headings or change the naming, if necessary. In other files the column headings are not included; therefore the human user must specify column headings. In mark-up files, XML *element* names arc used as headings. In general, for these types of files, the overhead is relatively low, since the user is only required to enter the names or make confirmations with a couple of button presses. There are some exceptional cases, but it was discovered in the aviation domain that this degree of human intervention was sufficient in 17 out of 19 relevant cases.

Exploiting semi-structured data (i.e. Delimited Formats in Non-Fixed Row Format) requires a relatively higher degree of interaction between the human user and the Data Integration Component. The C-KDD framework extends an existing approach referred to as *templating* to describe the semi-structured data schema to the components. With respect to the C-KDD approach, the specification of a template allows the user to *flatten* hierarchical data into row format. The template consists of several aspects. We define a *zone* to be the area of a template identified by delimination parameters (e.g. semicolon, space, or tab-delimited). Data can be delimited by a string delimiter and also by using fixed column locations. There are specialized attributes that describe the start and end of a zone. Other attributes allow the user to specify a zone by number of columns. It is not in the scope of this paper to describe the templating technique in detail but technical details can be found in related work (Blake, 2005).

Component-Mediated Processes for Data Transformation

The C-KDD framework includes a Data Transformation Component that generates a generalized, denormalized database. In the C-KDD framework, we introduce a process that generalizes the database schema into a model that C-KDD components can navigate. This is a reproducible process that is valid for any database with entities that share related columns. This process includes the creation of fact tables (Kimball, 1996; Kimball,

1998) that connect entities. With respect to the C-KDD framework, there is a *CorrelationSpace* entity that links multiple *CorrelationAttribute* entities. The CorrelationSpace table corresponds to the fact table in a star schema. The CorrelationAttribute entity corresponds to the dimension table in the star schema. Example CorrelationAttributes include time and location. Although the results will be discussed in a later section, Figure 2 contains an aviation-based model developed using this approach. There is a CorrelationSpace table, and the AreaSpace and TimeSpace tables are both CorrelationAttributes.

The process for creating the denormalized database in Figure 2 is as follows:

1. **Human domain specialist identifies related columns across multiple normalized tables.**

2. **The domain specialists identifies the specific range of data for the related columns/attributes**

   - This specification may consist of a range of time, a specific area, or a range of keyed information.

3. **Assuming columns are sorted, C-KDD components create generic Correlation-Attribute tables and preload records for data within that specified range.**

   - For example, if the user specifies the time between May and June, the component would build a CorrelationAttribute (i.e. TimeSpace) table that has a record for each time increment within that range.

4. **Components query the initial data tables and record-by-record create correlation records in the CorrelationSpace entities based on matching the record to the preloaded correlation attributes.**

Figure 2. The ASCEND Relational Database Schema

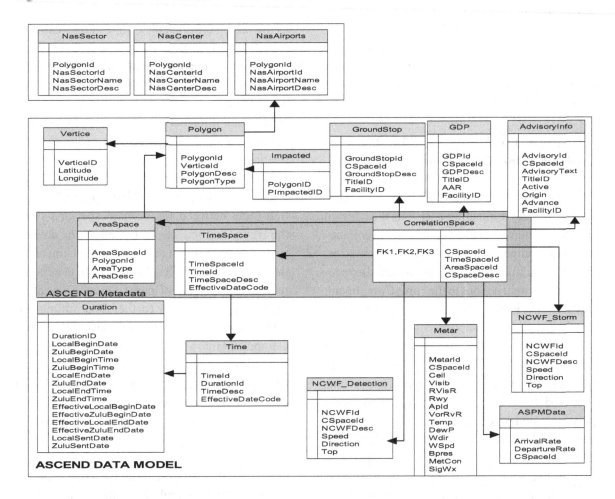

- Considering the earlier example in 3, the component would extract a record from the original table and search for the time increment corresponding to that record. The two individual records would be merged or 'joined' into a single composite record in the Correlation Space table.

5. **Additional detailed tables can be generated/connected to further describe the correlation attributes.** (This is not component-automated step.)

By using the generic CorrelationSpace and CorrelationAttribute table structures, component capabilities can be duplicated on any database containing these meta-information tables. The Data Mining Components are not limited by having to *hard-code* column names and table locations, instead queries can be managed based on pre-defined conditions. Also, this process essentially pre-loads entity joins into the database model. During loading, the Data Integration Components do not create duplicate correlation identifiers (i.e. CSpaceid in Figure 2), instead existing correlation records are reused. In this way, for example, when a weather record has the same correlation conditions (the same time and same airport) as a terminal performance record, both records have the same CorrelationSpace identification. This modeling approach separates the domain-specific information from the database semantics, an approach akin to the separation of concerns in software design. This separation allows the Data Mining Components to be able to perform basic text comparisons without knowledge of domain-specific concerns when generating data sets.

Component-Mediated Data Mining Routines using Extraction Hints

A major innovation in this work is the formal approach and corresponding user interface design that allows human domain specialists to collaborate with components on data mining scenarios. This approach uses a representation called *extraction hints* as instructions to the Hints Component. Domain specialists, at times, need to determine trends based on a composite list of constraints. In C-KDD framework, these constraints based on *qualifying events* are modeled as extraction hints. In the aviation domain, qualifying events can be defined as the combination of weather, processes, and performance conditions (i.e. "Give specified data when the temperature is greater than 70 degrees and the airport arrival rate is less than 15 per hour").

There are two major aspects of the extraction hint that human users can provide. The first aspect, called the *search criteria*, allows the input of a basic constraint. For example, a user might direct the component to explore situations where the cloud ceiling was greater than 1000 feet and temperature was greater than 90 degrees. This search criteria will specify records from the ASPMData table (Figure 2) where the values of the ceiling column is greater than 1000 and the temperature column is greater than 90.

Once a search criteria is set, the user can also suggest *information points*. An information point is defined as other information related to the search criteria, as constrained by the correlation attributes (in this case, time and airport).

For example, a user may specify an information point as the visibility at the same time and area as the search criteria constraint. A user can also specify an information point for a different location for a different time, perhaps at another airport and for the time 3 hours before the time captured when the search criteria is met. Both the search criteria and information points are composed of the correlation attributes represented in the correlation records.

The Hints Component has a specialized user interface that supports the collaboration of extraction hints between the domain specialists and the Hints Component. At initiation, the domain specialist suggests an initial extraction hint using this interface. Once results have been generated, the Hints Component can suggest a variation of the original hint for further data mining. In future work, the intent is to convert the Hints Component into a software agent to manage new, fully automated data mining scenarios. The Hints Component user interface as customized for the aviation domain is shown in Figure 3.

The search criteria is specified on the left side of the user interface. The *Table* textbox dynamically pulls table names from the C-KDD database. Once the table is chosen, the database columns are dynamically populated in the *Field* textbox. The domain specialist can designate a value (*Value* textbox) using any of the most common relational operators, that are populated in the *Relation* field. The *Preferred Name* textbox allows the user to associate a personalized heading for the search criteria. The information point is specified on the right side of the user interface, but was named *search information* for consistency. The domain specialist again can specify a preferred name, table, and field. In addition, the domain specialist can specify if there will be one data return correlated with the search criteria or multiple data returns (*Precision* textbox). The *CSpaceTimeType* and *CSpaceAreaType* textboxes and corresponding textboxes allows the domain specialist to

Figure 3. User interface for hints component

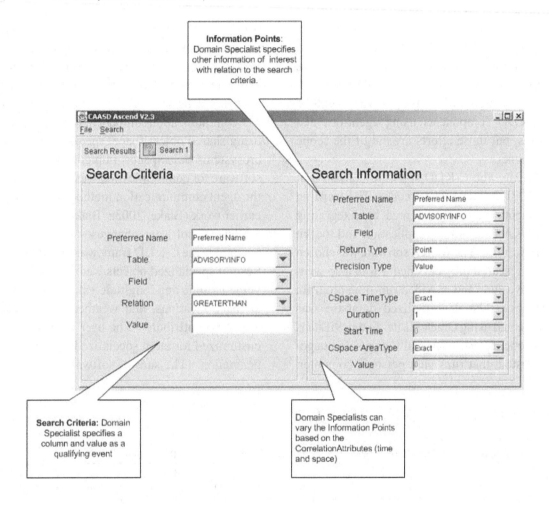

vary the correlation between the search criteria and search information. This user interface has been customized for the aviation domain so, in the case of this illustration, the correlation is based on time and location. However, it should be noted that the correlation attributes are not fixed, but that this implementation is just one embodiments of the approach. The user interface in Figure 3 shows one tab, but multiple tabs can be added on-demand by the domain specialist. Each tab has a new search criteria and information point (search information). Finally, the Hints Component creates an XML message that directs the Data Mining Component on how to extract datasets from the relational database. In the interest of space, there is just an overview of the capabilities of this user interface presented here.

ASCEND: C-KDD FOR ANALYSIS IN THE AVIATION DOMAIN

In evaluating the effectiveness of the C-KDD framework and approaches, the software was customized and deployed in an operational setting and used for an analysis on real data sources. The C-KDD framework and initial prototype was used in a joint project of the Center for Advanced Aviation System Development (CAASD) of The MITRE Corporation and the Department of Computer Science of Georgetown University. This joint project called Agent-Based Software for the Correlation of EN-route Data (ASCEND) was a customization of the C-KDD framework in the aviation domain. The ASCEND software was built predominantly using the C-KDD prototype. An additional goal of the project was to extend the C-KDD components using agent-oriented concepts, but those efforts are out of the scope of this paper.

Initially, the C-KDD software consisted of about 23,000 lines of Java code. The learning components were implemented by integrating the WEKA data mining application and toolkit (WEKA, 2005). The WEKA software was chosen for this research project, since it was also written in Java code and provided run-time program interfaces. The denormalized database was implemented using Oracle9iLite. Oracle9iLite is a fully operational relational database management system that runs on a personal computer.

This personal database was chosen to support the portability of the software and the database as one package. This ability made it possible to transfer the entire application and database from machine to machine on one CD. Both the C-KDD database and external databases (as data sources) were accessed using several JDBC interface software. The communication component was implemented using shared object space, specifically Sun Microsystems JavaSpaces implementation. The software for communication was an extension of the agent communication methods developed in earlier work (Blake, 2003a; Blake, 2003b).

Several software changes were required to customize the C-KDD framework for ASCEND. Several specialized objects were created to converge latitude and longitude values for airports, airspace locations, and weather locations into a common attribute. The user interfaces were customized for more specialized extraction hint generation. The sum of software changes was

Table 1. Data sources implemented in ASCEND

Data Source Name	Data Format Type	Source of Data	Description
Ground Stop (Order 7210.3S, 2003)	Microsoft Access Database (structured)	Federal Aviation Administration (FAA)	Procedure used to stop operations at a specific airport or group of airports with time and duration.
Ground Delay Program (GDP)	Microsoft Access Database (structured)	Federal Aviation Administration (FAA)	Procedure used to control the flow of arrivals into an airport or group of airports with a time and duration
Advisory Information	Delimited Text in *Non-Fixed* Row Format (unstructured)	Federal Aviation Administration (FAA)	Specific information about the status of the National Airspace System
ASPM Data (ASPM, 2005)	Delimited Text in Row Format	Federal Aviation Administration (FAA)	Airport performance metrics
National Convective Weather Forecast (NCWF) –STORM (National Weather Service, 2005)	Delimited Text in *Non-Fixed* Row Format (unstructured)	National Weather Service	Polygons representing areas of convective or inclement weather (prediction)
National Convective Weather Forecast (NCWF)-DETECTION	Delimited Text in *Non-Fixed* Row Format (unstructured)	National Weather Service	Polygons representing areas of convective or inclement weather (current forecast)
METAR	Delimited Text in Row (structured)	National Oceanic and Atmospheric Administration (NOAA)	Weather situation over a particular airport

less than 2000 lines of code which was favorable
with regards to the usability of C-KDD

The ASCEND Database

The ASCEND component-accessible database
populated with several data sources from multiple
heterogeneous sources as listed in Table 1. Access to these data sources was provided by The
MITRE Corporation. The final ASCEND data
model is closely related to the schema used for
the C-KDD approach. The final data model is
illustrated in Figure 2.

The data sources listed in Table 1 are shown
in the data model with direct association to the
CorrelationSpace entity. The CorrelationAttribute entities were given more specific names
expressed as database views. The names of the
two CorrelationAttribute entities are *AreaSpace*
and *TimeSpace*. The shaded area represents the
meta-data tables added for component navigation by the Data Integration Component. The
additional tables in the model are specialized
tables added to further describe the CorrelationAttribute entities. The additional specialized Java
code described in the previous section extended
the C-KDD framework to create and access the
additional entities (i.e. Vertice, Polygon, Time,
Duration entities).

Verifying C-KDD by Regenerating Known Aviation Rules

C-KDD was evaluated by performing aviation-
specific knowledge discovery routines using real
operational data. The ASCEND database was
populated with 6 months of data from May 2001
to October 2001 using the data sources described
in the previous section. This six month time-frame
is of great important to traffic flow management
in the United States because the convective
weather (i.e. thunderstorms) that occurs during
these months is the greatest cause of aviation

delay (Convective Weather PDT, 2005). The final
database was 600 megabytes in size.

The intention of the experimentation was
to verify the correctness of the framework by
performing studies that result in known rules.
The intention of the first study, involving Los
Angeles International Airport, was to verify
the C-KDD data mining tools and the second
study, involving Atlanta Hartsfield International
Airport focused on verifying the data transformation mechanisms. The rules resulting from both
studies would indicate trends that support several
well-known facts in aviation (i.e. when visibility
is bad, aviators are required to use their instruments also certain weather conditions negatively
affect the performance of airport departure and
arrival operations).

The first study was helpful in evaluating the
accuracy of the Data Mining Components by
re-generating known rules in real operational
data. The chosen experiment was to re-engineer
flight rules. From an aviation perspective, when
visibility is below a certain distance and ceiling
(cloud-level) is below a certain altitude, the FAA
institutes the instrument flight rules (IFR) restriction as opposed to the visual flight rules (VFR)
designation during normal conditions. During
IFR, any pilot flying an aircraft should be able
to operate the plane using solely the instruments.
In the MITRE-maintained METAR data source
(National Weather Service, 2005), the MetCon
(Flight Rule) field is determined by the value of
the Visib (visibility) and the Ceil (Cloud Ceiling)
columns. If the Visib field is less than 4 miles and
the Ceil field is less 700 feet, then the MetCon is
set to IFR. Otherwise, the MetCon is set to VFR.
There are other conditions, but it is not in the scope
of this paper to discuss the rules in detail. It is
more important to understand that the MetCon
column is a known function of the Ceiling and
Visibility. The study was executed on one data
source (i.e. METAR) to concentrate on the data
mining functions. In setting up this experiment,

the search criteria was set to Los Angeles airport and the information points were set to most of the METAR attributes (i.e. ceiling, visibility, flight rules, temperature, barometric pressure, wind speed, wind direction, and dew point). The relevant columns were not specified; therefore a successful experimental result could be shown in two outcomes. The first outcome would be that ceiling, visibility and flight rules should stand out as having the strongest correlation. A second successful outcome would be the determination of correct rules for flight rule designations. The experiment was successful from both aspects. Executing the experiment on all available METAR data for Los Angeles, the decision tree created using Data Mining Component (this component wraps the WEKA software (WEKA, 2005)) represented the known flight rule correlations. There were no significant deviations.

Using the same principle of discovering known rules, the second evaluation experiment was toward the verification of data integration processes and tools. In this experiment, the correlation between wind speed and airport performance was measured. Considering the fact that an aircraft lands against the wind and takes-off against the wind, excessively high wind speed tends to have a strong correlation to poor performance (low arrival/departure rates, high cancellation rates) in airports on a specific day. In this second experiment, we evaluated the affect of wind speed using the METAR data source with the airport performance using the ASPM data source (i.e. integration of separate data sources). As with the first experiment, the study contained many more columns than the columns with known correlation. The experiment was run on data for the Atlanta Hartsfield International Airport (ATL).

For a successful verification in this second evaluation, the expectation was that the high wind speed would result in low departure and arrival counts at Atlanta airport. Again, there were sufficient results to verify the tools ability to integrate the two data sources. The METAR and

ASPM data points were reported approximately twice a day during the period of time captured in this study. The Arrival and Departure counts were low in the majority of the cases when the wind speed was high. Several MITRE analysts were consulted to confirm that the results were consistent with the trends of weather-impacted operations at the facilities. The specific aviation-based results of the studies can be found in related literature (Blake, 2005).

DISCUSSION

In this paper, we describe a component-based framework that facilitates a human domain specialist in developing and executing KDD routines. This work represents a novel investigation of component capabilities for use in knowledge discovery. The C-KDD framework has been applied to the aviation domain and is currently in use for analysis purposes at The MITRE Corporation. We introduce the notion of a correlation space that enables us to generalize our components related to data preprocessing and data transformation. The innovation in the ASCEND project is the ability of the user to define the data mining scenario with the assistance of a general component-based framework. In addition, this is perhaps the first general-purpose framework that exploits KDD in the aviation domain. This paper presents an experience report of the C-KDD, but in-depth technical details can be found in related literature (Blake, 2005).

Although the current implementations have been deployed as a local workstation application, in future work we plan to distribute the C-KDD engine as a network accessible Web service. The underlying technologies (i.e. Java and Jini) would facilitate these future extensions. In other future work, we plan to evaluate to optimality our correlation modeling approach by recapturing our data model in other more standard formats. With regards to aviation studies, we plan to extend our current studies using a full year of aviation data. Although the May through October period (as analyzed in this work) is most relevant for traffic flow experimentation with respect to delays (Convective Weather PDT, 2005), other times during the year may be more valid for other concerns such as ground operations.

ACKNOWLEDGMENT

Our thanks to several undergraduate student developers, Lindsay Blohm, Todd Cornett, and Denitsa Apostolava. We thank David Hite, Urmila Hiremath, John Mack, and Joe Hoffman of the MITRE Corporation for their discussions in the evaluation of the framework and the interpretation of the data mining results. This work was produced for the U.S. Government under Contract DTFA01-01-C-00001 and is subject to Federal Aviation Administration Acquisition Management System Clause 3.5-13, Rights In Data-General, Alt. III and Alt. IV (Oct. 1996). The contents of this material reflect the views of the author and/or the Director of the Center for Advanced Aviation System Development. Neither the Federal Aviation Administration nor the Department of Transportation makes any warranty or guarantee, or promise, expressed or implied, concerning the content or accuracy of the views expressed herein.

REFERENCES

Agrawal, R. and Shim, K. (1996). Developing Tightly-Coupled Data Mining Applications on a Relational Database System. *Proceedings of the 2nd Int'l Conference on Knowledge Discovery in Databases and Data Mining*. Portland, Oregon

Blake, M.B. & Williams, A.B. (2003a). Developmental and Operational Processes for Agent-Oriented Database Navigation for Knowledge Discovery. 15th International Conference on Software Engineering and Knowledge Engineering (SEKE'03). San Francisco, CA

Blake, M.B. (2003b). Agent-Based Communication for Distributed Workflow Management using Jini Technologies. International Journal on Artificial Intelligence Tools.Vol. 12, No. 1, pp 81-99

Blake, M.B., Singh, L., Williams, A.B., Norman, W.N., and Sliva, A.L. (2005). A Component-Based Framework for Data Management and Knowledge Discovery. Georgetown Technical Report, http://daruma.georgetown.edu/techreports/techrep_data/blake_singh_%20C-KDD2005.pdf

Bueno, J.C. (1998). KDCOM: A Knowledge Discovery Component Framework. Masters Thesis, Spanish Council for Scientific Research

Callahan, M.B., De Armon, J., Cooper, A.M., Goodfriend, H., Moch-Mooney, D., & Solomos, G.H. (2001). Assessing NAS Performance: Normalizing for the Effects of Weather. 4th USA/Europe Air Traffic Management R&D Symposium,. Sante Fe

Chattratichat, J., Darlington, J., Guo, Y., Hedvall, S., Kohler, M. & Syed, J. (1999). An Architecture for Distributed Enterprise Data Mining. Proceedings of the 7th International Conference on High-Performance Computing and Networking.. Lecture Notes in Computer Science. Springer-Verlag. pp 573 – 582

Chawathe, S., Garcia-Molina, H., Hammer, J., Ireland, K., Papakonstantinou, Y., Ullman, J. & Widom, J. (1998). The TSIMMIS project: Integration of heterogeneous information sources. Proceedings of IPSJ Conference, Tokyo, Japan

Convective Weather Product Development Team (PDT), FAA Aviation Weather Research Program (2005): http://www.faa.gov/aua/awr/prodprog.htm

Engels, R. (1999) .Component-Based User Guidance in Knowledge Discovery and Data Mining. Volume 211 Dissertations in Artificial Intelligence-Infix, 1999

Fayyad, U., Piatetsky-Shapiro, G., and Smyth, P. (1996). Knowledge Discovery and Data Mining: Towards a Unifying Framework. Proceedings of the Second International Conference on Knowledge Discovery and Data Mining (KDD-96). AAAI Press

Kim, W., Park, S., Yong, H., Chae, K., Cho, D., Choi, B., Jeong, A., Kim, M., Lee, K., Lee, M., & Lee, S. (2002). The Chamois Component-Based Knowledge Engineering Framework. IEEE Computer, Vol 35, No 5, pp 44-52

Kimball, R. (1996). The Data warehouse Toolkit: Practical Techniques to Building Dimension Data Warehouses. New York: John Wiley

Kimball, R., Reeves, L., & Ross, M. (1998). The Data Warehouse Lifecycle Toolkit. New York: John Wiley

National Weather Service METAR/TAF Information (2005): http://205.156.54.206/oso/oso1/oso12/faq.htm

Nazeri, Z. & Jianping Z. (2002). Mining Aviation Data to Understand the Impacts of Severe Weather on Airspace System Performance. Proceedings of the International Conference on Information Technology:Coding and Computing (ITCC'02). IEEE Press

Netz, A., S. Chaudhuri, Fayyad, U. & Bernhardt, J. (2001). Integrating Data Mining with SQL Databases: OLE DB for Data Mining. Proceedings of the International Conference on Data Engineering (ICDE 2001). Heidelberg. Germany 2001

Nodine, M., J. Fowler, Ksiezyk, T., Perry, B., Taylor, M. & Unruh, A. (1998). Active Information Gathering in InfoSleuth. International Journal of Cooperative Information Systems 9:1/2, 3-28

Order 7210.3S, Facility Operation and Administration, Chapter 5 (Traffic Flow Management) (2003): http://www.faa.gov/atpubs/FAC/Ch17/chp17toc.htm

Sarawagi, S., Thomas, S., and Agrawal, R. (2000). Integrating Association Rule Mining with Databases: Alternatives and Implications. Data Mining and Knowledge Discovery Journal, 4(2/3)

Software Suites supporting Knowledge Discovery (2005): http://www.kdnuggets.com/software/suites.html

The Aviation System Performance Metrics (ASPM) (2005): http://www.apo.data.faa.gov/faamatsall.HTM

The National Convective Weather Forecast (NCWF) (2005): http://cdm.awc-kc.noaa.gov/ncwf/index.html

WEKA (2005) http://www.cs.waikato.ac.nz/~ml/weka/

This work was previously published in Int. Journal of Information Technology and Web Engineering, Vol 1, Issue 1, edited by G. Alkhatib and D. Rine, pp. 76-90, copyright 2006 by IGI Publishing (an imprint of IGI Global).

Chapter XVII
Agile Development of Secure Web–Based Applications

A. F. Tappenden
University of Alberta, Canada

T. Huynh
University of Alberta, Canada

J. Miller
University of Alberta, Canada

A. Geras
University of Calgary, Canada

M. Smith
University of Calgary, Canada

ABSTRACT

This article outlines a four-point strategy for the development of secure Web-based applications within an agile development framework and introduces strategies to mitigate security risks that are commonly present in Web-based applications. The proposed strategy includes the representation of security requirements as test cases supported by the open source tool FIT, the deployment of a highly testable architecture allowing for security testing of the application at all levels, the outlining of an extensive security testing strategy supported by the open source unit-testing framework HTTPUnit, and the introduction of the novel technique of security refactoring that transforms insecure working code into a functionally-equivalent secure code. Today, many Web-based applications are not secure, and limited literature exists concerning the use of agile methods within this domain. It is the intention of this article to further discussions and research regarding the use of an agile methodology for the development of secure Web-based applications.

INTRODUCTION

E-commerce and Web-based applications have quickly become a staple for many businesses, and in some cases represents an entire business itself. Success or failure in the online marketplace can, in fact, determine a company's fate. For example, in 2003, Dell Incorporated's U.S. home and home office divisions generated $2.8 billion or nearly 50% of its revenues through its online storefront (Dell Inc., 2003). Web-based applications are typically "always on," and although this allows customers to access products and services at all times, it also leaves the applications open to continuous access from malicious attackers. Security is therefore a major concern for Web-based applications, and a breach in security can lead to a significant loss in profit or the exposure of valuable information, such as trade secrets or confidential client information. Furthermore, security and privacy are listed as major concerns for customers utilizing e-commerce systems (Udo, 2001), and security is listed as one of the three most important quality criterion for Web-based application success (Offutt, 2002). According to a recent study, 75% of online security breaches occur at the application layer, not the transportation layer (Grossman, 2004a). Common exploits in modern Web-based applications are occurring due to security flaws within the Web-based application itself, regardless of protection from firewalls and Secure Socket Layer (SSL) communication channels. Malicious attackers appear to be concentrating on what they believe to be the weakest link—the application itself.

SQL injection, buffer overflows, cross-site scripting, file inclusion, URL injection, and remote code injection vulnerabilities have historically plagued Web-based applications developed by both the open-source and commercial communities. These vulnerabilities have been found in Web-based applications employed by organizations such as the FBI, CNN, Time Magazine, Ebay, Yahoo, Apple Computer, and Microsoft

(Cgisecurity.com, 2002). These vulnerabilities are not only extremely common in many Web-based applications, but can also be extremely costly. For example, an SQL injection vulnerability in the PetCo.com Website resulted in 500,000 customers' credit-card numbers and information being made vulnerable to anyone who could carefully construct a SQL query (Grossman, 2004b). Every month, 10 to 25 cross-site scripting security flaws are found within commercial Web-based applications (Cgisecurity.com, 2002). It is clear that the methodologies currently employed for the development of Web-based applications are not adequately meeting security needs.

The development of Web-based systems is often distinctly different from the development of traditional Information Technology (IT) systems as Web-based applications are typically much smaller than traditional IT applications, and consequently their production period is much shorter (Cusumano & Yoffie, 1999; Iansiti & MacCormack, 1997; Kirda, Jazayeri, Kerer, & Schranz, 2001; Ramesh, Pries-Heje, & Baskerville, 2002). Furthermore, these applications evolve at a much faster pace, and the development cycle is highly iterative in nature. Due to these factors, agile development methodologies are increasingly being used for the development of Web-based applications (Barnett & Narsu, 2005; Ramesh, Pries-Heje, & Baskerville, 2002). Until recently, agile development methodologies and traditional security engineering have been seen as orthogonal (Beznosov & Kruchten, 2004); however, recent discussions are beginning to harmonize the two seemingly different viewpoints (Beznosov, 2003; Beznosov & Kruchten, 2004). Discussions of agile security assurance to date have been at a very high level and although the works acknowledge the possibility of secure application development within an agile framework, they do not provide the necessary support infrastructure needed to develop secure applications for a specific domain. This paper will propose a strategy for the development of secure Web-based applications within an agile framework by adapting currently used and accepted agile development tools and techniques. The proposed strategy provides an appropriate level of technical detail to be translatable to agile software development, meanwhile remaining high-level enough to be extended and adapted to future Web-based application development.

Agile development methodologies are a group of software development methodologies that all ascribe to the Agile Manifesto (Beck et al., 2001). The Agile Manifesto, created in 2001 by 17 prominent figures in the then-lightweight software development field, is widely regarded as the canonical definition of an agile method. Today agile methods include extreme programming, scrum, and adaptive software development. Agile methodologies are generally characterized by close customer-developer collaboration and short, iterative development cycles. Compared to more traditional software development methodologies, agile methods rely on open, face-to-face communication between customer and developer, enabling the development team to react quickly to ever-changing customer requirements and expectations. The development process is broken down into short cycles typically lasting one to six weeks, allowing the development team to meet customer requirements iteratively. At the end of each cycle, the customer is provided with working code based on customer-prioritized functionality, which further facilitates the input of customer feedback in to the software development process.

Agile security engineering involves employing the same values that drive agile software engineering to the traditional practice of mitigating security risks in software. This includes using a highly iterative process for delivering the security solution and translating security objectives into automated security test cases. The security test cases should be described prior to completion of the target system; that is, they should be used to elaborate the security objectives and to characterize the secured behavior that would be classified

as "good enough security" from the customer's perspective. The role of a security engineer in this regard would be to advise and coach the customer on the foreseeable risks, with the customer ultimately deciding which ones would be of the greatest concern to them. This paper will outline a four-point strategy for the development of secure Web-based applications within an agile development framework. This strategy includes representing agile security requirements as test-cases, deploying a highly testable architecture, employing automatable security testing, and implementing security refactoring. This strategy will provide a basis for the negotiation of "good enough security" in the agile development of secure Web-based applications.

AGILE SECURITY REQUIREMENTS

One of the principle challenges in developing a secure Web-based application is that the target itself, security, is really an objective—a relatively abstract requirement as opposed to a functional requirement. The first step in a security testing protocol is to set the context for the tests; that is, to identify the security objectives. In more traditional development methodologies this may have been done as part of the requirements workflow of the project, but for many Web-based applications, functional requirements are often of the highest priority due to time-to-market pressures, and comprehensive security requirements are often left out of preliminary discussions. For many projects, security requirements become urgent only close to deployment time, and are often added as an afterthought and tested in an ad hoc fashion. From a traditional security engineering viewpoint, security requirements must be strictly defined from the beginning of the project and monitored and reviewed throughout the development process; however, the highly iterative and evolutionary nature of Web-based applications suggests that these ideas are simply not realistic for Web-based systems. Web-based applications are continually in transition; often one version of a Web-based application is deployed to the public while the next release is being finalized and tested on a private server. Techniques for harvesting and representing security requirements during iterative development cycles are necessary for the agile development of secure Web-based applications.

Within the agile development framework there are a number of methods for modeling requirements. Scott Ambler (2004), in his book "The Object Primer 3rd Edition: Agile Model Driven Development with UML 2", defines a number of requirement artifacts, one of which is a technical requirement. According to Ambler (2005), "a technical requirement pertains to a non-functional aspect of your system, such as a performance-related issue, a reliability issue, or technical environmental issue". Security requirements, although not explicitly mentioned in the definition of a technical requirement, can be modeled as technical requirements since they represent a non-functional aspect of the software system. Like other requirement artifacts such as features, user stories, and business rules, technical requirements are understood by the agile development community, and the modeling of security requirements as technical requirements can be comfortably integrated into current agile development practices.

A major force behind many agile development methodologies is test driven development (TDD) (Astels, 2003; Beck, 2002). TDD utilizes test cases to characterize customer requirements and to specify designs. Within an agile framework, security requirements captured as technical requirements must ultimately be expressed as test cases. Security test cases can be quite difficult to accentuate; however, a number of preliminary security test strategies specifically tailored to Web-based applications have been articulated. The Institute for Security and Open Methodologies has released the Open Source Security Testing

Methodology Manual (OSSTMM) version 2.1 (ISECOM, 2003). The OSSTMM provides a taxonomy of test facets for Web-based applications, but it does not provide any test implementation details. The taxonomy is very helpful in a discussion of what to test, and can be used by security engineers as a type of checklist in the negotiation of "good enough security" with customers. It does not however, help relate security requirements to specific test cases.

Modern agile development tools such as FIT (Cunningham, 2002) can be used to articulate tests of the application's ability to satisfy security requirements. FIT is a tool that enhances communication and collaboration between the customer and the developer by allowing customers to create test cases using tools such as Microsoft Office. The test cases are typically written in tabular form using Microsoft Word, then stored as HTML files. The programmer-created FIT-fixture can then interpret, test, and provide feedback to the customer and developer through the modification of the HTML files, alerting them to the results of each test case. FIT is especially suited to Web-based application security testing for two primary reasons. First, FIT is designed to interact with the application by bypassing complex GUI interactions; this is a perfect match for Web-based applications as a major component in their security testing is bypassing the client-side GUI. Secondly, utilizing the same tool for the security requirements that is used to elaborate and test the functional requirements makes the security requirements more approachable, and it is thus more likely that the security requirements will be built-in with the functional requirements. FIT can be used to capture both security and functional requirements, ensuring that both requirement sets are met from the start of the project or build cycle.

As an example, consider a database-backed Web-based application that has generic search capabilities. The application will typically have a search form that will permit the user to enter

Table 1. SQL injection fault testing with FIT

FixtureNamespace.FixtureName				
Remark	FirstName	LastName	Dept	Find()
Known single result	Michael	Stipe	*	1
Known multiple results	*	Smith	*	23
Try to inject some SQL	*	Smith'; drop table employees;'	*	0

their search criteria and then submit their search. An appropriate server-side component would then generate the SQL query to perform the search against the database and execute it as required. This search page would be an ideal candidate on which to perform a test for SQL injection faults, since the database query is ultimately generated from user input. If the user input is only validated on the client-side, then there is the likelihood of an SQL injection fault occurring. The security objective to be targeted is therefore to ensure that the underlying database is not accessible by exploiting SQL injection faults. To test this with FIT, a format similar to Table 1 may be used. This example is based on an enterprise phone directory that is accessible from the public Internet, and assumes that there is a base set of test data already in place.

In the example above, specially-placed single quotes and semi-colons may cause a susceptible application to execute the 'drop table' statement, clearly something that the target application should not permit. If the application developers only used client-side input validation, then this test would expose the SQL injection flaw. If the application

was built so that the server-side components also did input validation, then presumably the validation would clean the SQL query before executing it and the search would simply return 0 results. This type of test is possible because FIT bypasses the client-side functionality of the application and instead relies on fixtures that only emulate enough of the front-end to set up the appropriate tests.

A second example of security testing would be to run functional scenario tests but to annotate them with additional security information. These type of tests could target, for example, the typical role-based security that Web-based applications implement. In the example laid out in Table 2, an entry is being added to the enterprise phone directory, an application feature that only *PhoneDirectoryAdministrators* should be permitted to do. In this case, the FIT-fixture has been designed to return the data as inserted into the database with each field separated by a pipe (||) and a space. Note that this test again assumes that certain test data exists. Having an established base set of data is required for most automated testing situations in order to minimize the test setup/teardown code.

Table 2. Role-based security testing with FIT

FixtureNamespce.FixtureName						
Remark	FirstName	LastName	Dept.	User	Pass.	Add()
Valid user/pwd	Annabelle	Laxative	Hosiery	jib	job	Annabelle||Laxative||Hosiery
Valid user/invalid pwd	Frank	Lin	Home		jub	ERROR
Invalid user				jit	jot	ERROR
Valid user not in group				jat	jot	ERROR

Note that in the previous example, the error message could be even more precisely worded so that it could also be included as part of the test.

It is clear that security requirements can be captured and understood by the agile development community through the extension of the non-technical requirements artifact. These requirements can be gathered and translated into test cases through the use of emerging Web-based security testing strategies, and can be put on par with the functional requirements through the use of freely available tools such as FIT. Capturing security requirements in this fashion allows for security requirements to be built-in with functional requirements in an iterative, evolutionary fashion. Furthermore, the ability for security requirements to be added to the project at the beginning of every successive build cycle allows for the project to remain flexible and meet the changing customer requirements throughout the project. Through the use of tools such as FIT, both the customer and developers can view the status of the functional and security requirements concisely, providing up-to-date feedback as to the project's progress from both a functional and security viewpoint. Ultimately, this type of security requirements definition enables the communication of security requirements in the form of test cases, which can be used by an agile development team to explore the design space and produce a final product that satisfies the functional and security requirements.

HIGHLY TESTABLE ARCHITECTURE

Many Web-based applications today have increasingly complex functional requirements. This increase in complexity has a direct effect on the test effort required, and it is becoming more difficult to test these applications. Due to the increased complexity, manual testing, even with low-cost off-shore resources, is unlikely to

be cost-effective. The only cost-effective solution is to automate testing at all levels, not just at the unit testing level. Automated testing suites such as FIT, mentioned in the previous section, JUnit, PHPUnit, and HTTPUnit can be used to automate testing activities for Web-based applications (Cunningham, 2002; Gold, 2004b; Open Source Technology Group, 2005a, 2005b). It has also been indicated that both the customer and the developer may benefit from the inclusion of higher levels of testing in the test-first activities (Pancur, Ciglaric, Trampus, & Vidmar, 2003). In other words, organizations that build customer tests to characterize requirements, both functional and non-functional, and then subsequently use developer tests to specify design decisions, are in a better position than companies that only do developer testing. The net effect is that there is a need to develop highly testable software, and there are perceived security benefits to building that software using a test-driven process. The next section will outline the evolution of the traditional layered application architecture into a test-oriented application architecture, allowing for security testing of the Web-based application.

The Current State — Layered Architecture

Many Web-based applications are constructed using a variant of a *layered architecture*. Using this approach, the Web-based application's overall responsibilities are split amongst three or more layers: the data services layer, the business services layer, and the presentation layer (see Figure 1) (Microsoft Corporation, 2004).

The data services layer is responsible for data storage and retrieval, the business services layer is responsible for business workflow and logic, and the presentation layer is responsible for supporting interactions with the end-user through the Internet and ultimately through the Web browser. This layered architecture has a number of advantages, particularly given the heterogeneous nature

Figure 1. Standard layered architecture consisting of the presentation layer, business services and data access layer

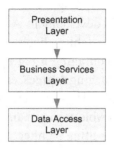

of the Internet. Similarly, there are advantages in using this architecture when more than one type of user interface might be needed. In this case, the same business logic and database, for example, could be accessed through a Web page, a desktop (thick client) application, touch-tone phone (IVR system), or a personal digital assistant (PDA). Given the increasing ubiquity and capabilities of cell phones, it also makes sense to consider that accessing the business logic from cell phones may be required in some business domains.

Figure 2. The class-type architecture is a variant of the standard layered architecture that organizes classes and objects based on their responsibilities

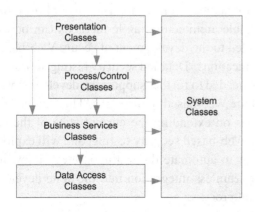

The Class Type Architectures

Scott Ambler (2002) extended the classical layered architecture in describing the class-type architecture, as shown in Figure 2. In the class-type architecture, the classical business services layer is further divided into two layers, one that contains only *business entities* and another that contains *business controllers*. A business controller class is responsible for the control and sequencing of one or more business scenarios, while business entities are the domain objects that are created or manipulated in the business scenarios (Ambler, 2002).

The class-type architecture maps particularly well to Web-based applications developed in Java and Microsoft .NET since in both cases a large set of classes are available for reuse. In Java, the presentation layer might be implemented as JavaServer Pages (JSP), and in the .NET environment the presentation layer would be implemented by Web Forms. The advantages of the class-type architecture over the classical layered architecture lie in splitting the business logic from the business entities. Entities tend to be constant in any given domain, yet the business processes in those same domains might be highly adaptive and change rapidly. Individuals shopping on the Internet, for example, still use a *shopping cart* to carry their *goods* to a *checkout*. Never mind that these objects are virtual objects—to the average shopper they are indistinguishable from the real thing. However, significant changes in retail business processes have been introduced because of the availability of the Web. Given that building Web-based applications based on the class-type architecture has proven to be successful in practice, and that there is an increased need for writing highly testable applications, it seems that there is an opportunity for merging these two trends. The intended result is an application architecture that retains the benefits of high testability and of the class-type architecture.

Proposed Architecture — Highly Testable Class-Type Architecture

This section will propose a revision of the representation of the class-type architecture shown in Figure 2 to include test layers (see Figure 3). This will allow for Web-based applications to utilize the benefits of a class-type architecture and also enable security testing at all levels. The test-cases and the testability of the target Web-based application are therefore put to the forefront of the design process. With the envisioned layers for both the Web-based application and the test-cases for that application in place, the design team has a foundation for iterative and evolutionary development. Security engineers can decide which of the test layers they propose to automate, what tools they propose to use for that automation, and how the test layers communicate with the product layers during the execution of tests, supporting the ability to test the Web-based application for security and functionality at all levels.

The addition of the test layers to the traditional class-type architecture highlights the testability

hooks that application developers should build into their applications. Furthermore, building the test layers becomes a purposeful pursuit, as they are no longer the afterthought that typically occurs under traditional development. At the same time, introducing the testability hooks does not necessarily mean encouraging a big up-front design effort, since to varying degrees, each of these test layers can be built alongside their target layers in an iterative and evolutionary manner (test-first or test-last). The resulting architecture is useful for security testing since various security test patterns can be employed within any number of the test layers. Security testing can target an individual layer (probably in conjunction with the use of mock objects to isolate the target layer) or also perform integration testing, targeting an upper layer and the layers that it depends on. The introduction of a highly testable architecture will support the execution of security-orientated test-cases, allowing security testing to be performed upon the application without the development of an extensive ad hoc security testing support infrastructure at the end of the project, by which time security is typically deemed to be a significant risk.

Figure 3. The highly testable architecture, identifying test layers for each of the layers within the class-type architecture except for the system classes

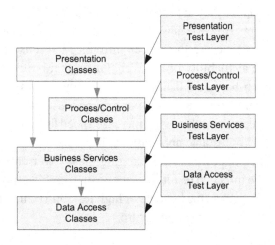

AUTOMATABLE SECURITY TESTING

With the ability to express security requirements as test cases through the use of tools such as FIT, and the ability to test the application at all layers of implementation through the use of a highly testable architecture, agile methods can be extended to the development of secure Web-based applications. Detailed security testing strategies are needed to further support the development of secure Web-based applications. This section will focus on extending the current state of the art for Web-based security testing, and will explore ways to automate the testing strategy allowing for seamless integration into the agile development process.

Current Strategies

SQL injection and bypass testing are two security testing strategies specifically intended for Web-based applications. SQL injection is a security testing strategy that attempts to access the backend database of a system through carefully crafted inputs into HTML forms (Chris, 2002; Finnigan, 2002; Grossman, 2004b; SPI Dynamics, 2002). SQL injection is both a testing strategy and an attack strategy that has been used to bypass security protocols, gain administrative privileges, access privileged information, and to simply manipulate back-end databases. This testing strategy involves the input of SQL-specific reserved characters and keywords into HTML forms in an attempt to alter database queries. This type of testing and test-case is very specific to SQL databases and only addresses one type of security breach; however, it has provided a basis for further work in the area of security testing for Web-based applications.

The idea of SQL injection has been further generalized, and a testing strategy outlined in the paper "Bypass Testing of Web Applications" (Offutt, Wu, Du, & Huang, 2004). The paper introduces the idea of bypass testing. Bypass testing attempts to test the robustness of the Web-based application by circumventing the client-side GUI restrictions and attempting to alter the application's behavior (Offutt, Wu, Du, & Huang, 2004). Bypass testing describes four categories of input-value testing. The first category, data type and value modification, calls for the input of invalid strings due to expected type restrictions. An example of this would be to provide the server with a real number instead of an integer. The second category, HTML built-in length violation, exploits client code that utilizes the built-in HTML form length restriction. This type of testing involves the input of longer-than-expected strings into the server. The third category, HTML built-in value violation, concentrates on modifying predefined input values that occur in check and radio boxes.

The final category, special input value, focuses on the input of reserved characters into text fields. The reserved characters attempt to violate server interactions with backend databases and XML communications.

Although bypass testing and SQL injection provide a good basis for security testing of Web-based applications, they face several limitations. Testing a Web-based application for security using SQL injection exclusively is far too limited to detect a number of security vulnerabilities. SQL injection only deals with one very specific component of a Web-based application—interactions with a backend database—and does not uncover common vulnerabilities such as URL injection or cross-site scripting vulnerabilities.

The bypass testing strategy outlined by Offutt et al. (2004) is limited to fundamental textual information provided to a Web-based application through HTML forms and does not address a number of other types of inputs that modern Web-based applications frequently use. Security breaches can come from a wide variety of sources including, but not limited to, those addressed by the bypass testing strategy. Many Web-based applications exchange information with users through cookies, files, and base64 encodings. Each of these vehicles for interaction are also being used by malicious attackers to target Web-based applications, and must be tested to ensure integrity.

Expanding Security Testing

All generic inputs to a Web-based application should be presumed compromised regardless of client-side verification, and subject to verification by the server. Many, if not all of the common security risks to Web-based applications can be mitigated by thorough server-side input verification. Generic inputs into a Web-based application primarily come from two sources: GET and POST requests. The length of each input must be verified by the server to prevent buffer overflow vulnerabilities. These inputs need to be checked against SQL and XML reserved characters, as outlined in the SQL injection and bypass testing strategies, but additional testing is still required. Inputs need to be verified and checked against UNIX, Windows, and JavaScript reserved characters, and invalid character sets, ASCII or Unicode. Furthermore, type checking is required for all inputs. Integers, naturals, and reals need to be verified of type, as well as being checked against the min/max and zero values. In short, all inputs into the software system must be considered tainted and subject to verification by the server.

Besides GET and POST requests, cookies have become a third staple input used in Web-based applications. Most Web-based applications utilize cookies for a variety of reasons, of which session management is one of the most common. Due to the extensive use of cookies and the security implications of a breached session management protocol, the security testing of cookies must be included in any testing strategy. Attackers can utilize cookies in three primary ways: by creation, modification, and deletion. Much like generic inputs, the information in cookies can be modified and should be subject to server-side verification. Web-based applications should be tested against cookie modification, spoofing, and deletion. The same principles outlined for the testing of generic inputs should be extended to the input data accepted from cookies, with further test cases generated to simulate the spontaneous creation, modification, or deletion of cookies at various states in the application control-flow. Further consideration should be given to the type of information stored in cookies, such as whether the information is valuable, whether it is encrypted, and whether an attacker can use the information stored in the cookie to attack the application. These types of considerations can and should be used in the generation of test cases to examine cookies placed on a machine by a Web-based application, as often an attacker, through a

single cross-site scripting vulnerability on another insecure Website, can obtain these cookies.

Many Web-based applications interact with users through the passing of files over the Internet. Online e-mail services, for example, provide the user with the ability to add attachments to outgoing e-mails, while online-dating services allow for the exchange of photographs and other privileged information between customers; in addition, defect tracking software often allows for the uploading of software patches. Although the ability to upload files is critical to the success of many Web-based applications, files can pose a serious threat to security. Images, documents, and all other file types are continuously being submitted to online services, and therefore need to be validated. Web-based applications must detect invalid or malicious images or documents before they are utilized by the application. This issue has been brought to the forefront by current computer viruses that can infect a user's system through the simple act of viewing a JPEG image (Microsoft Corporation, 2004). All told, files pose several threats to Web-based applications. File size and file name length must be verified by the system to ensure that the file does not cause a buffer-overflow, or utilize too many system resources or too much of the connection bandwidth. File type must also be validated, which requires more than just a simple extension check, as an attacker can often spoof the file extension. In short, thorough server verification of files needs to be performed on any Web-based application that accepts the uploading of user files.

Base64 encoding is a technique used to encode binary files as a set of ASCII characters (Freed, 1996; Linn, 1993). This encoding is frequently used on the Internet to transmit binary data over any communication channel that is limited to plaintext ASCII data, and is often used in conjunction with legacy e-mail applications. Web-based applications utilizing this type of input need to verify the incoming base64 encoding. This type of verification should focus primarily on the base64 encoding itself. Length and size of the input must be checked to mitigate the risk of a buffer overflow, and then the encoding itself should be verified for correctness. The alphabet used in the encoding must also be examined, to ensure that the characters transmitted as part of the encoding are within the accepted standard alphabet. Furthermore, in a base64 encoding, binary data is transmitted by sets of three ASCII characters; thus it should be verified that the encoding contains a multiple of three characters, to ensure that character addition or subtraction has not taken place. Test cases should focus on the introduction of invalid characters and the addition and subtraction of valid characters. It is important to note that once the base64 encoding is validated, the binary file transmitted using the base64 encoding must also be validated as described above.

It is clear that all inputs into a Web-based application need to be validated by the server.

Table 3. Summary of test inputs

Valid Input	Test Input	SQL Injection	Offutt et al.	Proposed Strategy
Generic Input	SQL reserved characters	X	X	X
	XML reserved characters		X	X
	Unix reserved characters		X	X
	Windows reserved characters			X
	Oversized string		X	X
	Non-ASCII characters			X
	Non-Unicode characters			X
	Null String		X	X
Integer Input	Min/max values		X	X
	Zero		X	X
	Real number		X	X
	Non-number		X	X
Real Number Input	Min/max values		X	X
	Zero		X	X
	Non-number		X	X
Cookies	Create/Modify/Destroy cookie			X
	Invalid cookie of the same name			X
	Invalid data types within the cookie (Generic, Real, Integer, etc)			X
Files	Different file type			X
	Invalid file of type			X
	Long file name			X
	Malicious file (script, image)			X
	Large file size			X
Base64 Encoding	Invalid Base64 encoding			X
	Improper Base64 alphabet			X
	Invalid underlying file			X

Inputs need to undergo checks for length, validity, character set (ASCII, Unicode, etc), reserved characters (SQL, XML, JavaScript, UNIX, Windows, etc), and type (string, integer, real, image, document, etc). These checks can eliminate many of the security vulnerabilities that affect Web-based applications. Table 3 below provides a summary of the input types and the test inputs used in the server input verification. The table also highlights the differences between the security testing strategy proposed in this paper and the strategies proposed by SQL injection (Chris, 2002; Finnigan, 2002; Grossman, 2004b; SPI Dynamics, 2002) and Offutt et al. (Offutt, Wu, Du, & Huang, 2004).

It is essential that any testing-based security strategy covers all of the aspects of Web-based security that are listed in Table 3. Without such rigorous efforts, a dynamic Web-based application can not be assured of its integrity. Table 3 provides a comprehensive list of security testing issues that can be used in discussions with the customer to define "good enough security" and can be used by the developers to translate security requirements into specific test cases. These test cases can then be defined within the FIT framework and used to ensure that the Web-based application meets the agreed security requirements.

Automated Security Testing

Automation is needed for any agile unit-level testing suite. Security requirements, just like functional requirements, must be translatable to not only test-cases, but to automatable test-cases. Although this goal is inherently supported by the highly testable architecture described in Section 3,

further integration with unit-level testing activities is needed for security requirements. This integration can be accomplished through a novel use of HTTPUnit to test for security. HTTPUnit is a unit-testing framework that provides the ability to bypass complex client-side GUI interactions and provide automated unit-level testing for Web-based applications (Gold, 2004b). Currently, HTTPUnit emulates HTML form submission, JavaScript, basic HTTP authentication, cookies, and automatic page redirection. This unit-test framework supports the analysis of returned HTML documents as plain text, an XML DOM, or containers of forms, tables, or links (Gold, 2004b). HTTPUnit is implemented in Java and is based on the JUnit framework, so it can be seamlessly integrated for use with other commonly used xUnit testing frameworks.

Hightower and Lesiecki (2002), in the book "Java Tools for Extreme Programming: Mastering Open Source Tools Including Ant, JUnit, and Cactus," provide an initial basis for the use of HTTPUnit within an agile development framework. The book proposes that HTTPUnit is a tool that can be used to perform functional and unit-level testing upon a Web-based application; however, this reflects a very traditional view of the relationship between the server and the client—a view which many attackers exploit when targeting Web-based applications. The remainder of this section will focus on the novel use of HTTPUnit to bypass not only the client-side GUI, but also the client-side input restrictions, allowing for the automated security testing of a Web-based application.

Although HTTPUnit was specifically designed to bypass complex GUI interactions, it was not

Figure 4. Creating an Invalidated Request Object Within HTTPUnit

```
WebRequest form = response.getForms()[0].newUnvalidatedRequest();
```

Figure 5. Example HTML Form For Posting Product Information

```
<form action="./" method="POST">
Product: <input type="text" name="product" size="20"
   maxlength="20"><p>
<TEXTAREA NAME="description" ROWS=6 COLS=40>
A Brief Description
</TEXTAREA> <p>
Contact E-mail Address: <input type="text" name="email" size="20"
   maxlength="20">
<input name="Submit" value="submit" type="submit">
</form>
```

originally intended to bypass the client-side input restrictions. HTTPUnit was designed to exactly mimic Web-browser behavior, including client-side input restrictions, to allow for traditional, functional, blackbox testing of Web-based applications. The first step in automating security testing then is to disable the client-side input verification. In HTTPUnit, this is done by creating a `WebRequest` object that contains an unvalidated request as shown in below in Figure 4.

The newly created `WebRequest` object will allow HTTPUnit to provide the server with input data that has not been restricted by the client, effectively bypassing not only the cumbersome GUI interactions, but also the client-side input restrictions. This type of testing will allow testers to provide the system with unexpected and invalid inputs that will test the robustness of the application under unexpected input values. The next two examples provide a basic outline for the creation of test-cases to check for cross-site scripting vulnerabilities and invalid cookie manipulation.

Cross-site scripting vulnerabilities are very common within Web-based applications that allow users to post messages to a trusted site. This example involves a typical Internet auction site. The site allows users to post or browse products for sale on the Website. The following HTML form, shown in Figure 5, enables a user to post a product to the Website.

This HTML form requires the user to specify and describe the product to be auctioned off by the application. This is a common situation in which a cross-site scripting vulnerability may surface. An attacker could place a malicious script within

Figure 6. An Example HTTPUnit Cross-Site Scripting Test Case

```
WebConversation wc = new WebConversation();
WebRequest request = new GetMethodWebRequest("http://usedcars.com/");
WebResponse response = wc.getResponse(request);

WebRequest form = response.getForms()[0].newUnvalidatedRequest();
form.setParameter("product","Laptop Computer");
form.setParameter("description","<script>alert(FAILED
   TEST)</script>");
form.setParameter("email","foo@foobar.com");

response = wc.getResource(form);

assertTrue(response.getText().matches("(?s).*<script>(?s).*"));
```

Figure 7. An Example HTTPUnit Test Case Modifying A Cookie's Value

```
WebConversation wc = new WebConversation();
WebRequest request = new
   GetMethodWebRequest("http://shop.com/cart.jsp");

wc.putCookie("ID","001");
WebResponse response = wc.getResponse(request);

wc.putCookie("ID","002");
WebLink link = response.getLinkWith("checkout");

link.click();
```

the description or title of the product. This script could redirect the browser to a dummy page asking for credit card information, or strip the user's machine of valuable cookies containing privileged information such as a username and password combination. The HTTPUnit test case, shown in Figure 6 will test the description field for a cross-site scripting vulnerability.

This test case attempts to insert a script into the description field. If the server does not check the description field for HTML reserved characters, namely the `<script>` meta tag, then this input will cause the Web-based application to produce a pop-up window for every visitor who accesses the description of the product. Although a pop-up window is harmless, the payload of this script could be much worse. Inputs into a Web-

based system that will be posted for the public to read must be checked and stripped of HTML meta tags and JavaScript. This type of server-side verification directly combats cross-site scripting and other common vulnerabilities.

A second example demonstrates the use of HTTPUnit to manipulate cookies for security testing. HTTPUnit provides the ability to manipulate cookies in two primary ways: by creation and deletion (Gold, 2004a). Creation of new cookies in order to overwrite existing ones is also a technique which may be used to effectively modify existing cookies. Creation and modification of cookies within the HTTPUnit framework is very straightforward. The HTTPUnit code segment provided in Figure 7 simulates an attacker at-

Figure 8. A Function To Remove A Specific Cookie

```
public void remove_cookie(String name, WebConversation wc) {
   HashMap cookieJar = new HashMap();
   String[] cookies = wc.getCookieNames();

   for(int i=0;i<cookies.length;i++)
      cookieJar.put(cookies[i], wc.getCookieValue(cookies[i]));

   wc.clearContents();

   for(int i=0;i<cookies.length;i++)
      if(!cookies[i].equals(name))
         wc.addCookie(cookies[i], (String)cookieJar.get(cookies[i]));
}
```

tempting to modify the value stored in a cookie in the middle of a checkout transaction.

The example initially accesses the Web-based application with the cookie ID set to the value 001. This could be reflective of a shopping cart based application. The example then modifies the value of the cookie from 001 to 002 in an attempt to assume the ID of another user. This example is over-simplified, as many Web-based applications utilize several cookies in conjunction rather than a single entity, but it demonstrates the ability to create and modify cookies within the HTTPUnit framework.

HTTPUnit also provides the ability to remove all the cookies from the test system. This is very useful in simulating test cases where a user accesses a Web-based application from a different machine, or where the cookies have been removed from the user machine due to the time-to-live mechanism. The framework does not, however, expressly provide the ability to remove a specific cookie from the test system, as this is not a typical user action. The following procedure, show in Figure 8, provides HTTPUnit with the ability to remove a specific cookie from the test system.

The function above can be added to test cases requiring the removal of specific cookies, or can be fitted into the HTTPUnit framework as a method within the WebConversation class.

HTTPUnit can also be outfitted to perform security testing for Web-based applications that utilize files and base64 encodings. The Upload-FileSpec and Form classes provide the ability to upload files to a Web-based application under test and the Base64 class provides the ability to encode and decode base64 encodings. Not only can HTTPUnit be retrofitted to perform all of the types of testing described in this section, as summarized in Table 3, but it can also be used in conjunction with FIT to bridge the gap between requirements and testing, and can be used to automate security test-cases at the Presentation and Process/Control test layers outlined in Agile Security Requirements section.

SECURITY REFACTORING

Security flaws within any application ultimately derive from human error, be that in the specification, design, implementation, or maintenance phase of any project. Furthermore, Web-based applications are frequently updated with new content, features and improvements, and each new line of code introduced to an application has the potential to create a security flaw. Utilizing the strategies from the previous three sections, an agile development team can express and explicitly test a Web-based application for security. Armed with the ability to detect security flaws, the ability to quickly react and patch potential security flaws is required to further support the

Figure 9. Escape output variables refactor

``Your message:
<?php
    print($_REQUEST["message"]);
?>```
	Initial Insecure Code

``Your message:
<?php
    print(htmlspecialchars($_REQUEST["message"]));
?>```
	Refactored Secure Code

Figure 10. Validate variables refactor

``php
<?php
    $result=mysql_query("SELECT * FROM users WHERE
        username=\"$_REQUEST["username"]\"");
?>
``
	Initial
	Insecure Code

``php
<?php
    if (isValidUsername($_REQUEST["username"])) {
        $result= mysql_query("SELECT * FROM users WHERE
            username=\"$_REQUEST["username"]\"");
    }
?>
``
	Refactored
	Secure Code

agile development of secure Web-based applications. The introduction of the novel technique of security refactoring will meet the need for agile development teams to quickly react to security flaws. Security refactoring provides the ability to address security flaws by merging the disciplined approach of refactoring with the current state of the art secure coding practices. This section will introduce security refactoring and present two security refactors that can be used to combat common security flaws that plague Web-based applications.

As stated by Martin Fowler (2005), "refactoring is a technique to restructure an existing part of the source code, that is, to alter the code's internal structure without changing its external behavior". Each refactor (transformation) represents a small, behavior preserving change to the source code. A sequence of refactors can result in a significant structural change to the code. Researchers assert that refactoring can lead to clearer, cleaner, simpler, and more reusable code (Opdyke, 1992; Thompson & Reinke, 2001). Refactoring is a technique accepted and understood by the agile community, and several catalogues of refactoring techniques are currently available (Fowler, Beck, Brant, & Opdyke, 1999; Thompson & Reinke, 2001). Although the notion of refactoring an application is standard practice within the agile

community, the notion of refactoring an application to enhance security is in its infancy and remains unexplored.

One proposed security refactor is the *Escape Output Variables* refactor. This refactor replaces special characters, such as <, >, or ', within strings outputted to the client with the benign equivalent. This constitutes a very simple refactor, but as mentioned earlier, many refactors are small transformations to source code. This refactor can directly combat cross-site scripting security vulnerabilities. Figure 9 shown below is an example of an insecure PHP code segment that displays a user-inputted message to the browser both before and after refactoring.

This code segment is very typical of the type of code developed for Web-based applications. Developers, often under intense time restrictions and pressure, simply do not escape output strings. Using the *Escape Output Variables* refactor, the vulnerable code in the above example is refactored to become secure. The change to the code is very minimal, the only difference is the addition of the `htmlspecialchars()` function to the print statement. This built-in PHP function simply converts any special HTML character into HTML entities which are subsequently displayed as text on the client browser. This function has equivalents in all major Web-development languages

Figure 11. An Example isValidUsername Function

```
function isValidUsername($input){

    return !ereg("[\\\";()=><]",$input);

}
```

currently in use, including PHP, JSP, .Net, and Rails. Despite the simplicity of this example, it is clear from the sheer number of cross-site scripting errors discovered in Web-based applications that this type of simple refactor is required to support the development of secure Web-based applications.

The second proposed security refactor is the *Validate Variables* refactor. This refactor attempts to verify variables used in dynamic database query generation before they are passed to the database. This refactor will directly combat SQL injection and will ensure that an attacker does not compromise the integrity of the backend database. Figure 10 below is an example of an insecure dynamic database query in PHP, generated from a user-defined variable, both before and after refactoring.

This code segment represents a typical SQL injection vulnerability within a Web-based application. The variable $ _ REQUEST["username"] represents a variable passed into the function from a GET request and can be modified to be any string that an attacker desires. This type of error is very common in many Web-based applications, and can often lead to stolen or modified information from a backend database. This type of error can be safe-guarded against by simply validating input variables before they are used within a database query. This is the goal of the *Validate Variables* refactor. Again, this change in the code is minimal; however, this refactor can effectively safeguard a Web-based application against SQL injection attacks. The refactor simply adds an if statement into the code to verify that the username is valid. In this example, the isValidUsername is not a pre-defined PHP

function. This function requires further development and must at a minimum ensure that the input variable does not contain any SQL special characters. An example of the minimum required functionality of the isValidUsername function is provided in Figure 11.

This function would check the input for the presence of special SQL characters used for SQL injection attacks. If the username does not contain those characters, than the input variable would be considered a valid input into the function. It is important to note that this example represents the minimum checking required, and that further integrity checks could be added to the function.

Other security refactors are currently under development. Security refactoring will focus on three primary areas—inputs, outputs, and external interactions. Security refactors for inputs will focus on inputs from traditional GET and POST sources, as well as cookies, environmental variables, and files. Output security refactors will primarily focus on variables used in print (or other functionally equivalent methods). Finally, external interaction refactors will be concerned with dynamically generated SQL queries, calls to external libraries, and system calls. Security refactoring will enable agile developers to refactor existing working code to meet security requirements in future build cycles, allowing the implementation of secure Web-based application development within an iterative framework.

CONCLUSION AND FUTURE WORK

Agile development methodologies and test driven development (TDD) are becoming increasingly popular as development methodologies for Web-based applications. This paper presents a novel strategy for the development of secure Web-based applications within an agile development framework. The paper presents four synergetic strategies that enable the development of secure Web-based applications within an agile framework. The four-point strategy outlined in this paper provides an effective way to capture, implement, and test security requirements for Web-based applications.

The first strategy extends the currently accepted requirements artifacts within agile development to included security requirements as technical requirements. The security requirements can then be expressed as test-cases and placed along side functional requirements within the FIT framework, allowing the agile development team to record and implement security requirements as though they were functional requirements. This ability enables the team to add-in both functional and security requirements at the beginning of each successive build cycle, and ensures that the team remains agile and able to quickly react to changing customer requirements, including changing customer security requirements.

The second strategy, the utilization of a highly testable architecture, further supports the ability for the development team to extend the principles of agile development and TDD to the realm of security engineering. Through the use of a highly testable architecture, the Web-based application developed will be testable at every level of implementation. This architecture supports both the functional and security development through the use of TDD, and also supports the ability to extensively test the system after development is complete for both functional and security defects. This architecture becomes the backbone for all testing activities, at both the unit- and system-level. With this type of architectural support, test-cases that support the development of secure applications can be developed quickly, without

the overhead of building testing infrastructure found within traditional software projects. The ability to quickly respond to customer security requirements in the form of test-case development is necessary for the creation of secure applications within an agile framework, and the presence of a highly testable architecture ensures that the ability to test the system for security at all levels will be present within the Web-based application.

The third strategy outlines an extensive testing strategy for Web-based applications. This strategy is paramount in the process of secure development within an agile framework. The importance of a security testing strategy is clearly reflected in the dependence of converting security requirements to test-cases within the first strategy. The third strategy outlines a number of test-cases that can be applied to a Web-based application to test for security. It also outlines an efficient open source solution that can be incorporated within current unit-level testing activities to provide unit-level testing of security requirements. This type of testing can be used in conjunction with the FIT framework outlined in the first strategy, and when utilized alongside a highly testable architecture, represents an incredibly powerful test suite for ensuring the functionality and security of a Web-based application.

The fourth and final strategy provides the ability for an agile development team to quickly respond to the security requirements added to a project at the start of any build cycle. Security requirements not being fulfilled (i.e. not passing specific security test-cases) can be quickly implemented using the novel technique of security refactoring. This technique, an extension of the commonly used agile technique of refactoring, defines a number of simple transformations that will enhance the security of existing code, without influencing the functionality of the code. The process of security refactoring is further supported by the ability to incorporate security requirements as test cases. The test cases recorded with the FIT and HTTPUnit frameworks not only constitute system requirements, but also a set of automated regressions tests that can be used to ensure that any refactor does not modify the functionality of the system.

A major challenge within the development of secure applications is that attackers are always developing new ways of attacking secure systems. This challenge requires that the software development teams developing the Web-based applications stay uwith the methods and types of attacks being used against Web-based applications. This paper is a snap-shot of the current situation, and simply cannot provide an extensive list of security measures for all time; however, this paper does outline a high-level strategy for the development of both current and future secure Web-based systems. With the development of new technologies and Web-based user interactions, the implementation of security within Web-based applications will change; however, the methods behind the development need not.

Future work in this area will focus on the further development of security testing strategies, security refactoring and empirical test studies. The security testing strategies outlined represent the current state of the art; however, as mentioned previously, technology and attack strategies are constantly changing, and future testing strategies must reflect these changes. There are a number of potential areas in which security refactoring can be explored. Initially there is a need for more security refactors. A number of new security refactors are currently under development. Further work is also being directed towards the development of a refactoring tool to aid programmers in security refactoring. Finally, there is a need for empirical results supporting this development strategy. Currently we are seeking industrial partners to provide case-studies and real world data to support the use of these techniques within an agile development framework. Initial reactions to the proposed development strategy are positive; however, empirical data is required to further validate the proposed strategy.

REFERENCES

Ambler, S. W. (2002). A Class Type Architecture For Layering Your Application. 2004, from http://www.ronin-intl.com/publications/classTypeArchitecture.htm

Ambler, S. W. (2004). *The Object Primer 3rd Edition: Agile Model Driven Development with UML 2*: Cambridge University Press.

Ambler, S. W. (2005). Agile Requirements Modeling. Retrieved March 14, 2005, from http://www.agilemodeling.com/essays/agileRequirements.htm

Astels, D. (2003). *Test Driven Development: A Practical Guide*: Prentice Hall PTR.

Barnett, L., & Narsu, U. (2005). Planning Assumption: Best Practices for Agile Development. Retrieved March 15, 2005, from http://www.forrester.com/Research/LegacyIT/Excerpt/0,7208,30193,00.html

Beck, K. (2002). *Test Driven Development: By Example*: Addison-Wesley Professional.

Beck, K., Beedle, M., Bennekum, A. v., Cockburn, A., Cunningham, W., Fowler, M., et al. (2001). Manifesto for Agile Software Development. Retrieved November 22, 2005, from http://agilemanifesto.org/

Beznosov, K. (2003). *Extreme Security Engineering: On Employing XP Practices to Achieve 'Good Enough Security' without Defining It*. Paper presented at the First ACM Workshop on Business Driven Security Engineering (BizSec), Fairfax, VA.

Beznosov, K., & Kruchten, P. (2004). *Towards Agile Security Assurance*. Paper presented at the New Security Paradigms Workshop, White Point Beach Resort, Nova Scotia, Canada.

Cgisecurity.com. (2002). The Cross Site Scripting FAQ. Retrieved May 20, 2005, from http://www.cgisecurity.com/articles/xss-faq.shtml

Chris, A. (2002). *Advanced SQL Injection In SQL Server Applications*: NGSSoftware Insight Security Research (NISR) Publication.

Cunningham, W. (2002). Framework for Integrated Test. Retrieved November 26, 2002, from http://fit.c2.com

Cusumano, M. A., & Yoffie, D. B. (1999). Software development on Internet time. *IEEE Computer, 32*(10), 60-69.

Dell Inc. (2003). New Industry Data Shows Dell Continues to Lead in Serving Customers Through Internet Commerce. Retrieved March 14, 2005, from http://www1.us.dell.com/content/topics/global.aspx/corp/pressoffice/en/2003/2003_10_20_rr_002?c=us&l=en&s=corp

Finnigan, P. (2002). SQL Injection and Oracle. Retrieved Jan. 10,, 2005, from http://www.securityfocus.com/infocus/1644

Fowler, M. (2005). Refactoring Home Page. Retrieved May 20, 2005, from http://refactoring.com

Fowler, M., Beck, K., Brant, J., & Opdyke, W. (1999). *Refactoring: Improving the Design of Existing Code*: Addison-Wesley.

Freed, N. (1996). *Multipurpose Internet Mail Extensions (MIME) Part One: Format of Internet Message Bodies*: RFC 2045.

Gold, R. (2004a). HTTPUnit 1.6 API. Retrieved Jan. 10,, 2005, from http://httpunit.sourceforge.net/doc/api/

Gold, R. (2004b). HTTPUnit Home. Retrieved Jan. 10, , 2005, from http://httpunit.sourceforge.net/

Grossman, J. (2004a). Insecure Web Sites. Retrieved May 20, 2005, from www.varbusiness.com/sections/news/dailyarchives.asp?articleid=48158

Grossman, J. (2004b). Thwarting SQL Web Hacks. Retrieved May 20, 2005, from www.varbusiness.com/showArticle.jhtml?articleID=18841325&flatPage=true

Hightower, R., & Lesiecki, N. (2002). *Java tools for extreme programming: mastering open source tools including Ant, JUnit, and Cactus* New York: John Wiley & Sons

Iansiti, M., & MacCormack, A. (1997). Developing Products on Internet Time. *Harvard Business Review, 75*(5), 108-117.

ISECOM. (2003). OSSTMM 2.1 - The Open Source Security Testing Methodology Manual. Retrieved May 20, 2005, from http://www.isecom.org/osstmm/

Kirda, E., Jazayeri, M., Kerer, C., & Schranz, M. (2001). Experiences in engineering flexible Web services. *IEEE Multimedia, 8*(1), 58 - 65.

Linn, J. (1993). *Privacy Enhancement for Internet Electronic Mail: Part I: Message Encryption and Authentication Procedures*: RFC 1421.

Microsoft Corporation. (2004). Microsoft Security Bulletin MS04-028. Retrieved January 10, 2005, from http://www.microsoft.com/technet/security/bulletin/MS04-028.mspx

Offutt, J. (2002). Quality attributes of Web software applications. *IEEE Software, 19*(2), 25 - 32.

Offutt, J., Wu, Y., Du, X., & Huang, H. (2004). *Bypass Testing of Web Applications*. Paper presented at the The Fifteenth IEEE International Symposium on Software Reliability Engineering, Saint-Malo, Bretagne, France.

Opdyke, W. F. (1992). *Refactoring object-oriented frameworks*. University of Illinois at Urbana-Champaign.

Open Source Technology Group. (2005a). JUnit. Retrieved Dec. 2, 2005

Open Source Technology Group. (2005b). PhpUnit. Retrieved Dec. 2, 2005, from http://sourceforge.net/projects/phpunit/

Pancur, M., Ciglaric, M., Trampus, M., & Vidmar, T. (2003) *Towards empirical evaluation of test-driven development in a university environment.* Paper presented at the EUROCON 2003. Computer as a Tool. The IEEE Region 8.

Ramesh, B., Pries-Heje, J., & Baskerville, R. (2002). Internet Software Engineering: A Different Class of Processes. *Annals of Software Engineering, 14*(1 - 4), 169.

SPI Dynamics. (2002). *SQL Injection: Are Your Web Applications Vulnerable:* SPI Dynamics Whitepaper.

Thompson, S., & Reinke, C. (2001). A Catalogue of Functional Refactorings. Retrieved May 21, 2005, from www.cs.kent.ac.uk/projects/refactor-fp/publications/refactoring-draft-catalogue.pdf

Udo, G. J. (2001). Privacy and security concerns as major barriers for e-commerce: a survey study. *Information Management & Computer Security, 9*(4), 165-174.

This work was previously published in Int. Journal of Information Technology and Web Engineering, Vol 1, Issue 2, edited by G. Alkhatib and D. Rine, pp. 1-24, copyright 2006 by IGI Publishing (an imprint of IGI Global).

Chapter XVIII
Web Data Warehousing Convergence:
From Schematic to Systematic

D. Xuan Le
La Trobe University, Australia

J. Wenny Rahayu
La Trobe University, Australia

David Taniar
Monash University, Australia

ABSTRACT

This paper proposes a data warehouse integration technique that combines data and documents from different underlying documents and database design approaches. The well-defined and structured data such as Relational, Object- oriented and Object Relational data, semi-structured data such as XML, and unstructured data such as HTML documents are integrated into a Web data warehouse system. The user specified requirement and data sources are combined to assist with the definitions of the hierarchical structures, which serve specific requirements and represent a certain type of data semantics using object-oriented features including inheritance, aggregation, association and collection. A conceptual integrated data warehouse model is then specified based on a combination of user requirements and data source structure, which creates the need for a logical integrated data warehouse model. A case study is then developed into a prototype in a Web-based environment that enables the evaluation. The evaluation of the proposed integration Web data warehouse methodology includes the verification of correctness of the integrated data, and the overall benefits of utilizing this proposed integration technique.

INTRODUCTION AND MOTIVATION

Currently, there are more and more techniques being provided to accommodate the high demand for exchanging and storing business information including Web and operational data. While the well-defined structured data are operated and stored in relational, object-oriented (Buzydlowski, 1998), object relational database environments, semi-structured data in XML or unstructured documents are stored in HTML. The problem of related information being separated and stored in multiple places happens quite often within an organization. Information from these applications is extracted and further developed into business analysis tools such as OLAP and data warehousing, which aim to support data analysis, business requirements, and management decisions.

Relevant business Web data have rapidly increased in significant amounts. Recently, XML has increased in popularity and has become a standard technique for storing and exchanging information over the Internet. The data integration (Breitbart, Olson, & Thompson, 1986) in the data warehousing has certainly received a lot of attention. There are three particular articles that are very close to the work in this article. Jensen, Moller and Pedersen (2001) allow an integration

of XML and relational data. Even though the object-oriented concept is used in this model, the semantic contribution in this work lacks object-oriented features. Therefore, the semantics of data have been only partially supported. Other systems (Golfarelli, Rizzi, & Birdoljak, 1998, 2001; Huang & Su, 2001) focus on supporting Web data at the schematic level. While their initial focus is to incorporate XML data, Relational data have also been mentioned but not yet been incorporated. They mostly concentrate on the creation of a logical model.

Hence, it is clear that there is yet to be developed a standard integration technique that provides a means of handling multiple data sources being integrated into a data warehouse system (Bonifati, Cattaneo, Ceri, Fuggetta, & Paraboschi, 2001), and allowing a full capture of semantics of data in the data source models.

The purpose of this article can be summarized as follows:

- To ensure the integration technique allows a meaningful uniformed integrated object-oriented data warehouse structure.
- To ensure the integrated data and their semantics are explicitly and fully represented.

Figure 1. Integration Web data warehouse overview

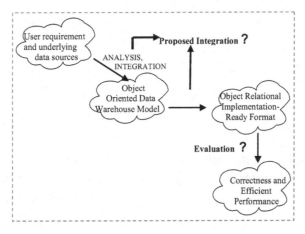

Table 1. Categorization and summary of existing work

Author(s)	Integration Methodology		
	Conceptual	Logical	Analysis and Comments
1. Integrated Relational Data in Data Warehousing			
Gupta and Mumick (1995)		Views	Map local source structures to global views to accomplish specific needs.
Calvanese et al. (1998)	Reasoning techniques	Declarative & procedural	Rewrite queries procedurally to declare relationships between data sources structure and data warehouse structure.
Cabibbo et al. (1998); Gopalkrishman et al. (1998)	Relational star schema and goal-driven analysis		Specify user-requirements on a *star* schema. Apply goal-driven analysis for selecting information to the target schema.
2. Integrated Relational and Object Data in Data Warehousing			
Chen, Hong, and Lin (1999); Filho, Prado, and Toscani (2000); Mohamah, Rahayu, and Dillon (2001)	Object-oriented model		Lack semantic representations. Use only an aggregation modeling feature to represent the data.
Miller, Honavar, Wong, and Nilakanta (1998); Serrano, Calero, and Piattini (2005)		Mapping object views	Extensive views allow various levels mapping. Develop a prototype to materialized views.
Gopalkrishman et al. (1998).	Object-oriented model		Lacked semantic representations. Use only inheritance modeling features to represent the data.
Huynh, Mangisengi, and Tjoa (2000).	Object-oriented model and mapping object methodology		The reversible mapping from object to relational environment causes possible lost of data semantics.
3. Integrated Relational, Object, and Web Data (HTML/XML) in Data Warehousing			
Golfarelli et al. (2001)	Attributes tree model		Integrate XML data based on DTD and XML schema.
Jensen et al., (2001).	UML model		Lack of data representation showing only aggregation relationship. Address both XML and relational data.
Byung, Han, and Song (2005); Nummenmaa, Niemi, Niinimäki, and Thanisch (2002)	Relational star schema		Enable query to distribute XML data in OLAP database. Address only XML data.
Nassis, Rahayu, Rajugan, and Dillon (2004)	UML Model		Specify user-requirement and XML structures on the object-oriented model.

- To ensure a proposed integrated data warehouse system with consistency and high quality.

- To ensure the correctness of integrated data and benefits such as usefulness of the proposed integrated data warehouse system.

Figure 1 shows an overview of the proposed works in this article. The integration technique starts with a conceptual integrated data warehouse model (Ezeife & Ohanekwu, 2005) where the user requirement and underlying data source structures are used to assist with the design. The integrated Web data warehouse conceptual model deals with class formalization and hierarchical structures. The specified conceptual integrated Web data warehouse model has created a need for an integrated Web data warehouse logical model where underlying source structures are then absorbed and specified onto the existing conceptual Web integrated Web data warehouse model. The proposed Web integrated data warehouse models are then translated into a suitable implementation format, which enables a prototype to be developed.

In order to confirm the efficiency of the proposed integration technique, a verification of integrated data is for the purpose of confirming the correctness and quality in the integrated data. This is done so that for each query requirement, a query is issued to access the integrated data warehouse system, and a set of queries access independent systems. The result that is obtained by the query that accessed the integrated data warehouse system is equivalent with the accumulative result that is obtained by queries that access one or more data source systems. The verification of the result would confirm the correctness and consistent quality of the integrated data alone, and the integration technique in general.

A SURVEY OF EXISTING DATA WAREHOUSE INTEGRATION APPROACHES

The existing approaches are classified into three categories. Table 1 briefly summarizes the existing approaches by category.

Category 1 includes the existing integration technique that can integrate only relational data into a data warehouse system. A data integration problem solved by proposing two approaches, namely, declarative and procedural can be found in the works of Calvanese, Giacomo, Lenzerini, and Rosati, (1998) and Lenzerini (2002) where as Cabibbo and Torlone (1998) and Gopalkrishman, Li, and Karlapalem (1998) propose different techniques to integrate data that are based on the requirements gathered from the user specification and also from studying the conceptual design of the operational source data. In order to create the model, a matching of requirements to sources is needed before creating fact and dimensions.

Category 2 shows techniques for handling complex information, which are different from the techniques that handle simple data types, which are available in the relational database. An object data warehouse approach allows an integration of both simple and complex data types. Its main function is to accomplish all important object-oriented concepts and additional features such as object ID and persistent object handling.

An object-oriented model extends the technique to handle the transition from relational data to object data (Filho et al., 2000; Gopalkrishman et al., 1998; Hammer, Garcia-Molina, Widom, Labio, & Zhuge, 1995; Huynh et al., 2000). However, the proposed model lacks a utilization of object-oriented features that result in insufficient representation of the semantics. Miller et al. (1998) introduce an object view in the mapping technique. They adopted the extensive view system to create views. However, views creation depends on the number of base classes.

Category 3 has allowed the data integration to move on to an advanced level where XML data is the main motivation. Web data nowadays can easily be found in XML structure, which has many possibilities for data modeling. This is because XML is well designed to support object-oriented modeling concept; the data semantics are very rich. Therefore, techniques for integrating XML data into a data warehouse system (Nassis et al., 2005; Rusu, Rahayu, & Taniar, 2004, 2005) needs to take more cautious because unlike relational and object data, XML data are classified as semi-structure.

While Golfarelli et al. (2001) try to deal with DTD and XML schema, Jensen et al. (2001) propose query to distribute XML data to an OLAP database according to the data representation. Part of our work is very much similar to the work of Jensen et al. (2001), we consider both XML and relational data for integration, and we also combine user requirements and underlying data structures to assist with the design. The difference between our work and the rest is that now we are handling three categories simultaneously. Not only are relational and XML data being considered, we also consider object data and other Web data structure such as HTML.

PROBLEM DEFINITION AND BACKGROUND

Identified Problems

Schemas

The most popular existing model in data warehousing is the star schema. The star schema allows business requirements to be organized and represented in a fact and dimensions surrounding fact. Dimensions are modeled on a flat level; therefore, it limits the data representations for both relationships and business requirements.

Unlike the star schema, the *snowflake* or *star flake* schema provides modeling of hierarchical relationships within the dimensions. The existence of hierarchies in the dimensions stores the whole attribute hierarchically and shows only one type of relationship, which is association. While it improves on the modeling representation, it creates more data-model complexity and therefore introduces implemental complexities.

The integration of the real world problems can be represented in a multidimensional model that consists of *dimensions* and *fact* using the hierarchical concept. Allowing for hierarchies in the dimensions would reduce the complexity of snowflake and star flake to a more efficient and clean integrated model while still being able to achieve a full data semantic capture.

Data Retrieval

The translation of the integrated data warehouse model into an implementation-ready format aims to address the adaptation of the object-oriented modeling concept into an implementation database environment where both object data and relational structures are maintained. Retrieved information must be correct and consistent in this proposed implementation when complex queries are specified in OLAP components. Performance of complex queries must be achievable in an efficient data accessing manner against the existing complex queries of the existing systems.

Background

We adopt object-oriented features, a semantic network diagram, and the TKPROF utility to assist with our strategy for solving the problem. They are briefly described as follows:

- **Object-oriented design concept:** The powerful features have allowed a problem to be modeled in much better semantics representations. Collection type allows the multi-values attribute to handle the storing of data in a more efficient manner using ROW, SET, and ARRAY. Features like aggregation allow a whole problem to be modeled as "part-of" where a lower hierarchy is part of the upper one, or part can be an existence-dependent or existence-independent.

When the part is considered as existence dependent, it means that the part cannot be shared with other classes or removed from the whole.

Whereas, Existence independent is where the part can be shared with other classes and can be removed independently of the whole.

An inheritance (Rahayu, 1999; Rahayu, Chang, Dillon, & Taniar, 2000) type is where the problem is modeled as a super class with sub-classes. The sub-class utilizes the information in the super-class and its own information to specialize itself.

An association relationship represents a connection between two objects. There are three types of association relationships such as one to one, one to many, and many to many. The type being used depends on the criteria of the problem.

- **Semantic Network Diagram:** If given an XML document as one of the data sources, we employ the semantic network diagram (Feng, Chang, & Dillon, 2002) to translate XML data into the proposed integrated model. The semantic network diagram is divided into the semantic level and schema level. The former developed a specific diagram from the XML document structure and the latter maps from this specific diagram into the target model, an integrated data model. The semantic network diagram is divided into four major components: nodes, directed edges, labels, and constraints. Suppose a semantic network diagram in Figure 1 is studied.

Based on the construction rules to formalize a semantic network diagram (Feng et al., 2002; Pardede, Rahayu, & Taniar, 2004), there are five nodes: A, B, X, Y, Z in the diagram. The first two nodes are the complex nodes while the rest are the basic nodes. There are four directed edges representing the semantic relationships between the objects. In our work, we use different labels to indicate the relationship corresponding to each edge. Different labels are interpreted as follows:

- *p* indicates "in-property"; *g* indicates generalization, *a* indicates aggregation; *c* indicates composition.

Various types of constraints such as uniqueness, cardinality, ordering, etc., can also be added to the nodes or edges. The modeling representation in Figure 2 presents a well-defined conceptual design from XML data. The attributes or elements declarations and simple or complex type (Pardede, Rahayu, & Taniar, 2005) definitions in XML schema are mapped into the four components or directed edges.

INTEGRATION PROPOSED TECHNIQUE

The structures of underlying data sources can be the combination of relational structures and structures that are available in XML documents and object databases.

- **Translation Technique of HTML Data into XML Structure:** Before conducting the integration of a Web data warehouse model, we adopt the mapping tool and technique that is proposed in the works of Bishay, Taniar, Jiang, and Rahayu (2000), and Li, Liu, Wang and Peng (2004) to map from HMTL data to XML data so that attributes can be identified. Figure 4 shows HTML data that are translated to XML schema using very basic and straight forward mapping steps. More information on the mapping and transforming techniques can be found in these two references.

1. **Mapping Rule:** Referring to Figure 3, let the content of table XYZ is a set of rows <TR> and each row contains a set of column <TD>; XYZ is mapped to an XML schema structure; <TR> is mapped to the <xsd:

Figure 2. Semantic network diagram

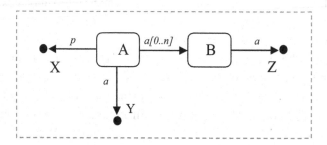

Sequence>; <TD> is mapped to the <xsd: elment> wihin the sequence.

2. **Motivation by a Case Study:** To provide a feasible example for this article, we illustrate the proposed approaches based on the need to build a data warehouse system for university enrolments. Information about the enrolments is stored in relational and Web forms. This is due to the fact that each individual faculty uses its own system and none is currently linked.

One faculty might have its own Web-based system while the others, for various reasons, might have just a normal database system to handle the enrolment of students. It is the goal of the university to construct a data warehouse system in order to analyze student enrolments in areas/subjects/degrees, and also the trend of enrolments in different years including semesters. The university is also interested in the analysis of degree enrolments for a particular area; for example, for the Masters degree, there might be more students enrolled in course work than in research. In some rare cases, a university may be limited in its ability to provide both research and coursework. Thus, it is interesting to see the relationship between these parties. A faculty may be formed by one or more schools, and a certain number of degrees belong to a particular school. A study of an advanced subject is required for some prerequisites. The university would like information about the prerequisites to be kept in

the warehouse system for future analysis. Points to consider are that a specific degree belongs to only one faculty. A subject can be attended by students across the degrees.

The methodology for specifying the conceptual integrated data warehouse model in two phases is as follows: phase (a) consists of the steps, which are temporarily referred to as *conceptual defined sequence*, to assist with the process of creating the conceptual integrated dimensions and fact; phase (b) is an extension of phase (a) to allow data structures of relational and HTML/XML data sources to be fully unified and incorporated in the integrated data warehouse model.

Conceptual Web Integrated Dimensions and Fact

Conceptually, starting with the assumptions of the user specified requirements and information related to underlying sources in relational and XML, we form a set of steps for defining our integrated Web data warehouse model. Please note that by this time, HTML data have been translated to XML structure. The methodology consists of the following steps, which we temporarily refer to as a *conceptual defined sequence*, to assist with the process of creating the model:

1. **Simplifying the requirements:** Structures of underlying data sources can also be simplified if possible.

2 **Defining integrated dimensions involves two sub steps**: (a) Specifying n classes where n ≥ 1; (b) classifying hierarchy: additional specified information by any other means is a great advantage. Suppose two classes A and B in a dimension, the relationship between A and B can either be a, b, or c.

a. **Aggregation:** Deals with the dependence between the classes. Considering the cardinality where needed, -to-one or to-many, between the base classes and sub-classes.

b. **Inheritance:** Categories subtypes and super-types.

c. **Collection:** Handles multi values in an attribute. This relationship in our approach is not for hierarchy building, but rather for storing data in a more efficient manner.

d. **Association:** Is when two classes have an association relationship, using a -to-one; -to-many to describe the association between classes

3. Defining Fact: A simple, single fact, which is surrounded by integrated dimensions. Hierarchy and cardinality should be identified.

The *conceptual defined sequence* is now used to specify the conceptual integrated Web dimensions and tact as follows.

*   **Inheritance Type Dimension:** Dimensional analysis is such "*…The university is also interested in the analysis of degree enrolments for particular type, for example, for a Masters degree, there may be more students enrolled in course work than in research but it may be that a university has a strong constraint in providing both research and coursework…,*" applying the **conceptual defined sequence,** a *conceptual degree* is specified as follows:

1. Simplifying requirements. A Degree can be further classified as a Research Degree or a Coursework Degree.

2. Identified Dimension {Degree}

Classes {Degree, Research, Coursework}

Hierarchy {Generalization} *additional formation: the same number of years applies to all Masters degrees. Extra information is needed to support*

Figure 3. Translating HTML data to XML structure

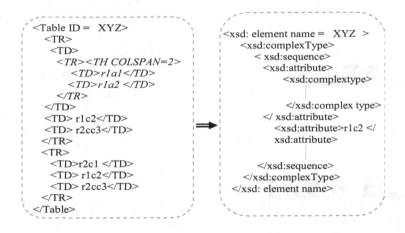

the specialization of a degree type. An inheritance type is an ideal modeling feature because a degree is a generalization and research or coursework is specialization. No cardinality.

A conceptual degree dimension is derived based on steps 1 and 2 shown in Figure 4.

- **Collection Type Dimension:** Dimensional analysis may be: "*...A study of an advanced subject is required for some prerequisites. The university would like information about the prerequisites to be kept in the warehouse system for future analysis...,*" applying the **conceptual defined sequence;** a *conceptual degree* is specified as follows.

1. Simplifying requirements. A subject needs to store its prerequisites. Each subject has two prerequisites at most.
2. Identified Dimension {Subject}
   Classes {Subject}
   Hierarchy{NIL} A collection type is an ideal modeling feature because it allows a prerequisite to be modeled as an attribute that stores multi-values using array, row, set. No cardinality.

A conceptual subject dimension is derived based on step 1 & 2 shown in Figure 5.

Figure. 4. A conceptual degree dimension

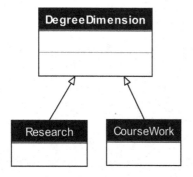

- **Aggregation Type Dimension:** As recalled earlier, we claim that aggregation is further grouped into two groups: *Non-shareable-existence dependent and shareable-existence dependent.*
- **Non-shareable Existence Independent Type Dimension:** Dimensional analysis is such "*...A faculty may be formed by one or more schools and a certain number of degrees belongs to a particular school...,*" applying the **conceptual defined sequence,** a *conceptual faculty* is specified as follows:

1. Simplifying requirements. A Faculty can own none or more than one school.
2. Identified Dimension {Faculty}
   Classes {Faculty, School}
   Hierarchy {Aggregation} *additional formation: a Faculty can be existed without a School.* One-to-many.

A conceptual faculty dimension is derived based on information above, shown in Figure 6.

- **Shareable Existence Independent Type Dimension:** Dimensional analysis is such "*...also the trend of enrolments in different years including semesters ...,*" applying the **conceptual defined sequence,** a *conceptual time* is specified in Figure 7.

1. Simplifying requirements. A time can also include semester. Semester is needed for enrollment.
2. Identified Dimension {Time}
   Classes {Time, Semester}
   Hierarchy {Aggregation} *additional information: A semester can be shared with other classes. Time has many months or years. And a year has more one or more semesters.*

Thus, it is a many-to-many as shown in Figure 7.

- **Fact Class:** Fact analysis is such "…compute student enrolment to timely analyze the trends and performance of subjects and degrees in faculties…." From *item 3* in section A, we have Class{Uni_Fact}; Hierarchy {Association}; one-to-many.

A conceptual fact class is derived in Figure 8 surrounding the support of the conceptual integrated dimensions:

Logical Web Integrated Dimensions and Fact

In this section, the rest of the integrated dimensions and facts are specified in greater detail to directly utilize the structures of underlying sources. It assumes that both relational data sources and HTML/XML documents are retrieved based on the user requirements and available structures in the sources.

- **Adding Attributes to Collection type Dimension:** A Semantic network diagram has not yet formalized a representation for a collection type. Thus, we propose a "C" label indicating a collection type that represents a semantic in the data complex type.

With reference to Figure 9, shows *relational data & semantic network diagram* Attrs{A, B, M1, M2..Mn} are simple data types; Attrs{M1, M2} are multi-valued attributes in relational table; And Attrs{M1, M2} sub-elements in Semantic Network Diagram; ComplexType (Type 1, Type 2}. Adding attributes to a collection type dimension consists of two steps:

- **Step 1:** For a relational data source table that has attributes {A, B, M1, M2}, which are required for analytical information. Attribute {A, B} are added to Dimension 1. Attributes { M1, M2} are stored as a {C} attribute that has a VARRAY type. Attribute

Figure 5. A conceptual subject dimension

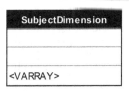

Figure 6. A conceptual faculty dimension

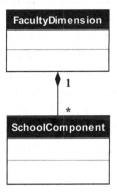

Figure 7. A conceptual time dimension

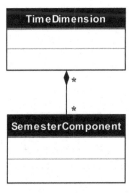

{C} is an array type that take two elements, which is also added to Dimension 1.

- **Step 2:** For two complex types namely Type 1 and Type 2 with elements {A, B} and {M1, M2} respectively, Type 2 is an inner complexType element in Type 1. Type 2 element contains sub-elements {M1, M2}. Thus, element {A, B} in Type 1 are mapped to attributes {A, B} in Dimension 1; sub-element{M1, M2} are mapped to an element

{C} in Dimension 1. Note element{C} is defined as a VARRAY type in step 1.

Example: Conceptual subject dimension in Figure 5 is now presented here to add appropriate attributes and data structures in order to complete the integration of a logical integrated subject dimension shown (Figure 10).

Step 1: For subject relational data table provided by health and science faculty with a set of attributes {Subjectid, Subjectname, Req1, Req2}, which are required for analytical information. Attributes {SubjectID, Subjectname} are added to the conceptual subject dimension. Attributes {Req1, Req2} are stored in a VARRAY element {Prerequisites}, which can take two elements in a single record. Attribute {Prerequisite} is

then also added to subject dimension. Refer to SubjectDimension in Figure 10.

Step 2: For an outer complex type, SubjectType and elements {Subjectid, Subjectname, Refsubject}. {Refsubjectprereq} is an inner complexType element of SubjectType. Refsubject complexType contains sub-elements {Req1,Req2}. Thus, elements {Subjectid, Subjectname} in SubjectType are mapped to attributes {Subjectid, Subjectname} in SubjectDimesnion, which are added in step 1. Elements { Req1, Req2} are mapped to element{Reprequisite}. And element {Reprequisite} can contain up to two sub-elements as formed in step 1.

A complete subject integration forms classes and attributes as follows:

Figure 8. Conceptual fact surrounded by integrated dimensions

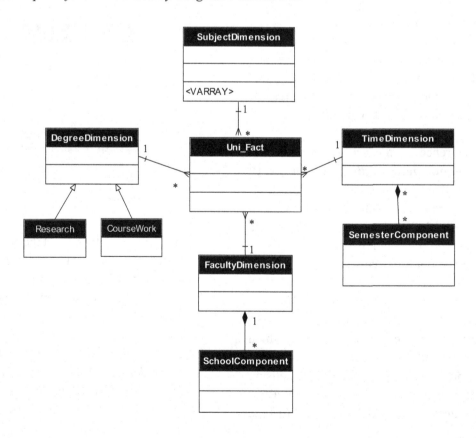

*SubjectDimension {**SubjectID**, Subjectname, prerequisite<Varray>}*

where SubjectID is primary key (OID)

- **Adding Attributes to Inheritance Dimension:** Figure 11 shows that relational data and semantic network diagram Attrs{A, B, D, E, F} are simple data types; Attrs{D} is a type attribute; generalized attributes{A,B} specialized Attrs{E, F}; ComplexType (Type 1, Type 2, Type 3...Type n). Adding attributes to an inheritance dimension consists of two steps:

Step 1: For a relational data source table that has attributes {A, B, D, E, F, E}, which are required for analytical information. Dimension 2 is a super-type, which has one or more sub-dimensions. Each sub-dimension has one or more specialized attributes. To complete an integration of inheritance dimension: add generalized attributes{A,B} to

Figure 9. Specifying data sources in dimension using collection type

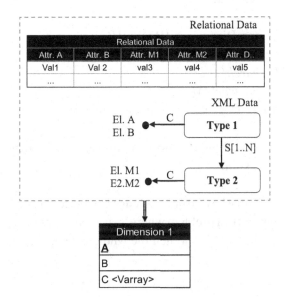

super-type Dimension 2; map a value group of type attribute {D} to a sub-dimension; add specialized attributes {E}, {F} or {E, F} to each sub-dimension.

Step2: For three complex types, namely Type 1, Type 2 and Type n with elements {A, B, D, E, F} are required analytical information. Type 1 is the base type where Type 2 and Type n are of the extension based Type 1. Element {A, B} in Type 1 are mapped to attributes {A, B} in Dimension 2. Extension base types Type 1 is mapped to sub-type of Value31; whereas Type n is mapped to Value32 respectively. An element such as {E} or {F} is mapped to its own class where appropriate.

Example: Conceptual degree dimension, in phase (i) Figure 4 earlier, is now presented in Figure 12 to add appropriate attributes and data structures in order to complete the integration of degree dimension.

Step1: For a relational degree source table that has attributes {DegreeID, Degreename, Degreetype, Area, Major}, which are required for analytical information. DegreeDimension is a super-type which can have two sub-dimensions, research, and coursework. Each sub-dimension has one or more specialized attributes such as {Area} or {Major}. To complete an integration of the inheritance DegreeDimension: add generalized attributes{Degreeid,Degreename} to DegreeDimension; mapping Research value of DegreeType to Research sub-type and Coursework value of DegreeType to Coursework sub-type; Area is an attribute to specialise the research degree and major is the attribute to specialize coursework degree. Thus, attribute {Area} is added to Research sub-type and {major} is added to Coursework sub-type.

Figure 10. Adding/mapping attribute data to the conceptual integrated subject dimension

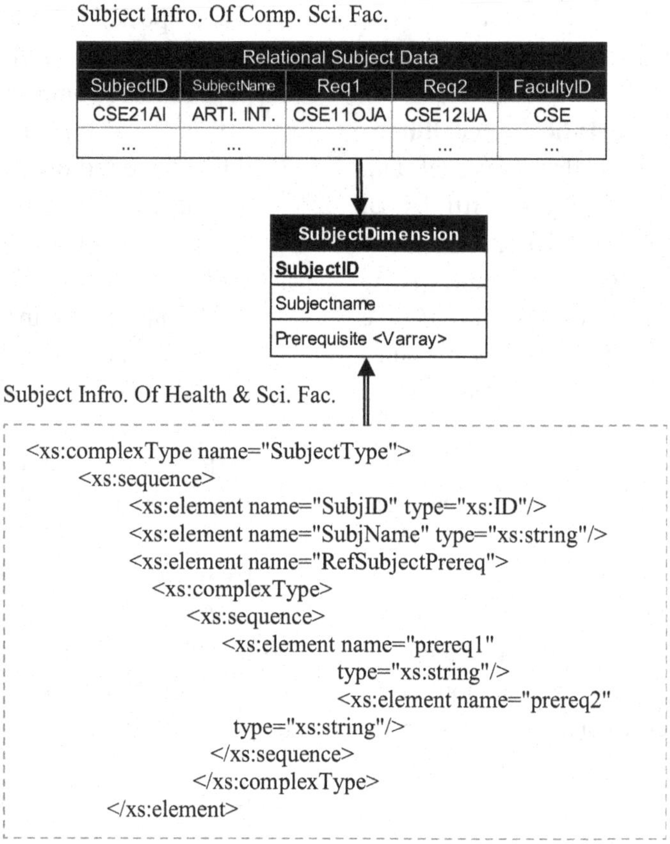

Subject Infro. Of Comp. Sci. Fac.

Relational Subject Data				
SubjectID	SubjectName	Req1	Req2	FacultyID
CSE21AI	ARTI. INT.	CSE11OJA	CSE12IJA	CSE
...	...	...	...	...

SubjectDimension

SubjectID

Subjectname

Prerequisite <Varray>

Subject Infro. Of Health & Sci. Fac.

```
<xs:complexType name="SubjectType">
    <xs:sequence>
        <xs:element name="SubjID" type="xs:ID"/>
        <xs:element name="SubjName" type="xs:string"/>
        <xs:element name="RefSubjectPrereq">
            <xs:complexType>
                <xs:sequence>
                    <xs:element name="prereq1"
                                type="xs:string"/>
                        <xs:element name="prereq2"
                    type="xs:string"/>
                </xs:sequence>
            </xs:complexType>
        </xs:element>
```

Step 2: For three complex types, DegreeType, ResearchType and CourseworkType with elements {DegreeID, Degreename, Area, Major}. DegreeType is the base type where ResearchType and CourseType are of the extension base DegreeType. Element {DegreeID, Degreename} in DegreeType are mapped to attributes {DegreeID, Degreename} in DegreeDimension. ComplexType of Research of extension base DegreeType is mapped to sub-type of Research; whereas ComplexType Coursework is mapped to sub-type Coursework. Element such as {Area} and {Major} is mapped to its own Research and Coursework respectively.

A complete degree integration forms classes and attributes as follows:

*DegreeDimension {**DegreeID**,*
Degreename, reprequisite<Varray>}
Research{Area}
Coursework{Major}
where DegreeID is primary key (OID)

• **Adding Attributes to Aggregation Dimension.**

Non-shareable Existence Dependent type is applied to a problem where "parts" are dependent on the "whole." When the whole is removed, its parts are also removed. With reference to Figure 13, Attrs{A, B, C, D, E, F} are simple data types; ComplexType (Type 1, Type 2). Adding attributes to aggregation dimension consists of two steps:

Step 1: For a relational data table 1 and relational data table 2 that have attributes {A, B, D, E}, which are required for analytical information. Relational data table 1 has a one-to-many relationship with relational data table 2. And relational data table 2 is composed of relational data table 1. Thus, relational data table 1 is a parent of relational data table 2.

Figure 11. Specifying data sources in dimension using inheritance type

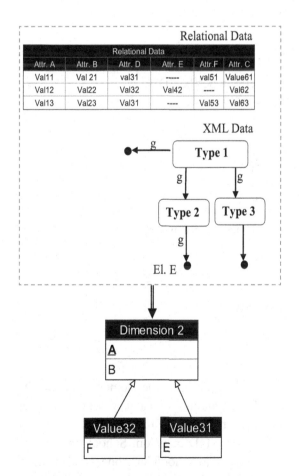

Step 2: For two complex types namely Type 1 and Type 2 with elements {A, D} and {E,F}. If Type 2 is composed by Type 1 then Type 1 is mapped to Dimension 3 and element {A, B} in Type 1 are added to attributes {A, B} in Dimension 3. Type 2 is also mapped to component of Dimension 3 and elements {E, D} are added to Component of Dimension 3. Note that element names in Type 2 are not matched with element names in Component. For the time being, presumably element {E} is matched with element {E} and element {D} is matched with element {F}.

Example: Conceptual faculty dimension, section (A) Figure 6 earlier, is now presented in Figure 14 to add appropriate attributes and data structures in order to complete the integration of the degree dimension.

Step 1: For the relational faculty data source table and relational school data tables that have attributes {FacultyID, Facultyname} and {SchoolID, Schoolname}, which are required for analytical information. Relational Faculty has a one-to-many relationship to the Relational School Table. And the Relational School Table comprises the Faculty Table. Thus, the Faculty Table is a parent of the School Table. On the other hand, FacultyDimension and SchoolComponent have a Part-Of relationship. On the other hand, the FacultyDimension is a parent of SchoolComponents. The SchoolComponent is a non-shareable part which means that when FacultyDimension is removed, SchoolComponents is also removed. To complete an integration of FacultyDimension: add attributes{FacultyID, Facultyname} in Faculty Relational table to FacultyDimension; add attributes {SchoolID, Schoolname) in Relational School table to the corresponding SchoolComponent.

Figure 12. Adding/mapping attribute data to the conceptual integrated degree dimension

Degree Infro. Of Comp. Sci. Fac.

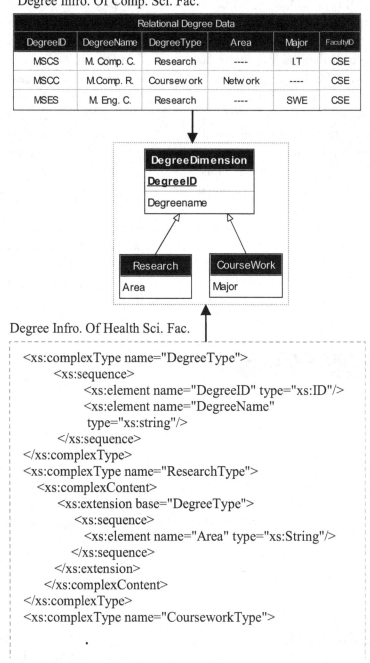

Relational Degree Data					
DegreeID	DegreeName	DegreeType	Area	Major	FacultyID
MSCS	M. Comp. C.	Research	----	I.T	CSE
MSCC	M.Comp. R.	Coursework	Network	----	CSE
MSES	M. Eng. C.	Research	----	SWE	CSE

Degree Infro. Of Health Sci. Fac.

```
<xs:complexType name="DegreeType">
    <xs:sequence>
        <xs:element name="DegreeID" type="xs:ID"/>
        <xs:element name="DegreeName"
        type="xs:string"/>
    </xs:sequence>
</xs:complexType>
<xs:complexType name="ResearchType">
  <xs:complexContent>
      <xs:extension base="DegreeType">
        <xs:sequence>
        <xs:element name="Area" type="xs:String"/>
        </xs:sequence>
      </xs:extension>
    </xs:complexContent>
</xs:complexType>
<xs:complexType name="CourseworkType">
```

Step 2: For two complex types, namely Faculty type and School type with elements {FacultyID, Facultyname} and {SchoolID,Schoolname}. If the School type comprises the Faculty type, then Faculty type is mapped to Fac-

ultyDimension. The elements {FacultyID, Facultyname} in Faculty type are added to attributes {FacultyID,Facultyname} in FacultyDimension. School type is also mapped to SchoolComponent and elements

Figure 13. Specifying data sources in dimension using non shareable existence dependent

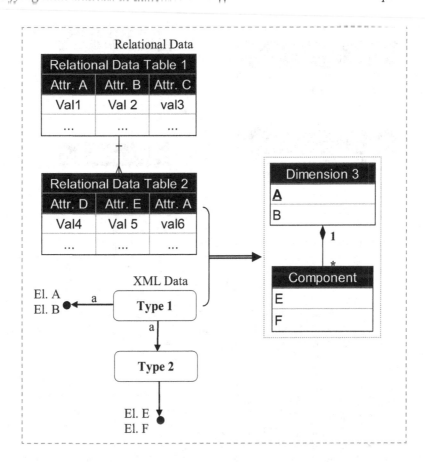

{SchoolID, Schooname} in School type are added to SchoolComponent.

A complete faculty integration forms classes and attributes as follows:

*FacultyDimension {**FacultyID**, Facultyname}*
*SchoolComponent{**SchoolID**, Schoolname}*

where *Faculty, SchoolID a*re primary keys (OIDs)

Shareable Existence Independent Type is applied where parts are independent of the whole. When the "whole" is removed, parts still remain.

The time conceptual dimension in Figure 7 now shows the process of specifying/mapping attributes in Figure 15. A complete time integration forms classes and attributes are formed.

*TimeDimension {**TimeID**,Description}*
*Semester {**SemesterID**,Description}*

where TimeID and SemesterID are primary keys

• **Adding Attributes Fact Class**

Figure 16 shows fact that is referenced to SubjectDimension, DegreeDimension, FacultyDimension and TimeDimention. Thus, keys of SubjectID, DegreeID, FacultyID and TimeID are

Figure 14. Adding/mapping attribute data conceptual faculty dimension

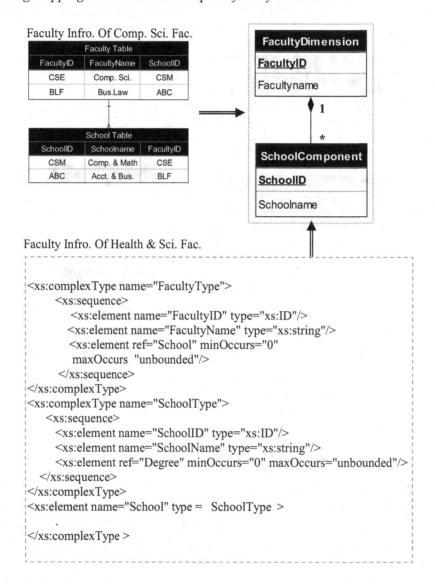

added to fact. Enrolment attribute is an aggregated value that is tracked by subject, degree, faculty, and times basis.

Figure 17 is a complete integrated university logical data warehouse model that is fully integrated with powerful object-oriented features where storing the hierarchy in a dimension table allows for the easiest browsing of subject, degree and faculty dimension data on yearly basis. In Figure 17, we could easily choose a class and then list all of that category's sub-classes. We would

drill-down into the data by choosing a specific type of degree and a general degree.

DISCUSSION AND ANALYSIS

We have successfully proposed an integration technique that allows data from different database design approaches to be integrated into a data warehouse model. The proposed data warehouse integration approach is clearly and simply pre-

Figure 15. Adding/mapping attribute data conceptual time dimension

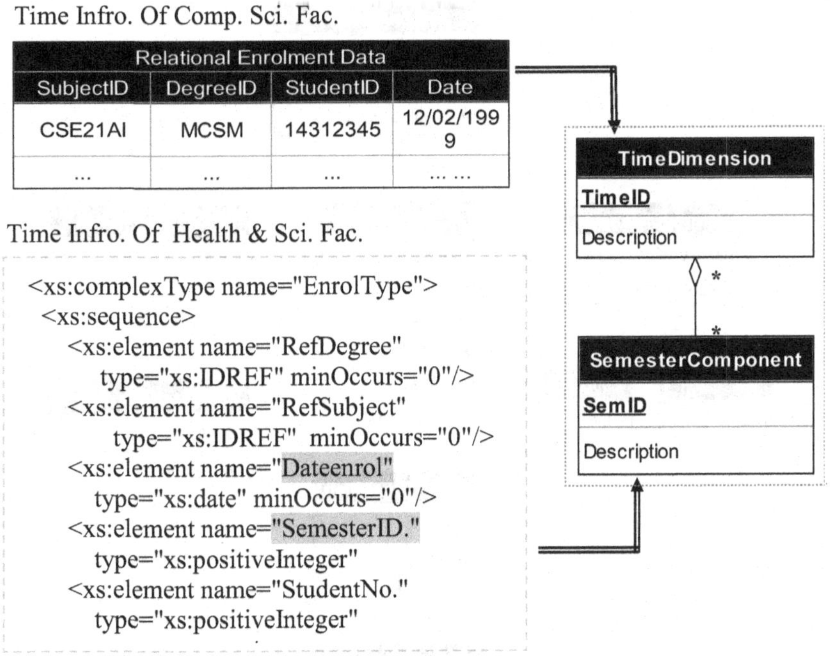

Time Infro. Of Comp. Sci. Fac.

Relational Enrolment Data			
SubjectID	DegreeID	StudentID	Date
CSE21AI	MCSM	14312345	12/02/1999
...	...	...	... ...

Time Infro. Of Health & Sci. Fac.

```
<xs:complexType name="EnrolType">
 <xs:sequence>
   <xs:element name="RefDegree"
       type="xs:IDREF" minOccurs="0"/>
   <xs:element name="RefSubject"
        type="xs:IDREF"  minOccurs="0"/>
   <xs:element name="Dateenrol"
       type="xs:date" minOccurs="0"/>
   <xs:element name="SemesterID."
       type="xs:positiveInteger"
   <xs:element name="StudentNo."
       type="xs:positiveInteger"
```

TimeDimension

TimeID

Description

*

*

SemesterComponent

SemID

Description

Figure 16. Specifying attributes to university fact class

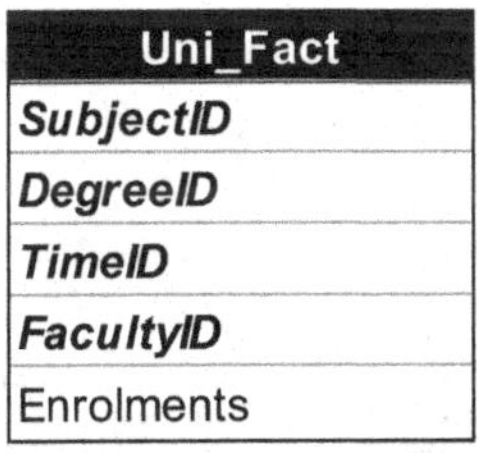

Uni_Fact
SubjectID
DegreeID
TimeID
FacultyID
Enrolments

sented in two sections. Section (A) allows user specified information to be established in a conceptual dimension. Each dimension is modeled with a different object-oriented feature which easily allows required attributes to be specified from different underlying data model sources in section (B).

The proposed integrated data warehouse model is a **simple** model that has a star schema structure in which hierarchies are modeled by a wide range of object-oriented features. The hierarchical dimensions aim to allow the easiest information browsing of the data detail at the lowest level possible. The **complete** range of data source models from different database design approaches, including well-structured data and semi-structured data, have been successfully integrated in the proposed model. Most importantly, large amounts of Web data such as HTML/XML are now formally handled in the proposed integrated data warehouse. The correctness of the proposed integrated data warehouse model is going to be evaluated in the next section.

EXPERIMENTATIONS AND ANALYSIS RESULTS

This section describes (i) the implementation of the proposed integrated data warehouse solution, using the case study, into a Web-based integrated data warehouse prototype. The prototype is then allowed us to carry out the analyses, which perform

Figure. 17. Object-oriented integrated data warehouse logical model

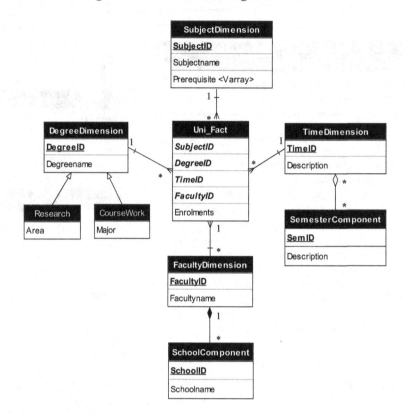

a validation of the correctness and consistency in the integrated data.

System Implementation

System Architecture

Figure 18 is an overview of the implementation that aims to create an integrated data warehouse system in which the front-end is the Web-based language to assist with the dimensional presentation and user interaction; the back-end is the Oracle 10g, which is used to store the physical database. While the front-end Web-based component allows the requests from the users and displaying of the results in dimensional forms, the back-end processes the user's requests in SQL statements and returns the retrieved results to the front-end platform for manipulation.

Figure 18. System architecture overview

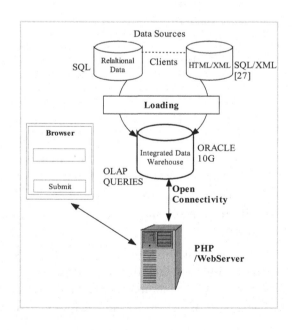

Data Source Creation includes the relational data source and XML data source, while a relational data source system for a faculty is developed including SQL for tables creation and sources generation. Source generation is simplified with the assistance of store procedures and functions. The XML data source system is developed including SQL/XML (Loney & Koch, 2000; Melton, 2003) with table creation and source generation. The source generation includes XML Spy for creating and validating the XML schemas. XML documents are then generated and validated using the created XML schema, both being done using XML Spy tool. The XML schema for validation is stored in Oracle and XML documents that contain XML data sources, and are then loaded into an XML database.

Integrated Data Warehouse Schema Creation and Data Source Loading consist of SQL queries to assist with tables and object types creation for hierarchical Dimensions and Fact classes that build an object relational data warehouse schema in SQL *PLUS.

Following each dimension and fact creation, a stored procedure is written for transforming data sources from a relational system and XML system into the integrated dimensions and fact table and types. The stored procedures use object relational (Taniar, Rahayu, & Srivastava, 2003) syntax for inserting data as object types into relational tables.

The transformation of data into the target integrated data warehouse schema is a critical task because of the data's multiple sources, for example, a subject may be taken by the degree students in different faculties. Therefore, the merging of the data may result in conflicts of subject information. An attempt to overcome the conflict problems that may cause abnormal system behavior and inconsistency in integrated data quality, our in-

Figure 19. Result based on integrated data

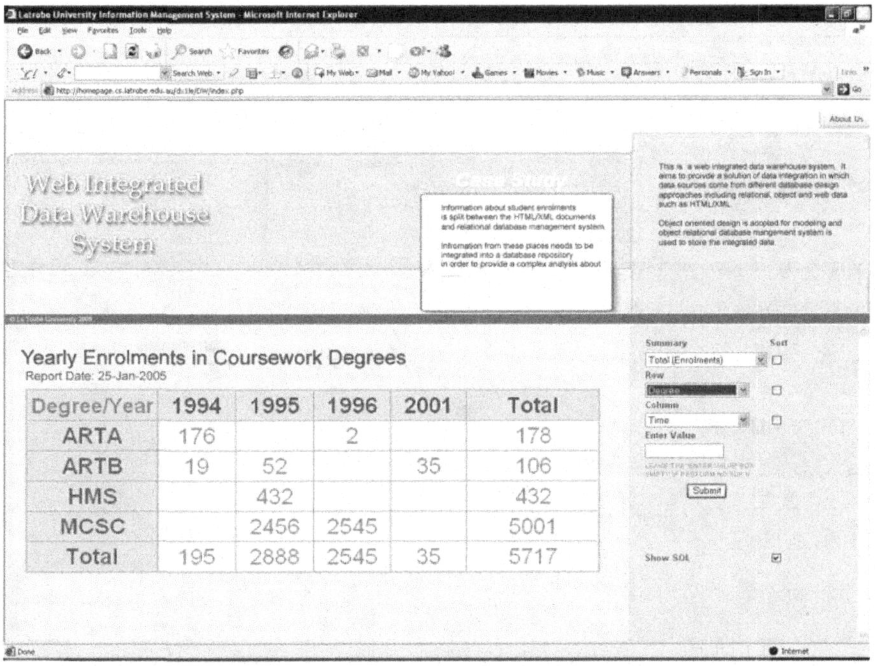

297

Figure 20. Result based on data in multiple source systems

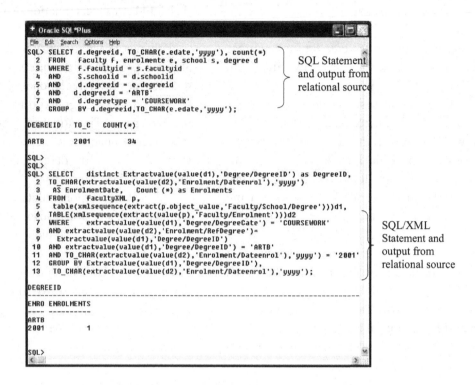

Figure 21. Result based on integrated data

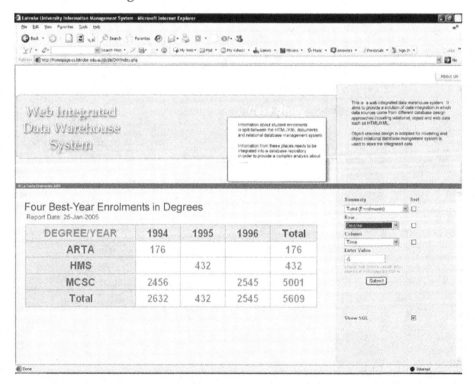

tegration technique also includes the checking of existing duplicate information and incorporation of techniques to handle such problems.

Analysis Results

Our query experimentation structure includes the validation of integrated data for ensuring the quality and consistency in the integrated data.

Category 1: *"The University is interested in the number of student enrolments in coursework degree on a yearly basis."*

As processed by the query for criteria in Category 1, the result shown in Figure 19, we recall that a degree has been modeled using an inheritance object-oriented feature. In this object relational integrated data warehouse query that

Figure 22. Result based on data in multiple source systems

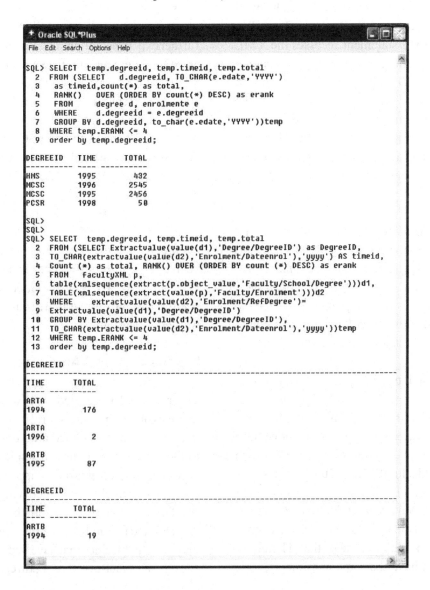

associates with the information of a specific degree type, it demonstrates the capture of information at the lower levels in the WHERE clause, in which the *IS OF* type is introduced to access the lower level's information without needing to use a join operation between the degree and its subtype, *coursework*, based selection in the object relational syntax.

Once the selection of values is made, the query processing next applies the aggregate function SUM on the Enrolment values and GROUP BY the *coursework* degree further by year.

Figure 20 shows the first SQL statement that accesses the relational system, which produces 34 enrolments for degree ARTB in year 2001. The second SQL/XML statement accesses the XML system, which produces one enrolment for degree ARTB in year 2001. The sum of results in first two statements for degree ARTB in 2001 is the 35. ARTB degree in year 2001 is 35 enrolments in Figure 19 and Figure 20 (sum of results). We may conclude that data have been consistently integrated in our integrated data warehouse system.

Category 2: An analytical requirement, which it demonstrates the ordering of the data result using rank function. *"Retrieve the enrolments in the degrees group by each year and display only the top four rows from the ranked results which have the most enrolments in the degrees and year."*

As processed by the query for criteria in Category 2, the result shown in Figure 21, the query for this criteria falls into an advanced OLAP query category. Apart from foundation syntax such as SUM() and GROUP BY which have been used, the RANK() function has also been used to handle the ranking concept based on the total measurement in the SQL statement. The Ranking () function assigns ranks from 1 to N and skips a rank in case of ties. Therefore, if two degrees have the same enrolments, a tie

ranking is applied to these two degrees. This is illustrated by the example below:

Raw	Rank	Enrolments	
3	3	2678	⟶ Tie for rank 3
4	3	2678	
5	5	2778	

As it can be seen, the result in Figure 21 that within a degree there are no enrolments in particular years, for instance the data of enrolments for the ARTA degree in 1994 is 176 enrolments and no enrolments in years 1995 and 1996. Now the question is: how many enrolments are there for ARTA degree in the year 1994 available in the source systems? Let's us prove the number of enrolments in degree ARTA in 1994 with a further experimentation. The verification involves an SQL statement to retrieve all the data in the relational data source system and an SQL/XML statement retrieves all data in the XML document as demonstrated in Figure 22.

Figure 22 shows the first SQL statement that accesses the relational system, which produces the coursework degrees grouped by year with their associated number of enrolments. The second SQL/XML statement accesses the XML system, which produces the 176 enrolments for degree ARTA in year 1994. ARTA degree in year 1994 is 176 enrolments in both Figure 21 and Figure 22. We may conclude that data have been consistently integrated in our integrated data warehouse system.

Discussion and Analysis

The proposed integrated data warehouse technique explicitly provides a fully integrated solution that includes a conceptual design extended to the logical design and an implementation for verification. Our integration approach is divided into phases, which are engaged with a very simple set of instructions to assist with the establishment of integrated fact and dimensions. The dimensions may have hierarchies that have been handled with a range of object-oriented features.

From the implementation experimentation, the system has been successfully developed with full relational data and XML data loaded into independent source systems. These source data are then integrated using stored procedures for extracting, transforming, and loading into the target system.

Query processing and data retrieval have been considered more efficient because of the leveling data representation. In the completion of query processing, the complex queries have utilized analytic functions, as demonstrated in the analysis results section, to successfully retrieved integrated data.

For a validation of the correctness and consistency of our integrated data, we perform two sets of queries processing—(i) a complex query is issued to access the integrated data system to retrieve the first result; (ii) and a set of queries to access the independent source systems to retrieve the one or more results and the sum of these results should be equivalent to the first result. This has been proven that the result of (i) and total result of (ii) are equivalent. We believe the integrated data in the proposed integrated object relational Web data warehouse system are successfully accessed and correctly integrated.

CONCLUSION AND FUTURE WORK

Our proposed Web integration data warehouse has utilized an object-oriented design concept to allow user requirements and underlying data source structures to be specified. It has successfully utilized a wider range of object-oriented features to model a **simple** integrated model that has a star schema structure in hierarchies. The hierarchies aim to allow the easiest information browsing of the data detail at the lowest level possible but at the same time fully capturing and representing data semantics in the underlying data source.

The **complete** range of data source models from different database design approaches, including well-structured data and semi-structured data, have been successfully integrated in the proposed model. Most importantly, large amounts of Web data such as HTML/XML are now formally handled in the proposed integrated data warehouse.

We have also implemented a prototype to allow an evaluation task performed on the integrated data and proposed technique. The correctness of the proposed integrated data warehouse model has been proved as well as the efficiency of performance among the queries has also been confirmed.

For future work, an immediate task could be to investigate the time performance of the queries. We would see an opportunity of using TKPROF trace tool to collect the statistics to analyze the processing time, fetching, and parsing of query.

REFERENCES

Bishay, L., Taniar, D., Jiang, Y., & Rahayu, W. (2000). Structured Web pages management for efficient data retrieval. *WISE 2000, IEEE* (pp. 97-104).

Bonifati, A., Cattaneo, F., Ceri, S., Fuggetta, A., & Paraboschi, S. (2001). Designing data marts for data warehouses. *TOSEM ACM* (pp. 452-481).

Breitbart, Y., Olson, Y., & Thompson, G. (1986). Database integration in a distributed heterogeneous data system. *ACM Data Engineering* (pp. 301-310).

Buzydlowski, J. W. (1998). A framework for object-oriented online analytic processing, data warehousing and OLAP. *ACM DOLAP* (pp. 10-15).

Byung, P., Han, H., & Song, Y. (2005). XML-OLAP: A multidimensional analysis framework for XML warehouses. *DaWak* (pp. 32-42).

Cabibbo, L., & Torlone, R. A. (1998). Logical multidimensional databases. *ACM Advances in Database Technology* (pp. 183-197).

Calvanese, D., Giacomo, G., De Lenzerini, M., & Rosati, D. N. (1998). Source integration in data warehouse. *DEXA, Springer* (pp. 192-197).

Chen, W., Hong, T., & Lin, W. (1999). Using the compressed data model in object-oriented data warehousing. *SMC, IEEE* (pp. 768-772).

Ezeife, C. I., & Ohanekwu, T. E. (2005). The use of smart tokens in cleaning integrated warehouse data. *International Journal of Data Warehousing and Mining, 1*(2), 1-22.

Feng, L., Chang, E., & Dillon, T. (2002). A semantic network based design methodology for XML documents. *ACM TOIS, 20*(4), 390-421.

Filho, A. H., Prado, H. A., & Toscani, S. S. (2000). Evolving a legacy data warehouse system to an object-oriented architecture. *SCCC, IEEE-CS* (pp. 32-40).

Golfarelli, M., Rizzi, S., & Birdoljak, B. (2001). Data warehousing from XML sources. *ACM DOLAP* (pp. 40-47), ACM Press.

Golfarelli, M., Rizzi, S., & Birdoljak, B. (1998). A conceptual design of data warehouses from E/R schema. *ACM HICSS* (pp. 334-344).

Gopalkrishman, V., Li, Q., & Karlapalem, K. (1998). Issues of object relational view design in data warehousing environment. *SMC, IEEE* (pp. 2732-2737).

Gupta, A., & Mumick, S. I. (1995). Maintenance of materialized views: Problems, techniques, and applications. *IEEE Data Eng. Bul, 18*(2), 3-18.

Hammer, J., Garcia-Molina, H., Widom, J., Labio, W., & Zhuge, Y. (1995). The Stanford data warehousing project. *IEEE Data Engineering Bulletin* (pp. 41- 48).

Huang, S. M., & Su, C. H. (2001). The development of an XML-based data warehouse system. *ACM DOLAP* (pp. 206-212), *ACM Press.*

Huynh, N., Mangisengi, O., & Tjoa, A. M. (2000). Metadata for object relational data warehouse. *DMDW, CEUR-WS* (pp. 3-1-3-9).

Hummer, W., Bauer, A., & Harde, G. (2003). XCube—XML for data warehouses. *ACM DOLAP* (pp. 33-44).

Jensen, M., Moller, T., & Pedersen, T. (2001). Specifying OLAP cubes on XML data. *SSDBM, IEEE* (pp. 101-112).

Lenzerini, M. (2002). Data Integration: A Theoretical Perspective. *ACM PODS*, 233-246.

Li, S., Liu, M., Wang, G., & Peng, Z. (2004). Capturing semantic hierarchies to perform meaningful integration in HTML tables. *APWeb, LNCS 3007* (pp. 899-902).

Loney, K., & Koch, G. (2000). *Oracle 9i: The complete reference.* Osborne McGraw-Hill.

Melton, J. (2003). Information technology—database languages—SQL—Part 14: XML-related specifications (SQL/XML). *ISO/IEC* (pp. 9075-14).

Miller, L. L., Honavar, V., Wong, J., & Nilakanta, S. (1998). Object-oriented data warehouse for information fusion from heterogeneous distributed data and knowledge sources. *IT, IEEE* (pp. 27-30).

Mohamah, S., Rahayu, W., & Dillon, T. (2001). Object relational star schemas. *IASTED, PDCS.*

Nassis, V., Rahayu, W., Rajugan, R., & Dillon, T. (2004). Conceptual design of XML document warehouses. *DaWak, Springer* (pp. 1- 14).

Nassis, V., Rajagopalapillai, R., Dillon, T. S., & Rahayu, W. (2005). Conceptual and systematic design approach for XML document warehouses.

International Journal of Data Warehousing and Mining, 1(3), 63-87.

Nummenmaa, J., Niemi, T., Niinimäki, M., & Thanisch, P. (2002). Constructing an OLAP cube on XML Data. *ACM DOLAP* (pp. 22-27).

Pardede, E., Rahayu, J. W., & Taniar, D. (2004). On using collection for aggregation and association relationships in XML object relational storage. *ACM SAC* (pp. 703-710).

Pardede, E., Rahayu, J. W., & Taniar, D. (2005). Preserving conceptual constraints during XML updates. *International Journal of Web Information Systems, 1*(2).

Rahayu, J. W. (1999). *Object relational transformation*. PhD Thesis of Computer Science and Computer Engineering, La Trobe University, Melbourne.

Rahayu, J. W., Chang, E., Dillon, T. S., & Taniar, D. (2000). A methodology of transforming inheritance relationships in an object-oriented conceptual model to relational tables. *Information Software Technology 42, Elsevier Science*, 571-

592, Intelligent Data Engineering and Automated Learning, Lecture Notes in Computer Science, vol. 3177, Springer-Verlag, 293-299.

Rusu, L. I., Rahayu, J. W., & Taniar, D. (2005). A methodology for building XML data warehouses. *International Journal of Data Warehousing and Mining, 1*(2), pp. 23-48.

Rusu, L.I., Rahayu, J.W., and Taniar, D. (2004). On building XML data warehouses.

Serrano, M., Calero, C., & Piattini, M. (2005). An experimental replication with data warehouse metrics. *International Journal of Data Warehousing and Mining, 1*(4), 1-21.

Taniar, D., Rahayu, W., & Srivastava P. (2003). *A taxonomy for object-relational queries, effective database for text & document management*. In S. A. Becker (Ed.), Hershey, PA: Idea Group Publishing.

Widom, J. (1995). Research problem in data warehouse. *Information Knowledge Management ACM* (pp. 25-30).

This work was previously published in Int. Journal of Information Technology and Web Engineering, Vol 1, Issue 4, edited by G. Alkhatib and D. Rine, pp. 68-80, copyright 2006 by IGI Publishing (an imprint of IGI Global).

Chapter XIX
Engineering Conceptual Data Models from Domain Ontologies:
A Critical Evaluation

Haya El-Ghalayini
University of the West of England (UWE), UK

Mohammed Odeh
University of the West of England (UWE), UK

Richard McClatchey
University of the West of England (UWE), UK

ABSTRACT

This paper studies the differences and similarities between domain ontologies and conceptual data models and the role that ontologies can play in establishing conceptual data models during the process of information systems development. A mapping algorithm has been proposed and embedded in a special purpose Transformation Engine to generate a conceptual data model from a given domain ontology. Both quantitative and qualitative methods have been adopted to critically evaluate this new approach. In addition, this paper focuses on evaluating the quality of the generated conceptual data model elements using Bunge-Wand-Weber and OntoClean ontologies. The results of this evaluation indicate that the generated conceptual data model provides a high degree of accuracy in identifying the substantial domain entities along with their relationships being derived from the consensual semantics of domain knowledge. The results are encouraging and support the potential role that this approach can take part in the process of information system development.

INTRODUCTION

In the last decade, ontologies have been considered as essential components in most knowledge-based application development. As these models are increasingly becoming common, their applicability has ranged from the artificial intelligence domain, such as knowledge engineering/representation and natural language processing, to different fields like information integration and retrieval systems, the semantic Web, and the requirements analysis phase of the software development process. Therefore, the importance of using ontologies in building conceptual data models (CDMS) (CDMs) has already been recognized by different researchers. In our approach, we claim that the differences and similarities between ontologies and CDMs play an important role in the development of CDMs during the information system development process. We indicate that CDMs can be enriched by modeling the consensual knowledge of a certain domain, which, in turn, minimizes the semantic heterogeneities between the different data models (El-Ghalayini, Odeh, McClatchey, & Solomonides, 2005). We chose to study ontologies represented by the Web ontology language (OWL), since it is the most recent Web ontology language released by the World Wide Web Consortium in February 2004 (W3C-World Wide Web Consortium, 2005), and its formal semantics are based on description logics (DL).

The remainder of this article is structured as follows. The next section provides relevant information related to ontologies, CDMs, and the so-called transformation engine (TE). Then the following section discusses the process of evaluating the TE and its parameters, in general, and the qualitative dimension in evaluating the quality of the generated CDM elements, using ontological rules. This evaluation is demonstrated by a real-life case study related to the transparent access to multiple bioinformatics information sources (TAMBIS) ontology; finally the conclusion and future work are presented.

ONTOLOGY VS. CONCEPTUAL DATA MODEL

This section informally explores ontologies and CDMs, including their similarities and differences. The literature shows many definitions of ontologies with the most popular definition proposed by Gruber (1995) as "a formal, explicit specification of a shared conceptualization" (p. 907). In general terms, an ontology may be defined as expressing knowledge in a machine-readable form to permit a common understanding of domain knowledge, so knowledge can be exchanged between heterogeneous environments.

On the other hand, conceptual data models capture the meaning of information for modelling an application and offer means for organizing information for the purposes of understanding and communication(Mylopoulos, 1998). The major role of the CDM is to model the so-called universe of discourse (UoD), entities and relationships in relation to particular user requirements independent of implementation issues. Hirschheim, Klein, and Lyytinen (1995) define the Universe of Discourse in the information systems (IS) world as "the slice of reality to be modelled" (p. 58). Therefore, there are some similarities and differences between ontologies and CDMs. Both are represented by a modeling grammar with similar constructs, such as classes in ontologies that correspond to entity types in CDMs. Thus, the methodologies of developing both models have common activities (Fonseca & Martin, 2005). While ontologies and CDMs share common features, they have some differences. According to Guarino's (1998) proposal of ontology-driven information systems, an ontology can be used at the development or run time of IS, whereas a CDM is a building block of the analysis and design process of an IS.

Moreover Fonseca and Martin (2005) define two criteria that differentiate ontologies from CDMs; the first is the *objectives of modeling* and the second *is objects to model*. Using the first criterion, an ontology focuses on the description of the "invariant features that define the domain of interest," whereas a CDM links the domain invariant features with a set of observations to be defined within an IS. Regarding the second criterion, objects to model, an ontology describes real or factual structures of a domain that enables information integration. Conversely, a CDM object represents a general category of a certain domain linked to its individual events, for example, linking the general category of gene with the size of its DNA sequence. The central question addressed in this research is: *"To what extent can domain ontologies participate in developing CDMs?"*

Having surveyed the literature, the differences between ontology and CDMs have been mainly explored using descriptive studies. Thus, in order to address the main research question, a two-phase approach has been devised to integrate both theoretical and empirical studies. In the first phase, the ontological model provided by Wand and Weber (1993), which is known as the Bunge-Wand-Weber ontology (BWW), has been utilized in interpreting the OWL ontology language. We note that ontology language constructs are related to the structural components of the problem domain.

Other constructs related to time dependency have not been represented in OWL. This result is in line with the observation of Bera and Wand (2004) that OWL concepts can be used to represent multiple BWW concepts. However, Bera and Wand focus on interpreting the basic concepts of OWL (i.e., classes, properties, and individuals), whereas our study is related to OWL constructs such as *owl:class or owl:objectTypeProperty.*

The second phase implements a new algorithm (implemented as a TE component) that maps a domain ontology expressed in OWL to a generated conceptual data model (GCDM) represented as a unified modeling language (UML) class model. The process of developing the CDM begins by selecting an OWL ontology of the domain of interest. Then, the TE applies the mapping rules onto the ontology concepts, thereby generating submodels that are integrated to construct the proposed CDM, as shown in Figure 1.

Briefly the TE mapping rules follow.

Rule 1: The ontology concept or class is mapped into the entity-type construct in the GCDM.

Rule 2: The ontology property is mapped to the relationship construct in the GCDM. In particular, property features such as *owl:inverseOf, owl:functional, owl:domain,* and *owl:range* determine the semantic constraints of the relationships.

Rule 3: The ontology restriction is decomposed to develop a relationship between two entity types, if the related property is a mutual type property. If the filler type of the restriction is a data type, then this relation should be refined to become an attribute of the source entity type.

Rule 4: Using an intrinsic type property, the restriction class is mapped to an attribute of the entity type with a proper data type range.

Rule 5: The subsumption relationship *(rdfs:subClassOf)* between ontology classes is mapped to generalization/specialization relationship between entity types in the GCDM.

Rule 6: The logical expression concept in the ontology language is decomposed into a generalization relationship between the entity types in the GCDM. For example, the *owl:intersectionOf* expression is translated to a multiple inheritance relationship between the operands of the logical expression (as superentity types) and the concept being studied as a subentity type, whereas the *owl:unionOf* expression partitions the concept being studied (i.e., the superentity type) into its operands as subentity types.

Figure 1. General architecture of the proposed approach

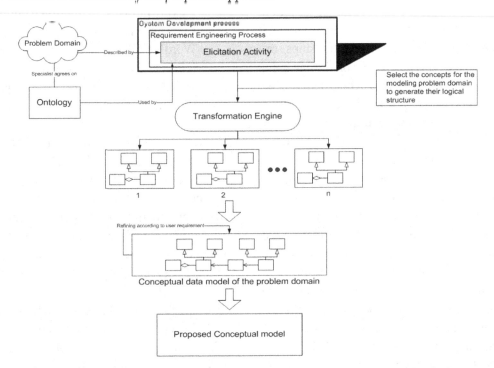

Conceptual data model of the problem domain

Proposed Conceptual model

Rule 7: A translation of the selected concepts from the domain ontology by the TE is followed by a refinement process of the GCDM (a) by searching for redundant concepts or relationships and removing them, and (b) by merging the same relationships having different cardinalities.

Therefore, to validate the significance of the above adopted approach, we propose a set of measures to evaluate the quality of the GCDM from a given domain ontology using the two prominent works of BWW (Wand & Weber, 1993) and OntoClean (Guarino & Welty, 2002).

THE EVALUATION PROCESS

The evaluation of the TE embodies two components, both qualitative and quantitative methods.

The quantitative dimension proposes a set of measures to evaluate the TE behavior and parameters when applied to different domain ontologies, and these are listed in the numbered sections below.

1. *TE performance* measures the effectiveness of a set of ontological constructs that have been used within the TE mapping algorithm on the GCDM elements.

To have a quantitative measure of the TE performance in mapping and decomposing the ontology constructs to CDM elements, a straight line regression analysis was used to develop the correlation between ontology constructs (classes, subsumption relation, mutual properties, and intrinsic properties) used in the TE and the GCDMs constructs (entity types, generalization/specialization, relationships, and attributes). The relationships (using R^2) are: 0.999, 0.9981, and 0.9645 for classes versus entity types, subsumption versus generalization/specialization, and mutual properties versus relationships, respectively. This means that on the one hand the TE performance was consistent for the different case studies; therefore, a best fit line can be produced for these constructs. On the other hand, the relationship is poor (0.0762 R^2) for intrinsic properties and attributes. This means that the proportion of the mapping of the attributes in the TE cannot be explained only with the intrinsic properties of the domain ontologies, and there must be some other variable participating in the mapping process. This is because in some domain ontologies intrinsic proprieties are expressed as mutual properties, so the TE refines the mapping of these properties to attribute constructs in the GCDM.

2. *GCDM accuracy* measures the "correct" answers in the GCDM compared to the models developed by human analysts. However, since there is no "gold standard" model for any given application requirements, we have selected a collection of data models, either available in databases texts or provided by the researcher working on different projects to be the gold models (GMs).

The results of comparing the GCDM by GM show that general knowledge about the domain has been extracted with an overall accuracy of 69% for entity types, 82% for generalization/specialization, and 35% for the relationships. The missing elements in the GCDM can be mainly attributed to modeling the application requirements in the GM that are not expressed in the domain ontologies.

3. *GCDM lexical correctness* measures the "correct" number of lexical names for elements of an ontology and the GCDM, using WordNet (Fellbaum, 1998), a lexical database for English developed at Princeton University. Since most of the terms in ontologies are phrases, we modified phrases, such as "AdministrativeStaff" before searching WordNet. The results of comparing the ontology and GCDM lexical correctness show that there is an overlap in the approaches used in developing a CDM and ontology.

Next, we present the qualitative dimension in evaluating the quality of the GCDM. This criterion addresses the question as to whether the GCDM components conform to the ontological-based rules, provided by philosophical ontologies of conceptual modeling. Consequently, it validates whether the domain ontology provides a proper ontological representation of the respective CDM elements. This will be investigated using a set of ontological rules that merges the BWW ontology and the OntoClean methodology (Guarino & Welty, 2002). The BWW ontology rules are used to validate the accuracy of the ontological meaning of the GCDM elements, whereas the OntoClean axioms are used to evaluate the correctness of the generalization/specialization relationships.

We agree with others that an ontological theory is essential for conceptual modeling, since ontological theories provide conceptual modeling constructs with the semantics of real-world phenomena (Weber, 2003). This impacts the quality of the CDM by reducing the maintenance cost if errors are discovered in the later stages of the software development process (Walrad & Moss, 1993) To describe our proposal, we introduce the main concepts in the BWW ontology followed by an overview of the OntoClean methodology in addition to introducing ontological rules to validate the ontological structure of the GCDM.

Overview of BWW Ontology

Wand and Weber (1993) are among the first researchers who initiated the use of ontology theories in information system analysis and design activity (ISAD). Based on their adaptation of Bunge's ontology, their ontology, the Bunge-Wand-Weber model or BWW, has led to fruitful research areas in ISAD, in general, and in evaluating modeling grammars in particular (Wand, Storey, & Weber, 1999; Guarino &Welty, 2004). For this reason, this ontology is considered as a benchmark ontology for evaluating the expressiveness of modeling languages, since it assists the modeler in constructing ontological CDMs with the maximum semantics about real-world phenomena (Weber, 2003).

In the BWW model, the world is made up of things. A thing can be either simple or composite, where the latter is made up of other things. Composite things possess emergent properties. Things are described by their properties. A property is either intrinsic, depending on only one thing, or mutual, depending on two or more things. A class is a set of things that possesses a common set of characteristic properties. A subclass is a set of things that possess their class properties in addition to other common properties. A natural kind describes a set of things via their common properties and laws connecting them. Properties are restricted by natural or human laws.

The aim of using these concepts is to validate whether the constructs used in the GCDM conform to their ontological meaning or not. For example, what is the proper representation for accession-number? and is it an entity type or an intrinsic property of protein entity type?

Overview of OntoClean

OntoClean is a methodology proposed by Guarino and Welty (2002, 2004) that is based on the philosophical notions for evaluating taxonomical structures. OntoClean mainly constitutes two major building blocks: (1) a set of constraints that formalizes the correctness of the subsumption relationship, and (2) an assignment of the top level unary predicates (concepts) of the taxonomical structure to a number of metaproperties. The four fundamental ontological notions of *rigidity*, *unity*, *identity*, and *dependence* are attached as

metaproperties to concepts or classes in a taxonomy structure describing the behavior of the concepts, i.e., these metaproperties clarify the way subsumption is used to model a domain by imposing some constraints (Evermann & Wand, 2001). We briefly and informally introduce these ontological/ philosophical notions.

1. *Rigidity* is based on the idea of an essential property that must hold for all instances of a concept or a class. Thus, a class or concept is rigid (+R) if it holds the essential property for all its instances. The nonrigid concept (-R) holds a property that is not essential to the entire concept instances, however it is necessary for some of the instances. The antirigid (~R) concept holds a property that is optional for all concept instances.

2. The notion of *identity* is concerned with recognizing a common property that identifies the individuals of a concept as being the same or different; and it is known as an identity condition or characteristics property in the philosophical literature. The identity metaproperty (+I) supplies or carries this property. If the class supplies this property then all subclasses carry it as an inherited property. On the contrary, if the concept does not provide the identity condition, then it will be marked with (-I).

3. *Unity* is defined if there is a common unity condition such that all the individuals are intrinsic wholes (+U). A class carries anti-unity (-U) if all its individuals can possibly be nonwholes.

4. *Dependence* (+D) is based on whether the existence of an individual is externally dependent on the existence of another individual with (-D), otherwise.

OntoClean classifies concepts into categories based on three metaproperties: identity, rigidity, and dependence. The basic categories are: type category, which describes (+R, ±D, +I); phased-sortal category, which describes (~R, -D, +I); role category, which describes (~R, +D, +I); and attribution category, which describes (-R, ±D, -I).

Also, the OntoClean methodology restricts the correctness of a given taxonomical structure by a set of axioms. The axioms related to identity, rigidity, and dependence metaproperties are:

1. An anti-rigid class cannot subsume rigid class;
2. A class that supplies or carries an identity property cannot subsume a class that does not hold this property;
3. A dependent class cannot subsume an independent class.

Merging OntoClean and BWW to Evaluate the GCDM

As a result of utilizing the BWW ontology for evaluating the expressiveness of different conceptual modeling languages, a set of rules are proposed as a theory of conceptual modeling practice. For example, Wand et al. (1999) derive a set of rules as a theory of constructing the relationships in conceptual modeling practice. Moreover, Evermann and Wand (2001) investigated the mapping between ontological constructs and UML elements; and this led them to suggest modeling rules, in general, and guidelines on how to use UML elements to model real-world systems, in particular.

In our approach, we utilize a set of these general rules in evaluating the quality of the GCDM. However, we suggest that the integration of these rules with the OntoClean methodology would improve the quality of the GCDM, especially in the generalization/specialization relationships. Therefore, the evaluation process has to prove the ontological appropriateness in representing the GCDM elements.

We have to mention here that the integration between different ontologies has been used recently by different researchers but for different purposes. Their purpose is to evaluate and develop an ontological UML and conceptual modeling language. For example, Guizzardi, Wagner, Guarino, & Sinderen (2004) use the general ontology language (GOL) and its underling upper-level ontology in evaluating the ontological correctness of the UML class model. Their approach is influenced by the OntoClean methodology, in addition to the psychological claims proposed by the cognitive psychologist John McNamara (1994). Also, Li (2005) studies the use of the Bunge ontology with the OntoClean methodology for the same objective. In our research, we integrate these prominent ontologies to evaluate the quality of the GCDM by studying the appropriateness of its ontological meanings. In the following sections, we propose a set of ontological rules inspired by BWW and OntoClean (Wand et al., 1999; Evermann & Wand, 2001; Guarino & Welty, 2002, 2004) in order to check the quality of the GCDM elements.

Rule 1: The BWW ontology models only substantial things in the world as entities, that is properties (attributes or relationships) or events cannot be modeled using entity type constructs. According to OntoClean, substantial things are recognized by their identity condition or characteristics property; therefore, substantial entities belong to type, phased-sortal, or role categories.

Rule 2: BWW's intrinsic properties are represented as attributes of an entity type that describe a property of one thing independent of any other entities. Therefore, the BWW property cannot be represented using an entity type construct. According to OntoClean, an attribute of an entity type is assigned (-R, -I, ±D) metaproperties.

Rule 3: Any BWW mutual property is represented as a relationship between two or more substantial things; therefore, it prescribes representing entity types as a mutual property.

Rule 4: A BWW aggregate or composite entity type must have emergent properties in addition to those of its components types; therefore, a composite thing should be recognized with an identity characteristic. Whilst a simple thing is composed of one thing, a composite or aggregate thing is made up of two or more things.

Rule 5: In the BWW ontology, a specialized entity type must define more properties than the general entity type. According to OntoClean, entities are recognized by their identity characteristics. In addition, the generalization/specialization relationship must conform to the OntoClean taxonomical structure axioms.

Applying the Evaluation Methodology Using the TAMBIS Ontology

The TAMBIS ontology contains knowledge about bioinformatics and molecular biology concepts and their relationships. It describes proteins and enzymes, as well as their motifs, and secondary and tertiary structure functions and processes (Goble et al., 2001). We use the TAMBIS ontology (TAO) to demonstrate our approach. TAO has 393 concepts and 94 properties, whereas the GCDM has 392 entity types, 259 relationships, 49 attributes, and 402 generalization/specialization relationships. In this case study, we have selected the concepts that are relevant to protein in order to generate the CDM using the TE. The GCDM has been translated to a set of Java files and reverse engineered to a class diagram by using a UML graphical tool.

In what follows, we present our observations of the GCDM (shown in Figure 2) with respect to the proposed ontological rules.

1. According to ontological Rule 1, protein structure and biological function are not substantial entities, since they do not have any identity property. Therefore, these concepts should not be represented as entity types. Protein structure is an intrinsic property that can be used in classifying protein type according to its internal structure, whereas a biological function can be used in classifying protein types according to their role with other existing entities.

2. According to OntoClean, protein name and accession number are assigned (-I-R+D) metasemantics, which means that these elements belong to the attribution category. By using ontological Rule 2, protein name and accession number are intrinsic properties that describe protein independent from any other entities; therefore, they cannot be represented as entity types, according to ontological Rule 1.

3. We consider an individual protein as a macromolecule of amino acid sequences linked by a peptide bond. We assume that these large molecules have their own essential properties, and their existence is independent of any other concepts. Therefore, +R+I-D seems to be an obvious assignment that classifies them as type category. The structure of a protein is considered as an intrinsic property that classifies proteins according to their internal structure. The primary structure or primary sequence is a linear sequence of amino acids; secondary structure involves the hydrogen bond that forms the alpha helix, beta sheet, and others; the tertiary structure is the three-dimensional structure of the molecule that consists of the secondary structure linked by covalent disulfide bonds and noncovalent bonds; and the quaternary structure is the association of separate polypeptide chains into the functional protein. Hence, each structure of a protein belongs to the phased-sortal category, since this classifier type allows an instance to change certain intrinsic properties while remaining the same entity. Also, according to the OntoClean axioms,

Figure 2. Excerpt of the GCDM for protein concept

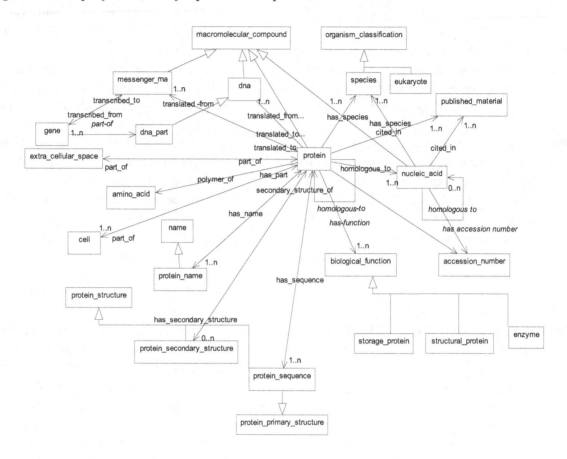

the generalization/specialization relation between protein and its different structures is correct.

4.   The function of the protein can be used as a classification property that classifies proteins according to their role with other existing entities.

Therefore, proteins can be classified according to their functions into, for example, enzyme, storage protein, and structural protein. Here we have to mention that these subentity types belong to the role category, since their existence depends on other entities, for example, each enzyme is catalyzed by one reaction.

5.   DNA and RNA are polymers of many nucleic acids (adenine, guanine, thymine, or cyto-

sine in DNA; adenine, guanine, uracil, or cytosine in RNA), whereas a protein is a large complex molecule made up of one or more chains of amino acids. According to this, we propose that the macromolecular-compound type specifies two types of compounds: a compound based on nucleic-acid blocks and a compound based on amino-acid blocks. In this case, nucleic-acids and amino-acid compounds belong to the type category with (+R+I-D). Also, DNA and m-RNA are subtypes of nucleic-acid compound, whereas protein is a subtype of amino-acid compound.

6.   We propose to replace the species type with the prokaryote type, since species type

Figure 3. The refined model of the protein concepts using the ontological rules

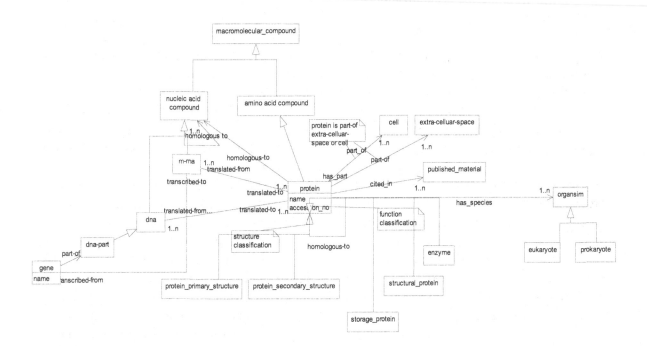

also can be classified into prokaryote and eukaryote.

Figure 3 presents the refined GCDM resulting from the application of the ontological rules. In addition it has been approved by a domain expert. However, evaluating the GCDM elements using the ontological rules leads to the following observations.

Firstly the TE achieves good agreement in automating the CDM development activity. This means that the invariant information about the domain can be extracted to a certain extent from the domain ontologies. In other words, the GCDM provides a high degree of accuracy in identifying the substantial entities along with their attributes and relationships. Therefore, the semantics of the CDM elements conform to the consensual knowledge about the interested domain.

Secondly there are some ontological issues that could not be built into the TE. For example, applying Rule 1 in the TE onto all named classes

in a domain ontology results in generating some entity types in the GCDM that lack the existence of the identity criteria that is considered an essential property for representing substantial things. For example, accession number and protein name are expressed as named classes in the ontology; thereby, they are mapped onto entity types using Rule 1, where these concepts are better mapped to attributes of protein type. Furthermore, the misinterpretation of Rule 1 in the TE for some ontology classes reflects on the rest of the rules in the TE. For example, Rule 5 in the TE is used to generate the generalization/specialization relation between biological function as a general entity type and enzyme, structural protein, and storage protein as subentity types. And according to the ontological rules, biological function is a mutual property that describes the role of protein kinds (enzyme, structural protein, and storage protein), depending on the existence of other entity types (i.e., the existence of an enzyme depends on the existence of a reaction). Therefore, the misinterpretation of biological function as an entity type leads to misinterpreting the generalization/specialization relationship.

This observation stems from the fact that, OWL class constructs are overloaded to represent all real-world characteristics (i.e., dynamic and static characteristics). This is the same construct used to represent a domain concept, event, process, or transformation. To overcome this problem, we propose extending the ontology language by adding more semantics to the class construct (metaconcept), in order to describe the nature of the represented real-world phenomena. Therefore, the "static" metaconcept represents domain concepts that identify and support the identity property of an entity type (i.e., substantial entities), whereas the "dynamic" metaconcept represents an event or transformation concept that captures the behavior of a given real-world phenomena.

CONCLUSION AND FUTURE WORK

The similarities and differences between ontologies and CDMs led us to study the possibility of engineering CDMs from domain ontologies. In this regard, a new approach has been developed to automate the derivation of CDMs from domain ontologies. The theoretical ontology of BWW has been used to interpret the OWL constructs, which have contributed to the development of a mapping algorithm to generate a CDM from the given domain ontology. An important aspect of this approach is that it accelerates the development of the CDM from an explicit and consensual knowledge model. In addition, a set of measures have been established to evaluate the capabilities and the effectiveness of this approach. The proposed measures in the quantitative dimension reveal that: (1) there is a strong correlation between the ontology and CDM constructs; (2) the domain ontology describes the invariant knowledge about

the domain; and hence the development of the GCDM elements, such as entity types, and that their relationships are independent of any application requirements; and (3) the development process of ontologies and CDMs conforms to the same lexical rules for naming their elements. In this work, a set of ontological rules, derived from the BWW and OntoClean ontologies, have been applied to serve the qualitative evaluation of the GCDM. The TAMBIS ontology has been used as the test case, and results have shown that the GCDM provides a high degree of accuracy in identifying the substantial entities along with their attributes and relationships.

However, to improve the quality of the GCDM, we suggest extending the definition of the class construct to incorporate a metaconcept element to distinguish between concepts related to the identity property and concepts representing the events and transformations of a given domain. Furthermore, as the functionality of the TE is restricted to decomposing and mapping domain ontology constructs to CDM constructs, the metaproperties of the OntoClean ontology can be used to validate the ontological correctness of the subsumption relations in the given domain ontology. This must be implemented as a part of the TE mapping algorithm, in order to improve the ontological appropriateness of the GCDM elements.

While this research has been focused on using one domain ontology to generate a possible and relatively appropriate CDM, further work needs to consider the possibility of using more than one related domain ontology to enable the development of a hybrid CDM, such as enterprise data models. This may even suggest enriching the process of ontology development with theoretical ontologies for the improved engineering of domain ontologies and, hence, CDMs.

REFERENCES

Bera, P., & Wand, Y. (2004). Analyzing OWL using a philosophy-based ontology. In *Proceedings of the 2004 Conference on Formal Ontologies in Information Systems FOIS* (pp. 353-362) .

El-Ghalayini, H., Odeh, M., McClatchey, R., & Solomonides, T. (2005). Reverse engineering domain ontology to conceptual data models. In *Proceedings of the 23rd IASTED International Conference on Databases and Applications (DBA), Innsbruck, Austria* (pp. 222-227).

Evermann, J., & Wand, Y. (2001). Towards ontologically-based semantics for UML constructs. In H. S. Kunii, S. Jajodia, & A. Solvberg (Eds.), *Conceptual modeling—ER* (LNCS no. 2224) (pp. 341-354). Springer.

Fellbaum, C. (1998). *WordNet: An electronic lexical database.* MIT Press.

Fonseca, F. and Martin, J. (2005). Learning the differences between ontologies and conceptual schemas through ontology-driven information Systems To appear in *a Journal of the Association of Information Systems Special Issue on Ontologies in the Context of Information Systems.* (fredfonseca@ist.psu.edu).

Goble, C. A., Stevens, R., Ng, G., Bechhofer, S., Paton, N. W., Baker, P. G., Peim, M., & Brass, A. (2001). Transparent access to multiple bioinformatics information sources. *IBM System Journal, 40*(2), 532-551.

Gruber, T. (1995). Toward principles for the design of ontologies used for knowledge sharing. *International Journal of Human and Computer Studies, 43*(5/6), 907-928.

Guarino, N. (1998). *Formal ontology and information systems.* Amsterdam, Netherlands: IOS Press.

Guarino, N., & Welty, C. (2002). Evaluating ontological decisions with OntoClean. *Communications of the ACM, 45*(2), 61-65.

Guarino, N., & Welty, C. (2004). An overview of OntoClean. In S. Staab & R. Studer (Eds.), *Handbook on ontologies* (pp. 51-159). Springer Verlag.

Guizzardi, G., Wagner, G., Guarino, N., & Sinderen, M. (2004). An ontologically well-founded profile for UML conceptual models. In *Proceeding of the 16th Conference on Advanced Information Systems Engineering- CAiSE04* (pp. 112-126).

Hischheim, R., Klein, H., & Lyytinen, K. (1995). *Information systems development and data modelling: Conceptual and philosophical foundations.* Cambridge: Cambridge University Press.

Li, X. (2005). Using UML in conceptual modelling: Towards an ontological xore. In *Proceeding of the 17th Conference on Advanced Information Systems Engineering-CAiSE05* (pp. 13-17).

McNamara, J. (1994). Logic and cognition. In J. McNamara & G. Reyes (Eds.), *The logical foundations of cognition* (Vo. 4) (pp.). Vancouver Studies in Cognitive Science.

Mylopoulos, J. (1998). Information modeling in the time of the revolution. *Information Systems, 23*(3/4), 127-155.

W3C-World Wide Web Consortium. (2005). OWL 1.1 Web Ontology Language Syntax. In P. F. Patel-Schneider (ed.). Retrieved May 2005 from from http://www-db.research.bell-labs.com/user/pfps/owl/syntax.html.

Walrad, C., & Moss, E. (1993). Measurement: The key to application development quality. *IBM Systems Journal, 32*(3), 445-460.

Wand, Y, Storey, V., & Weber, R. (1999). An ontological analysis of the relationship construct in conceptual modeling. *ACM Transactions on Database Systems, 24*(2), 494-528.

Wand, Y., & Weber, R. (1993). On the ontological expressiveness of information systems analysis and design grammars. *Journal of Information Systems, 3*(4), 217-237.

Weber, R. (2003). Conceptual modelling and ontology: Possibilities and pitfalls. *Database Management, 14*(3), 1-2

This work was previously published in Int. Journal of Information Technology and Web Engineering, Vol 2, Issue 1, edited by G. Alkhatib and D. Rine, pp. 57-70, copyright 2007 by IGI Publishing (an imprint of IGI Global).

Chapter XX
Modeling Defects in E-Projects

John D. Ferguson
University of Strathclyde, UK

James Miller
University of Alberta, Canada

ABSTRACT

It is now widely accepted that software projects utilizing the Web (e-projects) face many of the same problems and risks experienced with more traditional software projects, only to a greater degree. Further, their characteristics of rapid development cycles combined with high frequency of software releases and adaptations make many of the traditional tools and techniques for modeling defects unsuitable.

This paper proposes a simple model to explain and quantify the interaction between generic defect injection and removal processes in e-projects. The model is based upon long standing and highly regarded work from the field of quantitative ecological population modeling. This basic modeling approach is then subsequently tailored to fit the software production process within an e-project context.

INTRODUCTION

The Internet now forms a major platform supporting a wide range of commercial, educational, and social applications. While many of the early developments on the Web were based on client-server technology, the position has changed dramatically in the last few years with new technologies forming the basis of current applications.

Today, many of the software industry's current and new developments are destined for use either directly or indirectly, in sophisticated Web-based applications. Unfortunately, these developments have not come without cost, and industry is now faced with problems associated with verifying and maintaining Web-based applications. Current approaches to verification in the software industry are not succeeding. While systems grow evermore complex, the percentage of total costs consumed by verification continues to grow as defect rates increase (Tassey, 2002).

The characteristics of e-projects differ from traditional information technology projects in a number of ways. E-projects are characterized as any project which evolves software that is deployed via the World Wide Web (Offut, 2002; Ricca & Tonella, 2001). E-projects are typically much smaller than many traditional projects; correspondingly, their production period is much shorter with projects lasting from several weeks to a few months not uncommon. They also tend to evolve at a much faster rate (typically the "shelf life" of an e-project system may be only 3 months) and hence their production is nearly always highly iterative in nature. Starting from a largely descriptive overview of the required functionality they often move through a quick build and test cycle, to be immediately faced with perhaps another quick build and test cycle. This situation can become even more extreme when using modern development methodologies; for example, when using the SCRUM methodology (Schwaber, 2004), the project manager often aims for iteration cycles as short as every 2 weeks.

Many traditional production processes, such as the waterfall or spiral models, defer verification and validation activities until late in the life cycle, resulting in these components often being considered as an afterthought to the production component. Further, the testing activities often get disassembled into artificial sub-activities such as unit testing, integration testing and system testing. The popular "V model" of an integrated testing process is a good example of this type of structuring; This model results in the production team being forced into conducting these subactivities, regardless of the relative cost-benefit issues associated with each of these subactivities. Clearly, in any arbitrary project the costs and benefits associated with any verification and validation activity will be highly dependent on the domain of operation and the product under development. Since testing now accounts for more than half of the costs on many projects, any production methodology that fails to actively consider the costs and benefits of the testing activities is potentially wasting an extremely large amount of resources and failing to perfect the product for the marketplace. In contrast, e-projects systems with their short cycles tend to have a simpler, more time focused structure, typically comprising intertwined build and test components. For example, the recent rise of popularity of agile methodologies can be directly linked to the increasing number of e-projects in production. These methodologies often view the production processes in a different light from the traditional production methodologies; for example, in an XP production environment, the use of test-first programming (Beck, 2003) is extremely common.

Unfortunately, these differences in the production process of e-projects cause difficulties for many quantificational models of artifacts within the software processes or products, including approaches to modeling defects. Traditional views of modeling defects tend to assume that we are using explicit quality targets, which is less likely to be the case within these new types of systems where managing the risks to the project and product are a more common approach. In addition, traditional models often assume that existence of a production model such as the "V," where we have a long production period followed by a significant period of verification and validation. Commonly, we only model and analyze this verification and validation period. Again, this type of model will not translate effectively into the e-project domain. What is required is an alternative type of defect model which attempts to directly describe these frequent cycles of build and test processes. The principal aim and contribution of this article is to propose and construct such a model.

Motivation: Why Do We Need Defect Models for E-Projects?

Most software quality assurance processes deal with the conflict between processes that introduce defects into a software artifact or processes that seek to eliminate them. These deficiencies can be introduced at any, and all, stages of the development life cycle and similarly can be removed from each stage. Hence, we have a near continuous clash between these two opposing forces. A software quality assurance professional is interested in this situation for a variety of reasons; for example, its progress can be an indicator of current product quality and a pointer to project performance with regard to defects. Software engineering as a scientific discipline has an interest in modeling this confrontation in order to assist this group of professionals.

The principal reasons for constructing a model are to understand the processes at hand. Hence, this article takes the approach that both process types, which account for the presence or absence of defects in software artifacts, should be modeled. This is in contrast with many traditional approaches, which only model the impact of the removal process on the number of defects. This article argues that understanding the injectional processes is equally important. Regardless of the type of modeling, we would like to utilize the models to assist with, or to drive, economic decisions—in terms of the software produced and the production processes chosen for any particular project. Obviously, economic benefits can be derived from limiting the impact of the injectional processes and hence it is essential to model these aspects of the entire life cycle to allow a complete picture to be developed.

In addition, many approaches limit themselves to modeling the number of defects solely within the testing phase. However, this tends to limit the scope of the model; hence, they commonly deal with the specific quality control question: "Is the product ready for release?" This question is often answered by looking at the projected number of defects remaining within the software project against some deployment criteria. In this article, by modeling both types of processes it is hoped that the approach will eventually lead to models that are able to predict the potential economic impact, from a defect perspective, of the various options that exist when selecting a set of processes and approaches which will be utilized during the production of a software project—from its initial conception to its decommissioning.

Another driver towards modeling the entire process is the cost of defect removal. Boehm's (1981) classic text argues that the cost of removal spirals as we move through the life-cycle. Hence if we accept this argument then we will want to focus our modeling and economic decision making upon the start of the project, where removal activities are cheap, rather than at the end where the costs are soaring. This point is further underlined by many companies, especially in areas like embedded systems, which report that postrelease costs of fixing a defect are often greater than two orders of magnitude higher than prerelease costs.

ARE CURRENT MODELLING APROACHES APPLICABLE?

While it is tempting to assume that current approaches are applicable to this situation, it is believed that the realistic answer is no. Current approaches make several assumptions in a number of directions which imply that they are not effective modeling approaches to realistic formulations within this domain.

The most common class of models are parametric order-statistics models; a detailed overview of these models can be found in Lyu (1996). These models tend to derive parametric descriptions of the defects within a system, while making a number of assumptions and simplifications about the utilized development process and nature of the product. For example, a common assumption is that an explicit single testing phase exists that is the final stage before release and that we are only interested in producing and using our model during this analysis. This is believed to be an inappropriate assumption for most e-projects. Further, again, to simplify the model, many approaches assume that any software fault is fixed immediately upon detection and that this "rework" process is prefect. Again, this assumption is unrealistic as projects nearly always have a percentage of modifications requests left "open" during any phase of their life cycle. In fact researchers have empirically demonstrated that many faults encountered by customers are injected during this rework phase (Boland & Chuiv, 2002). This issue has recently been recognized by some researchers who have attempted to construct "richer" models; for example, Gokhale (2004) incorporate a rework component via the numerical solution of their model, and Schneidewind (2004) incorporates a constant rework rate into his previous models (Schneidewind, 1993). However, all current approaches still only provide a very limited picture of these back-end processes and present them in a simplified fashion. For example, these processes are often highly variable in real projects, due to cost and scheduling constraints whereas even these models see them as constants. Nonparametric variations of order statistic models are possible (e.g., Barghour, Abdel-Ghaly, & Littlewood, 1998); normally these are based upon transforming the model into a Bayesian framework; however, these approaches are only currently witnessed limited exploration.

The final class of approaches is pattern matching or computational intelligence approaches. Here we are not attempting to provide a casual explanation of the phenomenon rather we are trying to discover the underlying pattern in the data (e.g., Tian & Noore, 2005). This class of approaches provides a flexible approach which can, in theory, represent iterative processes. However, these approaches suffer from two fundamental limitations that we seek to address. Namely,

they offer no underlying causal explanation of the process, or processes, that they are modeling. This seriously limits the project managers ability to understand and explain the model and hence limits its application in areas where the rationale for the decision is considered an essential part of the decision-making process. Further, these approaches assume that the underlying processes are stationary over time. However, software production processes normally change requiring the modelers to regularly restart the pattern matching processes. Further, because of the lack of casual explanation we are in a limited position to understand when an event which introduces a "nonstationary" condition occurs; and instead of thinking through the casual implications of change, pattern matching approaches tend to rely on detecting them from changes in linear statistics. At best, this approach hopes to detect the nonstationary event after a delay, but often the event may not be able to identify the event, resulting in the disparate models, pre and post the event, being amalgamated. Software development processes are particular problematic for these techniques as the processes are regularly nonstationary, and their associated linear statistics are relatively unstable.

Defect Injection and Removal Processes

These processes are intrinsic within every component of the development life cycle. Every production process, whether it be requirements capture or documentation construction or the reworking of a defect reported by the customer base, can introduce defects. Since no production process is perfect, every process encompasses the possibility, if not the probability, of the introduction of errors and defects into the set of software artifacts that make up any real-world software project. Every time these artifacts are modified the possibility of transcription errors and oversights exist; these are often compounded by deficiencies introduced by poor interpersonnel communication processes between staff working upon the project. In turn, the background, or even the education of this staff, is likely to be less than perfect for the task at hand. Causes exist everywhere that can lead to the injection of defects and we are almost guaranteed that any and every attempt to evolve any of the artifacts will lead to the introduction of additional defects.

The opposite of the injection process is the removal process where the procedure is more obvious and well defined. The organization undertaking the software project will have explicitly decided to deploy various defect removal techniques as part of their project life cycle. The nature of these techniques will vary across the life cycle and across the different types of artifacts which make up the project. Typical examples are software testing, various forms of inspections and reviews, alpha and beta testing, usability evaluations, and so on. Each project will have its own life cycle and this life cycle will contain a variety of these components.

As the life cycle progresses, the two process types will have different impacts on the software project at various stages. Typically, a project goes through a construction phase (whether the construction is of a requirements document, code, a quality plan, or whatever is immaterial), during which the injection process will be in the ascendancy. This is commonly followed by a verification and validation phase where the removal process will be in the ascendancy. During both periods the other process will be operational (e.g., self-inspection during construction, and an oversight by a "test oracle" during system testing), but we can expect that its impact will be rather limited. Hence, we can anticipate that the balance will see-saw first in favor of the injection process and then reverse to become favorable to the removal process. Unfortunately, the exact nature of this oscillation between processes will be heavily dependent upon the type of processes deployed within the life cycle and hence is beyond the scope

of any attempt to produce a generic model.

Within this oscillation it can be seen that the two opposing forces are not symmetrical—as we would see in a traditional conflict. Instead, the situation exists where the output of the injection process becomes the input of the removal process and the injection process has no direct means of influencing the behavior of the removal process. This asymmetric behavior needs to be a cornerstone of any analytical model.

It then has to be considered what is known about the empirical nature of both types of processes. Unfortunately, there is no solid information to draw upon here. It might be possible to hypothesize various abstract probability density functions for the likelihood of defects occurring and being removed. However, since no solid information exists this would be highly speculative.

This article takes an alternative approach by asking if an initial model can be derived by analogy. If another field has a well-established theory for modeling this type of interaction, then this would provide a reasonable starting point for building such a model.

Choosing a Modeling Strategy by Analogy

It is believed that a realistic model of this situation must encompass the following six characteristics:

1. Be based upon an iterative development cycle as defined by either, or both, the domain of the application or the development methodology.
2. Must explicitly model both the defect injection and removal processes.
3. Must not include any unrealistic or restrictive assumptions about either points 1 or 2.
4. Must be flexible enough to accommodate the many or varied situations that are encountered during a variety of development situations potentially including "wicked

projects" components. This requirement places a constraint on any models ability to predict and absolutely model any single situation. The model should aim at providing reasonable performance across a wide range of circumstances rather than worrying about being optimized for any single situation.

5. Must not be inferred from a small number of potentially unrepresentative preexisting defect data sets. Rather it should be based upon common modeling ideas with wide applicability.

6. Must be suitable for a wide range project management tasks which often require a casual explanation of the decision and its derivation.

The discussion above has outlined the basic requirements for the model. While there are undoubtedly a multitude of different approaches to modeling these basic concepts, which will be mathematically valid, this article postulates that these approaches will vary in usability. Hence, this work has undertaken the approach of looking for a "tried and trusted" mechanism in other fields which has been utilized for modeling these types of systems. Fortunately, one exists within the field of quantitative population ecology; this field has a long history of modeling *'Predator and Prey'* systems. These systems provide a good analogy for the current situation, with defects being analogous to *Prey* and verification and validation activities being analogous to *Predators*. Other work

Figure 1. Lotka-Volterra: Phase diagram of defects(x) vs. validation-verification activities(y) for initial values of (x,y) at t=0 of [(0.1,0.1) (1.0,0.5) (1.2,1.2) (1.0,0.7)]; parameters [a:=1;b:=1;c:=1;d:=0.5]

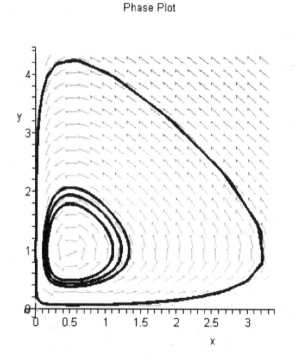

within software engineering has also borrowed models from quantitative population ecology; for example, the work using capture-recapture theory (Chao, Lee, & Jeng, 1992) to estimate the number of defects remaining after a software inspection activity. Eick et al. (1992) and Miller (1999) draw a similar population-oriented analogy.

MODELS FROM QUANTITATIVE POPULATION ECOLOGY

Lotka Volterra models (Lotka, 1925; Volterra 1931) have a long history within various branches of scientific endeavor and can still be seen as an active area of research in many scientific disciplines (e.g., Hernandez-Bermejo, 1998; Pekalski & Stauffer, 1998). The equations have also found several applications outside of the traditional sciences; for example, Ormerod (1994) uses them to describe the average Canadian unemployment rate since the second world war. The simplest of their models proves an excellent starting point for modeling the interaction between defects and their removal. Specifically, the simplest Lotka-Volterra system for modeling a two-entity interaction is given by

$$\frac{\partial x}{\partial t} = ax - bxy$$
$$\frac{\partial y}{\partial t} = cxy - dy$$

Where,

x = the remaining number of defects;
y = the amount of verification and validation activities;
a = the rate of growth of defects, assuming that no verification and validation activities exist;
b = the rate of decrease in the number of defects due to verification and validation activities;

c = the rate of growth in verification and validation activities in response to finding and removing defects 1;
d = the rate of decay in verification and validation activities; if there are few, or no defects to be found.

Figure 1 illustrates typical behavior of x and y when plotted on a phase diagram where the arrows indicate the flow of time. The plots are drawn for different starting values of (x, y) and indicate periodic solutions or oscillations.

The model forms a good mathematical fit for the defect injection and removal scenario outlined above. In addition, this approach has a long history and has been proven successful with a wide range of applications. Within this application, the model utilizes the amount of verification and validation activities as a variable quantity, unlike some projects that fix the amount of effort on these processes at the start of the project. One of the proposed advantages of this approach is the ability to optimize this quantity throughout the project and hence it is expressed as a function of time.

One further implication is the limiting cases of the two equations. Thus in the complete absence of validation and verification activities:
$$\frac{\partial x}{\partial t} = ax$$

This integrates to:

$$x_t = x_0 e^{at}$$

Also, in the complete absence of defects,
$$\frac{\partial y}{\partial t} = -dy$$

This integrates to:

$$y_t = y_0 e^{-dt}$$

This clearly shows that these models are built upon independent exponential growth and decay functions, and hence the models fit our final set of requirements.

RESTRICTING GROWTH AND DECAY RATES

Introduction of a Finite "Consumption" Rate for Defects

Although it can reasonably be expected that validation and verification activities will find more defects when defects are relatively bountiful compared with periods when defects are relatively scarce, the increase in performance will clearly have an upper bound. The obvious rationale for this limitation is that validation and verification activities take a finite amount of time. This time can be subdivided into four components:

- Searching and locating defects
- Familiarization and refamiliarization with the software artifacts
- Reporting or fixing defects
- Other activities associated with the verification and validation activities; for example, team meetings or briefings, periods of learning, and so on

Clearly, although the first component will be (positively) impacted by the quantity of defects (i.e., the average search time will decrease with an increase in the number of defects), the other components are independent of the quantity of defects. Hence, the number of defects found is strictly limited by these additional components. In addition, while the third and fourth components can be considered as constants, the total amount of time spent on the second component is clearly proportional to the number of defects found. Thus, the total amount of time can be characterized as

$$\sum_i T = \sum_i T_{search_i} + \sum_i T_{fix_i} + \sum_i T_{familiar} + T_{misc}$$

Hence, ignoring the constant components, the total amount of time spent on finding and processing defects can be approximately given by

$$T^* = T^*_{search} + T^*_{fix}$$

Where $*$ indicates summation over all defects found.

If we assume that that x_{T^*} defects are processed during duration T^*; then

$$T^*_{fix} = x_{T^*} . T_x$$

Where T_x is the average time spent on reporting and fixing any arbitrary defect.

If it is assumed that T^*_{search} can be modeled as a random process; and that the verification and validation activity is considered to search an "area" or "volume" (v) within a document or across several documents per unit of time.

Thus after time T^*, the activity will have searched an "area" vT^*_{search} and will discover vxT^*_{search} defects. Where x can also be thought of as the density of defects within the searched area. (This also assumes that the verification and validation process is assumed to be perfect; that is, all found defects would be corrected recorded allowing subsequent removal.)

Hence,

$$x_{T^*} = vxT^*_{search}$$

therefore,

$$T^* = x_{T^*} T_x + \frac{x_{T^*}}{vx}$$

and,

$$x_{T^*} = \frac{vxT^*}{1 + vxT_x}$$

This approach to limiting the behavior of the exponential growth and decay functions also exists in the ecological literature; see Holling (1959) for examples of this approach in the ecological arena.

Finally, the area (v) representing software artifacts must be finite. Possible models for v include function point estimates and lines of code measures from traditional software systems. Alternatively, as Web-based systems advance hopefully such measures can be replaced by more specific measures directly related to verification and validation coverage-oriented measures such as the number of HTTP requests or transactions, or an information-theory based measure of the amount of XML-data transferred. This obviously places restrictions on the possible growth of the defect population and hence defines a maximum density of defects, which can exist. This fact places a further restriction on the growth model, which will be introduced in a later section.

Increasing the Volume of Verification and Validation Activities

It is also reasonable to assume that many projects which experience a large and increasing defect population may seek to counter this by introducing further verification and validation processes and procedures into their production processes. This adjustment could take many forms, such as the introduction of code inspections to supplement current testing approaches or the change of some component within an already existing component, such as the adoption of checklists or scenarios into the existing inspection process. Existing verification and validation staff may also add to the increase by increasing efforts or durations spent on these activities, as their current undertaking is seen as highly fruitful due to the large number of defects being found during this period of abundant deficiencies.

Although these responses are probable, it is very difficult to quantitatively envisage the impact of the responses on the system. Hence, due to the lack of information it was decided to model this additional component in an extremely simple manner, namely by predicting that any increase in the response by verification and validation activities is simply proportional to the number of defects believed to exist within the system at any point in time.

Finally, with regard to the final perceived component within the model, namely the statistical independence or dependence of verification and validation activities, it has been decided not to model these potential effects. The principal reason behind this decision was the lack of understanding of the scale of impact of this phenomenon. Although it is difficult to believe that some level of dependence does not exist, currently no empirical knowledge exists to suggest that it will have any great impact upon existing numerical models. In fact, a recent empirical investigation into this effect by Miller (2002), in the area of software inspection, suggests that no appreciable level of dependence exists, supporting the decision not to include any dependence component into the proposed model.

If it was decided to add further components to model this dependence, then again ecological modeling may well provide suitable pointers to the shape of these components. In ecological systems, "predator and prey" models are often extended to include interspecies competition and cooperation. It is believed that this further set of models could be adapted to encode any dependence component requiring addition.

ADDING THE RESTRICTIVE COMPONENTS TO THE INITIAL MODEL

Recalling that the number of defects found and removed is given by

$$x_{T^*} = \frac{vxT^*}{1 + vxT_x}$$

Then the rate of reduction in the defect count by all of the verification and validation practitioners, per unit of time, is given by

$$\frac{vxy}{1 + vxT_x}$$

Further, as noted the system should also restrict the rate of growth of defects (assuming that no verification and validation activities exist) as this area will be bound by the finite size of the software artifact. While it could be argued that a software artifact could in fact be populated by an infinite amount of defects, it is considered that this argument is extreme, and a more conservative approach of restricting this component is in line with common experience.

Following the work of Verhulst (1838), a limit on the density of defects appearing in any software artifact (k) was introduced. The parameter a was reformatted so that as the population of defects increases, the rate of new introductions decreases. Verhulst's solution was to introduce a logistic term into the equation, specifically

$$1 - \frac{N}{k}$$

This term decreases as N (an arbitrary population) approaches the maximum k, reducing by an equal amount for each addition to the population, that is, the reduction is proportionate. This approach ensures that the behavior of the model is smooth and continuous and approaches the theoretical maximum asymptotically. Further, it incrementally penalizes the growth as it approaches the theoretical maximum modeling the increasing difficult of adding to the population when nearing saturation.

Figure 2. Introducing a limitation to the defect growth rate in the Lotka-Volterra Model: Phase diagram of defects(x) vs. validation-verification activities(y) for initial value of (x,y) at t=0 of (0.1,0.1); parameters [amax:=1;b:=1;k:=2;c:=1;d:=0.5]

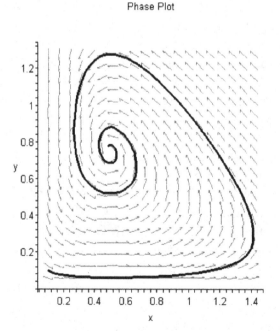

Therefore parameter a is now defined as

$$a = a_{max}(1 - \frac{x}{k})$$

Where *amax* is the maximum growth rate possible within the software artifact.

Hence, the fully restricted defect population dynamic equation is now given by

$$\frac{\partial x}{\partial t} = a_{max}(1 - \frac{x}{k})x - \frac{vxy}{1 + vxT_x}$$

Figure 2 shows the effect on the basic Lotka-Volterra model of introducing a limitation on the density of defects appearing within a software artifact. Placing a restriction on the rate of growth of defects has ensured that x never reaches a value exceeding the value of k. Further, the restriction on the growth of defects has led to a corresponding damping on the validation and verification activities as shown in Figure 3. If the value of k is reduced, the defect population will be further restricted and the validation and verification activities required to obtain equilibrium will effectively tend towards zero, Figure 4. This represents a potential single survivor equilibrium solution that is unlikely to be found with typical application data.

The population dynamics of the verification and validation activities also require to be restricted, as outlined earlier. Here the restriction is a result of the proportional linkage between the sizes of the two populations rather than a restriction on the size of the activities. Again, the introduction of a logistic term has been chosen to implement this restriction.

Hence, the equation for the rate of change of validation and verification activities becomes

$$\frac{\partial y}{\partial t} = (cx - d)y(1 - \frac{y}{wx})$$

Figure 3. Introducing a Limitation to the defect growth rate in the Lotka-Volterra Model: Plot of defects(x) and validation-verification activities(y) vs. t for initial value of (x,y) at t=0 of (0.1,0.1); parameters [amax:=1;b:=1;k:=2;c:=1;d:=0.5]

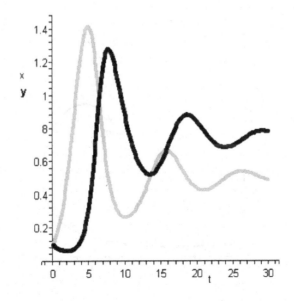

Figure 4. Reducing the value of k, the maximum defect population, drives the validation- verification activities towards zero: Phase diagram of defects(x) versus validation-verification activities(y) for initial value of (x,y) at t=0 of (0.1,0.1); parameters [amax:=1;b:=1;k:=0.5;c:=1;d:=0.5]

Phase Plot

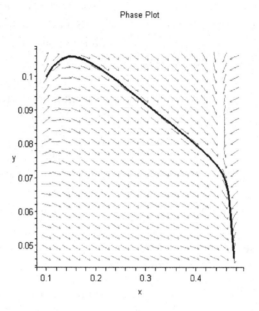

Figure 5. Introducing all restrictive components to the Lotka-Volterra Model: Phase diagram of defects(x) vs. validation-verification activities(y) for initial values of (x,y) at t=0 of [(0.1,0.1) (1.0,0.5) (1.2,1.2) (1.0,0.7)]; parameters [amax:=1;k:=2;w:=0.7;v:=2;T:=1;c:=1;d:=0.5]

Phase Plot

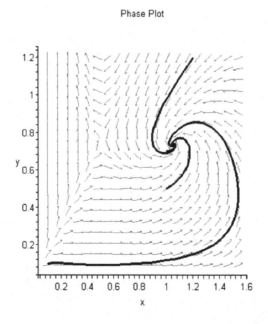

Where w is a weighting parameter to control the proportionality of the relationship between x and y.

With this approach, as the ratio of y/x tends towards w, the multiplying factor tends towards zero, limiting the growth in validation and verification activities. However, if y/x is much less than w the factor tends towards a value of one, giving normal Lotka-Volterra behavior.

Finally, the impact of introducing all three restrictive components to the model is shown in Figure 5. The consequences of restricting the proportionality relationship between x and y can be seen by the direction of the arrows to the left of the diagram. Overall, it can be seen that adding these restrictive components for growth and decay rates, with the parameters chosen in the examples, has had a damping effect on the oscillations within the model and led to a coexistence stationary equilibrium where the injected defects are being kept under control by a constant verification and validation effort.

CONCLUSION

To allow software professionals to develop well defined risk assessment and management strategies with regard to e-projects it is important to model the interaction between the processes that inject defects and the processes that remove them. Further, any model should be quantitative in nature and should support any arbitrary set of injectional and removal processes.

This article has developed a basic modeling framework based on the Lotka-Volterra predator prey interaction that allows a generic description of competing processes within the software production environment. The article has shown that the basic Lotka-Volterra model can be adapted to encode essential information about the interaction between processes and has the potential to give rise to a model appropriate to the interaction between injection and removal processes present within an e-project. The article has illustrated through example the effects of the restrictions on growth and decay rates introduced into the model, illustrating how they can lead to a coexistence stationary equilibrium between injection of defects and verification and validation activities. However, further work still has to be done to obtain suitable datasets that will allow estimates of model parameters that would lead to its application in predicting cost implications within the management of e-projects.

REFERENCES

Barghour, M., Abdel-Ghaly, A. A., & Littlewood, B. (1998). A non-parametric order statistics reliability model. *Journal of Software Testing, Verification and Reliability, 8*(3), 113-312.

Beck, K. (2003). *Test-driven development*. Addison-Wesley.

Boehm, B. W. (1981). *Software engineering economics*. Englewood Cliffs, NJ: Prentice Hall.

Boland, P. J., & Chuiv, N. (2001). Cost implications of imperfect repair in software reliability, *International Journal of Reliability and Application, 2*(3), 147-160.

Chao, A., Lee, S. M., & Jeng, S. L. (1992). Estimation of population size for capture-recapture data when capture probabilities vary by time and individual animal. *Biometrics, 48,* 201-216.

Eick, S., Loader, C., Long, M., Votta, L., & Vander Wiel, S. (1992). Estimating software fault content before coding. In *Proceedings of the 14th International Conference on Software Engineering* (pp. 59-65).

Gokhale, S. (2004). Software failure rate and reliability incorporating repair policies. In *Proceedings of the IEEE International Symposium on Software Metrics* (pp. 394-404).

Hernandez-Bermejo, B. (1998). Universality of the Generalized Lotka-Volterra equation. *CATHODE 2.*

Holling, C. S. (1959). The components of predation as revealed by a study of small mammal predation of the European pine sawfly. *Canadian Entomology, 91,* 293-320.

Lotka, A. J. (1925). *Elements of physical biology.* Baltimore: Williams & Wilkins.

Lyu, M. R. (1996). Software reliability modeling survey. In M. R. Lyu (Ed.),, *Handbook of software reliability engineering* (pp. 71-117). McGraw-Hill.

Miller, J. (1999). Estimating the number of remaining defects after software inspection, *Journal of Software Testing, Verification and Reliability, 9,* 167-189.

Miller, J. (2002). On the independence of software inspectors. *Journal of Systems and Software, 60*(1), 5-10.

Offutt, J. (2002). Quality attributes of Web software applications [Special Issue on software engineering of Internet software]. *IEEE Software, 19*(2), 25-32.

Ormerod, P. (1994). *The death of economics.* London: Faber and Faber Limited.

Pekalski, A., & Stauffer, D. (1998). Three species Lotka-Volterra model. *International Journal of Modern Physics C, 9*(5), 777-783.

Ricca, F., & Tonella, P. (2001). Analysis and testing of Web applications. *Proceedings of the 23rd International Conference on Software Engineering (ICSE 2001)* (pp. 25-34).

Scheidewind, N. (1993). Software reliability model with optimal selection of failure data. *IEEE Transactions on Software Engineering, 19*(11), 1095-1114.

Scheidewind, N. (2004). Fault correction profiles. In *Proceedings of the Eighth International Symposium on High Assurance Systems Engineering* (pp. 139-148).

Schwaber, K. (2004). *Agile project management with SCRUM.* Microsoft Press.

Tassey, G. (2002). *The economic impacts of inadequate infrastructure for software testing* (Tech. Rep.). National Institute of Standards and Technology.

Tian, L., & Noore, A. (2005). Evolutionary neural network modeling for software cumulative failure time prediction. *Journal of Reliability Engineering and System Safety, 87,* 45-51.

Verhulst, P. F., (1838). Recherches mathematiques sur la loi d'accrossement de la population. *Memoirs de l'Academie Royal Bruxelles, 18,* 1-38.

Volterra, V. (1931). *Animal ecology.* In R. N. Chapman (Ed.), (pp. 409-448). New York: McGraw-Hill.

This work was previously published in Int. Journal of Information Technology and Web Engineering, Vol 2, Issue 3, edited by L. Zhang, pp. 37-48, copyright 2007 by IGI Publishing (an imprint of IGI Global).

Chapter XXI
Tool Support for Model–Driven Development of Web Applications

Jaime Gomez
University of Alicante, Spain

Alejandro Bia
University of Alicante, Spain

Antonio Parraga
University of Alicante, Spain

ABSTRACT

This paper describes the engineering foundations of VisualWADE, a CASE tool to automate the production of Web applications. VisualWADE follows a model-driven approach focusing on requirements analysis, high level design, and rapid prototyping. In this way, an application evolves smoothly from the first prototype to the final product, and its maintenance is a natural consequence of development. The paper also discusses the lessons learned in the development of the tool and its application to several case studies in the industrial context.

INTRODUCTION

The rapid evolution of Internet in general and of the WWW in particular has promoted in recent years intensive research in the field of conceptual mod-eling of Web applications. This fact has induced a new research trend within Software Engineering known as Web Engineering. In this context, different methods, languages, tools and design patterns for Web modeling have been proposed.

Some of the most relevant studied so far are HDM (Garzotto & Paolini, 1993), WebML (Ceri, Fraternali, & Bongio, 2000), OOHDM (Schwabe, Rossi, & Barbosa 1996), UWE (Koch & Kraus, 2002), ADM (Atzeni, Mecca, & Merialdo, 1998), and OO-H (Gómez, Cachero, & Pastor, 2001). These methods are centered mainly in the definition of navigational and presentational aspects relative to the semantic of models to capture relevant properties of Web environments. However, few are the proposals that have tried to apply their methods to solve complex real cases to verify the effectiveness of their modeling approach. Much lesser have been the attempts (successful or not) of building specific purpose tools for Web Engineering. We can mention WebRatio (2000), developed at the Politecnico di Milano, Italy, under the technical direction of Professor Piero Fraternali, or ArgoUWE (Knapp, Koch, Moser, & Zhang, 2001), developed at the Luwdig Maximilians University of Munich, Germany, under the technical direction of Dr. Nora Koch.

This article describes the engineering foundations of VisualWADE (2003), a CASE tool for the design and automatic production of Web applications based on the OO-H method developed at the University of Alicante. The underlying idea behind VisualWADE consists of an appropriate combination of simple concepts (modeling elements) that allow the designer to model and automatically generate any type of Web-based system, from a Web portal or company intranet to a secure Web site for electronic commerce. VisualWADE follows a model-driven approach with emphasis on the requirements analysis, high-level design, and rapid prototyping. In this way, an application softly evolves from the first prototype to the final product. As new requirements (or changes in current requirements) appear, the designer only have to revise the conceptual model, establish the changes and finally, regenerate the implementation. VisualWADE exploits a group of very well-known concepts to capture the complexity of real

Web applications. The underlying method, OO-H (object oriented hypermedia), provides specific modeling elements to represent navigation maps based on a notation compatible with UML. The captured specification is compiled making use of model-based code generation techniques, and as a result, it produces a Web application with a default user interface. This user interface can be refined within the environment to obtain the final appearance of the Web application with the consequent increment of development productivity.

The article is organized as follows: The second section provides a brief introduction to the OO-H method to familiarize the reader with the modeling notation. The third section describes the basic aspects of modeling organized according to three different perspectives through which a Web application is modeled with VisualWADE (structure, navigation, and presentation). A running example (Web-based mail system) is used to describe the tool support. The fourth section presents advanced aspects of modeling, describing how the consistency between models is supported and giving a brief description of the model compilers that produce the final software artifacts. The fifth section describes the lessons learned by the development team that has created VisualWADE. These lessons are the result of the application of VisualWADE in the development of real Web engineering projects on various application domains (tax management, Internet banking, digital signatures). Finally, the article ends with some conclusions, based on our experience, about the evolution and the future of Web engineering methods, techniques and tools.

A BRIEF INTRODUCTION TO THE OO-H METHOD

The OO-H method (object-oriented hypermedia) is a generic method based on the object-oriented paradigm that provides a specific notation and semantics for the development of Web based applications. OO-H defines a set of diagrams, techniques, and tools that altogether comprise a complete approach for the modeling of Web application. The method includes: a design process, a navigational access diagram (NAD), an abstract presentation diagram (APD), and, finally, a CASE tool that supports and automates the development process. With OO-H, a traditional business application can be "converted" to a Web-compliant application by adding two new views (diagrams) that complement the structure (class diagram) and behavior views (interaction and state transition diagrams). The first of them, the NAD, is used to specify a navigation view. The second, the APD, captures concepts related to the final-interface presentation details. The NAD enriches a domain model with navigation and interaction characteristics. It also defines constraints about navigation and information, which should be showed to the Web user. For this purpose, OO-H uses the object constraint language OCL (Warmer & Kleppe, 1998). In this way, a precise navigation diagram can be obtained. On the other hand, the APD contains the definition of abstract pages (pages that are not attached to any specific Web language) based on a set of XML templates that capture the relevant presentational properties of the Web interface under construction. OO-H is a well-recognized Web design method in the field of Web Engineering, and several publications [5,6] provide detailed information about it. Due to fact that the focus of this article is to describe the OO-H tool (called VisualWADE), interested readers are redirected to the references commented above. In the next section, we describe the basic aspects to model a Web application with VisualWADE. A running example focused on a Web-based mail system is used to introduce the relevant concepts about the method.

VISUALWADE: BASIC ASPECTS

Domain Modeling

The starting point to approach the design of a Web application is the domain model represented with a class diagram (see Figure 1).

The notation of this diagram is based on UML which makes it quite intuitive for a designer familiarized with object oriented analysis and design. The application helps the designer throughout the whole edition process by means of a simple, but yet powerful and intuitive graphical interface. The creation of classes, attributes and relationships is carried out with simple mouse actions. The availability within the environment of zoom buttons and global views help the organization and management of complex diagrams comprised of several classes.

In Figure 1, a class diagram corresponding to the Web-based mail system can be observed. In this case, the *user* class and the *message* class are specified and between them two associations to capture the information corresponding to the messages *sent* and *received* by the user. Derived attributes can also be specified within the class diagram. Attributes stereotyped as "*derived*" has an associated OCL formula that specifies how the value of the attribute is obtained. This is the case of the attribute *receivedMsgs* of the *user* class, whose value is obtained by navigating through the *user2message1* role and calculating the number of instances of the *message* class (*size()* function). Obviously, we have implemented within the environment an OCL compiler that allows the syntactic and semantic validation of the OCL formulas.

Navigation Modeling

A navigation view shows the way in which attributes and services provided by the classes

Figure 1. A class diagram in VisualWADE

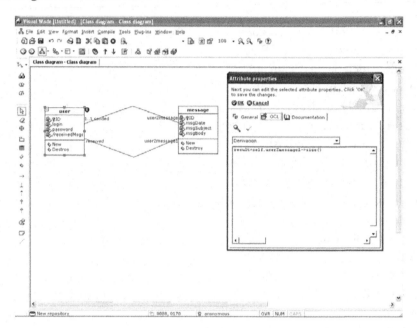

defined in the domain model are accessed. In Figure 2 a partial view of the NAD diagram for a Web user is shown.

The entry point is the *main* abstract page, which represents the navigation starting node. From *main* the Web user can navigate to the navigational class *user* through the *authenticate* link. Traversing the *authenticate* link requires the evaluation of filter (expressed as an OCL formula). In this case, the user must provide the *login* information (*dst.login*) and a *password* (*dst.password*) to check whether he/she is a valid user for the system. Depending on the success of this validation process the pre-conditions associated to links *LI2* and *LI3* will determine which of these links will be activated and therefore the destination abstract page (*menu* or *error*) to continue the navigation process. The *notEmpty()* and *isEmpty()* OCL functions provide the necessary information to know if a user is or not registered in the system. Continuing with the description of this navigation diagram, from the *main* abstract page and through the *LI4* link the *newUser* service of the navigational class

user is accessed. This modeling situation allow a Web user to activate the service *newUser* to register new users into the system.. Finally, from the *menu* abstract page the navigation continues to the navigational target *message management* while with the *error* abstract page it returns to the *main* starting page.

In Figure 2, the toolbar on the left contains the modeling elements that can be inserted in a NAD. By mouse selections, the internal properties of each element can be edited. For example, a link connects an origin element with a destination element. Link properties allow to specify whether the information of the origin element must be shown in the same page that the information of the destination element or not. The visual environment also includes very useful functions such as copy/paste, do/undo, zoom-in/zoom-out, quick element search and finally rules to check the model's consistency (model checking) and the corresponding warning messages. This last feature will be discussed later on.

Figure 2. Navigation diagram in VisualWADE

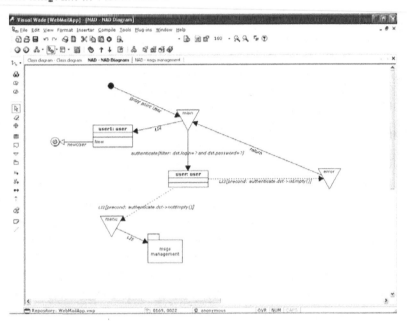

Presentation Modeling

Once the designer has specified a navigation diagram (completed or partially completed), this diagram can be compiled. As a result a set of XML (1999) pages that fulfills the navigation specifications are generated. The XML pages constitute the Web application and contains a preliminary Web user interface. One of the most powerful properties of the environment is the fact that this preliminary Web user interface can be refined within the environment to render the final look and feel of the Web application. The aspects that can be refined are those corresponding to the properties of styles, location, colors, inclusion of final components (images, presentations, Flash,...), just as it could be done with any authoring tool like Frontpage or Dreamweaver, but with the possibility of maintaining the consistency with the previous views (class and navigation diagrams). In this way, the incremental development of the Web application is achieved.

Figure 3 shows the abstract presentation diagram, result of compiling the NAD of Figure 2.

Several zones can be observed: on the left side the page viewer can be observed. It contains the abstract pages that have been generated, alphabetically ordered (*error, messages, menu, main, user, user1*). On the right side can be seen the editing area where the content of the abstract pages is visualized. The information of the *main* page is showed in this case. As a result of the compilation process from NAD to APD, a form has been generated with the fields *login* and *password* and the corresponding button to execute the action (*OK*). Also shown is the link *user1* which enables the navigation to register a *new user* into the system.

This preliminary Web user interface can be animated (within the environment) with the purpose of checking that indeed the appropriate solution is being designed. This can be done by means of the animation tool ✋.

When the animation tool is active, the links and buttons of the interface become sensitive to mouse selections, allowing the corresponding navigation jumps. While a model is being animated, it is still possible to select the edition tool to modify any

Figure 3. Presentation diagram in VisualWADE

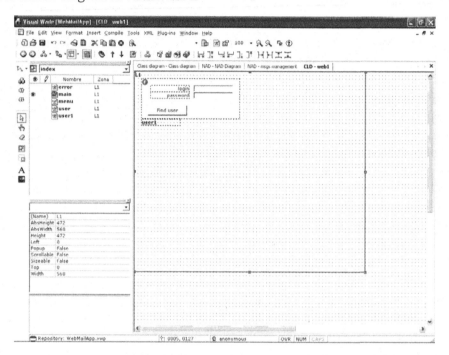

property of the elements of the interface. Figure 4 is the result of having activated the animation tool, having selected with the mouse the link *user1* of Figure 3, and finally having used the edition tool to modify the look of the page. It can be observed that within these refinements, a help text has been included and the position, size, and color of the users' creation form have been changed.

Once we have introduced the basic features of the VisualWADE environment, we continue describing advances features to support the creation of Web applications.

VISUALWADE: ADVANCED FEATURES

Automatic Model Checking

VisualWADE includes a powerful automatic model validation function. In this way, the captured specification is early verified with the consequent time saving in the code generation process.

The verification process takes place at three levels:

- Model checking: this function validates the construction of the structure and navigation views and presents any detected consistency problems as well as the necessary steps to fix them.

- Data-mapping checking: this function checks whether the elements of class diagrams are correctly represented in the generated database. Possible errors may be due to changes in the conceptual specification or class attribute renaming.

- Presentation checking: This process checks whether the representation of the abstract pages corresponds to the specification captured in the navigation diagram, providing the corresponding warnings to correct the error.

336

Figure 4. Refinement and animation in the APD

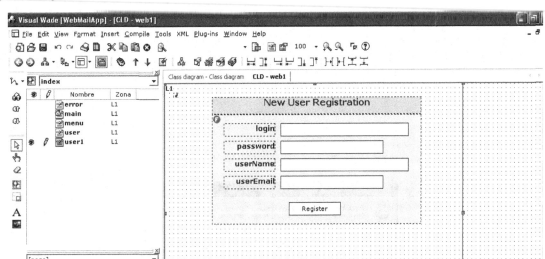

Figure 5 shows an environment warning of the model verification process. Concretely, it informs that the default APD cannot be generated because an error in the OCL formula associated to the "authenticate" link of the NAD view has been found. A further look will reveal that the formula refers to attributes that have not been declared in the class diagram.

Model Compilers

A model compiler compiles the conceptual model and produces as an output the source code for a concrete implementation technology. Visual-WADE integrates three compilers: user interface, navigation engine and database compilers. The structure of VisualWADE compilers follows a three-tiered architecture composed by user interface, navigation logic, and data layers respectively. Each compiler can be invoked independently to regenerate any desired layer leaving the rest unaltered. The structure of a project generated with VisualWADE is as follows:

User Interface

It is comprised of a set of pages that communicate with the navigation engine by means of an object (Object Mediator) to which each page makes its own programmed requests, such as services invocation, data request, or ask about the fulfillment of certain conditions. The interface pages can be based on templates, therefore they will contain a small logic to fill the contents of the templates and to visualize the result (the Visual-WADE Web site: VisualWADE, 2003) is a clear example of generation by means of templates). The pages of the interface layer do not have any business logic integrated into them, and they are simply devoted to query the Object Mediator, render the information to be showed and finally show the results.

Navigation Engine

It is comprised of the Object Mediator class and different function modules that will be invoked by the later at each interface request. Among the generated modules we can highlight:

Figure 5. Model checking in VisualWADE

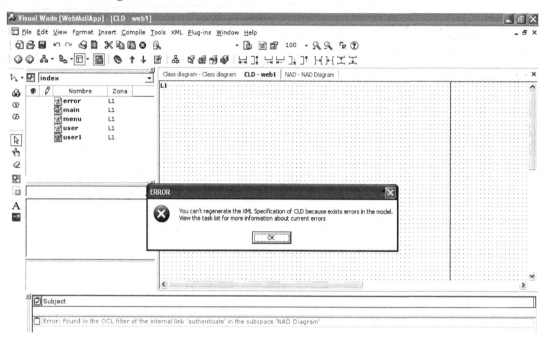

- **Query files:** Contains all the database queries and the corresponding logic to fill some proprietary data structures that the interface layer will know how to interpret to show the results.

- **Services file:** Contains the services defined in the NAD diagram. Basically, they carry out the insert, delete and update database operations.

- **Formulas file:** Contains the functions that manipulate data to transform them dynamically into other data as a result of the interpretation of derived attributes, NAD tags, and so on.

- **Context resolution file:** Contains the functions that allow the extraction of information from a user session such as the instances that were implied when a certain filter was executed, or whether the user has navigated or not through a certain link, and so on.

- **Conditions file:** Contains the functions to validate the preconditions defined in the model among other things. This file is similar to the formulas file, only that the domain of all the functions defined in this file is Boolean and that it simply serves for the Object Mediator to check whether the conditions defined by the user are fulfilled or not at any moment.

Database

The tool also includes a database generator that generates output for different relational database engines. The choice of database engine will make queries and services to be generated with the corresponding syntax (sometimes even optimized for the target engine), this being transparent to the rest of layers.

With all these functionalities we believe that VisualWADE constitutes a serious proposal of advanced tool for the design and automatic generation of Web application. VisualWADE and its underlying notation (OO-H) have been the result of four years of intense research in the field of Web Engineering at the University of Alicante. Next, we describe some of the relevant projects were we have applied the tool and interesting lessons learned.

VISUALWADE: LESSONS LEARNED

Application Scope

VisualWADE has been used in such different environments as: the Autonomous Organization of Tax Administration of the Province of Alicante (SUMA, 2003), the Mediterranean Savings Bank (CAM, 2003), the Association of Industrial Technical Engineers of the Province of Alicante (COITI) (PROVE, 2003) , as well as to create VisualWADE's own Web site (VisualWADE, 2003). In this section we will present some of the characteristics of the systems that have been designed with VisualWADE within these companies.

In SUMA Tax Administration, several Web applications have been developed, most of which are data-oriented. Among them, we highlight in chronological order: an inventory management system, SUMA's intranet and its Internet portal. The inventory management system is an application to manage the computer material inventory, which is distributed along its 250 offices in the province of Alicante. Actually, inventory management can be seen as a traditional desktop application with a Web user interface. This was the first application that we completely designed using VisualWADE and also the one where more design errors were made. The reason was that we were strongly influenced by the type of user interfaces that the company was accustomed to use, and we were forced to carry out an "unnatural" design for a Web environment. Few Web visualization patterns were used so that the navigation was not intuitive and it was directed by the set of services offered from the interface (the same as in their traditional applications). Inventory management had more than 150 available services in the application. The experience of this development made both the SUMA team and the VisualWADE team to mature very much in a parallel way, and to realize that doing design like this prevented us from taking advantage of all the benefits of Web

environments. The second project carried out at SUMA was its intranet. Basically, the intranet provides the necessary functionality to manage the group of news, events, tools and internal documents of the company through an intuitive and user-friendly Web interface. It is the first application that was designed for several user profiles, among them the administrator whose fundamental role is to supervise the information entered to the system from the different departments. Currently, the intranet of SUMA provides services to more than 400 users, and by the third month of operation it had increased its visits by more than 300% compared to the same period of the previous year. The last project carried out was the portal of SUMA. With a navigation design similar to that of the intranet, this application offers new and interesting services to citizens and city councils. In its design, some of the advanced characteristics provided by VisualWADE have been used, like multilanguage support and template-based interface generation. In fact, the graphic design was developed by a subcontracted external company. Later, this graphic design was adapted to the generated navigation model.

Regarding the Mediterranean Savings Bank (CAM, 2003), the use of VisualWADE was more limited there, mainly for reasons of security, which are described in the next section. Coordinated with the team of the CAM-directo service, whose responsibility is to maintain the group of applications to provide bank service through Internet, we used VisualWADE only to design the user interface navigation of the CAM-directo system itself. In this case, none of the capabilities of VisualWADE to generate predefined services was used, since the functionality already existed and had to be simply invoked from the navigation environment. To do so, we used the VisualWADE Web services integration modules (not described in this article) that "encapsulated" the calls to the different necessary operations through a WSDL specification. The most difficult part was to adapt the return of parameters from the services to the navigation engine for later presentation on the Web interface. Regrettably, this task of integration with Web services still has to be made by hand. The experience was very positive, but we also realized that much of the potential use of VisualWADE is lost, since only a few of the characteristics of the environment like the interface generator were used. The need for privacy and security demanded by bank environments forced us to modify the Web design environments so that these security requirements are treated as first level elements. In this sense, we have created a workgroup with the CAM-directo team to identify and propose a set of modeling primitives that should be incorporated to a security model of Web applications.

The PROVE (proyecto visados electronicos) project developed in the COITI (industrial engineer association of the province of Alicante) has been another system where VisualWADE has been applied successfully. The aim of this project is to provide a Web-based application to manage electronic documents following the digital signature standards. PROVE makes an intensive use of Web services to offer digital signature services provided by the public key infrastructure (PKI) of the Generalitat Valenciana (PKI, 2004). PROVE, is the first system developed with VisualWADE that connects three different information systems; the PKI Web server, the CAM-directo system and the COITI system. Conceptually, an industrial engineer can send through the PROVE system a digitally signed electronic document (pdf file that contains the description of a project), pay the corresponding administrative rates through the CAM-directo system, and submit it automatically to the department of COITI for registration. Just like the case of SUMA, the integration with Web services had to be carried out by hand. This is therefore a pending area for improvement in future versions of the tool. PROVE currently serves more than 1,350 members, processing more than 15,000 projects per year.

Finally, the conceptual design and generation of the VisualWADE Web site itself has been car-

ried out using the tool. The VisualWADE portal is also based on templates and provides a set of very interesting navigation functionalities. All these functionalities have been fully generated using the properties of VisualWADE. For instance, the possibility to register at the Web site to access the free download of the tool, or to participate in discussion forums, or even to execute a project's task-management application example. Contrary to the systems that have been presented previously, in the VisualWADE portal there is no use of any functionality from third-party developers. In this sense, we could have used any free software for forum management available in Internet, but we preferred to build it from scratch to demonstrate the power and ease of use of the environment. The VisualWADE portal is open since November 2004. Currently it manages a transfer rate of more than 15 Gb per month, and more than 600 downloads of the tool from all over the world have already taken place.

Although all these systems that have been briefly presented here constitute a real fact about the usability of advanced Web development environments, our current purpose is to make VisualWADE available to the highest number of possible interested users with the objective of exploring new uses and development experiences. We are sure that this new phase will highlight interesting experiences yet to discover. Next we present some of our experiences acquired during the development of the Web information systems described.

Experiences in the Development of Real Applications

In this subsection, we intend to provide some of the experiences of the VisualWADE team in the application of the tool for the resolution of real cases. As common denominator, all these cases required Web-based solutions for their information systems. Most of these solutions (85%, approximately) did not require new developments, but adaptations of existent information systems to the new Web environment, while only the remaining (15%, approximately) could be considered as new developments, although in fact they were small extensions of functionalities not available until then.

As mentioned before, VisualWADE provides, on one hand, predefined operations to support the design of date-intensive Web applications. This type of operations has demonstrated to be enough to provide basic business logic in applications like the inventory management or the intranet of SUMA. In fact, a great number of the Web applications demanded by companies are data-oriented. Therefore, it is particularly important to provide CRUD services for the great majority of Web environments that companies require, particularly companies that possess organizational information systems.

On the other hand, the ability to specify and to use Web services in VisualWADE has facilitated the integration of functions that, in the form of legacy software, were needed in the new environment. For reasons dealing with security, privacy and complexity among others, these inherited functions could not be rewritten again but rather they had to be integrated into the new solutions. Consider that many of these companies have invested heavily in the past so that their information systems could reach the maturity and reliability desired. Therefore, what these companies need are not tools for the construction of Web software from scratch, but tools that facilitate the migration of their systems to the new environment, preserving the highly reliable existent functionality.

Regarding the primitives and navigation patterns, our experience shows the necessity of an intensive use of structures like index, show-all and guided-tours in the designed and generated applications. Also, the great volume of information managed by them often requires information to be presented by pieces. Therefore, it became indispensable to offer constructors to paginate the results. In VisualWADE such constructors are an implicit part of the navigation primitives, allowing the designer to enable or disable the pagination property as well as the number of objects per page.

We have also identified some lacks related to navigation primitives of particular usefulness that unfortunately VisualWADE does not support at this time, among them, the nested indexes and the multiple attribute selection. It has been detected that with these two navigation primitives some pending modeling situations, which were not possible to specify or had to be specified in another less efficient way, could have been covered in a satisfactory way.

The animation capabilities provided within the presentation diagram proves to be highly productive in several senses. On one hand, it helps to reduce the learning curve of the tool by 25%, approximately, especially on navigation diagram concepts, since from the animation environment the effect of a modeling specification on the end-user interface can be seen at a glance. On the other hand, the development speed is increased by a factor of 10 by providing specific model compilers that faithfully reproduce the appearance and the behavior of the animated interface.

In all the companies where VisualWADE has been applied we had to carry out periods of computer personnel's training. Our experience in this sense shows that an important update is required by most of the personnel, especially regarding object oriented analysis and design techniques, which we found quite surprising. The computer personnel of these companies possess an adequate knowledge of data modeling, and therefore to understand or to specify a class diagram was not a problem for them. However, we had to struggle to explain the navigation diagram and particularly its most advanced concepts such as the use of OCL to specify filters and preconditions on links and services. In the case of the CAM project, this situation did not happen and the transfer of knowledge was much more agile due to the personnel's high training.

Another thing that we have learned is that it is very important that the navigation models take into account temporal data about the navigated information. Unfortunately, the great majority of the existent Web design methods and tools do not keep in mind this dimension when specifying a navigation space. When modeling the SUMA intranet project, we needed to support navigational requirements to maintain the expiration period of news and events that were generated within the intranet itself and we realized that we needed some means to deal with time in the navigation model of VisualWADE. In this case, we opted for a solution based on extending the OCL language of VisualWADE by adding time primitives. This allowed us to consider operations between dates and so on within the environment.

The experience of working with VisualWADE in the CAM-directo team has been very productive. Especially, to learn both restrictions of the environment and situations that would have been impossible to realize without this experience. For example, the CAM team did not like that VisualWADE's model compilers produce a fixed generation skeleton (architecture). They said that anyone who knew how the different artifacts generated communicate to each other had a very valuable information to attempt against the security of the generated code. For this reason, our efforts to improve model compilers are directed to provide mechanisms based on MDD/MDA to produce different generation skeletons based on a set of architecture templates.

CONCLUSION

Web developers should improve the productivity and quality to satisfy market needs and reduce delivery times and costs. Regrettably, the methods and standard techniques that are used for Web development still present several deficiencies:

- Models and tools for analysis and design lack appropriate concepts to capture the development properties in this type of environments. As a consequence most of the application code is written by hand and difficult to reuse.
- Documentation is scarce and of low quality, especially for user interfaces.
- Costs and development time are difficult to predict and quickly get out of control during the maintenance and evolution phases of the application.

Web development tools still limit their scope to the implementation phase, or they are centered in concrete vertical solutions (often based on components), which are difficult to personalize and integrate.

From our experience, the use of CAWE techniques (Computer-Aided Web Engineering) in the design or implementation of Web applications provides the following benefits:

- Higher productivity: up to 80% due to the powerful model compilers that generate the code in an automatic way from the conceptual specification.
- Rapid Prototyping: from 1 to 3 days are enough to produce a high-quality prototype. In this way, the time to market is improved considerably.
- Customer satisfaction: the exchange of information with the customer is much more agile and the response to demanded changes can be shown quickly, thanks to rapid prototyping. In this way, it is possible to gain the customer's trust.
- Reduced learning curve: in 5 days, a designer can produce complete high-quality Web applications without the need for programming skills.
- Effort distributed along the life cycle: the possibility of devoting more time to the

user is causes an increment in the quality of the application regarding system requirements.

As a consequence of these considerations and of our experience during the last four years, we believe that in a near future there will be development tools that will simultaneously offer:

- The possibility of visually modeling a Web application using high-level modeling constructors, together with model compilers that facilitate the automatic generation of portable and efficient code from the captured conceptual specification.
- Support of the whole life cycle of the application, including analysis, prototyping, design, deployment, and maintenance.
- Integration of preexistent logical modules (legacy software) in an optimized development process.

VisualWADE, in its current state, solves some of these demands, and at present, is being used for the resolution of complex real cases in institutions like SUMA Tax Administration (Alicante), Mediterranean Savings Bank (CAM, 2003), and the Association of Industrial Technical Engineers of the Province of Alicante. VisualWADE and OO-H are under permanent development. Our next challenge is to integrate the new development paradigm based on MDD/MDA into the environment. We invite the interested reader to download the latest version of the tool and to experience the benefits of advanced Web development environments.

REFERENCES

Atzeni P., Mecca G., & Merialdo P. (1998). Design and maintenance of data-intensive Web sites. *Advances in Database Technology,* 436-449.

CAM. (2003) *Mediterranean Savings Bank.* Retrieved from http://www.cam.es

Ceri S., Fraternali, P., & Bongio, A. (2000). Web modeling language (WebML): A modeling language for designing Web sites. Proceedings from the Ninth International Conference on the WWW, (pp. 15-27).

Garzotto, F., & Paolini, P. (1993). HDM: A model-based approach to hypertext application design. *ACM Transactions on Information Systems (TOIS), 11*(1), 1-26.

Gómez J., Cachero, C., & Pastor, O. (2000). Extending a conceptual modelling approach to Web application design. *CAiSE 2000,* 79-93.

Gómez J., Cachero, C., & Pastor, O. (2001). Conceptual modeling of device-independent Web applications. *IEEE Multimedia 8*(2), 20-32.

Knapp, A., Koch, N., Moser, F., & Zhang, G. (2001). *ArgoUWE: A CASE Tool for Web applications.* Retrieved from http://www.pst.informatik.uni-muenchen.de/~kochn

Koch, N., & Kraus, A. (2002). The expressive power of UML-based Web engineering. In

Proceedings of the Second IWWOST, CYTED. (pp. 105-119).

PKI. (2004). *Generalitat Valenciana.* Retrieved from http://pki.gva.es

PROVE. (2003). Retrieved from http://www.copitial.org

Schwabe, D., Rossi, G., & Barbosa, D. J. (1996). Systematic hypermedia application design with OOHDM. In *Proceedings of the Seventh ACM Conference on HYPERTEXT '96*, (pp. 166-168).

SUMA. (2003). *Gestion tributaria.* Retrieved from http://www.suma.es

VisualWADE. (2003). Retrieved from http://www.visualwade.com

XML. (1999). eXtensible markup language (XML). Retrieved from http://www.w3.org/XML/

Warmer, J., & Kleppe, A. (1998). *The object constraint language: Precise modeling with UML.* Addison-Wesley.

WebRatio. (2000). Retrieved from http://www.Webratio.com

ENDNOTE

[1] This article has been supported by the MEC through the METASIGN project, reference number: TIN2004-00779

This work was previously published in Int. Journal of Information Technology and Web Engineering, Vol 2, Issue 3, edited by L. Zhang, pp. 65-78, copyright 2007 by IGI Publishing (an imprint of IGI Global).

Compilation of References

Abrams, M., Standridge, C. R., Abdulla, G., Williams, S., & Fox, E. A. (1995). Caching proxies: Limitations and potentials. In *Proceedings of the 4th International World Wide Web Conference,* Boston, (pp. 119-133).

Adams, P., Boldyreff, C., Nutter, D., & Rank, S. (2005, May 17). *Adaptive reuse of libre software systems for supporting on-line collaboration.* In *Proceedings of the 5th Workshop on Open Source Software Engineering,* St. Louis, Missouri.

Adusei, I. K., et. al. (2002). Mobile positioning technologies in cellular networks: An evaluation of their performance metrics. *MILCOM 2002,* California, USA.

Agrawal, D., & Bernstein, A. J. (1991). A nonblocking quorum consensus protocol for replicated data. *IEEE Transactions on Parallel and Distributed Systems, 2*(2), 171-179.

Agrawal, R. and Shim, K. (1996). Developing Tightly-Coupled Data Mining Applications on a Relational Database System. *Proceedings of the 2nd Int'l Conference on Knowledge Discovery in Databases and Data Mining.* Portland, Oregon

Albert, R., & Barabasi, A.-L. (2002). Statistical mechanics of complex networks. *Reviews of Modern Physics, 74,* 47–97.

Albert, R., Barabási, A.-L., Jeong, H., & Bianconi, G. (2000). Power-law distribution of the World Wide Web. *Science, 287.*

Albitz, P., & Liu, C. (2001). *DNS and BIND* (4th ed.). O'Reilly & Associates.

Alexander Barmouta & Rajkumar Buyya (2003), "Grid-Bank: A Grid Accounting Services Architecture (GASA) for Distributed Systems Sharing and Integration ", Parallel and Distributed Processing Symposium, Nice, France, IEEE Computer Society.

Aljadhai, A., & Znati, T. (2001). Predictive mobility support for QoS provisioning in mobile wireless environments. *IEEE JSAC, 19*(10), 1915-30.

Altheim, M., & Shane McCarron, S. (Eds.). (2001). *XHTML 1.1 - Module-based XHTML.*

Altheim, M., Boumphrey, F., McCarron, S., Schnitzenbaumer, S., & Wugofski, T. (Eds.). (2001). *Modularization of XHTML.*

Al-Zoubi, K. (2006). *Hierarchical scheduling in grid systems.* Unpublished master's thesis, Carleton University, Ottawa, Canada.

Ambler, S. W. (2002). A Class Type Architecture For Layering Your Application. 2004, from http://www.ronin-intl.com/publications/classTypeArchitecture.htm

Ambler, S. W. (2004). *The Object Primer 3rd Edition: Agile Model Driven Development with UML 2*: Cambridge University Press.

Ambler, S. W. (2005). Agile Requirements Modeling. Retrieved March 14, 2005, from http://www.agilemodeling.com/essays/agileRequirements.htm

Anastasopoulos, M., & Gacek, C. (2001). Implementing Product Line Variabilities. *ACM SSR '01,* 109-117.

Anderson, T., Breitbart, Y., Korth, H. F., & Wool, A. (1998). Replication, consistency and practicality: Are these mutually exclusive? *ACM SIGMOD'98,* Seattle.

Anthonisse, J. (1971). The rush in a directed graph (Tech. Rep.). Amsterdam: Stichting Mathemastisch Centrum.

Anthony Sulistio & Chee Shin Yeo & and Rajkumar Buyya (2003), Visual Modeler for Grid Modeling and Simulation (GridSim) Toolkit, International Conference on Computational Science (ICCS) 2003: Saint Petersburg, Russia / Melbourne, Australi .

Apers, P. G. M. (1998). Data allocation in distributed database systems. *ACM Transactions on Database Systems, 13*(3), 263-304.

Ardagna, C.A., Damiani, E., De Capitani di Vimercati, S., Frati, F., & Samarati, P. (2006). CAS++: An open source single sign-on solution for secure e-services. In *Proceedings of 21st IFIP International Information Security Conference "Security and Privacy in Dynamic Environments"*, Karlstad, Sweden.

Ardagna, C.A., Damiani, E., Frati, F., & Montel, M. (2005). Using open source middleware for securing e-gov applications. In *Proceedings of the First International Conference on Open Source Systems (OSS 2005)*, Genova, Italy.

Ardagna, C.A., Damiani, E., Frati, F., & Reale, S. (2006). Adopting open source for mission-critical applications: A case study on single sign-on. In *Proceedings of the Second International Conference on Open Source Systems (OSS 2006)*, Como, Italy.

Arends, R., Austein, R., Larson, M., Massey, D., & Rose, S. (2005a). *DNS security introduction and requirements*. Internet RFC 4033.

Arends, R., Austein, R., Larson, M., Massey, D., & Rose, S. (2005b). *Protocol modifications for the DNS security extensions*. Internet Request for Comments (RFC) 4035.

Arends, R., Austein, R., Larson, M., Massey, D., & Rose, S. (2005c). *Resource records for the DNS security extensions*. Internet RFC 4034.

Arun A. Somasundara & Aditya Ramamoorthy & Mani B. Srivastava (2004), Mobile Element Scheduling for Efficient Data Collection in Wireless Sensor Networks with Dynamic Deadlines, 25th IEEE International Real-Time Systems Symposium (RTSS'04) .

Astels, D. (2003). *Test Driven Development: A Practical Guide*: Prentice Hall PTR.

Ateniese, G., & Mangard, S. (2001). A new approach to DNS security (DNSSEC). In *Proceedings of the Eighth ACM Conference on Computer and Communications Security* (pp. 86-95). New York: ACM Press.

Atsuko Takefusa (2001) , A Study of Deadline Scheduling for Client-Server Systems on the Computational Grid, 10th IEEE Symposium on High Performance and Distributed Computing (HPDC'01), San Francisco, California.

Atzeni P., Mecca G., & Merialdo P. (1998). Design and maintenance of data-intensive Web sites. *Advances in Database Technology,* 436-449.

Aubry, P., Mathieu, V., & Marchal, J. (2004). ESUP-Portal: Open source single sign-on with CAS (Central Authentication Service). In *Proceedings of EUNIS04 - IT Innovation in a Changing World*, Bled, Slovenia.

Bac, C., Berger, O., Deborde, V., & Hamet, B. (2005, July 11-15). *Why and how to contribute to libre software when you integrate them into an in-house application? In Proceedings of the First International Conference on Open Source Systems*, Genova.

Baker, S. M., & Moon, B. (1999). Scalable web server design for distributed data management. In *Proceedings of the 15th International Conference on Data Engineering*, Sydney, (pp. 96-110).

Bao, L., & Garcia-Luna-Aceces, J. J. (2001). A new approach to channel access scheduling for ad hoc networks. *ACM MOBICOM,* 210-221.

Barak, B., Herzberg, A., Naor, D., & Shai, E. (1999). The proactive security toolkit and applications. In *Proceedings of the Sixth ACM Conference on Computer and Communications Security* (pp. 18-27).

Barghour, M., Abdel-Ghaly, A. A., & Littlewood, B. (1998). A non-parametric order statistics reliability model. *Journal of Software Testing, Verification and Reliability, 8*(3), 113-312.

Barnett, L., & Narsu, U. (2005). Planning Assumption: Best Practices for Agile Development. Retrieved March 15, 2005, from http://www.forrester.com/Research/LegacyIT/Excerpt/0,7208,30193,00.html

Basili, V. (1995). Applying the goal/question/metric paradigm. Experience factory. In *Software quality assurance and measurement: A worldwide perspective* (pp. 21-44). International Thomson Publishing Company.

Bauer, A., & Pizka, M. (2003). The contribution of free software to software evolution. In *Proceedings of the International Workshop on Principles of Software Evolution (IWPSE)*.

Beaulieu, M. (2002). Wireless Internet Applications and Architecture, Addison-Wesley.

Beck, K. (1999). Extreme Programming Explained: Embrace Change. Addison-Wesley.

Beck, K. (2002). *Test Driven Development: By Example*: Addison-Wesley Professional.

Beck, K. (2003). *Test-driven development*. Addison-Wesley.

Beck, K., Beedle, M., Bennekum, A. v., Cockburn, A., Cunningham, W., Fowler, M., et al. (2001). Manifesto for Agile Software Development. Retrieved November 22, 2005, from http://agilemanifesto.org/

Behrens, H., Ritter, T., & Six, H.-W. (2003). Systematic Development of Complex Web-Based User Interfaces. *Computer Science in Perspective, 2598*, 22-38.

Bellovin, S. M. (1995). Using domain name system for system break-ins. In *Proceedings of theFifth Usenix UNIX Security Symposium*. Salt Lake City, UT.

Bensaou, B., Wang, Y., & Ko, C. C. (2000). Fair medium access in 802.11 based wireless ad-hoc networks. *IEEE/ACM MobiHOC, Boston, MA*.

Bera, P., & Wand, Y. (2004). Analyzing OWL using a philosophy-based ontology. In *Proceedings of the 2004 Conference on Formal Ontologies in Information Systems FOIS* (pp. 353-362) .

Berstis, V. (2002). *Fundamentals of grid computing.* Retrieved from http://www.redbooks.ibm.com/redpapers/pdfs/redp3613.pdf

Bestavros, A. (1995). Demand-based document dissemination to reduce traffic and balance load in distributed information systems. In *Proceedings of the IEEE Symposium on Parallel and Distributed Processing*, pp. 338-345.

Bettini, C., Jajodia, S., Sean Wang, X., & Wijesekera, D. (2002). Provisions and obligations in policy management and security applications. In *Proceedings of the 28th VLDB Conference*, Honk Kong, China.

Beznosov, K. (2003). *Extreme Security Engineering: On Employing XP Practices to Achieve 'Good Enough Security' without Defining It.* Paper presented at the First ACM Workshop on Business Driven Security Engineering (BizSec), Fairfax, VA.

Beznosov, K., & Kruchten, P. (2004). *Towards Agile Security Assurance.* Paper presented at the New Security Paradigms Workshop, White Point Beach Resort, Nova Scotia, Canada.

Bharghavan, V., Demers, A., Shenker, S., & Zhang, L. (1994). MACAW: A media access protocol for wireless LAN's. In *Proceedings of the Conference on Communications Architectures, Protocols and Applications* (pp. 210-225).

Bishay, L., Taniar, D., Jiang, Y., & Rahayu, W. (2000). Structured Web pages management for efficient data retrieval. *WISE 2000, IEEE* (pp. 97-104).

Bishop, M. (2002). *Computer security: Art and science.* Addison-Wesley.

Blake, M.B. & Williams, A.B. (2003a). Developmental and Operational Processes for Agent-Oriented Database

Navigation for Knowledge Discovery. 15th International Conference on Software Engineering and Knowledge Engineering (SEKE'03). San Francisco, CA

Blake, M.B. (2003b). Agent-Based Communication for Distributed Workflow Management using Jini Technologies. International Journal on Artificial Intelligence Tools. Vol. 12, No. 1, pp 81-99

Blake, M.B., Singh, L., Williams, A.B., Norman, W.N., and Sliva, A.L. (2005). A Component-Based Framework for Data Management and Knowledge Discovery. Georgetown Technical Report, http://daruma.georgetown.edu/techreports/techrep_data/blake_singh_%20C-KDD2005.pdf

Blankenhorn, K., & Jeckle, M. (2004). A UML Profile for GUI Layout. *Net.ObjectDays*, 110-121.

Boehm, B. W. (1981). *Software engineering economics.* Englewood Cliffs, NJ: Prentice Hall.

Boland, P. J., & Chuiv, N. (2001). Cost implications of imperfect repair in software reliability, *International Journal of Reliability and Application, 2*(3), 147-160.

Bolchini, D., & Paolini, P. (2004). Goal-driven requirements analysis for hypermedia-intensive Web applications. *Requirements Engineering, 9*, 85-103.

Boneh, D., & Franklin, M. (1997). Efficient generation of shared RSA keys. In *Proceedings of the Advances in Cryptology (Crypto '97)* (pp. 425-439).

Bonifati, A., Cattaneo, F., Ceri, S., Fuggetta, A., & Paraboschi, S. (2001). Designing data marts for data warehouses. *TOSEM ACM* (pp. 452-481).

Bononi, L., Budriesi, L., Blasi, D., Cacace, V., Casone, L., & Rotolo, S. (2004). A differentiated distributed coordination function MAC protocol for cluster-based wireless ad hoc networks. In *Proceedings of the 1st ACM International Workshop on Performance Evaluation of Wireless Ad Hoc, Sensor, And Ubiquitous Networks* (pp. 77-86).

Booch, G., Rumbaugh, J., & Jacobsen, I. (2000). The Unified Modeling Language User Guide, Addison-Wesley.

Booch, G., Rumbaugh, J., & Jacobson, I. (1999). *The Unified Modeling Language User Guide*: Addison Wesley Longman, Inc.

Bos, B., Celik, T., Hickson, I., & Lie, H. W. (Eds.). (2004). *Cascading Style Sheets, level 2 revision 1 CSS 2.1 Specification. W3C Candidate Recommendation. Available online: http://www.w3.org/TR/2004/CR-CSS21-20040225.*

Braford, P., Bestarov, A., Bradley, A., & Crovella, M. (1999). Changes in web client access patterns: Characteristics and caching implications. *WWW Journal, 2*(1), 15-28.

Breitbart, Y., Olson, Y., & Thompson, G. (1986). Database integration in a distributed heterogeneous data system. *ACM Data Engineering* (pp. 301-310).

Buell, D.A., & Sandhu, R. (2003, November-December). Identity management. *IEEE Internet Computing, 7*(6), 26-28.

Bueno, J.C. (1998). KDCOM: A Knowledge Discovery Component Framework. Masters Thesis, Spanish Council for Scientific Research

Burkhardt, J, Henn, H., Hepper, S., Rintdorff, K., & Schack, T. (2002). Pervasive Computing Technology and Architecture of Mobile Internet Applications, Addison-Wesley.

Buttyan L., & Hubaux, J. (2003). Simulating cooperation in self-organizing mobile ad hoc networks. *ACM/Kluwer Mobile Networks and Applications, 8*(5)

Buzydlowski, J. W. (1998). **A framework for object-oriented online analytic processing,** data warehousing and OLAP. *ACM DOLAP* **(pp. 10-15).**

Byung, P., Han, H., & Song, Y. (2005). XML-OLAP: A multidimensional analysis framework for XML warehouses. *DaWak* (pp. 32-42).

Cabibbo, L., & Torlone, R. A. (1998). Logical multidimensional databases. *ACM Advances in Database Technology* (pp. 183-197).

Cali, F., Conti, M., & Gregori, E. (1998). IEEE 802.11 wireless LAN: Capacity analysis and protocol enhancement. In *Proceedings of INFOCOM'98, San Francisco,* (pp. 142-149).

Callahan, M.B., De Armon, J., Cooper, A.M., Goodfriend, H., Moch-Mooney, D., & Solomos, G.H. (2001). Assessing NAS Performance: Normalizing for the Effects of Weather. 4th USA/Europe Air Traffic Management R&D Symposium,. Sante Fe

Calvanese, D., Giacomo, G., De Lenzerini, M., & Rosati, D. N. (1998). Source integration in data warehouse. *DEXA, Springer* (pp. 192-197).

CAM. (2003). *Mediterranean Savings Bank.* Retrieved from http://www.cam.es

Campbell, D.T., & Stanley, T.D. (1990). *Experimental and quasi-experimental design.* Houghton Mifflin Company.

Cardellini, V., Colajanni, M., & Yu, P. S. (1999). Dynamic load balancing on web-server systems. *IEEE Internet Computing, 3*(3), 28-39.

Catalano, D., Gennaro, R., & Halevi, S. (2000). Computing inverses over a shared secret modulus. In Proceedings of *Advance in Cryptology (Eurocrypt 2000)* (pp. 190-206).

Central Authentication Service. (2003). Retrieved June 16, 2006, from http://tp.its.yale.edu/tiki/tiki-index. php?page= CentralAuthenticationService

Ceri S., Fraternali, P., & Bongio, A. (2000). Web modeling language (WebML): A modeling language for designing Web sites. Proceedings from the Ninth International Conference on the WWW, (pp. 15-27).

Ceri, S., Martella, G., & Pelagatti, G. (1982). Optimal file allocation in a computer network: A solution method based on knapsack problem. *Computer Networks, 6*(11), 345-357.

CERT. (2001). Advisory CA-2001-19: Code Red Worm. Retrieved June 15, 2006, from http://www.cert.org/advisories/CA-2001-19.html

Cgisecurity.com. (2002). The Cross Site Scripting FAQ. Retrieved May 20, 2005, from http://www.cgisecurity. com/articles/xss-faq.shtml

Chang, S. K., & Liu, A. C. (1982). File allocation in distributed database. *International Journal of Computer Information Science, 11*(2), 325-340.

Chao, A., Lee, S. M., & Jeng, S. L. (1992). Estimation of population size for capture-recapture data when capture probabilities vary by time and individual animal. *Biometrics, 48,* 201-216.

Chastek, G., Donohoe, P., Kang, K. C., & Thiel, S. H., A. (2001). *Product Line Analysis: A Practical Description (CMU/SEI-2001-TR-001).* Pittsburgh, PA: Software Engineering Institute, Carnegie Mellon University.

Chattratichat, J., Darlington, J., Guo, Y., Hedvall, S., Kohler, M. & Syed, J. (1999). An Architecture for Distributed Enterprise Data Mining. Proceedings of the 7th International Conference on High-Performance Computing and Networking..Lecture Notes in Computer Science. Springer-Verlag. pp 573 – 582

Chawathe, S., Garcia-Molina, H., Hammer, J., Ireland, K., Papakonstantinou, Y., Ullman, J. & Widom, J. (1998). The TSIMMIS project: Integration of heterogeneous information sources. Proceedings of IPSJ Conference, Tokyo, Japan

Chen, M. (2004) A methodology for building mobile computing applications. International Journal of Electronic Business, Vol. 2, No. 3, pp. 229-243.

Chen, W., Hong, T., & Lin, W. (1999). Using the compressed data model in object-oriented data warehousing. *SMC, IEEE* (pp. 768-772).

Chen, X., Mohapatra, P., & Chen, H. (2001). An admission control scheme for predictable server response time for Web accesses. In *Proceedings of the 10th WWW Conference,* Hong Kong, (pp. 45-54).

Chiu, M. H., & Bassiouni, M. A. (2000). Predictive schemes for handoff prioritization in cellular networks based on mobile positioning. *IEEE JSAC, 18*(3), 510-522.

Choi, S., & Shin, K. G. (1998). Predictive and adaptive bandwidth reservation for handoffs in QoS-sensitive cellular networks. In *Proceedings of ACM SIGCOMM '98* (pp. 155-166),

Chris, A. (2002). *Advanced SQL Injection In SQL Server Applications*: NGSSoftware Insight Security Research (NISR) Publication.

Clarke, A.E. (2003). Situational analysis: Grounded theory mapping after the postmodern turn. *Symbolic Interaction, 26*(4), 553-576.

Clements, P., & Northrop, L. (2002). *Software Product Lines: Practices and Patterns.* (2nd ed.): Addition-Wesley.

Cockburn, A. (2001). *Writing effective use cases*. New York: Addison-Wesley.

Cohen, S. G., Stanley, J. J. L., Peterson, A. S., & Krut Jr., R. W. (1992). *Application of Feature-Oriented Domain Analysis to the Army Movement Control Domain* (CMU/SEI-91-TR-28). Pittsburgh, PA: Software Engineering Institute, Carnegie Mellon University.

Colajanni, M., & Yu, P. S. (1988). Analysis of task assignment policies in scalable distributed Web server systems. *IEEE Trans. on Parallel and Distributed Systems, 9*(6), 585-600.

Conklin, M. (2004, July 30). Do the rich get richer? The impact of power laws on open source development projects. In *Proceedings of the Open Source Conference (OSCON),* Portland, Oregon.

Conklin, M., Howison, J., & Crowston, K. (2005, May 17). Collaboration using OSSmole: A repository of FLOSS data and analyses. In *Proceedings of the Mining Software Repositories Workshop (MSR2005) of the 27th International Conference on Software Engineering (ICSE 2005),* St. Louis, Missouri,

Convective Weather Product Development Team (PDT), FAA Aviation Weather Research Program (2005): http://www.faa.gov/aua/awr/prodprog.htm

Conway, M. (1968). How do committees invent? *Datamation, 14*(4), 28–31.

Cousin, E., Ouvradou, G., Pucci, P., & Tardieu, S. (2002). *PicoLibre: A free collaborative platform to improve students' skills in software engineering.* In *Proceedings of the IEEE International Conference on Systems, Man and Cybernetics.*

Crowston, K., & Howison, J. (2003). The social structure of open source software development teams. In *Proceedings of the ICIS.*

Crowston, K., & Howison, J. (2004). The social structure of open source software development teams. *First Monday, 10*(2). Retrieved from http://firstmonday.org/issues/issue10_2/crowston/.

Crowston, K., Howison, J., & Annabi, H. (2006). Information systems success in free and open source software development: Theory and measures. *Software Process: Improvement and practice, 11*(2), 123148.

Crowston, K., Scozzi, B., & Buonocore, S. (2003). An explorative study of open source software development structure. In *Proceedings of the ECIS*, Naples, Italy.

Cunningham, W. (2002). Framework for Integrated Test. Retrieved November 26, 2002, from http://fit.c2.com

Curtis, B., Krasner, H., & Iscoe, N. (1998). A field study of the software design process for large systems. *Communications of the ACM, 31*(11), 1268-1287.

Cusumano, M. A., & Yoffie, D. B. (1999). Software development on Internet time. *IEEE Computer, 32*(10), 60-69.

Damiani, E., Grosky, W., & Khosla, R. (2003). Human-centered e-business. MA: *Kluwer Academic Publishers.*

Dandamudi, S. (2003). *Hierarchical scheduling in parallel and cluster systems*. Kluwer Academic Publishers.

Daniel Nurmi & Rich Wolski & John Brevik (2004), ModelBased Checkpoint Scheduling for Volatile Resource Environments, University of California Santa Barbara, Department of Computer Science, Technical Report, Santa Barbara.

Dantong Yu (2003), Divisible Load Scheduling for Grid Computing, Conference on Parallel and Distributed Computing and Systems (PDCS 2003).

De Clercq, J. (2002, October 1-3). Single sign-on architectures. In G.I. Davida, Y. Frankel, & O. Rees (Eds.), *Proceedings of the International Infrastructure Security Conference* (p. 4058), Bristol, United Kingdom. Lecture Notes in Computer Science 2437. Springer-Verlag.

Dell Inc. (2003). New Industry Data Shows Dell Continues to Lead in Serving Customers Through Internet Commerce. Retrieved March 14, 2005, from http://www1.us.dell.com/content/topics/global.aspx/corp/pressoffice/en/2003/2003_10_20_rr_002?c=us&l=en&s=corp

Desmedt, Y. (1988). Society and group oriented cryptography: A new concept. In *Proceedings of Advances in Cryptology (Crypto '87)* (pp. 120-127).

Desmedt, Y. (1994). Threshold cryptography. *European Trans. on Telecommunications, 5*(4), 449-457.

Desmedt, Y. (1997). Some recent research aspects of threshold cryptography. In *Information security* (pp. 158-173).

Desmedt, Y. G., & Frankel, Y. (1994). Homomorphic zero-knowledge threshold schemes over any finite abelian group. *SIAM Journal on Discrete Mathematics, 7*(4), 667-679.

Desmedt, Y., Di Crescenzo, G., & Burmester, M. (1994). Multiplicative nonabelian sharing schemes and their application to threshold cryptography. In *Proceedings of Advances in Cryptology (Asiacrypt '94)* (pp. 21-32).

Dicks, B., & Mason, B. (1998). Hypermedia and ethnography: Reflections on the construction of a research approach. *Sociological Research Online, 3*(3). Retrieved June 9, 2006, from http://www.socresonline.org.uk

Diffie, W., & Hellman, M. E. (1976). New directions in cryptography. *IEEE Transactions on Information Theory, 22*(6), 644-654.

Dinh-Trong, T.T., & Bieman, J.M. (2005). The FreeBSD project: A replication case study of open source development. *IEEE Transactions on Software Engineering, 31*(6), 481–494.

Dowdy, L., & Foster, D. (1982). Comparative models of the file assignment problem. *Computer Surveys, 14*(2), 287-313.

Drane, C. R., Macnaughtan, M., & Scott, C. (1998). Positioning GSM telephones. *IEEE Commun. Mag., 36*(4), 46-59.

Dridi, F., & Neumann, G. (1999, June). How to implement Web-based groupware systems based on WebDAV. In *Proceedings of the IEEE 8th International Workshops on Enabling Technologies: Infrastructure for Collaborative Enterprises.*

Droms, R. (1997). *Dynamic host configuration protocol.* Internet RFC 2131.

Dubinko, M. (2003). *XForms Essentials*: O'Reilly & Associates, Inc.

Dubinko, M., Leigh, L., Klotz, J., Merrick, R., & Raman, T. V. (2002). *XForms 1.0.* Available: http://www.w3.org/TR/xforms/.

Eastlake D. (2000). *DNS request and transaction signatures (SIG(0)s).* Internet RFC 2931

Eastlake, D. (1997). *Secure domain name system dynamic update.* Internet RFC 2137.

Eastlake, D. (1999a). *DNS security operational considerations.* Internet RFC 2541.

Eastlake, D. (1999b). *DSA KEYs and SIGs in the domain name system (DNS).* RFC 2536.

Eastlake, D. (1999c). *RSA/MD5 KEYs and SIGs in the domain name system (DNS).* Internet RFC 2537.

Eastlake, D. (2001). *RSA/SHA-1 SIGs and RSA KEYs in the domain name system (DNS).* IETF Internet RFC 3110.

Eckstein, R., Loy, M., & Wood, D. (1998). *Java Swing.* (1st. ed.). Sebastopol, CA: O'Reilly and Associates, Inc.

Eick, S., Loader, C., Long, M., Votta, L., & Vander Wiel, S. (1992). Estimating software fault content before coding. In *Proceedings of the 14th International Conference on Software Engineering* (pp. 59-65).

El-Gamal, Y., El-Abd, A. E., & Khader, O. H. S. (2003). Improving FSR protocol using the optimal performance operational parameters. In *ICCTA' International Conference on Computer Theory and Application,* (pp. 38-45).

El-Ghalayini, H., Odeh, M., McClatchey, R., & Solomonides, T. (2005). Reverse engineering domain ontology to conceptual data models. In *Proceedings of the 23ʳᵈ IASTED International Conference on Databases and Applications (DBA), Innsbruck, Austria* (pp. 222-227).

Elliott, M., & Scacchi, W. (2003, November). Free software developers as an occupational community: Resolving conflicts and fostering collaboration. In *Proceedings of the ACM International Conference on Supporting Group Work* (pp. 21-30), Sanibel Island, Florida.

Elliott, M., & Scacchi, W. (2004). Mobilization of software developers: The free software movement (Tech. Rep.). Retrieved June 16, 2006, from http://opensource. mit.edu/papers/elliottscacchi2.pdf

Elliott, M., & Scacchi, W. (2005). Free software development: Cooperation and conflict in a virtual organizational culture. In S. Koch (Ed.), *Free/open source software development* (pp. 152-172). Hershey, PA: Idea Group Publishing.

Engels, R. (1999) .Component-Based User Guidance in Knowledge Discovery and Data Mining. Volume 211 Dissertations in Artificial Intelligence-Infix, 1999

Erbas, F., Kyamakya, K., Steuer, J., & Jobmann, K. (2002). On the user profiles and the prediction of user movements in wireless networks. In *Proceedings of PIMRC 2002.*

Eriksson, H.-E., Penker, M., Lyons, B., & Fado, D. (2004). *UML 2 Toolkit*: Wiley Publishing, Inc.

Everitt, K., & Lederer, S. (2001). *A usability comparison of Sun StarOffice Writer 5.2 vs. Microsoft Word 2000.* Retrieved June 15, 2006, from http://www.sims.berkeley. edu/courses/is271/f01/projects/WordStar/

Evermann, J., & Wand, Y. (2001). Towards ontologically-based semantics for UML constructs. In H. S. Kunii, S. Jajodia, & A. Solvberg (Eds.), *Conceptual modeling—ER* (LNCS no. 2224) (pp. 341-354). Springer.

Ezeife, C. I., & Ohanekwu, T. E. (2005). The use of smart tokens in cleaning integrated warehouse data. *International Journal of Data Warehousing and Mining, 1*(2), 1-22.

F. Berman & H. Casanova (2005), "New Grid Scheduling and Rescheduling Methods in the GrADS Project", International Journal of Parallel Programming.

Fall, K., & Varadhaa, K. (2002). NS notes and documentation. *The V l N l Project.* University of California-Berkeley.

Fang, Z., Bensaou, B., & Wang, Y. (2002). Performance evaluation of a fair backoff algorithm for IEEE 802.11 DFWMAC. *International Symposium on Mobile Ad Hoc Networking & Computing,* (pp. 48–57).

Fayyad, U., Piatetsky-Shapiro, G., and Smyth, P. (1996). Knowledge Discovery and Data Mining: Towards a Unifying Framework. Proceedings of the Second International Conference on Knowledge Discovery and Data Mining (KDD-96). AAAI Press

Feitelson, D. (2005). *Parallel workloads archive.* Available from http://www.cs.huji.ac.il/labs/parallel/workload/

Feldman, S. (2000). The changing face of e-commerce. *IEEE Internet Computing, 4*(3), 82–84.

Fellbaum, C. (1998). *WordNet: An electronic lexical database.* MIT Press.

Feller, J., & Fitzgerald, B. (2001). *Understanding Open Source Software development.* Addison-Wesley.

Feng, L., Chang, E., & Dillon, T. (2002). A semantic network based design methodology for XML documents. *ACM TOIS, 20*(4), 390-421.

Fenton, N.E., & Pfleeger, S.L. (1997). *Software metrics: A rigorous and practical approach* (2nd ed.). PWS Publishing Company.

Filho, A. H., Prado, H. A., & Toscani, S. S. (2000). **Evolving a legacy data warehouse system to an object-oriented architecture.** SCCC, IEEE-CS (pp. 32-40).

Finkelstein, A.C.W., Gabbay, D., Hunter, A., & Nuseibeh, B. (1994). Inconsistency handling in multi-perspective specifications. *IEEE Transactions on Software Engineering, 20*(8), 569-578.

Finnigan, P. (2002). SQL Injection and Oracle. Retrieved Jan. 10,, 2005, from http://www.securityfocus. com/infocus/1644

Fisher, M. K., & Hochbaum, D. S. (1980). Database location in computer networks. *Journal ACM, 27*(10), 718-735.

Fonseca, F. and Martin, J. (2005). Learning the differences between ontologies and conceptual schemas through ontology-driven information Systems To appear in *a Journal of the Association of Information Systems Special Issue on Ontologies in the Context of Information Systems.* (fredfonseca@ist.psu.edu).

Foster, I. (2001). The anatomy of the grid: Enabling scalable virtual organizations. In *Proceedings of the 1st International Symposium on Cluster Computing and the Grid.* Retrieved from http://csdl2.computer.org/comp/ proceedings/ccgrid/2001/1010/00/10100006.pdfFoster, I., & Kesselman, C. (2004). *The grid: Blueprint for a new computing infrastructure.* Morgan Kaufmann.

Fowler, M. (2005). Refactoring Home Page. Retrieved May 20, 2005, from http://refactoring.com

Fowler, M., Beck, K., Brant, J., & Opdyke, W. (1999). *Refactoring: Improving the Design of Existing Code*: Addison-Wesley.

Frankel, Y., & Desmedt, Y. (1992). *Parallel reliable threshold multisignature* (Tech. Rep. Nos. TR–92–04–02). Milwaukee: University of Wisconsin–Milwaukee, Deptartment of EE & CS.

Frankel, Y., Gemmell, P., MacKenzie, P. D., & Yung, M. (1997). Proactive RSA. In *Advances in Cryptology (Crypto '97)* (pp. 440-454).

Frankel, Y., MacKenzie, P. D., & Yung, M. (1998). Robust efficient distributed RSA-key generation. In *Proceedings of the 30th Annual ACM Symposium on Theory of Computing* (pp. 663-672). Dallas, TX.

Franklin, M. J., & Zdonik, S. B. (1998). Data in your face: push technology in perspective, *ACM SIGMOD Conference on Management of Data,* Seattle, (pp. 29-34).

Freed, N. (1996). *Multipurpose Internet Mail Extensions (MIME) Part One: Format of Internet Message Bodies*: RFC 2045.

Freeman, C. (1977). A set of measures of centrality based on betweenness. *Sociometry, 40,* 35-41.

Frontier (2004), The Premier Internet Computing Platform, Whitepaper, http://www.parabon.com/clients/clientWhitePapers.jsp.

Fuggetta, A. (2003). Open source software: An evaluation. *Journal of Systems and Software, 66*(1), 77–90.

Galbraith, B., et al. (2002). *Professional Web services security.* Wrox Press.

Gamma, E., Helm, R., Johnson, R., & Vlissides, J. (1995). *Design Patterns* (1st ed.): Addison-Wesley Professional.

Gans, G., Jarke, M., Kethers, S., & Lakemeyer, G. (2003). Continuous requirements management for organisation networks: A (dis)trust-based approach. *Requirements Engineering, 8,* 4-22.

Gartner Inc. (2003). *Distributed computing chart of accounts.* Retrieved June 15, 2006, from http://www.gartner.com/4_decision_tools/modeling_tools/costcat.pdf

Garzotto, F., & Paolini, P. (1993). HDM: A model-based approach to hypertext application design. *ACM Transactions on Information Systems (TOIS), 11*(1), 1-26.

Gasser, L., Scacchi, W., Penne, B., & Sandusky, R. (2003, December). Understanding continuous design in OSS projects. In *Proceedings of the 16th International Conference on Software & Systems Engineering and their Applications,* Paris, France.

Gavish, B., & Sheng, O. R. L. (1990). Dynamic file migration in distributed computer systems. *Comm. of ACM, 33*(1), 177-189.

Gennaro, R., Jarecki, S., Krawczyk, H., & Rabin, T. (1996a). Robust and efficient sharing of RSA functions. In *Advances in Cryptology (Crypto '96)* (pp. 157-172).

Gennaro, R., Jarecki, S., Krawczyk, H., & Rabin, T. (1996b). Robust threshold DSS signatures. In *Advances in Cryptology (Eurocrypt '96)* (pp. 354-371).

Gennaro, R., Jarecki, S., Krawczyk, H., & Rabin, T. (2001). Robust threshold DSS signatures. *Information and Computation, 164*(1), 54-84.

Gennaro, R., Rabin, M. O., & Rabin, T. (1998). Simplified VSS and fast-track multiparty computations with applications to threshold cryptography. In *Proceedings of the 17th annual ACM symposium on Principles of Distributed Computing* (pp. 101-111).

Germán, D. (2004a). An empirical study of fine-grained software modifications. In *International Conference in Software Maintenance.*

Germán, D. (2004b). Decentralized open source global software development, the GNOME experience. *Journal of Software Process: Improvement and Practice, 8*(4), 201-215.

Germán, D.M., & Hindle, A. (2006). Visualizing the evolution of software using softChange. *Journal of Software Engineering and Knowledge Engineering, 16*(1), 5-21.

Ghosh, R.A., & Prakash, V.V. (2000). The Orbiten free software survey. *5*(7). Retrieved from http://www.orbiten.org/ofss/01.html

Gilboa, N. (1999). Two party RSA key generation. In *Advances in Cryptology (Crypto'99)* (pp. 116-129). Santa Barbara, CA:

Gîrba, T., Kuhn, A., Seeberger, M., & Ducasse, S. (2005). How developers drive software evolution. In *Proceedings of the International Workshop on Principles in Software Evolution* (pp. 113–122), Lisbon, Portugal.

Glaser, B., & Strauss, A. (1967). *The discovery of grounded theory: Strategies for qualitative research.* Chicago: Aldine Publishing Co.

Goble, C. A., Stevens, R., Ng, G., Bechhofer, S., Paton, N. W., Baker, P. G., Peim, M., & Brass, A. (2001). Transparent access to multiple bioinformatics information sources. *IBM System Journal, 40*(2), 532-551.

Godfrey, M.W., & Tu, Q. (2000). Evolution in open source software: A case study. In *Proceedings of the*

International Conference on Software Maintenance (pp. 131–142), San Jose, California

Gokhale, S. (2004). Software failure rate and reliability incorporating repair policies. In *Proceedings of the IEEE International Symposium on Software Metrics* (pp. 394-404).

Goland, Y., Whitehead, E., Faizi, A., & Jensen, D. (1999). HTTP extensions for distributed authoring. In *Proceedings of WEBDAV*. Retrieved June 16, 2006, from http://Webdav.org/

Gold, R. (2004a). HTTPUnit 1.6 API. Retrieved Jan. 10,, 2005, from http://httpunit.sourceforge.net/doc/api/

Gold, R. (2004b). HTTPUnit Home. Retrieved Jan. 10, , 2005, from http://httpunit.sourceforge.net/

Golfarelli, M., Rizzi, S., & Birdoljak, B. (1998). A conceptual design of data warehouses from E/R schema. *ACM HICSS* (pp. 334-344).

Golfarelli, M., Rizzi, S., & Birdoljak, B. (2001). Data warehousing from XML sources. *ACM DOLAP* (pp. 40-47), ACM Press.

Gomaa, H. (2004). *Designing Software Product Lines with UML : From Use Cases to Pattern-Based Software Architectures*: Addison-Wesley Professional.

Gomaa, H., & Gianturco, M. (2002). Domain Modeling for World Wide Web Based Software Product lines with UML. *IEEE ICSR-7, LNCS, 2319*, 78-92.

Gómez J., Cachero, C., & Pastor, O. (2000). Extending a conceptual modelling approach to Web application design. *CAiSE 2000*, 79-93.

Gómez J., Cachero, C., & Pastor, O. (2001). Conceptual modeling of device-independent Web applications. *IEEE Multimedia 8*(2), 20-32.

Gómez, J., & Cachero, C. (2003). OO-H Method: Extending UML to Model Web Interfaces, *Information Modeling for Internet Applications* (pp. 144-173). Hershey, PA, USA: Idea Group Publishing.

González-Barahona, J.M., López-Fernández, L., & Robles, G. (2004). Community structure of modules in the Apache project. In *Proceedings of the 4th Workshop on Open Source Software*.

Goodman, J., Albert G. Madras, N., & March, P. (1985). Stability of binary exponential backoff. *Journal of the ACM, 35*(3), 579–602.

Gopalkrishman, V., Li, Q., & Karlapalem, K. (1998). Issues of object relational view design in data warehousing environment. *SMC, IEEE* (pp. 2732-2737).

Grinter, R. E. (2003). Recomposition: Coordinating a web of software dependencies. *Computer Supported Cooperative Work, 12*(3), 297-327.

Grossman, J. (2004a). Insecure Web Sites. Retrieved May 20, 2005, from www.varbusiness.com/sections/news/dailyarchives.asp?articleid=48158

Grossman, J. (2004b). Thwarting SQL Web Hacks. Retrieved May 20, 2005, from www.varbusiness.com/showArticle.jhtml?articleID=18841325&flatPage=true

Gruber, T. (1995). Toward principles for the design of ontologies used for knowledge sharing. *International Journal of Human and Computer Studies, 43*(5/6), 907-928.

Guarino, N. (1998). *Formal ontology and information systems.* Amsterdam, Netherlands: IOS Press.

Guarino, N., & Welty, C. (2002). Evaluating ontological decisions with OntoClean. *Communications of the ACM, 45*(2), 61-65.

Guarino, N., & Welty, C. (2004). An overview of OntoClean. In S. Staab & R. Studer (Eds.), *Handbook on ontologies* (pp. 51-159). Springer Verlag.

Guimera, R., Danon, L., Diaz-Guilera, A., Giralt, F., & Arenas, A. (2003). Self-similar community structure in a network of human interactions. *Physical Review E 68, 065103(R)*.

Guizzardi, G., Wagner, G., Guarino, N., & Sinderen, M. (2004). An ontologically well-founded profile for UML conceptual models. In *Proceeding of the 16th Conference on Advanced Information Systems Engineering- CAiSE04* (pp. 112-126).

Gupta, A., & Mumick, S. I. (1995). Maintenance of materialized views: Problems, techniques, and applications. *IEEE Data Eng. Bul, 18*(2), 3-18.

Haas, Z. J. (1997). A new routing protocol for the reconfigurable wireless networks. In *Proceedings of IEEE ICUPC'97* (pp. 562-566). San Diego

Haas, Z. J., & Pearlman, M. R. (2000). Determining the optimal configuration for the zone routing protocol. *IEEE Journal on Selected Areas in Communications,* 1395-1414.

Hammer, J., Garcia-Molina, H., Widom, J., Labio, W., & Zhuge, Y. (1995). The Stanford data warehousing project. *IEEE Data Engineering Bulletin* (pp. 41- 48).

Hastad, J., Leighton, T., & Rogoff, B. (1987). Analysis of backoff protocols for multiple access channels. In *Proceedings of the Nineteenth Annual ACM Conference on Theory of Computing* (pp. 241-253).

Healy, K., & Schussman, A. (2003). *The ecology of open-source software development.* (Tech. Rep.). University of Arizona.

Heddaya, A., & Mirdad, S. (1997). Web wave: Globally load balanced fully distributed caching of hot published documents. In *Proceedings of the 17th IEEE International Conference on Distributed Computing Systems,* (pp. 160-168).

Hellebrandt, M., & Mathar, R. (1999). Location tracking of mobiles in cellular radio networks. *IEEE Trans. On Vehicular Technology, 48*(5).

Hellebrandt, M., Mathar, R., & Scheibenbogen, M. (1997). Estimating position and velocity of mobiles in a cellular radio network. *IEEE Trans. On Vehicular Technology, 46*(1).

Hennicker, R., & Koch, N. (2001). *Modeling the User Interface of Web Applications with UML.* Paper presented at the In Practical UML-Based Rigorous Development Methods - Countering or Integrating the eXtremists, Workshop of the pUML-Group at the UML 2001, Gesellschaft für Informatik, Köllen Druck+Verlag.

Hernandez-Bermejo, B. (1998). Universality of the Generalized Lotka-Volterra equation. *CATHODE 2.*

Hightower, R., & Lesiecki, N. (2002). *Java tools for extreme programming: mastering open source tools including Ant, JUnit, and Cactus* New York: John Wiley & Sons

Hine, C. (2000). *Virtual ethnography.* Newbury Park, CA: Sage Publications.

Hischheim, R., Klein, H., & Lyytinen, K. (1995). *Information systems development and data modelling: Conceptual and philosophical foundations.* Cambridge: Cambridge University Press.

Hofmann-Wallehnhof, B., Lichtenegger, H., & Collins, J. (1997). *Global positioning system: Theory and practice.* New York: Springer-Verlag.

Holling, C. S. (1959). The components of predation as revealed by a study of small mammal predation of the European pine sawfly. *Canadian Entomology, 91,* 293-320.

Holly Dail & Henri Casanova & Fran Berman (2002), A Decoupled Scheduling Approach for the GrADS Program Development Environment, IEEE/ACM SC2002 Conference.

Hotovy, S. (1996). Analysis of the early workload on the Cornell theory. *ACM SIGMETRICS, 272-273.*

Howison, J., & Crowston, K. (2004). The perils and pitfalls of mining sourceforge. In *Proceedings of the Mining Software Repositories Workshop at the International Conference on Software Engineering (ICSE 2004),* Edinburgh, Scotland.

Httperf. citeseer.nj.nec.com/mosberger98httperf.html.

HttpUnit. http://httpunit.sourceforge.net.

Huang, S. M., & Su, C. H. (2001). The development of an XML-based data warehouse system. *ACM DOLAP* (pp. 206-212), *ACM Press.*

Huang, Y., Rine, D., & Wang, X. (2001). A JCA-based implementation framework for threshold cryptography. In *Proceedings of the 17th Annual Computer Security Applications Conference* (pp. 85-91). New Orleans, LA: IEEE Computer Society Press.

Hummer, W., Bauer, A., & Harde, G. (2003). XCube—XML for data warehouses. *ACM DOLAP* (pp. 33-44).

Huynh, N., Mangisengi, O., & Tjoa, A. M. (2000). Metadata for object relational data warehouse. *DMDW, CEUR-WS* (pp. 3-1-3-9).

Iansiti, M., & MacCormack, A. (1997). Developing Products on Internet Time. *Harvard Business Review, 75*(5), 108-117.

IEEE, ANSI/IEEE Standard 802.11. (1999). *Edition (R2003), Part 11: Wireless LAN medium access control (MAC) and physical layer (PHY) specifications* (pp. 138-153)

ISECOM. (2003). OSSTMM 2.1 - The Open Source Security Testing Methodology Manual. Retrieved May 20, 2005, from http://www.isecom.org/osstmm/

ITU. (1994). *Information technology – abstract syntax notation one (ASN.1) – specification of basic notation* (ITU–Telecommunication Standardization Sector, Recommendation X.680).

Jacobsen, I., Booch, G., & Rumbaugh, J. (2000). The Unified Software Development Process. Addison-Wesley.

Jacobson, I., Christerson, M., Jonsson, P., & Overgaard, G. (1992). *Object-Oriented Software Engineering: a Use Case Driven Approach.* Reading, MA: Addison-Wesley.

Jacobson, I., Griss, M., & Jonsson, P. (1997). *Software Reuse: Architecture, Process, and Organization for Business Success.* Reading, MA: Addison-Wesley Longman.

James Frey (2001), Condor-G: A Computation Management Agent for Multi-Institutional Grids, IEEE.

Jang-uk In & Paul Avery (2004), "Policy Based Scheduling for Simple Quality of Service in Grid Computing", 18th International Parallel and Distributed Processing Symposium (IPDPS 2004), Santa Fe, New Mexico, USA. IEEE Computer Society.

Java Open Single Sign-On Project. (2005). Retrieved June 16, 2006, from http://www.josso.org

Jayaputera, J., & Taniar, D. (2005). Data retrieval for location-dependent queries in a multi-cell wireless environment. *Mobile Information Systems, 1*(2), 91-108.

JBoss, Open Source Application Server. (2003). Retrieved June 16, 2006, from http://www.jboss.org

Jensen, C., & Scacchi, W. (2005a, January). Collaboration, leadership, control, and conflict management in the NetBeans.org community. In *Proceedings of the 38th Hawaii International Conference on Systems Science,* Waikola Village, Hawaii.

Jensen, C., & Scacchi, W. (2005b, July-September). Process modeling across the Web information infrastructure. *Software Process--Improvement and Practice, 10*(3), 255-272.

Jensen, M., Moller, T., & Pedersen, T. (2001). Specifying OLAP cubes on XML data. *SSDBM, IEEE* (pp. 101-112).

Jonny Axelsson, Beth Epperson, Masayasu Ishikawa, Shane McCarron, Ann Navarro, & Steven Pemberton (Eds.). (2003). *XHTML™ 2.0. W3C Working Draft 6 May 2003.*

Kaliski, B. S., Jr. (1998). Emerging standards for public-key cryptography. In *Lectures on Data Security* (pp. 87-104). Springer.

Kalpakis, K, Dasgupta, K., & Wolfson, O. (2001). Optimal placement of replicas in trees with read write and storage costs. *IEEE Trans. on Parallel and Distributed Systems, 12*(6), 628-637.

Kang, S., Song, M., Park, K., & Hwang, C. (2005). Semantic prefetching strategy to manage location dependent data in mobile information systems. *Mobile Information Systems, 1*(3), 149-166.

Kangasharju, J., Roberts, J., & Ross, K. W. (2002). Object replication strategies in content distribution networks. *Computer Communications, 25*(4), 367-383.

Kaplan, E. D. (1996). *Understanding GPS: Principles and applications.* Artech House Inc.

Kaplan, E. D. (1996). *Understanding the GPS: Principles and applications.* Boston: Artech House.

Karlsson, M., & Karamanolis, C. (2004). Choosing replica placement heuristics for wide-area systems. *International Conference on Distributed Computing Systems (ICDCS) 2004.* Retrieved from http://www.hpl.hp.com/personal/Magnus_Karlsson

Karn, P. (1990). MACA—A new channel access method for packet radio. *ARRL/CRRL Amateur Radio 9th Computer Networking Conference,*(pp. 134–140).

Khare, R. (2000). Can XForm Transform the Web? Transcending the Web as GUI, Part II. *IEEE Internet Computing*(March-April), 103-106.

Kim, W., Park, S., Yong, H., Chae, K., Cho, D., Choi, B., Jeong, A., Kim, M., Lee, K., Lee, M., & Lee, S. (2002). The Chamois Component-Based Knowledge Engineering Framework. IEEE Computer, Vol 35, No 5, pp 44-52

Kimball, R. (1996). The Data warehouse Toolkit: Practical Techniques to Building Dimension Data Warehouses. New York: John Wiley

Kimball, R., Reeves, L., & Ross, M. (1998). The Data Warehouse Lifecycle Toolkit. New York: John Wiley

Kirda, E., Jazayeri, M., Kerer, C., & Schranz, M. (2001). Experiences in engineering flexible Web services. *IEEE Multimedia, 8*(1), 58 - 65.

Kitchenham, B.A., Dyba, T., & Jorgensen, M. (2004). Evidence-based software engineering. In *Proceedings of the 26th International Conference on Software Engineering* (pp. 273-281), Edinburgh, Scotland. IEEE Computer Society.

Kleinrock, L., & Stevens, K. (1971). *Fisheye: A lenslike computer display Transformation* (Tech. Rep.) UCLA, Computer Science Department.

Knapp, A., Koch, N., Moser, F., & Zhang, G. (2001). *ArgoUWE: A CASE Tool for Web applications.* Retrieved from http://www.pst.informatik.uni-muenchen.de/~kochn

Koc, C. K. (1994). *High-speed RSA implementation* (Tech. Rep.). RSA Laboratories.

Koch, N., & Kraus, A. (2002). The expressive power of UML-based Web engineering. In

Koch, S., & Schneider, G. (2002). Effort, cooperation and coordination in an open source software project: GNOME. *Information Systems Journal, 12*(1), 27–42.

Kovacevic, S. (June 1998). *UML and User Interface Modeling.* Paper presented at the UML'98, Mulhouse, France.

Krishnamurthy, S. (2002). Cave or community? An empirical examination of 100 mature open source projects. *First Monday, 7*(6). Retrieved from http://www.firstmonday.org/issues/issue7_6/krishnamurthy/

Krishnamurthy, S. (2002). Cave or community? An empirical investigation of 100 mature open source projects. *First Monday, 7*(6).

Kumar, R., Raghavan, P., Rajagopalan, S., & Tomkins, A. (2002). The Web and social networks. *IEEE Computer, 35*(11), 32–36.

Kwan, T. T., Mcgrath, R. E., & Reed, D. E. (1995). NCSA's World Wide Web server: Design and performance. *IEEE Computer, 28*(11), 68-74.

Kyamakya, K. et al. (2002). A navigation system using Cell-ID-based positioning and signal strength-based movement detection in cellular systems. *International Conference on Wireless Networks (ICWN 2002)*, Las Vegas.

Landeshauptstadt München. (2003). *Clientstudie der Landeshauptstadt München.* Retrieved June 15, 2006, from http://www.muenchen.de/aktuell/clientstudie_kurz.pdf

Langford, S. K. (1995). Threshold DSS signatures without a trusted party. In *Proceedings of Advances in Cryptology (Crypto '95)* (pp. 397-409).

Latora, V., & Marchiori, M. (2003). Economic small-world behavior in weighted networks. *Euro Physics Journal, B32*, 249-263.

Laurie, B., Sisson, G., Arends, R., & Blacka, D. (2006). *DNSSEC hashed authenticated denial of existence.* Retrieved from IETF Internet-Draft draft-ietf-dnsext-nsec3-08

Lee, D. L., Zhu, M., & Hu, H. (2005). When location-based services meet databases. *Mobile Information Systems, 1*(2), 81-90.

Lee, S.-W. (2004). *Proxy viewpoints model-based requirements discovery.* Unpublished doctoral, George Mason University, Fairfax, VA. U.S.A.

Leite, J.C.S.P., & Freeman, P.A. (1991). Requirements validation through viewpoint resolution. *IEEE Transactions on Software Engineering, 17*(12), 1253-1269.

Lenzerini, M. (2002). Data Integration: A Theoretical Perspective. *ACM PODS*, 233-246.

Li, B. (1999). Content replication in a distributed and controlled environment. *Journal of Parallel and Distributed Computing, 59*(2), 229-251.

Li, Q. Z., & Moon, B. (2001). Distributed cooperative Apache web server. In *Proceedings of the 10th International World Wide Web Conference, Hong Kong* (pp. 555-564).

Li, S., Liu, M., Wang, G., & Peng, Z. (2004). Capturing semantic hierarchies to perform meaningful integration in HTML tables. *APWeb, LNCS 3007* (pp. 899-902).

Li, X. (2005). Using UML in conceptual modelling: Towards an ontological xore. In *Proceeding of the 17th Conference on Advanced Information Systems Engineering-CAiSE05* (pp. 13-17).

Liberty Alliance Project. (2004). Retrieved June 16, 2006, from http://www.projectliberty.org/

Lie, H. W., & Bos, B. (1999). *Cascading Style Sheets, level 1* (11 Jan 1999). Available: http://www.w3.org/TR/REC-CSS1 [2003, June 28, 2003].

Lilly, S. (2000). *How to Avoid Use-Case Pitfalls.* Available: http://www.sdmagazine.com/print/ [2005, April 9, 2005].

Linn, J. (1993). *Privacy Enhancement for Internet Electronic Mail: Part I: Message Encryption and Authentication Procedures*: RFC 1421.

Liu, C. (1999). *Securing an Internet name server.* Retrieved from http://www.acmebw.com/papers/securing.pdf

Liu, T., Bahl, P., & Chlmtac, I. (1998). Mobility modeling, location tracking, and trajectory prediction in wireless ATM networks. *IEEE JSAC, 16*(6), 922-36.

Loikopoulos, T., & Ahmed, I. (2000). Static and dynamic data replication algorithms for fast information access in large distributed systems. In *Proceedings of the 20th IEEE Conference on Distributed Computing Systems, Taipei*, (pp. 385-392).

Loney, K., & Koch, G. (2000). *Oracle 9i: The complete reference.* Osborne McGraw-Hill.

Lopez, L., Gonzalez-Barahona, J.M., & Robles, G. (2004). Applying social network analysis to the information in cvs repositories. In *Proceedings of the International Workshop on Mining Software Repositories, 26th International Conference on Software Engineering*, Edinburg, Scotland.

Lotka, A. J. (1925). *Elements of physical biology.* Baltimore: Williams & Wilkins.

LTTR (2000). *Long term technology review of the science & engineering base*. Available from http://www.rcuk.ac.uk/lttr/

Lynch, C. L. (1999). *A Methodological Framework For Interface Requirements Identification and Specification*. Unpublished Doctoral, George Mason University, Fairfax, VA, U.S.A.

Lyu, M. R. (1996). Software reliability modeling survey. In M. R. Lyu (Ed.),, *Handbook of software reliability engineering* (pp. 71-117). McGraw-Hill.

MacKenzie, P., & Reiter, M. (2001). Two-party generation of DSA signatures (Extended abstract). In *Proceedings of Advance in Cryptology (Eurocrypt 2001)* (pp. 137-154).

Madey, G., Freeh, V., & Tynan, R. (2002). The open source development phenomenon: An analysis based on social network theory. In *Proceedings of the Americas Conference on Information Systems (AMCIS2002)* (pp. 1806–1813), Dallas, Texas.

Mahmood, A. (2005a). Object grouping and replication algorithms for World Wide Web. *Informatica, 28*(3), 347-356.

Mahmood, A. (2005b). Object replication algorithms for World Wide Web. *Computing and Informatics, 24,* 371-390.

Mahmoud, Q. (2002). MobiAgent: An Agent-based Approach to the Wireless Internet. Journal of Internet Computing, special issue on Wireless Internet, pp. 156.162.

Manaseer, S., & Ould-Khaoua, M. (2005). A new backoff algorithm for MAC protocol in MANETs. *21ˢᵗ Annual UK Performance Engineering Workshop,* (pp. 159-164).

Marcus, A. (2002). Dare We Define User-Interface Design? *Interactions, 9*(5), 19–24.

McNamara, J. (1994). Logic and cognition. In J. McNamara & G. Reyes (Eds.), *The logical foundations of cognition* (Vo. 4) (pp.). Vancouver Studies in Cognitive Science.

Melton, J. (2003). Information technology—database languages—SQL—Part 14: XML-related specifications (SQL/XML). *ISO/IEC* (pp. 9075-14).

Meyer, E. A. (2000). *Cascading Style Sheets: The Definitive Guide*. USA: O'Reilly & Associates, Inc.

Meyer, E. A. (2003). *Eric Meyer on CSS: Mastering the Language of Web Design* (2nd ed.): New Riders Publishing.

Meyer, E. A. (May 2000). *Cascading Style Sheets: The Definitive Guide*: O'Reilly

Mi, P., & Scacchi, W. (1996). A meta-model for formulating knowledge-based models of software development. *Decision Support Systems, 17*(4), 313-330.

Microsoft Corporation. (2004). Microsoft Security Bulletin MS04-028. Retrieved January 10, 2005, from http://www.microsoft.com/technet/security/bulletin/MS04-028.mspx

Miller, J. (1999). Estimating the number of remaining defects after software inspection, *Journal of Software Testing, Verification and Reliability, 9,* 167-189.

Miller, J. (2002). On the independence of software inspectors. *Journal of Systems and Software, 60*(1), 5-10.

Miller, L. L., Honavar, V., Wong, J., & Nilakanta, S. (1998). Object-oriented data warehouse for information fusion from heterogeneous distributed data and knowledge sources. *IT, IEEE* **(pp. 27-30).**

Miyazaki, S., Sakurai, K., & Yung, M. (1999). On threshold RSA-signing with no dealer. In *Proceedings of the Second International Conference on Information Security and Cryptology (ICISC99)* (pp. 197-207). Seoul, Korea: Springer.

Mockapetris, P. (1987a). *Domain names—Concepts and facilities*. Internet RFC 1034.

Mockapetris, P. (1987b). *Domain names—Implementation and specification*. Internet RFC 1035.

Mockapetris, P. V., & Dunlap, K. J. (1995). Development of the domain name system. *ACM SIGCOMM Computer Communication Review, 25*(1), 112-122.

Mockapetris, P., & Dunlap, K. (1986). Implementation of the domain name system. In *Proceedings of the ACM SIGOPS European Workshop on Making Distributed Systems Work* (pp. 1-2). Amsterdam, The Netherlands:

Mockapetris, P., & Dunlap, K. J. (1988). Development of the domain name system. *ACM SIGCOMM Computer Communication Review, 18*(4), 123-133.

Mockus, A., Fielding, R.T., & Herbsleb, J.D. (2002). Two case studies of open source software development: Apache and Mozilla. *ACM Transactions on Software Engineering Methodology, 11*(3), 309-346.

Mockus, A., Fielding, R.T., & Herbsleb, J.D. (2002). Two case studies of open source software development: Apache and Mozilla. *ACM Transactions on Software Engineering and Methodology, 11*(3), 309–346.

Mohamah, S., Rahayu, W., & Dillon, T. (2001). Object relational star schemas. *IASTED, PDCS*.

Monk, A., & Howard, S. (1998, March-April). The rich picture: A tool for reasoning about work context. *Interactions, 5*(2), 21-30.

Morisio, M., & Oivo, M. (2003). Guest Editors Introduction: Software Engineering for the Wireless Internet. IEEE

Motorola Application Certification Program. http://qpqa.com/motorola/iden.

Murthy, S., & Garcia-Luna Aceves, J. J. (1996). An efficient routing protocol for wireless networks. *ACM/Baltzer Mobile Networks and Applications, 1*(2), 183-197.

Mustafa Sanver & Sathya Priya Durairaju & Ajay Gupta (2004), "Should one incorporate Mobile-ware in Parallel and Distributed Computation?", 10th International Conference on High Performance Computing (HiPC 2003), Hyderabad, India.

Myers, B. A. (1989). User-Interface Tools: Introduction and Survey. *IEEE Interface Systems*(January 1989), 15-23.

Mylopoulos, J. (1998). Information modeling in the time of the revolution. *Information Systems, 23*(3/4), 127-155.

Nabrzyski, J., Schopf, J., & Weglarz, J. (2004). *Grid resource management: State of the art and future trends*. Kluwer Academic Publishers.

Nadeem, T., & Agrawala, A. (2004). IEEE 802.11 DCF enhancements for noisy environments. *The 15th IEEE international Symposium on Personal, Indoor, and Mobile Radio Communications (PIMRC'04), Barcelona*.

Narayanan, N.H., & Hegarty, M. (2002). Multimedia design for communication of dynamic information. *International Journal on Human-Computer Studies, 57*, 279-315.

Nassis, V., Rahayu, W., Rajugan, R., & Dillon, T. (2004). Conceptual design of XML document warehouses. *DaWak, Springer* (pp. 1- 14).

Nassis, V., Rajagopalapillai, R., Dillon, T. S., & Rahayu, W. (2005). Conceptual and systematic design approach for XML document warehouses. *International Journal of Data Warehousing and Mining, 1*(3), 63-87.

National Weather Service METAR/TAF Information (2005): http://205.156.54.206/oso/oso1/oso12/faq.htm

Navrati Saxena & Kalyan Basu & Sajal K. Das & Christina M. Pinotti (2005), "A Dynamic Hybrid Scheduling Algorithm with Clients' Departure for Impatient Clients in Heterogeneous Environments" , 19th IEEE International Parallel and Distributed Processing Symposium (IPDPS'05), April - Rhodes Island, Greece.

Navrati Saxena (2005), New Hybrid Scheduling Framework for Asymmetric Wireless Environments with Request Repetition , Third International Symposium on Modeling and Optimization in Mobile, Ad Hoc, and Wireless Networks.

Nazeri, Z. & Jianping Z. (2002). Mining Aviation Data to Understand the Impacts of Severe Weather on Airspace System Performance. Proceedings of the International Conference on Information Technology:Coding and Computing (ITCC'02). IEEE Press

Netcraft Survey. (2005). Retrieved June 15, 2006, from http://news.netcraft.com/archives/web_server_survey.html

Netz, A., S. Chaudhuri, Fayyad, U. & Bernhardt, J. (2001). Integrating Data Mining with SQL Databases: OLE DB for Data Mining. Proceedings of the International Conference on Data Engineering (ICDE 2001). Heidelberg. Germany 2001

Newman, M.E.J. (2001a). Scientific collaboration networks: I. Network construction and fundamental results. *Physical Review, E64, 016131.*

Newman, M.E.J. (2001b). Scientific collaboration networks: Ii. Shortest paths, weighted networks, and centrality. *Physical Review, E64, 016132.*

Newsforge. (2002). *Largo loves Linux more than ever.* Retrieved June 15, 2006, from http://www.newsforge.com/print.pl?sid=02/12/04/2346215

Nichols, D.M., & Twidale, M.B. (2003, January). The usability of Open Source software. *First Monday, 8*(1). Retrieved June 15, 2006 from http://www.firstmonday.org/issues/issue8_1/nichols/

Nikkanen, M. (2004). User-centered development of a browser-agnostic mobile e-mail application. Proceedings of the third Nordic conference on Human-computer interaction, Tampere, Finland, pp. 53-56.

NIST. (2000). *Digital signature standard (DSS)*. FIPS 186–2.

NIST. (2002). *Secure hash standard (SHS)*. FIPS 180–2.

Nodine, M., J. Fowler, Ksiezyk, T., Perry, B., Taylor, M. & Unruh, A. (1998). Active Information Gathering in InfoSleuth. International Journal of Cooperative Information Systems 9:1/2, 3-28

Noll, J., & Scacchi, W. (2001). Specifying process-oriented hypertext for organizational computing. *Journal of Network & Computer Applications, 24*(1), 39-61.

Noy, N.F., Sintek, M., Decker, S., Crubezy, M., Fergerson, R.W., & Musen, M.A. (2001, March-April). Creating semantic Web contents with Protégé-2000. *IEEE Intelligent Systems, 16*(2), 60-71.

Nummenmaa, J., Niemi, T., Niinimäki, M., & Thanisch, P. (2002). Constructing an OLAP cube on XML Data. *ACM DOLAP* (pp. 22-27).

Nunes, N. J. (2003). Representing User-Interface Patterns in UML. *Lecture Notes in Computer Science,, 2817,* 142 - 151.

Nuseibeh, B., & Easterbrook, S. (2000). Requirements engineering: A roadmap. In A. Finkelstein (Ed.), *The future of software engineering.* ACM and IEEE Computer Society Press.

Ocampo, A., Boggio, D., Munch, J., & Palladino, G. (2003): Towards a Reference Process for Developing Wireless Internet Services. IEEE Transactions on Software Engineering, Vol. 29, No. 12, pp. 1122 – 1134.

Odlyzko, A. (2003). Internet traffic growth: Sources and implications. *Proceedings of the SPIE, 5247,* 1-15. Retrieved from http://www.dtc.umn.edu/~odlyzko/doc/itcom.internet.growth.pdf

Offutt, J. (2002). Quality attributes of Web software applications. *IEEE Software, 19*(2), 25 - 32.

Offutt, J. (2002). Quality attributes of Web software applications [Special Issue on software engineering of Internet software]. *IEEE Software, 19*(2), 25-32.

Offutt, J., Wu, Y., Du, X., & Huang, H. (2004). *Bypass Testing of Web Applications.* Paper presented at the The Fifteenth IEEE International Symposium on Software Reliability Engineering, Saint-Malo, Bretagne, France.

OMG. (2002). *Meta Object Facility (MOF) Version 1.4.* Available: http://www.omg.org/technology/documents/formal/mof.htm.

OMG. (2003a). *UML 2.0 OCL Specification, ptc/03-10-14*: Object Management Group.

OMG. (2003b). *Unified Modeling Language: Infrastructure, version 2.0 (3rd revised submission to OMG RFP ad/00-09-01)*: Object Management Group.

OMG. (2004). *Unified Modeling Language: Superstructure, version 2.0. ptc/04-10-02.*

Opdyke, W. F. (1992). *Refactoring object-oriented frameworks.* University of Illinois at Urbana-Champaign.

Open Mobile Alliance. http://www.wapforum.org.

Open Source Technology Group. (2005a). JUnit. Retrieved Dec. 2, 2005

Open Source Technology Group. (2005b). PhpUnit. Retrieved Dec. 2, 2005, from http://sourceforge.net/projects/phpunit/

Order 7210.3S, Facility Operation and Administration, Chapter 5 (Traffic Flow Management) (2003): http://www.faa.gov/atpubs/FAC/Ch17/chp17toc.htm

Ormerod, P. (1994). *The death of economics.* London: Faber and Faber Limited.

Östergren, M., & Juhlin, O. (2005). Road talk: A roadside location-dependent audio message system for car drivers. *Journal of Mobile Multimedia, 1*(1), 047-061.

Oza, M., Nistor, E., Hu, S. Jensen, C., & Scacchi, W. (2004, February). A first look at the Netbeans requirements and release process. Retrieved June 9, 2006, from *http://www.ics.uci.edu/cjensen/papers/FirstLookNetBeans/*

Pancur, M., Ciglaric, M., Trampus, M., & Vidmar, T. (2003). *Towards empirical evaluation of test-driven development in a university environment.* Paper presented at the EUROCON 2003. Computer as a Tool. The IEEE Region 8.

Pardede, E., Rahayu, J. W., & Taniar, D. (2004). On using collection for aggregation and association relationships in XML object relational storage. *ACM SAC* (pp. 703-710).

Pardede, E., Rahayu, J. W., & Taniar, D. (2005). Preserving conceptual constraints during XML updates. *International Journal of Web Information Systems, 1*(2).

Park, V. D., & Corson, M. S. (1997). A highly adaptive distributed routing algorithm for mobile wireless net works. In *Proceedings of IEEE INFOCOM'97* (pp. 1405-1413). Japan: Kobe.

Pashalidis, A., & Mitchell, C.J. (2003). A taxonomy of single sign-on systems. In *Proceedings of ACISP 2003* (pp. 249-264). LNCS 2727.

Pathirana, P. N., Svkin, A. V., & Jha, S. (2004). Location estimation and trajectory prediction for cellular networks with mobile base stations. *IEEE Transactions of Vehicular Technology, 53*(6), 1903-1913.

Pedro A. Szekely, Piyawadee Noi Sukaviriya, Pablo Castells, Jeyakumar Muthukumarasamy, & Salcher, E.

(1996). *Declarative Interface Models for User Interface Construction Tools: the MASTERMIND Approach*. Paper presented at the In Engineering for Human-Computer Interaction, Chapman & Hall, London, UK.

Pekalski, A., & Stauffer, D. (1998). Three species Lotka-Volterra model. *International Journal of Modern Physics C, 9*(5), 777-783.

Perkins, C. E., & Bhagwat, P. (1994). Highly dynamic destination sequenced distance vector routing (DSDV) for mobile computers. *Proceedings of ACM SIGCOMM'94, London, UK,* (pp. 234-244).

Perkins, C. E., & Royer, E. M. (1999). Ad hoc on-demand distance vector routing. In *Proceedings of IEEE WMCSA'99* New Orleans, LA (pp. 90-100).

Perkowitz, M., & Etzioni, O. (1998). Adaptive web sites: Automatically synthesizing web pages. In *Proceedings of the AAAI'98,* 722-732.

Peter Gradwell (2003) ,Overview of Grid Scheduling Systems, Located at http://www.peter.me.uk/phd/writings/computing-economy-review.pdf

Phillips, C., Kemp, E., & Kek, S. M. (2001). Extending UML Use Case Modelling to Support Graphical User Interface Design. *Proceedings of Software Engineering Conference,* 48 – 57.

PKI. (2004). *Generalitat Valenciana*. Retrieved from http://pki.gva.es

Postel, J. (1994). *Domain name system structure and delegation*. Internet RFC 1591.

Powell, T. (2003). *HTML & XHTML: The Complete Reference* (4th ed.): McGraw-Hill/Osborne.

Pressman, R. S. (2004). 15 Product Metrics for Software, *Software Engineering: A Practitioner's Approach* (6th ed.): McGraw-Hill.

Pressman, R.S. (2005). Software Engineering: A Practitioner's Approach. Sixth Edition, McGraw Hill.

Proceedings of the Second IWWOST, CYTED. (pp. 105-119).

PROVE. (2003). Retrieved from http://www.copitial.org

Public-Key Infrastructure (X.509), The Internet Engineering Task Force. (2003). Retrieved June 16, 2006, from http://www.ietf.org/ html.charters/pkix-charter.html

Quisquater, J.-J., & Couvreur, C. (1982). Fast decipherment algorithm for RSA public-key cryptosystem. *Electronic Letters, 18*(21), 905-907.

Rabin, T. (1998). A simplified approach to threshold and proactive RSA. In *Proceedings of Advances in Cryptology (Crypto'98)* (pp. 89-104).

Radoslavov, P., Govindan, R., & Estrin, D. (2001). Topology informed internet replica placement. *Proceedings of the 6th International Workshop on Web Caching and Content Distribution, Boston,* Retrieved from http://www.cs.bu.edu/techreports/2001-017-wcw01-proceedings

Raggett, D., Hors, L. E., & Jacobs, I. (1999). *HTML 4.01 Specification*. Available: http://www.w3.org/TR/REC-html40/.

Rahayu, J. W. (1999). *Object relational transformation*. PhD Thesis of Computer Science and Computer Engineering, La Trobe University, Melbourne.

Rahayu, J. W., Chang, E., Dillon, T. S., & Taniar, D. (2000). A methodology of transforming inheritance relationships in an object-oriented conceptual model to relational tables. *Information Software Technology 42, Elsevier Science,* 571-592. Intelligent Data Engineering and Automated Learning, Lecture Notes in Computer Science, vol. 3177, Springer-Verlag, 293-299.

Rajkumar Buyya & Manzur Murshed (2002), GridSim: a toolkit for the modeling and simulation of distributed resource management and scheduling for Grid computing, The Computing Research Repository (CoRR).

Rajkumar Buyya & David Abramson & Jonathan Giddy (2002), Economic Models for Resource Management and Scheduling in Grid Computing, The Journal of Concurrency and Computation: Practice and Experience (CCPE).

Rajkumar Buyya & Manzur Murshed & and David Abramson (2003), A Deadline and Budget Constrained Cost-Time Optimization Algorithm for Scheduling Task Farming Applications on Global Grids, The Computing Research Repository (CoRR).

Ramesh, B., Pries-Heje, J., & Baskerville, R. (2002). Internet Software Engineering: A Different Class of Processes. *Annals of Software Engineering, 14*(1 - 4), 169.

Rao, R. (2003, November). From unstructured data to actionable intelligence. *IT Pro,* pp. 29-35.

Raymond, E.S. (1997). The cathedral and the bazar. *First Monday, 3*(3).

Ricca, F., & Tonella, P. (2001). Analysis and testing of Web applications. *Proceedings of the 23rd International Conference on Software Engineering (ICSE 2001)* (pp. 25-34).

Riska, A., Sun, W., Smilui, E., & Claulu, O. (2002) ADATPTLOAD: Effective load balancing in clustered web servers under transient load conditions. *Proceedings of the 22nd International Conference on Distributed Systems, Austria*, (pp. 89-97).

Rivest, R., Shamir, A., & Adleman, L. (1978). A method for obtaining digital signature and public key cryptosystems. *Communications of the ACM, 21*(2), 120-126.

Robert Frances Group. (2002). *Total cost of ownership for Linux Web servers in the enterprise.* Retrieved June 15, 2006, from http://www.rfgonline.com/subsforum/LinuxTCO.pdf

Robles, G. (2005, May 17). Developer identification methods for integrated data from various sources. In *Proceedings of the International Workshop on Mining Software Repositories (MSR2005) of the 27th International Conference on Software Engineering (ICSE2005)*, St. Louis, Missouri.

Robles, G., Amor, J.J., Gonzalez-Barahona, J.M., & Herraiz, I. (2005a). Evolution and growth in large libre software projects. In *Proceedings of the International Workshop on Principles in Software Evolution* (pp. 165–174), Lisbon, Portugal.

Robles, G., González-Barahona, J.M., & Michlmayr, M. (2005b). Evolution of volunteer participation in libre software projects: Evidence from Debian. In *Proceedings of the 1st International Conference on Open Source Systems* (pp. 100–107), Genoa, Italy.

Robles, G., Koch, S., & Gonzalez-Barahona, J.M. (2004). Remote analysis and measurement of libre software systems by means of the cvsanaly tool. In *Proceedings of the 2nd ICSE Workshop on Remote Analysis and Measurement of Software Systems (RAMSS), 26th International Conference on Software Engineering*, Edinburg, Scotland.

Rosenberg, D., & Scott, K. (2001). *Top Ten Use Case Mistakes.* Available: http://www.sdmagazine.com/print/ [2005, April 1, 2005].

Rossi, B., & Succi, G. (2004). *Analysis of dependencies among personal productivity tools: A case study.* Undergraduate Thesis, Free University of Bolzano-Bozen.

RSA Laboratories. (1999). *PKCS #1 v2.1: RSA cryptography standard.*

Rumbaugh, J., Jacobson, I., & Booch, G. (2005). *The Unified Modeling Language Reference Manual* (2nd ed.): Addison Wesley.

Rusu, L. I., Rahayu, J. W., & Taniar, D. (2005). A methodology for building XML data warehouses. *International Journal of Data Warehousing and Mining, 1*(2), pp. 23-48.

Rusu, L.I., Rahayu, J.W., and Taniar, D. (2004). On building XML data warehouses.

Sabidussi, G. (1996). The centrality index of a graph. *Psychometrika, 31*, 581-606.

Safar, M. (2005). K nearest neighbor search in navigation systems. *Mobile Information Systems, 1*(3), 207-224.

Sakakibara, K., Sasaki, M., & Yamakita, J. (2005). Backoff algorithm with release stages for slotted ALOHA systems. *ECTI Transactions on Electrical Engineering, Electronics, and Communications, 3*(1), 59-70.

Saltzer, J., & Schroeder, M. (1975). The protection of information in computer systems. *Proceedings of the IEEE, 23*(9), 1278-1308.

Samar, V. (1999). Single sign-on using cookies for Web applications. In *Proceedings of the 8th IEEE Workshop on Enabling Technologies: Infrastructure for Collaborative Enterprises* (pp. 158–163), Palo Alto, California.

Sandhu, R., Bellare, M., & Ganesan, R. (2002). Password enabled PKI: Virtual smartcards vs. virtual soft tokens. In *Proceedings of the First Annual PKI Research Workshop* (pp. 89-96).

Sandhu, R., Bhamidipati, V., & Munawer, Q. (1999). The ARBAC97model for role-based administration of roles. *ACM Transactions on Information and Systems Security, 2*(1), 105-135.

Sandhu, R., Coyne, E., Feinstein, H., & Youman, C. (1996). Role-based access control models. *IEEE Computer, 29*(2), 38-47.

Sang-Min Park & Young-Bae Ko & Jai-Hoon Kim (2003) , Disconnected Operation Service in Mobile Grid Computing, International Conference on Service Oriented Computing ICSOC 2003: Trento, Italy.

Sarawagi, S., Thomas, S., and Agrawal, R. (2000). Integrating Association Rule Mining with Databases: Alternatives and Implications. Data Mining and Knowledge Discovery Journal, 4(2/3)

Satoh, I. (2003). A Testing Framework for Mobile Computing Software. IEEE Transactions on Software Engineering, Vol. 29, No. 12, pp. 1112-1121.

Sauer, C., & Mac Nair, E. (1983). *Simulation of computer communication systems.* Prentice-Hall, Inc.

Sauers, M., & Wyke, R. A. (2001). *XHTML essentials.* New York: Wiley Computer Publishing.

Sayal, M., Breitbart, Y., Scheurermann, P., & Vingralek, R. (1998). Selection of algorithms for replicated web sites. *Performance Evaluation Review, 26*(1), 44-50.

Scacchi, W. (2002, February). Understanding the requirements for developing open source software systems. *IEE Proceedings on Software, 149*(1), 24-39.

Scacchi, W. (2004, January). Free/open source software development practices in the computer game community. *IEEE Software, 21*(1), 59-67.

Scacchi, W. (2005). Socio-technical interaction networks in free/open source software development processes. In S.T. Acuña & N. Juristo (Eds.), *Peopleware and the software process (*pp. 1-27*).* World Scientific Press.

Scheidewind, N. (1993). Software reliability model with optimal selection of failure data. *IEEE Transactions on Software Engineering, 19*(11), 1095-1114.

Scheidewind, N. (2004). Fault correction profiles. In *Proceedings of the Eighth International Symposium on High Assurance Systems Engineering* (pp. 139-148).

Schengili-Roberts, K. (2004). *Core CSS: Cascading Style Sheets* (2nd ed.): Prentice Hall PTR, NJ.

Schmitt, C. (2003). *Designing CSS Web Pages* (2nd ed.): New Riders Publishing.

Schuba, C. (1993). *Addressing weaknesses in the domain name system protocol.* Unpublished master's thesis, Purdue University, West Lafayette, IN.

Schwabe, D., Rossi, G., & Barbosa, D. J. (1996). Systematic hypermedia application design with OOHDM. In *Proceedings of the Seventh ACM Conference on HYPERTEXT '96,* (pp. 166-168).

Schwaber, K. (2004). *Agile project management with SCRUM.* Microsoft Press.

Schwarz, K. P., & El-Sheimy, N. (1999). Future positioning and navigation (POS/NAV) technologies technical study. Study performed under Scientific Services Agreement with U.S. Topographic Engineering Center, Fort Belvoir, VA.

Scogings, C., & Phillips, C. (2001). A method for the early stages of interactive system design using UML and Lean Cuisine+. *Proceedings. Second Australasian User Interface Conference, 2001. AUIC 2001,* 69 -76.

Scott, K. (2004). *Fast Track UML 2.0: UML 2.0 Reference Guide*: Springer Verlag.

Scott, S. (2003). *The JBoss Group: JBoss administration and development* (3rd ed., 3.2.x Series). JBoss Group, LLC.

Seaman, C.B. (1999). Qualitative methods in empirical studies of software engineering. *IEEE Transactions on Software Engineering, 25*(4), 557-572.

Security Assertion Markup Language, OASIS Security Services (SAML) TC. (2003). Retrieved June 16, 2006, from http://www.oasis-open.org/committees/tc_home.php?wg_abbrev=security

SEI. (2005a). *A Framework for Software Product Line Practice, Version 4.2.* Software Engineering Institute. Available: http://www.sei.cmu.edu/productlines/framework.html [2005, March 23].

SEI. (2005b). *Software Product Lines.* Available: http://www.sei.cmu.edu/productlines/ [2005, March 23, 2005].

Serrano, M., Calero, C., & Piattini, M. (2005). An experimental replication with data warehouse metrics. *International Journal of Data Warehousing and Mining, 1*(4), 1-21.

Shamir, A. (1979). How to share a secret. *Communications of the ACM, 22*(11), 612-613.

Shan, H., Smith, W., Oliker, L., & Biswas, R. (2004). *Job scheduling in a heterogeneous grid environment.* Retrieved from http://www-library.lbl.gov/docs/LBNL/549/06/PDF/LBNL-54906.pdf

Shapiro, C., & Varian, H.R. (1999). *Information rules: A strategic guide to the network economy.* Harvard Business School Press.

Shibboleth Project. (2004). Retrieved June 16, 2006, from http://shibboleth.internet2.edu/

Shin, E. M. (2002). *Evolution in Multiple-View Models of Software Product Families.* George Mason University, Fairfax, VA.

Shoup, V. (2000). Practical threshold signatures. In *Proceedings of Advance in Cryptology (Eurocrypt 2000)* (pp. 207-220).

Sillitti, A., Janes, A., Succi, G., & Vernazza, T. (2003, September 1-6). Collecting, integrating and analyzing software metrics and personal software process data. In *Proceedings of EUROMICRO 2003,* Belek-Antalya.

Silva, P. P. d. (2002). *Object Modelling of Interactive Systems: The UMLi Approach.* Unpublished Doctoral, University of Manchester, United Kingdom.

Silva, P. P. d., & Paton, N. W. (2003). User Interface Modeling in UML i *IEEE Software* (July/August 2003), 62-69.

Simple Object Access Protocol (SOAP), The World Wide Web Consortium (W3C). (2003). Retrieved June 16, 2006, from http://www.w3.org/TR/soap/

Single Sign-On, The Open Group. (2003). Retrieved June 16, 2006, from http://www.opengroup.org/security/sso/

Software Suites supporting Knowledge Discovery (2005): http://www.kdnuggets.com/software/suites.html

Soh, W. S., & Kim, H. S. (2001). Dynamic guard bandwidth scheme for wireless broadband networks. In *Proceedings of the IEEE INFOCOM'01* (pp. 572-581), Anchorage, AK.

Soh, W. S., & Kim, H. S. (2003). QoS provisioning in cellular networks based on mobility prediction techniques. *IEEE Communication Magazine, 41*(1), 86-92.

Sommerville, I. (2001). Chapter 15 User Interface Design, *Software Engineering*: Addison-Wesley.

Song, M., Kang, S., & Park, K. (2005). On the design of energy-efficient location tracking mechanism in location-aware computing. *Mobile Information Systems, 1*(2), 109-127.

SourceID, Open Source Federated Identity Management. (2005). Retrieved June 16, 2006, from http://www.sourceid.org/index.html

SPI Dynamics. (2002). *SQL Injection: Are Your Web Applications Vulnerable*: SPI Dynamics Whitepaper.

Spinuzzi, C., & Zachry, M. (2000, August). Genre ecologies: An open system approach to understanding and constructing documentation. *ACM Journal of Computer Documentation, 24*(3), 169-181.

Stadt Nürnberg. (2004). *Strategische Ausrichtung im Hinblick auf Systemunabhängigkeit und Open Source software*. Retrieved June 15, 2006, from http://online-service.nuernberg.de/eris/agendaItem.do?id=49681

Stadt Wien. (2004). *Open Source software am Arbeitsplatz im Magistrat Wien*. Retrieved June 15, 2006, from http://www.wien.gv.at/ma14/pdf/oss-studie-deutsch-langfassung.pdf

Stinson, D. R. (1995). *Cryptography: Theory and practice*. Boca Raton, FL: CRC.

SUMA. (2003). *Gestion tributaria*. Retrieved from http://www.suma.es

Sun Microsystems J2ME Wireless Toolkit: http://java.sun.com/products/j2mewtoolkit.

Sun Microsystems J2ME: http://java.sun.com/j2me.

Sun Microsystems. (2004a). *How to implement a provider for the Java cryptography architecture*. Retrieved from http://java.sun.com/j2se/1.5.0/docs/guide/security/How-ToImplAProvider.html

Sun Microsystems. (2004b). *Java cryptography architecture API specification & reference*. Retrieved from http://java.sun.com/j2se/1.5.0/docs/guide/security/CryptoSpec.html

Sundaresan, K., & Sivakumar, R. (2004). A unified MAC layer framework for ad-hoc networks with smart antennas. In *Proceedings of the 5th ACM international symposium on mobile ad hoc networking and computing* (pp. 244–255).

Syrjärinne, J. (2001). *Studies of modern techniques for personal positioning*. Doctor of Technology thesis work, Tampere University of Technology.

Takefusa, A. (2001). Bricks: A performance evaluation system for scheduling algorithms on the grids. *JWAITS,* .

Taniar, D., Rahayu, W., & Srivastava P. (2003). *A taxonomy for object-relational queries, effective database for text & document management*. In S. A. Becker (Ed.), Hershey, PA: Idea Group Publishing.

Tassey, G. (2002). *The economic impacts of inadequate infrastructure for software testing* (Tech. Rep.). National Institute of Standards and Technology.

Tellis, W. (1997a). Application of a Case Study Methodology. *The Qualitative Report, 3*(3).

Tellis, W. (1997b). Introduction to Case Study. *The Qualitative Report, 3*(2).

Tenzakhti, F., Day, K., & Olud-Khaoua, M. (2004). Replication algorithms for the word-wide web. *Journal of System Architecture, 50*, 591-605.

Tewfik Ziadi, Loïc Hélouët, & Jézéquel, J.-M. (May 2004). Towards a UML Profile for Software Product Lines. *Lecture Notes in Computer Science, 3014*, 129 - 139.

The Aviation System Performance Metrics (ASPM) (2005): http://www.apo.data.faa.gov/faamatsall.HTM

The National Convective Weather Forecast (NCWF) (2005): http://cdm.awc-kc.noaa.gov/ncwf/index.html

The Sourceforge Project. (2002). Retrieved June 16, 2006, from http://sourceforge.net/

The Yankee Group. (2005). 2005 *North American Linux TCO survey.* Retrieved June 15, 2006, from http://www.yankeegroup.com

Thompson, S., & Reinke, C. (2001). A Catalogue of Functional Refactorings. Retrieved May 21, 2005, from www.cs.kent.ac.uk/projects/refactor-fp/publications/refactoring-draft-catalogue.pdf

Tian, L., & Noore, A. (2005). Evolutionary neural network modeling for software cumulative failure time prediction. *Journal of Reliability Engineering and System Safety, 87,* 45-51.

Tobagi, F., & Kleinrock, L. (1975a). Packet switching in radio channels: Part I—Carrier sense multiple-access modes and their throughput-delay characteristics. *IEEE Transactions on Communications, 23*(12), 1400-1416.

Tobagi, F., & Kleinrock, L. (1975b). Packet switching in radio channels: Part II—The hidden terminal problem in carrier sense multiple-access and the busy-tone solution. *IEEE Transactions on Communications, 23*(12), 1417-1433.

Tony Griffiths, Peter J. Barclay, Jo McKirdy, Norman W. Paton, Philip D. Gray, Jessie B. Kennedy, Richard Cooper, Carole A. Goble, Adrian West, & Smyth, M. (September 1999). *Teallach: A Model-Based User Interface Development Environment for Object Databases.* Paper presented at the UIDIS'99, Edinburgh, UK.

Transactions on Software Engineering, Vol. 29, No. 12, pp. 1057-1058.

Truex, D., Baskerville, R., & Klein, H. (1999). Growing systems in an emergent organization. *Communications of the ACM, 42*(8), 117-123.

UCLA Parallel Computing Laboratory, University of California. *About GloMoSim.* Retrieved from http://pcl.cs.ucla.edu/projects/glomosim/

Udo, G. J. (2001). Privacy and security concerns as major barriers for e-commerce: a survey study. *Information Management & Computer Security, 9*(4), 165-174.

Verhulst, P. F., (1838). Recherches mathematiques sur la loi d'accrossement de la population. *Memoirs de l'Academie Royal Bruxelles, 18,* 1-38.

Viller, S., & Sommerville, I. (2000). Ethnographically informed analysis for software engineers. *International Journal Human-Computer Studies, 53,* 169-196.

VisualWADE. (2003). Retrieved from http://www.visualwade.com

Vixie, P. (1995). DNS and BIND security issues. In *Proceedings of the Fifth Usenix Security Symposium.* Salt Lake City, UT.

Vixie, P., Gudmundsson, O., Eastlake, D., III, & Wellington, B. (2000). *Secret key transaction authentication for DNS (TSIG).* Internet RFC 2845.

Vixie, P., Thomson, S., Rekhter, Y., & Vound, J. (1997). *Dynamic update in the domain name systems (DNS update).* Internet RFC 2136.

Volterra, V. (1931). *Animal ecology.* In R. N. Chapman (Ed.), (pp. 409-448). New York: McGraw-Hill.

W3C. (2002). XHTML 1.0: The Extensible Hypertext Markup Language (second edition).

W3C. *The Extensible Stylesheet Language (XSL).* Available: http://www.w3.org/Style/XSL/ [2003, May 3].

W3C-World Wide Web Consortium. (2005). OWL 1.1 Web Ontology Language Syntax. In P. F. Patel-Schneider (ed.). Retrieved May 2005 from from http://www-db.research.bell-labs.com/user/pfps/owl/syntax.html.

Wagstrom, P.A., Herbsleb, J.D., & Carley, K. (2005). A social network approach to free/open source software simulation. In *Proceedings of the 1st International Conference on Open Source Systems* (pp. 100–107), Genoa, Italy.

Wainer, G. (2002). CD++: A toolkit to develop DEVS models. *Software: Practice and Experience, 32*(13), 1261-1306.

Walrad, C., & Moss, E. (1993). Measurement: The key to application development quality. *IBM Systems Journal, 32*(3), 445-460.

Waluyo, A. B., Srinivasan, B., & Taniar, D. (2004). Allocation of data items for multi channel data broadcast in mobile databases. *Embedded and Ubiquitous Computing, Lecture Notes in Computer Science* (Vol. 3207, pp. 409-418), Springer-Verlag.

Waluyo, A. B., Srinivasan, B., & Taniar, D. (2005a). Efficient broadcast indexing scheme for location-dependent queries in multi channels wireless environment. *Journal of Interconnection Networks (JOIN), Special Issue on Advanced Information Networking: P2P Systems and Distributed Applications, 6*(3), 303-321.

Waluyo, A. B., Srinivasan, B., & Taniar, D. (2005b). Indexing schemes for multi channel data broadcasting in mobile databases. *International Journal of Wireless and Mobile Computing, 1*(6).

Waluyo, A. B., Srinivasan, B., Taniar, D., & Rahayu, J. W. (2005). Incorporating global index with data placement scheme for multi channels mobile broadcast environment. *Embedded and Ubiquitous Computing, Lecture Notes in Computer Science* (Vol. 3824, pp. 755-764), Springer-Verlag.

Wand, Y, Storey, V., & Weber, R. (1999). An ontological analysis of the relationship construct in conceptual modeling. *ACM Transactions on Database Systems, 24*(2), 494-528.

Wand, Y., & Weber, R. (1993). On the ontological expressiveness of information systems analysis and design grammars. *Journal of Information Systems, 3*(4), 217-237.

Wang, X., Huang, Y., Desmedt, Y., & Rine, D. (2000). Enabling secure online DNS dynamic update. In *Proceedings of the 16th Annual Computer Security Applications Conference* (pp. 52-58). New Orleans, LA: IEEE Computer Society Press.

Wang. J., et al. (2000). Integrating GPS and Pseudolite signals for position and attitude determination: Theoretical analysis and experiment results. *Proceedings of ION GPS 2000, 13th International Technical meeting, Satellite Division* (pp. 19-22), Institute of Navigation, Salt Lake City, UT.

Warmer, J., & Kleppe, A. (1998). *The object constraint language: Precise modeling with UML.* Addison-Wesley.

Watts, D.J. (2003). *Six degrees.* New York: W.W. Norton & Company.

Watts, D.J., & Strogatz, S. (1998). Collective dynamics of small-world networks. *Nature, 393,* 440-442.

Webber, D. L. (2001). *The Variation Point Model For Software product Lines.* George Mason University, Fairfax, VA, U.S.A.

Weber, R. (2003). Conceptual modelling and ontology: Possibilities and pitfalls. *Database Management, 14*(3), 1-2

WebRatio. (2000). Retrieved from http://www.webratio.com

Weiss, D. (2005). Quantitative analysis of open source projects on SourceForge. In *Proceedings of the First International Conference on Open Source Systems (OSS 2005),* Genova, Italy.

WEKA (2005) http://www.cs.waikato.ac.nz/~ml/weka/

Wellington, B. (2000). *Secure domain name system (DNS) dynamic update.* Internet RFC 3007.

Wellington, B., Massey, D., Blacka, D., Lewis, E., Akkerhuis, J., Schlyter, J., et al. (2002). *Secure dynamic DNS howto.* Retrieved from http://ops.ietf.org/dns/dynupd/secure-ddns-howto.html

Wheeler, D.A. (2005). Why open source software/free software (OSS/FS, FLOSS, or FOSS)? Look at the numbers! Retrieved June 16, 2006, from http://www.dwheeler.com/oss_fs_why.html

Widom, J. (1995). Research problem in data warehouse. *Information Knowledge Management ACM* (pp. 25-30).

Wolfson, O, Jajodia, S., & Huang, Y. (1997). An adaptive data replication algorithm. *ACM Trans. Database Systems, 22*(2), 255-314.

Wu, C., & Li, V. O. (1987). Receiver-initiated busy-tone multiple access in packet radio networks. In *Proceedings of the ACM workshop on frontiers in computer communications technology* (pp. 336–342).

Wu, T., Malkin, M., & Boneh, D. (1999). Building intrusion tolerant applications. In *Proceedings of the Eighth Usenix Security Symposium* (pp. 79-91).

Xiaoshan He (2003), A QoS Guided Scheduling Algorithm for Grid Computing, Journal of Computer Science and Technology, Special Issue on Grid Computing, 18(4).

XML. (1999). eXtensible markup language (XML). Retrieved from http://www.w3.org/XML/

Xu, J., Gao, Y., Christley, S., & Madey, G. (2004). A topological analysis of the open source software development community. In *Proceedings of HICSS 2005,* Hawaii.

Xu, J., Gao, Y., Christley, S., & Madey, G. (2005). A topological analysis of the open source software development community. In *Proceedings of the 38th Hawaii International Conference on System Sciences,* Hawaii.

Xu, J., Li, B., & Lee, D. L. (2002). Placement problems for transparent data replication proxy services. *IEEE Journal on Selected Areas in Communications, 20*(7), 1383-1398.

Xu, K., Gerla, M., & Bae, S. (2002). How effective is the IEEE 802.11 RTS/CTS handshake in ad hoc networks. *IEEE Global Telecommunications Conference, 1,* 72-76.

Xu, K., Hong, X., & Gerla, M. (2002). An ad hoc network with mobile backbones. In *Proceedings of IEEE ICC,* New York.

Yin, R. K. (2003). *Case Study Research: Design and Methods* (3rd ed. Vol. 5). Thousand Oaks: Sage Publications, Inc.

You, T., & Hassanein, H. (2002). Infrastructure-based MAC in wireless mobile ad-hoc networks. *27th Annual IEEE Conference on Local Computer Networks,* 821-830.

ZDNet. (2005). *Extremadura Linux Migration case study.* Retrieved June 15, 2006, from http://insight.zdnet.co.uk/software/linuxunix/0,39020472,39197928,00.htm

Zhai, H., & Fang, Y. (2003). Performance of wireless LANs based on IEEE 802.11 protocols. In *Proceedings of the 14ᵗʰ IEEE International Symposium on Personal, Indoor and Mobile Radio Communication,* 2586-2590.

Zhao, Y. (1997). *Vehicle, location, and navigation systems: Intelligent transportation systems.* Boston; London: Artech House Publishers.

Zhao, Y. (2002). Standardization of mobile phone positioning for 3G systems. *IEEE Commun. Mag.,* 108-16.

Zhong, Y., & Yuan, D. (2003). Dynamic source routing protocol for wireless ad hoc networks in special scenario using location information. In *Communication Technology Proceedings, ICCT, International Conference, 2,* (pp. 1287-1290).

Zhuo, L., Wang, C-L., & Lau, F. C. M. (2002). *Document replication and distribution in extensible geographically distributed web servers.* Retrieved from http://www.cs.hku.hk/ ~clwang/papers/ JPDC-EGDWS-11-2002.pdf

Zhuo, L., Wang, C-L., & Lau, F. C. M. (2003). Document replication and distribution in extensible geographically distributed web servers. *Journal of Parallel and Distributed Computing, 63*(10), 927-944.

Zimmermann, T., & Weißgerber, P. (2004). Processing CVS data for fine-grained analysis. In *Proceedings of the International Workshop on Mining Software Repositories* (pp. 2–6), Edinburg, Scotland.

Zimmermann, T., Weißgerber, P., Diehl, S., & Zeller, A. (2005). Mining version histories to guide software changes. *IEEE Transactions on Software Engineering, 31*(6), 429–445.

Zipf, G. K. (1949). *Human behavior and the principle of least-effort.* Cambridge: Addison-Wesley.

Index

A

agile security 259
annotated artifacts 55
Apache 28
Apache Web server 68
ASCEND 253
authentication 87
authorization 87
automatable security testing 264
aviation studies 244–256

B

Bugzilla 21
business Web data 279
butterfly algorithm 147
BWW ontology 308

C

C-KDD 245
census, conducting a 19
centralized identity management 87
class-type architecture 263
closeness centrality 34
clustering 33
commiter network 46
communication 215
conceptual data model 305
cookie 89
corporate data sets 244
cryptography 189

D

data cleaning 21
data mining 245
data retrieval 282
data warehouse integration technique 278
defect injection 320
defect removal 319
desktop software 98
directed resource flow graph 57
distance centrality 34
distributed Web-server system (DWS) 158, 159
DNS Security Extension (DNSSEC) 185
domain modeling 333
domain name system (DNS) 185–202
domain ontologies 304

E

e-commerce 258
e-projects 317
extraction hints 250

F

fallback algorithm 147
Firefox 68
fisheye, and message reduction 206
FLEA 72
FLOSSmole 18–27
FLOSSmole, requirements of 22
free, libre, and open source software (FLOSS) 18
free/open source software development (F/OSSD) 52

G

GET public research portal 3
global positioning system (GPS) 114
Grid characteristics 144
Grid systems, and hierarchical scheduling 143–157
Groupe des Écoles des Télécommunications1 (GET) 1

H

HIPAA 84

I

infrastructured networks 175
Internet 317

J

Java cryptography architecture 193
JOSSO 93

K

key share 194
knowledge discovery in databases (KDD) 245

L

laptop 203
Libre software 1–17, 30

M

MANET 174, 205
Manet routing protocols 204
message latency 102
micro browser 100
MIDlet 100
mobile ad-hoc network 203
mobile computing model 98
mobile device 129
mobile device, and computational grid 129
mobile device movement path 136
modeling strategy, choosing by analogy 321
modified backoff algorithm 177
multimode process modeling 53

N

navigation engine 337
navigation modeling 333
navigation systems 114

O

object grouping 158–173, 163
object replication model 162
OntoClean 309
OntoClean ontologies 304
OO-H method 332
Open Data Standards (ODS) 67
OpenOffice.org 66–82
open source software (OSS) 66

P

PicoLibre 4
prediction 113
process ontology 58
ProGET 1
PRO Metrics 71
public key cryptography 194
public Web portal 3

R

rich pictures 55
rigidity 309
road topology-based prediction algorithm flowchart 118

S

Sarbanes Oxley (SOX) 84
schemas 282
secure DNS architecture 191
Secure Socket Layer (SSL) 258
secure Web-based applications, development of 257–277
security 102, 186, 259
security flaws 271
security refactoring 271
security testing 265
security testing, automated 268
Self-Ranking Algorithm (SRA) 127–142
Shibboleth 93
single sign-on 83
single sign-on system, requirements 87
single sign-on technology 86
social network 31
software product line (SPL) 213–243
source code management repositories 28
Sourceforge 19

T

TAMBIS ontology 311
Task Farming Engine (TFE) 132
test driven development 260
threshold cryptography 189
ticket granting cookie 89
total cost of ownership (TCO) 67
trust 91

U

Unified Modeling Language (UML) 213
universe of discourse (UoD) 305
UNIX 98
user interface 215

V

verification 325
virtual desktop 6
VisualWADE 331–344
VisualWADE, class diagram 334
VisualWADE, navigation diagram 335

W

Web-based systems 113
Web data warehousing convorgence 278–303
weighted clustering 33
wireless applications 98–112, 100
wireless environment 207
wireless software engineering 103
World Wide Web (Web), growth in 158
WUIML 216
WUIML, basic elements 217

X

XML 278

Z

zone-security servers 188